3 1299 00387 4741

D0076009

DATE			
7/6			

EXPERIMENTALPSYCHOLOGY

Third Edition

EXPERIMENTALPSYCHOLOGY

Third Edition

ANNE
MYERS

CHRISTINE
H. HANSEN
Oakland University

Brooks/Cole

Publishing

Company

Pacific Grove, CA

Brooks/Cole Publishing Company
A Division of Wadsworth, Inc.

© 1993, 1987, 1980 by Wadsworth, Inc., Belmont, California 94002. All rights reserved. No part of this book may be reproduced, stored in a retrieval system, or transcribed, in any form or by any means—electronic, mechanical, photocopying, recording, or otherwise—without the prior written permission of the publisher, Brooks/Cole Publishing Company, Pacific Grove, California 93950, a division of Wadsworth, Inc.

Printed in the United States of America

10   9   8   7   6   5   4   3   2   1

Library of Congress Cataloging in Publication Data

Myers, Anne.
    Experimental psychology / by Anne Myers and Christine Hansen. —
3rd ed.
        p.   cm.
    Includes bibliographical references and index.
    ISBN 0-534-16758-6
    1. Psychology, Experimental.   I. Hansen, Christine.   II. Title.
BF181.M85   1992
150'.724—dc20   92-4364
                                                                              CIP

Sponsoring Editors: *Vicki Knight, Marianne Taflinger*
Marketing Representative: *David Leach*
Editorial Assistant: *Heather L. Graeve*
Production Editor: *Linda Loba*
Manuscript Editor: *Candace Demeduc*
Permissions Editor: *Karen Wootten*
Interior and Cover Design: *Lisa Berman*
Cover Photo: *Lee Hocker*
Art Coordinator: *Lisa Torri*
Photo Editor: *Larry Molmud*
Typesetting: *GTS Graphics*
Cover Printing: *Phoenix Color Corporation*
Printing and Binding: *Arcata Graphics—Fairfield*

To my Dad, for many postcards.
A. M.

To R. D. H., my favorite colleague.
C. H.

Goals of the Text

Experimental Psychology, Third Edition, is an introduction to the basic principles of research in psychology. It explains the key principles of research, particularly experimental research, clearly and within the context of concrete examples. It teaches students how to design and execute an experiment, analyze and interpret the results, and write a research report. Although the main focus is on experimentation, alternative approaches are discussed as important complements to controlled laboratory experiments.

This text was designed to be as comprehensive as possible—without overwhelming the beginning researcher. The principles of experimentation and the skepticism of the scientific approach are new concepts that run counter to students' commonsense notions about causal inference; for most psychology students experimental methods require a quantum leap from their original ideas of what psychology is all about. For students, experimentation requires learning an entirely new language. This text has been designed with empathy for these problems as well as practical solutions to address them. It was written with flexibility in mind for the instructor as well. Each chapter can stand on its own, and instructors can select text assignments to match individual course content.

Special Features of the Text

This text introduces the experimental process in a structured way that allows students to better grasp scientific method. First, it is organized to carry the student through the entire process of conducting an experiment. The major sections—Introduction, Method, Results, and Discussion—parallel the major sections of the research report to clarify the relationship between designing the experiment, conducting, and reporting it.

Second, many practical aids are provided. Research ethics are discussed in detail, as are specific techniques for developing a research hypothesis. In presenting research methods, we have stressed the integral relationship between the experimental hypothesis and the research design. The process of selecting a design has been broken down into basic steps to provide more structure for the student. A detailed chapter on report writing includes a sample journal article to illustrate reporting conventions. (The manuscript version of this article is reproduced in Appendix C.) The rationale behind procedures is explained to help students apply them. Important terms are introduced in boldface type throughout the text and listed at the end of each chapter. Each chapter also includes a summary and a list of review and study questions. At the end of the book, a random number table, glossary, and index are included.

Third, examples are drawn from a variety of research areas to emphasize the importance of experimental procedures throughout psychological research. A few nonpsychological examples are included too, to encourage an appreciation of the experimental approach as a general thinking style. Both classic and current examples are given. The examples provide clear, concrete illustrations of the concepts at hand. The eclectic choice of examples creates a text that can be supplemented easily with content-oriented readings in areas of the instructor's choice.

Finally, to help students to interpret research findings, statistical material is included. The results section of the text provides the student with a conceptual overview of the process of statistical inference and step-by-step instructions for selecting and carrying out some of the tests commonly used in simple experiments. Basic terms are reviewed, and statistical tables are included so that all the required information is available in this single source. The process of interpreting the results is also discussed.

Organization of the Third Edition

Those of you who used the text in its second edition will find that the overall plan and focus of the book remain unchanged. Many interesting new examples have been included throughout. Many topics have been updated and expanded in light of reviewer and user feedback. New topics have been added. Chapter 2, for example, contains broadened coverage of nonexperimental approaches and new discussion of popular correlational methods. Chapter 4 now includes a section on scale construction. The use of deception in psychological research has been given extended coverage in Chapter 5. The concept of power has been introduced in Chapters 13 and 14. There is more classic methodology from Cook and Campbell[1] interspersed among the later chapters. We think you will find the Third Edition even more comprehensive than before—but still quite "user-friendly."

[1] Cook, T. D., & Campbell, D. T. (1979). *Quasi-experimentation: Design and analysis for field settings.* Chicago: Rand-McNally.

Acknowledgments

Many people contributed to the development of this manuscript. We would like to thank our colleagues and students, who offered comments, suggestions, and encouragement. We are especially grateful to Robert D. Nye, who served as an untiring sounding board. Howard Cohen, James Halpern, David Schiffman, Mark Sherman, and Jodi Solomon deserve special mention for reading portions of the original manuscript. Phyllis Freeman, Joanne Green, Zanvel Liff, Barbara Novick, David Morse, Robert Presbie, Richard Sloan, and Carol Vazquez were also helpful.

Special thanks to Deanna Hall, Cynthia Shantz, and Donna Kiehle, who read and commented on the current edition from a student's point of view. Thanks, also, to three methodological wizards: Bill Crano, Randy Hansen, and Larry Messé. We are also deeply indebted to the many researchers whose work inspired much of this text and to the many authors and publishers who permitted reproduction of portions of their works. They are cited throughout the text. We are grateful to the Literary Executor of the late Sir Ronald A. Fisher, F.R.S., to Dr. Frank Yates, F.R.S., and to Longman Group, Ltd., London, for permission to reprint portions of Tables III and XXXIII (Tables B2 and B1 in our Appendix B) from their *Statistical Tables for Biological, Agricultural, and Medical Research* (6th edition, 1974).

We gratefully acknowledge the contributions of Dr. Paul Koch, Saint Ambrose University; Dr. Charles Samuelson, Texas A & M University; and Dr. Roland Siiter, Montclair State College, who reviewed this third edition. Their constructive suggestions improved the book considerably. We are particularly indebted to Roland Siiter, who reviewed both revisions, for his many helpful recommendations.

We would also like to thank the people at Brooks/Cole Publishing Company for their careful handling of the revision, particularly Marianne Taflinger, acquisition editor, Heather Graeve, editorial assistant, Linda Loba, production editor, Karen Wootten, permissions, and Candace Demeduc, copyeditor. Deborah Hoffman, Henie Lentz, Alice Edelman, and Robert Rossini also played special roles.

Anne Myers
Christine Hansen

Contents

EXPERIMENTALPSYCHOLOGY

Third Edition

Introduction

**Experimental
Psychology
and the
Scientific
Method**

**Alternatives to
Experimentation**

**Formulating
the Hypothesis**

1

Experimental Psychology and the Scientific Method

The Need for Scientific Methodology

The Characteristics of Modern Science
The Scientific Mentality
Data Gathering
Seeking General Principles
Good Thinking
Self-Correction
Publicizing Results
Replication

Applying the Scientific Method
Observation
Measurement
Experimentation

Scientific Explanation and the Psychology Experiment

The Experimental Process

Summary
Plan of the Text

Key Terms

Review and Study Questions

References

P sychology is the science of behavior; as psychologists, we take a scientific approach. We work to explain and predict behavior through scientific methods: We specify the conditions under which we make our observations; we observe in a systematic or orderly way; we accept or reject alternative explanations of behaviors on the basis of what we observe. In short, we do a great deal of research.

In this text we will examine some of the basic tactics of research in psychology. We will study **methodology,** the scientific techniques used to collect and evaluate psychological *data* (facts and figures). All areas of psychology use scientific research methods. For example, researchers studying perception collect data through formal laboratory experiments designed to provide the most precise information. Psychologists interested in understanding attitudes and social behavior sometimes gather data under controlled laboratory conditions; at other times they conduct opinion polls in the community or observe and record people's behavior in natural settings. Clinicians may collect data in the form of impressions of personality functioning from a variety of sessions with a variety of patients. But whether their data come from laboratory experiments, everyday settings, or treatment sessions, all psychologists use scientific criteria to evaluate them.

THE NEED FOR SCIENTIFIC METHODOLOGY

All of us collect and use psychological data in our daily lives. You notice that your roommate is upset, so you decide to postpone the news that your rent check is about to bounce. You do not invite Chris and Lee to the same party because you know they do not like each other. You let your significant other choose the movie tonight because you selected the last three and you are worried about appearing selfish. You can probably think of many more examples of situations in which you used psychological data. The kind of everyday data gathering that we do may work well enough in a casual way. We may hit upon the "best" time to break some bad news to our roommates or to assert our movie preferences.

At other times though, nonscientific data gathering can leave us up in the air. For example, your significant other has just announced that she has been accepted for a university summer program at the Sorbonne in Paris.

Should you be worried? Some of the scientific data you gather about absent partners is reassuring ("absence makes the heart grow fonder"), but some is not ("out of sight, out of mind"). Knowing how studious she can be, you may decide that most of your data supports the former conclusion, and you see her off in good spirits. Driving home from the airport, you remember all the stories you have heard about Paris nightlife and handsome Parisian men . . . Without knowing which outcome is *really* more probable in this specific situation, you are likely to spend an anxious summer. If we want to have confidence in our conclusions and if we want to use them as general principles to predict behavior across many settings and conditions, we need to proceed more systematically.

Scientific methods provide us with just such systematic, reliable, general principles of behavior. The data we collect in psychological research must be evaluated and interpreted according to scientific criteria. For example, were the data gathered in a *systematic* and *unbiased* way? Are they *representative* of what we would see if we studied many more people? Can our findings be *replicated*? We seldom worry about these questions as we form our day-to-day impressions. But these issues are critical to the value of all psychological research.

In this text we will focus primarily on one research method—the psychology experiment, or the **experimental method**. We will explore several kinds of basic experimental research designs. However, because psychologists use other scientific research methods too, we will also look at some of the nonexperimental approaches to research. The experimental method has certain advantages over other methods (and some disadvantages too), as you will see in later chapters.

When we do an experiment, we make a controlled test of a hypothesis about behavior. Throughout the text we will examine experimental techniques in a wide variety of areas. Experimentation might be used, for example, to study learning in rats and to specify the reinforcement contingencies that will lead to a particular behavior. We can also use experimental techniques to evaluate the effectiveness of a particular type of psychotherapy or to learn what personality traits distinguish a good therapist from a mediocre one. Do anxious people spend more time with others? Does smiling make you feel better? Does adversity build character? Do attractive people earn higher salaries? These and many other questions can be studied through experimental methods. In the following chapters, we will discuss the details of setting up and running experiments and evaluating the findings. By the time you have read the entire text, you will know why experimentation is important, and you will be able to formulate a research hypothesis, design an experiment to test it, and analyze and interpret the results.

You will also be a more sophisticated judge of others' findings. You will be able to evaluate the procedures and results of published experiments for yourself, and you will understand what goes into the citations that fill textbooks like this one. You will learn the *pros* and *cons* of different research designs and be able to judge for yourself whether an experiment was well conducted. Last but not least, you will be a better consumer of information in everyday life. The news media regularly communicate research findings because we are naturally interested in what the "experts" say about things that are important to us—like human behavior! And we are subjected all the time to research claims made by advertisers: "Painaway relieved my headache pain faster than my old brand." "Deodoroma keeps you a lot drier than the other antiperspirants." Eating Yog-O has been found to be related to a long life." Each of these claims implies a different research design, and each design has its own strengths and limitations.

Before we begin to examine specific methods of research, it will be helpful to look more closely at what we mean in psychology by science, the scientific method, and scientific explanation.

THE CHARACTERISTICS OF MODERN SCIENCE

When you think of **science,** you probably think first of biology, chemistry, or physics. We all take some of these science courses. The word *science* comes from the Latin word *scientia,* which means knowledge. As the word is used today, it has two connotations—content and process. The *content* of science is *what* we know, such as the facts we learn in our biology, chemistry, and physics courses. Science is also a *process*—that is, an activity that includes the systematic ways in which we go about gathering data, noting relationships, and offering explanations. The steps we take to gather and verify information, answer questions, explain relationships, and communicate this information to others is known as the *scientific method*. Just like biologists, chemists, and other scientists, psychologists use the scientific method to add to the body of psychological knowledge.

As psychologists, our ultimate goal is to understand behavior well enough to predict the behavior that will occur in a specific situation, much as a chemist may predict the outcome of combining two elements. Our goal is to understand psychological phenomena well enough to be able to predict what is most likely to happen in particular instances (Will the rat learn the maze after ten reinforced trials? Will the young woman remain faithful?). Some psychologists, especially those whose work involves helping people with psychological or behavioral problems, are interested in using predictability to change or control behavior. Once we can predict behavior accurately, we can often change it. We can increase the number of desired behaviors and decrease the number of harmful ones.

The Scientific Mentality

The psychologist's goal of prediction rests on an important assumption: Behavior must follow a natural order; therefore it can be predicted. This assumption seems simple enough. Most of us share the belief that there are specifiable (although not necessarily simple or obvious) reasons for the way people behave. However, this elementary assumption lies at the heart of what Alfred North Whitehead called "the scientific mentality." Whitehead was a philosopher of science who traced the development of science in his now classic book *Science and the Modern World* (1925). He postulated that "faith" in an organized universe is essential to science. If there were no inherent order, there would be no point in looking for one. Hence, there would be no need to develop methods for doing so.

Modern scientists have faith in a natural order of things, and so they seek examples and explanations of it. Their assumption is that the universe "makes sense" in ways that can be discovered through research. Because each human being possesses many more unique qualities than do physical elements or lower organisms (experience, consciousness, and free will, for example), psychologists may never be able to achieve the goal of perfect prediction. But research psychologists believe that there is a natural order to even complex human behavior that can be understood and predicted for similar classes of people and situations, if not, perhaps, for every person in every situation.

Data Gathering

Whitehead saw the forerunner of modern science in the works of Aristotle, the ancient Greek philosopher. Aristotle, like the contemporary scientist, assumed that order exists in the universe, and he set about to describe that order in a systematic way. Others followed his example. Still, there was little scientific progress until the 16th century. What was missing from Aristotle's approach was a second key feature of the scientific mentality: reliance on empirical—that is, *observable*—data. Aristotle argued that heavy objects fall faster than light objects because their "natural" place is down. When Galileo (1564–1642) finally performed observations to test Aristotle's reasoning, ideas about acceleration owing to gravity were finally changed. Galileo's observations led to the inescapable conclusion that light objects fall just as fast as heavy ones, providing we set up the proper testing condition. This condition is a vacuum, which is needed so that air currents and resistance are eliminated.

Seeking General Principles

Modern scientists go beyond cataloging observations to proposing general principles—laws or theories—that will explain them. We could observe endless pieces of data, adding to the content of science. But our observations would be of limited use without general principles to structure them. When these principles have the generality to apply to all situations, they are called **laws.** Scientific laws are useful because they help us explain our universe and predict events. For example, astronomer Tycho Brahe painstakingly gathered observations of the stars for nearly a lifetime. But it was

Johannes Kepler who made these observations useful by explaining them through a system of equations now known as Kepler's laws.

Often, we do not have enough information, or perhaps insight, to state a general law. We may then propose an interim explanation, commonly called a **theory.** Theories pull together, or unify, diverse sets of facts into an organizing scheme, such as a set of rules, that can be used to predict new examples of behavior. Theories can explain many, but not all, instances of a situation or behavior—the more it can explain, the better the theory. But theories are always subject to change to accommodate data that remains unexplained, and sometimes old theories are replaced by new theories with greater explanatory power. Since laws are seldom determined outside the physical sciences, the behavioral sciences like psychology largely progress by developing better and better theories. Theories also guide the course of future observations: "We must remember that what we observe is very much determined by what theory suggests should be observed; and we must remember also that the way in which observation will be reported and interpreted is a function of the theory that is in the observer's mind" (Schlegel, 1972, p. 11). Many scientists, including Einstein, have sought data consistent with their theories (Sagan, 1979).

Good Thinking

Another characteristic of the scientific method is **good thinking**. Our approach to the collection and interpretation of data should be organized and rational. Our thinking must remain *open-minded* and *objective*. The scientist avoids letting private beliefs and expectations influence observations or conclusions. Good thinking means being open to new ideas and avoiding *"woodenheadedness."* Woodenheaded thinking is "assessing a situation in terms of preconceived fixed notions while ignoring or rejecting any contrary signs" (Tuchman, 1984, p. 7). Good thinking also follows the rules of logic. Conclusions will follow from the data, whether we are in agreement with our findings or not.

An important aspect of good thinking is the **principle of parsimony,** sometimes called Occam's razor. William of Occam was a 14th-century philosopher who cautioned us to stick to a basic premise: Entities should not be multiplied without necessity. Parsimony usually refers to stinginess: Scrooge was parsimonious—at least until he met up with some persuasive Christmas ghosts. But parsimony in science has a more positive meaning. What Occam had in mind was simplicity, precision, and clarity of thought. We must avoid making *unnecessary* assumptions to support an argument or hypothesis. The simplest explanation is preferred until it is ruled out by conflicting data.

Lewis (1978) applied the idea of parsimony to some developmental findings in an interesting way. He reported that infants in poor families spent more time in their mothers' laps than middle-class infants did. Infants in poor families also tended to vocalize less than infants in middle-

"IT'S UNIFIED AND IT'S A THEORY, BUT IT'S NOT THE UNIFIED THEORY WE'VE ALL BEEN LOOKING FOR."

FIGURE **1-1** Courtesy of Sidney Harris.

class families. We could speculate on all sorts of differences in attitudes, cultural factors, or parental expectations that might lead to differences in mothers' behaviors, which in turn might affect infant development. But Lewis's more parsimonious explanation made a compelling case for a simpler environmental difference:

> Even though the mother's lap is the most frequent place for the infant, the child is less likely to make sounds there than in any other situation. Mothers tend to vocalize more with their children in their arms and their vocalization inhibits their infants from making sounds. Surprisingly, some of the least frequent situations—such as in the playpen and the floor—account for the highest percentage of infant vocalization.

When we analyzed the data by social class, the importance of situational differences became even more clear. . . . No low-income mother ever put her infant on the floor, but middle-class babies spent three percent of their time there. Why? If, for example, the floors of the poor are unsafe—cold, lacking rugs, and with the added danger of attacking rodents—a poor mother would be unlikely to allow her child to play on the floor. Therefore, if infant vocalization is greater when the child is out of the mother's arms, then social class differences in infant vocalization may not be a function of different attitudes or desires of mothers of different classes, but of situational differences as mundane as what shape the floor is in. (p. 22)[1]

It is more parsimonious, or *simpler,* to explain the findings in terms of the physical conditions in poor homes than attitudes or desires of different classes.

Self-Correction

Modern scientists accept the uncertainty of their own conclusions. The content of science changes as we acquire new information, and old information is reevaluated in light of new facts. Changes in scientific explanations and theories are an important part of scientific progress. Sir Karl Popper (1959), a modern philosopher of science, wrote that science progresses only through *falsification*—not verification. What this means is that scientists challenge existing explanations by testing hypotheses that follow logically from them. (We will discuss some of the details of this hypothesis-testing process in later chapters.) If the test shows a hypothesis is false, the original explanation should be modified or abandoned for one that explains the new findings. Hypotheses that have not been proved false are not, however, necessarily true. Perhaps our testing methods are not sufficiently sensitive to accomplish this critical test. Science can only demonstrate that, at a given point in time, a hypothesis is not false. Experience favors a "weight-of-evidence" approach: The more evidence that accumulates to support a particular explanation or theory, the more confident we can be that the theory is correct. Old explanations often give way simply because the weight of supporting evidence tips the scales in favor of a different scientific explanation.

Publicizing Results

Because of the dynamic nature of modern science, it has become a highly public activity. Scientists meet frequently through professional and special-interest groups and attend professional conferences to exchange information about their current work. The number of scientific papers published each year in scientific journals is growing, and new publications are constantly being added in specialized disciplines. This continuous

[1] From "A New Response to Stimuli," by M. Lewis, 1978, *Readings in Psychology 78/79 Annual Editions.* Copyright © 1978 by Dushkin. Reprinted by permission.

exchange of information is vital to the scientific process. It would do little good for scientists to work in isolation. The opportunity to incorporate the most recent findings of others would be missed. There would be much wasted effort as researchers duplicate failures as well as successes.

Replication

Replication is another important part of the scientific approach. It should be possible to repeat our procedures and get the same results again. If we have gathered data objectively and if we have followed good thinking, we should be able to replicate our original findings. It should also be possible for other researchers to follow our procedures and get the same results. Findings that can be obtained by only one researcher have limited scientific value. For example, people sometimes report dreams that seem to predict the future. A woman dreams of a stranger and meets him the following day; a man dreams of a car accident and then hears of the fatal crash of a friend. Have these people seen into the future through their dreams? We cannot provide a scientific answer to that question. It is impossible to re-create the original conditions that led to these events. We cannot replicate these experiences. It is also difficult to evaluate them objectively, since the dreamer is the only observer of the dream.

In contrast, a researcher predicts that children will hit a doll after they have seen an adult hitting the doll. The prediction is confirmed. In this instance we can apply scientific criteria to the researcher's findings. We can replicate the findings by setting up the same or similar conditions and observing whether the outcome is the same. Replication of research findings by others can be important; we have a great deal more confidence that we have explained something if the predicted effects are repeatable by other researchers. Generally, replication is more common in the physical than the behavioral sciences. For example, a recent experiment in which investigators in Texas reported that they had created nuclear fusion in the laboratory without heat (a monumental scientific discovery) has led to worldwide attempts to replicate their experiment in other laboratories. To date, the claim for "cold fusion" has not been substantiated by other researchers. As in other sciences, published replications of psychological research are more common when the reported findings either have important implications or when reported results directly contradict current conventional wisdom.

APPLYING THE SCIENTIFIC METHOD

Let us continue our discussion of science by focusing on three samples of behavior:

Harry Houdini, the world-famous escape artist and magician, died of complications from acute appendicitis in Detroit, Michigan, on October 31, 1926.

Houdini had captivated his audiences for years with his death-defying escapes and astounding illusions. But, in fact, he was equally well known for debunking famous spiritualists and mediums across the United States (much like the Amazing Randi today). Houdini believed in the possibility of life after death, and he promised to attempt to return from the dead (if it were humanly [?] possible). For years, his wife attended séances Halloween night—the anniversary of his death—in the hope of aiding Harry to cross back over to the world of the living. (Fitzsimons, 1980)

Imagine the bewilderment of the group if on one evening their vigil was interrupted by not one, but three, visitors:

First man: "I am Harry Houdini."

Second man: "No, you are a liar. *I* am Harry Houdini."

Third man: "You are *both* lying. *I* am Harry Houdini."

What would we do if the group approached us and asked us to deal with these three gentlemen? We have before us three men, all claiming to be Harry Houdini. Our task is to discover which of the three (if any) is the real Harry.

As psychologists, we study the science of behavior. At a minimum, we ought to be able to tell whether similar-appearing behaviors are really the same or not. The three behaviors look the same—each man is claiming to be Harry Houdini—but is each man really engaging in the same behavior? Are they all lying? Is one telling the truth, while the other two are lying? Or are some or all of the men suffering from a delusion? Let us examine our evidence.

Three people have claimed to be Harry Houdini. There are several possible suppositions about their behavior. First, we might assume that in fact we *are* faced with three people whose real name is Harry Houdini. In this case the observed behaviors could be interpreted as three people reporting a fact. Second, we might assume that there is in reality only *one* real Harry Houdini, world-famous magician, and he has returned. Hence, two of the three must be lying. Third, we might assume that there is only *one* Harry Houdini, but he has not returned from the dead. Hence, all three people are either lying or mentally ill. You can probably think of several other alternatives.

Although we have observed three people doing the same thing, it is clear that the explanations for their behavior may be quite different. How might we go about deciding which alternative is the best explanation? We could approach the problem from the standpoint of the philosophy of ethics. We might then argue the likelihood that one or more people would be motivated to lie in this situation. Or we could approach the problem from the philosophy of metaphysics. We might then debate the possibility that someone could return from the dead after more than six decades. Or we could take a scientific approach by formulating a systematic plan to gather information relevant to all plausible, alternative explanations. We might continue to observe the three people, looking for additional behaviors that would tend to confirm or disconfirm our possible explanations. We might set up special conditions in which to observe.

Harry Houdini was famous for his illusions as well as his death-defying escapes. We could set up a test: Each man would be required to attempt the famous and difficult "saw-a-woman-in-half" illusion. If all three did poorly on the illusion test, we might conclude that the real Houdini was probably not present. In addition, we might attempt to rule out the mental illness hypothesis by subjecting each man to a psychological evaluation. Whether we could *ever* identify the real Harry with certainty could be debated. However, the scientific approach requires that we gather information objectively and systematically and that we base our conclusions on the evidence we obtain.

Let us look now at the main tools of the scientific approach: observation, measurement, and experimentation. These are also the basic tools of the experimental psychologist.

Observation

Observation is the systematic noting and recording of events. Only events that are observable can be studied scientifically. At this point it may seem as though we are restricting what we can study in psychology to a very narrow range of events. Many behaviors are observable (smoking, posture, head nods), but what about internal processes like thinking and problem solving? How can we explore those areas? The key is the way we apply the scientific method. It is perfectly legitimate to study events that go on inside the person, such as thinking, feeling, and dreaming. But in order to make a scientific study of those events, we must develop observable signs of them. Although we cannot see "hunger," for example, we *can* observe that an animal deprived of food for 24 hours eats more when food is presented than an animal deprived for 12 hours, and we can assume that the first animal was "hungrier." The key to studying internal processes is defining them in terms of events that can be observed: the time it takes a person to solve a problem; how long a patient takes to respond to an ink blot; a person's answers to a questionnaire; the amplitude of someone's palmar skin conductance responses. (Finding a suitable definition is one of the problems we will discuss in Chapter 4.)

Within the scientific framework, observations must be made systematically—the researcher must devise a system for observing, and the same system must be applied consistently to each observation. And of equal importance, observations must be made objectively. We must avoid distorting data by allowing our preconceived notions of the nature of events to alter our records. The good scientist avoids merging with the data. Personal feelings, thoughts, and expectations must remain separate from the external events being recorded. One criterion of such objectivity is the basic understanding that another objective observer viewing the same events would produce a similar record of them. So observation must be objective (we record only what in fact happens) as well as systematic (we do it the same way each time).

Measurement

Measurement is the systematic estimation of the quantity, size, or quality of an observable event. We usually try to quantify estimates by assigning numerical values to them according to conventional rules. We are all familiar with physical dimensions like length, width, and height. Rather than relying on global impressions ("It was really big!"), we use standardized units, agreed-upon conventions that define such measures as the minute, the meter, and the ounce. Standards are not always as clear-cut for dimensions of human behavior. We have standardized intelligence tests and a variety of standardized personality measures that we use. However, very often our standards are determined by the context of a particular study. We often wish to describe the behaviors of individuals in a predetermined situation (How much did they talk with others in a stressful situation?). Other times we want to measure individuals' reactions to the situation we have created (How happy did they feel at the time?). Or we may wish to quantify their evaluations of an object or another person (In a stressful situation, is a stranger judged more favorably on dimensions like attractiveness and intelligence?). We are typically interested in comparing individuals exposed to different sets of conditions. But regardless of what we choose to measure, we must be able to quantify subjects' behaviors by assigning standard amounts to any dimension we are measuring (How *much* did they converse with the stranger? How *much* did they report liking the stranger?). Because statistics are used to evaluate our results objectively, we need to be able to assign numerical values, or scores, to different levels or amounts. As you will see in upcoming chapters, we often compare the average scores of all subjects exposed to one set of conditions with scores from other groups of subjects exposed to different conditions.

Measurement is a way of describing our observations, and it too must be systematic and objective. To make data comparable, we take our measurements as consistently as possible. The reasons behind systematic measurement are the same reasons a dieter weighs in at the same time and on the same scale each day—if you weigh in at different times of day or use a different scale, measurement of your weight loss cannot be accurately determined. A 2-pound loss might be the result of the scale, not your diet. Nor would you change the units of measurement—you would not use pounds one day and inches off your waist the next, because they are not directly comparable. Similarly, the psychologist compares people who have all been assessed with the same procedures. For example, if we chose to use psychological evaluations to rule out the explanation that one or all of the would-be Houdinis was suffering from delusions, we would want to give all three people the same evaluation under the same conditions. Or if we were measuring changes within a single individual (like decreases in the anxiety level of an arachnophobic after repeated exposures to a spider), we would also need to use the same measurement procedure and the same units of measurement each time. If measurement is inconsistent, we cannot compare our measured observations directly, and comparing measured observations is the way we determine the existence of predictable relationships between observable events. (We will learn more about the ways in which these comparisons are made in later chapters.) Finally, measurements must also be made objectively; our expectations should not interfere with our conclusions. We record measurements as exactly as possible, even if they do not support our predictions.

Experimentation

Experimentation is a process undertaken to discover something new or to demonstrate that events that have already been observed will occur again under a particular set of conditions. When we experiment, we systematically manipulate aspects of a setting to verify our predictions about behavior under particular conditions. Experimentation is not always possible. To do an experiment, our predictions must be **testable**. Two minimum requirements must be met: First, we must have procedures for manipulating the setting. Second, the predicted outcome must be observable.

Suppose we have predictions about the observable effects on human travelers of making a 20-year journey through space. Our predictions are not testable because we do not have the technology to make that long a journey. Some hypotheses that cannot be tested now may become testable in the future.

Now consider the prediction that you are allergic to a particular shampoo. Ever since you switched to Suds-Oh, you have had an itchy scalp. You might try a simple experiment: Do not use Suds-Oh for two weeks. If all your symptoms disappear by the end of that time, you may conclude you are probably allergic to Suds-Oh. As a further check, you might use Suds-Oh again for a few days to see if your symptoms return. Your hypothesis is testable: The procedures for manipulating the situation are available (you either use or do not use Suds-Oh); the predicted outcome is observable (allergy symptoms are either present or absent).

To use experimentation, we must have procedures to manipulate the environment, and we must make predictions about observable outcomes. Experimentation must also be objective. Ideally, we do not bias our results by setting up situations in which our predictions can always be confirmed. We do not stack the deck in our favor by giving subjects subtle cues to respond in the desired way. Nor do we prevent them from responding in the nonpredicted direction. For example, if we believe that the real Harry Houdini is not present, the three imposters should do poorly at "sawing a woman in half." Having made this prediction, it would be unscientific to test the men under poor conditions. For instance, if we allow too little time for the test, all three may indeed do poorly and we may confirm our prediction, but the finding will have little value.

Sometimes experimentation is possible but it cannot be carried out for *ethical* reasons. For example, we would not test the effects of smoking on fetal development in pregnant women by asking a group of nonsmoking women to smoke during their pregnancy. We would not induce migraines to test whether hypnosis can reduce headache pain. We would not peep through windows to study sexual behavior. We would not change students' exam grades to learn about how people respond to success and failure. In a moral society, there are simply many experiments that should never be conducted because it would be unethical to do so. (We will explain the ethical guidelines for research psychologists in detail in Chapter 5.)

SCIENTIFIC EXPLANATION AND THE PSYCHOLOGY EXPERIMENT

In a scientific context, **explanation** is best defined as specifying the antecedent conditions of an event or behavior (McGuigan, 1983). **Antecedent conditions,** or antecedents, are the circumstances that come before the event or behavior that we wish to explain. In psychology some examples of antecedent conditions are stressful events, food deprivation, watching an adult hit a doll, or the number of other people around to help at the scene of an accident. If we can identify all the antecedents of a behavior, we can explain that behavior in the following way: We can say that when XYZ is the set of antecedent conditions, the outcome is a particular behavior. This explanation allows us to make predictions about future behaviors. If the XYZ set of antecedents occurs again, we expect the same outcome. This is analogous to explanation and prediction in the physical sciences.

For example, if a steel ball of a given volume is lowered into a measured container of water, we can predict the exact amount that the water will rise. In effect, the volume of the ball and the dimensions of the container of water are antecedents to the rising of the water; they are preexisting conditions. If we use a larger ball, the water will rise more.

In psychology we are dealing with organisms that are a great deal more complex than steel balls and beakers of water, so our explanations and predictions are not always that precise. It is virtually impossible to identify all the antecedents that affect a particular *subject* (the term given to a research participant) at a particular time. But although we cannot identify all the antecedent conditions, we may focus on particular antecedents that we believe have an effect on behavior. In the psychology experiment, we create specific sets of antecedent conditions that we call **treatments**. We compare different treatments so that we may test our explanations of behaviors systematically and scientifically. Keep in mind that the word *treatment,* as used in experimentation, does not necessarily mean that we must *actively* do something to "treat" each subject (although it can in some experiments). Rather, it means that we *treat some subjects differently than we do others*: We expose them to different antecedent conditions. Sometimes we test our explanations of behavior by creating treatment conditions in which some people are exposed to a particular set of antecedent conditions (hypnotherapy or TV violence, for instance) while others are not exposed to them at all. When we are able to specify the antecedents, or treatment conditions, leading to a behavior, we have essentially explained that behavior.

The **psychology experiment** is a controlled procedure in which at least two different treatment conditions are applied to subjects. The subjects' behaviors are then measured and compared in order to test a hypothesis about the effects of those treatments on behavior. Note that we must have at least two different treatments: We compare behavior under varied conditions so that we can observe the way behavior changes as treatment conditions change. Note also that the procedures in the psychology experiment are carefully controlled: Control is necessary so we can be sure we are *measuring what we intend to measure.* For this reason, characteristics of subjects receiving different treatments are also controlled by special techniques (explained in Chapter 6). We want to ensure that people who receive one kind of treatment are *equivalent* (as similar as possible) to subjects receiving a different treatment. If subjects who received one treatment had different characteristics than subjects who received a different treatment, we would have no way of knowing whether we were measuring behavioral differences produced by differences in the antecedent conditions we had created or whether we were just measuring behavioral differences that already existed! The need for control in psychology experiments is like the need for control in the physical sciences.

When you were a child did anyone ever ask you: "Which falls faster, a feather or a stone?" If so, you probably said, "A stone." And of course, you would have been right if the test were made under uncontrolled conditions. Stones *do* fall faster than feathers, unless we control the effects of air currents and air resistance by measuring how fast they fall in a vacuum. As Galileo discovered, the acceleration due to gravity is really the same for all objects.

We achieve the greatest degree of control with experiments that are run in the laboratory. In a laboratory the psychologist can insulate subjects from factors that could affect behavior and lead to incorrect conclusions. However, many people feel that laboratory experiments are too artificial. Critics argue that laboratory situations can be unrealistic and that laboratory results might not be applicable to everyday life. But then, not many stones fall to earth in vacuums. We sometimes sacrifice a certain amount of realism and generalizability to gain precision. The value of the psychology experiment is that, within the experiment, we may infer a **cause and effect relationship** between the antecedent conditions and the subjects' behaviors. If the XYZ set of antecedents is always linked with a particular behavior, whereas other treatments are not, we infer that XYZ *causes* the behavior. For example, with all other factors constant, if you begin to show allergy symptoms after using Suds-Oh shampoo, you would conclude that Suds-Oh causes your allergy symptoms. If you use the shampoo again and get the same symptoms, you would be even more sure the shampoo caused the problem. However, in Chapter 11 we will discover that our inferences about cause and effect relationships are stated in the form of probabilities—never certainties.

As we search for cause and effect relationships, it is extremely important that we maintain control over the environment and know what aspects of it have varied. You may be allergic to Suds-Oh, but perhaps by chance you also ate strawberries on the days you used that product. Controlled tests would be needed to rule out the strawberries as the cause of your symptoms.

The causal relationship you suspect between Suds-Oh and your allergy symptoms falls into the category of a *temporal* cause and effect relationship. First you use the shampoo, then the symptoms occur. There is a time difference that regularly holds in this relationship. You do not get symptoms *before* you use the shampoo. If you did, you would most likely look for another cause.

There are other kinds of cause and effect relationships too. In a mystery movie, we might see the heroine holding a gun and standing over a body. A *spatial* relationship—namely, the heroine and corpse together in the same room—suggests a cause and effect relationship between them. But did she really commit the murder?

We also use *logical* relationships to establish cause and effect: Did our heroine have a motive for the murder? If not, she will seem a less likely suspect. Last week one of the authors awoke to discover an ugly hole in the wall above the living room sofa that had not existed the previous evening. Given that only two relatively sedate adults, one tiny cat, and one very large (and rambunctious) golden Labrador reside in the house, the cause could be identified through logic. Neither adult had thrown anything at the wall (or at each other) lately, and her small size probably ruled the kitten out. The dog, however, has his own way of getting his daily exercise if he has not been walked. At some internal signal, he will start to run full speed up and down the length of the house for several minutes, carrying as many of his prized, wolf-sized, plastic bones as he can fit into his mouth at a time. Then he immediately falls asleep, exhausted. For some reason, running across the sofa is part of this ritual. Most of the time, he runs the course with great agility. But he *has* been known to run full force into walls, furniture, or people who happen to be in his way. Logically then, he seemed the most likely perpetrator. Even though no one witnessed the crime, we can be reasonably sure how it happened. We have found the most logical explanation.

As we search for cause and effect relationships through our research, we generally look for temporal relationships. We build these relationships into our experiments. We give subjects various instructions, then see how they behave. We show children various cartoons, then observe their play. There is always a component of inference in the conclusions we draw from these kinds of manipulations. Philosopher David Hume (1711–1776) argued that we can never establish causality in this way. (According to Whitehead, the logical conclusion of Hume's philosophy is that there can be no science. For that reason, scientists are not Hume's disciples.)

Hume's objections were based on the fact that because one event precedes another, it does not necessarily mean that the first causes the second. For example, in 16 of 18 years, the stock market has risen in the years when an original NFL team won the Super Bowl and has declined in the years when an original AFL team won (*Wall Street Journal Report,* 1984). Few people would want to say that stock prices are set on the football field. Obviously, many other factors exist that could have an impact on the economy. The advantage of the experiment in bringing us closer to establishing cause and effect relationships is that in the experiment only *one* factor is allowed to change. If every year were the same *except* for who won the Super Bowl, investors might have to pay closer attention to the gridiron.

As we seek cause and effect relationships in science and psychology, we try to identify the conditions under which events will occur. We can distinguish between *necessary* and *sufficient* conditions. For example, if the relative humidity reaches 100%, it will rain. Thus we can say that relative humidity of 100% is a *sufficient* condition of rain. But in reality, it sometimes rains even when the relative humidity is less than 100%. We therefore know that 100% relative humidity is not a *necessary* condition of rain. In contrast, an automobile will not run without fuel. Therefore fuel is a necessary condition for running an automobile.

The cause and effect relationships established through scientific research commonly involve identifying sufficient conditions. Many psychological studies have shown that being in a good mood increases helpfulness to others (Isen, 1987). But we know that many other things, such as characteristics of the person who needs help and the number of other potential helpers around, can also determine whether we will help or not (Latané & Darley, 1970). So being in a good mood is not a necessary condition to increase helpfulness. When we seek causes, we rarely seek conditions that are *both necessary and sufficient.* To do so would involve a search for the first or primary cause—*Cause* with a capital *C*! Given the complexity of our universe, we would make slow progress in our search for order if we refused to settle for anything less than causes that were both necessary and sufficient. Helping researchers would probably still be trying to trace the Cause of altruistic behavior, right down to the molecular chain that produces the biochemical changes associated with helping. How that chain got there, the Cause's Cause, would lengthen their search even further. The scientific approach to causality is more practical, relying on sufficient causes as explanations for events that go together. Let us now turn to a brief description of the experimental process through which we confirm cause and effect relationships.

THE EXPERIMENTAL PROCESS

As experimenters, we proceed through an orderly series of steps in conducting an experiment. We begin by reviewing the available psychological literature on the area to be studied. Through our review we arrive at a hypothesis or conjecture about what might happen under a given set of conditions. Next, we design a procedure to test our hypothesis in a systematic way. We record our observations of what occurs and then analyze these data using statistical procedures. We then decide whether the data confirm our hypothesis and evaluate our findings in relation to prior studies. We also reevaluate our procedures to be sure we have accomplished what we intended. Finally, we may write a research report of our experiment so that others in the field will know what has been found.

Each research report begins with a descriptive title and an abstract (summary) of the experiment. The body of the report is divided into four major sections that parallel the process of conducting the experiment: introduction, method, results, and discussion. The introduction includes a review of the pertinent psychological literature, along with an explanation of how the hypothesis was derived. The method section includes a detailed description of the subjects tested, as well as all the materials and procedures used. Enough information is given to allow others to replicate the study. A summary description of the observed data and the results of statistical analyses are presented in the results section. In the discussion section, the experimenter evaluates what was found and relates the findings to the existing psychological literature in the area. Problems in the design of the experiment may be included here, along with suggestions for improvements or modifications and ideas for further research. References indicating the sources of material cited in the text are included at the end of the report.

SUMMARY

Ultimately, scientists aim to explain and predict (and sometimes control) events. Psychology is the science of behavior, and as such, its goal is the same: explanation and prediction of behavior. Explanation and prediction provide psychologists with the tools for controlling or changing problem behaviors. Psychology shares the key features of all modern science: an emphasis on gathering observable, objective data and the search for general *laws* or *theories* to organize and explain the relationships among isolated bits of data.

The scientific approach requires *good thinking,* thinking that is organized and rational. Our explanations of behavior should be *parsimonious*—that is, as simple as possible. Scientists constantly engage in *self-correction,* challenging their findings through tests of new hypotheses that follow logically from them. Therefore, science is dynamic and ever-changing. The results of science are communicated through journals and professional meetings, stimulating *replication*. It should be possible to repeat our procedures and obtain the same findings again. Other researchers should be able to do the same.

The scientific approach is applied through observation, measurement, and experimentation. *Observation* is the systematic noting and recording of events. We can only make a scientific study of events that are observable. In order to make a scientific study of internal processes like feeling and thinking, we must be able to define those events in terms of observable signs. *Measurement* is quantifying an event or behavior. We try to measure in standardized units so that our measurements will be meaningful. *Experimentation* is a process undertaken to discover something new or to demonstrate that already observed events will occur again under a particular set of conditions.

Objectivity is essential in all phases of the scientific process; we cannot allow our personal feelings or expectations to influence the data we record. One criterion for objectivity is that impartial observers can produce the same record.

A scientific *explanation* specifies the antecedent conditions of an event or behavior. If we can specify all the circumstances that come before a behavior, we say that we have explained that behavior, and we can predict the outcome when the same set of antecedents occurs again. Psychologists generally look for the *sufficient conditions* that explain behavior rather than the ultimate causes of behavior.

In the psychology experiment, we create specific sets of *antecedent conditions* called *treatments*. The *psychology experiment* is a controlled procedure in which at least two different treatment conditions are applied to subjects. The subjects' behaviors are then measured and compared in order to test a hypothesis about the effects of those treatments on behavior. We may also infer a *cause and effect relationship* between the antecedent treatment conditions and the subjects' behaviors; we may say that the particular treatment causes the behavior.

The experimental process begins with a review of the research literature to suggest a hypothesis about behavior. Next, we design a procedure to test that hypothesis in a systematic way. We often use statistical procedures to analyze our observations. Through our analysis we decide whether the data confirm the hypothesis. We then reevaluate our procedures and write a research report of the findings.

Plan of the Text

This text is divided into four major parts: "Introduction," "Method," "Results," and "Discussion." These sections parallel both the process of conducting an experiment and the corresponding sections of a research report. Part 1, "Introduction," gives an overall orientation to the field of experimental methods, much as a literature review gives an overall picture of the state of research in a particular content area. Chapter 2 and later chapters focus on the differences between experimental and other research methods in psychology to help develop your understanding of experimentation. The section ends with a chapter on formulating a hypothesis. In short, Part 1 will provide you with all the information you need to begin thinking about an experiment in a particular area.

Part 2, "Method," includes all the basic procedures used in conducting simple experiments, including information on selecting subjects and collecting data in a scientific way. It includes chapters on controlling for potential problems. Part 3, "Results: Coping with Data," explains the common statistical procedures used to analyze data. Examples of experiments and actual computations are included to help you understand how these procedures are used and what they mean. Part 4, "Discussion," looks at the major issues involved in drawing conclusions from data. It examines problems of generalizing from a laboratory experiment to the real world. The chapter on report writing includes information on how to locate reference materials, as well as how to write each section of a research report.

KEY TERMS

Antecedent conditions   All circumstances that occur or exist before the event or behavior to be explained; also called "antecedents."

Cause and effect relationship   The relation between a particular behavior and a set of antecedents that always precedes it—whereas other antecedents do not—so that the set is inferred to *cause* the behavior.

Experimental method   The controlled test of a hypothesis about behavior.

Experimentation   The process undertaken to discover something new or to demonstrate that events that have already occurred will occur again under a specified set of conditions; a principal tool of the scientific method.

Explanation   The specifying of the antecedent conditions of an event or behavior.

Good thinking   Organized and rational thought, characterized by open-mindedness and objectivity, and including application of the principle of parsimony; a principal tool of the scientific method.

Laws   General scientific principles that explain our universe and predict events.

Measurement   The systematic estimation of the quantity, size, or quality of an observable event; a principal tool of the scientific method.

Methodology   The scientific techniques used to collect and evaluate psychological data (facts and figures).

Observation   The systematic noting and recording of events; a principal tool of the scientific method.

Principle of parsimony   An aspect of good thinking, stating that the simplest explanation is preferred until ruled out by conflicting evidence; also known as "Occam's razor."

Psychology experiment   A controlled procedure in which at least two different treatment conditions are applied to subjects whose behaviors are then measured and compared to test a hypothesis about the effects of the treatments on behavior.

Replication   The process of repeating research procedures to verify that the outcome will be the same as before; a principal tool of the scientific method.

Science   The systematic gathering of data to provide descriptions of events taking place under specific conditions, enabling researchers to explain, predict, and control events.

Testable   Capable of being tested; typically used in reference to a hypothesis. Two requirements must be met in order to have a testable hypothesis: procedures for manipulating the setting must exist, and the predicted outcome must be observable.

Theory   A set of general principles that attempts to explain and predict behavior.

Treatment   A specific set of antecedent conditions created by the experimenter and presented to subjects to test its effect on behavior.

REVIEW AND STUDY QUESTIONS

1. What is science?
2. Why do we need scientific methods?
3. What are the characteristics of modern science?
4. What do we mean by objectivity? How does objectivity influence each aspect of the scientific method?
5. a. Define an experiment.
   b. Make up an experiment to test the saying, Absence makes the heart grow fonder.
   c. Make up your own experiment.
6. What are antecedent conditions and how are they used in scientific explanation?
7. Professor Green made the following statement on the first day of class: "In order to pass this course, you must attend every class and receive a minimum grade of 75 on each exam." Is class attendance a necessary or sufficient condition for a passing grade?
8. What are treatment conditions?
9. What is the purpose of using at least two treatment conditions in an experiment?
10. Name and describe each of the four main sections of the experimental report.
11. For each of the following examples, explain which basic principles of the scientific method have been violated:
    a. J. R. wanted to do a little experiment on gas mileage to see whether the name brands give better mileage. She filled her tank with Fuel-Up one week and with a well-known brand the following week. At the end of that time, she thought things over and said, "Well, I didn't notice much difference between the brands. I filled the car with Fuel-Up on a Tuesday and needed gas again the following Tuesday. It was the same story with the big-name brand, so they must be about the same."

b. B. T. has been telling all his friends that his 2-year-old son Joe can read. One evening B. T. invites some of his friends over for coffee and offers to give a demonstration of his son's remarkable skill. Joe then appears to read a small storybook that B. T. keeps on the coffee table. One of the friends is not convinced and asks the boy to read a page from a different but equally simple storybook. Joe remains silent. B. T. explains Joe's behavior by saying, "He's just shy with strangers."

c. An author advocates the use of large doses of vitamins to prolong life. In an interview he says he has tried this treatment only on himself.

d. A researcher reports that plants respond to the verbal threat of being burned with a match. Others try unsuccessfully to reach the same findings. The researcher argues that skeptical critics are insensitive to the plants' responses.

REFERENCES

FITZSIMONS, R. (1980). *Death and the magician: The mystery of Houdini*. London: H. Hamilton.

ISEN, A. (1987). Positive affect, cognitive processes, and social behavior. In L. Berkowitz (Ed.), *Advances in experimental social psychology* (Vol. 20, pp. 203–253). New York: Academic Press.

LATANÉ, B., & DARLEY, J. M. (1970). *The unresponsive bystander: Why doesn't he help?* New York: Appleton-Century-Crofts.

LEWIS, M. (1978). A new response to stimuli. In *Readings in psychology 78/79, Annual Editions.* Guilford, CT: Dushkin. (Original work published 1977.)

McGUIGAN, F. J. (1983). *Experimental psychology* (4th ed.). Englewood Cliffs, NJ: Prentice-Hall.

POPPER, K. R. (1959). *The logic of scientific discovery*. New York: Basic Books.

SAGAN, C. (1979). *Broca's brain*. New York: Ballantine.

SCHLEGEL, R. (1972). *Inquiry into science: Its domain and limits*. New York: Anchor.

TUCHMAN, B. W. (1984). *The march of folly: From Troy to Vietnam*. New York: Knopf.

WALL STREET JOURNAL REPORT. March 3, 1984. New York: WPIX-TV.

WHITEHEAD, A. N. (1925). *Science and the modern world*. New York: Free Press.

2

Alternatives to Experimentation

Describing Research Activities

Nonexperimental Approaches
Phenomenology
Case Studies
Field Studies
Correlational Studies
Ex Post Facto Studies

Summary

Key Terms

Review and Study Questions

References

In the traditional psychology experiment, we *create* specific sets of antecedent conditions, or treatments, to test a hypothesis about behavior. To use the experimental approach, the researcher must be able to set up these conditions for *any* individual who ends up as a subject in the experiment. Many times, this requirement cannot (and sometimes should not) be met. For example, we may wish to study characteristics of the participants (like gender, intelligence, or music preferences) to see how they affect behavior. In these situations we cannot create the antecedent conditions, so we need to gather data in other ways. Sometimes the conditions a researcher wants to study (like pregnancy or smoking) cannot be created for ethical reasons.

Other questions cannot be answered experimentally because it is not practical to create the treatment conditions necessary to test them. Questions such as "What are the long-term effects of TV violence on aggressiveness?" fall into this category. To find the answer experimentally, it would be necessary for researchers to manipulate childrens' exposure to TV violence for many years while controlling for other potential influences on aggressiveness—clearly an impossible (and unethical) task. You could not simply allow subjects to choose their own level of exposure and wait to see which kids grow up to be more aggressive, because it is plausible that innate or learned differences in aggressiveness might determine what kind of television children like to watch. More aggressive kids might enjoy watching a lot of violent TV, while less aggressive kids might gravitate toward nonviolent fare. Finding that kids who chose to watch more violent TV while they were growing up were more aggressive as teenagers would be inconclusive. Differences in teenage aggressiveness could simply reflect different personalities. The apparent differences may be completely unrelated to television. You can probably think of many other similar questions that would never be answerable if psychologists were limited to the experimental approach. Fortunately, there are several alternatives to doing experiments.

Nonexperimental approaches are used in situations in which an experiment is not feasible. They are also used whenever testing a hypothesis in an existing real-life situation is necessary or important. Each nonexperimental approach provides useful data, and it is important to understand the scope of various nonexperimental approaches as they are applied in psychological research. The strength of the experimental approach is its ability to specify precise sets of antecedent conditions that affect behavior. Nonexperimental approaches can show relationships between sets of conditions and behavioral effects (like the relationship between smoking and lung cancer in humans), but as you will see, it is much more difficult to establish cause and effect relationships using nonexperimental designs. However, because there are many things that can never be studied in an experiment, researchers rely on a wealth of nonexperimental approaches to understand phenomena that could not be approached if they relied solely on the experimental method.

As we discussed in the first chapter, the primary purpose of an experiment is to establish a causal relationship between a specified set of antecedent conditions (treatments) and the subsequent observed behavior. The degree to which a researcher is able to do this is referred to as the **internal validity** of the experiment. An experiment is considered internally valid if we can say with certainty that the treatments caused the observed differences in behavior among the various groups of subjects in the experiment. Laboratory experiments are popular with researchers in part because they are potentially high in internal validity. (We say "potentially" because there are a variety of ways in which experiments may fall short of this goal. These will be discussed in later chapters.)

Still, experiments are often criticized—in the media, by students, by laypersons, and by seasoned professionals—for being artificial and unrealistic. If we could only take subjects out of the laboratory and observe them as they really are, say the critics, we could discover the truth about behavior. To some extent this criticism may be justified. True experiments often seem to lack **external validity**—that is, applicability to situations outside the actual experiment. Alternatives to experimentation are often preferred because they may have greater external validity. Their *generalizability* to the real world is often more apparent. There is, however, some trade-off. What we gain in external validity we may lose in internal validity. A study that is fetchingly realistic may bring us no closer to the "truth" than one that seems painfully contrived.

With these points in mind, we will discuss five major nonexperimental approaches. We will look at examples of how they are used and compare them to true experiments. These alternatives to laboratory experiments may increase external validity. But it is important to recognize that experimental and nonexperimental approaches to research have in common the fact that they can both be described along two main dimensions.

DESCRIBING RESEARCH ACTIVITIES

The two main dimensions that describe both experimental and nonexperimental research are (1) the degree of manipulation of antecedent conditions and (2) the degree of imposition of units (Willems, 1969). The degree of manipulation of antecedents theoretically varies from low to high, from letting things happen as they will to setting up carefully controlled conditions. As you already know, the manipulation of antecedent conditions is one of the most desirable features of the psychology experiment. For example, a study might simply involve tracking behavior along with subjects' normal diets (low manipulation of antecedents). At the other extreme, we might choose to place subjects on fixed diets where all meals are provided (high manipulation of antecedents). If we selected a high degree of manipulation, we could then vary meals in predetermined ways and evaluate subsequent changes in behavior.

The degree of imposition of units is an equally important dimension. It refers to the degree to which the researcher constrains, or limits, the responses a subject may contribute to the pool of data to be studied. For example, in a study of teenagers, we might simply watch a group of teenagers and record whatever they say or do (low imposition of units). With such a plan, we would be imposing relatively little constraint on the teens' behaviors. But suppose that, instead, we were interested only in a particular behavior, such as the amount of time they listen to rock music. We might then limit our subjects' responses to the answer to the question "How much time do you spend listening to rock music each day?" Our study would then score high on the dimension of imposed units. As you will see in later chapters, most experiments limit subjects' inputs to a narrow range of responses, placing such experiments high on the scale of imposed units.

Antecedent conditions and imposed units can change independently, and we can represent the various research approaches visually as shown in Figure 2-1. As the figure illustrates, there exists a range of possible research approaches. Laboratory experiments, which tend to fall in the

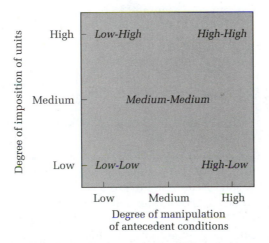

FIGURE **2-1** A space for describing research activities. From "Planning a Rationale for Naturalistic Research," by E. P. Willems. In E. P. Willems and H. L. Raush (Eds.) 1969, *Naturalistic Viewpoints in Psychological Research.* Copyright © 1969 Holt, Rinehart and Winston. Reprinted by permission.

high-high range, represent only one approach. As we discuss the alternatives to laboratory experiments, we will refer to this figure again.

The approaches discussed in this chapter fall outside the high-high portion of the graph: In contrast to laboratory experiments, nonexperimental approaches involve less direct manipulation of antecedents. Sometimes they place few constraints on subjects' responses; other times they are high in the imposition of units. Keep in mind, however, that the dimensions represented are continuous. Examples of the same research approach may fall in different portions of the graph. Each study must be evaluated independently.

NONEXPERIMENTAL APPROACHES

Let us now discuss five common nonexperimental approaches used by psychologists: (1) phenomenology, (2) case studies, (3) field studies, (4) correlational studies, and (5) ex post facto studies. Together, these approaches form an important source of data on human as well as animal behavior. They permit us to gather information and gain understanding when experimentation cannot or should not be used.

Phenomenology

So far we have discussed the scientific method in terms of observing and recording events that are assumed to be external to the observer. The phenomenological approach is an important supplement to the scientific method. **Phenomenology** is the description of one's own immediate experience. Rather than looking at behaviors and events that are external to us, we begin with our own experience as a source of data.

As a research approach, phenomenology often falls near the low-low end on our graph of research activities (Figure 2-1). Antecedents are not manipulated, and the data may consist of any immediate experience. No constraints are imposed.

Much early work in psychology was based on the phenomenological approach. Boring (1950) cites Purkinje as a good example of the phenomenologically based researcher. Purkinje was interested in the physiology of vision. He noticed that colors seemed to change as twilight deepened: Reds appeared black; blues retained their hue. This observation (now called the Purkinje phenomenon) eventually led to our understanding of the spectral sensitivity of the rods and cones of the eye.

William James (Figure 2-2) also used the phenomenological approach. In his *Principles of Psychology* (1950, original 1890), James dealt with basic psychological issues, including habits, emotions, consciousness, and the stream of thought. James approached many ideas from the perspective of his own experience. One of his most appealing passages deals with his

FIGURE **2-2** William James (1842–1910). National Library of Medicine.

own difficulty in getting up in the morning. He pointed out that our resistance to getting up inhibits our movement. While we concentrate on the pleasure of warm sheets and the dread of a cold floor, we are paralyzed. Said James, "If I may generalize from my own experience, we more often than not get up without any struggle or decision at all. We suddenly find that we have got up" (p. 524). Thus if we do not resist, we ought to be able to rise without effort.

The phenomenological approach precludes experimental manipulation: Comparison of behaviors under different treatment conditions is not required. When using this approach, we simply attend to our own experience. As Boring (1950) explained: "Since phenomenology deals with immediate experience, its conclusions are instantaneous. They emerge at once and need not wait upon the results of calculations derived from measurements. Nor does a phenomenologist use statistics, since a frequency does not occur at an instant and cannot be immediately observed" (p. 602).

Thus the phenomenological approach is applied to a small sample of subjects—a sample of one. We cannot be sure that the process we are observing in ourselves is not altered in some way by our attention to it. Since the observer is also the person whose process is observed, we may not be able to achieve the degree of accuracy and objectivity through phenomenology that we might achieve through other methods. Also, our private experience is not publicly observable; it will be difficult for others to replicate our experiences and apply scientific criteria to our findings. Since comparisons of subjects under different conditions are not made, the phenomenological approach does not permit us to make cause and effect statements about our experience. Purkinje could not know absolutely that his experience of altered color was due to an external change (a change in the amount of light) that would affect all observers in a similar manner. Had he not been a scientist, he might have explained his experience in terms of a demon that had taken possession of his sense organs. In the absence of further evidence, one explanation would have been as good as the other.

Although phenomenology does not yield cause and effect statements, it can be a useful source of information that may lead us to formulate hypotheses suitable for experimentation. Experimentation is still required to determine which antecedent conditions produce the behavior or experience. It is also necessary since, as James noted, it may not be legitimate to generalize from one's own experience to everyone else's. If Purkinje had been color-blind, his experience at sundown would have been very different from that of most people. We may wish to experiment on a larger sample of people to discern whether they report the same experience under the same or different conditions.

Phenomenology may lead us into areas of discovery that might otherwise go unnoticed. Phenomenological data often have high heuristic value, meaning that they help us discover new knowledge by suggesting hypotheses for further research. In short, they may raise more questions than they answer. Phenomenology is an approach that can be combined with experimentation. In fact, that is probably one of the most common uses of the approach today. Much of contemporary perception research relies on phenomenological, or *self-report,* data to study the effect of various experimental manipulations. However, unlike James's traditional approach, antecedent conditions are manipulated and subjects' responses are typically constrained (that is, some degree of units is imposed) in modern studies: tell which line seems longer, which light brighter, and so on. Thus elements of phenomenology can be found in many studies that are truly experimental. We will return to phenomenology again when we discuss means of formulating a hypothesis for an experiment.

Case Studies

Like phenomenology, the case study method involves no manipulation of antecedent conditions. The **case study**[1] is a descriptive record of an individual's experiences and/or behaviors kept by an outside observer. It may be used in a variety of ways: to make inferences about developmental processes, the impact of life events, a person's level of functioning, and the origin of disorders. Such a record may be produced by systematically recording experiences and behaviors as they occur over time.

There are generally no restrictions on the type of data to be included in a case study. Thus case studies would be expected to fall in the low-low

---

[1] Research produced using any of the nonexperimental or experimental approaches is often referred to as a "study." Only true experiments, however, are accurately called "experiments."

portion of our graphic scheme. The exact procedures used to produce a case study will depend on the purpose of the study. Sometimes, as in the clinical case, we may work from a record made after the fact: The client or other knowledgeable source provides information concerning events in the client's life and the client's reactions and behaviors. An excerpt from a clinical case is presented in Box 2-1 to illustrate the kind of information that may be found in a case study.

This information may be used in a variety of ways. First, we may use a case study to make inferences about developmental processes: We may observe whether progressive changes in functioning occur as the person ages. This approach provided the first systematic data on the development of children's motor and linguistic abilities. By making extensive records of the behaviors of individual children, early researchers like Velten (1943) arrived at descriptions of normal developmental sequences. Psychodynamic development may be inferred from case studies. Freud's case of Hans (Freud, 1962, original 1909) is an example of the way in which an individual case may suggest a developmental process. Hans was afraid of horses. Freud's analysis of Hans's conversations with his father and the dreams he reported suggested that the fear of horses was a symbol for Hans's fear of his father and anxiety about castration. Such case studies led to Freud's formulation of the theory of the Oedipus complex. The case study provides information from which we may draw conclusions about the impact of significant events in a person's life. We may evaluate whether changes occurred in the individual's adjustment following critical events

---

BOX **2-1**
Case study: An example of involutional paranoid reaction

A. S. was admitted to the hospital at the age of 59. The patient was born in Latvia. Little is known concerning her childhood experiences and the emotional climate of the home. She came to the United States at the age of 19 to marry a man who had preceded her to this country. She and her husband returned to Latvia, where the husband took over his father's farm and attained considerable success and status. At this point the farm buildings were destroyed by fire, and the patient was so seriously burned that she required hospital care for three months. They returned to the United States and the husband established an upholstering business in which the patient assisted until this business failed. The husband then began to drink, and he committed suicide by hanging, a casualty discovered by the patient.

When she was approximately 54 years of age, the patient began to complain that people were talking about her, that her son-in-law was maritally unfaithful, that nearly all persons, especially the clergy of a different religious faith, were sexually immoral. She expressed a fear that she would be "signed away for experimental purposes." She stated that a physician who had treated her at the menopause had given her cancer. Finally, after having complained to the police on several occasions that her food was being drugged and that a "society of science" was plotting against her, she was committed. *(continued)*

BOX **2-1**
(continued)

Following the patient's admission to the hospital, her daughter, in describing her mother's personality pattern, reported that she had always been a meticulous, hardworking person who was critical, suspicious, stubborn, uncompromising, and domineering. The daughter described her mother as an immaculate housekeeper who also did "beautiful sewing."

On arrival at the hospital, her sensorium was clear, and she was fully oriented. She was suspicious, and when her abdominal reflexes were tested, she asked if the physician was going to operate on her. At times she became quite agitated and hostile and insisted that she be permitted to leave. Someone, she said, was trying to secure possession of her home and to kill her; she must therefore appeal to the police to help her. She complained that the nurses tried to compel her to perform unpleasant tasks because they were members of a religious organization that was persecuting her.

Because of an electrocardiogram suggestive of coronary involvement and myocardial damage, it was decided not to give the patient electroshock treatment. After seven months of hospital residence, the patient became much less tense, was pleasant and cooperative, and was regarded as one of the most faithful and capable workers in the hospital cafeteria. Within a year after her admission, she was given freedom of the hospital grounds and was to spend weekends with friends. Unless questioned, she expressed no delusional ideas. Upon inquiry, however, it was found that there had been no fundamental change in her paranoid ideation. Fifteen months after her admission the patient was permitted to leave the hospital. A year later her employer wrote: "Mrs. S. is cheerful and pleasant and I am very satisfied with her work."

So little is known about this woman's emotional relations with parents and siblings during childhood and any early traumatizing experiences that it is not easy to construct a desirably complete genetic-dynamic formulation of her psychotic personality disturbance. Her daughter's report that the patient was a meticulous, critical, suspicious, stubborn, dominating, and uncompromising person suggests that, because of a basic feeling of insecurity, she had developed these personality characteristics to serve as defenses. In spite of a long series of threats, these defenses proved adequate for many years until the involutional period, with its various accompanying psychological factors, became so menacing that life-long traits were no longer able to control anxiety-producing threats. As a further defense, therefore, the patient resorted to projection to a reality-sacrificing, or psychotic, degree.

Although the problems that the patient had found too difficult to meet must remain a matter of speculation, one suspects, in view of the nature of her personality traits and the character of her delusions, that a deeply seated hostility, the fear of economic insecurity, and a weakening in the repression of instinctive sex drives may have been important ones.*

* From *Modern Clinical Psychiatry,* by L. C. Kolb, 1973, pp. 365–366. Copyright © 1973 by W. B. Saunders Co. Reprinted with permission.

like the loss of a job or the birth of a child. Knowledge about these events may lead to a better understanding of the psychodynamics of experience. For example, the fact that an early loss, like the death of a parent, is associated with depression in later life is indicated by many cases (Jacobson, 1971). As we understand the impact of such events more fully, we may be able to devise more appropriate treatment techniques, as well as preventative measures.

In addition, the case study is used to evaluate an individual's overall level of functioning. We compare our case against some hypothetical standard of "normal" behavior. Based on this comparison, we may suspect some form of psychopathology. We may then compare our case against other cases to assess the degree of similarity or difference. This is the process underlying psychological diagnosis. The development of standard diagnostic criteria for categories of mental disorders appearing in the *Diagnostic and Statistical Manual of Mental Disorders, Third Edition, Revised* (1987; abbreviated as *DSM-III-R*) reflect groupings of many case histories of many different patients. Clinicians have noted similarities among different patients that permit their problems to be classified into groups. For example, the records of persons previously diagnosed with an "antisocial personality disorder" have certain important similarities (see Box 2-2). Thus in making a diagnosis, the clinician compares the behaviors of an individual patient with those of many other patients who have displayed similar behaviors.

The **deviant case analysis** (Robinson, 1976) is an extension of the evaluative case study in which deviant individuals are compared with those who are not. By examining the histories of these different types of individuals, we may be able to isolate the significant variations between them. These variations may have implications for the etiology, or origin, of the deviance in question. This was the procedure used by Sarnoff Mednick to study the etiology of schizophrenia. He found that autonomic nervous system functioning differed between schizophrenic and normal children (Mednick, 1969; Mednick, Schulsinger, & Venables, 1981). Now research using other nonexperimental approaches is in progress that is designed to test whether these differences may be used to predict which children will become schizophrenic.

Clearly, the case study is a useful source of information. It is especially useful when we cannot experiment because of practical or ethical reasons. Obviously, we would not subject an individual to a stressful life experience, such as loss of a parent, simply to observe the outcome. However, this approach has limitations that make it undesirable in situations in which experimentation is possible. First, since we are working with only one or perhaps a few subjects, we cannot be sure the people we are evaluating are representative of the general population: We would obtain a very distorted picture of language development if we studied one exceptional child. Second, if we are not able to observe the individual directly all the time, we cannot be sure that we are aware of all the relevant aspects of the individual's life. Third, subjects or others providing data for case studies may neglect to mention points they believe are irrelevant or embarrassing.

BOX **2-2**

Antisocial
personality disorder

It is estimated that about 3% of adult American men and 1% of adult American women could be diagnosed as having an antisocial personality disorder. Another term for the disorder is *sociopathy*. These individuals were formerly called "psychopaths." Diagnosis of this category of personality disorder requires that the individual meet several criteria. The diagnostic criteria were determined by the clinical judgments of experts in psychiatry and psychology and evolved from many, many case studies. When we think of the term *sociopath* or *psychopath,* convicted serial killers like Ted Bundy typically come to mind. However, psychologists Davison and Neale (1986) describe an important fact about people with an antisocial personality disorder—they can be found anywhere! "Business executives, politicians, and physicians, plumbers, salespeople, carpenters, and bartenders—they are to be found in all walks of life. Prostitutes, pimps, confidence men, murderers, and drug dealers are by no means the only sociopaths" (p. 233).

It can be said that some individuals with aspects of an antisocial personality disorder are quite a bit more successful at managing not to break the law than others. What all these people have in common is that their personal histories will reflect similar kinds of behaviors and life events. Sociopathy always begins in childhood or adolescence with occasions of truancy, aggression, vandalism, stealing, lying, physical cruelty, or other antisocial behaviors. Before the age of 18, such individuals would be diagnosed as having a "conduct disorder." Their behavior rarely goes unnoticed; they often find themselves in trouble with the authorities.

After age 18, a diagnosis of antisocial personality disorder is made if individuals fulfill specific behavioral criteria associated with the disorder. These individuals carry over the pattern of childhood antisocial behavior into adulthood, where they are seen to engage in repeated instances of behaviors that are assaultive, destructive, irresponsible, or illegal. In addition, sociopaths do not suffer from (true) remorse for their actions. From collections of case studies, several predisposing childhood factors have also been identified: inconsistent parental discipline, substance abuse, attention-deficits, and hyperactivity, for example. Sociopathy is also more likely if one or both parents had the disorder.

While *DSM-III-R* is the standard for diagnosing mental disorders, not all experts agree with the diagnostic criteria. For example, many psychologists believe that sociopaths are also characterized by a superficial veneer of charm that can make them quite charismatic. Underneath it all, though, they feel little or nothing for others (Cleckley, 1976). Part of the problem with compiling information from case studies on individuals diagnosed with antisocial personality disorder is that generally the individuals available for study are the extreme cases—typically incarcerated criminals or psychiatric patients. One can argue, as have Davison and Neale (1986), that the data base for sociopathy is probably missing valuable information about the most successful sociopaths.

An additional problem is that the case studies frequently rely on **retrospective data.** Retrospective data are data collected now that are based on recollections of past events. Information collected long after the fact is apt to be inaccurate for several reasons. First of all, people often cannot accurately remember all that happened at a particular point in time. We also know that human memories become altered or "reconstructed" over time by the cognitive system. Retrospective data can also be easily biased by the situation in which it is collected. The mood of the data provider, for example, will affect recollections; we tend to recall more positive events when we are in a good mood and more negative events when we are in a bad mood. In addition, particular kinds of recollections can be "triggered" by aspects of the situation. Something that seems as innocuous as a reproduction of the Mona Lisa on the therapist's wall might bring to mind past experiences with enigmatic, dark-haired women that otherwise would not have been recalled at all. And even unintended hints from a researcher that certain kinds of data are more interesting than others can bias the kind of information that is brought to mind. For these reasons, reliance on retrospective data is a shortcoming. Records made at the time of an event are always much preferred. The use of retrospective data is not limited to case studies but frequently occurs in this method.

Even more important, since we have not created the antecedent conditions in case studies, we cannot make cause and effect statements about the behaviors we observe. The manipulation has already taken place. Since we cannot know everything about our subjects, we have no way of knowing that what we hypothesize as the cause is the *only* attribute of the groups that differs. For example, we cannot say that an early loss causes later depression; we can merely say that there seems to be a relationship between the two occurrences. It is just as plausible that some related factor, such as moving or changing schools because of a parent's death, explains later depression.

Field Studies

Field studies are nonexperimental approaches used in the field or in real-life settings. Researchers doing field studies often combine various types of data gathering to capitalize on the richness and range of behavior found outside the laboratory. Antecedent conditions are not manipulated in field studies, but the degree of constraint on responses varies considerably from study to study. Depending on the measures used, field studies may fall anywhere along the continuum of low-low to low-high in our graphic scheme (see Figure 2-1). We will now discuss some different types of field studies.

Naturalistic observation. Naturalistic observation is the technique of observing behaviors as they occur spontaneously in natural settings. It is a *descriptive* method: Like phenomenology and the case study method, it involves no manipulation of antecedent conditions. Subjects' responses are free to vary; few constraints are imposed by the researcher (Sackett, 1978). The naturalistic approach has been used most extensively in animal research, but it may be applied to human behavior as well. During naturalistic observation, the observer remains unobtrusive (for example, behind a duck blind) so that the behaviors observed are not altered by the presence of the observer. Every attempt is made to keep the setting as natural as possible, so that the naturally occurring events will not be altered in any way. "The primary feature of such research is that human perceptual and judgmental abilities are necessary to extract quantitative data from the flow of responses" (Sackett, 1978, p. 2). This creates special challenges for the field study. In a typical laboratory experiment, the researcher has only a small set of behaviors to record. In contrast, researchers who conduct field studies must contend with a vast array of responses, often including unanticipated, unconventional responses. Deciding who and when to observe and what to record and analyze draws heavily on both the researcher's judgment and observational skills.

With all the added demands of naturalistic observation, would it not just be simpler to stick with the tried-and-true laboratory experiment? With a field study, we can only describe behaviors that occur, but if we manipulate antecedents and constrain our subjects' responses, we optimize our chances of being able to explain behaviors and predict outcomes. Perhaps this is true. But the use of direct, naturalistic observation is often essential and even preferable. Psychological phenomena are rarely simple. In an experiment a researcher can fail to take all the important antecedent conditions into account. Years of experiments on helpfulness are a case in point. There are so many factors that influence our helpfulness that it would be impossible to manipulate all of them in a single experiment so that we could look at their combined effects. In a field study, researchers are only limited by their ability to keep track of everything at once! Imposing a great deal of constraint on subjects' responses is not always desirable either. A simple constrained response—a yes/no answer on a questionnaire, measuring only certain kinds of actions, a test score—may not address the complexity of the research question very well. If we wanted to study interpersonal dynamics in a classroom, for example, we would be hard pressed to develop a scoring procedure that would take into account the variety of activities and combinations of participants (number of interactants, gender composition, ages, personality styles, and so on) in even a small class. The field researcher accepts the larger challenge of dealing with data as they occur in real-life settings.

Naturalistic observation is occasionally carried out in the laboratory. At times it is necessary to compare laboratory findings with behavior in natural settings to confirm the usefulness of the laboratory setting for a particular research topic. Some behaviors may be distorted by bringing them into the laboratory setting. Such behaviors are best observed where they occur naturally. Naturalistic observation remains important even when experimentation is possible. According to Miller (1977), there are at least five good reasons for using naturalistic observation: (1) studying nature for its own sake; (2) using nature as a starting point from which to develop a program of laboratory research; (3) using nature to validate or add substance to previously obtained laboratory findings; (4) obtaining information about species differences that will subsequently increase the efficient use of animals in the laboratory; and (5) using the field as a naturalistic "laboratory" to test some hypothesis or theoretical concept.

Naturalistic observation will be more useful in some situations than others. For example, if we are interested in the mating behavior of wild ducks, naturalistic observation is a sensible way to proceed. However, the data we obtain are descriptive—not explanatory. Through naturalistic observation we could obtain a good description of mating in ducks, but we would not know why ducks mated. We would be unable to separate out the effects of different aspects of the environment that govern mating behavior. Suppose we observed a courtship dance, a display of feathers, and an unusual call. We would not be able to tell whether any of these behaviors are necessary (or sufficient) for mating to occur. In other words, we would not be able to specify the relevant antecedent conditions that affect mating. As Miller (1977) suggests, naturalistic observation provides a description of behaviors and the setting in which they occur and can be used as the starting point for a series of experiments to test hypotheses about these behaviors. In the laboratory we might choreograph a puppet duck to do a courtship dance without a display of feathers and without a mating call. This would enable us to see whether the dance alone would elicit mating behavior from other ducks.

A further limitation of naturalistic observation is that we are dealing with particular samples of time that may or may not contain the behaviors we wish to observe. We must wait for mating, fighting, or any other behavior of interest to occur within our viewing range. If we bring our study into the laboratory, we may be able to create conditions to elicit the behavior of interest within a circumscribed time and space. But when we do bring our subjects into the laboratory, we must be aware of the possibility that their behaviors in the laboratory setting may not be the same as they are in the wild. Particularly with human subjects, we may find that behaviors become very different when the subjects know they are being watched. We may even find that subjects try to guess the purpose of the experiment so that they may either confirm the researcher's expectations or sabotage the results. (We will discuss these issues further in later chapters.)

Interviews and questionnaires.   In addition to naturalistic observation, the techniques of interviews and questionnaires are used in field settings. The researcher may observe the subjects initially, then interview them to get their opinions. In other situations, the researcher may choose not to observe behaviors at all but to make inferences about behaviors solely from interview or questionnaire data.

Interviews and questionnaires commonly include an assortment of open and closed questions. Closed questions take the form of "Do you use Tide?" "Should there be a ban on nuclear energy?," and "On a scale from 1 to 10, how much do you like Madonna?" They are questions to be answered by one of a limited number of alternatives. Open questions solicit information about opinions and feelings by asking the question in such a way that the person must respond with more than a yes, no, or 1–10 rating. Examples of open questions are "Why do you prefer powdered detergents over liquids?" and "What made you decide to come for treatment now?" By asking a combination of questions, the interviewer may gather a great deal of useful information. The interview is an important aspect of field research. Especially when dealing with feelings, beliefs, and attitudes, observation may not always suffice.

Unobtrusive measures. In addition to interviews, the researcher may make inferences about behavior from observations of aspects of the environment. Many indexes of behavior can be observed without the subject's knowledge. Such indicators are called **unobtrusive measures**. For example, a researcher could study the traffic pattern in a supermarket by assessing the frequency of replacement of floor tiles in each aisle (or even the wear and tear on tiles in different parts of the store). The subjects—shoppers—would never know their behaviors were being observed. Unobtrusive measures are often preferred over conspicuous measurement techniques, *obtrusive measures,* because unobtrusive measures yield data that are unbiased and objective. Subjects may behave very differently if they know they are being observed. (Do you know someone who would skip certain aisles, like the junk food or candy aisle, if they knew a researcher was watching? We do!)

Conducting a field study. A study by Bechtol and Williams (1977) is a good example of the range of techniques that may be used in a field study. Bechtol and Williams were interested in California litter. They noted that unregulated coastline areas attract large numbers of beachgoers, even though the supervised state beaches are considerably cleaner. They set out to determine who were the users of the unregulated beaches, whether there was a pattern to the littering that occurs on such a beach, and how users of the beach feel about sunbathing in the midst of debris. They employed several of the techniques common in field studies.

Bechtol and Williams spent two years observing activities on an unregulated beach in Southern California. They used *naturalistic observation* to determine who used the beach: They simply watched and recorded what sorts of people appeared. They saw that young people were the principal users. By using an *unobtrusive measure* to assess the pattern of littering— collecting and counting all the cans left on the beach—they assessed behavior without their subjects' knowledge. From the number of cans in the sand, they inferred that people litter the beach. There was no need to see anyone litter. As we might expect, Bechtol and Williams found that littering was greatest during the summer, when beach use was greatest.

In addition to observation, Bechtol and Williams approached people on the beach and asked them how they felt about the condition of the beach. At this point the researchers deviated from naturalistic observation. Instead of continuing to remain inconspicuous, the researchers interviewed people to get their views. Their findings were quite interesting.

First, users of the beach reported being disturbed about its littered condition. And second, all the people interviewed reported that *they* always took their own trash with them when they left; although in two years of observation, the researchers never saw a single person do so. This is an excellent example of why interview and questionnaire data should be supplemented with objective observations, including unobtrusive measures, whenever possible.

As with the other approaches we have discussed so far in this chapter, the field study does not involve any direct manipulation of conditions. Behaviors are observed and recorded as they occur in the natural setting. Subjects may be interviewed in the "wild," where the contaminating effects of a laboratory setting are absent. It is a useful way of gathering many types of data, particularly when the researcher is studying behavior like littering, which we might not see in the laboratory. Note that a field study is not to be confused with a *field experiment*. A field experiment is a true experiment (with manipulated antecedent conditions) that is conducted outside the laboratory.

An interesting example of a field experiment, conducted in seven suburban Chicago-area bars, is provided by Cunningham (1989). Cunningham trained several college students to approach opposite-sex bar patrons at random, delivering one of several different kinds of conversation-starters ("lines"). The positivity of each patron's response to the line was surreptitiously measured. Cunningham discovered that women were much more sensitive to the kind of line an opposite-sex person delivered than were men. Women responded more positively to lines that were either self-disclosing or ordinary, like a simple "Hi," than they did to a flippantly delivered line, like "You remind me of someone I used to date" or "Bet I can outdrink you." Men, however, did not appear to care which kind of conversational gambit a woman used; they responded equally positively to all three. It is sometimes possible to achieve high degrees of both external and internal validity, as Cunningham did, by conducting actual experiments "in the field." We will return to field experiments in later chapters about experimental approaches.

Correlational Studies

All the methods described thus far can yield useful information. But as psychologists we often wish to go beyond describing our observations to provide a quantitative summary of what we have seen. Rather than listing each subject's score on each questionnaire item, for example, we may prefer to talk in terms of overall trends.

There are a great many ways to describe the data of nonexperimental studies; we will discuss a few of them. One approach, correlation, is so common in nonexperimental studies that it is often discussed as a research method in its own right. However, correlation is really a technique for summarizing data that could be used in studies falling in any portion of our graphic scheme.

The correlation technique can be used with both laboratory and field data. A **correlational study** is one that is designed to determine the **correlation,** or degree of relationship, between two or more traits, behaviors, or events. Researchers often use correlational studies to explore behaviors that are not yet well understood. By measuring many behaviors and seeing which go together, we begin to see possible explanations for behaviors. With the widespread availability of computers, researchers can measure and analyze the relationships among countless numbers of variables in a single study. (Incidentally, a *variable* is any observable behavior, characteristic, or event that can vary or have different values.) Although this "shotgun approach" is not always the most elegant research strategy, it may have heuristic value. Correlational data may serve as the basis for new experimental hypotheses, as we shall see in the next chapter.

In a correlational study, the traits or behaviors of interest are measured first. Numbers are recorded that represent the subjects' behaviors. Next, the degree of relationship, or correlation, between the numbers is determined through statistical procedures. In the correlational study, the researcher measures events without attempting to alter the antecedent conditions in any way; she or he is simply asking how well the measures go together. Correlational studies thus fall in the low-high portion of Figure 2-1. Once the correlation is known, it can be used to make predictions. If we know a person's score on one measure, we can make a better prediction of that person's score on another measure that is highly related to it. The higher the correlation, the more accurate our prediction will be.

Suppose a researcher wonders whether there is a relationship between television viewing and the size of people's vocabularies. The researcher could gather data to determine whether such a relationship exists. First, he or she would devise an objective measure of vocabulary. Either a standardized test or an improvised procedure might be used. For instance, the researcher might ask subjects to go through a dictionary and check off all the words that are familiar. One approach might be preferred to another, depending on time, resources, and the subjects' patience. The researcher would also carefully measure daily television viewing time. The degree of relationship, or correlation, between the two measures would then be assessed through statistical procedures.

Relationships between pairs of scores from each subject are known as *simple correlations*. The Pearson Product Moment Correlation Coefficient (r) is the most commonly used procedure for calculating simple correlations. Determining the intercorrelation of three or more scores from each individual requires other procedures (see Box 2-3). But you will see the Pearson r reported in most correlational studies. When r is computed, three general outcomes are possible: a positive relationship, a negative relationship, or no relationship.[2] These are illustrated in Figure 2-3. Because of the way the statistic is computed, the values of a correlation coefficient can only vary between -1.00 and $+1.00$. The sign (plus or

---

[2] This discussion is limited to linear (or straight-line) relationships. The Pearson r does not measure nonlinear relationships.

BOX **2-3**
Exploring
relationships among
more than two
variables

Sometimes we wish to see whether there is a relationship among a number of measured behaviors. Intercorrelations among three or more behaviors can be computed with a statistic known as *multiple correlation* (represented by R). Conceptually, R is quite similar to r. Multiple correlations are particularly useful to augment information gained from simple correlations. For example, let us say that we took three measurements (age, amount of television viewing, and vocabulary) for a large sample of children, whose ages varied from a few days old to 10 years old. We might find that a large multiple correlation was obtained ($R = +.61$), showing that age, television viewing, and vocabulary are interrelated. Not too surprising, really, because infants do not watch TV or know any words, but as children get older they watch more TV and also learn more words. But this multiple correlation would tend to put a damper on a hypothesis that watching TV increases vocabulary, wouldn't it? More likely, both television time and vocabulary are age-related changes. The multiple correlation does not explain why the three measures are related, but it suggests the hypothesis that age is an important third variable that could be explored in subsequent research.

Another common correlational procedure that is used when many behaviors are measured from each individual is called *factor analysis,* which allows us to see the degree of relationship among many traits or behaviors at the same time. Now that computers are available for statistical data analysis, researchers quite frequently use complicated statistical procedures, like multiple correlations and factor analysis. When many measures are taken, those measures that are most strongly intercorrelated are grouped together by the analysis as "factors." Factor analysis is commonly used in personality research. Over the years hundreds of trait dimensions (warm/cold, shy/sociable, dominant/submissive) have been measured by researchers, but factor analysis routinely groups them into only a few basic factors (Cattell, 1946), such as sociability, agreeableness, conscientiousness, emotionality, and culture. Many researchers now believe that a few basic factors underlie all human personality structure.

Another correlational method that handles multiple behavioral measures is *path analysis.* In path analysis, the researcher creates models of possible causal sequences of related behaviors. For example, Serbin and her colleagues (1990) were interested in trying to explain differences between boys' and girls' academic performance in elementary school. They suspected that different things could influence girls and boys. Through path analysis, they confirmed that the best models to predict school performance differed for boys and girls. Socioeconomic and parental education factors were important for predicting success in all the children. But beyond these factors, girls' performance in the lower grades seemed to be better accounted for by social responsiveness and willingness to follow directions. Boys' academic performance, however, was better predicted by their level of visual/spatial skills. Obviously, path analysis is another descriptive method, but it generates important information for

(continued)

BOX **2-3**
(continued)

experimental hypotheses. It is limited, however, in an important way. The models can only be constructed using the behaviors that have been measured. If a researcher omits an important behavior, it will be missing in the model too.

---

minus) tells us the positive or negative *direction* of the relationship; the absolute value of *r* (the unsigned value) tells us the *strength* of the relationship. Correlation coefficients can be depicted on a number line going from −1.00 to +1.00 (we always carry correlation coefficients out to two decimal points).

You will notice that a collection of dots is shown in each section of Figure 2-3. These dots illustrate what researchers call **scatterplots,** which are visual representations of the scores belonging to each subject in the study. Each dot stands for one subject. Each subject has two scores—one for TV viewing time and one for vocabulary. One score is used to place the dot along the *X* (horizontal) axis. The second score is used to place the dot along the *Y* (vertical) axis.

Scatterplots are often the researcher's first step toward analyzing correlational data. As you can see, the arrangement of dots gives a rough indication of both the direction and strength of relationship that has been measured. Figure 2-3 depicts three possible correlational outcomes for the TV viewing and vocabulary study. In Figure 2-3(a), the scatterplot shows that as viewing increased, vocabulary also increased (a positive relationship). In Figure 2-3(b), as viewing increased, vocabulary declined (a negative relationship). In Figure 2-3(c), the dots form no particular pattern (no strong relationship). This is reflected in the value of the computed *r,* which is quite small (+.02).

The lines drawn on the scatterplots are called **regression lines,** or lines of best fit. They illustrate the mathematical equation[3] that best describes the relationship between the two measured scores. The direction of the line corresponds to the direction of the relationship. As you can see, the position of the line changes as the correlation changes.

When the computed value of *r* is positive, there is a **positive correlation** between vocabulary and TV viewing time: The more a person watches television, the larger his or her vocabulary. This is also called a *direct relationship.* The absolute (unsigned) value of *r* tells us how strong the relationship is. If $r = +1.00$, we have a perfect positive correlation, and we can predict the value of one measure with complete accuracy if we know a subject's score on the other measure. Positive values of *r* that are less than +1.00 (for example, +.52) tell us there is a direct relationship between our two measures, but we cannot predict the value of one from the other with complete accuracy because the relationship between them is imperfect. If the value of *r* is relatively small (for example, +.02), our prediction may be

---

[3] These equations are called *regression equations,* and they are used as formulas to predict one score from the other.

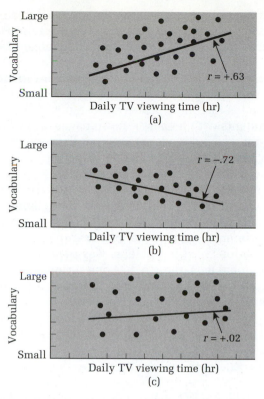

FIGURE **2-3** Some hypothetical relationships between size of vocabulary and length of daily TV viewing: (a) a positive (direct) relationship; (b) a negative (inverse) relationship; (c) no strong relationship.

no more accurate than any random guess. In that event the correlation would not be very useful.

A second possibility is a **negative correlation** between vocabulary and TV viewing time (that is, *r* is negative). This would mean that the more a person watches television, the smaller his or her vocabulary. This is also called an *inverse relationship*. One of the most difficult concepts to grasp about correlations is that the direction of the relationship (positive or inverse) does not affect our ability to predict scores. We could predict vocabulary just as well from a negative correlation as from a positive one, provided that the strength of the relationships was the same. You will recall that the strength of the relationship is indexed by the absolute (or unsigned) value of *r*. A correlation of *r* = −.34 actually represents a stronger relationship than *r* = +.16. The sign merely tells us whether the relationship is direct or inverse; the absolute value tells us how strong it is. As the absolute value gets larger, we can make more and more accurate predictions of a person's score on one measure when we know the person's score on the other.

A third possibility is no relationship between vocabulary and TV viewing time (*r* is near zero). In that event we would not learn anything about a person's vocabulary through knowledge of his or her television habits.

It is easy to see that correlations provide information that can be quite useful. The reason that universities ask for SAT or ACT scores from entering freshmen is that these scores show a positive correlation with college grades. Students with higher admissions test scores tend to also get better grades in college. But obviously the predictive power is not perfect—you may even know someone with outstanding SAT scores whose college course grades are only mediocre (or worse).

Because they are so useful and are relatively easy to conduct, correlational studies are used by researchers in every branch of psychology. They have become indispensible in many areas that cannot be investigated using experimental approaches. For example, the link between smoking and many serious health problems was revealed from correlational studies. Correlational data, though, has one serious drawback.

When we are dealing with correlational data, we cannot make causal inferences: *Correlation does not prove causation*. In other words, even though a relationship exists between two measures, we cannot say that one causes the other, even when such a statement appears reasonable. The fact that two measures are strongly related does not prove that one is responsible for the occurrence of the other. Over the last hundred years, there has probably been a correlation between the number of automobiles and the number of airplanes in the world. But it would be illogical to say that automobiles cause airplanes or vice versa.

Another look at the earlier example of studying the effects of TV violence on aggressiveness illustrates the limitations of trying to explain the cause of behavior from correlational studies. It would not be difficult to correlate the amount of time a person spends watching television violence with some measure of trait aggressiveness (indeed, similar studies have been done many times since the advent of TV!). Let us imagine that we actually carried out this study and found that exposure to TV violence and aggressiveness were strongly related. Can we say that violent TV causes aggressiveness? No.

No matter how reasonable this hypothesis sounds, we have not established that TV violence causes aggression. Why not? Because, in addition to our hypothesis that aggression is produced by exposure to TV violence, there are three alternative possibilities. First (as we noted earlier in the chapter), innate aggressiveness may determine a preference for violent TV—not the other way around. Second, some third agent may actually be causing the two behaviors to seem to be related. (Could this explain the automobile/airplane relationship?) This is known as the "third-variable" problem. Perhaps a preference for violent TV and a tendency toward aggressiveness both result from underactive autonomic nervous system functioning. Violence produces negative arousal in many individuals, and so does aggressiveness, but it may be that some people are less aversely affected than others. Less arousable individuals may be able to both watch more violent TV and behave more aggressively. A third causal alternative is also plausible with correlated behaviors like TV violence and aggressiveness. It is possible that innate aggressiveness results in more exposure to TV violence, but at the same time, the more exposure a person has, the more aggressive she or he becomes. The behaviors may affect each other. This is called "bidirectional causation." Because either of these alternatives is possible, inferring that TV violence is the cause of aggression would have been an unjustified conclusion. But even though a causal statement is not justified, it *would* be appropriate to predict an individual's aggressiveness by how much violent TV the person watched.

In an experiment we are able to establish causality by setting up at least two different treatment conditions and evaluating their effects on behavior. If we can specify exactly the conditions that will lead to a particular behavior, we have explained the occurrence of that behavior and may say that a particular set of conditions caused that behavior. This is not possible in the correlational study because we do not manipulate the conditions under which we are testing; we simply measure what occurs and ask whether two dimensions are related to each other. It is important to remember that correlational studies are limited by the way data are obtained—not by the statistical methods used to analyze them. Like the other nonexperimental methods we have discussed, correlational studies aid us in setting up hypotheses suitable for experimental study, they can suggest meaningful explanations of behavior, and they can help us to predict one behavior from another.

Ex Post Facto Studies

Often, researchers are interested in the effects of traits, behaviors, or naturally occurring events that cannot or should not be manipulated by a researcher. In those cases the researcher may choose to do an **ex post facto study**—that is, a study in which the researcher systematically examines the effects of subject characteristics (often called *subject variables*) but without actually manipulating them. The researcher forms treatment groups on the basis of differences that already exist between subjects (Kerlinger, 1973).

Ex post facto means "after the fact." In effect, the researcher capitalizes on changes in the antecedent conditions that occurred before the study. The result is a study that looks a great deal like an experiment, with the important exception that the antecedent conditions have not been manipulated by the experimenter. The experimenter also has no direct control over who belongs to each of the treatment groups of the study. These studies generally fall in the low-high portion of Figure 2-1.

Preexisting differences define membership in different treatment groups in the study: Shirley's father died last year, so Shirley is placed in a group of subjects who have experienced the loss of a parent. Subjects come into an ex post facto study with attributes that already differ from one subject to another. The differences are used as the basis for separating them into groups (for example, extroverts, introverts), and the researcher then looks for differences in behavior that are related to group membership.

The ex post facto approach has some special advantages. Like the correlational study, it deals with things as they occur. There is no manipulation of the conditions that interest the researcher. However, the ex post facto study allows a researcher to zero in on those occurrences in a more systematic way. Instead of studying the whole range of people along a particular dimension (extremely introverted to extremely extroverted), the focus can be on a carefully chosen subset. Typically, the ex post facto researcher studies the extremes, the subjects who rank highest and lowest on the dimension of interest. This increases the likelihood that the researcher will be able to see the effects of changes along that dimension more clearly.

In addition, ex post facto studies are generally done with many of the same rigorous control procedures used in experiments. The researcher makes a prediction in advance and attempts to test it in the most objective way. We may think of the ex post facto approach as a bridge between nonexperimental and experimental approaches. Systematically forming groups based on differences in preexisting characteristics is a critical feature of an ex post facto study, but it also prevents such a study from being classified as a true experiment.

In a true experiment, there should be no systematic differences between people in different treatment conditions. As we will see in Chapter 6, guarding against these kinds of systematic differences is an important benchmark of true experiments. Experimenters typically use a method known as *random assignment of subjects* to create treatment groups in which any preexisting differences in people are distributed evenly across all the treatment groups. In an ex post facto study, those preexisting differences become the "manipulation," and measuring the effects they produce is the objective of the research.

Franklin, Janoff-Bulman, and Roberts (1990) were interested in studying the potential effects of divorce on attitudes and beliefs of children. Using an ex post facto study, they assessed whether college-age children of divorced parents held different beliefs about themselves and other people than college students who came from intact families. Franklin et al. were interested in measuring these subjects' beliefs about the world in general, about people in general, about their own self-worth, and about interpersonal relationships. Interestingly, they found no differences between the two groups of college students on any of the first three kinds of beliefs. Both groups reported similar beliefs about the world, others, and themselves. Differences *were* found, though, on beliefs about relationships—especially on issues related to love and marriage. As a group, the students from divorced families reported more accepting attitudes toward divorce and more pessimistic beliefs about their own success in a marriage. Students with divorced parents believed that they were less likely to have a long and successful marriage than the students whose parents had stayed together. Using an ex post facto study, the researchers were able to thus demonstrate that a life event, the divorce of parents, does not *seem* to have global, negative effects on children's belief systems. Instead, divorce *seemed* to influence only a narrow range of beliefs, those related to the possibility of divorce in their own future.

A strong word of caution. Because the kinds of effects Franklin et al. (1990) found were very closely related to the event used to classify subjects into groups, it would be tempting to make a causal inference—to say that divorce *alters* beliefs about marriage and divorce. However, because the researchers did not create the group differences but instead relied on a naturally occurring event, there is no way to be certain that the effects were actually produced by the *ex post facto variable* and not by something else. It is always possible that something other than divorce was the actual cause: Perhaps the parents held similar pessimistic attitudes about marriage before the divorce. The parents' negative expectations may have caused both the divorce and their children's pessimistic attitudes about marriage. You may have noticed that this is the same problem that we encountered with correlational studies—that nemesis of nonexperimental designs—the third variable. Therefore we cannot explain behavior from an ex post facto study. We can, however, learn a great deal of useful information.

In addition to studying physical attributes (like gender or handedness) and life events (like divorce or the loss of a limb), researchers often use ex post facto studies to learn more about the behavioral ramifications of individual differences in psychological functioning and personality processes. As you can probably guess, we cannot study mental illness or personality in a strictly experimental manner. How would we go about manipulating antisocial personality disorder, Type A behavior, or agoraphobia to create the tendency we want to study? If we *could* devise procedures that would accomplish that goal, would we really want to use them?

The ex post facto approach enables us to explore many dimensions that we could not or would not choose to study experimentally. For that reason, it is a very useful source of information. For example, using an ex post facto design, researchers recently discovered that a person's coping style when faced with a negative experience could be important in the treatment of cancer patients (Ward, Leventhal, & Love, 1988). Ward et al. studied cancer patients who had been identified as either repressors or nonrepressors. Repressors are individuals who minimize negative emotional experiences. (You may remember the theory of repression from studying Sigmund Freud.) A repressive or nonrepressive coping style can be reliably identified by a personality questionnaire.

Using interviews and questionnaires to measure the patients' symptom-related behavior, the researchers found important differences between the two kinds of people. Repressors were much less likely than nonrepressors to report awareness of either cancer treatment side effects or symptoms of their illness. Even though these differences cannot be explained, the information may be very important for the prevention and treatment of cancer. As the researchers noted, repressors may be less likely to notice cancer symptoms and seek early treatment. Once the disease is diagnosed, however, repressors may actually cope better with cancer treatment.

Despite its limitations, the ex post facto approach is a useful technique that allows us to demonstrate that certain predictable relationships exist. We can establish, for instance, that gender, or personality traits, or mental disorders are associated with particular patterns of behavior. In some respects, ex post facto studies are more useful than certain kinds of experimental studies because they provide more realistic data. However, when it is possible to experiment, the experiment is preferred because it allows us to draw conclusions about cause and effect that we cannot make on the basis of ex post facto data.

The nonexperimental approaches are *descriptive* rather than *explanatory,* because they focus on naturally occurring events. No attempt is made to manipulate or control antecedent conditions systematically. Subjects cannot always be observed under carefully specified treatment conditions. This can make replication difficult. For these reasons, the nonexperimental approaches cannot be used to establish cause and effect explanations of behavior. When we wish to confirm cause and effect relationships, experimentation is required. Despite their limitations, these approaches are important adjuncts to experimentation. Without attention to our own experience and the ongoing activities around us, we would miss a great deal of relevant psychological data. The nonexperimental approaches lack the artificiality that is sometimes criticized in experimental research. In fact, they are often used as the sources of experimental hypotheses that lead to further research. We will return to some of them again in our next chapter, which deals with formulating a hypothesis.

SUMMARY

Research activities may be described along two dimensions: degree of manipulation of antecedent conditions and degree of constraint on subjects' responses. Laboratory experiments tend to fall at the high end of both dimensions, representing only a small portion of the possible research options.

We have looked at five major nonexperimental approaches to data collection: phenomenology, case studies, field studies, correlational studies, and ex post facto studies. Although these approaches differ in detail, they share certain features that distinguish them from the experimental approach.

Phenomenology is the description of one's own immediate experience. Rather than looking out at behaviors in the world, the phenomenological approach requires that we begin with our own experience as a source of data. Phenomenological data are limited in two main respects: Since we do not compare subjects under different conditions, we cannot make cause and effect statements about our experience. We also have no way of knowing whether attending to our experience alters it. What we observe may not be completely accurate or objective.

The *case study* is used to study individuals. It is a descriptive record made by an outside observer of an individual's experiences and/or behaviors that may be used to make inferences about developmental processes, the impact of life events, a person's level of functioning, and the origin of disorders. The record may be made systematically over a period of time or after the fact, as is often the case in clinical practice. This approach enables us to study a variety of life events we would not study experimentally.

Field studies are studies done in real-life settings. They allow us to explore behavior that we probably would not see in the laboratory. But these studies have some limitations. We cannot make inferences about cause and effect relationships on the basis of a field study because we do not manipulate the conditions.

Field studies include a variety of techniques for collecting data. *Naturalistic observation* is the technique of observing events as they occur in their natural setting and is a common component of field research. It is a descriptive method. During naturalistic observation, the observer remains unobtrusive so that the behaviors being observed are not altered by the presence of an intruder. This approach allows us to study behaviors that would be distorted or absent in the laboratory. It also gives us the chance to verify the accuracy of findings that were obtained in the laboratory.

In addition to observing behaviors, the researcher may interact with the subjects in a field study. Interviews may be conducted. Various *unobtrusive measures* may be used to assess behavior without subjects' knowledge.

Correlational studies may be run in the laboratory or in the field. A correlational study is done to determine the *correlation,* or degree of relationship, between two or more traits, behaviors, or events. First, the variables of interest are measured; then the degree of relationship between them is established through statistical procedures. When two measures are correlated, we can more accurately predict the value of one if we know the value of the other. But we cannot infer cause and effect from a correlation. Relationships between three or more measures can also be investigated using more complicated correlational methods, such as multiple correlation, factor analysis, and path analysis.

Ex post facto studies are a bridge between the nonexperimental and the experimental methods. In an ex post facto study, the researcher uses preexisting characteristics to separate subjects into groups. The researcher then looks for differences in behaviors as a function of group membership. Typically, the ex post facto study involves factors that cannot or should not be studied experimentally. Predictions are made and tested through many of the same techniques that are used in experiments.

KEY TERMS

Case study   The descriptive record of an individual's experiences and/or behaviors kept by an outside observer that may be used to make inferences about developmental processes, the impact of life events, a person's level of functioning, and the origin of disorders.

Correlation The degree of relationship between two or more traits, behaviors, or events.

Correlational study A study designed to determine the correlation between two or more traits, behaviors, or events.

Deviant case analysis An extension of the evaluative case study in which deviant individuals are compared with those who are not to isolate the significant variations between them and perhaps explain the origin of the deviance.

Ex post facto study A study in which a researcher systematically examines the effects of preexisting subject characteristics (often called "subject variables") by forming treatment groups on the basis of the differences that already exist between subjects.

External validity The degree to which the findings of an experiment apply to situations not tested directly; their generalizability to the real world.

Field study A nonexperimental research method used in the field or in a real-life setting, typically employing a variety of techniques including naturalistic observation, unobtrusive measures, and interviews.

Internal validity The degree to which a researcher is able to establish a causal relationship between a specified set of antecedent conditions (treatments) and the subsequent observed behavior; the soundness of the procedures within an experiment.

Naturalistic observation A descriptive technique used in nonexperimental research of observing behaviors as they occur spontaneously in natural settings.

Negative correlation The relationship existing between two variables such that an increase in one is associated with a decrease in the other; also called an "inverse relationship."

Phenomenology A nonexperimental method of gathering data by attending to and describing one's own immediate experience.

Positive correlation The relationship between two measures such that an increase in the value of one is associated with an increase in the value of the other; also called a "direct relationship."

Regression line The line of best fit; represents the equation that best describes the mathematical relationship between two variables measured in a correlational study.

Retrospective data The data collected in the present based on recollections of past events; apt to be inaccurate because of faulty memory, bias, mood, and situation.

Scatterplot A graph of data created by plotting the value of one variable on the X (horizontal) axis and the other variable on the Y (vertical) axis for each subject in a correlational study.

Unobtrusive measure A procedure used to assess subjects' behaviors without their knowledge; used to obtain more objective data.

REVIEW AND STUDY QUESTIONS

1. Describe each of these nonexperimental approaches and give an example of how each might be used: (1) phenomenology, (2) case study, (3) field study, (4) correlational study, (5) ex post facto study.
2. What is meant by external validity? Why does it concern researchers?
3. What are some advantages and disadvantages of the nonexperimental approaches?
4. What is retrospective data? Why is the use of retrospective data a shortcoming?
5. For each of the research topics listed below, indicate the type of nonexperimental approach that would be most useful and explain why. (You may find more than one approach potentially useful for some topics.)
   a. Pushing ahead in line
   b. Daydreaming
   c. Locating the most popular painting in an art gallery
   d. Determining if hot weather is associated with higher rates of violence in the streets
   e. Studying whether first-born children are more likely to help others than later-born children
   f. Determining whether a particular patient has improved with psychotherapy
   g. Predicting the outcome of an election
   h. Predicting schizophrenia from autonomic arousal in childhood
6. For each of your answers to question 5, explain whether an experiment would generate more useful information than the nonexperimental method you selected. Would it be possible to set up experiments to explore all these problems? If not, why not?
7. What are unobtrusive measures?
8. Devise an unobtrusive measure to establish each of the following:
   a. Which professor at the university is the most popular?
   b. What are the most popular library books?
   c. Do people prefer to sit on the left or the right side of the theater when they go to the movies?
   d. If people find addressed letters with stamps on them, will they mail them?
9. Explain the meaning of the statement "Correlation does not prove causation."
10. Jack just computed the Pearson Product Moment Correlation Coefficient for two sets of data. He got $r = +2.3$. Jack is thrilled, marveling at what a large relationship he found. What can he conclude from his findings?
11. A college administrator has located a new aptitude test that is correlated with academic achievement ($r = -.54$). The admissions committee of the college now uses a screening test also correlated with aca-

demic achievement, but the correlation is $r = +.45$. Which test would be a better choice if the admissions committee is interested in predicting how well prospective students would do at the school?

REFERENCES

BECHTOL, B., & WILLIAMS, J. (1977). California litter. *Natural History, 86*(6), 62–65.

BORING, E. G. (1950). *A history of experimental psychology* (2nd ed.). New York: Appleton-Century-Crofts.

CATTELL, R. B. (1946). *Description and measurement of personality.* New York: World Book.

CLECKLEY, J. (1976). *The mask of sanity* (5th ed.). St. Louis, MO: C. V. Mosby.

CUNNINGHAM, M. R. (1989). Reactions to heterosexual opening gambits: Female selectivity and male responsiveness. *Personality and Social Psychology Bulletin, 15*(1), 27–41.

DAVISON, G. C., & NEALE, J. M. (1986). *Abnormal psychology: An experimental clinical approach.* New York: Wiley.

Diagnostic and statistical manual of mental disorders, third edition, revised. (1987). Washington, DC: American Psychiatric Association.

FRANKLIN, K. M., JANOFF-BULMAN, R., & ROBERTS, J. E. (1990). Long-term impact of parental divorce on optimism and trust: Changes in general assumptions or narrow beliefs? *Journal of Personality and Social Psychology, 59*(4), 743–755.

FREUD, S. (1962). Analysis of a phobia in a five-year-old boy. In *The complete psychological works of Sigmund Freud* (Vol. X). London: Hogarth. (Original work published 1909.)

JACOBSON, E. (1971). *Depression.* New York: International Universities Press.

JAMES, W. (1950). *Principles of psychology.* New York: Dover. (Original work published 1890.)

KERLINGER, F. N. (1973). *Foundations of behavioral research* (2nd ed.). New York: Holt, Rinehart and Winston.

KOLB, L. C. (1973). *Modern clinical psychiatry* (8th ed.). Philadelphia: Saunders.

MEDNICK, S. A. (1969). A longitudinal study of children with a high risk for schizophrenia. In M. Zax & G. Stricker (Eds.), *The study of abnormal behavior.* London: Macmillan.

MEDNICK, S. A., SCHULSINGER, F., & VENABLES, P. H. (1981). The Mauritius project. In S. A. Mednick, A. Baert, & B. P. Bachmann (Eds.), *Prospective longitudinal research* (pp. 314–316). Oxford: Oxford University Press.

MILLER, D. (1977). Roles of naturalistic observation in comparative psychology. *American Psychologist, 32*(3), 211–219.

ROBINSON, P. W. (1976). *Fundamentals of experimental psychology.* Englewood Cliffs, NJ: Prentice-Hall.

SACKETT, G. P. (1978). *Observing behavior (vol. II): Data collection and analysis methods.* Baltimore: University Park Press.

SERBIN, L. A., ZELKOWITZ, P., DOYLE, A., GOLD, D., & WHEATON, B. (1990). The socialization of sex-differentiated skills and academic performance: A mediational model. *Sex Roles, 23*(11/12), 613–628.

VELTEN, H. V. (1943). The growth of phonemic and lexical patterns in infant language. *Language, 19,* 281–292.

WARD, S. E., LEVENTHAL, H., & LOVE, R. (1988). Repression revisited: Tactics used in coping with a severe health threat. *Personality and Social Psychology Bulletin, 14*(4), 735–746.

WILLEMS, E. P. (1969). Planning a rationale for naturalistic research. In E. P. Willems & H. L. Raush (Eds.), *Naturalistic viewpoints in psychological research.* New York: Holt, Rinehart and Winston.

3

Formulating the Hypothesis

The Characteristics of an Experimental Hypothesis
Synthetic Statements
Testable Statements
Falsifiable Statements
Parsimonious Statements
Fruitful Statements

The Inductive Model

The Deductive Model

Combining Induction and Deduction

Building on Prior Research

Serendipity and the Windfall Hypothesis

Intuition

When All Else Fails

Summary

Key Terms

Review and Study Questions

References

The term *hypothesis* has appeared a number of times in the preceding chapters. You now know that the psychology experiment is designed to test hypotheses about the effect of different treatment conditions on behavior. In this chapter we will concentrate on the experimental hypothesis in detail. We will look at the differences between experimental and nonexperimental hypotheses and then turn our attention to hypotheses for experimental designs—the major focus of the chapter. We will look at the characteristics of the experimental hypothesis and discuss several ways of arriving at hypotheses suitable for experimental study: induction, deduction, building on prior research, serendipity, and intuition.

The hypothesis represents the end of the long process of thinking about a research idea. The **hypothesis** is the thesis, or main idea, of an experiment. It is a statement about a predicted relationship between at least two variables. Some nonscientific synonyms are *inkling, conjecture, guess,* and *hunch.*

The statement of a research hypothesis is designed to fit the type of research design that has been selected. You know from Chapter 2 that nonexperimental designs are used to demonstrate relationships between sets of behaviors, but they may not be used to infer a cause and effect relationship between them. For this reason, a **nonexperimental hypothesis** is a statement of your predictions of how events, traits, or behaviors might be related—not a statement about cause and effect. In a true experiment, the hypothesis predicts the effects of specific antecedent conditions on some behavior that is to be measured.

Some nonexperimental designs, particularly those that do not restrict subjects' responses, do not typically include a hypothesis. Phenomenology, naturalistic observation, and case studies, for instance, are primarily intended to explore and describe behaviors as they occur naturally. And it would be difficult to make guesses about behaviors or events that may or may not occur.

Other nonexperimental designs, like correlational and ex post facto studies, generally include hypotheses about predicted relationships between variables. The following sentences are examples of nonexperimental hypotheses: "The amount of television viewing will be directly related to vocabulary size." "College grades should be related to subjects' SAT scores." "Repressors will report fewer treatment-related side effects than nonrepressors." Nonexperimental hypotheses are straightforward predictions of the relationships the researcher expects to find between variables.

THE CHARACTERISTICS OF AN EXPERIMENTAL HYPOTHESIS

Every experiment has at least one hypothesis. Complicated experimental designs that compare several treatments at the same time may test various hypotheses simultaneously. Each **experimental hypothesis** is a tentative explanation of an event or behavior. It is a statement that predicts the effects of specified antecedent conditions on a measured behavior.

By the time you are ready to formulate your hypothesis, you have already thought a great deal about a behavior. You may have discarded several improbable explanations of it and are ready to propose one particular explanation that seems plausible.

Suppose you began to make a list of all the conditions that could affect a particular behavior. Say the behavior is the speed at which you are reading this book. The factors that affect your reading speed include the style in which this text is written and your average reading speed. Your pace might also be affected by the amount of noise outside, the amount of light in the room, and whether or not you have eaten lunch. Perhaps it is even affected by the number of people who are now singing in Tibet or the number of shrimp in the ocean. Clearly, an enormous number of factors might affect your behavior at any given time. Before doing an experiment to determine which factors were critical to your reading speed, you would obviously want to narrow down the possibilities.

Things far removed from one another are not likely to be causally related. Thus we would not consider the shrimp population as a likely explanation for reading speed. Similarly, we would not spend much time on the people in Tibet. However, factors such as writing style, your normal reading speed, and lighting probably do determine your speed. If you have not had lunch, your images of food will certainly reduce your speed.

This process of whittling away at the number of possible factors affecting your reading speed is the key to formulating a hypothesis. Now that we have selected a small, finite number of possibilities, we are ready to propose an explanation for your reading speed. We are ready to state a hypothesis.

In order to be scientific, each hypothesis should meet certain basic criteria. As you will see, the criteria have very little to do with personal beliefs or attitudes. Believing that something is true or interesting is not enough to make it a useful hypothesis. Hypotheses must be synthetic statements that are testable, parsimonious, and we hope fruitful.

Synthetic Statements

Synthetic statements are those that can be either true or false. Psychologists have borrowed the terminology from the field of logic. Each experimental hypothesis must be a synthetic statement so there is some chance it is true and some chance it is false. "Hungry students read slowly" is a synthetic statement that can be supported or contradicted. An experiment designed to test it will yield information we can use to decide between the two possibilities; deciding whether we believe the statement "Hungry students read slowly" is true or false will add to our knowledge.

Nonsynthetic statements should be avoided at all costs. These fall into two categories: analytic or contradictory. An **analytic statement** is one that is always true; for example, "I am pregnant or I am not pregnant." Clearly, even the best constructed experiment could not disprove that statement because the statement itself can explain all possible outcomes. Sometimes we inadvertently generate analytic-type statements by failing to state our predictions adequately: "The weight of dieters will fluctuate." "Working mothers will have various relationships with their children." These are essentially analytic statements because they are sufficiently vague to be true for everyone. Everyone's weight fluctuates a bit, whether dieting or not. Unless all working mothers and all children are the same and live in identical environments, the mother/child relationships will undoubtedly vary. When stating a hypothesis, we want to be concise enough to be proven wrong. Fence-sitting will not do.

Similarly, we want to avoid making **contradictory statements**; that is, statements that are always false. "I have a brother and I do not have a brother" is an example of a contradictory statement.

If we propose hypotheses in the form of analytic or contradictory statements, our experiments will provide no useful information. Since analytic statements are always true and contradictory statements are always false, we do not need to conduct experiments to test them: We already know what the outcome will be.

In order to ensure that a hypothesis is a synthetic statement, we must evaluate its form. A hypothesis meets the definition of a synthetic statement when it can be stated in what is known as the "If . . . then" form. This form is another way of expressing the potential relationship between the antecedents and the behaviors to be measured:[1] "If you look at an appealing photograph, then your pupils will dilate" is such a hypothesis. It expresses a potential relationship between a particular antecedent condition (being shown an appealing photograph) and a behavior (pupil dilation). The statement can be true or false. Perhaps the content of a photograph has no effect on the pupils. Similarly, consider the saying, "Adversity builds character." This might be considered a hypothesis concerning the way in which life experiences affect character development. Is this a synthetic statement? Yes, it is. This statement can be easily translated into the "If . . . then" form: "If you have experienced difficult life circumstances, then you will have character." Again, this statement may be true or false. Difficult experiences do not necessarily guarantee positive character development.

---

[1] Ex post facto hypotheses can also be stated in this form, as illustrated by the following: "If people are repressors, then they report few treatment side effects."

Testable Statements

An experimental hypothesis must also be **testable.** That is, the means for manipulating antecedent conditions and measuring the resulting behavior must exist. There are many interesting hypotheses that are currently of no scientific use because they do not meet this criterion. For example, have you ever wondered whether your dog dreams? Some people hypothesize that dogs dream because they exhibit behaviors that resemble the behaviors associated with dream reports in humans—rapid eye movements, muscle twitches, even occasional vocalizations. Suppose we propose a research hypothesis in the "If . . . then" form: "If dogs display rapid eye movements, muscle twitches, and vocalizations during sleep, then they must be dreaming."

We now have a hypothesis in proper form. How do we proceed? We might observe dogs sleeping under various conditions. We could manipulate any number of antecedents to encourage sleep. We might start with a simple comparison of dogs fed warm food versus those fed food at room temperature. Some might sleep more than others. But how will we know if they are dreaming? We can ask them, of course, although we cannot expect any useful answers. The difficulty here is that we have an interesting but alas untestable hypothesis. The means for observing and recording the behavior of interest—namely, dreaming in dogs—does not exist.

Still, untestable hypotheses are not necessarily useless. Scientists who speculated on what it would be like to walk on the moon probably generated quite a few untestable hypotheses at the start. But there is always the hope that new technology will open new areas of discovery. Some day perhaps dreams will be projected on televisions. We will then know not only whether dogs dream but—if they do—what they are dreaming about. In the meantime, if you are reading this book as part of a course assignment, it will be to your advantage to work with hypotheses you can test.

Falsifiable Statements

Statements of research hypotheses must be *falsifiable* (disprovable) by the research findings. Hypotheses need to be constructed so that failures to find the predicted effect *must* be considered evidence that the hypothesis is indeed false. Consider the following (purely illustrative) "If . . . then" statement: "If you read this book carefully enough, then you will be able to design a good experiment." Suppose you carefully read the book, spending hours on each chapter, and after you finish we ask you to design an experiment. You come up with an experiment, but your design is not very good. Given the wording of the statement (it contains the qualifier *enough*), would we be willing to accept this evidence that our book did not teach experimental methods very well? More likely, we would be tempted to say that you simply did not read it carefully *enough*. As the hypothesis was worded, it simply is not falsifiable, because any failures to produce the predicted effect can be explained away by the researcher.

Parsimonious Statements

A research hypothesis should also be *parsimonious*. You will recall from Chapter 1 that parsimony means that the simplest explanation is preferred. Thus a simple hypothesis is preferred over one that requires many supporting assumptions. The hypothesis "If you look at an appealing photograph, then your pupils will dilate" would be preferred over "If you look at an appealing photograph, then your pupils will dilate if it is a warm Saturday in June."

Fruitful Statements

Ideally, a hypothesis is also fruitful; that is, it leads to new studies. It is often difficult to know in advance which hypotheses will be the most fruitful.

There is some indication that a hypothesis is fruitful when we can think of new studies that will become important if the hypothesis is supported. An example of a fruitful hypothesis is Watson and Rayner's 1920 study of classical conditioning. They hypothesized that fear of otherwise neutral objects could be acquired through learning. Their hypothesis might be stated in the "If . . . then" form as follows: "If a child, Albert, is repeatedly exposed to a loud, cry-inducing noise in the presence of a harmless furry animal, then Albert will begin to cry at the sight of the animal alone." This hypothesis and its confirmation led to a multitude of studies on classical conditioning in human subjects that continue today.

We have considered what may seem like an overwhelming number of criteria for a good hypothesis. The good hypothesis is a synthetic statement of the "If . . . then" form. It is testable, falsifiable, parsimonious, and fruitful. With so many criteria and so many areas of research, how does an experimenter ever arrive at a hypothesis? According to Bertrand Russell (1945), "As a rule, the framing of hypotheses is the most difficult part of scientific work, and the part where great ability is indispensable. So far, no method has been found which would make it possible to invent hypotheses by rule" (p. 545).

A number of general approaches describe the way in which hypotheses are most often formed. Although there are no rules that can be used to generate hypotheses, an understanding of these approaches will help you to think about the psychological issues you might like to study experimentally.

THE INDUCTIVE MODEL

The **inductive model** of formulating a hypothesis, the process of reasoning from specific cases to more general principles, is often used in science and mathematics. By examining individual instances, we may be able to construct an overall classification scheme to describe them.

Has something like this ever happened to you at a party? A stranger comes over to you and says: "You must be a Libran. I can tell by your beautiful clothes, your meticulous grooming, and the birthstone ring you're wearing." The stranger has tried a somewhat overworked conversation-starter—but it illustrates the basics of inductive thinking. He or she has taken certain specific facts about you (your style of dress and your manner) and used them to reach a more general conclusion about you—your birth sign. People of different signs are said to have different personality traits that are dependent on the sign of birth, as well as the positions of the planets at the exact time of birth. A person familiar with astrology may take certain specific facts about you and arrive at a hypothesis about your birth sign through induction.

Research hypotheses often come from the use of inductive reasoning. While in line at the dorm cafeteria, you may have noticed many instances of athletes (who tend to wear clothes advertising their sport) cutting to the front of the food line. You also notice that no one seems to challenge their behavior. You come up with your own explanation for this: Being identified as an athlete allows you privileges not available to nonathletes. This is a hypothesis that came about through induction. You observed several specific instances of behavior and used these instances to form a general principle to explain the behavior. You might be able to come up with an interesting idea for testing it experimentally.

B. F. Skinner (1904–1990) was a convincing advocate for inductive research in psychology. Skinner studied operant conditioning in rats and pigeons extensively. In operant conditioning, the organism is reinforced or rewarded when it produces a particular response, such as bar-pressing, which has been selected by the experimenter for reinforcement. Skinner studied many variations of the basic operant procedures, keeping careful records of what happened to behavior under various conditions. He tried giving reinforcement on some but not all occasions when the animal emitted the required response. He tried new reinforcement contingencies based solely on the number of responses emitted (one pellet of food for each three bar-presses) or on the elapsed time (one pellet of food per minute for one or more bar-presses). He tried withholding reinforcement after the response was well established. From the results of numerous experiments, Skinner developed the concepts of partial reinforcement and extinction, along with reliable descriptions of the way intermittent reinforcement alters behavior (Ferster & Skinner, 1957). Concepts essential to understanding the learning process grew out of Skinner's inductive approach.

Induction is the basic tool of theory building. A *theory* is a set of general principles that can be used to explain and predict behavior. Through induction, researchers construct theories by taking bits of empirical data and forming general explanatory schemes to accommodate those facts. While we may not put much faith in it, the 12 astrological signs represent a theory of behavior. Some scientific theories have been constructed on the work of a single researcher, such as Skinner. Other times, theories come about by assimilating the research of many experimenters into general explanatory principles. For instance, the theory of the "mere-exposure"

FIGURE **3-1** B. F. Skinner (1904–1990).
Brooks/Cole photo

effect came about as a result of reviewing the published results of many past experiments that seemed to zero in on the same conclusion: The more we are exposed to something, the more we like it (Zajonc, 1966). Over the years Zajonc and his students have refined the theory through experimentation, and its success can be seen by how often the theory is used as the basis of advertising and political campaigns.

THE DEDUCTIVE MODEL

The **deductive model** of formulating a hypothesis is the converse of the inductive model. Deduction is the process of reasoning from general principles to make predictions about specific instances. The deductive model is most useful when we have a well-developed theory with clearly stated basic premises. Then it is possible to deduce predictions about what should happen in new situations in which the theory would apply. Testing such predictions provides a test of the value of the theory.

An excellent example of the deductive method in psychology is research that stemmed from predictions generated by "equity theory" (Walster, Walster, & Berscheid, 1978). These psychologists were not the first to consider equity (or perceived fairness) an important determinant of behavior in human relationships. Philosophers like Aristotle also believed it was important. But Walster, Walster, and Berscheid provided a comprehensive and useful theory of equity in interpersonal situations. They proposed that the behavior of individuals could be predicted by three simple propositions:

1. Individuals will try to optimize their outcomes (outcomes = rewards minus costs).
2. When individuals believe they are in an inequitable relationship, they will feel distress in direct proportion to the perceived degree of inequity.
3. The more distress they feel, the harder they will work to restore equity.

The theory has been used by many researchers to predict behavior. It has successfully predicted outcomes in a great number of interpersonal circumstances: victimization, helping, employment, and love are a few. Apparently, whether we feel overbenefited or underbenefited in a relationship, we will do what we can to restore a sense of fairness. For example, Pritchard, Dunnette, and Jorgenson (1972) found that workers who *felt* they were overpaid relative to others doing the same job actually worked harder than other workers who believed they were paid less than others. (In actuality, the researchers manipulated the antecedent conditions so that everyone was really being paid the same wage.)

COMBINING INDUCTION AND DEDUCTION

We have looked at induction and deduction as two separate approaches to formulating a hypothesis. In practice, these approaches are not so neatly separated. As you might imagine, theorists like Walster, Walster, and Berscheid did not formulate equity theory without some reference to specific cases. They formulated the theory on the basis of their own and others' observations. In fact, the list of references used for the book describing their theory included over 500 such observations, which were used as evidence for the theory. Thus their propositions were formed initially through induction from specific cases. Later tests of the propositions were based on predictions derived from the propositions through deduction. Box 3-1 illustrates the importance of these processes in the work of the chemist Dmitri Mendeleyev.

Researchers in the field of memory have used a combination of inductive and deductive thinking to find an explanation for data that conflict with the multistage model of memory, which describes three distinct stages of human memory: sensory, short term, and long term. Each stage was assumed to have distinct characteristics. The multistage model was developed inductively on the basis of many experiments (for example, Peterson & Peterson, 1959; Sperling, 1960; Glanzer & Cunitz, 1966). Once the model was in place, researchers used deduction to formulate research hypotheses to test predictions from the model in specific instances.

One feature of the model was the premise that short-term memory, the kind of memory we use when rehearsing a phone number we just looked

BOX **3-1**
Dmitri Mendeleyev
and the periodic
table

The work of Dmitri Mendeleyev illustrates the use of induction to generate scientific hypotheses. Mendeleyev was a 19th-century chemist interested in devising a meaningful classification scheme for all 66 elements known at that time. He reviewed the atomic weight (the weight of a single atom as compared to a standard) and the typical properties of all the elements. Mendeleyev saw a pattern, a general relationship now known as the periodic law: When arranged according to their atomic weights, the elements show a periodical change in properties. From the patterns he observed, Mendeleyev was able to predict the discovery of a number of elements, as well as their properties (Partington, 1964). Although his classification scheme has been revised to incorporate newly discovered elements (there are now 109 in all), Mendeleyev's basic work remains a cornerstone of chemistry and physics.

Although we have discussed Mendeleyev as an example of an inductive thinker, his work also illustrates the complementary nature of induction and deduction. Mendeleyev saw a pattern in the atomic numbers of the elements and their properties. However, he also saw that some elements did not exactly fit this pattern. Having arrived at the general pattern through induction, Mendeleyev deduced that some of the atomic numbers on record were inaccurate. The probable course of Mendeleyev's thinking is represented schematically by Figure 3-2.

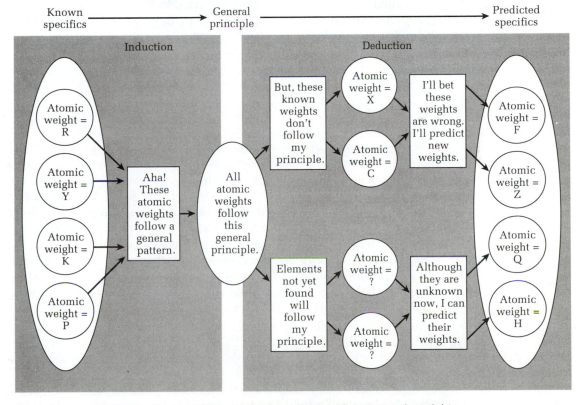

FIGURE **3-2**   Schematic representation of Mendeleyev's thinking on atomic weights.

up in the directory, encodes mainly acoustic information. That is, the sound of the items to be remembered is what is contained in short-term memory, which lasts about 15–20 seconds. Long-term memory is used to store semantic information (meaning), which lasts beyond 20 seconds and contains items such as recollections of our first days at school and what we did last Thursday.

One prediction that follows deductively from the multistage model is that it should be easier to recognize words that sound alike (homonyms) for items in short-term storage; conversely, it should be easier to recognize words with the same meaning (synonyms) for items in long-term storage. In fact, subjects were able to recognize homonyms and synonyms for words stored in both long- and short-term memory (Shulman, 1970; 1972): Acoustic and semantic information are encoded in both long-term and short-term memory. Shulman's studies are among several that have failed to confirm predictions based on the multistage model. More recent memory models (Craik & Lockhart, 1972; Cermak & Craik, 1979) favor a "levels-of-processing" explanation of memory: The more we do with incoming information, the better we remember it. Predictions based on the levels-of-processing explanation are in turn being tested, and so the research process continues.[2]

Both induction and deduction are important in research. Both are useful in formulating hypotheses for study. Through induction we devise general principles and theories that can be used to organize, explain, and predict behavior until more satisfactory principles are found. Through deduction we rigorously test the implications of those theories.

BUILDING ON PRIOR RESEARCH

So far we have discussed global approaches that can be applied to a variety of research topics. Now we will look at how the researcher narrows down the field of possibilities enough to formulate a single hypothesis. The most useful way of finding hypotheses is by working from research that has already been done. The nonexperimental studies we discussed in Chapter 2, for example, are a good source of ideas for experimentation. We may use nonexperimental studies to help narrow down the alternatives. However, to establish convincing cause and effect inferences, we must experiment; that is, we must manipulate the antecedents and observe the resultant change in behavior. Nonexperimental studies often *suggest* cause and effect explanations that can be translated into experimental hypotheses.

---

[2] For a more detailed discussion of memory research and the scientific process, see Lachman, R., Lachman, J. L., & Butterfield, E. C. (1979). *Cognitive psychology and information processing: An introduction*. Hillsdale, NJ: Erlbaum.

We will look briefly at two examples of the way in which this might be done.

The Bechtol and Williams (1977) study of California litter (discussed in Chapter 2) was a field study. Bechtol and Williams observed people on an unregulated beach in California to see who would litter. They concluded that everyone littered. Since the litter problem was more serious on this unregulated beach than on the state-operated beaches, we can ask a number of experimental questions about littering. The fact that everyone on the unregulated beach left trash suggests two possibilities.

First, perhaps the people who choose to use unregulated beaches are systematically different from people who do not. Perhaps they are more rebellious and hence more likely to flaunt convention by littering. Through their interviews Bechtol and Williams found that the users of the nonregulated beach were there because they could do things such as drink and make bonfires that were prohibited in the regulated areas. Thus we may state a hypothesis in the "If . . . then" form: "If people have rebellious personalities, then they will litter." We can explore different sets of antecedents through an ex post facto study. We can select two groups of people varying in personality. One group would have rebellious personalities, the other group would be conformists. If we took these groups to the beach, we would expect to find that those in the rebellious group litter more than those in the conformist group. We would then conclude that the antecedents (the personality differences) are related to differences in littering behavior. Notice that the Bechtol and Williams study suggests this explanation. Our ex post facto study clarifies the existence of the relationship. However, a true experiment (that is, creating rebellious and conformist subjects) would be required to establish a cause and effect relationship.

A second explanation for littering suggested by Bechtol and Williams is that there were no trash baskets on the unregulated beach. From this observation we may state another hypothesis about littering: "If there are no trash baskets, then people will litter." In this case, we *can* set up different antecedent conditions to test the hypothesis experimentally. We set up one beach with trash baskets and an identical beach without trash baskets. Let us assume that the people who use the two beaches are comparable. (You will learn more about why this is a critical assumption for all true experiments in Chapter 6.) Given our hypothesis, we would expect to find less litter on the beach that has trash baskets. If trash baskets have no effect on littering, we would find the same amount of litter accumulating on both beaches. If there is the predicted difference in litter for the two beaches, we conclude that the lack of trash baskets causes littering.

The other nonexperimental approaches may also lead to experimental hypotheses. One very important example is the research on cigarette smoking and cancer. At first, only correlational and ex post facto data were available. Researchers noted a positive correlation between smoking and lung cancer. In ex post facto studies, smokers had higher rates of lung cancer than nonsmokers. This suggested the hypothesis that smoking causes cancer. Stated in the "If . . . then" form: "If people smoke, then they will get cancer." Experimenters test the hypothesis under controlled conditions. Because of ethical issues, the subjects in these experiments are animals rather than humans: If smoking really does cause cancer, scientists would not want to expose human subjects to smoking. The experiments begin with the creation of different antecedent conditions—groups of rats are exposed to varying amounts of cigarette smoke. If rats who "smoke" develop higher rates of cancer than rats that do not, the conclusion is that smoking causes cancer. Again, the systematic manipulation of the antecedent conditions permits us to make cause and effect inferences that cannot be made on the basis of nonexperimental data alone.

It is also possible to get ideas for new hypotheses from prior experimental research. If you do not already have a specific hypothesis in mind, you will find the experimental literature useful in focusing your thinking on important issues. As you read more and more studies in an area, you may begin to see points that other researchers have missed or new applications for previously tested hypotheses. These may form the basis for new experiments. For instance, if you are interested in equity theory, reading what others have done can trigger ideas for new applications of the theory—perhaps feelings about the fairness of course grades would predict how many hours students are willing to put into a course. Other times, past research will suggest additional variables that could mediate an effect demonstrated in an experiment—perhaps littering is not directly caused by rebelliousness, but instead is mediated by the amount of alcohol consumed by rebellious sunbathers. By reading prior studies, you will also see the kinds of problems others have had in researching a topic. This will help you to anticipate difficulties you might not have thought of alone.

A literature search is facilitated by reference books like *Psychological Abstracts*.[3] Available in most university libraries, they contain abstracts (summaries) of previous research that has been published on your topic in the major psychological journals. Many university libraries now have computer-generated literature searches, making this job easier. You can now type in the topic that interests you, and the computer will generate a printout of the relevant *abstracts*. You still have to select the abstracts that seem most relevant to you, locate the journal articles, and read them.

Also, be on the lookout for edited volumes that contain chapters written by experts in your topic area. They often contain "review articles," chapters written to summarize research in a topic area. A particularly good source of information is a "meta-analysis" conducted on your topic, which can be found in journals or books. Meta-analysis is a statistical reviewing procedure that utilizes data from many similar studies to summarize research findings about individual topics. A meta-analysis has the added benefit of quantification of past findings—it uses special statistical procedures to measure how "strong" the cause and effect relationship between the antecedent conditions and measured behaviors appears to be. And,

---

[3] There are many other useful reference sources: *Social Science Citation Index; Education Resources Information Center;* and *Dissertation Abstracts* are a few. Reference librarians are happy to help you find the library sources you need.

Computers occupy a central place in contemporary technology. But although computers were first designed for routine data processing, psychologists are using them as a powerful heuristic device, a tool for generating not only understanding but also new hypotheses. By studying the way computers process incoming information and solve problems, researchers hope to gain insight into the way the human mind works. The assumption is that the way computers solve problems and process information is analogous—that is, functionally similar—to the way humans handle these tasks. Thus what is true of computer operations ought to be true of human thinking as well. We have here the potential source of countless new hypotheses about behavior.

The computer analogy has already been applied to the study of memory (Loftus, 1980). Large computer systems can update files overnight. They reorganize the day's input to make it easier to find. Loftus suggested that a similar process "might be represented in some form of the human dreaming process" (p. 177). Loftus also pointed out that, like computer memory, human memory must have an index. The question of how such an index is organized and used forms the basis for many new experiments.

Similarly, computers have been applied to perceptual problems. What does it take to make a machine that will "read" printed numbers on a check or the pricing code on a can of peas? Development of such machines led to the "template-matching model" (Neisser, 1967), which suggests that we recognize incoming visual information by matching it to prior stored representations (templates or patterns). This explanation is inadequate for many reasons. For one thing, we can recognize and identify things even if some of the features have changed from those in our representation: Dave has grown a beard since we saw him last, but we still recognize him easily. Thus we can recognize T, t, and *t*, as the same letter. Each has the same features, a vertical component crossed by a horizontal.

As the technology of machine readers advances, so may our understanding of human information processing. The computer may ultimately replace the laboratory animal as the most popular research subject.

because they are statistically derived, conclusions from a meta-analysis can be more objective than review articles.

A good review of the literature available on your topic is important in designing a good experiment and essential to writing an effective report. Regardless of where an experimental hypothesis originates, a literature review is still a necessary component of report writing. As you will see in Chapter 15, one goal of report writing is to integrate your findings into existing facts. In addition, a good literature review will help you avoid duplicating someone else's work. Research in fields other than psychology can sometimes open fruitful new avenues for research, as explained in Box 3-2.

SERENDIPITY AND THE WINDFALL HYPOTHESIS

All the approaches we have looked at so far are purposeful; the experimenter is usually looking for a new hypothesis on which to base an experiment. However, at times a discovery has been made where none was intended; such discoveries may be attributed to serendipity. The word comes from the 18th-century tale of "The Three Princes of Serendip" by Horace Walpole, which describes the adventures of the three princes who found many valuable things they were not seeking. **Serendipity** is the knack of finding things that are not being sought. Discoveries through serendipity have been made in the physical sciences as well as in psychology.

An element of serendipity appeared in the work of Ivan Pavlov (1927), a Russian physiologist whose main interest was the digestive glands (Figure 3-3). His studies involved feeding dogs and observing the changes that occurred in their stomach secretions. Through his work Pavlov became interested in salivation. He asked such questions as "If I feed the dog, how long will it be before the dog begins to salivate?" The questions seemed straightforward enough until Pavlov began to notice some distracting things. As the dogs became familiar with the bread Pavlov fed them, they began to salivate even before they were actually fed. Seeing the food seemed to produce salivation. Indeed, in a short while the dogs began to salivate as soon as he entered the room. Pavlov found these observations so interesting that he began to study the "psychic secretions" that he hypothesized were the result of the dogs' mental activity. His unplanned observations pulled him in a most unexpected direction.

What Pavlov observed was the phenomenon of classical conditioning.

FIGURE **3-3** Ivan Pavlov (1849–1936).
National Library of Medicine

Initially, salivation was elicited only by eating the food. After repeated pairings, the sight of the food, as well as the sight of Pavlov, elicited salivation. Pavlov won the Nobel Prize for his work on digestion, but he also made an unplanned contribution to the psychological study of learning.

Are such happy accidents really achievements? Didn't animal trainers and many parents know about conditioning already? Couldn't anyone have made the same contribution as Pavlov, if not with salivation, then with some other response? The answer is probably no. What distinguishes a scientist like Pavlov is that he was able to differentiate between a commonplace incident and something of great importance. Another person might have abandoned the salivation research as hopeless. Pavlov continued his research, performing many new experiments and offering unique interpretations of his findings. Serendipity can be useful in generating new hypotheses only when we are open to new possibilities (remember woodenheadedness). The good scientist takes note of all potentially relevant observations and analyzes and evaluates them: Are they interpretable? Do they explain something that was previously unexplained? Do they suggest a new way of looking at a problem? Serendipity is not just a matter of luck; it is also a matter of knowing enough to use an opportunity.

INTUITION

Intuition is another approach we will discuss in this chapter. It is not discussed in most experimental psychology texts. Psychology is a science. As such, it should be governed by formal, logical rules. But using intuition is not necessarily unscientific; rather, the inferences drawn from intuition often violate scientific criteria.

Intuition may be defined as knowing without reasoning. As such, it is probably closest to phenomenology. We acquire phenomenological knowledge simply by attending to our own experience. However, intuition may take us beyond mere apprehension of our own experiences. We may feel by intuition that a close relative has died. Because what the feeling is cannot be specified in observable, quantifiable terms, it seems out of place in a scientific context.

Although it is difficult to be concrete about what we mean by intuition, intuition is probably a very common basis for experimentation. We have a hunch about what might happen in a particular situation, so we set up an experiment to test it. Intuition guides what we choose to study. Of course, our experiments are still conducted in the context of prior research. We review the experimental literature to avoid carrying out experiments that are pointless given what is already known. For example, we may believe intuitively that dogs can see colors, but a review of the prior work on perception shows that they cannot.[4] Knowing this, we would not begin a new series of tests to check color vision in dogs.

[4] Dogs are able to discriminate brightness. Such discriminations sometimes appear to be based on color, but dogs do not have color vision.

When is intuition likely to be most helpful? According to Herbert Simon (1967), a psychologist and computer scientist who won a Nobel Prize, intuition is most accurate if it comes from experts. He believes that good hunches are really an unconscious result of our own expertise in an area—not a form of clairvoyance at all! The more we know about a topic, the better our intuitive hypotheses are likely to be.

We must be careful to remain within the bounds of science when we use our intuition. By intuition, we may have a tentative explanation for behavior or events. But such an explanation is truly tentative; it cannot be accepted as valid until it has been translated into a hypothesis and subjected to empirical tests. Intuition is just that—and it should not be confused with fact. If we were going on vacation and knew only by intuition that the plane leaves at noon, it would be risky to go to the airport without first checking to verify the flight schedule. Furthermore, intuition should not turn into woodenheadedness and destroy objectivity. Even though we believe intuitively that something is true, we must be prepared to change our thinking if the experimental evidence does not confirm our belief. Unless we find flaws in the experiment that would account for why our expectations were not confirmed, the observable data take precedence over intuition. Box 3-3 contains an example of some results that don't match what our intuition tells us.

WHEN ALL ELSE FAILS

If you are reading this text as part of a course requirement, you may be required to design an experiment of your own. You realize by now that you must have a hypothesis. Perhaps you also realize that our discussion of the ways in which others derive hypotheses has not been particularly helpful. As Russell said, there are no rules that can be used to generate hypotheses. If you feel completely at sea, here are some suggestions that have helped other students.

You are least likely to come up with a hypothesis by trying to think about everything you know about psychology. Begin by focusing on one or two broad areas that interest you. Perhaps you like learning and memory. If so, that is the place to start.

Once you select some broad areas of interest, take out a general psychology text and reread the sections on these areas. You may now be able to narrow down the number of possible topics even further. Perhaps you are most interested in the work on learning lists of words. Now locate the latest research that has been done in this area. You may have to do quite a bit of reading before you can derive a hypothesis of your own. Try to structure your reading in terms of the approaches we have discussed. Do you find any specific instances that suggest general principles? Is there a study that sets out a theory leading to deductions that are testable? Were there nonexperimental studies that can be redone as experiments to test cause and effect inferences? You may hit upon something by accident, or you

BOX **3-3**
The home field
disadvantage*

Sports fans often mention the "home field advantage" when predicting the chances of their favorite team in a sports championship. We typically assume that playing at home gives a team the edge. The presence of the cheering fans spurs players on to do their best. Or does it? Baumeister and Steinhilber (1984) put the question to an empirical test through a creative application of the ex post facto approach.

The researchers read through the sports archives and analyzed data on home and away victories during each World Series from 1924 through 1982. They found that the home team enjoyed a clear advantage during the early games of a series. However, during decisive last or seventh games (pressure situations), the visitors won significantly more often. The results are summarized in Table 3-1.

TABLE **3-1**

World Series game results 1924–1982			
	Winners		
Games	Home	Visitor	Home %
1 and 2	59	39	.602
Last game	20	29	.408
7	10	16	.385

NOTE: *Tabulations exclude ten Series in which the same team won all the games.*

Similar results were found for fielding errors committed during World Series games. Analysis of basketball (NBA) championship and semifinal playoff series showed comparable patterns.

Baumeister and Steinhilber had predicted these findings on the basis of prior research on self-presentation and self-attention. The self-presentation model suggests that thinking about our image distracts us from doing what needs to be done. "To give a crude but relevant example, the (baseball) shortstop who is busy imagining himself celebrated as a World Series hero in a victory parade may misjudge the ball bouncing toward him and make a fielding error" (p. 86).

The self-attention model suggests that paying too much attention to skills that have become automatic may disrupt them and hamper performance: "The shortstop who monitors the arm and hand muscle movements by which he throws the baseball to first base, after years of doing it automatically, may alter the skillful execution and make an error" (p. 86). Baumeister and Steinhilber did not try to determine which explanation works better for their findings. It is clear, however, that contrary to popular belief, the home field advantage is nothing to cheer about.

* Table 3-1 and quotes from "Paradoxical Effects of Supportive Audiences on Performance Under Pressure: The Home Field Disadvantage in Sports Championships," by R. F. Baumeister and A. Steinhilber, 1984, *Journal of Personality and Social Psychology, 47,* 85–93. Copyright © 1984 by the American Psychological Association. Reprinted by permission.

may develop a hunch about what might happen in a slightly new experimental setting.

Here is another suggestion: try observation. Some very good hypotheses come from observing how people behave in public places. In graduate school an early class assignment of one of the authors was to go to a public place and observe the people until a testable experimental hypothesis was found. It worked. Forming hypotheses about the kinds of antecedent conditions that affect people's behavior comes naturally—we do it all the time. These hypotheses are called "causal attributions" (Kelley, 1971). We search for a cause to which we can attribute someone's behavior. Has the following ever happened to you? You are driving behind a slow automobile on a one-lane road, and it seems to you that the driver speeds up whenever it is legal to pass and slows down in the no-passing areas. You can form a hypothesis about this (and you probably will). You might decide that the cause of the slowing down is "internal" (dispositional)—the person is a bad driver, or worse, a real blockhead. Or you could decide that the cause is "external" (situational)—the no-passing lanes are always on hills, and some cars have trouble maintaining their speed on hills. Either causal attribution could be a research hypothesis.

Finally, if all else fails, turn your attention to a real-world problem and try to figure out what causes it. An added benefit of this approach is that once the cause can be determined, a solution often suggests itself. A psychologist studying vision noticed that the elderly have more trouble than others reading road signs. He hypothesized that the problem was caused by the spatial frequency of letters and numbers typically placed on the signs. Experimentation confirmed this hypothesis and led to subsequent research to find a spatial frequency (width of line contours) that was more easily read by all drivers (Schieber, 1988). Attempting to discover causes of littering, vandalism, or shoplifting would be other examples of real-world problems to explore.

Since there are no rules, it is usually impossible to predict how long it will take to develop a good hypothesis. Remember that the work you will do in a single course is not expected to alter the course of psychology. Set realistic goals for yourself. Work from hypotheses that can be tested in the time frame you have available. You will probably need all the time you can get, which means that it is not a good idea to wait until the last minute to begin thinking about a hypothesis.

SUMMARY

Every experiment is designed to test a hypothesis about the effects of different treatment conditions on behavior. Every experiment must have a hypothesis. The *hypothesis* represents the end of the process of thinking about a behavior and zeroing in on one particular explanation that seems plausible.

The *experimental hypothesis* has several characteristics. First, it must be a *synthetic statement.* A hypothesis meets the definition of a synthetic statement if it can be stated in the "If . . . then" form. Second, the experimental hypothesis must be *testable:* The means for manipulating the antecedent conditions and measuring the resulting behavior must exist. The hypothesis must be disprovable or *falsifiable.* The hypothesis must also be *parsimonious:* The simplest hypothesis is preferred until it is ruled out by conflicting evidence. Ideally, the hypothesis is also *fruitful* and will lead to new research.

Hypotheses may be found through induction, deduction, serendipity, or intuition. *Induction* is the process of reasoning from specific cases to more general principles. *Deduction* is the process of reasoning from general principles to predictions about specific instances. In practice, induction and deduction are often used together. Through induction we may devise general principles, or theories, that may be used to organize, explain, and predict behavior until more satisfactory principles are found. Through deduction, we may rigorously test the implications of a premise or theory. Regardless of which method we use, we are generally *building on prior research*. Ex post facto and other nonexperimental studies may suggest experiments to test cause and effect relationships. We may also experiment to replicate prior findings and to test new predictions that follow from them.

Hypotheses occasionally grow out of *serendipity,* the knack of finding things that are not being sought. Researchers occasionally make unexpected observations that lead them in surprising directions. *Intuition* may also lead to hypotheses. We may have a hunch that something is true and carry out an experiment to test that notion. Hypotheses may also arise out of systematic searches through the research in specific areas of interest. Finally, hypotheses may come from *everyday observation* of behaviors and real-world problems.

KEY TERMS

Analytic statement   A statement that is always true.

Contradictory statement   A statement that is always false.

Deductive model   The process of reasoning from general principles to specific instances; most useful for testing the principles of a theory.

Experimental hypothesis   A statement that predicts the effects of specified antecedent conditions on a measured behavior.

Fruitful statement   A statement that leads to new studies.

Hypothesis   The thesis, or main idea, of an experiment consisting of a statement that predicts the relationship between at least two variables.

Inductive model   The process of reasoning from specific cases to more general principles to form a hypothesis.

Intuition The development of ideas from hunches; knowing directly without reasoning from objective data.

Nonexperimental hypothesis A statement of predictions of how events, traits, or behavior might be related, but not a statement about cause and effect.

Serendipity The knack of finding things that are not being sought.

Synthetic statement A statement that can be either true or false, a condition necessary to form an experimental hypothesis.

REVIEW AND STUDY QUESTIONS

1. What is a hypothesis?
2. What are the characteristics of a good hypothesis?
3. Which of the following are synthetic statements? Why?
    a. If I am cold, then it is December.
    b. Out of sight, out of mind.
    c. Virtue is its own reward.
    d. A statement that is always true is always true.
4. Explain what is meant by induction and deduction. How are they different?
5. What is serendipity?
6. Is a discovery made through serendipity just a matter of luck?
7. a. What is the role of intuition in research?
    b. Is intuition scientific?
    c. Why are our hunches often correct?
8. Before you set up an experiment, you should make a review of the research literature. What is the purpose of such a review?
9. Dr. P has just completed a study that shows a correlation between the amount of time children watch television and their attention span. Assume the correlation was $-.34$. State an experimental hypothesis based on this finding and devise a simple procedure for testing it.
10. Explain the way in which an ex post facto study could be used to generate an experimental hypothesis.
11. Mary is lost: She just cannot think of a hypothesis. Give her some advice on how to proceed.
12. Select one of the research areas listed below. Review some of the prior work in that area and formulate a new experimental hypothesis based on your review.
    a. Paired-associate learning
    b. The influence of a set in problem solving
    c. Solving anagrams (scrambled words)
    d. Bystander apathy
    e. The mere-exposure effect
13. Sit in a public place and observe people for an hour. Write down all the hypotheses that come to mind to explain their behaviors.

REFERENCES

BAUMEISTER, R. F., & STEINHILBER, A. (1984). Paradoxical effects of supportive audiences on performance under pressure: The home field disadvantage in sports championships. *Journal of Personality and Social Psychology, 47*(1), 85–93.

BECHTOL, B., & WILLIAMS, J. (1977). California litter. *Natural History, 86*(6), 62–65.

CERMAK, L. S., & CRAIK, F. I. (Eds.) (1979). *Levels of processing in human memory.* Hillsdale, NJ: Erlbaum.

CRAIK, F. I., & LOCKHART, R. S. (1972). Levels of processing: A framework for memory research. *Journal of Verbal Learning and Verbal Behavior, 11,* 671–684.

FERSTER, C. B., & SKINNER, B. F. (1957). *Schedules of reinforcement.* New York: Appleton-Century-Crofts.

GLANZER, M., & CUNITZ, A. R. (1966). Two storage mechanisms in free recall. *Journal of Verbal Learning and Verbal Behavior, 5,* 351–360.

KELLEY, H. H. (1971). *Attribution in social interaction.* Morristown, NJ: General Learning Press.

LOFTUS, E. (1980). *Memory.* Reading, MA: Addison-Wesley.

NEISSER, U. (1967). *Cognitive psychology.* New York: Appleton-Century-Crofts.

PARTINGTON, J. R. (1964). *A history of chemistry: Vol. IV.* London: Macmillan.

PAVLOV, I. (1927). *Conditioned reflexes* (G. V. Anrep, Trans.). London: Oxford University Press.

PETERSON, L. R., & PETERSON, M. J. (1959). Short-term retention of individual verbal items. *Journal of Experimental Psychology, 58,* 193–198.

PRITCHARD, R. D., DUNNETTE, M. D., & JORGENSON, D. O. (1972). Effects of perceptions of equity and inequity on worker performance and satisfaction. *Journal of Applied Psychology, 56,* 75–94.

RUSSELL, B. (1945). *A history of western philosophy.* New York: Simon & SCHUSTER.

SCHIEBER, F. (1988). Vision assessment technology and screening older drivers: past practices and emerging techniques. In National Research Council (Eds.), *Transportation in an Aging Society, Vol. 2* (pp. 270–293). Washington, D.C.: Transportation Research Board.

SHULMAN, H. G. (1970). Encoding and retention of semantic and phonemic information in short-term memory. *Journal of Verbal Learning and Verbal Behavior, 9,* 499–508.

SHULMAN, H. G. (1972). Semantic confusion errors in short-term memory. *Journal of Verbal Learning and Verbal Behavior, 11,* 221–227.

SIMON, H. A. (1967). Motivational and emotional controls of cognition. *Psychological Review, 74,* 29–39.

SPERLING, G. (1960). The information available in brief visual presentations. *Psychological Monographs, 74*(74, Whole No. 11).

WALSTER (HATFIELD), E., WALSTER,

G., & BERSCHEID, E. (1978). *Equity: Theory and research.* Boston: Allyn & Bacon.

WATSON, J. B., & RAYNER, R. (1920). Conditioned emotional reactions. *Journal of Experimental Psychology, 3,* 1–14.

ZAJONC, R. B. (1966). Attitudinal effects of mere exposure. *Journal of Personality and Social Psychology, 9,* 1–27.

PART**TWO**

Method

4

The Basics of Experimentation

Independent and Dependent Variables
Some Research Examples
Identifying Variables

Operational Definitions
Defining the Independent Variable: Experimental
Operational Definitions
Defining the Dependent Variable: Measured Operational
Definitions
Defining Constructs Operationally
Defining Nonconstruct Variables
Defining Scales of Measurement
Selecting Levels of Measurement

Evaluating Operational Definitions
Reliability
Validity

Evaluating the Experiment: Internal Validity
Control Groups
Experiments Without True Control Groups
Extraneous Variables and Confounding

Summary

Key Terms

Review and Study Questions

References

O nce you have formulated a hypothesis, you may want to set up an experiment to test it. As you saw in Chapter 2, there are several useful nonexperimental approaches to research. Each demands special skills, and each could form the basis of an entire text. However, the remainder of this book deals primarily with experimentation. Much of the research currently done in the field of psychology is experimental. In addition, an understanding of the principles of experimentation strengthens any researcher's potential for success.

When it is feasible, psychologists prefer experiments over other research methods, because a properly conducted experiment allows us to draw causal inferences about behavior. To review briefly, the psychology experiment has these main features: We manipulate the antecedent conditions to create at least two different treatment conditions. At least two treatments are required so that we can make statements about the impact of different sets of antecedents. If we used only one treatment, there would be no way to evaluate what happens to behaviors as the conditions change. We expose subjects to different treatment conditions so that we can measure the effects of those conditions on behavior. We record the responses or behaviors of subjects under various conditions and then compare them. We can then assess whether our predictions are confirmed.

Doing an experiment allows us to draw causal inferences about behavior. If behavior changes as the antecedent conditions change, we may say that the differences in antecedent conditions caused the difference in behavior. However, such an inference is justified only when a carefully controlled test of our predictions has been made. The chapters in this section of the text deal with the basic methods and problems involved in planning a good experiment.

In this chapter you will begin to see how researchers move from the general idea expressed in a hypothesis to the specific actions required to carry out an experiment. For the purposes of scientific research, the experimenter must clearly define what is being studied, and how, so that the research can be evaluated as well as replicated.

By the end of this chapter, you will be familiar with the basic components of experiments: the independent variable, the dependent variable, operational definitions, and control groups. We will examine these concepts in the context of particular experiments. We will also discuss some issues involved in evaluating definitions and experiments: reliability, validity, and confounding. The concepts presented in this chapter are fundamentals of experimental design; we will return to them again and again throughout the book.

INDEPENDENT AND DEPENDENT VARIABLES

An experimental hypothesis states a potential relationship between two variables: If *A* occurs, then we expect *B* to follow. Variables are aspects of an experiment that vary, things that can take on different values along some dimension. To be more precise, the experimental hypothesis expresses a potential relationship between two kinds of variables, the independent and the dependent variable. We will begin with some text-book definitions of these terms and then look at some concrete examples from actual research.

The **independent variable** (**IV**) in an experiment is the dimension that the experimenter intentionally manipulates; it is the antecedent the *experimenter* chooses to vary. It is "independent" in the sense that its values are created by the experimenter and are not affected by anything else that happens in the experiment. Independent variables are often simply aspects of the physical environment that can be brought under the experimenter's direct control. We call these **environmental variables.** Illumination (bright or dim), typeface size (large or small), and noise levels (loud or soft) are some examples.

Aspects of a given task may also become independent variables. We call these **task variables.** Complexity (easy, moderate, or difficult), mode of presentation (auditory versus visual), and meaningfulness (nonsense syllables versus real words) are some examples.

There must be at least two different treatment conditions to meet the definition of an experiment; thus the IV must be given at least two possible values in every experiment. The researcher decides which values of the IV to use. These values are also called the *levels* of the IV in the experiment. The researcher varies the IV by creating different treatment conditions within the experiment. Each treatment condition represents one level of the IV. If the IV is to have two levels, there must be two different treatment conditions. If three values of the IV are to be used, there must be three different treatment conditions, and so on. Be careful not to confuse the levels of the IV with the IV itself. For example, suppose a professor tries giving tests on either blue or yellow paper to see if the color of the paper influences the scores. Blue and yellow represent two levels of the one IV, color. We could add other levels such as pink, green, and orange. We would still have only one IV—color.

In an ex post facto study (Chapter 2), the researcher may explore the way behavior changes as a function of changes in variables outside the researcher's control. These are typically **subject variables,** characteristics of the subjects themselves (age, personality characteristics, sex) that cannot be manipulated experimentally. It is common for researchers to refer to these variables as "independent variables" too. Although they are not manipulated by the researcher, they are often "independent" in the sense that the researcher selects the particular values that will be included in the study. For instance, in their study of cancer patients' reactions to chemotherapy, Ward, Leventhal, and Love (1988) selected patients who showed repressor or nonrepressor coping styles.

Ex post facto studies are also sometimes called *quasiexperimental research.* Quasi means "in a sense" or "as if." Researchers using the quasiexperimental approach behave as if they were doing true experiments: They have treatments and measured observations (Cook & Campbell, 1979). However, the "independent variable" is not manipulated the way it is when we study something under our direct control, such as a drug dose or the brightness of a light. In quasiexperiments, the researcher *selects* rather than creates the levels of the IV by assigning subjects to treatment groups on the basis of a subject variable. In an ex post facto study, individuals in various treatment groups are supposed to differ on a subject variable because the subject variable is the one we are testing.

In a true experiment, we test the effects of a manipulated independent variable—not the effects of different kinds of subjects. Therefore, in a true experiment, we have to make certain that our treatment groups do *not* consist of people who are different on a preexisting characteristic. If we simultaneously varied *both* a subject variable and a manipulated independent variable, there would be no way of knowing whether effects we observed were due to differences between subjects or to the IV. For example, if we gave introverts their exams on blue paper and extroverts their exams on yellow paper, we would not know whether differences in their exam grades were due to the color of the paper or to personality differences. This problem is known as "confounding," and we will return to it later in the chapter.

How will we know whether changes in the levels of the IV have altered behavior? We measure the dependent variable to determine whether the independent variable had an effect. The **dependent variable (DV)** is the particular behavior we expect to change as a result of our experimental intervention; it is the behavior we are trying to explain. Sometimes it helps to think of it this way: In an experiment, we are testing effects of the IV *on* the DV.

If the hypothesis is correct, different values of the independent variable should produce changes in the dependent variable. The dependent variable is "dependent" in the sense that its values are assumed to depend on the values of the independent variable: As the independent variable changes value (as we look at behavior under different treatment conditions), we expect to see corresponding changes in the value of the DV.

Selecting appropriate independent and dependent variables is an important part of setting up every experiment. If we expect to understand the causes of behavior, we need to focus on the pertinent antecedents. Remember, if we can specify the antecedents that lead to a particular behavior, we have explained that behavior from a scientific viewpoint.

We also need to accurately assess the impact of our treatment conditions. In an experiment we cannot rely solely on our overall impression of whether the independent variable has some effect. We need more precision than that in a scientific study: We need an objective measure of the effect of the independent variable. We do not want the evaluation of the outcome of the experiment to depend on our subjective judgment, which might be somewhat biased. In addition, our findings will have more widely understood meaning if they are presented in terms of an observable dimension that can be measured again and again. By clearly defining the way we are measuring the effect of the independent variable, we make it easier for others to replicate our research. Let us turn now to some specific examples of independent and dependent variables in the research literature.

Some Research Examples

Schachter.   Consider this hypothesis, tested by Schachter (1959): If people are anxious, then they will want to affiliate, or be, with others. Put another way, misery loves company. The hypothesis states a potential relationship between two variables—anxiety and affiliation. To test the hypothesis, Schachter did the following experiment: Subjects were brought into a room with an experimenter wearing horn-rimmed glasses and a white laboratory coat. The experimenter introduced himself as Dr. Gregor Zilstein of the Departments of Neurology and Psychiatry. He explained that this was an experiment on the effects of electric shock. The subjects were split into two groups. One group was shown some elaborate electrical equipment and led to expect painful shocks: "These shocks will hurt, they will be painful. As you can guess, if, in research of this sort, we're to learn anything at all that will really help humanity, it is necessary that our shocks be intense" (p. 13). The other group received instructions leading them to believe they would feel no pain: ". . . do not let the word 'shock' trouble you; I am sure that you will enjoy the experiment. . . . I assure you that what you feel will not in any way be painful. It will resemble more a tickle or a tingle than anything unpleasant" (p. 13).

Thus both groups were told that they would receive electric shock, but one group expected pain whereas the other did not. The group that expected pain was assumed to be more anxious than the group that did not. The experimenter then explained that there would be a delay while the experiment was being set up and asked the subjects to indicate on a questionnaire whether they preferred to wait for the next part of the experiment alone, with other subjects, or had no preference. Based on the hypothesis, those subjects who were more anxious would be more likely to want to wait with others. This was the end of the experiment. The real purpose of the study was then explained, and no one ever actually received electric shock.[1]

---

[1] Although no one was ever shocked in Schachter's experiment, the ethics of the procedure may be questioned by some psychologists. We will return to this experiment when we discuss the ethics of research in Chapter 5.

FIGURE **4-1** Stanley Schachter.

In his hypothesis Schachter stated a potential relationship between two variables, anxiety and affiliation: If subjects are anxious, then they will want to affiliate with others. The hypothesis expresses the relationship between the independent and the dependent variables.

The independent variable in any experiment is the antecedent condition (the treatment) deliberately manipulated by the experimenter. Its values are represented by the various treatment conditions of the experiment. Schachter created two levels of anxiety (high and low) by using different sets of instructions. He manipulated anxiety by giving subjects varying instructions, leading them to believe that they either would or would not be exposed to painful shock; anxiety was the independent variable in this experiment. It was "independent" in the sense that its values were set by Schachter. It was not affected by anything else that occurred in the experiment.

The dependent variable is the variable measured to determine whether the independent variable had the expected effect on behavior. It was "dependent" in the sense that its values were assumed to depend on the values of the independent variable. In Schachter's experiment the dependent variable was affiliation. According to the hypothesis, whether subjects choose to wait alone or with others depends on how anxious they are:

Anxious subjects will be less likely to want to wait alone. If anxiety has no effect on affiliation, all the subjects, whether anxious or not, will be equally willing to wait alone. In fact, Schachter's experiment supported his hypothesis; he found that the subjects who expected painful shocks were less likely to want to wait alone.

Hess.   Let us look at another research example of testing the effects of an independent variable on a dependent variable. Hess (1975) tested the following hypothesis: Large pupils make people more attractive. Throughout history there has been popular support for this notion. Women once used the drug belladonna to make themselves more beautiful; one of its effects is dilation (widening) of the pupils. Candlelight dinners seem to flatter everyone; aside from masking minor imperfections, dim light also causes pupils to dilate.

To test his hypothesis, Hess asked male subjects to rate four photographs of two women. The photographs were retouched so that each woman had small pupils in one photograph and large pupils in another. Thus the two photographs were identical except for pupil size. (Examples resembling Hess's photographs are shown in Figure 4-2.) Subjects were asked to select which woman in a series of pairs of these photographs appeared to be more friendly, charming, and so on.

The independent variable in this experiment was pupil size. Hess deliberately varied the size of the pupils in order to test the effects of pupil size on attractiveness. The two treatment conditions were two different values, or levels, of the independent variable: large and small pupils. The dependent variable, of course, was attractiveness. If the hypothesis is correct, measures of attractiveness should depend on size of pupils. And in fact, Hess found that his subjects were likely to attribute more of the positive traits to the women with large pupils.

Identifying Variables

You will have little difficulty identifying the independent and dependent variables in an experiment if you take the time to think about what the experimenter did. Ask yourself the following questions: What did the experimenter manipulate? Is this what I am calling the independent variable? What was used to assess the effect of the independent variable? Is this what I am calling the dependent variable? Suppose we are designing an experiment to test our own hypothesis. How will we identify the independent and dependent variables? Since the experiment has not been done, we cannot examine the procedures that were used. There is no simple rule for deciding which variable is the independent variable in a hypothesis. To make this determination, we must think about the hypothesis and the way we would go about testing it.

When you are working with your own hypothesis, you must ask the same types of questions you ask about an experiment that has already been

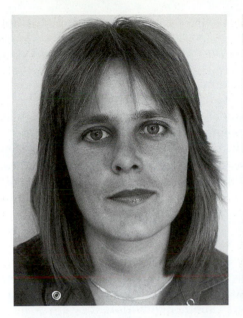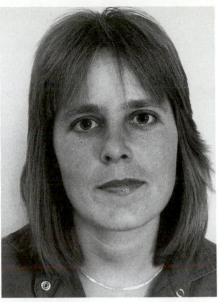

FIGURE **4-2**   Photographs of a woman retouched so that she has small pupils in one photograph and large pupils in the other. Brooks/Cole photo

done: What will you manipulate or vary to test the hypothesis? (This is your independent variable.) What behavior are you trying to explain; what will you measure to find out whether your independent variable had an effect? (This is your dependent variable.) Keep in mind that if you do not need to manipulate the antecedent conditions by creating different treatment conditions (if you will simply measure behaviors as they occur), you do not have an experimental hypothesis.

Suppose this is your hypothesis: People learn words faster when the words are written horizontally than when they are written vertically. You have come to this hypothesis through your review of research on the effects of practice. Since English-speaking people customarily see words printed horizontally, you suspect that words oriented vertically might seem more unfamiliar and thus be harder to learn. What are the independent and dependent variables in this hypothesis?

First, what will be manipulated? To test the hypothesis, you must manipulate the way the words are presented. You must present some words vertically and some horizontally. The independent variable is *word orientation.* You could run the experiment with two treatment conditions, horizontal and vertical presentation. Note again the distinction between the IV and its levels. The IV is the general dimension that is manipulated—in this case, word orientation. There are a great number of possible word orientations along the many diagonal lines that could be drawn between horizontal and vertical. We have, however, selected to use only two of the possible values. Horizontal and vertical are our two levels of the single IV, word orientation.

What will you measure to evaluate the effect of word orientation? According to the hypothesis, the orientation of the words will affect the rate of learning. *Rate of learning* is the dependent variable. If the hypothesis is correct, subjects will learn words faster if they are presented horizontally. You are predicting that the rate of learning depends on the way the words are presented.

The independent variable in one experiment may function as the dependent variable in another. Whether a particular variable is an independent variable, a dependent variable, or neither depends on the particular hypothesis being tested. In Schachter's experiment, the independent variable was anxiety and the dependent variable was affiliation. Schachter found that subjects who were made anxious wanted to wait for the next part of the experiment with others.

Based on Schachter's findings, we might suggest a new hypothesis. Perhaps people want to be with others when they are anxious because being with others causes them to become less anxious. How would we go about testing this hypothesis? We might place subjects in one of two conditions. In one condition, subjects are asked to spend 20 minutes waiting alone in a room. In another condition, they are asked to spend 20 minutes waiting in a room with another person. At the end of the waiting period, the subjects' anxiety levels are measured. If the hypothesis is correct, subjects who wait alone should be more anxious than subjects who wait with another person. The independent variable in *this* experiment is affiliation. We manipulate affiliation by assigning subjects to wait either alone or with others. The dependent variable is anxiety. According to the hypothesis, anxiety level depends on whether subjects wait alone or with another person. In Schachter's original experiment, anxiety was the independent variable, and affiliation was the dependent variable. As you can see, we changed the status of these variables when we turned to another hypothesis.

OPERATIONAL DEFINITIONS

So far we have talked about IVs primarily in everyday language. We all have a conceptual notion of what we mean by "brightness" or "rate of learning," for example. However, because one criterion of science is replicability, it is not enough to have only conceptual definitions. Earlier we talked about color as an IV and blue and yellow as treatment levels. However, for scientific purposes, we would have to be much more precise in our designation of these colors. There are many shades and hues of blue and yellow (one source—Judd and Kelly, 1965—identified 7500 different colors). In our experiment we would have to specify which blue we are using by giving a standardized definition. Psychologists use the Munsell color chart. The chart, developed by Albert Henry Munsell, describes colors by hue, saturation (purity), and lightness or brightness.

Similarly, what I mean by "anxiety" may actually be quite different from what you mean by "anxiety." And so, in addition to giving conceptual, everyday labels to our variables, we also need to specify what they mean in the context of each experiment.

The definition of each variable may change from one experiment to another. When we run an experiment, we naturally want to be sure that others will understand what we have done. Many concepts have more than one meaning, and those meanings are often vague. If we study variables without defining them exactly, the meaning of our findings will be unclear. As scientists, we also want to be sure that our procedures are stated clearly enough to enable other researchers to replicate our findings.

Thus each IV and each DV has two definitions—one conceptual definition that is used in everyday talk and one **operational definition** that is used in carrying out the experiment. An operational definition specifies the precise meaning of a variable within an experiment: It defines a variable in terms of observable operations, procedures, and measurements. It is called an operational definition because it clearly describes the "operations" involved in manipulating or measuring the variables in an experiment. Operational definitions are essential because many variables of interest to psychologists cannot be observed directly. Operational definitions describe variables in terms of observable reality. We include operational definitions in written reports of experiments so that other researchers will understand exactly what was done and will be able to replicate it. Operational definitions are sets of instructions that tell others how to carry out an experiment. They are statements of the operating procedures.

Operational definitions are quite different from ordinary dictionary definitions. A dictionary may define anxiety as "a state of concern or painful uneasiness about a future or uncertain event." Learning may be defined as "acquiring skill or knowledge." Although both definitions may be adequate for everyday use, neither will do in the context of an experiment. With these definitions we do not know how to produce different levels or values of the variables. They do not give us procedures we could follow to make people feel anxious or nonanxious or to have more or less learning. Similarly, they contain no information on how to measure or quantify the variables. How would we determine who has more anxiety or more learning? Operational definitions include both of those types of information.

Defining the Independent Variable: Experimental Operational Definitions

We can distinguish between two kinds of operational definitions, experimental operational definitions and measured operational definitions (Kerlinger, 1973). **Experimental operational definitions** explain the meaning of independent variables; they define *exactly* what was done to create the various treatment conditions of the experiment. An experimental operational definition includes all the steps that were followed to set up each value of the independent variable. Schachter gave experimental operational definitions of high and low anxiety. The high-anxiety condition was defined in terms of the electronic equipment set up in the room, the ominous behavior of Dr. Zilstein, and the explicit statement that the subjects should expect painful shocks. The low-anxiety condition was defined by the absence of equipment, Dr. Zilstein's more relaxed manner, and the explicit statement that the shocks would not be painful. If we were to replicate Schachter's experiment, we would be able to follow all these procedures in setting up each of the two treatment conditions. Note that if Schachter had merely said, "I set up a high-anxiety condition and a neutral condition," we would not know how to go about repeating his experiment. We would also have difficulty interpreting his findings, since we would have no way of judging just how "anxiety producing" his conditions may have been.

If we were constructing an experiment to test our hypothesis about the learning of words presented horizontally or vertically, we would need to specify the precise nature of the experimental procedures and stimuli. We would need to provide a detailed description of how we set up our treatments: the procedure used to present the words; the size of the words; the type of printing; the level of illumination in the room; the distance and location of words in the subject's visual field; and the duration of presentation of the words. We would need to provide all this information in order for others to evaluate our procedures and replicate our work.

In the case of quasiexperimental studies, the experimental operational definition is somewhat different. It is essentially the procedure used to select subjects who fit the required levels of the independent variable. In the Ward, Leventhal, and Love (1988) study described earlier, the researchers selected subjects on the basis of a written test of repressive coping style. A description of the test and the cutoff scores used to place people into different groups make up the operational definition of the quasi-independent variable used in the study.

Defining the Dependent Variable: Measured Operational Definitions

Dependent variables are defined by **measured operational definitions,** which describe what we do to measure the variables. Measured operational definitions of the dependent variable describe exactly what procedures we follow to assess the impact of different treatment conditions. They include exact descriptions of the particular behaviors or responses recorded. They also explain how those responses are scored. If we are using scores on a standardized test to measure our dependent variable, we identify the test by name: "scores on the Wechsler Adult Intelligence Scale," not simply "scores on an intelligence test." If our measure is not standardized, we describe it in enough detail to allow other researchers to repeat our procedures. In Schachter's experiment the dependent variable, affiliation, was given a measured operational definition. Schachter scored the desire to affiliate by having subjects check off their preferences on a questionnaire. The questionnaire is described in detail in his report. Again, it would be easy to replicate his procedures for measuring affiliation: We would simply administer the same questionnaire in the same way.

Defining Constructs Operationally

The need for operational definitions is apparent when we zero in on variables, like anxiety, that are actually **hypothetical constructs** or ideas, which are unseen processes postulated to explain behavior. Many psychological variables are hypothetical constructs; that is, constructs that cannot be observed directly. We infer their existence from behaviors that we can observe: An ordinarily good student panics and does poorly on an important exam. An actor has stage fright and forgets his lines. From these observations, we infer the existence of "anxiety." Now, we could say that "anxiety" is a peculiar feeling of queasiness that inhibits behavior. Unfortunately, that definition also neatly fits the first time one of the authors ate raw clams. She was not anxious. But she was definitely queasy, and she has not eaten clams since. Furthermore, what we mean by "anxiety" may be quite different if we are talking about a person's experience before taking a test compared to waiting in line for a roller-coaster ride.

Typically, several different definitions may be formulated for the same construct. Schachter's experiment illustrated one kind of operational definition for anxiety. In effect, Schachter said that "high anxiety" is the feeling experienced in a particular kind of situation—namely, one in which the person expects pain. In the low-anxiety condition, the subjects saw no equipment and did not expect pain. By definition, the feeling they experienced in this setting is "low anxiety." You may or may not agree with Schachter's decision to define anxiety in this way, but you do know what definitions apply in this particular experiment.

Operational definitions for constructs like anxiety are also important for another reason; namely, effects produced on behavior may differ from one operational definition to another. When anxiety is defined in another way, its effects on the desire to affiliate may be very different. Another research example shows that this is indeed the case. Sarnoff and Zimbardo (1961) conducted a study in which anxiety was operationally defined very differently. Undergraduate men were told that they would be participating in a study of sensory stimulation of the skin around the mouth. Subjects in a "high-anxiety" condition were told that the procedure would require them to suck for 2 minutes on various objects while physiological sensations around the mouth were being measured. An experimenter showed them several different objects they would be sucking on: things like baby bottles, oversized nipples, pacifiers, and breast shields (sometimes worn over a woman's breast while nursing). They were also shown vivid slides of a man demonstrating the sucking procedure on each of the objects. You may have guessed by now that Sarnoff and Zimbardo were trying to create a different sort of high anxiety than that manipulated by Schachter! In a "low-anxiety" condition, a similar procedure was used; but subjects were told instead that they would be placing objects (whistles, kazoos, and the like) in their mouths for 10 seconds while their skin sensations were recorded. To make the waiting period seem natural, all subjects were told that they would need to wait in another room while their preexperimental (*baseline*) physiology was recorded. As in the Schachter experiment, they were given the option of waiting alone or with others. Do you think the high-anxiety men in this experiment wanted to wait with others or alone? Not surprisingly, men exposed to the high-anxiety condition showed much *less* desire to affiliate than did men in the low-anxiety condition—a reversal of what Schachter had found. You can see from this amusing example how important an experimental operational definition is for defining construct variables.

Similarly, there are many possible measured operational definitions of anxiety. We need a measured operational definition when a construct variable like anxiety is a dependent variable. One such definition might be "a heartbeat in excess of 120 beats per minute following 5 minutes rest on a sofa." This definition could be used to explain what we mean by "anxiety" in a particular experiment. Notice that the components of the definition are observable dimensions; we can readily determine a person's pulse. We would expect to get good agreement on whether or not a person is "anxious" according to this definition.

We can also define anxiety by a score on a written test like the Taylor Manifest Anxiety Scale, or TMAS (Taylor, 1953). This test includes a variety of items that are assumed to index different degrees of anxiety, such as the frequency of nightmares, fear of spiders, worries about work, and so on. In using the test, we assume that people who express many of these concerns are more anxious than those who express few of them. We use predetermined cutoff scores to determine who is anxious and who is not. Again, we have an objective, observable set of measures (the subjects' responses to a series of test items) to define anxiety. To say that anxiety is "feeling queasy" is not acceptable. We cannot observe queasiness directly, nor can we be sure that subjects will know what we mean if we simply ask them whether they are "anxious."

Learning is also a construct. Like anxiety, it cannot be observed directly; it must be operationally defined by objective criteria. We can define learning in terms of performance on a written test, in a maze, or on a bicycle. We can count up the number of correct responses or errors. We can also use the time taken to complete a task as an index of learning. In an experiment to test our word-orientation hypothesis, we can define learning as the number of words that subjects are able to remember and write down, or as their scores on a written recognition test that we devise. Although the operational definitions vary, they all specify learning in observable terms. We cannot measure learning directly, but we can infer its occurrence from these objective measures; and we can state our procedures clearly enough to permit other researchers to measure learning in the same way.

Defining Nonconstruct Variables

It is easy to see why operational definitions are required when we are dealing with constructs. Something that cannot be seen must be defined by observable dimensions before we can deal with it scientifically. However, operational definitions are equally important when we are working with variables that can be observed more directly. Suppose we wish to test the effects of lighting on newborn babies. We may wish to compare crying among babies in light rooms versus crying in dark rooms, as did Irwin and Weiss in 1934. The comparison seems straightforward enough, but before it can be made we must operationally define what we mean by "light" versus "dark" rooms. Is a "light" room as bright as a sunny day? Is a "dark" room completely shielded from any source of light, or one in which the shades are drawn? To make a legitimate comparison, we must define what we mean by "light" and "dark" as objectively as possible, ideally by the use of a photometer or light meter.

The dependent variable, crying, must also be defined. It must be done in such a way that independent observers would reliably agree on its occurrence. Do intermittent sounds constitute "crying," or must the sound be sustained for a given period of time? Is a whimper also a cry or must the sound reach a certain level of intensity (some decibel level)? All these decisions must be made before the experiment is conducted. Otherwise, the results may not mean anything to anyone except the experimenter.

Defining Scales of Measurement

In setting up experiments and formulating operational definitions, researchers also consider the available **scales of measurement** for each variable. You may have noticed that in our examples of independent variables, some of the levels we specified were simply comparative labels (bright or dim illumination, large versus small typeface). However, it might have been possible to make them precise quantitative measurements, such as 50 versus 100 luxes (standard units of illumination) and 10-point versus 14-point typeface.

Many variables can be measured in more than one way. The measurement alternatives differ in the degree of information they provide. Setting treatment levels at 5 versus 10 milligrams of a drug, for example, is more precise than dividing subjects simply on the relative basis of low versus high doses. Stating the level of room illumination in luxes is going to allow other researchers to more thoroughly evaluate and replicate an experiment than knowing only that a room was bright or dim.

Dependent variables can also be measured in more than one way, and the amount of information provided will depend on how the variable is measured. The two experiments that tested the effects of "anxiety" on affiliation used the same dependent variable (desire to affiliate), but the way affiliation was measured differed somewhat. In the Schachter (1959) experiment, subjects simply stated whether they wished to wait with others, alone, or had no preference. But Sarnoff and Zimbardo (1961) had subjects rate the intensity of their preference on a scale from 0 (very weak preference) to 100 (very strong preference). The second type of measurement provides the researcher with additional information and uses a different level of measurement.

The **level of measurement** is the kind of scale used to measure a variable. There are four levels of measurement: nominal, ordinal, interval, and ratio. The simplest level of measurement is called a **nominal scale,** which classifies items into two or more *distinct* categories on the basis of some common feature. A nominal scale groups items together into categories that can be named (the term *nominal* comes from the Latin word for *name*). But it does not quantify the items in any way. Classifying subjects into boys or girls uses the nominal level of measurement; a subject can either be a boy or a girl but not both. Nominal scaling is sometimes called the lowest level of measurement because it provides the least information; however, for some subject variables, it is the only type of scale that can be used. Political affiliation is a commonly used nominal measurement. You may be a Democrat, Republican, Independent, or Other. There is no difference in magnitude among these categories; you are not more or less affiliated if you belong to one party rather than another.

In Schachter's (1959) experiment, a nominal scale was used to assess affiliation. Subjects selected a response from one of three categories: wait alone, with others, or no preference. See Figure 4-3 for an another example. Nominal scales place responses into categories but do not provide the researcher with any information about differences in magnitude between the items.

The next level of measurement is called an **ordinal scale,** which is a rank ordering of items. The magnitude of each value is measured in the form of ranks. Placing first, second, or third in a track event is an example of an ordinal scale. The winner's time is faster than the runner-up's time; the runner-up's time is faster than the time of the third-place finisher. Here, an ordinal scale gives us some idea about the *relative* speed of the three racers, but it does not tell us the precise speed of any single racer. A researcher interested in studying the effects of aggressive cartoons on children's aggressiveness might rank order different cartoons in terms of how violent they are. "Teenage Mutant Ninja Turtles" might be ranked higher than "New Kids on the Block," but we would not know *how much* higher. In order to quantify the magnitude of differences between events, we turn to higher levels of measurement.

An **interval scale** measures magnitude or quantitative size using measures with equal intervals between the values. However, an interval scale has no "true" zero point. The Fahrenheit and centigrade temperature scales are interval scales. Although both have zero points, neither has an absolute zero. Neither 0° F nor 0° C represent true zero points (the absence of *any* measurable temperature): Temperatures below zero are possible on both scales. For that reason, we cannot say 40° is twice as hot as 20°. But because the intervals between values (between degrees) are equal, we can

FIGURE **4-3** An example of nominal scaling. Drawing by Koren; © 1982 *The New Yorker Magazine, Inc.* Reprinted by permission.

say that the difference between 40° and 20° is the same as the difference between 20° and 0°.

Sarnoff and Zimbardo's (1961) 0–100 scale is an example of the type of interval scale commonly used by researchers to measure a dependent variable. Some statisticians question whether number scales like this truly meet the criteria for an interval scale, but the value of the information that can be obtained from them and their common acceptance among psychologists argue strongly for using them. Some common methods of constructing interval-scale questions are described in Box 4-1.

The highest level of measurement is called a **ratio scale,** which has equal intervals between all values *and* a true zero point. Measures of physical properties, like height and weight, are variables whose quantity or magnitude can be measured along ratio scales. Time (measured in seconds, minutes, or hours) is another common ratio-scaled variable. The values of a ratio scale are expressed by numbers such as 3 feet, 18 kilograms, or 24 hours. Clearly, the intervals between scale values (feet, kilograms, hours) are equal. Measures of feet, kilograms, and hours also have a true zero point—values of 0 feet, 0 kilograms, and 0 hours represent the true absence of height, weight, or time. These attributes enable us to express relationships between values on these scales as ratios: We can say 2 meters are twice as long as 1 meter.

Selecting Levels of Measurement

Variables may be measured by using one of the four types of scales. At times it is possible to measure a variable by more than one of these scales. Hamburgers, for example, could be categorized by fast-food restaurant

If we wanted to discover people's attitudes about scientific research, how could we go about soliciting their opinions? Well, we could just ask them, "What do you think about scientific research," and let them answer in their own words. But then we would have to determine what they meant by those words. For example, imagine that one person answered, "Well, it's okay, I suppose," and another said, "I don't have a real strong opinion about that." Do these people have the same or a different opinion? Is one more favorable than the other? If so, how much more favorable?

Because it is convenient, psychologists who solicit attitudes standardize both the questions asked and the answers available to the respondents. *Scaling* is an example of this practice. There are many different scaling techniques, but we are going to focus on three: semantic differential, Likert, and Thurstone.

The semantic differential was devised by Osgood, Suci, and Tannenbaum (1957). If we were to use their semantic-differential technique for measuring people's attitudes toward scientific research, we would ask respondents to indicate their attitude toward scientific research by evaluating it on a number of dimensions. Each dimension would consist of two adjectives separated by a scale, usually consisting of 7 points. The adjectives on each scale are antonyms (having opposite meanings), so the semantic differential is comprised of *bipolar adjective scales*. Our semantic differential might look like the following example:

Scientific Research

Positive — — — — — — Negative

Worthless — — — — — — Valuable

Wise — — — — — — Foolish

Unethical — — — — — — Ethical

Helpful — — — — — — Destructive

We would ask our subjects to indicate their attitude toward scientific research by placing a check mark on each scale. To quantify each person's attitude, we could score each scale from 1 (most negative) to 7 (most positive) and then sum the person's score across all the scales.

The Likert scaling procedure (Likert, 1932) takes a different approach. If we were to use this technique to measure attitudes toward scientific research, we would present people with some positively worded statements and some negatively worded statements about scientific research. We would arrange the possible responses to each statement in a multiple-choice format. Most often, researchers give respondents five answer options: "strongly disagree," "disagree," "undecided" (or "neutral"), "agree," and "strongly agree." With this technique we could ask people to indicate the degree of their agreement or disagreement with each of the following statements:

Scientific research has produced many advances that have significantly enhanced the quality of human life.

____ strongly disagree
____ disagree
____ neutral
____ agree
____ strongly agree

Scientific research has frequently produced confusing results, based on statistics that are biased in the direction of the researcher's beliefs.

____ strongly disagree
____ disagree
____ neutral
____ agree
____ strongly agree

We would quantify each person's attitude by scoring each question and then summing their scores across all the questions. We want higher numbers to indicate more positive attitudes, so we would have to make strong *agreement* with a *positively* worded statement (for example, the first question above) worth 5 points. We also would make strong *disagreement* with a *negatively* worded statement (for example, the second question above) worth 5 points. Strong disagreement with a positively worded statement or strong agreement with a negatively worded statement would each be worth 1 point.

A slightly different Likert-type technique is also employed to assess individuals' evaluations of people, ideas, or things. If you were asked to rate the value of scientific research on a scale from 0–10 (0 is your least positive rating and 10 your most positive), a researcher would be measuring your answer using a common Likert-type scale. This type of rating scale can also be used to measure the strength of either the positive or negative attitudes an individual holds toward scientific research, as in the following example:

How do you feel about scientific research? (Circle a number on the scale below.)

Strongly Against	Somewhat Against	Neutral	Somewhat For	Strongly For
−2	−1	0	+1	+2

The third technique—Thurstone scaling—is the oldest procedure (Thurstone, 1928). If we were constructing a Thurstone scale for measuring people's attitudes toward scientific research, we would begin by composing as many statements as we could think of to express an attitude about scientific research. Some statements would be as negative as we could
(continued)

BOX **4-1**
(continued)

make them ("Scientific research is evil, and there is no doubt that it will cause the destruction of all life on this planet"), and some would be as positive as we could make them ("Scientific research is the greatest achievement of humankind"). Our goal would be to compose statements that expressed attitudes across the whole range from the most favorable to the least favorable, including every level in between. We would need a great many; 100 statements is not unusual for researchers constructing a Thurstone scale.

A panel of judges would read each of our 100 statements and rate each one on a scale, indicating the positivity or negativity of the attitude expressed by the statement. Typically, judges rate the statements on 11-point scales (higher numbers indicate greater positivity and lower numbers indicate greater negativity). The average of our judges' ratings for each statement will be the *value* for that statement. Very negative statements will have very low values and very positive statements will have very high values.

The next step is to select the 20 or 30 statements that we are going to use in our final Thurstone scale. After eliminating all the items on which our judges did not agree, we would decide which of the remaining statements to use. We would select them to accomplish two goals. First, we want statements that cover the whole range of opinions: some that are very negative, some that are moderately negative, some that are moderately positive, and some that are very positive. Second, we want to select statements with values that are about equally distant from one another: We could select one statement with a value of 1.0, another with a value of 1.5, another with a value of 2.0, and so on, until we reach statements with values of 10.5 and 11.0.

We can now construct the scale by arranging the statements in order of their negativity or positivity. We would ask people to read all the statements and to circle the two or three that best reflect their attitude about scientific research. The average value of their answers is used as their score on the question. You will probably agree with most researchers that the Thurstone technique is very precise—and very time-consuming. The semantic-differential and Likert techniques are easier, and for that reason, they are used most often by researchers.

(nominal data), ranked in order of taste (ordinal data), or measured for exact calorie counts (ratio data). The best type of scale to use will depend on two things: the nature of the variable you are studying and how much measurement precision you desire. The level of measurement needs to "fit" the variable being measured. Sometimes a nominal scale is sufficient. If we were interested in measuring marital status, for example, knowing whether someone is unmarried or married (nominal data) may be all the information that we need. A different kind of study might require knowing how many years subjects have been married (ratio data).

Often, psychological variables lend themselves to different levels of measurement because they represent a **continuous dimension.** Traits, attitudes, and preferences can be viewed as continuous dimensions. The trait of sociability, for example, can be conceptualized as a continuous dimension that ranges from very unsociable to very sociable—each person falls somewhere on that dimension. Attitudes can range from strongly negative to strongly positive, and preferences from very weak to very strong. Multiple scales are possible for these dimensions. Attitudes toward issues like animal experimentation, which will be discussed in the next chapter, could be measured using a nominal scale ("for" or "against") or an interval scale ("On a scale of 1–10, how strongly do you favor using animals in psychological research?").

Researchers generally use the following rule of thumb for selecting a level of measurement: When different levels of measurement will "fit" equally well, choose the highest level possible because it provides more information about a variable. In subsequent chapters we will also learn that various levels of measurement are analyzed with different statistical techniques, and the statistical tests we can use for interval or ratio data are more *powerful* than those for nominal and ordinal data. Thus ratio and interval scales tend to be preferred over ordinal and nominal measurements.

EVALUATING OPERATIONAL DEFINITIONS

Since there may be many definitions for the same variable, how is it possible to know which definition is best? There are no hard and fast answers to this question. As with many other aspects of experimentation, what works well in one experiment may simply not be appropriate in another. Our definition must be objective and precise so that others can evaluate and duplicate the procedures. In addition, there are more general criteria. We can group these under the general headings of reliability and validity.[2]

Reliability

Reliability means consistency and predictability. Good operational definitions are reliable: If we apply them in more than one experiment, they ought to work in similar ways each time. Suppose we have specified all the operations that must be performed to create two treatment conditions, hungry and not hungry. If our operational definition is reliable, every time we apply the definition (each time we create these two conditions), we should obtain similar consequences. Subjects in the "hungry" condition

---

[2] The issues of reliability and validity also affect our ability to make statements that go beyond the experiment we did. We will return to them in a later chapter.

should consistently show signs of hunger—increased activity, food-seeking behavior, or a verbal report of hunger if our subjects are people. If our "hungry" subjects show signs of hunger only occasionally, our operational definition is not reliable. The procedures we have specified to define the various levels of the independent variable work haphazardly: Sometimes we produce hunger and sometimes not. Better definitions are needed.

Measured operational definitions should also be reliable. If we took several sets of measurements according to our operational definition of the dependent variable, we should get the same results each time. When possible, we select measuring devices, like standardized tests, that have been shown to be reliable. When not using standardized measures, we make sure our measurement procedures are clearly and simply defined. The more accurate they are, the more likely they are to be reliable. There are several procedures for checking the reliability of measurement techniques.

Interrater reliability.   One way to assess reliability of measurement procedures is to have different observers take measurements of the *same* responses; the agreement between their measurements is called **interrater reliability.** Typically, this method is used when the qualitative content of subjects' responses must be scored by raters (for example, several raters might score all subjects' essays for "assertiveness"). This scoring method is called a "content analysis." When two or more raters score each response, scores given by different raters can be statistically compared.[3] If there is little agreement between them, the chances are good that the measuring procedure is not reliable. There are other types of measurement reliability that can be assessed through statistical techniques.

Test-retest reliability.   Reliability of measures can also be checked through repeated testing using the same measuring instrument. This is called **test-retest reliability.** If people consistently get the same scores on a personality test, the test is considered reliable. Standardized intelligence tests, like the Wechsler Adult Intelligence Scale, have been shown to have good test-retest reliability; people's scores do not change very much from one testing session to another.

Interitem reliability.   A third way of checking the reliability of measurement procedures is to assess the degree to which different items measuring the same variable attain the same results, called **interitem reliability.** Scores on different items designed to measure the same construct should be highly interrelated (correlated). This type of interitem reliability is called "internal consistency." A test of internal consistency is most often used when a researcher has created a multiple-item questionnaire to measure a construct variable like intelligence, need for achievement, or anxi-

[3] Statistical tests of reliability provide reliability coefficients (similar to correlation coefficients) that range from 0.0 (only chance levels of agreement) to 1.0 (perfect agreement). For a more detailed presentation of methods for assessing reliability and validity, see Crano, W. D., & Brewer, M. B. (1986). *Principles and methods of social research.* Newton, MA: Allyn & Bacon.

ety. The individual items on a standardized test of anxiety, such as the TMAS (Taylor, 1953) will show a high degree of internal consistency if they are reliably measuring the same variable.

Validity

A second important problem in formulating definitions is stating definitions that are valid. Valid definitions are sound; they can withstand criticism. More specifically, **validity** in experiments refers to the principle of actually studying the variables that we wish to study. We can formulate precise, objective definitions that may even be reliable. But if they are not valid, we have not accomplished the goals of our experiment.

Often, several procedures can be used to manipulate the same variable. Construct variables like hunger, for example, can be approached in a variety of ways. Is one definition more valid than another? We may define hunger in terms of hours of food deprivation: An animal that has been without food for 24 hours is hungry. We can also define it in terms of body weight: An animal maintained at 90% of its normal body weight is hungry. Other definitions, such as stimulating appropriate parts of the brain, may also be used. But which is the most valid? Which represents what we want to call "hunger"?

One approach to the problem is a comparison of the consequences of the various procedures. If they all produce "hunger," they should all lead to the same observable signs of hunger. Hungry animals will be more active, will eat foods they refuse when they have a choice, and so on. Researchers make these kinds of comparisons to develop the best procedures. Comparing all the available procedures is not always feasible, particularly in the course of a single experiment. However, it should be clear that we need to evaluate the validity of our experimental manipulations. We must ask whether we really manipulated what we intended to manipulate. Validity can be determined in several ways.

Face validity. Validity of operational definitions is least likely to be a problem with variables that can be manipulated and measured fairly directly. For instance, in studying the effects of pupil size, it is reasonably easy to know whether we are using a valid experimental operational definition of pupil size. We simply use a standard measuring device—for instance, a ruler—to define the treatment conditions. Defining pupil size by the marks on a ruler has **face validity.** The procedure is self-evident; we do not need to convince people that a ruler measures width. Face validity is the least stringent type of validity.

Similar issues arise in evaluating definitions of the dependent variable. The validity of a measured operational definition centers around the question of whether we measured what we intended to measure. As with experimental definitions, there should be some consensus that our procedures yield information about the variable we had in mind when we started the experiment. But because many psychological variables require indirect measures, the validity of a measured definition may not be self-evident—but it may still be good measure. Response time is considered to be a valid measure of attitude importance (judgments about important attitude objects are made more quickly), even though the connection between time and attitude strength is not readily apparent (Fazio, 1990). Aside from using common sense in selecting appropriate measures, two other kinds of validity are important as we develop measures: content validity and predictive validity. Measures that appear to have face validity do not necessarily meet these criteria.

Content validity. Content validity depends on whether we are taking a fair sample of the quality we intend to measure. When we evaluate **content validity,** we are asking: Does the content of our measure reflect the content of the thing we are measuring? The questions students might raise about an exam are often questions of content validity. An exam is supposed to measure what students have learned. However, students sometimes feel an exam includes *only* questions about the things they did not understand. Winston Churchill had the same feeling when he wrote the following:

> I had scarcely passed my 12th birthday when I entered the inhospitable regions of examinations, through which, for the next seven years, I was destined to journey. These examinations were a great trial to me. The subjects which were dearest to the examiners, were almost invariably those I fancied least. I would have liked to be examined in History, Poetry, and writing essays. The examiners, on the other hand, were partial to Latin and Mathematics. And their will prevailed. Moreover, the questions which they asked on both these subjects were almost invariably those to which I was unable to suggest the satisfactory answer. I should have liked to be asked to say what I knew. They always tried to ask what I did not know. When I would willingly have displayed my knowledge, they sought to expose my ignorance. This sort of treatment had only one result: I did not do well in examinations.[4]

Whether a particular measure has content validity is often a matter of judgment. Teachers and students sometimes disagree on whether particular tests or particular questions are fair representations of the course material. However, for experimental purposes we try to obtain some consensus on the content validity of our measures. For areas in which a lot of research is conducted, like intelligence, content validity of measures is often the topic of books by experts (Lutey, 1977).

Suppose you have devised a questionnaire to measure racial attitudes. You have a series of questions about whether people would live in integrated neighborhoods, whether they would help a person of another race who was in trouble, and so on. You could simply administer the questionnaire. However, you would have a better idea of whether your questionnaire has content validity if you obtained ratings of the items from objective judges. Each judge would be asked to rate each item for its measurement of racial attitudes. You would then have the opportunity to include items that are most representative of that variable, according to the

[4] Churchill, W. (1930). *My early life.* New York: Scribner's.

raters' judgments. If the raters do not agree on the items, you will have to rework the questionnaire.

The degree of content validity we can achieve depends on the particular variable we want to measure. The more specific the variable, the easier it will be. Clearly, it would be relatively easy to define weight gain in a way that would have high content validity. Measuring the size of a mental image poses more difficult problems. Other times, it is difficult to attain high content validity because the circumstances you wish to measure are very infrequent. Researchers studying the content validity of tests used to assess combat readiness in the military, for example, find it difficult to achieve a high level of content validity because most tests are simulations conducted in peacetime (Vineberg & Joyner, 1983).

Predictive validity. We can also ask whether our measures of the dependent variable have **predictive validity.** Do our procedures yield information that enables us to predict what subjects will do in another situation? They should, if we are measuring what we intend to measure. Schachter (1959) defined the desire to affiliate in terms of subjects' responses to a questionnaire. You will recall that they were asked to indicate whether they preferred to wait alone, with others, or had no preference. This definition has face validity. It seems to have something to do with people's desire to be together. It seems to have content validity too; part of the desire to affiliate is a wish to be with other people. When we raise the question of predictive validity, however, we are asking this: Can we use people's responses to this questionnaire to predict a particular behavior? If people have the desire to affiliate, it is reasonable to predict that they will stay near others when they have the opportunity. In Schachter's study we could evaluate the predictive validity of the affiliation measure by changing the procedures slightly. Instead of telling subjects that the experiment was over after they completed the questionnaire, we could take them all into a large waiting room. If the affiliation measure has predictive validity, the subjects who said they wanted to wait with others will seat themselves closer together and perhaps talk to each other more than subjects who preferred to wait alone. If we do not observe these overt signs of the desire to affiliate, we may have to conclude that the written measure does not have predictive validity: It does not predict what people will do.

Construct validity. The fourth, and perhaps most important, aspect of validity is **construct validity.** Somewhat different from the other forms of validity we have discussed, construct validity deals with the transition from theory to research application. We start with a conceptual notion of a relationship between behavior and a trait or characteristic; we then seek to find ways of putting our idea to an empirical test. The issue of construct validity arises when we ask, "Have I succeeded in creating a measuring device that measures what I think it does? Am I really testing the hypothesis I started with? What do my test data really mean? Are my operational definitions tapping only the construct I want to test?"

The specific modern methods for evaluating construct validity are largely statistical and highly theoretical. Basically, researchers ask whether the data make sense in the context of the overall theoretical framework in which they operate. One way of doing this is to see whether the data follow expected patterns in relation to other concepts. Although we cannot look at the details of how a construct validity analysis might be done, a description of two simple applications will help clarify the essence of what is involved.

First, suppose we wish to study intelligence. Depending on our hypothesis, intelligence could be either an independent or dependent variable. If intelligence were the IV, we might separate subjects into groups on the basis of high or low intelligence test scores (a quasiexperimental approach). Or if intelligence were the DV, we might introduce some environmental change (for example, better nutrition) and observe its impact on subsequent IQ scores. In either case we would want to be sure that our intelligence test truly measures only "intelligence," and that we have not inadvertantly measured another construct.

From a scientific standpoint, we are faced with a construct validity question. Does the test we use actually measure the hypothetical construct we call "intelligence"? Perhaps the test measures something else, such as test-taking skills, cultural background, or motivation. There is extensive research literature dealing with such issues, and testing experts have tried to create tests that minimize the influence of these other factors. The Ravens Progressive Matrices Test is one example of a test that is considered relatively culture-fair. Figure 4-4 illustrates the type of items found on such a test.

As a student, it is unlikely that you would get heavily involved in construct validation. The experts who have created standardized intelligence tests have already addressed the problem for you. Your task would be to select the most appropriate test on the basis of the research literature. When constructing tests, experts work with many sources of data as they assess validity. Computer applications have made much of this work feasible. To the extent that the tests measure intelligence, test scores ought to show certain predictable relationships with other related variables, such as school achievement and reading level. Test results should also correlate highly with scores on other intelligence tests. A valid intelligence test should also be able to appropriately classify "known groups" of people with high and low levels of intelligence. It should have no trouble discriminating between members of Mensa (a society admitting only high-IQ individuals) and mentally retarded individuals. Thus, the validation process focuses on *how well* the test scores fit in an overall theoretical network of understanding how the concept of intelligence works in human functioning.

There are many other examples concerning construct validity in the psychological literature. Researchers do not always have standardized tests to work with and therefore have to solve their own validation problems. How they go about establishing construct validity is illustrated in an article by Marsh and Parker (1984). They assessed the construct validity of

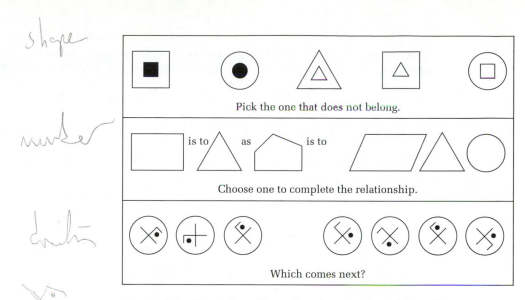

FIGURE **4-4** Examples of items found on a *culture-fair* intelligence test.

the Self Description Questionnaire (SDQ), an instrument that was intended to measure self-concept. Sample items from the 76-item questionnaire are shown in Table 4-1.

As in the case of intelligence testing, Marsh and Parker looked for predictable relationships between SDQ scores (presumably self-concept) and other variables. They were able to do that through sophisticated statistical procedures, including factor analysis and path analysis. They evaluated the relationships between SDQ scores and other variables, such as teacher ratings of student self-concept and academic achievement. They were able to show that self-concept, as measured by the SDQ, actually has two distinct components—academic and nonacademic self-concept.[5] Basically, how people perform in school does not necessarily affect the way they view their abilities in other areas. Winston Churchill probably would have agreed.

EVALUATING THE EXPERIMENT: INTERNAL VALIDITY

So far we have focused on the notion of validity in connection with operating procedures. We want to develop procedures that define our variables in valid ways. However, a more general evaluation is also required: Is the experiment valid? Have we made valid measurements of the effects of the independent variable? We can talk about two kinds of validity when we look at the experiment as a whole. The first is **internal validity,** the sound-

[5] Paradoxically, they also found that students in educationally disadvantaged schools had higher self-concepts than those in better schools. Although students in better schools achieved more academically, Marsh and Parker raised the question of whether it is preferable "to be a relatively large fish in a small pond even if you don't learn to swim as well."

TABLE **4-1**

			Sometimes False, Sometimes		
	False	Mostly False	True	Mostly True	True
I like the way I look	☐	☐	☐	☐	☐
I get good marks in all SCHOOL SUBJECTS	☐	☐	☐	☐	☐
My parents like me	☐	☐	☐	☐	☐
I do lots of important things	☐	☐	☐	☐	☐
I am dumb at READING	☐	☐	☐	☐	☐

NOTE: *From Self Description Questionnaire by H. W. Marsh and I. D. Smith, 1981. Copyright © 1981 by H. W. Marsh and I. D. Smith, The University of Sydney. Reprinted by permission.*

ness of the procedures within the experiment. Later in the book we will discuss **external validity,** how well the findings of the experiment apply to situations that were not tested directly (for example, real life). But before we can talk about the external validity of an experiment, we must first evaluate its internal validity.

When we set up an experiment, we plan procedures to measure the effects of various treatment levels. We are trying to assess the impact of the independent variable. We can ask whether we have achieved that goal in the context of the experiment: *An experiment is internally valid if we can be sure that the changes in behavior observed across the treatment conditions of the experiment were actually caused by the independent variable* (Campbell, 1957). If other explanations are possible, the experiment is not internally valid; we cannot identify the impact of the independent variable with certainty. We cannot make any correct generalizations from an experiment that is not internally valid. In the following sections, we will look at three important concepts that are tied to the problem of internal validity: control groups, extraneous variables, and confounding. These factors affect our ability to understand the effects of our treatment conditions.

Control Groups

In order to assess the impact of the independent variable, we must have at least two different treatment conditions so that we can compare the effect of different values of the independent variable. We cannot draw valid conclusions about the effect of the independent variable without this comparison.

In the simplest experiments, we have only two treatment conditions. Often, one condition is an experimental condition and the other is a control condition. In the **experimental condition,** we apply a particular value of our independent variable to the subjects and measure the dependent variable. The subjects in an experimental condition are called an **experimental group.** The **control condition** is used to determine the value of the dependent variable without an experimental manipulation of the independent variable. The subjects in a control condition are called a **control group.** In the control condition, we carry out exactly the *same* procedures that are followed in the experimental condition, except for the experimental manipulation. Sometimes the control condition is a "no-treatment" condition. We simply measure subjects' responses without trying to alter them in any way. A no-treatment control condition tells us how subjects *ordinarily* perform on the dependent measure. We can use this control condition as a point of comparison; we can see whether subjects' performance in the experimental condition was better, worse, or the same as subjects who were not exposed to our experimental manipulation. For instance, we could compare test performance of students who engaged in 15 minutes of aerobic exercise prior to the exam with the performance of students who did not exercise. Without the no-treatment control group, we cannot say whether the experimental subjects did better or worse than usual.

However, often a control group does receive treatment—in the sense that in the control condition, subjects engage in the same behaviors *except* for some level of the independent variable of interest. An example will explain the difference. Suppose we are interested in the effects of televised violence on kids. We decide to look at violence in music videos to see if it produces the same kinds of increased aggressiveness that other kinds of TV violence appear to produce. Our hypothesis is that violence in music videos will increase aggressiveness. We plan an experiment on the effects of violent music videos on early adolescents' aggressive behavior during their school lunch recess. Naturally, we would need to operationally define both our IV and DV. If we used a no-treatment control condition as one level of the IV, we would show one group of students but not the other a music video that had been rated by objective judges as very violent. Then we would record the aggressiveness of both groups of kids (counting the number of arguments they begin, perhaps). Let us say that we found that kids exposed to the violent video were indeed more aggressive. We could say that a violent video caused an increase in aggression. But did we really construct a good test of our hypothesis about violent content? Perhaps *any* music video increases aggression because the music is physiologically arousing—a reasonable hypothesis. A better control condition for the music video experiment would be to expose the control group to a nonviolent but equally arousing music video and then measure aggressiveness during recess. If we still found that kids who watched the violent music video were more aggressive, then we could say that the increased aggression was due to the *violent* content of the video (which was really what we set out to demonstrate). A research example illustrating the importance of a control group is given in Box 4-2.

The type of control group you select will depend on what you want to show. If you simply want to compare the presence of a treatment with the absence of a treatment (like the difference between exercise and no exer-

BOX **4-2**
A research example

Doob et al. (1969) were interested in the effect on final sales of the initial selling price of an item. Manufacturers will often introduce new products at special low prices and provide free samples or coupons to induce consumers to try the products. The hope is that shoppers will continue to buy the product. Doob et al. tested this notion by introducing new products at low prices in a chain of discount houses. The initial low prices were later raised to the regular selling prices. If the marketers' notion is correct, shoppers should continue to buy the product after the price increases. A variety of items was tested, including mouthwash, toothpaste, aluminum foil, and light bulbs. In most cases the researchers found that, predictably, sales dropped off after the price increase but continued at a reasonable level. On the surface it seems that the low price was a useful device to encourage people to try the products, since at least some buyers continued to use them.

Nevertheless, as you can see, the experiment requires a control group. In order to establish normal sales for each product, Doob et al. introduced the products at their regular prices in a comparable set of stores. That is, they included a control condition in which there was no price reduction. This is an essential part of the experiment. Without knowing what sales are when a product's initial price is the regular price, we cannot say whether the lower price affects sales at all. Some buyers will try any new product regardless of its price. Thus initial sales might be explained by curiosity. Since a product usually has some merits, at least some buyers will remain after the price increase. In fact, Doob et al. found that the low initial selling price actually reduced overall sales of the products. After periods ranging from 4 to 20 weeks, depending on the product, they found that in stores where the initial price was the usual selling price, sales were higher than in stores where an initially low price was later increased to the normal selling price. They explain their paradoxical findings in terms of cognitive dissonance theory: When customers pay more for a product, they must come to like it more in order to reduce their dissonance, or conflict, over buying the item at that price. Then, because they like it more, they buy it again. On the other hand, a cheap item does not need to be as good to be worth the price; there is little need to justify buying it or to buy it again.

cise), you could use a no-treatment control condition. But a word of caution about no-treatment control conditions: You always need to think about what the subjects in the control group are doing while subjects in the experimental group are being treated. For instance, in the exercise experiment, you would need to make sure that the subjects in the no-treatment control condition were not spending their 15 minutes studying for their exam, while the other students were exercising! Remember what we said in the beginning of this section: In the control condition, we carry out exactly the *same* procedures that are followed in the experimental condition, except for the experimental manipulation. Very often, control conditions involve carefully arranging conditions that *control* for what control-group subjects are doing. In the exercise experiment, we might decide to create a situation in which the control group is engaged in some (nonaerobic) activity that would not be expected to have any effect on how well they will perform on the upcoming test.

Experiments Without True Control Groups

It may not always be possible or even desirable to use a treatment condition in which subjects are not exposed to some value of the IV. Often, experiments are conducted without a control group at all. Control-group experiments are particularly useful in the first stages of experimentation. Once it has been established that an IV produces some effect not ordinarily present, researchers often begin to look at behavioral differences that occur when subjects are exposed to different treatment levels of the IV. For example, we could test whether a highly violent music video produces more aggressiveness than a music video with a low level of violence. Or we could investigate whether 15 minutes of aerobic exercise is better than 10 minutes. These experiments also require at least two experimental conditions, because we must always have data to evaluate behavior under different values or levels of our independent variable.

Holloway and Hornstein (1976) carried out a well-designed experiment without a control group. They suggested that the news influences our view of human nature. In one experiment they tested the effect of hearing good or bad news. Subjects were brought into a waiting room one at a time. They thought they were waiting for the experiment to begin, but in reality it had already started. While they were in the waiting room, a radio played music for a time. The music was then interrupted by the voice of a newscaster who read one of two "news items." Half the subjects heard the report of a man whose life would be saved because of a kind donor who would provide the organ needed for an emergency kidney transplant. The remaining subjects heard a very different story. This one reported the murder of an elderly woman. The murderer was identified as a respected clergyman and neighbor of the victim. After these reports the radio returned to music until one of the researchers casually turned it off and ostensibly began the experiment.

In the next part of the experiment, subjects were asked to make ratings concerning human nature. They were asked questions like "What percentage of people try to apply the Golden Rule even in today's complex society?" Holloway and Hornstein found that "the people who heard the tale of the woman's murder thought much less of their fellows than those who heard the good news about the kidney donor. The former estimated that fewer members of their community were decent, honest, and altruistic" (p. 76).

In this experiment the independent variable was news (good versus bad). The dependent variable was the opinion of humankind—that is, how honest, decent, and upright the subjects rated other people. The experiment had only two groups of subjects, those who heard "good news" and those who heard "bad news." Good news was operationally defined as a news story in which one person helps another. Bad news was operationally defined as a news story in which one person harms another. The dependent variable was operationally defined in terms of subjects' answers to a series of questions about the morals and attitudes of others. The Holloway and Hornstein experiment is a well-designed experiment that has no control group. All subjects heard some news, either good or bad. Holloway and Hornstein concluded the following: "The good news produces more favorable views of humanity's general moral disposition than bad news does—despite the fact that the news deals only with certain special cases and not at all with human nature on the grand scale" (p. 76). The conclusion is worded carefully. Since there was no group that received no news at all, Holloway and Hornstein could only make statements about the relationship between the different values of the independent variable that were actually tested—good and bad news.

Still, it is possible that hearing any news will alter people's attitudes or feelings. Folklore tells us, No news is good news. Does this mean that even good news might produce some negative effects? Perhaps the highest ratings of humanity would be obtained from subjects who heard no news at all. Indeed, we might speculate that although the "good" news story in the Holloway and Hornstein experiment has a "happy" ending, it is not a particularly good story at all. Both men must endure the pain and risk of major surgery; each will have to function for the rest of his life with only one kidney. This story could cause some subjects to focus on human frailty, which in turn might cast doubt on others' ability to resist temptation and abide by ethical and moral standards. Of course, there is no way of verifying any of these speculations without a control group. *The conclusions that may be drawn from an experiment are restricted by the scope and representativeness of the treatment conditions.*

As you design your own experiments, you will want to focus on the hypothesis you are testing. You must decide in advance which and how many treatment conditions will be necessary to make an adequate test of your hypothesis. Since Holloway and Hornstein focused on the differences produced by good versus bad news, the absence of a control group does not invalidate their study. However, using a control group would have increased the amount of information about the effect of the independent variable. Sometimes deciding whether or not to use a control group becomes an ethical decision. We will discuss this problem in Chapter 5.

Extraneous Variables and Confounding

From an experiment we can draw a causal inference about the relationship between the independent and dependent variables. If the value of the dependent variable changes significantly as the independent variable changes, we may say that the independent variable *caused* changes in the dependent variable.[6] But this inference is justified only when the experiment is well controlled. Many things other than the independent and dependent variables may be changing throughout an experiment—time of day, the experimenter's level of fatigue, the particular subjects who are being tested. Such variables are called **extraneous variables;** they are factors that are not the main focus of the experiment. They are neither intentionally manipulated independent variables nor dependent variables measured as indexes of the effect of the independent variable. They can include differences among subjects, equipment failures, inconsistent instructions—in short, anything that varies. Extraneous variables can affect results: Experimental subjects may be tired if they are in an experiment at the end of the day; equipment breakdowns can change the results produced by an independent variable during a treatment session; differences in the way instructions are presented can alter subjects' responses. In a well-controlled experiment, we attempt to recognize the potential for extraneous variables and use procedures to control them. Realistically though, even the most well-controlled experiment will be influenced from time to time by extraneous variables that cannot be controlled in advance. As long as these influences are infrequent, *random* events, they do not necessarily invalidate an experiment. However, random influences from extraneous variables do introduce errors into the scores obtained from subjects, so it is important to control for them as carefully as possible. These influences will obscure the effects we are really interested in and make it more difficult to detect significant treatment effects.

The real gremlin that wreaks havoc on an experiment is an extraneous variable that changes in a *systematic* way along with the independent variable. In a well-controlled experiment, the variation in the independent variable must be the *only* systematic variation that occurs across treatment conditions. If an extraneous variable occurs in one treatment condition but not another, an experiment cannot be internally valid. *If uncontrolled extraneous variables are allowed to change along with the independent variable, we may not be able to tell whether changes in the dependent variable were caused by changes in the independent variable or by extraneous variables that also changed value across conditions.*

When the value of an extraneous variable changes systematically across different conditions of an experiment (that is, when it changes *along with* the independent variable), we have a situation known as **confounding.** A good experiment must be free of confounding. Box 4-3 presents a hypothetical experiment in which confounding is a serious problem. When there is confounding, experimental results cannot be interpreted with certainty. Causal relationships between the independent and depen-

---

[6] *Significance* is a statistical term we will return to many times. In an experiment there is always some probability that observed effects were produced by chance and hence not by our treatment. A significant effect is one in which the odds of this effect occurring by chance have been virtually ruled out by statistics.

BOX **4-3**
Confounded
experiment

With the increasing concern about food additives, we might hypothesize that the average consumer would now be more likely to select a product with fewer food additives than a similar one with more additives. Suppose we set up an experiment to be conducted in a local supermarket.

We approach every third customer who enters the market and ask that person to participate in a study of consumer preferences. We show the subject two containers of potato chips. The first container (labeled "Crunchy Chips" in bright, cheerful colors) lists the following ingredients: potatoes, oil, salt. The second container (labeled "Gumshoe Chips" in dull, unattractive colors) lists these ingredients: potatoes, oil, salt, monosodium glutamate, calcium silicate, disodium inosinate, disodium guanylate, polymorphosperversinate, artificial flavor, and artificial color. We now ask our subjects to examine both packages and indicate the one they would be more likely to buy, assuming the price of the two items is equal.

Suppose that of the 236 shoppers who agree to participate, 232 select the first as the product they would be most likely to buy. May we conclude that, consistent with our original hypothesis, shoppers prefer products with less additives? Definitely not.

This experiment contains a confounding variable. The independent variable is the number of additives listed on the food package. The dependent variable is desirability, measured by the subjects' reports of which product they would be more likely to purchase. There are two conditions in the experiment: a control condition in which the product has no additives and an experimental condition in which the product has many additives. Were subjects avoiding the experimental food that contains many additives? Based simply on reported preferences, we might be tempted to conclude that shoppers avoid foods that contain many additives. However, in addition to the number of additives, the names of the products also varied across conditions. The name "Crunchy Chips," which suggests a crispy product, may be more appealing than "Gumshoe Chips." The package labeling also differed across conditions—"Crunchy Chips" had a more attractive package than "Gumshoe Chips." Since the names of the products and their packaging as well as the ingredients are different, we cannot conclude with certainty that subjects chose one product over the other because of the ingredients and not the names or the packaging.

In order to establish that subjects prefer one product over another on the basis of ingredients, we must eliminate the names of the products and the packaging.* We might relabel both products simply "Potato Chips." We would also want to use two containers of the same color and size, keep the price of the two items constant, and refrain from smiling as subjects examine the labels. With all other factors held constant across conditions, if subjects still showed a clear preference for one product over the other, we might then conclude that subjects preferred one to the other because of the ingredients.

* In a later chapter you will learn about a more complex design in which it is possible to explore the effects of both the names and the ingredients at the same time.

dent variables cannot be inferred. In effect, confounding sabotages the experiment because the effects we see can be explained equally well by changes in the extraneous variable or in the independent variable; our experiment is not internally valid. In subsequent chapters we will study some of the basic techniques used to avoid confounding.

Our goal is always to set up an experiment in such a way that the independent variable is the only variable (besides the dependent variable) that changes value across conditions. In order to draw causal inferences about the effects of the independent variable, we must be sure that no extraneous variables change along with the independent variable.

For example, suppose a researcher was interested in the effects of age on communicator persuasiveness. She hypothesized that older communicators would be more persuasive than younger communicators—even if both presented the same arguments. She set up an experiment with two experimental groups. Subjects listened to *either* an 18-year-old man or a 35-year-old man presenting the same 3-minute argument in favor of gun control. After listening to one of the communicators, subjects rated how persuaded they were by the argument they had just heard. As the researcher predicted, subjects who heard the older man speak were more persuaded. Would she be justified in stating that a speaker's age influences persuasiveness. Definitely not. Too many extraneous variables could have changed along with the independent variable (age): The older speaker may have seemed more attractive, better educated, more intelligent, or more self-confident (all these variables can influence our persuasability). Even though the researcher believed she was manipulating only the age of the speaker, several other extraneous variables may also have systematically varied along with the IV. Therefore we cannot say with assurance that age (and not one of the other variables) influenced persuasion. What might she have done to control for these potential sources of confounding?

You can see that it is difficult to control all the sources of possible confounding in an experiment. We must often compromise in setting up our experimental design by focusing on the variables most likely to affect the dependent variable we are measuring. For example, in a study of learning in the classroom, we would be more concerned about finding classes of comparable intelligence than classes containing equal numbers of brown- and blue-eyed students. Just as we narrow down the number of possible independent variables we want to explore, we narrow down the number of extraneous variables we choose to control. The rule of thumb is to *control as many variables as possible.* If a variable can be held constant in an experiment, it makes sense to do so even when any impact of that variable on the results may be doubtful. In the hypothetical persuasion experiment, for example, the researcher did control some potential confounds (sex of the speaker and content of the speech). However, we often find that as we control one variable, another changes value and is out of control. Many of the design problems you will face can be described as "finding the least worst alternative."

SUMMARY

In this chapter we have examined a number of basic experimental concepts. The *independent variable* is the antecedent condition (the treatment) that is deliberately manipulated by the experimenter to assess its effect on behavior. We use different values or levels of the independent variable in order to determine how changes in the independent variable alter the value of the dependent variable, our index of behavior. The *dependent variable* is an indicator of change in behavior. Its values are assumed to depend on the values of the independent variable.

Both independent and dependent variables must be defined operationally. An *operational definition* specifies the precise meaning of a variable within an experiment: It defines the variable in terms of observable operations, procedures, and measurements. Operational definitions establish what operations and procedures constitute each of the different values needed to test the effect of the independent variable. They also specify the procedures used to measure the impact of the independent variable.

The researcher must define the *level of measurement* of each variable. There are four levels of measurement: nominal, ordinal, interval, and ratio. A *nominal scale,* the lowest level of measurement, measures a variable by establishing categories, which are not measures of size but are mutually exclusive: An item cannot belong to more than one nominal category at the same time. An *ordinal scale* reflects differences in magnitude by rank ordering values of a variable. An *interval scale* has magnitude, equal intervals between values of a variable, but no absolute zero point. A *ratio scale,* the highest level of measurement, has magnitude, equal intervals between its values, and an absolute zero point. We generally use the highest level of measurement that is feasible.

Operational definitions are developed according to criteria of *reliability* and *validity.* Reliable procedures have consistent and predictable outcomes. Valid definitions are sound and sensible. If our definitions are valid, we will be manipulating and measuring the variables we intend to study. *Face validity* is the simplest criterion for evaluating validity. We may also evaluate the *content* and *predictive validity* of our dependent measures. Researchers are also concerned with *construct validity,* the fit between data and theory.

An experiment is *internally valid* if we can be sure that the changes in behavior that occurred across treatment conditions were caused by the independent variable. To make valid statements about the effect of the independent variable, we must use at least two treatment conditions. One may be a *control condition* that tells us how subjects do on the dependent variable when the independent variable is not manipulated. Other conditions are *experimental conditions* in which different values of the independent variable are applied.

Ideally, the independent variable is the only variable that changes value in the different treatment conditions of the experiment. However, sometimes we find that *extraneous variables,* variables that are neither independent nor dependent variables in the experiment, also change across conditions. When extraneous variables change value from one treatment condition to another along with the independent variable, we have a situation known as *confounding*. When there is confounding, we cannot say for sure whether the changes we see in the dependent variable from one condition to another were caused by the changes in the values of the independent variable or by an extraneous variable that was also changing: The experiment is not internally valid.

KEY TERMS

Confounding An error that occurs when the value of an extraneous variable changes systematically along with the independent variable in an experiment.

Construct validity The degree to which a measurement device accurately assesses the hypothetical construct it is intended to measure.

Content validity The degree to which the content of a measure reflects the content of what is measured.

Continuous dimension The concept that traits, attitudes, and preferences can be viewed as continuous dimensions (for example, sociability can be viewed as a continuous dimension ranging from very unsociable to very sociable).

Control condition The determination of the value of a dependent variable without the presence of the independent variable.

Control group The subjects in a control condition.

Dependent variable (DV) The particular behavior that a researcher tries to explain in an experiment.

Environmental variable An independent variable that the experimenter can bring under direct control.

Experimental condition A treatment condition in which the researcher applies a particular value of an independent variable to subjects and then measures the dependent variable.

Experimental group The subjects in an experimental condition.

Experimental operational definition The explanation of the meaning of independent variables; defines *exactly* what was done to create the various treatment conditions of the experiment.

External validity How well the findings of an experiment apply to situations that were not tested directly.

Extraneous variable A variable other than an independent or dependent variable; a variable that is not the main focus of an experiment and that may confound the results if not controlled.

Face validity The degree to which a measurement technique is self-evident.

Fruitful statement A statement that leads to new studies.

Hypothetical construct   Unseen processes, such as hunger or learning, postulated to explain observable behavior.

Independent variable (IV)   The variable (antecedent condition) that the experimenter intentionally manipulates.

Interitem reliability   The degree to which different items measuring the same variable attain the same results.

Internal validity   The soundness of the procedures within an experiment; the determination that the changes in behavior observed across treatment conditions in the experiment were actually caused by the independent variable.

Interrater reliability   The degree of agreement among different observers or raters.

Interval scale   The measurement of magnitude or quantitative size having equal intervals between values but no true zero point.

Level of measurement   The type of scale of measurement used to measure a variable.

Measured operational definition   The description of *exactly* how a variable in an experiment is measured.

Nominal scale   The simplest level of measurement; classifies items into two or more distinct categories on the basis of some common feature.

Operational definition   The specification of the precise meaning of a variable within an experiment; defines a variable in terms of observable operations, procedures, and measurements.

Ordinal scale   A measure of magnitude in which each value is measured in the form of ranks.

Predictive validity   The degree to which a measure, definition, or experiment yields information that allows prediction of behavior.

Ratio scale   A measure of magnitude having equal intervals between values and having an absolute zero point.

Reliability   The consistency and predictability of experimental procedures and measurements.

Scale of measurement   The type of precise, quantitative measurement used to measure variables.

Subject variable   The characteristics of the subjects in an experiment that cannot be manipulated; an independent variable, in the sense that a researcher can select subjects for their particular values.

Task variable   An aspect of a task that the experimenter intentionally manipulates.

Testable   Capable of being tested; that is, the means for manipulating antecedent conditions and measuring the resulting behavior exist.

Test-retest reliability   Consistency between an individual's scores on the same test taken at two or more different times.

Theory   A set of general principles that can be used to explain and predict behavior.

Validity   The soundness of a statement; its ability to withstand criticism; in experiments, the principle of actually studying the variables intended to be measured.

REVIEW AND STUDY QUESTIONS

1. Define each of the following terms:
   a. Independent variable
   b. Dependent variable
   c. Extraneous variable
2. Identify the independent and dependent variables in each of the following hypotheses:
   a. Absence makes the heart grow fonder.
   b. It takes longer to recognize a person in a photograph seen upside down.
   c. People feel sadder in rooms painted blue.
   d. Smoking cigarettes causes cancer.
3. What is an operational definition?
4. Formulate an experimental operational definition for each independent variable in question 2.
5. Formulate a measured operational definition for each dependent variable in question 2.
6. For each hypothesis in question 2, discuss three extraneous variables that might interfere with making a valid test of that hypothesis.
7. Define and give an example to illustrate each of these terms:
   a. Interrater reliability
   b. Test-retest reliablity
   c. Interitem reliablity
   d. Content validity
   e. Predictive validity
   f. Construct validity
8. a. Discuss the requirements of a good operational definition.
   b. What specific criteria are applied to measure operational definitions?
9. What is internal validity? Why is it important?
10. Summarize the characteristics of each of the following levels of measurement and give an example of each:
    a. Nominal
    b. Ordinal
    c. Interval
    d. Ratio
11. What type of scale is being used in each of these instances:
    a. A researcher measures the brand of car purchased by subjects who heard one of three advertising campaigns.
    b. A counselor assesses the divorce rate among couples who had marriage counseling.
    c. A seamstress estimates how much fabric will be needed to make a coat.
    d. Three racks of sweaters are labeled "small," "medium," and "large."

e. In Murphy's Hardware, all the latex paints are on the top shelf; all the oil-base paints are on the bottom shelf.

f. A researcher asks subjects to reproduce the length of a line they have just seen.

g. On a scale from 0–10 (0 = not at all; 10 = extremely), how hungry are you right now?

12. In their news study, Holloway and Hornstein (1976) did not use a control group. Design two different control conditions that they might have used. Design one to be a no-treatment condition and the other to *control* for being exposed to any kind of news.

13. An ambitious graduate student wanted to collect all the data for his thesis in one day. His project involved subjects' ability to solve word problems. The student began by testing all the subjects in his experimental group first, beginning at noon. Unfortunately, the testing took far longer than he had expected. By the time he finished testing the first group of subjects, it was nearly midnight. But he did not let that stop him. He knocked at dormitory doors and woke the occupants. Before the drowsy student could protest, the experiment was completed according to the procedures of the control condition. Without knowing more about the experiment, what can you say about any conclusions this researcher might draw?

14. A researcher wanted to test the effect that riding the subway has on mental health. She formed two groups of subjects, an experimental group and a control group. The experimental group rode the subway for 60 minutes every morning. The control group jogged for an equal period of time. At the end of 1 month, both groups were measured on a scale of adjustment and well-being. The control group was found to be better adjusted than the experimental group. Do you accept the conclusion that riding the subway damages mental health? Why or why not?

15. How could you change the study described in question 13 to set up an experiment that would be internally valid?

REFERENCES

CAMPBELL, D. T. (1957). Factors relevant to the validity of experiments in social settings. *Psychological Bulletin, 54,* 297–312.

COOK, T. D., & CAMPBELL, D. T. (1979). *Quasi-experimentation: Design and analysis issues for field settings.* Boston: Houghton Mifflin.

DOOB, A. N., CARLSMITH, J. M., FREEDMAN, J. L., LANDAUER, T. K., & TOM, S. (1969). Effect of initial selling price on subsequent sales. *Journal of Personality and Social Psychology, 11,* 345–350.

FAZIO, R. H. (1990). Multiple processes by which attitudes guide behavior: The mode model as an integrative framework. In M. P. Zanna (Ed.), *Advances in experimental social psychology* (Vol. 23, pp. 75–109). New York: Academic Press.

HESS, E. (1975). Role of pupil size in communication. *Scientific American, 233*(5), 110*ff.*

HOLLOWAY, S. M., & HORNSTEIN, H. A. (1976). How good news makes us good. *Psychology Today, 10,* 76*ff.*

IRWIN, O. C., & WEISS, L. A. (1934). Differential variations in the activity and crying of newborn infants under different intensities of light: A comparison of observational with polygraph findings. *University of Iowa Studies in Child Welfare, 9,* 139–147.

JUDD, D. B., & KELLY, K. L. (1965). The ISCC-NBS method of designating colors and a dictionary of color names. *U.S. National Bureau of Standards Circular, 553* (2nd ed.).

KERLINGER, F. N. (1973). *Foundations of behavioral research* (2nd ed.). New York: Holt, Rinehart and Winston.

LIKERT, R. (1932). A technique for the measurement of attitudes. *Archives of Psychology,* No. 140.

LUTEY, C. L. (1977). *Individual intelligence testing: A manual and sourcebook.* Greeley, CO: Carol L. Lutey Publishing.

MARSH, H. W., & PARKER, J. W. (1984). Determinants of student self-concept: Is it better to be a relatively large fish in a small pond even if you don't learn to swim as well? *Journal of Personality and Social Psychology, 47*(1), 213–231.

OSGOOD, C. E., SUCI, D. J., & TANNENBAUM, P. H. (1957). *The measurement of meaning.* Urbana, IL: University of Illinois Press.

SARNOFF, I., & ZIMBARDO, P. G. (1961). Anxiety, fear, and social affiliation. *Journal of Abnormal and Social Psychology, 62,* 356–363.

SCHACHTER, S. (1959). *The psychology of affiliation.* Stanford, CA: Stanford University Press.

TAYLOR, J. A. (1953). A personality scale of manifest anxiety. *Journal of Abnormal and Social Psychology, 48,* 285–290.

THURSTONE, L. L. (1928). Attitudes can be measured. *American Journal of Sociology, 33,* 529–554.

VINEBERG, R., & JOYNER, J. N. (1983). Performance measurement in the military services. In F. Landy, S. Zedeck, & J. Cleveland (Eds.), *Performance measurement and theory* (pp. 233–250). Hillsdale, NJ: Erlbaum.

WARD, S. E., LEVENTHAL, H., & LOVE, R. (1988). Repression revisited: Tactics used in coping with a severe health threat. *Personality and Social Psychology Bulletin, 14*(4), 735–746.

5

Research Ethics

The American Psychological Association Guidelines
Deception and Full Disclosure
Anonymity and Confidentiality
Ethical Dilemmas in Human Research

Protecting the Welfare of Animal Subjects

Plagiarism

Summary

Key Terms

Review and Study Questions

References

So far we have focused on the basic principles for setting up an experiment to make the best possible test of the relationship between the independent and dependent variables. But any research project also involves decisions concerning the subjects who will participate in the study. Who will they be and how will we test them? In Chapter 1 we discussed the general concept of objective, data-based science. Science deals with facts, with truth seeking, and with understanding our universe. Science is commonly thought of as *amoral:* Facts discovered through science are neither moral nor immoral. Facts imply no standards of right and wrong. Whatever facts are discovered or technology developed, they are neither right nor wrong from a *scientific* point of view—they just happen to exist.

Thus science per se does not include values. However, as scientists, we do bring our values, ethics, and sense of right and wrong to the work we do. We report our findings truthfully (whether we like them or not). We must also deal with the ethical and moral questions that arise: Is it right to discover ways to build more efficient weapons? Is it right or prudent to create new life forms through genetic experiments? Is it right to postpone death through the use of artificial life supports? Is there a limit to what we can or should know? Do we have the right to perform any experiment imaginable simply for the sake of new knowledge?

In this chapter we will focus on the last question. We will discuss the ethics of the researcher's relationship with human and nonhuman subjects and the researcher's responsibilities in every experiment.

RESEARCH ETHICS

The researcher's foremost concern in recruiting and using subjects is treating them ethically and responsibly. Whether we work with animals or humans, we must consider their safety and welfare. Responsible psychological research is not an attempt to satisfy idle curiosity about other people's innermost thoughts and experiences. Rather, responsible research is aimed at advancing our understanding of feelings, thoughts, and behaviors in ways that will ultimately benefit humanity. But the well-being of the individual subject is no less important than the search for general knowledge: Research that is harmful to subjects is undesirable even though it may add to the store of knowledge. For instance, early experience is an important aspect of child development—but we would not raise children in isolation just to assess the effects of deprivation. There is no way we can justify such a study, no matter how important the knowledge we might gain.

A researcher is legally responsible for what happens to the subjects of a study. He or she is liable for any harm that comes to subjects, even if it occurs unintentionally. This means a researcher could be sued for damages if an experiment hurt someone, whether the injury was physical or psychological, intentional or accidental.

In order to protect the subjects of psychological research, several specific legal and ethical guidelines have been formulated. From a legal standpoint, human subjects are protected by a federal law (Title 45, Section 46.106[b]). This law requires that each institution set up a review committee to evaluate every proposed study. The committee's first task is to decide whether the proposed study puts the subjects "at risk." According to the regulations,

> "subject at risk" means any individual who may be exposed to the possibility of injury, including physical, psychological, or social injury, as a consequence of participation as a subject in any research, development, or related activity which departs from the application of those established and accepted methods necessary to meet his needs, or which increases the ordinary risks of daily life, including the risks inherent in a chosen occupation or field of science. (Department of Health, Education, and Welfare, 1975, p. 11854)

In essence, the regulations say that a subject **at risk** is one who is more likely to be harmed in some way because of the nature of the research.

Another task of the review committee is to ensure that the safety of the subjects is adequately protected, that any risks to the individual are outweighed by potential benefits or the importance of the knowledge to be gained, and that each subject at risk gives informed consent to participate.

Informed consent means that the subject agrees to participate after having been fully informed about the nature and purpose of the study. Several aspects of informed consent are particularly relevant to psychological research. First, individuals must exercise free will when agreeing to participate in an experiment: They must give their consent freely, without the use of force, duress, or coercion. They must also be free to drop out of the experiment at any time. Second, researchers must give subjects a full explanation of the procedures to be followed and offer to answer any questions about them. Third, researchers must make clear the potential risks and benefits of the experiment. If there is any possibility of pain or injury to subjects, researchers must explain this in advance, so that subjects know what they are getting into.

Consent should be given in writing. When the subject is a minor or is impaired, researchers should obtain consent from a parent or legal guardian. Even in these cases, however, subjects should still be given as much explanation as they can understand and be allowed to refuse to participate, even though permission has been given by the parent or guardian.

Box 5-1 shows an example of the kind of written *informed-consent form* typically used in psychological experiments. You will see that sub-

**INFORMED CONSENT FOR PARTICIPATION OF
HUMAN SUBJECTS IN A RESEARCH PROJECT**

Name of Participant: _____

Project Title: _____

I voluntarily agree to participate in this study. I understand that I can terminate my participation at any point and that termination will in no way jeopardize my standing at (name of university).

The investigation has been described to me by the experimenter, who has answered all my questions. I hereby authorize this person to measure certain aspects of my person. I understand that I will be asked to (specific procedures of study).

My participation is subject to the following conditions:

1. That adequate safeguards be provided to maintain the privacy and confidentiality of my responses.

2. That my name and my family's name not be used to ultimately identify said material; instead, code numbers are to be used.

3. That my individual scores not be reported; that data be reported as aggregate or group scores.

_____

(participant's signature)

_____

(investigator's signature)

jects are provided with information relevant to their participation in the experiment: the nature of the experiment, an overview of the procedures that will occur, and what they will be required to do. The specific hypothesis of the experiment, however, is not disclosed. If subjects are made aware of the expectations of the researcher, their reactions during the experiment may be unintentionally or intentionally altered by this information. (We will talk about this and other "demand characteristics" in

Chapter 10.) The purpose of informed consent is to give subjects enough information about the experiment so that they can make an *informed decision* about whether they want to participate.

THE AMERICAN PSYCHOLOGICAL ASSOCIATION GUIDELINES

Although the law contains specific provisions for the way research is to be conducted, questions may still arise in actual situations. For this reason, the American Psychological Association (APA) has published its own set of ethical principles (1990). The code applies to psychologists and students who assume the role of psychologists by engaging in research or practice. The APA principles include the same general requirements for ensuring the subjects' welfare as in the law, as well as help in evaluating specific cases.

The APA principles applying to research with human subjects are reproduced in Box 5-2 and with animal subjects in Box 5-3 (later in this chapter).

The guidelines require that whenever there is any question concerning the ethics of an experiment or procedure, the researcher should seek advice from others and employ all possible safeguards for the subjects (principle *a*). Institutions engaging in research are required by law to have a research review board that makes decisions on each study. (Check with your instructor or supervisor to clarify the procedures that apply in your institution. Always obtain approval for an experiment from an instructor or review committee before you begin.)

Even after procedures have been approved, the individual researcher has the final responsibility for carrying out the study in an ethical way (principle *c*). Obtaining informed consent is considered especially important.

Fully informed consent is required from all subjects who are at risk because of the nature of the research. In some cases subjects are considered to be **at minimal risk** (principle *b*). Basically, this means that the research does not alter the participants' odds of being harmed. For example, a study of what proportion of the population uses soap and water to wash their hands in a public restroom could probably be considered minimal-risk research: The participants are engaging in a public activity in a public place. Whether or not their behavior is recorded as part of a study is unlikely to affect them in any way. There is a small chance they could be injured during the study (for example, by falling on a slippery floor). However, the research does not increase the chances of this happening.

In cases in which the research has no conceivably harmful impact, subjects are said to be at minimal risk and informed consent is not mandatory (principle *d*). As a safeguard, however, it is usually desirable to obtain informed consent for all studies.

BOX **5-2**
Ethical principles for
research with human
participants*

The decision to undertake research rests upon a considered judgment by the individual psychologist about how best to contribute to psychological science and human welfare. Having made the decision to conduct research, the psychologist considers alternative directions in which research energies and resources might be invested. On the basis of this consideration, the psychologist carries out the investigation with respect and concern for the dignity and welfare of the people who participate *and with cognizance of federal and state regulations and professional standards governing the conduct of research with human participants.*

a. In planning a study, the investigator has the responsibility to make *a careful evaluation of its ethical acceptability.* To the extent that the weighing of scientific and human values suggests a compromise of any principle, the investigator incurs a correspondingly serious obligation to seek ethical advice and to observe stringent *safeguards to protect the rights of human participants.*

b. Considering whether a participant in a planned study will be a *"subject at risk"* or a *"subject at minimal risk,"* according to recognized standards, is of primary ethical concern to the investigator.

c. The investigator always retains the responsibility for *ensuring ethical practice in research.* The investigator is also responsible for the ethical treatment of research participants by collaborators, assistants, students, and employees, all of whom, however, incur similar obligations.

d. Except in minimal-risk research, the investigator establishes a *clear and fair agreement* with research participants, prior to their participation, that clarifies the obligations and responsibilities of each. The investigator has the obligation to honor all promises and commitments included in that agreement. The investigator *informs the participants of all aspects of the research that might reasonably be expected to influence willingness to participate* and explains all other aspects of the research about which the participants inquire. Failure to make full disclosure prior to obtaining informed consent requires additional safeguards to protect the welfare and dignity of the research participants. Research with children or with participants who have impairments that would limit understanding and/or communication requires special safeguarding procedures.

e. Methodological requirements of a study may make the use of concealment or deception necessary. Before conducting such a study, the investigator has a special responsibility to (1) determine whether the use of such techniques is *justified* by the study's prospective scientific, educational, or applied value; (2) determine whether *alternative procedures* are available that do not use concealment or deception; and (3) ensure that the participants are provided with *sufficient explanation* as soon as possible.

f. The investigator *respects the individual's freedom to decline to participate in or to withdraw from the research at any time.* The obligation to protect this freedom requires careful thought and consideration when the

(continued)

BOX **5-2**
(continued)

investigator is in a position of authority or influence over the participant. Such positions of authority include, but are not limited to, situations in which research participation is required as part of employment or in which the participant is a student, client, or employee of the investigator.

g. *The investigator protects the participant from physical and mental discomfort, harm, and danger* that may arise from research procedures. If risks of such consequences exist, the investigator informs the participant of that fact. Research procedures likely to cause serious or lasting harm to a participant are not used unless the failure to use these procedures might expose the participant to risk of greater harm, or unless the research has great potential benefit and fully informed and voluntary consent is obtained from each participant. The participant should be informed of procedures for contacting the investigator within a reasonable time period following participation should stress, potential harm, or related questions or concerns arise.

h. After the data are collected, the investigator provides the participant with information about the nature of the study and attempts to *remove any misconceptions* that may have arisen. Where scientific or humane values justify delaying or withholding this information, the investigator incurs a special responsibility to monitor the research and to ensure that there are *no damaging consequences* for the participant.

i. Where research procedures result in *undesirable consequences* for the individual participant, the investigator has the responsibility to detect and remove or correct these consequences, including *long-term effects*.

j. Information obtained about a research participant during the course of an investigation is *confidential* unless otherwise agreed upon in advance. When the possibility exists that others may obtain access to such information, this possibility, together with the plans for protecting confidentiality, is explained to the participant as part of the procedure for obtaining informed consent.

* From American Psychological Association. (1990). *Ethical principles of psychologists* (amended June 2, 1989). *American Psychologist, 45,* 390–395. Reprinted by permission. Emphasis added.

Subjects are free to refuse to participate, or to discontinue participation, at any time (principle *f*).

The responsibilities of both subject and experimenter must be agreed upon in advance, and the experimenter must honor all commitments made to subjects (principle *d*). Commitments include things such as promises to pay subjects and to share the results of the study with them.

Deception and Full Disclosure

The relationship between researcher and participants should be as open and honest as possible. In many psychological studies, however, the true purpose of the study is disguised. Currently, some form of deception is used in approximately 60% of psychological studies (Christensen, 1988). For instance, Holloway and Hornstein (1976) did not tell subjects that the experiment began as soon as they came into the waiting room. Subjects sat and listened to a radio that broadcast music and a fictitious news report. Whether subjects heard good news or bad news was the main focus of the study. Subjects later rated others on traits such as honesty. The purpose of the experiment was to determine whether good news would make subjects rate others more favorably. In fact, it did. Holloway and Hornstein clearly used deception in their experiment; subjects had no way of knowing that the experiment began in the waiting room or that the reports they heard were contrived to test the effects of news on attitudes.

How do research subjects feel about being deceived? Many studies have actually been conducted in order to determine the answer to this question. In a recent review of these studies, Christensen (1988) reports that most research subjects are apparently not bothered by deception.

> This review of the literature, which has attempted to document the impact of deception on research participants, has consistently revealed that research participants do not perceive that they are harmed and do not seem to mind being misled. In fact evidence exists suggesting that deception experiments are more enjoyable and beneficial than nondeception experiments. (p. 668)

Interestingly, Christensen also reports that research professionals are much more bothered by deception than subjects. The consensus among researchers, however, seems to be that the use of deception is justified by the knowledge that is gained (Suls & Rosnow, 1988). Many important psychological problems cannot be studied without the use of deception, and it may be argued, as Christensen has, that to fail to study important problems is even less justifiable.

When we consider the principles concerning full disclosure of experimental procedures, we must also consider the impact of disclosure on the outcome of the study. If Holloway and Hornstein had told subjects that the news reports were fictitious, would the subjects have responded in the same way? There is no way to be sure without actually running such an experiment. But it is possible that the impact of the reports would have been different if subjects had known they were phony. Similarly, in Schachter's (1959) study of anxiety and affiliation, subjects probably would not have become anxious if they had known they would not actually be shocked; they probably would have behaved differently.

Sometimes a small omission, or outright deception, seems necessary to make an appropriate test of the experimental hypothesis. How can this be reconciled with the principles of informed consent? According to the APA guidelines: "The investigator informs the participants of all aspects of the research that reasonably might be expected to influence willingness to participate, and explains all other aspects of the research about which the participants inquire" (principle *d*). In other words, if the subjects are misled, the deception must be such that subjects would not refuse to participate if they knew what was really happening. For instance, it would not be ethical to recruit subjects for a learning experiment without telling them we intend to punish their incorrect responses by exposing them to the sound of scratching nails on a blackboard. Since many subjects might decline to participate in such a study, our deception would be unethical. In contrast, as far as we know, Holloway and Hornstein's subjects would probably have consented to hearing a fictitious newscast, just as Schachter's subjects would have agreed to be in a study in which they would not be shocked. Furthermore, in both studies the researchers adhered to the principle of full disclosure by completely **debriefing** subjects at the end of the experiment—that is, explaining the nature and purpose of the studies (principles *e* and *h*).

Debriefing, however, can mean other risks. We assume that debriefing will undo the effects of the deception. Is this assumption justified? Is it possible that an explanation of what was done may not relieve subjects' fears? Bramel's (1963) study of projection is an example of a study in which debriefing may have been insufficient. Bramel was interested in studying attributive projection, which is the process of projecting traits onto another person. The traits projected are traits the person is consciously aware of having, making it different from the classical projection Freud described. (In classical projection, the traits projected are those the person is not consciously aware of possessing.) To ensure that subjects were aware of possessing a trait they might project, Bramel employed a procedural deception. Male subjects were shown photographs of males in various stages of nudity. Subjects were given false feedback about their degree of sexual arousal to the pictures, which led them to believe they possessed homosexual tendencies. Bramel then tested the subjects for projection of sexual arousal onto others. He asked them to estimate how aroused other people would be when they saw the pictures. Bramel found that subjects projected arousal onto people who were similar to themselves (other students) but not onto people who were unlike themselves (criminals).

Of course, Bramel debriefed all his subjects at the end of the experiment: He told them the feedback had been false and that there was no indication of homosexual tendencies in their responses, since this was not even being measured. Was the explanation sufficient? It is possible that for subjects who had doubts about their sexual identity the bogus feedback aroused considerable anxiety and discomfort. It is also possible that subjects may have doubted Bramel's final full disclosure. If he admitted deceiving them about the feedback, perhaps he was also deceiving them about their real responses. At the very least, subjects may have felt cynical about research and perhaps foolish at having been duped by the experimenter. Whether the effects of deception can ever be fully reversed by debriefing remains a serious ethical question. Regardless of any later explanation, the subjects' anxiety and discomfort during the experiment are real. Once done, these experiences cannot be undone.

Consider this example of an experiment concerning classical conditioning and extinction in human subjects. Campbell, Sanderson, and Laverty (1964) established classical conditioning in a single trial through the use of a traumatic event. Classical conditioning, first studied in Pavlov's laboratory, involves the pairing of an initially neutral conditioned stimulus (CS) with an unconditioned stimulus (UCS) that always leads to a specific unconditioned (unlearned) response (UCR). After repeated pairings, the originally neutral conditioned stimulus will lead to a response that resembles the unconditioned response. This response is known as the conditioned response (CR), since its occurrence is dependent upon the success of the conditioning procedure. Campbell, Sanderson, and Laverty used a drug, succinylcholine chloride dihydrate ("Scoline") to induce temporary paralysis and cessation of breathing in their subjects. Although the paralysis and inability to breathe were not painful, according to subjects' reports the experience was "horrific." "All the subjects in the standard series thought they were dying" (p. 631). The effect of the drug (UCS) led to an intense emotional reaction (UCR). The drug was paired with a tone (CS). Subjects became conditioned to the tone in just one trial. After a single pairing of the tone with the drug, the tone alone was sufficient to arouse emotional upset (CR) in most subjects. The emotional reaction persisted (that is, failed to extinguish) and actually increased with repeated presentations of the tone. Whether they were debriefed or not, these subjects went through a very upsetting experience.

Since we cannot always reverse our experimental effects, it makes sense to avoid procedures that are potentially harmful, painful, or upsetting to subjects (principle g). In addition to their dubious ethical standing, such procedures often add little to our understanding of behavioral processes. For instance, we already know that high anxiety has debilitating effects on many behaviors. What would it *add* to our understanding of the thinking process to find that subjects learn nursery rhymes or solve riddles less efficiently after they are made extremely afraid by a noxious laboratory procedure? When experimental procedures lead to undesirable consequences for subjects, the experimenter has the responsibility to correct these consequences (principle i). This could mean holding additional debriefing sessions or providing continuing counseling or psychotherapy to correct the upset.

The importance of using extensive debriefing to remove undesirable consequences can be illustrated by the consequences of being involved in studies of violent pornography and what researchers are doing to remove these harmful effects. When subjects (typically male undergraduates) are exposed to violent pornography in psychology experiments, they become more accepting of the "rape myth" than nonexposed men (Donnerstein, Linz, & Penrod, 1987). They are more likely to report callous attitudes toward women, such as "women really want to be raped." They are also more likely to say that they would consider raping a woman if they knew they would not be caught. Unfortunately, these attitudes do not seem to disappear quickly on their own. Extensive postexperimental debriefings that detail the unreality of the themes and images in violent pornography, however, do seem to help. In one experiment, a follow-up study was conducted 2 to 4 months after men had participated in a violent pornography study. The researchers wanted to assess the impact of debriefing on removing the harmful consequences. They found that an extensive debriefing helped to remove the harmful beliefs created by the films; 2 to 4 months later, men who had not yet been debriefed showed significantly more accepting attitudes about the rape myth than men who had received an extensive debriefing (Donnerstein & Berkowitz, 1981).

Anonymity and Confidentiality

One final consideration is the importance of maintaining anonymity and confidentiality (principle *j*). The researcher has the responsibility to protect subjects' privacy. When possible, data should be given anonymously and identified only by code numbers. Thus subjects would indicate only a number on a questionnaire, not a name. And there would rarely be a reason to identify subjects by name—most psychological research uses "aggregated" or group data and reports results as average scores for each treatment group (as you will learn later, in the chapters on statistics).

Data collected are also confidential. They must be stored in a secure place to which the public does not have access. They may not be used for any purpose not explained to the subject. They do not become items of gossip to be shared with friends. When shared with colleagues, data must also be treated with discretion and subjects' identities protected. Fictitious names or numbers (such as subject #17) should be used. Identifying details should be disguised if there is a chance that a subject will be recognizable.

Ethical Dilemmas in Human Research

Researchers use the guidelines provided by law and by APA to guide their ethical decisions. Institutional review boards serve as watchdogs by reviewing and agreeing to written proposals of experiments. But the researcher who conducts the experiment will ultimately determine whether subjects are being treated ethically by the way he or she carries out the research. We have already discussed some of the ethical decisions that must be made: whether to use deception; whether the information gained from an experiment justifies the risk of harm to participants. Sometimes researchers face another kind of ethical decision. In some experiments the need for a control group actually creates an ethical dilemma.

Testing the efficacy of psychotherapeutic procedures and medical and drug treatments often requires a control group so that effects of the treatment can be compared with the absence of treatment. In drug-testing experiments, a special type of control group (called a **placebo group**) is used. The placebo group is the prototype of a good control group: a control condition in which subjects are treated exactly the same as subjects who are in the experimental group, except for the presence of the IV. Subjects in the experimental group get some dosage of a drug, but subjects in the placebo group get something that looks like a drug but is actually a placebo (a pill containing an inert substance or an injection of a saline solution). Physiological effects on both groups of subjects are measured and compared to see whether the drug produced the effects.

However, at some time the drug needs to be tested on people who have the medical problem the drug is designed to help. This creates the ethical dilemma. When the placebo procedure is carried out on people who are actually in need of the benefits expected from the medication, the researcher in effect may be *denying* treatment to people who need it for the sake of scientific advancement. A partial solution is to compare a new drug with one that is currently being used. If the new drug performs as well or better, then positive results have been obtained.

A similar problem occurs in psychological research. Testing the efficacy of a psychotherapeutic treatment for depression sometimes requires comparing its results against a group of depressed people who have received no treatment. The control group for a psychotherapy study is usually a "waiting-list control group"—people who are waiting their turn for treatment. If the therapy proves beneficial, does the researcher then have the responsibility to treat the control group as well? It is often argued that the control group would not normally be receiving treatment, so they are not being denied a benefit. But it is an ethical decision that the researcher must make.

The AIDS epidemic has brought these kinds of ethical dilemmas to the forefront. Similar questions are being asked both of drug testing and psychological experiments. Kelly, St. Lawrence, Hood, and Brashfield (1989) were faced with this decision when they used a waiting-list control group in an experiment to test a behavioral intervention to reduce risky sexual practices in gay men. A 12-week program that combined education, social support, and assertiveness training to counteract coercive sexual situations was successful in reducing high-risk behaviors when measured in a follow-up 8 months later. Without a control group, there would have been no way of knowing whether men receiving the intervention were being helped by it. A much greater dilemma would have been created if the control group had been comprised of people who would ordinarily have been receiving some kind of treatment.

PROTECTING THE WELFARE OF ANIMAL SUBJECTS

The principles governing informed consent, debriefing, anonymity, and confidentiality are clearly important aspects of ethical research involving human subjects. There are other standards that must be applied to research involving animals. Questions about animal rights are not new. Evans addressed the issue in 1898 and summarized one position: "[A]nimals have no more rights than inanimate objects, and it is no worse from an ethical point of view to flay the forearm of an ape or lacerate the leg of a dog than to rip open the sleeve of a coat or rend a pair of pantaloons" (p. 99). Clearly, few if any contemporary researchers would agree with this position.

More recently, the Animal Welfare Act of 1966, as amended in 1970 (Public Law 91-579), was passed specifically to protect research animals. The Animal Welfare Act deals with general standards for adequate animal care, including the use of drugs and anesthesia. The act was recently reamended by Congress (*Federal Register,* February 15, 1991) to include new regulations that address the psychological well-being of higher animals. It requires, for example, that all dogs receive exercise and that primates are housed along with others of their species. There are several professional organizations around the country that also encourage ongoing monitoring of care of laboratory animals through self-policing by members of the scientific community. The American Association for Laboratory Animal Science (AALAS), for example, publishes detailed training manuals that include information on adequate housing, sanitation, and nutrition for animals used for research.

The American Association for Accreditation of Laboratory Animal Care (AAALAC) also promotes uniform standards. AAALAC uses the *Guide for the Use and Care of Laboratory Animals*[1] as its principal set of guidelines. That publication provides specific standards for cage sizes, food and bedding, waste disposal, drugs and anesthesia, and many other aspects of animal care. One of the guide's aims is to create standards for keeping animals in comfortable, safe conditions. It also addresses issues of safety and sanitation for the benefit of animal handlers working in the labs.

The American Psychological Association includes animal care among its ethical principles (see Box 5-3). APA's Committee on Animal Research and Ethics (CARE), established in 1925, has been influential in establishing national guidelines for psychological research that protect animal welfare. We will review the most important points of the APA guidelines here.

Animals do not have the understanding of human subjects, so the notion of informed consent is irrelevant. Animals cannot give consent, and they cannot walk out on procedures. Most animal research is done with animals raised in laboratories so they will be available for study. The animals are typically raised in cages and are totally dependent on the experimenter or lab assistant for food, water, and healthy conditions. When using animals for study, the experimenter is responsible for providing adequate care. The animals must be sheltered in clean cages of adequate size. Except when food or water deprivation is a variable for study, they must receive sufficient nourishment. When surgical procedures are required, the animals should be anesthetized and given good postoperative care to ensure the minimum amount of pain and discomfort. If it is necessary to sacrifice an animal, the procedure should be done by a researcher trained to carry it out in a humane fashion. As with human subjects, our concern is to avoid any unnecessary pain or risk to the subject. Research involving any procedure that might be painful to the animals, such as surgery, drug use, or shock, must be closely supervised by a researcher specially trained in the field.

Despite the existence of legal guidelines and the ethical standards of professional societies, controversy continues to surround the area of animal research. Basic custodial care is usually not the issue. Animal rights activists charge that laboratory animals are needlessly tortured and sacrificed in the name of Science. To what extent are these charges justified in

[1] Department of Health, Education, and Welfare Publication, NIH 78-23 (1978).

BOX **5-3**
Ethical principles for
care and use of
animals*

An investigator of animal behavior strives to advance understanding of basic behavioral principles and/or to contribute to the improvement of human health and welfare. In seeking these ends, the investigator ensures the welfare of animals and treats them humanely. Laws and regulations notwithstanding, an animal's immediate protection depends upon the scientist's own conscience.

a. The acquisition, care, use, and disposal of all animals are in *compliance* with current federal, state or provincial, and local laws and regulations.

b. A psychologist trained in research methods and experienced in the care of laboratory animals *closely supervises* all procedures involving animals and is responsible for ensuring appropriate consideration of their comfort, health, and humane treatment.

c. Psychologists ensure that all individuals using animals under their supervision have received *explicit instruction* in experimental methods and in the care, maintenance, and handling of the species being used. Responsibilities and activities of individuals participating in a research project are consistent with their respective competencies.

d. Psychologists make every effort to *minimize discomfort, illness, and pain of animals.* A procedure subjecting animals to pain, stress, or privation is used only when an alternative procedure is unavailable and the goal is justified by its prospective scientific, educational, or applied value. Surgical procedures are performed under appropriate anesthesia; techniques to avoid infection and minimize pain are followed during and after surgery.

e. When it is appropriate that the animal's life be terminated, it is done *rapidly and painlessly.*

* From American Psychological Association. (1990). *Ethical principles of psychologists* (amended June 2, 1989). *American Psychologist, 45,* 390–395. Reprinted by permission. Emphasis added.

the field of psychology? Are psychologists guilty of violating the ethical rights of animals? In his book *Animal Liberation* (1975), Peter Singer chronicled numerous cases of possible violations of the ethical rights of animals during psychology experiments. Many of the examples dealt with studies involving electric shock or food deprivation. (An even greater portion of the book dealt with the treatment of animals being raised for food or used to test consumer products.)

Singer described more studies than we can here. However, two of his examples are of special interest, since you will come across them later as examples of particular experimental concepts. Brief descriptions of them will give you a clear idea of the kind of research Singer and others find objectionable.

The first example comes from the work of Joseph V. Brady (1958). For several years he studied the emotional behavior of rhesus monkeys. The monkeys were kept in restraining chairs; these allowed them to move their heads and limbs but not their bodies (see Figure 5-1). They were placed in the chairs so that they could be trained through various conditioning procedures involving electric shock. The experimental setup, according to Brady, seemed to be quite stressful for the animals. Many of them died during the preliminary study. Autopsies showed that many of the dead subjects had developed ulcers, which are unusual in laboratory animals. Restraint alone was not the explanation; some animals had been kept in the restraining chairs for 6 months, received no shock, and did not develop ulcers. Therefore, in subsequent work Brady explored the effect of the conditioning procedures. Brady trained two monkeys, designating one an executive and one a control. Both monkeys were given brief shocks on the feet. However, the executive monkey could prevent shock by pressing a lever. Unless the executive acted appropriately, it (and its partner, the control monkey) would be shocked on the feet once every 20 seconds.

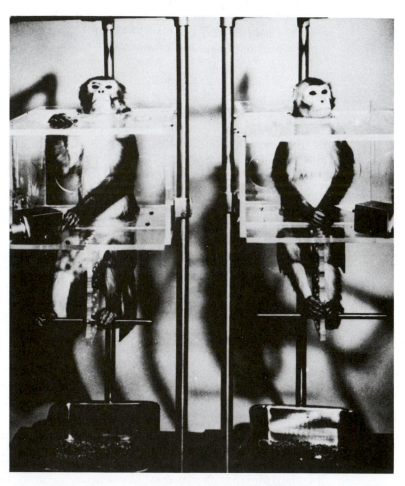

FIGURE **5-1** Rhesus monkeys being kept in restraining chairs. Used with permission of Walter Reed Research Institute, Washington, D.C.

The monkeys were exposed to alternating 6-hour periods of shock avoidance and rest (no shock). This procedure continued for 23 days, after which the executive monkey collapsed and was sacrificed. Subsequent experiments were conducted with different pairs of monkeys and with different time intervals.

There are several ethical objections to this line of research. First, the use of the restraining chairs alone is probably quite distressing to the animals, even though that by itself did not produce ulcers. Rhesus monkeys, like other monkeys, are very active and agile animals. Although we must be careful not to attribute human qualities to animals without justification, it is not very farfetched to assume that these normally active animals would prefer some alternative to the restraining chairs Brady used. Bear in mind that some animals spent 6 months in these chairs.

Second, the use of electric shock concerns many critics of animal research. Brady's original article (1958) does not contain the specific level of shock used in the experiment. We are told only that the shocks were brief. Most of us try to avoid electric shock of any magnitude, no matter how brief. Monkeys apparently share this preference, since they quickly learn to work to avoid shock. Some of the animals were so distressed physiologically by Brady's experiment that they actually developed ulcers and other gastrointestinal problems. Many died or were sacrificed so that their tissues could be studied for signs of ulcers. Is this justified based on what was learned from the experiment?

Before we try to frame an answer to this last question, let us look at a second example of animal abuse cited by Singer. This research also involved animals learning to avoid electric shocks. Solomon and Wynne (1953) tested avoidance learning in dogs. They set up a box divided into two compartments. A dog was placed in one side of the box, the floor of which was an electrified grid that could be used to shock the dog's feet. The dog's task was to learn to jump over a barrier between the two compartments to escape the shock and, later, to avoid it. Some animals were prevented from escaping the shocks; later they were unable to learn to avoid them. They had acquired what is now known as learned helplessness, a state that some researchers believe is linked to depression.

The shocks used by Solomon and Wynne were fairly intense (10.0–12.5 milliamperes). They also lasted up to 2 minutes. There were five training sessions per dog, with ten trials per session. Dogs yelped, shrieked, defecated, and urinated during the experiment.

Clearly, in both the Brady and Solomon and Wynne experiments, animals experienced discomfort and even outright pain. However, both these studies (and many others cited by Singer) predate the ethical guidelines that currently apply to research psychologists. The levels of shock used in the Solomon and Wynne study, for instance, are considerably stronger than those commonly used by psychologists today.

Coile and Miller (1984) wanted to evaluate the more recent allegations of animal abuse in psychological research. To do so, they reviewed all 608 articles reporting animal research that appeared in the psychology journals published by the American Psychological Association between 1979 and

TABLE **5-1**

Accusations of animal abuses by psychologists and the percentage of articles in which such treatments and/or results were reported	
Allegation	*Percentage of Articles in Which Reported*
"Animals are given intense repeated electric shocks which they cannot escape, until they lose the ability to even scream in pain any longer."	0.0%
"They are deprived of food and water to suffer and die slowly from hunger and thirst."	0.0%
"They are put in total isolation chambers until they are driven insane, or even die, from despair and terror."	0.0%
"They are subjected to crushing forces which smash their bones and rupture their internal organs."	0.0%
"Their limbs are mutilated or amputated to produce behavioral changes."	0.0%
"They are the victims of extreme pain and stress, inflicted upon them out of idle curiosity, in nightmarish experiments designed to make healthy animals psychotic."	0.0%

NOTE: *Adapted from "How Radical Animal Activists Try to Mislead Humane People" by D. C. Coile and N. E. Miller, 1984,* American Psychologist, 39, *pp. 700–701. Copyright © 1984 by the American Psychological Association.*

1983. (These are the major journals in which psychologists publish.) Table 5-1 summarizes a portion of the findings with respect to recent allegations.

Overall, the psychology research literature for a 5-year period does not support the accusations of radical animal activists. Although shock and food deprivation were used in some studies, the manipulations were by no means as extreme as reported by the critics of animal research. In reality, *none of the specific extreme allegations was supported by the literature.* Shock was used in 10% of the studies; inescapable shocks stronger than .001 ampere[2] were used in 3.9% of all the studies and in just 0.2% of the studies involving monkeys, dogs, or cats. The longest period of food or water deprivation reported was 48 hours. Less than 1% of the deprivation studies left animals without food or water for more than 24 hours. Most used 24 hours of deprivation, which corresponds to feeding once a day as is recommended for most house pets.

Nor were any studies done out of idle curiosity. As Coile and Miller (1984) noted: "Experiments involving inescapable shock . . . were aimed at understanding mechanisms believed likely to be involved in human depression, a condition that often causes its victims such intense suffering that they are driven to suicide. For young adults, suicide is the third leading cause of death" (p. 700).

Several objections might be raised about Coile and Miller's findings. First, abuse by psychologists may occur but not be reported in APA jour-

[2] "A strength that most experimenters can easily endure on their fingers" (Coile & Miller, 1984, p. 700).

nals. This is certainly possible, since many articles that are submitted to professional journals are rejected and never printed. Keep in mind that Coile and Miller only reviewed psychology journals—not medical or biomedical journals. Second, it is possible that 1979–1983 were simply good years for animals in psychological experimentation. That is why it is important to have an ongoing review of animal research practices. Abuses may occur occasionally, but they are by no means encouraged or condoned by the vast majority of professional psychologists.

Or are they? The basic premise of the APA guidelines for animal research is that animal research is acceptable in order to further the understanding of behavioral principles and to promote the welfare of humans.[3] Inherent in this premise is the assumption that the best interests of humans automatically take precedence over the rights of animals. The essence of this assumption was highlighted on October 26, 1984, when the heart of a healthy baboon was transplanted into a dying newborn baby. Many questions were subsequently raised about whether the baby's parents had given truly informed consent. But an equally controversial issue was whether humans have the right to take the life of another animal (Mainardi, 1984). Most of us make the decision, consciously or not, that we do have that right. We decide yes each time we eat a steak or a drumstick (Regan, 1983). We also decide yes every time we open a can of pet food (Herzog, 1991). Although we might not want to give up our pets or become vegetarians, we may still question the ethics of animal research. Do animals suffer needlessly? Singer made a strong case for this point of view. Other writers share his opinion:

> Many research projects are pointless, gratuitously repetitive, fatally flawed, or concerned with the obvious or the trivial. If animal suffering is of any significance whatsoever, its infliction can only be justified for clearly-defined goals. But many experiments are ill-conceived or actually unconceived in that no hypothesis has been formulated before conducting the experiment. One or a very few repetitions of an experiment may be needed to confirm the results, but some experiments are repeated time and again with no epistemological[4] justification. (Miller & Williams, 1983, p. 326)

The situations causing the grievances of the past cannot be undone. However, the picture for the future is hopeful. Only a few years ago, ethics was not even included as a topic in books such as this. Before 1987 the *E* in CARE stood for "experimentation." It now stands for "ethics." Currently there are strong efforts to formalize the teaching of ethics within psychology curricula at all educational levels (Mills, 1984). The charges of animal rights activists, although at times perhaps exaggerated and overly dramatic, do serve to heighten our awareness of the issues. There are still no clear-cut rules about what constitutes acceptable animal research. Who will make these decisions and on what basis? Keehn (1981), for example, found that human and animal experiments are judged differently. The results of Keehn's survey showed that "for humans, the principal consid-

[3] Keehn (1977) noted that many animal studies benefit animals too.
[4] *Epistemological* refers to the gathering of knowledge.

FIGURE **5-2** Demonstration for animal rights. Bruce Young/UPI/Bettmann

erations were for the protection and safety of the subjects while for animals they pertained to the design and conduct of the experiment'' (p. 81).

There are currently animal rights activists who favor a total ban on research with animals as subjects. An AALAS policy statement represents the other side of this issue:

> The use of experimental animals has been shown to be essential to the development of an understanding of many biochemical, behavioral, physiological, and disease processes. Many of the factors that affect both animal and human life can only be studied in intact animal systems by systematically manipulating specific research variables. Given an incomplete knowledge of biological systems, it is inconceivable that animal experimentation can be replaced, in the foreseeable future, by mechanical models or other incomplete biological systems.[5]

As long as animal research continues, researchers have an obligation to behave responsibly. Rollin (1981) argued that researchers need to pay more attention to the three *R*s: replacement, reduction, and refinement. When possible, as in many consumer product tests, live animals should be replaced by alternatives, such as tissue cultures or bacteria. There is evidence that fewer animals are, in fact, being used in research each year (Rowan & Andrutis, 1990). Some cosmetic companies, for example, have stopped testing their products on animals because of public pressure. Ani-

[5] American Association for Laboratory Animal Science. Policy Statement on Biomedical Research (news release, October 26, 1984).

FIGURE **5-3**   A close relationship can develop between researchers and their non-human subjects. UPI/Bettmann

mal suffering should be reduced by using fewer animals whenever possible and by avoiding needless duplication of effort and endless replication of prior findings. Research procedures should continue to be refined to shorten experiments, to use anesthetics and painkillers, and to make experiments less stressful for the animals.

The challenge to contemporary researchers is to ensure that each human or animal subject contributes something worthwhile to scientific knowledge. In the chapters that follow, we will return to ethical questions regarding human and animal subjects when pertinent in our examples of actual research projects.

PLAGIARISM

So far we have discussed the ethical concerns of researchers designing experiments involving human or animal subjects. Reporting on research is a necessary part of the scientific process. It is also an ethical matter. We report our procedures and findings honestly and accurately. We must also be careful in the way we draw upon the work of others in our presentation.

To **plagiarize** means to represent *someone else's ideas, words, or written work as your own.* Plagiarism is a serious breach of ethics and can result in legal action. It is not only "borrowing" facts and figures from someone else; it includes using someone else's ideas without giving proper credit. A well-known author was sued by a former professor who claimed the ideas in the author's best-selling book came directly from his lectures. The professor won his suit and now receives a share of the royalties.

Although some forms of plagiarism are intentional, others occur through simple oversights. It would be a rather large oversight to forget to give authors credit for direct quotations used, but what about paraphrasing their work—using their ideas but changing the words around? Paraphrasing without giving credit is representing someone else's idea as your own; it is plagiarism. Even if you believe that the information you wish to use is "common knowledge," if you have read it in someone else's book, give the author credit. If you have done a thorough review of the literature, your research report should contain many "citations."[6] Also, this is the only way the reader will know that you have read the important research in your topic area.

Unfortunately, it is easy to plagiarize without being aware of it. We read many things, jot down notes, and later forget where we got the information. If we use that information elsewhere, we may inadvertently forget or be unable to name the source. In preparing any research report, several guidelines should be followed to avoid the possibility of plagiarism (these guidelines also apply to works that are unpublished or not yet published).

1. Take complete notes, which include a complete citation of the source: author's name, title of article, journal name, volume number, year of publication, and page numbers. For books, include the publisher's name and city.

2. Within your report, identify the source of any ideas, words, or information that are not your own.

3. Identify any direct quotes by quotation marks at the beginning and end of the quotes and indicate where you got the quotes.

4. Be careful with paraphrasing (restating someone else's words). There is a great temptation to lift whole phrases or catchy words from another source. Use your own words instead or use quotes. Be sure to give credit to your source.

5. Include a complete list of references at the end of the report. References should include all the information listed in item 1.

6. If in doubt about whether a citation is necessary, cite the source anyway. You will do no harm by being especially cautious.

Throughout this book you will find figures, passages, and photographs used with the written permissions of the original authors, artists, and publishers.

[6] The citation given for Regan's (1983) idea that eating meat and poultry is a decision that goes against the best interests of animals is a good example of this. Everyone has probably heard this argument (and so have we), but we came upon Regan's published article as we reviewed the literature on ethics, so we cited this source because it gave us the idea to write about it.

SUMMARY

A well-planned experiment includes careful treatment of the subjects who participate. Today some aspects of psychological research are regulated by federal law. An institution must, for example, have a review board to approve each study. Many of the law's provisions are reflected in the ethical guidelines of the American Psychological Association. Most important is the *informed consent* of all those who will be subjects in an experiment. This consent must be given freely, without force or coercion. The person must also understand that he or she is free to drop out of the experiment at any time. In addition, subjects must be given as much information about the experiment as possible so that they can make a reasonable decision about whether to participate.

Sometimes a researcher may need to disguise the true purpose of the study so that subjects will behave naturally and spontaneously. In experiments that require some deception, subjects must be *debriefed.* But because simply debriefing subjects does not guarantee that we can undo any upset we caused them, researchers try to avoid exposing subjects to any unnecessary pain or risk. When possible, data should be collected anonymously and identified only by code numbers. Data collected are kept confidential; they may not be used for any purpose not explained to the subject. When they are reported, data should be identified by code numbers or fictitious names to protect subjects' identities.

Ethical principles apply in research with animals. Since animals have no choice about being subjects, researchers have a special responsibility to look out for their welfare. Animal subjects must receive adequate physical care to keep them healthy and comfortable. If drugs, surgery, or any potentially painful procedures are involved, the animals must be closely supervised by a researcher who is specially trained in the field. Despite allegations by animal rights activists, there is little evidence to support accusations of widespread abuse in psychological research. Educational efforts to heighten awareness of animal rights issues, as well as other ethical issues, are becoming increasingly widespread in the field.

Plagiarism, representing someone else's work as your own, is considered a serious breach of ethics. Researchers must be careful to give proper credit to others who contributed words and ideas to their published work.

KEY TERMS

At minimal risk   The subject's odds of being harmed are not increased by the research.

At risk   The likelihood of a subject being harmed in some way because of the nature of the research.

Debriefing   The principle of full disclosure at the end of an experiment; that is, explaining to the subject the nature and purpose of the study.

Informed consent   A subject's voluntary agreement to participate in a research project after the nature and purpose of the study have been explained.

Placebo group   A control condition in which subjects are treated exactly the same as subjects who are in the experimental group, except for the presence of the independent variable.

Plagiarism   The representation of someone else's ideas, words, or written work as one's own; a serious breach of ethics that can result in legal action.

REVIEW AND STUDY QUESTIONS

1. What is informed consent?
2. What is the principle of full disclosure?
3. At the end of the semester, all students in one section of a general psychology course are told they will not receive credit for the course unless they take part in the instructor's research project. Students who refuse to participate are given incompletes and do not get credit for the course. Is this approach unethical? Does it violate any principles of the APA guidelines?
4. An experimenter studying the effects of stress gave subjects a series of maze problems to solve. The subjects were led to believe that the problems were all quite easy. In fact, several had no solution. Some of the subjects were visibly upset by their inability to solve the problems. At the end of the study, the experimenter gave no explanation of the procedures. What ethical principles apply in this case? What *should* the experimenter have done?
5. In a study of sexual attitudes, a student experimenter finds that Pat, a friend's spouse, has responded yes to the question, "Have you ever had an extramarital affair?" The student is sure that the friend is unaware of Pat's behavior. The student decides to show Pat's answers to the friend. What ethical principles have been violated? How could this situation have been avoided?
6. Have you ever been a subject in a research project? If so, how were ethical principles applied in that study?
7. What ethical principles apply when we do research with animals?
8. In order to study the effect of a new drug to reduce depression, researchers must sacrifice animal subjects and dissect their brains. Discuss the ethical pros and cons of this line of research.
9. Lee had put off doing a lab report until the end of the term. He was badly pressed for time. His roommate said, "No problem. I took that course last year. You can use my report. Just put your name on it." Lee decides it is all right to use the paper since he has the author's consent. Do you agree? Why or why not?

REFERENCES

AMERICAN PSYCHOLOGICAL ASSOCI-
ATION (1990). Ethical principles
of psychologists (amended June
2, 1989). *American Psychologist,
45*, 390–395.

BRADY, J. V. (1958). Ulcers in executive monkeys. *Scientific American, 199*(4), 95–100.

BRAMEL, D. (1963). Selection of a
target for defensive projection.
*Journal of Abnormal and Social
Psychology, 66,* 318–324.

CAMPBELL, D., SANDERSON, R. E., &
LAVERTY, S. C. (1964). Characteristics of a conditioned response
in human subjects during extinction trials following a single traumatic conditioning trial. *Journal
of Abnormal and Social Psychology, 68,* 627–639.

CHRISTENSEN, L. (1988). Deception
in psychological research: When
is its use justified? *Personality
and Social Psychology Bulletin,
14,* 664–675.

COILE, D. C., & MILLER, N. E. (1984).
How radical animal activists try
to mislead humane people.
American Psychologist, 39, 700–
701.

DEPARTMENT OF HEALTH, EDUCA-
TION, AND WELFARE (1975, March
13). Protection of human subjects. *Federal Register, 40*(50),
Part II.

DONNERSTEIN, E., & BERKOWITZ, L.
(1981). Victim reactions in
aggressive erotic films as a factor
in violence against women. *Journal of Personality and Social
Psychology, 41,* 710–724.

DONNERSTEIN, E., LINZ, D., & PEN-
ROD, S. (1987). *The question of
pornography: Research findings
and policy implications.* New
York: Free Press.

EVANS, E. P. (1898). *Evolutional
ethics and animal psychology.*
New York: D. Appleton.

HERZOG, H. A. (1991). Conflicts of
interests: Kittens and boa con-
strictors, pets and research.
American Psychologist, 46, 246–
248.

HOLLOWAY, S. M., & HORNSTEIN,
H. A. (1976, July). How good
news makes us good. *Psychology
Today,* pp. 76*ff.*

KEEHN, J. D. (1977). In defence of
experiments with animals. *Bulletin of the British Psychological
Society, 30,* 404–405.

KEEHN, J. D. (1981). To do or not to
do: Dimensions of value and
morality in experiments with
animal and human subjects.
Social Science & Medicine, 15f,
81–84.

KELLY, J. A., ST. LAWRENCE, J. S.,
HOOD, H. V., AND BRASHFIELD,
T. L. (1989). Behavioral interven-
tion to reduce AIDS risk activi-
ties. *Journal of Consulting and
Clinical Psychology, 50,* 60–67.

MAINARDI, D. (1984, November 1).
E il babbuino che ne dice?
[Doesn't the baboon have some-
thing to say?] *Espresso,* p. 29.

MILLER, H. B., & WILLIAMS, W. H.
(1983). *Ethics and animals.* Clif-
ton, NJ: Humana Press.

MILLS, D. H. (1984). Ethics education and adjudication within
psychology. *American Psychologist, 39,* 669–675.

REGAN, T. (1983). *The case for animal rights.* Berkeley: University
of California Press.

ROLLIN, B. E. (1981). *Animal rights and human morality.* Buffalo, NY: Prometheus Books.

ROWAN, A. N., & ANDRUTIS, K. A. (1990). Animal numbers: Up, down and swing them all around. *Psychologists for the Ethical Treatment of Animals Bulletin, 9*(2), 3–5.

SCHACHTER, S. (1959). *The psychology of affiliation.* Stanford, CA: Stanford University Press.

SINGER, P. (1975). *Animal liberation.* New York: New York Review, Random House.

SOLOMON, R. L., & WYNNE, L. C. (1953). Traumatic avoidance learning: Acquisition in normal dogs. *Psychological Monographs, 67*(4, Whole No. 354).

SULS, J., & ROSNOW, J. (1988). Concerns about artifacts in behavioral research. In M. Morawski (Ed.), *The rise of experimentation in American psychology* (pp. 163–187). New Haven, CT: Yale University Press.

6

Basic Experimental Designs (Between-Subjects Designs)

In order to test an experimental hypothesis, a researcher must develop a basic plan or design for the experiment. The **experimental design** is the general structure of the experiment. It is analogous to the floor plan of a building, which specifies how many rooms there are and how they are connected but says nothing about what is inside the rooms and how they are used. Just as a floor plan describes rooms that can serve many different purposes, an experimental design can be used to answer many different research questions.

As we discussed various examples in earlier chapters, you may have noticed that some experiments resembled others in their overall structure. For instance, both Schachter's (1959) experiment on anxiety and affiliation and Holloway and Hornstein's (1976) study of good and bad news included two groups of subjects and two values of the independent variable. Experiments that test different hypotheses may have the same design. Then again, the same hypothesis may sometimes be approached through more than one design. The design is the *general structure* of the experiment, *not* its specific content. It is made up of things such as the number of treatment conditions and whether the subjects in all conditions are the same or different individuals. The particular design used in an experiment is determined mainly by the nature of the hypothesis. However, prior research, the kind of information the researcher is seeking, and practical problems in running the experiment also influence choice of design.

Although there is an infinite variety of potential hypotheses, a few basic designs may be used for the majority of research questions. Three aspects of the experiment play the biggest part in determining the design: (1) the number of independent variables, (2) the number of treatment conditions needed to make a fair test of the experimental hypothesis, and (3) whether the same or different subjects are used in each of the treatment conditions. We will look at basic research designs in terms of these aspects. In this chapter and the next, we will look at designs in which different subjects take part in each condition of the experiment. These are called **between-subjects designs.** The name is based on the fact that we draw conclusions from between-subjects experiments by making comparisons between the behavior of different groups of subjects. In Chapter 8 we look at within-subjects designs, in which the same subjects take part in more than one treatment condition of the experiment. In those designs we look for changes in behavior within the same group of subjects. But before we discuss the details of specific designs, let us look at the researcher's first decision—how to select subjects for the experiment.

SELECTING SUBJECTS

Populations and Samples

Selecting subjects is an important part of any experiment, regardless of its design. First, the researcher must decide who or what the subjects will be. The type of subject needed will depend on what is being studied. If we are doing an experiment on the attitudes of college students, we will obviously want to use college students as subjects. To study the effects of a drug, white rats or monkeys might be more desirable. Ideally, when we conduct an experiment, we would include all the members of the population we wish to study. The **population** consists of all people, animals, or objects that have at least one characteristic in common—for example, all undergraduates form one population; all jelly beans form another.

Before making statements about "students," "baboons," or "fathers," we ought to examine all the individuals who belong to these populations. But in practice this is rarely possible: An experiment on adult human learning would go on forever if we tried to test all adult humans. It would also be enormously expensive—and what if we missed some people? Would the results be invalid? Because of these problems, the researcher usually tests only a *sample*—a part of something assumed to be representative of the whole. Manufacturers sometimes distribute samples of new products. A small portion of the product gives us an idea of what the product is like so that perhaps we will buy a larger size later.

A **sample of subjects** is a group that is a part of the population of interest. The researcher uses a sample of subjects to get an idea of how all members of the population would behave. Data collected from a sample of subjects can be used to draw inferences about a population without examining all its members. In this way pollsters like Gallup are able to make predictions about the outcome of important elections. Not everyone in the country is questioned in the poll, but we get an idea of how the voting will go on the basis of the responses of those who are sampled.

The way in which the sample is selected is important. Different samples may produce very different data. How accurately we can predict from a given sample depends on its **representativeness,** meaning how closely the sample mirrors the larger population; or more precisely, how closely the *sample responses* we observe and measure reflect those we would obtain if we could sample the entire population. *The less the sample resembles the whole population, the less likely it is that the behavior of the sample mirrors that of the population.* We would be very wrong about the percentage of votes going to a candidate if we based our predictions on a preelection sample that included only Democrats. The representativeness of a sample poses problems for the way in which we will interpret the results of an experiment. Can we generalize the findings to the entire population? Thus representativeness affects an experiment's *external validity*. Suppose the sample does not reflect what is true of the population; the data we collect may give us an inaccurate picture of the effect of the experimental treatments on the population at large.[1] We will return to validity issues when we discuss the ways in which members of the sample are assigned to treatment conditions and again when we explore the interpretation of experimental results in later chapters. For now let us look at two general sampling approaches—probability and nonprobability sampling.

Probability Sampling

Probability refers to the study of the likelihood of events. What are your chances of rolling a 7 with a pair of dice? What are your chances of winning the lottery today? Probability is a quantitative discipline; to study probabilities, we must be able to count events and possible outcomes.

From a theoretical standpoint, some form of probability sampling is the preferred means of selecting subjects for research. **Probability sampling** involves selecting subjects in such a way that the odds of their being in the study are known or can be calculated. To use probability sampling, we must therefore begin by defining the population we wish to study. For example, our target population might be all females born in 1965 and now living in East Lansing, Michigan. If we wanted to count the members of this population, we could, although it would take time.

A second condition for probability sampling is that the researcher uses a means of selecting subjects without bias. The choice of participants is made through chance procedures such as flipping a coin or drawing a number out of a hat. This process is called **random selection,** meaning that the outcome of the sampling procedure cannot be predicted ahead of time by any known law (Kerlinger, 1973). As you will see in later chapters, random selection is also a common assumption of the statistical tests used most often to analyze data. Now let us look at *three* types of probability samples—simple random sample, stratified random sample, and cluster sample.

Simple random sampling. The most basic form of probability sampling is the **simple random sample,** whereby a portion of the whole population is selected in an unbiased way. Huff (1954) described the basic procedure in these colorful terms:

> If you have a barrel of beans, some red and some white, there is only one way to find out exactly how many of each color you have: Count 'em. However, you

---

[1] Keep in mind, though, that representativeness does not directly affect the *internal validity* of an experiment. As long as other proper control procedures are used, we can still be confident that the measured effects produced by an IV are correct; however, they may be correct only for this sample—not for the larger population for whom we wish to predict.

PROBABILITY

IF YOU HAVE 5 DOGS, 3 WILL BE ASLEEP

FIGURE **6-1** Courtesy of Sidney Harris.

can find out approximately how many are red in much easier fashion by pulling out a handful of beans and counting just those, figuring that the proportion will be the same all through the barrel. (p. 13)

Through random sampling we can find out about what the population is like without studying everyone. To obtain a simple random sample, *all members of the population being studied must have an equal chance of being selected to participate in the experiment.* A truly random sample is formed in such a way that there is no bias in favor of selecting one member over another. If there are one million people in the population, the chance of any particular person being selected should equal one in a million.

Even then, using random selection procedures does not guarantee that our sample will be truly representative of the whole population. Suppose someone put all the white beans into Huff's barrel first. If he took his sample from the top, he might conclude incorrectly that the barrel contained only red beans. When we use random sampling, we must keep in mind that each sample yields an estimate of what is *likely* to be true. The only way to guarantee 100% accuracy would be to measure the whole population. If that were feasible, however, we would not need a sample.

Stratified random sampling.   Researchers often prefer another variation of probability sampling known as stratified random sampling. A **stratified random sample** is obtained by randomly sampling known subsets, or subgroups, of the population. As you know, some samples can be poor reflections of the population's overall makeup. Stratified sampling can improve the representativeness of the sample and increase the accuracy of generalizing our experimental results to the entire population.

Stratified random sampling would be preferred in any sampling situation involving distinct subgroups within the same population. A study in a city, for example, might use it to mirror ethnic differences. A college administrator might choose it to ensure equal participation by upper and lower classmates. A market researcher might choose it to incorporate the preferences of various age and income groups.

There are two advantages to stratified sampling: First, the subsets can be sampled separately so that important minorities are represented in the total. Second, different procedures can be used with different subsets to maximize the utility of the data (Warwick & Lininger, 1975). This is desirable when the various subgroups are likely to respond differently. Let us look closely at one example.

A particular factory is made up of 10% managers and 90% production workers. If you wanted to measure employee morale in this plant, it would be desirable to use stratified random sampling. Managers and production workers may not have the same feelings about the company. If you wanted a stratified sample of 100 employees, you could randomly select 90 production line workers and 10 managers. Your sample would then reflect the makeup of the entire staff. A simple random sample might result in a sample that included only production line workers. By using stratified random sampling to include management, you ensure that their views are represented in the data.

Suppose we suspect that the morale problems in this factory are a direct result of the attitudes of management. In this case we might wish to **oversample** the group of managers—select a greater proportion of them to participate in the experiment—in order to increase our understanding of their behavior. Notice that the selection of the people within each stratum is done at random. All forms of probability sampling require random selection procedures at some stage of the process.

Cluster sampling.   When the population of interest is very large, it is often too costly or impractical to randomly select subjects one by one. In such cases researchers may use another form of probability sampling called **cluster sampling.** Instead of sampling individuals from the whole population or from specified strata, they sample from *clusters,* or bunches, that occur within the population.

For example, a person studying attitudes toward the postal service might use cluster sampling, because it would be very expensive and time-consuming to randomly sample the entire population of millions of postal users. However, each postal user has a zip code. Basically, the post office has mapped out clusters for us. The first digit of the zip code represents one of ten geographic areas of the country. The second and third digits represent one of the approximately ten areas into which each state is divided. The researcher could begin by selecting a group of zip codes from which to sample. He or she might choose to build stratification into the study at this point, too, by selecting codes for a cross section of geographic areas across the country. Once the codes have been selected, the researcher would randomly sample clusters of postal patrons within those zip code areas, using whole city blocks or perhaps entire mail routes.

The main advantage of cluster sampling is that the researcher can sample data efficiently from relatively few locations. As with all forms of probability sampling, participants are randomly selected; but in this method they are *selected in groups rather than individually*. A potential disadvantage of this approach is that subjects within clusters may resemble one another. The people on the same postal route, for instance, may be quite similar in economic status, education, race, and even age. For that reason, it is desirable to sample many clusters and to obtain as large a sample as possible.

Some variation of probability sampling is generally preferred for research purposes because subjects can be selected in an unbiased way. There are, however, other ways of selecting samples, which fall under the heading of nonprobability samples.

Nonprobability Sampling

It is sometimes impossible to use the kinds of procedures we have just described, despite their advantages. Even though random selection of subjects is accepted as a cornerstone of good research, many studies are based on nonprobability samples. As the name implies, with **nonprobability sampling** the subjects are not chosen at random. The likelihood that any particular member of the population will be selected is not known and cannot be calculated. Let us look at two common examples of nonprobability samples—quota and accidental.

Quota sampling. In a quota sample, researchers may select samples through predetermined quotas that are intended to represent the makeup of the population. It is up to the individual collecting the data (often someone other than the researcher) to fill the specified quotas. For example, a newspaper may wish to document campus attitudes toward nuclear arms. A reporter is sent to a university with instructions to interview 40 students, half male, half female, since the college body is roughly half men, half women.

As defined, the reporter's task is to fill the specified quotas. There are no constraints on how she or he does it. Because the selection is left to the reporter's discretion, the resulting sample may or may not be a good representation of the college community. The researcher may arrive early in the morning and approach students gathered around the vending machines in the student union building. There are many sources of potential bias in this approach—students who have late classes are missing; those who have money for the vending machines may be overrepresented; the reporter may want to approach only those who appear most friendly and cooperative. Such samples have human interest value and are often used in public opinion surveys. However, quota sampling generally lacks the rigor required in scientific research.

> The operation of a poll comes down in the end to a running battle against sources of bias, and this battle is conducted all the time by all reputable polling organizations. What the reader of the reports must remember is that the battle is never won. No conclusion that "sixty-seven per cent of the American people are against" something should be read without the lingering question, Sixty-seven per cent of which American people? (Huff, 1954, p. 22)

Accidental sampling.   An accidental sample is obtained by using any groups who happen to be convenient—for example, a church choir, an English class, a bowling league, or a supermarket checkout line. For this reason, it is also called a "convenience sample." This is considered a weak form of sampling because the researcher exercises no control over the representativeness of the sample. Despite this drawback, accidental sampling is probably done more often than any other kind. It is convenient, it is certainly less expensive than sampling the whole population at random, and it is usually faster. Researchers who rely on accidental samples must be cautious in the conclusions they draw from their data. Accidental samples limit the external validity of their results. It may not be valid to generalize their findings beyond the group they studied. Whatever distinguishes choir members, classmates, or bowlers from the rest of the population may also lead to atypical results. We will return to these issues in later chapters. For now keep in mind that it is always preferable to use some form of probability sampling *if that can be done*. Through random selection we have our best chance of obtaining a sample that is representative of the whole population. Let us turn now to look more closely at the process of random selection.

Using Random Selection

Suppose we want to do an experiment on the use of learning strategies among elderly people. Such research with children (for example, Wolff & Levin, 1972) indicates that learning is better when the researcher provides the child with a strategy for remembering. Would this procedure benefit the elderly, who sometimes have difficulty recalling information? The population we are interested in studying is the population of elderly people, which we might operationally define as all people over age 65. Clearly, we cannot study the entire population; what we want is a sample representative of the population. In practice, we often find that even this goal cannot be achieved. We may, for example, only have access to the residents of one nursing home. Thus the "population" available for study is already a select group. Although we would ultimately like to make statements about the general population of elderly people, our sample must be taken from this smaller group. Suppose we have access to the 32 residents of a local home for the aged, and our experiment requires only 20 subjects. Assuming that all the residents are willing to participate in the experiment, how do we decide which 20 will take part?

We could simply ask everyone to report to the testing room and allow the first 20 arrivals to be in the study. But some residents may arrive at the testing room later than others for a variety of reasons. Those who are new to the home might not know their way around the grounds and might take more time to find the correct room. General health may be a factor. Individuals who do not feel well may not want to walk to the testing room. Furthermore, there may be significant personality differences between those who get up early and those who sleep late. Thus a sample of subjects based on arrival time may not be representative of the group as a whole. It would be biased to include a disproportionate number of healthy early risers who know their way around the building.

Suppose, instead, that we simply test the 20 people who happen to be sitting in the solarium at a given moment. We have now restricted our sample of nursing home residents to the entire group of people in one room. This approach also poses problems. People who sit in the solarium may be different from those who do not. The solarium may provide more opportunity for conversation; residents who stay in their rooms may be more introverted than those who choose to come out. Such a difference could affect the outcome of our experiment. Perhaps extroverted subjects are more likely to develop rapport with the experimenter and use the suggested strategies. The behavior of introverted subjects might be quite different. A bias in favor of including only extroverted subjects would limit our ability to make statements about nursing home residents or elderly people in general because we would expect to find both introverts and extroverts in these populations.

Techniques for random selection.   We can get a fairly good random sample of the nursing home residents if we write all the prospective subjects' names on small pieces of paper, put them into a hat, mix well, and draw them out one by one until we have as many as we need. To simplify the procedure for ourselves, we can assign numbers to each individual and draw numbers from the hat instead of using names. The hat method is usually adequate, but it is not foolproof: A small variation in the size of the papers may bias the selection. The papers may not be mixed enough, so you draw out only names beginning with X or only the last numbers you wrote.

If you need many subjects, you may not want to spend your time drawing names or numbers out of hats. For this reason, you should become familiar with the **random number table** (see Appendix B), which is a table of numbers generated by a computer so that every number to be used (in this case 00 to 99) has an equal chance of being selected for each position in the table. Unlike the hat method, the computer-generated table is totally unbiased.

How do we use the random number table? We begin by assigning code numbers to all members of our subject pool. At the nursing home, we might

BIZARRE SEQUENCE OF COMPUTER-GENERATED RANDOM NUMBERS

FIGURE **6-2**   Courtesy of Sidney Harris.

simply number the subjects in the order they appear on an alphabetical list. If there are 32 people available, we assign them numbers 1 through 32. If we need only 20 subjects, we go through the random number table in an orderly manner (such as by reading vertically down each successive column of numbers) to find the first 20 numbers between 1 and 32 that appear in the table. Look at Appendix B, Table B1. Beginning at the top of the first column and reading down, we find the numbers 03, 16, and 12. All are between 1 and 32. So subjects 3, 16, and 12 will be in our sample. (The numbers 97 and 55 also appear in the first column, but since they are greater than 32, we ignore them.) We continue going through the table systematically until we have a total of 20 subjects. This group of 20 is a random sample of the 32 people available for the experiment. To form this group of 20, we arbitrarily began with the first number in the first column. To avoid using the same subject numbers over and over again in our experiments, we start at a different point in the table for each study. The starting point for each study should be decided in a blind manner. For instance, you might close your eyes and put your finger on a part of the table. You would begin your selection there.

Practical limits.   Ideally, when we take a random sample, every individual in the population has an equal chance of being selected. In practice, this ideal is rarely achieved. Our samples must be drawn from subsets of the population, such as the residents of one nursing home. Typically, we do not have access to all college students. We can sample only the airline passengers at the terminal nearest us. Our nursing home example dealt with a situation in which we have more individuals available than are needed. However, this is not always the case: People are often reluctant to participate in an experiment because they feel it will take too much time.[2] Unfortunately, they also are often wary of psychological research. At times individuals seem fearful that the experimenter will uncover very private information. This attitude stems partly from the popularization of Freud's ideas, especially the idea that every action contains an important hidden meaning known only to the trained psychologist. This makes it especially important that we follow ethical guidelines and keep subjects informed of what we are doing.

Rosnow and Rosenthal (1976) offered some suggestions for encouraging prospective subjects to volunteer: Make your appeal interesting, nonthreatening, and meaningful. Get someone known to the subjects to ask them, preferably a woman of high status. Emphasize the responsibility of people to aid in research that can help others and point out that lots of people do it. Pay them if you can and give token gifts (a stick of gum would do) for taking time to hear you out. Assess whether you should ask publicly (show of hands) or privately (fill out a form). Try to put yourself in the others' place and ask what would make you most likely to say yes.

As you recruit subjects, you may find that you have to use procedures that do not guarantee a random sample. You may have to recruit all your subjects from a single class or location, resulting in an accidental sample. Students in our classes have found that the lobby of the college library and outside the bookstore can sometimes be good places to find willing subjects. In desperation, they have also resorted to asking their friends to participate. However, asking friends is risky on three counts: First, it can dissolve a friendship. Second, friends may not be totally ignorant about the purpose of an experiment that you have been talking about for 2 weeks. They may also be sensitive to your subtle cues to behave in particular ways. These cues may influence the way they respond in the experiment and may lead to erroneous data. Third and most important, they may feel obliged to participate. This raises ethical questions concerning free choice. But even when we have the time, energy, and resources to do extensive sampling, another difficulty remains. Since it is unethical to coerce people into participating in an experiment, there is no way of knowing whether those who choose to participate are essentially different from those who do not. Perhaps we would obtain very different data if we tested everyone regardless of personal choice. Without resorting to coercion, there is no way we can ever guarantee a truly random sample.

---

[2] One of the authors recalls scouting for subjects to take part in a brief, on-the-spot perception experiment that lasted about a minute. Prospective subjects often provided elaborate explanations of why they had no time to participate. Their stories usually lasted longer than the actual experiment.

Reporting Procedures

In reporting an experiment, researchers pay special attention to selection of subjects. Usually, it is not enough to say that a sample was randomly selected; the report must give enough information to enable another researcher to replicate the experiment. The details of the type of subject and the selection process are important parts of the procedure.

The way a sample is chosen also affects what can be concluded from the results. The report must explain recruitment procedures so that the results from an experiment can be interpreted properly (as well as replicated). After all, college students in the library lobby might respond differently in many circumstances than nursing home residents in the solarium, and results obtained from one convenience sample might not be expected to generalize to everyone. So we need to tell the reader exactly how the sample was obtained. This includes identifying the specific population sampled (for example, college students), as well as giving an exact description of where and how subjects were obtained (for example, "The subjects were 60 undergraduates, 30 men and 30 women, at the University of Oregon who responded to an ad in the college newspaper"). Any details that might have influenced the type of subject participating in the study must be included. If subjects were paid for participating, that fact should be noted. If subjects were recruited from a class and their participation fulfilled a course requirement, readers should be told that too. In our nursing home example, we might say: "The subjects were 20 (8 male and 12 female) randomly selected residents of the Valley Nursing Home in Elmtown, Ohio. Subjects ranged in age from 67.2 years to 73.4 years. The average age was 69.3 years." Note that this statement immediately tells readers that although we are discussing learning in the "elderly," our subjects are drawn at random from a very small pool—namely, the residents of a single nursing home. It also tells readers that we tested both men and women who fell within a particular age range.

Any limitations on who could participate should also be noted. For instance, of the people who responded to the newspaper ad, we may choose to include only those with 20/20 vision or only those over age 18. We must report whatever restrictions we imposed so that readers know exactly what sorts of subjects we tested. Occasionally, some subjects who are selected are not included in the report: They dropped out, their data were discarded because they could not follow the instructions, and so on. These facts should also be reported.

How Many Subjects?

How many subjects are enough for an experiment? Ten? One hundred? There is no simple answer to this question. In later chapters we will discuss experiments that require only one or two subjects and others that require many more. Usually, we want to have more than one or two subjects in each treatment condition. Remember that we use samples of subjects to make inferences about the way the independent variable affects the population. Too small a sample can lead to erroneous results. For instance, if we wanted to know the height of the "average" American adult, we would want a large sample. Samples of two or three people would probably be inadequate even if they were randomly selected. We would hesitate to make statements about millions of people on the basis of such a small sample. Similarly, in an experiment we might hesitate to make great claims for our independent variable on the basis of a few subjects.

Of course, if everyone were exactly the same, if everyone behaved exactly the same way, we could use samples of one or two subjects with confidence. We would know that the experimental results reflect what we would find if we tested everyone in the population. But we know that, in reality, subjects are not all the same. Different subjects will get different scores. Our independent variable may affect different subjects in different ways. The more responses can vary, the harder it is to get a sample that reflects what goes on in the population. If individuals in the population are all very similar to one another on the dependent variable, small samples are adequate. However, when individuals are likely to be quite different, larger samples are needed. *If we take larger samples, we are more likely to obtain individuals who represent the full range of behaviors on the dependent variable*—some people who score high, some who score low, and some who score in between. Thus a larger sample is more likely to mirror the actual state of the population.

Typically, we get slightly different responses from different subjects in an experiment because of individual differences. Subjects' scores should also differ because of the treatment conditions. We expect the behavior of subjects under different treatment conditions to be noticeably different. We use statistical tests to make comparisons between the behavior of subjects under different treatment conditions. When we discuss test results (Part 3), you will see exactly how these procedures work. As we choose our samples, though, certain general characteristics of the statistical procedures shape our decisions. The statistical procedures we will discuss in this text require computing averages of the results under different treatments. In effect, we ask whether, *on the average,* our independent variable had an effect. We evaluate the effect in terms of the amount of fluctuation we would expect to see among *any* samples measured on our dependent variable. We are not especially interested in the performance of individual subjects in the experiment; we know that individual scores will differ. The question is whether or not we see more of a difference if we look at responses obtained under different treatment conditions.

We use statistical procedures to decide whether the differences we see between responses under different treatment conditions are *significant differences:* Are they larger than the differences we would probably see between *any* groups that we measure on the dependent variable? Are they so unlikely to have happened accidentally that they are noteworthy and require a scientific explanation? From a statistical standpoint, it is much harder to show that differences between treatment groups are significant when we use a small number of subjects. This is especially true when individual responses are apt to vary a great deal from one subject to another under any circumstances. For that reason, we usually try to have a reasonably large number of subjects in each treatment group. If the effects of the independent variable are strong, we should be able to detect them with about 10 to 20 subjects per group. A moderate size effect should show up with about 20 to 30 subjects per group. Weaker effects may be detected in larger groups. Of course, these are only rough estimates. Other factors besides the number of subjects and the impact of the independent variable influence the outcome; a larger sample is no guarantee that an experiment will turn out as you expect.

Practical considerations also affect the total number of subjects to be used. You may plan to have 50, but if you can only get 30, that may have to do. If the experiment requires lengthy individual testing sessions, it may not be feasible to run large numbers of subjects. You can use the review of prior research as a guide. If other researchers have had success with 20 subjects, that is a reasonable number. As a rule of thumb, it is advisable to have at least 10 subjects in each treatment group. Smaller numbers make it very difficult to detect an effect of the independent variable unless the effect is enormous.

ONE INDEPENDENT VARIABLE: TWO-GROUP DESIGNS

The simplest experiments are those in which there is only one independent variable. As you know, an experiment must have at least two treatment conditions: The independent variable is manipulated in such a way that at least two levels or treatment conditions are created. When only two treatment conditions are needed, the experimenter may choose to form two separate groups of subjects. This approach is known as the **two-group design.** Sometimes one group is a control group, which receives the "zero value" of the independent variable (for example, the placebo group in a drug study). The other group, the experimental group, is exposed to a nonzero value of the independent variable. At other times the experimenter might design an experiment with two experimental groups: both treatment groups may receive some nonzero level of the IV (good or bad news; 5 versus 10 mg of a drug). In every two-group experiment, both groups are then measured on the dependent variable and their behavior compared. If the independent variable has an effect, there should be differences between the two groups on the dependent variable.

There are two variations of the two-group design: One is the two-independent-groups design, the other is the two-matched-groups design. Both use two treatment conditions, but they differ dramatically in the way the researcher decides *which* subjects will take part in each treatment condition.

TWO INDEPENDENT GROUPS

In the **two-independent-groups design**, randomly selected subjects are placed in each of two treatment conditions through random assignment. The first step is to choose subjects through an unbiased selection procedure, as discussed previously. We may draw names out of a hat or use the random number table to decide which individuals will be in the experiment. Ideally, each member of the population we study should have an equal chance of being selected for our experiment. If it is not possible to select subjects entirely at random, the two-independent-groups design can still be used, but the researcher will have to settle for conclusions with less *external validity*. However, since a two-group design involves two treatment conditions, we also need to make decisions about which individuals will take part in each treatment condition. We do that by using another procedure, random assignment. Even if a researcher cannot use true random selection in deciding who the subjects of an experiment will be, he or she *always* uses random assignment to treatment conditions.

Random Assignment

Random assignment means that every subject has an equal chance of being placed in any of the treatment conditions. When we use an independent-groups design, we use the same unbiased procedures for assigning subjects to groups that are used in random selection of subjects for an experiment. Putting subject 3 in the control group should not affect the chances that subject 4 will also be assigned to that group. In an independent-groups design, the groups are "independent" of each other. The makeup of one group has no effect on that of the other.[3]

If subjects are not assigned at random, confounding may occur. We may inadvertently put all our witty subjects in the control group and so distort the outcome of the experiment. Random assignment gives us a better chance of forming groups that are *roughly* the same on all the extraneous variables that might affect our dependent variable. Assigning subjects at random controls for the differences that exist between subjects before the experiment. In short, it controls for subject variables. Our separate treatment groups will not consist of identical individuals, of course, but any potential differences will be spread out randomly across the conditions of the experiment. Thus random assignment guards against the possibility that subjects' characteristics will vary *systematically* along with the independent variable. When there are two treatment conditions, as in the two-independent-groups design, assignment may be made by simply

---

[3] Sometimes we may have to deviate from this ideal plan. For practical reasons, we may want to have equal numbers of subjects in all treatment groups. That may mean that we have to throw our last few subjects into one particular group to even up the numbers. We call this "random assignment with constraints." The assignment is random, except for our limitations on number per group, equal numbers of men and women per group, and so on.

flipping a coin. When there are more than two conditions, we may use the random number table. These methods eliminate bias; they reduce the chances that our experiment will be confounded because treatment groups are already different when we start the experiment.

Remember that random selection and random assignment are two separate procedures. It is possible to select a random sample from the population but then assign the subjects to groups in a biased way. The reverse is also possible. We can start out with a nonrandom, biased sample of subjects and randomly assign those subjects to our different treatment groups. But the original sample is still biased and may not represent the population we are trying to study. Nonrandom selection affects the external validity of an experiment—that is, how well the findings can be applied to the population and other situations. Random assignment, however, is critical to internal validity. If subjects are not assigned at random, confounding may occur. The experiment will not be internally valid because we will not be sure that the independent variable caused the differences observed across treatment conditions. It could be that the differences we see were created by the way we assigned the subjects to the groups.

In Box 6-1 we return to Brady's (1958) study of ulcers in monkeys. You will recall from Chapter 5 that this study raised several ethical concerns. It also raised methodological questions, since the researcher failed to assign subjects at random to the two treatment conditions.

Even though the researcher attempts to assign subjects at random, without objective aids the assignments may be biased in subtle ways. For instance, without being aware of it, the experimenter may put all the subjects he or she dislikes into the control condition because it is the most tedious. The treatment groups would then be different even before the experiment begins. If the groups are already different at the start, it might look as though the experimental manipulation is having some effect, even if it is not. The opposite can also happen. Differences in the treatment groups can mask the effect of the independent variable. Either way, the experiment leads to false conclusions about the effects of the independent variable.

Randomization was also important in a classic study by Kelley (1950). Kelley was interested in the effects of people's expectations on their impressions of others. He carried out a two-independent-groups experiment. Introductory psychology students were given one of two descriptions of a guest lecturer before he came to class. Half the students were told the visitor was "warm," half were told he was "cold." Kelley was careful to hand out the descriptions of the lecturer at random. The guest came and led a 20-minute class discussion. After that, students were asked to report their impressions of him. Their ratings differed in ways that indicated that students who expected the lecturer to be warm reacted more favorably to him.

Why was it important to hand out the descriptions of the lecturer at random? What might have happened if, say, all the "warm" descriptions were given out first? For one thing, students who sit in different parts of the classroom might be different. If we gave out all the "warm" descrip-

BOX **6-1**
Ulcers in executive
monkeys

Brady's (1958) study of ulcers in executive monkeys has received a great deal of publicity. Recall that the monkeys were divided into two groups. An executive group was given control of a button connected to an apparatus that produced electric shock. The executive's task was to prevent a painful electric shock by hitting the control button at least once every 20 seconds. Each nonexecutive was coupled (or yoked) with an executive. If the executive failed to hit the button in time, the nonexecutive would also receive a shock. The nonexecutives had no control over the shock; only the executives could prevent it.

The independent variable in Brady's experiment was control over the shock. The executives had control; the nonexecutives had none. The dependent variable was the development of gastrointestinal ulcers. Brady hypothesized that monkeys that had the responsibility of remaining vigilant and preventing the shock would be more apt to develop ulcers. In other words, their "executive" responsibilities in the experiment would be stressful; they would develop ulcers just as a hard-driving human executive might. After the experimental phase of the experiment ended, Brady sacrificed the monkeys and studied their tissues for signs of ulcers. As predicted, the executives had many ulcers; the nonexecutives did not.

On the face of it, his experimental procedure appears sound. Brady devised a controlled task that would presumably be more stressful to one treatment group than the other. Executives and nonexecutives were coupled together so that both received the same total number of shocks. The only difference was the degree of control the monkeys had over the shocks. Nevertheless, the study has been severely criticized. Weiss (1972) pointed out that Brady's treatment groups were not formed at random. Brady had used a pretest to determine which monkey in each pair could learn to avoid the shock more quickly, and this monkey was then made the executive. Therefore the study was not internally valid: The way the treatment groups were formed introduced a confounding variable. We cannot be sure that the requirements of the executive job produced ulcers. The executive monkeys may have been more sensitive to the shock, or they may have differed in other ways from the nonexecutives before the experiment began. They may, for example, have been more prone to ulcers under any circumstances. In fact, in another study using rats as subjects, Weiss (1972) demonstrated that lack of control over the shocks was apt to be more stressful than being in charge of things—if subjects were assigned to the treatment conditions at random. The number of coping attempts and the amount of appropriate or "relevant" feedback were also identified as important variables.

tions first, they might go to all the students who sit in the front of the class. Perhaps these students sit up front because they are more interested in the material or because they arrive earlier. In any case, their reactions to the class may be different from those of people who sit in the back. When it comes time to rate a guest speaker, these attitudes could alter the ratings as much as the descriptions that were given. Again, differences among subjects could confound the results of the experiment.

Forming Independent Groups

Let us look a little more closely at the randomization procedures used to form two independent groups in an experiment.

Zajonc, Heingartner, and Herman (1969) tested the hypothesis that cockroaches would run faster through a simple maze when other roaches were present than when they had to run alone. The hypothesis is based on the principle of social facilitation: In the presence of an audience, the performance of some behaviors improves. Cockroaches should do better in some mazes when other roaches are present. We can test this hypothesis ourselves using two independent groups.[4] One group, the experimental group, runs through the maze in the presence of an audience. The control group runs with no one watching. The dependent variable is the average time it takes each group to run the maze. Just like human subjects, the cockroaches must be assigned at random to each condition.

We begin by assembling our roaches for the experiment. As we take each roach out of its cage, we flip a coin to decide whether it goes into the experimental or the control group. By assigning subjects at random, we hope to create two groups that are roughly equivalent on important subject variables that could influence the outcome of the experiment. One such variable is the weight of each individual subject; heavy subjects might run more slowly than light ones under any circumstances. Weight, then, is a potential source of confounding in this experiment. Table 6-1 shows the hypothetical weights of our subjects assigned at random to the two treatment conditions. As you can see, the weights of individual subjects differ. We would expect this, since subjects differ from one another. If we look at the groups on the whole, however, we find that their *average* weights (represented by $\overline{X}$) are about the same. Even though individual roaches in each group weigh different amounts, the average weight of the groups is about equal. If we chose to, we could evaluate whether the small difference between the groups is statistically significant. We would find that although the groups are not identical, the difference between them is not significant; that is, it is not enough to merit concern. We can accept the groups as *equivalent* enough for our purposes. Assigning our subjects to the groups at random, we created two groups that are equivalent on an important subject variable. We will not have confounding due to weight in this experiment.

When we assign subjects at random, we expect to form groups that are roughly the same on any subject variables that could affect our dependent variable. This is important because we may not always be aware of every

---

[4] Zajonc, Heingartner, and Herman's actual experiment had a more complicated design to include a test of the effect of drive level as well as the presence of an audience.

FIGURE **6-3** Robert Zajonc.

variable that should be controlled. Sometimes we are aware of variables but do not have the tools, the time, or the resources to measure them. *Assigning subjects at random controls for differences we have not identified but that might somehow bias the study.*

The more subjects we have available to assign to treatment conditions, the better the chances that randomization will lead to equivalent groups of

TABLE **6-1**

Cockroaches randomly assigned to treatment conditions: Hypothetical weights			
Experimental Group		*Control Group*	
Subject Number	*Hypothetical Weight (gm)*	*Subject Number*	*Hypothetical Weight (gm)*
S_1	1.59	S_6	3.52
S_2	1.26	S_7	1.57
S_3	1.34	S_8	2.31
S_4	3.68	S_9	1.31
S_5	2.49	S_{10}	1.18
$N = 5$		$N = 5$	
$\overline{X}_E = 2.072$		$\overline{X}_C = 1.978$	

NOTE: *Randomization produced two groups of very similar average weight ($\overline{X}_E$ is about the same as $\overline{X}_C$).*

subjects. For example, if we have only two cockroaches available, one light and one heavy (like S_2 and S_4 in Table 6-1), there is no chance at all of forming similar groups. We will always have one heavy group and one light group. With ten cockroaches (as in Table 6-1), our chances of attaining groups with similar weights is increased. As we add additional subjects, the odds are even better that random assignment will produce similar groups. This becomes particularly important when we consider humans. We expect people to differ on many characteristics that could potentially affect their responses on the dependent variable. The more subjects we have, the better our chances of achieving groups that are equivalent on a number of different characteristics.

Block Randomization

Ideally, when we select a random sample, each member of the population we wish to study will have an equal chance of being selected for the experiment. However, as you know, we cannot force people to be in an experiment; they must volunteer. This means that we may have only a limited number of people available for our study. How then do we deal with the problem of assigning subjects to several treatment conditions in such a way that no bias results? One way would be to use a random number table. Suppose we are set to run an experiment with *three* different treatment conditions. We could first pick a spot in the random number table in an unbiased way, for instance, by closing our eyes and pointing. Wherever we land is the place we begin. We then look for the numbers 1, 2, and 3 in the table. Whatever order they appear in (2, 3, 1, 3, for example) would be the order in which we assign subjects to the three treatment conditions. The first volunteer would be assigned to treatment condition 2; the second volunteer would be assigned to treatment condition 3, and so on. We could proceed this way until we have assigned all the available subjects to the conditions of the experiment.

This method works fairly well from the standpoint of randomizing the assignment of subjects among the various conditions. However, because we have followed a random sequence, the number of subjects in each treatment group will not necessarily be the same. For a total of 30 subjects, we might find 14 in condition 1, 9 in condition 2, and only 7 in condition 3. The precise numbers would vary depending on where we entered the random number table to begin the process. From a practical standpoint, it is easier to analyze experimental data when the number of subjects in each treatment group is the same. That is, we would generally prefer to have ten subjects in each of the three conditions of this experiment. How can we deal with this practical problem and still apply the principles of random assignment?

In order to obtain equal numbers of subjects in all treatment conditions, psychologists use a sophisticated procedure called **block randomization.** Basically, the researcher begins the process of randomization on paper by creating *treatment blocks.* If there are three different treatment

TABLE **6-2**

Example of block randomization in a three-condition experiment				
Block A	Block B	Block C	Block D	Block E
S_1 2	S_4 2	S_7 3	S_{10} 1	S_{13} 2
S_2 1	S_5 1	S_8 2	S_{11} 3	S_{14} 1
S_3 3	S_6 3	S_9 1	S_{12} 2	S_{15} 3

NOTE: *Here we have five subjects per condition. To have more subjects per condition, successive blocks are filled as subjects (S_n) sign up for the experiment. The order of treatments within blocks is random.*

conditions in the experiment, each treatment block contains the three conditions listed in random order. As subjects sign up for the experiment, the researcher fills each successive treatment block. The more blocks he or she can fill, the more subjects there will be in each treatment condition.

Table 6-2 shows a block randomization scheme created to guarantee five subjects per condition for an experiment with three treatment conditions. Note that there are five blocks, and each condition is represented once per block. The order of the treatments within each block comes from the random number table. To set up a block, pick a spot at random from the random number table. Look for the number 1, 2, or 3. Whichever occurs first is the first treatment in that block. Continue down the table until you find a different number between 1 and 3. This will be the second treatment in the block. Since each treatment can be used only once per block, the last number is the one we have not used yet. Then create a second treatment block in exactly the same way. Repeat the process for each treatment block. Every additional block we can fill with subjects adds one subject to each treatment condition. Through block randomization we thus create a scheme by which subjects can be assigned to conditions at random while still ensuring equal numbers across conditions.

Here we have described the process for an experiment with three conditions. However, the same procedures apply for any number of treatment conditions. Simply set up blocks in which each treatment occurs once in a random order. For an experiment with four conditions, each block must contain the four conditions in random order. A five-condition experiment would have five conditions per block, and so on. The total number of blocks determines the number of subjects in each treatment group. The more blocks you fill, the larger your treatment groups.

When to Use a Two-Independent-Groups Design

How do we decide whether the two-independent-groups design is appropriate for an experiment? We begin by looking at the hypothesis. If there is only one independent variable, the two-independent-groups approach may work if the hypothesis can be tested with two treatment conditions.

In an experiment such as the one on cockroaches, two groups made sense. We simply wanted to see whether cockroaches would run better with (condition 1) or without (condition 2) an audience. When we run the experiment, we carefully assign subjects to the treatment conditions at random.

When we use the two-independent-groups design, we assume that randomization is successful. We assume that when we start the experiment, the treatment groups are about the same on all the extraneous subject variables that might affect the outcome. Unfortunately, this is not always the way things turn out.

In our cockroach experiment, we assigned subjects to the treatment groups at random. As you saw in Table 6-1, the random assignment produced two groups of very similar average weight. But suppose we do the experiment again. We again take the roaches from their cages and flip a coin to decide which group to put them in. The hypothetical weights of these new groups are shown in Table 6-3. What is wrong? We assigned our subjects at random, but the control group looks much heavier than the experimental group. How can this be? Well, you know that random assignment means every subject has an equal chance of being assigned to either treatment condition. There is always a chance that treatment groups will end up being very different on some subject variables, and this is particularly true when we have a small number of subjects in each condition.[5] Here, our random assignment did not produce comparable groups. Just by chance, the control group turned out to be quite heavy compared to the experimental group. Since the dependent variable in this experiment is running speed, the difference in weight may contaminate the results. The way things turned out here, the weight of the two groups is a confounding variable. If there is a difference in the running speed of the two groups, we cannot be sure whether it is due to the audience or to the difference in weight. The difference in running speed can be explained equally well by either variable.

TWO MATCHED GROUPS

Randomization does not guarantee that treatment groups will be comparable on all the relevant extraneous subject variables. Researchers therefore sometimes use the second of the two-group procedures, the **two-matched-groups design.** In this design there are also two groups of sub-

---

[5] You can test this principle, called Bernoulli's "law of large numbers," by flipping a coin. The laws of chance predict equal odds (50/50) for heads or tails each time you flip; this means that half your flips should end up heads and half tails. But if you flipped a coin only four times, it would not be unusual to get three heads and one tails or even four heads and zero tails. However, as you increase the number of coin flips, your chances of getting an equal number of heads and tails go up. If you flipped a coin one hundred times, your chances of getting an equal number of heads and tails is much better than if you only flipped it four times. The same law applies to random assignment to treatment conditions: The likelihood that treatment groups will be equivalent on extraneous subject variables increases as the number of subjects increases.

TABLE **6-3**

Cockroaches randomly assigned to treatment conditions			
Experimental Group		**Control group**	
Subject Number	Hypothetical Weight (gm)	Subject Number	Hypothetical Weight (gm)
S_{10}	1.18	S_4	3.68
S_2	1.26	S_6	3.52
S_3	1.34	S_8	2.31
S_9	1.31	S_5	2.49
S_7	1.57	S_1	1.59
$N = 5$		$N = 5$	
$\overline{X}_E = 1.332$		$\overline{X}_C = 2.718$	

NOTE: *Randomization produced two groups of very different weights.*

jects, but the researcher assigns them to groups by matching or equating them on a characteristic that will probably affect the dependent variable. The researcher forms the groups in such a way that they are sure to be comparable on an extraneous variable that might otherwise produce confounding.

Matching Before and After an Experiment

In order to form matched groups, subjects must be measured on the extraneous variable that will be used for the matching. Table 6-4 shows the way our cockroaches might be divided into two groups matched on weight.

TABLE **6-4**

Cockroaches assigned to two groups matched on weight					
	Experimental Group			**Control Group**	
Pair	Subject Number	Hypothetical Weight (gm)		Subject Number	Hypothetical Weight (gm)
a	S_2	1.26		S_{10}	1.18
b	S_3	1.34		S_9	1.31
c	S_1	1.59		S_7	1.57
d	S_8	2.31		S_5	2.49
e	S_6	3.52		S_4	3.68
	$N = 5$			$N = 5$	
	$\overline{X}_E = 2.004$			$\overline{X}_C = 2.046$	

NOTE: *The matched groups have very similar average weights ($\overline{X}_E$ is about the same as $\overline{X}_C$). Within each pair, the members are assigned to the treatment conditions at random. One member of each pair is randomly chosen to be in the control group; the other member is placed in the experimental group.*

Once the roaches have been weighed, we separate them into pairs. The members of each pair are selected so that they have similar weights. For instance, the first pair is made up of subjects 2 and 10. Subject 2 weighs 1.26 grams; subject 10 weighs 1.18 grams. Although members of each pair are not exactly equal in weight, they are closer to each other than to any other roaches in the sample. *When it is not possible to form pairs of subjects that are identical on the matching variable, the researcher must decide how much of a discrepancy will be tolerated.* A difference of 0.8 grams might be acceptable, but a difference of 2 grams might not. According to Underwood (1966), the decision is arbitrary. However, we obviously want to make good enough matches to ensure that our groups are not significantly different on the matching variable. If there is no suitable match for an individual in the sample, that individual must be eliminated from the study. After all the pairs have been formed, we randomly assign one member of each pair to a treatment condition. We can do this simply by flipping a coin. It is very important to put the members of each pair into the treatment conditions at random. If we do not, we may create a new source of confounding—exactly what we are trying to avoid.

In our cockroach example, the matching is done before the experiment is run. In some experiments it may not be feasible to do the matching beforehand. Suppose we need to match our subjects on intelligence. We may not be able to give an intelligence test, score it, match and assign subjects to groups, and run the actual experiment in a single block of time. Since we must know the test scores before we can do the matching, we might need a separate testing session just to give the test. In these situations we may proceed differently. We make the initial assignment to conditions at random and run the experiment with two randomly assigned groups of subjects that may or may not be comparable on our matching variable. Our subjects take part in the treatment conditions as usual. However, we also give them the intelligence test (that is, we measure them on the matching variable).

When the experiment is over, we use the intelligence test scores to match the subjects across the two groups, discarding those subjects in each group who cannot be matched. There are three ways to go about doing this. We may use **precision matching,** in which we insist that the members of the matched pairs have identical scores. A more common procedure is **range matching,** in which we require that the members of a pair fall within a previously specified range of scores. The process of range matching subjects after the experiment is run is illustrated in Table 6-5.

In the table you can see that subjects are considered matched if their scores fall within 3 points of each other. The choice of range is arbitrary. However, the smaller the range, the more similar the subjects must be on the matching variable. If we set the range at 50 points on an intelligence test, we would obviously gain little through matching.

As you can see from the table, range matching after the experiment is run may create problems. We cannot be sure there will be a suitable match for each subject in our sample. Some subjects will have to be discarded if no match is available. This could raise questions about the representative-

TABLE **6-5**

Matching subjects after the experiment: Pairing of scores on the matching variable, intelligence			
Experimental Group		*Control Group*	
Subject Number	*IQ*	*IQ*	*Subject Number*
S_1	109	91	S_6
S_2	94	100	S_7
S_3	116	111	S_8
S_4	102	63	S_9
S_5	133	115	S_{10}

NOTE: *Connecting lines represent final pairs of subjects. Subjects 5 and 9 must be discarded because there are no suitable matches for them in the sample.*

ness of the remaining subjects. Subjects who can or cannot be matched may differ in important ways that will affect their scores on the dependent variable. When using matching, it is therefore advisable to sample as many subjects as possible. This will minimize the chances that no match will exist within the sample. If we must discard subjects, the net result is that the total number available for analysis is smaller than we had planned. Having less data reduces the chance of detecting the effect of the independent variable. For this reason, matching before running the experiment is preferable to matching after it.

A third matching procedure, **rank-ordered matching,** is sometimes used. The subjects are simply rank ordered on the basis of their scores on the matching variable. Subjects with adjacent scores then become a matched pair. With rank-ordered matching, we do not specify an acceptable range between members of each pair. The benefit of rank-ordered matching is that unless you have to discard a subject because you have an uneven number of scores, all subjects are typically used. The down side is that there may be unacceptably large differences between members of a pair on the matching variable. This would certainly have been the case if we had used rank-ordered matching to form pairs from subjects in Table 6-5.

When to Use Two Matched Groups

Whether to match at all is another question. The advantages are clear: By matching on a variable that is likely to have a strong effect on the dependent variable, we can eliminate one possible source of confounding. We do not need to *assume* that our treatment groups are comparable on an important extraneous variable; we can make them comparable through matching.

In some cases, matching can also make the effects of the independent variable easier to detect even if random assignment has worked successfully and confounding is not a concern. When we match, we use statistical procedures that differ from those used with independent groups. We will look at these procedures in some detail in Part 3 of the book; it is enough to say here that the matched-groups procedure allows us to make comparisons based on the differences between the members of each of our matched pairs of subjects. Because some of the effects of individual differences are controlled within each pair, the impact of the independent variable is clearer.[6] We are able to compare the responses of rather similar subjects who were tested under different treatment conditions. Procedures for independent groups, however, require that we combine, or "pool," all the data from each treatment group and make comparisons between group averages. This makes it somewhat harder to detect the effect of our independent variable: We are forced to look at treatment effects along with the effects of individual differences. If our independent variable has an effect, we are more likely to detect it in our data if we have used matching.

Matching procedures are especially useful when we have very small numbers of subjects because there is a greater chance that randomization will produce groups that are dissimilar. This risk is not so great when we have large numbers of subjects available. As pointed out before, the larger the treatment groups, the better the chances that randomization will lead to similar groups of subjects and the less need there may be for matching.

Since there are advantages in using the matched-groups design, why not always use it? By matching on a variable such as weight, we can guarantee that our treatment groups will be similar on at least one extraneous variable. Unfortunately, there are potential disadvantages in this procedure—disadvantages related to the statistical techniques used to analyze the data from two-group experiments.

When we match, it is essential that we match on the basis of an extraneous variable that is highly related to the dependent variable of the experiment. In an experiment on weight loss, it would make sense to begin by matching subjects on weight. Subjects who are already heavy may be more likely to lose weight during the experiment. It would not make sense to match subjects on weight in an experiment on how to teach spelling to 12-year-olds because it is difficult to see any clear connection between weight and spelling ability. It would be more appropriate to match on another variable, such as intelligence; intelligence does affect the ability to spell. We would want to match on intelligence to avoid getting two groups of subjects with different IQs who would learn spelling at different rates regardless of the teaching method. Unfortunately, it is not always easy to know what variables are the best to use for matching. If we match on a variable that is *not* highly correlated with the dependent variable, it will be much more difficult to detect the effect of experimental manipulations. This is true because of the special statistical procedures used for data from matched groups. We will discuss those procedures in Chapter 12, and you

---

[6] Because matching makes treatment effects easier to detect, the statistical procedures used to test for significant differences between treatment groups are more *powerful* in matched than independent-groups designs.

BOX **6-2**
Using a two-group
design: Guidelines

Use a two-group design whenever two values of the independent variable are needed to test a hypothesis. Sometimes one group will be a control or no-treatment group, and the second will be an experimental group that is given some value of the independent variable. Other times both groups will be experimental groups given different levels of the independent variable. In addition to selecting subjects at random, you must assign your subjects to the treatment conditions at random: Each subject must have an equal chance of being assigned to each of the two conditions. If subjects are not assigned at random, there may be confounding in the experiment: The two treatment groups may be different before the experiment begins. If they are different to start with, you will not be able to tell whether differences in the dependent variable across conditions are due to the experimental manipulation or to the initial difference between the groups.

To avoid confounding because of subject variables, you may want to form matched groups of subjects. Matched groups are used when we do not want to assume that randomization alone was enough to produce two equivalent groups. We form matched groups by first measuring subjects on the variable that will be used for matching. Then we divide the subjects into pairs. The pairs are formed so that the members are roughly the same on the matching variable (for example, subjects with similar personalities). Then we randomly assign one member of each pair to condition 1; the other member of each pair is placed in condition 2. This guarantees that the final groups of subjects are about the same on the matching variable. If we cannot do the matching before the experiment, we can randomly assign the subjects to the treatment conditions first. Then we carry out the experiment and measure the subjects on the matching variable. After the experiment, we form our pairs. But if range matching is used, we can lose data this way, so it is a good idea to do the matching before the experiment begins.

will see then exactly how matching can be disadvantageous. For now, Box 6-2 summarizes the guidelines for setting up two-group designs.

SUMMARY

The *design* of an experiment is its general structure—the experimenter's plan for testing the hypothesis—not the experiment's specific content. The researcher decides on the *experimental design* mainly on the basis of three factors: (1) the number of independent variables in the hypothesis, (2) the number of treatment conditions needed to make a fair test of the hypothesis, and (3) whether the same or different subjects are used in each of the treatment conditions.

A basic assumption behind each experimental design is that subjects in the experiment are typical of the population they represent. Researchers use a variety of procedures to obtain the most *representative* samples; ideally, they use *random samples,* in which each member of the *population* has an equal chance of being selected for the experiment. Random samples can be obtained through some form of *probability sampling,* through which the odds of any individual being selected are known or can be calculated. *Simple random sampling, stratified random sampling,* and *cluster sampling* are the most frequent examples of this approach.

For practical reasons, researchers often use *nonprobability samples. Quota samples* and *accidental samples* are the most common examples. However, experimenters must be extremely cautious in generalizing their results from samples, particularly when the samples were not chosen at random.

After subjects have been selected for the experiment, they are assigned to treatment conditions in various ways. *Between-subjects designs* are those in which different subjects take part in each condition of the experiment. The name comes from the fact that we draw conclusions from between-subjects experiments by making comparisons between the behavior of different groups of subjects. We have looked at two main types of between-subjects designs: two independent groups and two matched groups.

The *two-independent-groups design* is used when one independent variable must be tested at two treatment levels or values. Sometimes one of the treatment conditions is a control condition in which the subjects receive the zero value of the independent variable. The other condition is an experimental condition in which the subjects are given some nonzero value of the independent variable. Other times both groups are experimental groups. Each experimental group receives a different (nonzero) value of the independent variable. The independent-groups design is based on the assumption that subjects are assigned at random. If treatment groups are different on a variable related to the dependent variable of the experiment, the result may be confounding. When we use an independent-groups design, we assume that randomization was successful. Sometimes, however, especially when the total number of subjects is small, we do not want to rely on randomization. Even with *random assignment,* sometimes treatment groups start out being different from each other in important ways. These differences can affect the dependent variable, and we may not be able to separate the effects of the independent variable from the effects of the initial differences between the groups.

Instead of relying on randomization, we may want to use the *two-matched-groups design,* in which we select a variable that is highly related to the dependent variable and measure subjects on that variable. For a two-group experiment, we form pairs of subjects having similar scores on the matching variable and then randomly assign one member of each pair to one condition of the experiment. The remaining member of each pair is placed in the other treatment condition. Matching is advantageous because we can guarantee that groups start out the same on variables that matter. It can also make treatment effects easier to detect because statistics used with matched designs look at effects of the IV on each matched pair, where it can be more easily detected. However, there are also disadvantages: We do not always know what we should use as our matching variable. Because of the statistical tests used for matched groups, we have to be sure that our matching variable is really related to our dependent variable. If it is not, matching can actually work against us—making it more difficult to see whether the independent variable had an effect.

KEY TERMS

Accidental sampling   A form of nonprobability sampling that selects subjects from any available group.

Between-subjects design   A design in which different subjects take part in each condition of the experiment.

Block randomization   The procedure used to assign equal numbers of subjects at random to each treatment condition of an experiment. Subjects are assigned to treatment blocks, where each block represents the condition of the experiment listed in random order.

Cluster sampling   The random selection of subjects by groups that occur in the population of interest; used when the population is very large.

Experimental design   The general structure of an experiment (but not its specific content).

Nonprobability sampling   A selection of subjects that is not random; the probability of selecting any individual subject is unknown.

Oversampling   In stratified random sampling, the selection of a larger than actual proportion of a particular subgroup in a population.

Population   In psychology experiments, all people, animals, or objects that have at least one characteristic in common.

Precision matching   Creating pairs whose subjects have identical scores on the matching variable.

Probability   The study of the likelihood of events; a quantitative discipline that counts events and possible outcomes.

Probability sampling   The selection of subjects in such a way that the odds of their being in a study are known or can be calculated.

Quota sampling   A form of nonprobability sampling that selects subjects by preset target numbers intended to reflect the makeup of the population of interest.

Random assignment   The technique of assigning subjects to treatments so that each subject has an equal chance of being assigned to each treatment condition.

Random number table   A table of numbers generated by a computer so that every number has an equal chance of being selected for each position in the table.

Random selection   The selection of subjects without bias; the outcome of the sampling procedure cannot be predicted ahead of time by any known law.

Range matching Creating pairs of subjects whose scores on the matching variable fall within a previously specified range of scores.

Rank-ordered matching Creating matched pairs by placing subjects in order of their scores on the matching variable; subjects with adjacent scores become pairs.

Representativeness How closely the responses of a sample of subjects reflect those responses that would be obtained if the entire population were sampled.

Sample of subjects A part of a population of interest assumed to be representative of the whole.

Simple random sample The most basic form of probability sampling; all members of a population have an equal chance of being selected.

Stratified random sampling The random sampling of known subsets, or subgroups, of the population; can improve the representativeness of the sample and increase the accuracy of the experimental results for the entire population.

Two-group design The simplest experimental design, used when only two treatment conditions are needed.

Two-independent-groups design An experimental design in which randomly selected subjects are placed in each of two treatment conditions through random assignment.

Two-matched-groups design An experimental design with two treatment conditions and with subjects who are matched on a subject variable thought to be highly related to the dependent variable. Generally, subjects are first measured on the matching variable, then divided into pairs having the most similar scores; members of each pair are then assigned to treatment conditions at random.

REVIEW AND STUDY QUESTIONS

1. What is the design of an experiment?
2. What features of the experimental hypothesis affect the choice of a design?
3. Discuss the logic behind random selection and why it is important in research.
4. For each of the following populations, outline three different sampling approaches that would yield random samples:
   a. College seniors
   b. Readers of *Time* magazine
   c. Assembly-line workers
   d. Computer owners
5. Discuss the potential advantages and disadvantages of each approach outlined in your answer to question 4.
6. Explain random assignment.
7. How does random assignment differ from random selection?

8. Why is it important to assign subjects to each treatment condition at random?
9. Describe a matched-groups design. How is the matching done?
10. A watched pot never boils. What design can you use to test this notion? How many treatment conditions do you need?
11. You are planning an experiment to test whether students learn better with or without a radio playing while they study.
    a. What will be your independent and dependent variables?
    b. How will you define them operationally?
    c. What type of design will you use?
    d. Is more than one design possible?
    e. What subject variables will you need to control?
12. A skeptical student tells you that it's silly to bother with a control group. After all, you're really only interested in what the experimental group does. How would you convince the student otherwise?
13. A researcher would like to match subjects on weight for an experiment on weight control. The weights of each subject in the sample are shown in the table below. Match them into pairs and form one experimental and one control group by using random assignment. Carry out the procedure using precision matching, range matching, and rank-ordered matching.

Subject Number	Weight	Subject Number	Weight
S_1	115	S_9	122
S_2	185	S_{10}	160
S_3	163	S_{11}	159
S_4	122	S_{12}	154
S_5	165	S_{13}	143
S_6	183	S_{14}	143
S_7	184	S_{15}	138
S_8	115	S_{16}	137

14. Referring back to question 13, how did the outcomes of precision, range, and rank-ordered matching differ? What are the pros and cons of using each procedure?
15. Evaluate each of the following as a technique for obtaining a random sample of subjects.
    a. An experimenter obtains subjects by asking every third driver stopping at the light on Hollywood and Vine to be in an experiment.
    b. A researcher places an ad in a local paper asking for volunteers for a psychology experiment.
    c. An experimenter calls every fourth number in the phone book and asks for volunteers for a research project.
    d. A wealthy graduate student posts signs on the university bulletin boards offering $5 per hour for participating in a 2-hour perception experiment.
16. What is a random number table? How do you use it?

17. Using the random number table in Appendix B of this book, select a random sample of 10 subjects from a subject pool of 20.

REFERENCES

BRADY, J. V. (1958). Ulcers in "executive" monkeys. *Scientific American, 199*(4), 95–100.

HOLLOWAY, S. M., & HORNSTEIN, H. A. (1976, July). How good news makes us good. *Psychology Today,* pp. 76*ff.*

HUFF, D. (1954). *How to lie with statistics.* New York: Norton.

KELLEY, H. H. (1950). The warm-cold variable in the first impressions of persons. *Journal of Personality, 18,* 431–439.

KERLINGER, F. N. (1973). *Foundations of behavioral research* (2nd ed.). New York: Holt, Rinehart and Winston.

ROSNOW, R., & ROSENTHAL, R. (1976). The volunteer subject revisited. *Australian Journal of Psychology, 28,* 97–108.

SCHACHTER, S. (1959). *The psychology of affiliation.* Stanford, CA: Stanford University Press.

UNDERWOOD, B. J. (1966). *Experimental psychology.* New York: Appleton-Century-Crofts.

WARWICK, D. P., & LININGER, C. A. (1975). *The sample survey: Theory and practice.* New York: McGraw-Hill.

WEISS, J. M. (1972). Psychological factors in stress and disease. *Scientific American, 226*(6), 104–113.

WOLFF, P., & LEVIN, J. R. (1972). The role of overt activity in children's imagery and production. *Child Development, 43,* 537–548.

ZAJONC, R. B., HEINGARTNER, A., & HERMAN, E. M. (1969). Social enhancement and impairment of performance in the cockroach. *Journal of Personality and Social Psychology, 13,* 83–92.

Experiments With More Than Two Groups

In the last chapter, we saw how we can test a variety of hypotheses by using two groups of subjects. We run subjects through two sets of treatment conditions so that we can see how their behaviors differ when the independent variable has different values. We can use groups of subjects who are assigned to the treatment conditions at random or are matched on a relevant subject variable. In this chapter we will study two additional types of designs—multiple-group and factorial designs. Like the two-group designs, they can be carried out using the between-subjects approach: Different groups of subjects participate in the different treatment conditions of the experiment. But we use these designs when two conditions are not enough to tell us what we want to know.

MULTIPLE-GROUP DESIGNS

Sometimes it takes more than two treatment conditions to make a good test of a hypothesis: In an experiment to test the effectiveness of a new drug, we might need to test several different dosages. A simple comparison between the presence or absence of the drug would be too crude to assess its effects adequately; the amount of a drug makes a difference in how well it works. In situations in which the amount or degree of the independent variable is important, we usually need a **multiple-group design**—a design in which there are more than two groups of subjects and each group is run through a different treatment condition. Often, one of the treatment conditions is a control condition in which subjects receive the zero value of the independent variable. The most commonly used multiple-group design is the **multiple-independent-groups design,** in which the subjects are assigned to the different treatment conditions at random. It's also possible to use multiple groups and matched subjects. The basic procedures are the same as those used in the two-matched-groups design, except that there are more than two treatment conditions.

Because most researchers use the randomized approach, we will do the same here.

Suppose we want to test the hypothesis that coffee drinking enhances productivity. Everyday experience tells us that some people simply cannot function without a morning cup of coffee. We suspect that some amount of coffee is (temporarily, at least) beneficial—but how much? If one cup of coffee is beneficial, perhaps two or more might be even better. Because we are interested in the effects of different levels of the independent variable, we could test our hypothesis with three groups of subjects, one control group and two experimental groups.

The experiment would be quite simple to conduct. Coffee drinking is our independent variable and productivity is our dependent variable. A cup of coffee could be operationally defined as one level teaspoon of Instant Maxwell House dissolved in one cup of boiling water. The operational definition here is important. The proportion of coffee to water is critical, since the strength of the coffee probably determines its effect. There may be differences between the effects of brewed versus instant coffee or between Maxwell House and other brands that might need to be explored in the future. Whether we allow subjects to use cream and sugar in their coffee is an issue we would need to consider. Do we want to allow these extraneous variables to exert potential influences on productivity? No. So we will require our subjects to drink the coffee black. Our dependent variable, productivity, can be operationally defined as the number of o's a subject crosses out on a page of newsprint in 10 minutes.

The control group (C) drinks no coffee; the first experimental group (E_1) drinks one cup; the second experimental group (E_2) drinks two cups. Assume that the hypothesis is confirmed: The more coffee the subjects drink, the more productive they are. Our hypothetical results are illustrated in Figure 7-1, which reflects a gradual increase in productivity as the amount of coffee consumption increases.

We may be convinced that coffee enhances productivity. But let us try just one more experiment. This time we will have four groups, one control

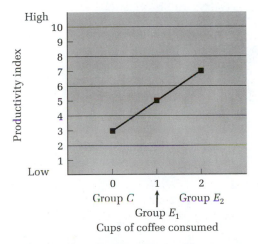

FIGURE **7-1** Productivity as a function of the amount of coffee consumed (fictitious data from a three-group experiment).

and three experimental groups. The hypothetical outcome of this experiment is illustrated in Figure 7-2. Again, we see that moderate amounts of coffee appear to enhance productivity. However, something different seems to be happening to group E_3: It received the largest amount of coffee, but its productivity is *low* relative to the other groups. Although the smaller amounts of coffee seem to increase productivity, the larger amount seems to inhibit it. These fictitious results resemble some actual research findings. Broadhurst (1959), for example, reported that subjects perform best on complicated tasks when they have a moderate amount of drive (that is, motivation). This is paradoxical; when we have little motivation, we do not accomplish much. But too much motivation interferes with performance. Think about taking a test: The stimulation of a little anxiety helps you to do better. But if you are extremely anxious, you may not remember anything; your mind goes blank, and you do not do very well.

Because different values of the same independent variable can produce different effects, researchers often test more than two levels of an independent variable. By using more than two conditions, they can often get a better idea of how the independent variable operates. They need to test such variables across a wide range of values to get an understanding of how the variables work.

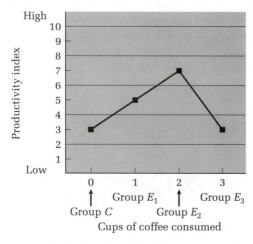

FIGURE **7-2** Productivity as a function of the amount of coffee consumed (fictitious data from a four-group experiment).

Choosing Treatments

What if we decide that we need more than two treatment conditions? How do we know how many to use? Some variables have an infinite number of possible values; we could not test them all even if we wanted to. We might be able to create many different conditions, but using all of them might not make sense. Let us look at an actual experiment that illustrates how an experimenter can zero in on the appropriate number of conditions.

Lassen (1973) was interested in what happens during a patient's initial interview with a therapist. In particular, she thought that seating arrangements might affect the amount of anxiety patients showed during their first session. Lassen used a multiple-group design to test the hypothesis that patients would show more anxiety with increasing distance from the therapist. Three groups of patients were randomly assigned to each of three experimental conditions. In the first condition, patients were seated 3 feet away from the therapist. In the second condition, patients were seated 6 feet away, and in the third condition they were 9 feet away. The sessions were audio taped. Later, the tapes were used by raters who evaluated the amount of anxiety displayed by each of the patients during the sessions. Lassen found that patients seated 3 feet away from the therapist showed less anxiety than patients seated 6 feet away. Patients who were seated 9 feet away showed the most anxiety. The therapists who ran the sessions, however, unanimously preferred the 6-feet condition, although they adapted to the 3-feet condition "unless a patient was particularly flirtatious, hostile, odorous, or fat" (p. 231). Like their patients, therapists were less comfortable in the 9-feet condition, feeling out of touch.

Lassen's independent variable, the distance between patient and therapist, can take on an infinite number of values. Some, of course, are obviously inappropriate for this experiment. We would not seat patients and therapists in the same chair. A distance of a mile would be just as ridiculous. Still, there are many other real possibilities. Lassen could have placed patients at 1 foot away. She could have used 18 or even 100 feet. Why did she restrict the conditions to 3, 6, and 9 feet? Let us try to imagine some of the thinking that might go into the choice of these three conditions:

I want to see the effect of different distances between patient and therapist in the first session. I know there are an infinite number of possible distances. Which ones make the most sense? Well, in our culture strangers usually don't stand too close to one another to have a conversation. Most people think it's rude for a stranger to come very close to ask a question—we prefer to have a little distance between us. From what I've seen of people's behavior, 3 feet seems to be about as close as people want to stand when they are talking to someone they don't know very well. Patients and therapists would rarely want to get closer than this. If we look at how furniture is arranged in therapists' offices, the closest chairs seem to be about 3 feet apart. So it makes sense to use 3 feet as the smallest distance I will test.

Now I'll have to decide about the greatest distance. I can eliminate distances over about 20 feet because patient and therapist would probably have difficulty hearing each other if they were that far apart. Anyway, most consultation rooms aren't that large. People seem to feel that more than 20 feet isn't appropriate. What about 20 feet? Even that seems too great. It's just not comfortable to talk to someone that far away. The chairs in consultation rooms seem to be placed no more than 10 feet apart. Since I've decided to use 3 feet as my smallest distance, I'll use 9 feet as my largest distance. That way I'll have two conditions that are proportional to one another: Nine feet is exactly three times as far as 3 feet. I'd also like to test a distance in between these two extremes so that I'll have a better idea of how distance affects patients' behavior. I could use several conditions between 3 and 9 feet, but one is probably enough to give me a good idea of how distance affects anxiety. So I'll use one more condition. Since my extremes are 3 and 9 feet, I'll make the middle condition 6 feet. That way I'll have three conditions that are all proportional to one another. Six feet is twice as far as 3 feet, the smallest distance. Nine feet is three times as far as the smallest distance.

Actually, if you consult Lassen's article, you will find that her decisions were dictated by prior research. She cites Hall's (1966) space dimensions as the source of her choices. Hall described a number of space categories, including personal distance-far (2½ to 4 feet), social distance-close (4 to 7 feet), and social distance-far (7 to 12 feet). As you can see, Lassen set up her treatment conditions to fit these categories. But notice that Lassen chose conditions that are *proportional* to one another. Given Hall's categories, she could have used distances of 3, 5, and 12 feet. Instead she chose to use 3, 6, and 9 feet. Why? You will find that research involving quantitative variables is usually done this way. You may see an experimenter using drug doses of, say, 5, 10, and 15 milligrams. You are less likely to see one in which the experimenter uses randomly chosen doses such as 2, 9, and 14 milligrams. It is possible to do experiments with conditions that are selected at random rather than planned. Sometimes that is the only possible way. However, many researchers prefer to be able to make statements about conditions that are proportional. For instance, Lassen could see very clearly from her study whether doubling the distance between the patient and the therapist also doubled the patient's rated anxiety.

When you think about using a multiple-group design, always think in terms of the hypothesis you are testing. The principal question you should ask is this: *What will I gain by adding these extra conditions to the experiment?* Lassen was interested in evaluating the usefulness of Hall's categories. Since there were several categories, it made sense for her to use more than two treatment conditions. It is also reasonable from a commonsense viewpoint. The effect of distance, like motivation or coffee drinking, might be complex. Instead of simply increasing as the distance increases, the patient's anxiety might increase to a point and then decline. For instance, at a very great distance, patients might feel out of touch and uninvolved with their sessions. Using three conditions gave Lassen a better idea of how distance from the therapist works within its usual range of values.

Let us return to an experiment in which the researchers decided *not* to use the multiple-group approach. Holloway and Hornstein (1976) used a two-independent-groups design to test "good" versus "bad" news, but they could have used a multiple-group design instead. What would they have gained by adding more groups? For example, what information would be gained by adding a control group? If the researchers had wanted to know about people's opinions of human nature without any news at all, they could have added a group of subjects that listened to the same music broadcast but without a news interruption. Maybe opinions are the most positive without *any* news! Or, in terms of our judgments of human nature, maybe no news *is* good news; if so, opinions would have been equally positive for subjects in either the good- or no-news conditions. With a control condition, we would have gained useful information.

Alternatively, they could have added an intermediate value of news ("neutral" news) to act as a starting point, or baseline, for comparisons with their two conditions. The two-group design allowed the researchers to say that opinions were more positive after good news than after bad news, but it did not tell us whether opinions after good or bad news were any different than opinions after hearing any news at all. It would be more informative if we knew whether good news *increases* positivity over neutral news or whether bad news *decreases* positivity. In general, people have a "positivity bias" toward others (Zajonc, 1968). We tend to think of people as basically good. Maybe any news—except bad news—will produce generally positive evaluations of others.

Holloway and Hornstein could also have included additional levels of bad and good news. For instance, they might have used "super," "very good," "slightly good," "slightly bad," "very bad," and "horrid" as additional treatments. Additional levels could have added to our understanding of the effects of news. But Holloway and Hornstein used only those levels that were critical to *their* hypothesis. Since the hypothesis dealt with the effects of good versus bad news, it was perfectly appropriate to test *only* these contrasting levels. Other values of the independent variable could be explored in future experiments. Notice that the levels chosen were at *opposite* ends of the continuum. They used good versus bad rather than good versus very good. Researchers try to use values of a variable that are extreme enough to bring out differences on the dependent variable. They do this to maximize the possibility of seeing a change across conditions. The effects of good versus very good stories might be about the same. If we test values that are further apart, we are more likely to find a difference if one exists.

However, researchers also want to use values that are realistic. If Holloway and Hornstein had tested only news that was horrid versus super, their results would have only limited generalizability, because people seldom hear news this extreme in real life. As mentioned in the discussion of Lassen's (1973) experiment, it *is* possible to use values that are too extreme to be meaningful. But as long as we select appropriate levels of the independent variable, two groups may be all that are necessary to test our hypothesis. Then it is more economical to use a two-group design, even though a multiple-group design is possible. As a general rule of thumb, *select the simplest design that will make an adequate test of your hypothesis.*

Practical Limits

As you set up experiments, you will make decisions about which comparisons will provide the most appropriate test of the hypothesis. An experiment that includes several levels of the independent variable can often yield more information than one that includes only two groups. However, practical considerations also affect choice of design. The multiple-group procedures assume that treatment groups are formed by random assignment. Thus there will be as many different treatment groups in the experiment as there are levels of the independent variable. If you have five levels of the independent variable, you will need five groups of subjects. It may be difficult to find enough subjects to make this design feasible. Running additional levels also takes more time, and the statistical procedures are more complicated than those used with the two-group design. Thus it makes sense to think through all the advantages and disadvantages of the multiple-group design before you begin your experiment. A review of the experimental literature in the area should guide you. If prior researchers have consistently used two-group designs to compare only opposite values of the independent variable, you may want to do the same. However, if others have used additional levels to gather information, this may be the most appropriate strategy.

Sometimes researchers conduct a *pilot study* to pretest selected levels of an independent variable before conducting the actual experiment. A pilot study is like a miniexperiment, in which the treatments are tested on a few subjects to see whether the levels seem to be appropriate or not. Pilot studies are also a good way to work out any bugs in the procedures of an experiment before the real experiment is under way. A pilot study allows you to make changes before you invest the time and resources in a large-scale experiment.

MORE THAN ONE INDEPENDENT VARIABLE: FACTORIAL DESIGNS

All the designs we have looked at so far had only one independent variable. But in real life, variables rarely occur alone. It often seems most appropriate to look at more than one variable at a time. Suppose we wanted to see whether talking to plants actually makes them grow better. Like any other hypothesis, this one would have to be tested in a rigorous, controlled fashion. We could set up a simple experiment in which talking is the independent variable. But we might also want to know whether music is beneficial to plants. We could run another experiment in which music is the independent variable. *This approach is very inefficient:* We may need twice as many plants and perhaps twice as much time to carry out two experiments rather than one. It also has another disadvantage. There may be a relationship between the effects of music and talking. Perhaps plants that get conversation do not need music. Maybe they prefer music to conversation. There is no way to look for these kinds of relationships if we study music and conversation separately. We need another kind of experimental design, one that enables us to look at the effects of more than one independent variable at a time. Because experiments with multiple independent variables are efficient and provide more information than experiments with one independent variable, they are the preferred design of many experimental psychologists.

Designs in which we study two or more independent variables at the same time are called **factorial designs.** The independent variables in these designs are called **factors.** The simplest factorial design has only two factors; it is called a **two-factor experiment.**

The data we get from a factorial experiment give us two kinds of information: First, they give us information about the effect of each independent variable in the experiment. These are called "main effects." Second, they enable us to answer this question: How does the operation of one independent variable affect the operation of another in the experiment?

Looking for Main Effects

A **main effect** is the action of a single independent variable in an experiment. When we measure a main effect, we are asking: How much did the changes in this one independent variable change subjects' behaviors? When we look more closely at statistical tests, we will look at this definition again in a more quantitative way. However, keep in mind that a main effect is simply a change in behavior associated with a change in the value of a single independent variable.

When we have only one independent variable in an experiment, we do not usually talk about main effects, although we could. There is only one main effect in an experiment with one independent variable. When there is more than one independent variable, there is a main effect for each one. *There are as many main effects as there are factors.* These main effects may or may not be statistically significant. To tell if they are, we need to carry out statistical tests. When we do those tests, we first evaluate the impact of each independent variable in the experiment separately. We test whether each main effect is statistically significant or not. For example, in our plant study, there would be two factors—talking and music. We would want to know about the main effects of both factors. How much did changes in talking affect plant growth? How much did changes in music affect plant growth? We would conduct statistical tests to determine if either independent variable or both produced any *significant* main effects.

Looking for Interactions

Factorial designs are particularly useful because they allow us to look at the effects of more than one independent variable at a time. This is more efficient than running several different experiments, but it also has another advantage. The factorial design gives us the chance to test for relationships between the effects of different independent variables. Earlier we posed the notion that plants that get conversation might not need music. Alternatively, of course, plants that get both might show truly spectacular growth. This is one example of how effects produced by two (or more) variables might influence each other. When this kind of relationship exists, we have an interaction.

An **interaction** is present if there is a change in the effect of one independent variable when another independent variable in the experiment changes value. For instance, we could suppose that music might be helpful to plants that are always ignored. But the same music might have no effect on plants exposed to speech. In other words, there would be an interaction between these two variables. Let us look at more realistic examples.

Your roommate sometimes teases you about how dumb you are, and you usually laugh it off or respond in kind. However, if you just received a poor grade on an important exam, you may become angry or depressed by those same teasing remarks. The impact of the teasing is altered by an important variable, your recent exam grade.

A few drinks at a party can make you feel relaxed and happy. If you are upset or anxious, a sleeping pill may help you to sleep. By themselves, a little alcohol or a sleeping pill may not be especially harmful. But take the two together and you may end up dead or in a coma. There is an *interaction* between these two substances: The effect of sleeping pills is altered by the presence of alcohol.

The number of possible interactions depends on the number of independent variables in the experiment. When there are two independent variables, there is usually only one possible interaction.[1] The two independent variables may interact with each other. When there are more than two independent variables, the picture becomes more complex. We can get **higher-order interactions** that involve more than two variables at a time. For instance, in a three-factor experiment, it is possible to get an interaction between all three independent variables: The action of each independent variable could be influenced by the values of the other two. For example, driver experience, alcohol, and degree of darkness may interact in causing traffic accidents. In an experiment with three independent variables, it is also possible that any two factors, but not the third, could interact just as they might in a two-factor experiment.

Like main effects, we measure interactions quantitatively through statistical tests—we evaluate their significance. It is possible to run an experiment and find that an interaction between variables is significant even though the main effects are not. We may also get significant main effects with no significant interaction. It is also possible to have an interaction along with one or more significant main effects. All possible combinations of outcomes can occur. We will look at some of these possibilities more closely in our discussion of statistical procedures. Box 7-1 presents an actual research problem that can be approached through a factorial design.

---

[1] The picture is more complicated when we have the same subjects in more than one treatment condition of the experiment.

BOX **7-1**
Dichotic listening: A
factorial approach

To understand the nature of the problem, try to imagine this situation: You are at a large party and the room is crowded. On every side of you, people are carrying on conversations. But in spite of all the noise and confusion, you are able to follow one voice saying, "Hi. I'm Chris. I'm a silversmith. Didn't I see you at the crafts fair last week?" Cherry (1953) called this the "cocktail party phenomenon." In spite of all the distracting noises, voices, and competing messages, we are able to select just one voice to listen to. Cherry's observations led him and other researchers into the study of *selective attention*, the process by which we pay attention to some of the available input and reject the rest.

The technique Cherry developed for studying this phenomenon is called "dichotic listening": The subject listens with both ears, but each ear gets a different verbal message. It is a bit like trying to listen to two telephone conversations at the same time. Most of us are not able to do that very well, so we listen on one line and put everyone else on "hold." Of course, we need an objective measure to judge how well subjects can separate incoming messages in the dichotic listening task. We do not want to rely on subjects' general impressions of how well they do. (Often, people believe they can do two things at once, when they really can't.) Cherry asked his subjects to "shadow" one of the two messages—that is, to repeat one of the messages as it was presented. How accurate a subject is in shadowing one message is a clear indication of how well that subject is able to separate the two messages that are presented. Many variables may affect our ability to separate two incoming messages. Treisman, noted for her work in this area, explored the effects of a number of physical and linguistic variables (see, for example, Treisman, 1964). Our example is based on some of her work. One thing that we want to know about dichotic listening is whether the voices that carry the messages are important. Is it easier to separate two messages spoken by dissimilar voices? It seems likely that it would be. It might be harder for subjects to disentangle words spoken by similar voices—say, two deep male voices. We can explore changes in the speaker's voice as a single independent variable: We simply manipulate the speaker's voice in a two-group experiment. For half the subjects, two similar incoming messages are spoken by similar voices. For the remaining subjects, the messages are spoken by two voices that differ along specified dimensions—say, the sex of the speaker. For this experiment we would have two levels of our voice variable, similar and different.

We may also want to study the effects of the content of the non-shadowed message. The content of the message is probably important. (How often has your attention shifted from one speaker to another when you heard your name mentioned?) If both messages have similar content—that is, they deal with the same subject matter—will it be harder for subjects to separate them? Now, we could run a second two-group experiment to test this notion. One group of subjects would hear two messages that have similar content—perhaps passages from the same story. The other group would hear two messages that have different content—perhaps pas-
(continued)

sages from different stories. We would measure our dependent variable (shadowing) to assess the effect of changing the message content. As you can guess, running two separate experiments may not be the most efficient way to handle our questions about these variables: Two experiments can be time-consuming. Also, if we run two experiments, we cannot answer any questions about the relationship between effects produced by the two variables. After all, in reality, the speaker's voice and the content will often change together. Does the effect of the speaker's voice make a difference depending on whether the content of the messages is the same or different? Will the content be more critical when the voices are similar? In short, do these variables interact with each other in some way? We can only assess the way our variables operate together if we do one experiment that enables us to study the impact of both variables at the same time. To do this, we need a factorial design.

LAYING OUT A FACTORIAL DESIGN

We can use a factorial design to approach the research problem outlined in Box 7-1. We can study the effects of speaker's voice and message content on shadowing in the same study. Speaker's voice is one factor; message content is another. We will use only two levels (values) of each factor. It helps to look at our design graphically as we set it up. If you can translate your thinking about an experiment into a simple diagram, called a "design matrix," you will find it easier to understand what you are testing and what kind of design you are using.[2] Figure 7-3 illustrates our two-factor experiment. Your diagram will be more complex if you are working with more than two factors or more than two levels of each factor.

We begin by diagramming the basic components of the design, the two factors (Figure 7-3, step 1). Notice that we label each factor with a number—message content is factor 1 and speaker's voice is factor 2. These numbers may be used later as a shorthand way of referring to the factors in the final report. We predicted that the type of message content has an effect. We will select values that are on opposite ends of the continuum for each of our two variables. Since we want only the two opposite values of message content, we can use "same" and "different" to label our treatment levels, just as we would in a two-group design. We indicate "same" and "different" in our diagram (Figure 7-3, step 2). We are also planning to use two opposite levels of the voice factor. Our question about the effect of the voice at this point is simply whether or not the type of voice has any effect on shadowing. It makes sense to use "similar" and "dissimilar" as the two levels of this factor. We can always explore more subtle differences in

---

[2] You can use the diagram later as you do the appropriate statistical tests. Values of the dependent variable—say, the average percentage of words correctly shadowed in each treatment condition—would be recorded in the cells. (See also Part 3.)

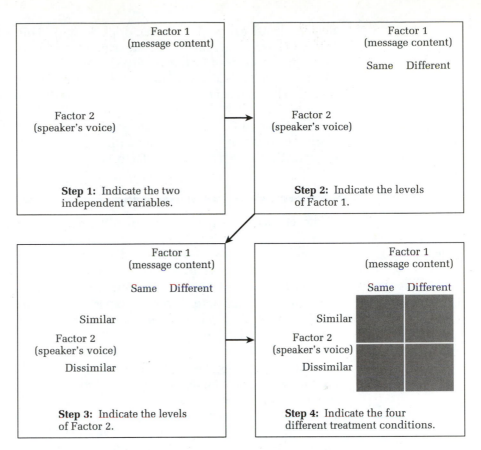

FIGURE **7-3** Diagramming a matrix design for the two-factor experiment described in Box 7-1.

future studies. This is exactly what we would do if we were setting up a two-group design with the speaker's voice as our single independent variable. We may indicate the two levels of the voice factor in the diagram simply by "similar" and "dissimilar" (Figure 7-3, step 3). We now draw the four separate *cells* of the matrix that represent the four treatment conditions needed in the experiment (Figure 7-3, step 4). If we assign our subjects to the conditions at random, each cell also represents a different group of randomly assigned subjects. Some subjects will hear similar voices speaking the same content; others will hear similar voices speaking different content, and so on.

Describing the Design

We know this is a two-factor experiment because there are two independent variables. However, there is another common way of describing factorial designs. It is a shorthand method that actually gives us more information. The design we are looking at here is called a "2 × 2 factorial design" (read as two-by-two factorial design). This **shorthand notation** tells us several things about the experiment it describes. First, the numbers tell us the number of factors involved. Here, there are two numbers (2 and 2). Each number refers to a different factor. Hence, this experiment has two factors. The value of each number tells us how many levels each factor has. If we have a 2 × 2 design, we automatically know there are two levels of each of the two factors of the experiment. We also know that the experiment has four different conditions (the product of 2 × 2). Box 7-2 shows other methods used to describe factorial designs.

BOX **7-2**
Additional methods for describing design variables

When factorial designs are described in research reports, the shorthand notation system is often expanded to include the variable names. This system makes it much easier to understand the complete research design at a glance. There are several ways to do this, and you will find examples of each of them in the research literature. For simplicity, we will illustrate how the 2 × 2 dichotic listening experiment would be described using each different method. The same methods can also be used to describe larger factorial designs.

Factor-Labeling Method. The names of each factor are placed in parentheses following the numerical notation. The name of the factor represented by the first digit would be the first name you would list; the name of the second factor would be the second. Just like the shorthand notation, the factor labels are separated by "×." Because different subjects have been assigned to each of the four treatment conditions, the experiment is a between-subjects factorial design.

Example 1: 2 × 2 (message content × speaker's voice) between-subjects factorial design

Factor and Levels Methods. There are two procedures for this method, and you can use either. These give the most complete information about the experimental design because they also list the levels of each factor. The first method places the factor name and its levels immediately following the shorthand notation for the entire design. This simply extends the factor-labeling method to include the factor levels. The second method places the names for the individual levels of each variable immediately following its number in the shorthand notation.

Example 2: 2 × 2 (message content: same, different × speaker's voice: similar, dissimilar) between-subjects factorial design
Example 3: 2 (same or different message content) × 2 (similar or dissimilar speaker's voice) between-subjects factorial design

---

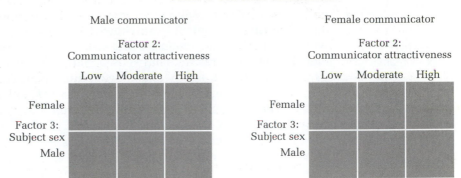

FIGURE **7-4**   Diagram of a 2 × 3 × 2 factorial design. The diagram represents an experiment in which there are three independent variables: the sex of the person delivering a persuasive communication, the attractiveness of that communicator, and the sex of the subjects being exposed to the communication. The hypothesis of this experiment is as follows: Subjects will be more persuaded by a message delivered by a more attractive communicator, but only when the communicator is the opposite sex from the subject.

Although our example involves only two factors, it is possible to design factorial experiments with any number of factors. The number of factors will determine the way the design is labeled—an experiment involving three independent variables, for example, is called a three-factor experiment. The shorthand notation indicates additional information. If an experiment is referred to as a "2 × 3 × 2 factorial design," we immediately know several things about it. Since three digits are mentioned (2, 3, and 2) we know this experiment involves three independent variables. The numerical value of each digit tells us the number of levels of each of the factors. We know that the first factor has two levels; the second has three; and the third has two. We also know that this experiment has 12 separate conditions (the product of 2 × 3 × 2). Figure 7-4 presents a sample diagram of a 2 × 3 × 2 experiment.

An experimental example of a 2 × 2 factorial experiment is shown in Box 7-3. This experiment produced one significant main effect along with a significant interaction. Main effects and interactions can be difficult to understand. When possible, it is helpful to look at the data from these kinds of experiments in graphic form to get a true picture of what they represent.

Figure 7-5 illustrates the actual outcome of the experiment done by Pliner and Chaiken (1990; see Box 7-3 on the following page). However, a variety of other patterns of results might be observed in a factorial experiment, and each would require a different interpretation. Figure 7-6 presents some additional possibilities to help you understand the difference between main effects and interactions. Keep in mind that these do not represent actual data.

BOX **7-3**

Eating in women and
men: A factorial
experiment with a
significant main
effect and an
interaction

Pliner and Chaiken (1990) were interested in the relationship between gender and eating behavior. It is well known that, in our culture at least, young women show a greater concern with eating lightly and being slim than do men. Even though research has shown that young men do not really prefer slim over average-weight women, being thin seems to obsess many American women. Anorexia and bulimia, potentially life-threatening eating disorders, can be an end product of this distorted view of the "ideal" female body image.

Pliner and Chaiken believe that thinness and light eating have come to be viewed as appropriate sex-role behaviors for women, making them appear more feminine than their heavy-eating counterparts. If this is the case, women should be especially prone to eat lightly in situations where they want to appear most feminine—when they are with an attractive person of the opposite sex. Young men, the authors argue, don't worry about how much they eat in front of others because it does not affect the kind of impression they will make.

The authors conducted an experiment that tested the following hypothesis: Women will eat less in the presence of an opposite-sex partner than in the presence of another of the same sex, but men's eating behavior will not be influenced by their partner's gender. Pliner and Chaiken have predicted that two variables—subject sex and partner sex—will interact in their effects on eating behavior. Let us look at the variables in their experiment.

What must be manipulated to test the hypothesis? First, the behavior of women must be compared with that of men. The first independent variable is the sex of the subject. Notice that the first factor in the experiment is an ex post facto variable, or subject variable. The "manipulation" is simply the selection process; subjects are automatically assigned to an experimental group on the basis of their gender. Second, the sex of the subject's partner must be manipulated. The second independent variable is the gender of a second person with whom the subjects are paired: a partner of the same or opposite sex. Here, the experimenters manipulate which type of partner subjects will get.

Individual subjects in the experiment were led to believe that they and a partner were taking part in a study on the effects of hunger on task performance. They had been asked not to eat anything the day of the experiment, so they would be hungry when they arrived. Each subject was told that he or she and the partner had been assigned to the "full" condition of the experiment and would be asked to eat as much as it took for them to feel comfortably full while working on the experimental task. Crackers with various toppings were provided. Early in the session, the subject and partner were interviewed together by the experimenter. This interview was designed to give the subject the impression that her or his partner was single and socially attractive.*

The dependent variable in this experiment was eating behavior. The researchers measured eating by counting how many crackers each subject ate. To make sure that the partner's eating did not confound the experiment, the partner always ate 15 crackers (about 315 calories). The researchers' hypothesis would be supported if a significant interaction between the two factors were obtained: if women ate fewer crackers in the presence of an opposite-sex partner than with a same-sex partner, but men's eating did not differ. Their findings are depicted graphically in Figure 7-5. However, before we explore an interaction between the factors, let us look at the effects produced by each factor alone.

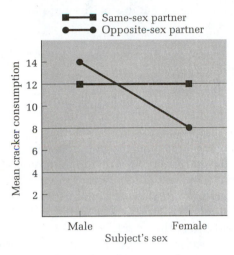

FIGURE **7-5** Cracker consumption by women and men in the presence of a same-sex or an opposite-sex partner. From results reported by Pliner and Chaiken (1990).

Remember that in a factorial experiment, we always look at the effect of each independent variable separately as well as looking for an interaction. These main effects explore each factor by itself, ignoring the other. (These are like the effects we would get if we had conducted two separate experiments—one testing the effect of subject sex on eating and one testing the effect of partner sex on eating.)

Did the first factor, subject sex, produce any effects on eating? Yes. The experiment produced a significant main effect for this factor. If we just consider how many crackers men and women tended to eat in the experiment, we find that men ate more crackers on the average than women (about 13.5 versus 10.9). This is not too surprising; we expect men to eat more than women. Did the second factor, same- or opposite-sex partner, have any effect by itself on eating? No, it did not. If we combine the data for all subjects in the experiment, we find that, on average, people ate about the same amount of crackers whether their partners were the same sex or the opposite sex. There were a few more men than women in the experiment, which brought the average for the entire group up slightly, so the average number of crackers eaten in the presence of either type of partner was about 12.3.

(*continued*)

BOX **7-3**
continued

Finally, we look at the interaction. The interaction describes the effects of one factor (male vs. female subjects) at different levels of the other (same-sex vs. opposite sex partners). The interaction asks whether men's or women's eating habits change with different kinds of partners. Was Pliner and Chaiken's hypothesis supported? Yes, there was a significant interaction between subject sex and type of partner. Men ate about the same amount whether their partner was the same or the opposite sex. But, as expected, women varied their eating depending on the gender of their partner. If their partner was the same sex, they ate more than if their partner was the opposite sex.

* For simplicity, we are including only effects that occurred when subjects actually perceived their partner to be socially attractive.

In Figure 7-6(a), the experimental data show no significant main effects or interactions. This is the way the data would look when graphed if the subject's sex had not influenced eating, and subjects ate about the same amount regardless of the type of partner they had. This would mean that the experimenters' hypothesis was wrong or that the procedures used were inadequate to detect the effect.

Figure 7-6(b) illustrates the outcome if there were a significant main effect for type of partner, but the main effect for subject sex and the interaction were not significant. The figure depicts an outcome in which both male and female subjects ate less in the presence of an opposite-sex partner. And, in fact, this finding was actually reported in an earlier experiment by Mori, Chaiken, and Pliner (1987).[3]

What would the graph look like if a significant main effect for type of partner indicated that both male and female subjects ate less in the presence of a same-sex partner than they did in the presence of an opposite-sex partner? The two lines would be reversed; the line for same-sex partners would be lower than the line for opposite-sex partners.

A significant main effect for sex of subject is illustrated in Figure 7-6(c). The graph would look like this if men ate more than women regardless of who their partners were. In this graph, neither the main effect for type of partner nor the interaction is significant. What would the graph look like if a main effect for sex of subject showed that women ate more than men? The points on the left would be lower than the points on the right.

Figure 7-6(d) shows one possible outcome when there are two significant main effects in the data but no interaction. As shown in the figure,

[3] In a second experiment reported by Pliner and Chaiken (1990), both men and women also ate less in the presence of an opposite-sex partner. The authors suggested that eating can be influenced by the kinds of personal and social motives that are important at the time. Wishing to appear socially desirable, cooperative, or similar to their opposite-sex partner may have reduced eating among men in the presence of women.

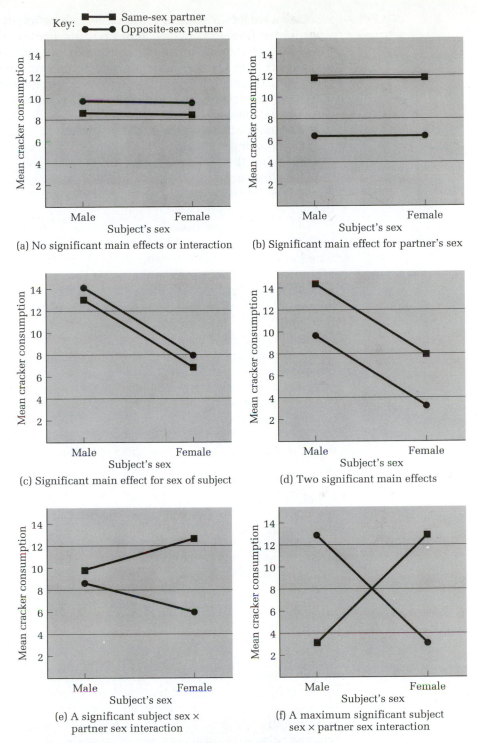

FIGURE **7-6** Examples of various hypothetical outcomes of Pliner and Chaiken (1990). Keep in mind these do not represent actual data.

whether a subject is male or female affects how much they eat. However, whether the partner is the same or opposite sex also makes a difference. Men in all conditions eat more than women, *and* everyone eats more with a same-sex partner than when they have an opposite-sex partner. Both independent variables exert an influence on eating, but they do not interact; the influence of one variable does not depend on the level of another.

Figures 7-6(e) and (f) depict two examples of significant interactions in the absence of any significant main effects. (You saw an example of an interaction along with a significant main effect earlier in Figure 7-5.) The graphs of data that reflect an interaction always show a characteristic pattern: The lines are not parallel. Graphs showing an interaction can *diverge* (spread out, as in Figure 7-6[e]), *converge* (come together), or *intersect* (as in Figure 7-6[f] and the earlier Figure 7-5).

Measuring interactions is one of the key reasons for doing factorial research. By looking at two (or more) variables together, we can assess whether the effect of one variable depends on the level of another variable. When we have an interaction, knowing the value of just one IV will not necessarily enable us to predict the performance of subjects with any degree of accuracy. For instance, suppose the data came out like the graph in Figure 7-6(e), which represents an outcome in which men ate the same amount regardless of type of partner, but women varied their eating with different partners. Women ate more with a same-sex partner than with an opposite-sex partner. Because there is an interaction, eating depends on both factors. If we want to predict accurately how many crackers would be eaten by any subject, we would need to know both the subject's sex and the type of partner.

This is even more apparent in Figure 7-6(f), which represents the maximum interaction possible: The effect of type of partner on eating is exactly opposite for male and female subjects. To predict for any subject in the experiment, we would need to know whether the subject was male or female and what type of partner the subject had.

Main effects and interactions are quantified and evaluated through statistical tests. Chapter 13 contains additional information on these concepts and the procedures required to evaluate them.

CHOOSING A BETWEEN-SUBJECTS DESIGN

As you begin planning your first experiments, you will probably experience the temptation of trying to do everything in one experiment. You may try to set up studies with as many as five or six different factors. But if you try to do too many things at once, you may lose sight of what you are trying to accomplish. A simple set of hypotheses that zeros in on the most important variables is better than a more elaborate set that includes everything from astrological signs to zest for life. Keep your first experiment simple.

Although the factorial designs make it possible to look at many different variables at a time, do not get carried away. Focus on the variables that are critical. Once again, a review of the experimental literature will be a helpful guide. If other researchers have simply controlled time of day by testing all their subjects together, there is no need to vary time of day in your study so that you can include it as an independent variable—unless you have strong reasons for doing so. You will develop a better understanding of the experimental process by starting with simple designs and working up to more complex ones.

There are several practical reasons for keeping factorial designs simple. First, subjects are usually assigned to each of the treatment conditions at random. This means you will need as many groups of subjects as you have treatment conditions. It is not always easy to find subjects. More treatment conditions also means more time to run the experiment and more time to do the statistical analysis. Moreover, the results of complicated designs may be virtually uninterpretable. It is very difficult to describe the interaction of three factors, let alone explain why it happened. A significant three-way interaction (like the outcome predicted for the experiment in Figure 7-4) is rarely a predicted result. Four-way interactions are practically impossible to conceptualize and explain. There is not much point in collecting data that we cannot understand. It is just not practical to include unnecessary factors and conditions. Use your review of prior research in the area to help you decide what variables and what levels to include.

So far we have covered four different kinds of between-subjects designs. We looked at two-group designs that had either independent or matched groups. We also looked at multiple-group designs and factorial designs. You may still feel a bit uneasy about trying to select the appropriate design for your own between-subjects experiment. To make things easier, you should always begin with some basic questions. Your design will be determined to a large extent by the number of independent variables you have and by the number of treatment conditions needed to test your hypothesis. You should also use your literature review to get an idea of the kinds of designs others have used for similar problems. To help make your search more systematic, we summarize the basics of the decision-making process in Figure 7-7 on the following page. Simply begin at the top and work down, answering the questions in terms of your experiment.

In the next two chapters, we will look at another important type of experimental strategy—within-subjects designs. In the four designs we have already covered, each subject participates in only one treatment condition and is measured on the dependent variable after the experimental manipulation has taken place. In a within-subjects experiment, subjects participate in more than one treatment condition of an experiment, and a measurement is taken after each treatment is given. Factorial experiments can also be conducted using a within-subjects design. In a within-subjects factorial design, subjects receive all conditions in the experiment instead of receiving only one.

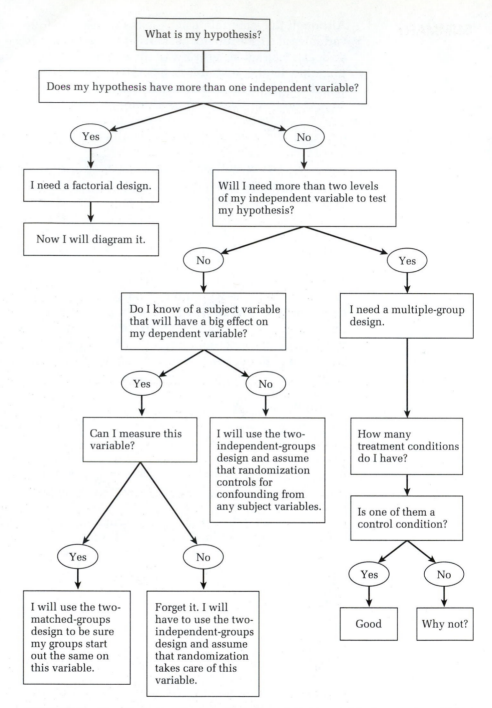

FIGURE **7-7** Questions to ask when designing a between-subjects experiment (start at the top and work down).

SUMMARY

In between-subjects designs, a comparison of two values of the independent variable is sometimes not enough; we may need more than two treatment conditions to test an experimental hypothesis. A *multiple-group design* serves this purpose. In a *multiple-independent-groups design,* there are more than two levels of the independent variable, and subjects are assigned to treatment conditions at random. With several treatment conditions, researchers can look at the effects of several different values of the independent variable and see whether low, medium, and high values of a variable produce increasing changes in the dependent variable. They can also detect more complex patterns. For instance, some variables may produce little change at extreme values but a lot of change at middle values. Although we can get additional information from a multiple-group design, it is not always practical or necessary to do so. For some experimental hypotheses, a comparison of just two values of the independent variable is sufficient.

The *factorial design* has two or more independent variables, which are called *factors*. By studying more than one factor at a time, we can measure *main effects*—the action of each independent variable in the experiment. We can also measure *interactions*—a change in the effect of one independent variable when another independent variable changes value.

Factorial designs are described with *shorthand notation*. If we are told that an experiment has a $3 \times 2 \times 4$ design, we know it has three independent variables because three numbers are given. The value of each number tells us how many levels each factor has. The first factor has three, the second has two, and the third has four levels, or values. We also know there are 24 treatment conditions, the product of $3 \times 2 \times 4$. There are practical limitations on using factorial designs: They often require many subjects. They can be time-consuming, and they require more complicated statistical procedures than the other designs we have discussed. However, they also provide valuable information that other types of experiments cannot.

KEY TERMS

Factor   An independent variable in a factorial design.

Factorial design   An experimental design in which more than one independent variable is manipulated.

Higher-order interaction   An interaction effect involving more than two independent variables.

Interaction   The change in the effect of one independent variable when another independent variable in the experiment changes value.

Main effect   The action of a single independent variable in an experiment; the change in the dependent variable produced by the various levels of a single independent variable.

Multiple-group design A between-subjects design with one independent variable, in which there are more than two treatment conditions.

Multiple-independent-groups design The most commonly used multiple-group design in which the subjects are assigned to the different treatment conditions at random.

Shorthand notation A system that uses numbers to describe the design of a factorial experiment.

Two-factor experiment The simplest factorial design, having two independent variables.

REVIEW AND STUDY QUESTIONS

1. Explain the meaning of the terms *experimental design* and *between-subjects design*.
2. Describe a multiple-independent-groups design. When do we need this type of design?
3. Explain the advantages of using a multiple-group design rather than a two-group design.
4. If people stand closer together, they will communicate better. How would you test this hypothesis? How many treatment conditions would you need? Would it be possible to test this hypothesis with more than one design?
5. People who have known each other for a long time may communicate better than people who have known each other for a short time. Imagine you are carrying out the study suggested in question 4. All your subjects know each other, but for varying lengths of time. How can you make sure that the length of time that subjects have known each other will not be a confounding variable in your study? What design do you need?
6. What is a factorial design?
7. Explain what we mean by the terms *main effect* and *interaction*.
8. What are the advantages of running experiments with a factorial design?
9. After watching a group of nursery school children, we get the idea that some toys are more popular with children than others. We would like to test the difference in time spent playing with toys that are used for building (for example, blocks) and toys that are not (for example, stuffed animals). Since there are many differences between boys and girls, we would also like to look at sex as an independent variable. What kind of design do we need?
10. Diagram the experiment suggested in question 9.
11. Describe the design in the diagram in question 10 using the factor-labeling method and the factor and level methods.
12. You are told that an experiment has a $3 \times 3 \times 3$ design.
    a. How many independent variables does it have?
    b. How many different treatment conditions does it have?
    c. Make a diagram of it.
13. A researcher decides to run an experiment to study the effects of three

independent variables on learning. (1) She will vary background noise by playing or not playing a radio while subjects study a list of words. (2) She will vary smoking: Half the subjects (all regular smokers) will have a cigarette before the experiment and half will not. (3) She will vary the length of the list to be learned: Half the subjects will try to learn a short list; half will try to learn a long list in the same amount of time. The dependent variable is the percentage of words recalled. Take this hypothetical experiment and do the following:

a. Describe this experiment using shorthand notation for factorial designs.

b. Diagram the experiment.

c. In addition to defining the subject population as "regular smokers," what other subject variables might be important to the outcome of this study? How can they be controlled?

d. Identify three nonsubject variables you think might affect the outcome of this study.

14. A new student in class says: "I'm not going to bother thinking about the design of my experiment in advance. I'll just go ahead and run it and then figure out what it is later." How would you convince this student that this approach will not work?

15. What features of an experimental hypothesis are important in selecting a design?

16. In a study of age and recognition of advertised products, Stoneman and Brody (1983) reported that children who saw a video presentation (viewing commercials without hearing the sound track) or audiovisual presentation (TV picture plus sound) recognized more products than children who heard only the sound. They also found that second-grade children later recognized more of the products than kindergarten children did; and kindergarten children scored better than preschoolers.

a. What is the design of this experiment? Describe it using shorthand notation. Diagram it.

b. How many main effects were reported?

c. Using a simple graph, illustrate the pattern of the overall results of this experiment.

REFERENCES

BROADHURST, P. L. (1959). The interaction of task difficulty and motivation: The Yerkes-Dodson Law revived. *Acta Psychologica, 16*, 321–328.

CHERRY, E. C. (1953). Some experiments on recognition of speech, with one, and with two ears. *Journal of the Acoustical Society of America, 25*, 975–979.

HALL, E. T. (1966). *Hidden dimensions.* Garden City, NY: Doubleday.

HOLLOWAY, S. M.; & HORNSTEIN, H. A. (1976, July). How good news makes us good. *Psychology Today*, pp. 76*ff*.

LASSEN, C. L. (1973). Effect of proximity on anxiety and communication in the initial psychiatric interview. *Journal of Abnormal Psychology, 81,* 226–232.

MORI, D., CHAIKEN, S., & PLINER, P. (1987). "Eating lightly" and the self-presentation of femininity. *Journal of Personality and Social Psychology, 53,* 693–702.

PLINER, P., & CHAIKEN, S. (1990). Eating, social motives, and self-presentation in women and men. *Journal of Experimental Social Psychology, 26*(3), 240–254.

STONEMAN, Z., & BRODY, G. H. (1983). Immediate and long-term recognition and generalization of advertized products as a function of age. *Developmental Psychology, 19*(1), 56–61.

TREISMAN, A. M. (1964). Verbal cues, language, and meaning in selective attention. *American Journal of Psychology, 77,* 206–219.

ZAJONC, R. B. (1968). Cognitive theories in social psychology. In G. Lindzey & E. Aronson (Eds.), *The handbook of social psychology* (2nd ed., Vol. 1, pp. 320–411). Reading, MA: Addison-Wesley.

8

Within-Subjects Designs

A Within-Subjects Experiment: Optical Illusions

Advantages of Within-Subjects Designs

Disadvantages of Within-Subjects Designs
Practical Limitations
Interference Between Conditions

Small *N* Designs
A Small *N* Design: Talking to Plants
When to Use Small *N* Designs
When to Use Large *N* Designs

***ABA* Designs**

Pretest/Posttest Designs

How Can You Choose?

Summary

Key Terms

Review and Study Questions

References

U p to now, we have focused on four main types of designs: two-independent-groups, two-matched-groups, multiple-group, and factorial designs. All our examples of these designs had one underlying assumption—that the subjects in each of the different treatment conditions were different, randomly selected individuals. We assumed that each subject would be in only one treatment condition. These are called "between-subjects designs." Conclusions are based on comparisons between different subjects (that is, the different groups of the experiment). This approach usually works well, but only in certain cases. Others call for a different type of design, as the following example illustrates.

Let us consider dreams and how we would design an experiment to find out about them. A person might say, "I had the strangest dream last night." Even if the person tells you all about it, it still may not make much sense to you. Dreams are highly personal experiences, and their study continues to fascinate psychologists.

Gackenbach and Schillig (1983) were especially interested in the phenomenon of lucid dreams, dreams in which the dreamer "feels he is suddenly in possession of his normal waking memories and thoughts but knows that he is actually asleep and dreaming" (p. 1). They wanted to compare subjects' ratings of the qualities of lucid dreams to ratings of dreams that lack lucidity. As part of the experiment, subjects were asked to rate their dreams on various dimensions. The plan was to compare subjects' ratings of different kinds of dreams along several dimensions.

If you take an informal survey among the people you know, you will most likely find that reports about dreams vary a great deal. The content of dreams is very different from one dream to the next, and the way people report them varies a great deal too. Some people seem to recall many dreams and in great detail. Others remember few dreams and little detail. Suppose both types of dreamers report having lucid dreams. For subjects with good recall, lucid dreams might seem quite vivid and real. For others, they might be totally forgotten.

Suppose we used a between-subjects approach for this research, which would pool the data from very diverse types of subjects. Half would describe lucid dreams; half would describe nonlucid dreams. We would then compare the ratings obtained from these two groups. The chances are that this procedure would yield little in the way of understanding lucid dreams: Subjects' reports of their dreams would differ so much in content and intensity that it would not make sense to compare the responses of groups of different people. Such large differences exist among people's reports of their dreams that a difference between lucid and nonlucid dreams is likely to be undetectable among all the diverse ratings. Whenever we expect responses from different subjects to be extremely dissimilar, finding effects from an independent variable is like looking for a needle in a haystack.

Obviously, a between-subjects design will not work for this type of research. That is why Gackenbach and Schillig (1983) chose to use a **within-subjects design**—a design in which each subject serves in more than one condition of the experiment. In their case, Gackenbach and Schillig asked subjects to report all their dreams over a 28-day period and to indicate which of them were lucid. They then compared the reported qualities of the two types of dreams for the same subjects. They found that lucid dreams were reported as being more perceptual in content: They received significantly higher ratings on visual, color, sound, and other sensations (see Table 8-1).

By having the same subjects describe both lucid and nonlucid dreams, the researchers improved their chances of detecting the differences between the two kinds of dreams. From a statistical viewpoint, we refer to this as increasing the *power* of the experiment. Increased power means a greater chance of detecting a genuine effect of the independent variable.

TABLE **8-1**

Means and *F* values for perceptual items on A.R.E.[†] dream tally sheets			
	Type of Dream		
Variable	Lucid	Nonlucid	F Value
Vision	1.66	1.10	115.15*
Color	1.27	0.85	53.95*
Sound	0.78	0.29	115.49*
Voice	1.12	0.64	97.06*
Taste-smell	0.11	0.08	2.41*
Kinesthetic	0.75	0.32	92.81*

[†] A.R.E. stands for the Association of Research and Enlightenment, which sponsored a phase of this research. The ratings shown are group averages (means). The *F* values represent the outcome of statistical tests done to evaluate the results. They indicate that, with the exception of the taste-smell dimension, perceptions reported in this study were more vivid in lucid than in nonlucid dreams.
* $p < .0001$.
NOTE: From "Lucid Dreams: The Content of Conscious Awareness of Dreaming During the Dream," by J. Gackenbach and B. Schillig, 1983. Journal of Mental Imagery, 7(2), 1–14. Copyright © by Brandon House, Inc. Reprinted by permission.

As you already know, this example is based on a quasiexperiment. The researchers did not create the various types of dreams that were reported.[1]

Some hypotheses and research topics naturally require a within-subjects approach: Does a family's perception of itself change over the course of family therapy? Do you improve each time you take the same intelligence test? Do additional reviews of class notes yield better exam scores? Let us turn to an actual laboratory experiment in which a within-subjects approach was used.

A WITHIN-SUBJECTS EXPERIMENT: OPTICAL ILLUSIONS

We can set up a variety of within-subjects designs. The basic principles remain the same: Each subject takes part in more than one condition of the experiment. We make comparisons of the behavior of the same subjects under different conditions. If our independent variable is having an effect, we are often more likely to find it if we use a within-subjects design. In a between-subjects design, the effects of our independent variable can be masked by the differences between the groups on all sorts of extraneous variables. A comparison within groups is more precise. If we see different behaviors under different treatment conditions, the differences are more likely to be linked to our experimental manipulation. Remember that the whole point of an experiment is to set up a situation in which the independent variable is the only thing that changes systematically across the conditions of the experiment. In a between-subjects design, we change the independent variable across conditions. However, we also use different subjects in the different conditions. We can usually assume that randomization controls for extraneous variables that might affect the dependent variable. But we have even better control with a within-groups design, because we use the same subjects over and over.

Coren and Girgus (1972) used a within-subjects design to study optical illusions, configurations like those in Figure 8-1. They are deceptive figures; we see things in them that do not really exist. For instance, in the Müller-Lyer illusion, the two horizontal lines are actually the same length, but the top one, the one with the arrows pointing outward, appears to be shorter.[2] Coren and Girgus wanted to see whether the amount of illusion

---

[1] In addition, only 68 of 99 subjects reported having lucid dreams during the course of the study. This raises some questions about the representativeness of the sample. Perhaps people who have lucid dreams less frequently would also describe them differently. Gackenbach and Schillig also studied differences among reports of lucid, vivid, and ordinary dreams. The above arguments in favor of within-subjects analysis apply to those comparisons as well.

[2] Favreau (1977) showed that in many textbook illustrations of the Müller-Lyer illusion, one line actually *is* shorter than the other. Textbook figures are often drawn to maximize the illusion. Favreau postulates the existence of a conspiracy to disillusion beginning psychology students, but you can try drawing your own honest Müller-Lyer figure using identical lines. You will find that even without exaggeration, the illusion is powerful.

(a) The Müller-Lyer illusion. Both horizontal lines are actually the same length.

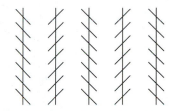

(b) The Poggendorf illusion. Will the diagonals meet if extended across the parallel lines?

(c) The Ponzo illusion. Which horizontal line is longer?

(d) The Zöllner illusion. A new slant on parallel lines.

FIGURE **8-1**   Examples of optical illusions.

people saw would change if they looked at the figures several times. They suggested that our perceptions correct themselves as we become more familiar with the figures.

The amount of illusion that subjects see in a figure varies. One person sees very little distortion; another reports a large effect. Thus it would be hard to see whether several exposures to the optical illusions made a difference if we compared data from different subjects. We stand a better chance of detecting the effect of repeated exposures if we compare the reports of the same subjects as they see the figures again and again. Coren and Girgus did exactly that. They used a within-subjects design to measure the changes in the illusions over a series of trials. Each subject saw each of the illusions several times. The more times the subjects saw the figures, the less illusion they saw. The effect of repeated exposures probably would have been muddled if Coren and Girgus had done the experiment with a between-groups design.

The within-subjects design works better when there are large individual differences in the way subjects react to treatment conditions. Changes in the responses of different subjects across different conditions could be caused by the independent variable, differences between the subjects, or both. By getting responses from the same subjects again and again, Coren and Girgus got a more accurate idea of how their independent variable worked. They made their data more precise by comparing responses of the same subjects under different conditions, which eliminated the error from differences between subjects. The responses of the same subjects are likely to be more consistent from one measurement to another. Therefore if responses change across conditions, the changes are more likely to be caused by the independent variable.

So far we have talked about within-subjects designs that tested a single independent variable. However, these designs can also be set up as factorial designs. Suppose a researcher was interested in measuring how long it takes to identify different facial expressions. She might decide to show subjects slides of people displaying four different expressions—perhaps anger, fear, happiness, and sadness—and measure how quickly people can recognize each one. She could use a within-subjects design, showing each subject all four kinds of faces and timing how long it takes each subject to identify each expression. She also suspects that the gender of the person displaying an emotion might have an effect on subjects' reaction time, so she also wants to show subjects both male and female faces. In this case, she can use the sex of the person in the slide as an additional within-subjects factor. The design would be a 4 × 2 *within-subjects factorial;* each subject would take part in eight separate conditions (4 × 2 = 8). Subjects would see and identify eight different faces: a man and a woman displaying each of the four expressions.[3] It is easy to see that a within-subjects factorial can require many fewer subjects than a between-subjects factorial design that is testing the same hypothesis.

It is also possible to use a factorial design that combines one factor that is manipulated within subjects (like the four types of expressions) with a between-subjects factor (often a variable, like sex or age, that cannot be manipulated by an experimenter). A design that combines within- and between-subjects variables in a single experiment is called a **mixed design.** Suppose the researcher who conducted the facial-expression experiment found that some expressions were indeed identified more quickly than others, but it did not matter whether the person in the slide was male or female. She might continue investigating facial expressions along other lines. For instance, she may wonder whether men or women are faster at identifying these facial expressions. Testing this hypothesis would require a 2 × 4 mixed design. Subjects would be divided into two groups on the basis of their gender. Subjects in both groups would see and identify slides of all four different expressions. Mixed designs are quite common in psychology, but the statistical procedures for analyzing mixed designs are more complex than those for within-subjects or between-subjects factorial designs, and we will not cover them in this book.

ADVANTAGES OF WITHIN-SUBJECTS DESIGNS

In within-subjects experiments, we use the same subjects in different treatment conditions. This is a big help when we cannot get many subjects; we can actually run an entire experiment with only one subject if we must. If

[3] As you will discover later in the chapter, the experimenter would also need to use a special control procedure, called "counterbalancing"; different subjects would see the eight faces in different orders to prevent confounding. Methods for counterbalancing will be presented in the next chapter.

we have four treatment conditions and want 10 subjects in each condition, we need only 10 subjects if we run the experiment within subjects. Each of the 10 subjects runs through all four conditions. However, if we run the same experiment between subjects, we need 40 subjects, 10 in each condition.

A within-subjects design can also save us time when we are actually running the experiment. If subjects must be trained, it is more efficient to train each subject for several conditions instead of for just one.

We usually have the best chance of detecting the effect of our independent variable if we compare the behavior of the same subjects under different conditions. The within-subjects design controls for **subject variables,** the ways in which subjects differ from one another. That way, if we see differences in behavior under different conditions, we know that they are not likely to be simply the differences that occur because the subjects in one group do not act like the subjects in another.

The responses recorded for a group of subjects tend to overlap from one occasion to another, as long as the conditions remain the same. Responses of different groups of subjects are likely to show less consistency and less overlap than responses from the same group. Different subjects act in different ways. The less overlap there is between subjects' behaviors, the more we need a within-subjects design. When we run an experiment, we usually do not care much about how individual subjects differ from one another. We really want to measure the changes in behavior that are caused by different levels of the independent variable. From a statistical standpoint, we have a better chance of detecting the effect of our experimental manipulation if we use a within-subjects design. The reasons parallel the reasons we discussed in connection with the matched-groups procedures.

In a sense, the within-subjects design is the most perfect form of matching we can have. The influence of subject variables across different treatment conditions is controlled because the same subjects take part in all the treatment conditions. *Each subject serves as his or her own control in the experiment.*

In a within-subjects design, the subject is measured after each treatment condition; therefore, subjects are measured more than once on the dependent variable. For this reason, this type of design is also often called a **repeated-measures design.** We repeat the measurements of the impact of the different values of the independent variable on the same subjects.

Since we are looking at the responses of the same people under different conditions, we expect their responses to be about the same—*unless our treatment conditions affect their behaviors.* If we have the same subjects in all our conditions (or matched subjects who are also somewhat similar), any differences in behavior produced by the experimental intervention will be more apparent. These differences will not be buried among the variability that is created by testing different subjects. We have increased the power of the experiment.

In a within-subjects experiment, we can also get an ongoing record of subjects' behaviors over time. This gives us a more complete picture of the way the independent variable works in the experiment. We have both practical and methodological gains with this approach. Since there are so many advantages to a within-subjects design, why not always use it?

DISADVANTAGES OF WITHIN-SUBJECTS DESIGNS

Practical Limitations

There are several reasons why within-subjects designs do not always work. Sometimes they actually are not practical. Within-subjects designs generally require each subject to spend more time in the experiment. For instance, the various conditions of an experiment might require the subjects to read and evaluate several stories. A researcher may need to schedule several hours of testing if this experiment is run with a within-subjects design: Each subject must spend several hours reading and scoring several stories. The same experiment might be run with a group of subjects in only an hour using a between-subjects design: Each individual subject would spend just one hour reading and evaluating one story.

If a procedure involves testing each subject individually, a great deal of time can be taken up by resetting equipment for each condition. That could lead to extra hours of testing per subject. In a perception experiment that requires calibrating several sensitive electronic instruments for each condition, the researcher and subjects are in for some tedious testing sessions. As an alternative, several subjects in a row could be tested in each condition, requiring fewer changes to the equipment.

Experiments can easily become tedious for subjects. Subjects who are expected to perform many tasks may get restless during the experiment and begin to make hasty judgments to hurry the process along—leading to inaccurate data. For the most part, these limitations are really just inconveniences. We can seek out subjects who are willing to invest a lot of time in a study. We can spend an additional 10, 20, or even 100 hours testing subjects if it is essential to the value of the experiment. Sometimes it is, and experimenters may spend hours or even days testing each subject. But more serious problems, linked to the independent variable, limit the within-subjects approach.

Interference Between Conditions

Often, each subject can be in only one condition of the experiment. Taking part in more than one condition would be either impossible or useless or would change the effect of later treatments.

Imagine that we are doing a study on car-buying preferences. We hypothesize that the type of car people first learned to drive will influence their own purchasing choices later. For simplicity, let us say that people who learn to drive in small cars (compact or smaller) will be more likely to buy small cars than people who learn to drive in full-sized cars. With the cooperation of a local driving school, we randomly assign half our subjects to each treatment condition (small or full-sized car).

We suspect that car-buying preferences are influenced by a wide range of other factors too, including financial status, parents' choice of car, advertising, and perhaps even unidentified genetic differences in personality that influence our choices. The numerous makes and models on the market attest to the diversity of tastes. People differ a great deal in what they want in a car. Since so many subject variables are involved, perhaps a within-subjects design would be a better choice.

Actually, in this experiment our choice is simple: We cannot do a within-subjects experiment. Once a person learns to drive in a small car, he or she can never learn to drive again as a beginner in a full-sized car. Even if we put subjects through the same sets of lessons again, they would not respond to them in the same fashion because they are not novices any more. The first training condition would interfere with all later attempts. If one treatment condition precludes another, as it does in this kind of experiment, we will do better with a between-subjects design.

Sometimes it is possible to run all subjects through all treatments, but it does not make sense to do it. What if we want subjects to learn a list of words? In one condition, we tell the subjects to learn the words by forming mental pictures (images) of them. In the other condition, we ask subjects to repeat the words over and over. We want to use the same list in both conditions so that the difficulty of the list will not be a confounding variable. But once the subjects have practiced the list in one condition, they will recall it more easily in the next condition. If they formed pictures of elephants sitting on flagpoles, they will remember elephants and flagpoles. Bower (1972), a well-known researcher in the field of memory, understood this and therefore used between-subjects designs in similar experiments.

The interference between different conditions of an experiment is the biggest drawback in using within-subjects designs. If the treatments clash so badly that we cannot give them to the same subjects, we need a between-subjects design. Whenever we consider a within-subjects design, we also need to consider the possibility that effects on the dependent variable might be influenced by the order in which we give the treatments. Subjects' responses might differ from one treatment to another just because of the position, or order, of the treatments. In a within-subjects experiment, order is always a *potential* confound. For instance, if we were asking people to watch a series of television commercials and rate how much they liked each one, the order in which we presented the commercials might affect ratings. The first commercial they saw might always get a higher rating than it deserves simply because it is novel. By the third or fourth one, ratings of any commercial may be lower than they should be because subjects have tuned out. Advertisers know about this kind of order effect and keep their fingers crossed that their commercial will be placed first in any long commercial break. In a within-subjects design, we use special counterbalancing procedures to offset interference and to control for potential order effects between conditions. We will look at those procedures in detail in the next chapter.

SMALL *N* DESIGNS

Since subjects get more than one treatment condition in a within-subjects experiment, we can run experiments with very few subjects. The clearest examples of the within-subjects approach are experiments with only one subject. The basic idea for these experiments was developed and used extensively by B. F. Skinner, the famous behavioral psychologist. Skinner thought there was often more to gain by careful, continuous measurement of the behavior of a single subject than by using statistical tests to compare data obtained from different groups of subjects. Skinner's approach is called a **small *N* design,** a special case of a within-subjects experiment in which we use just one or two subjects (*N* stands for the number of subjects needed in the experiment). This approach can be very useful in exploratory research; if we see that a variable affects the behavior of one subject, we can expand the research to larger groups later. Running an experiment with one subject requires special measurement procedures. Let us look at them in a simple hypothetical experiment.

A Small *N* Design: Talking to Plants

We want to test the notion that talking to a plant makes it grow better. Of course, we want to approach this hypothesis in a rigorous, scientific way. As you know, we can set this up as a two-group experiment. We can compare different groups of plants—we talk to one group but not to the other. We measure their growth and see how the groups compare. Or we might plan a multiple-group experiment and use varying amounts of talking as our treatment conditions. We might even choose to look at a second variable (like music) and set up a factorial design. These designs, which require groups of subjects, are usually called **large *N* designs.**

Instead of sacrificing our entertainment budget for a whole year in order to purchase enough plant subjects to conduct a large *N* study, we could use a small *N* design to do our experiment on talking to plants. First, we carefully choose our subject. Cactus grows too slowly to be of much use; bamboo grows very quickly but needs a temperate climate. After some library research, we settle on the hardy *ficus elastica,* better known as the rubber plant. We begin with the control condition of the experiment (condition *A*): For a time, we do not talk to the plant at all. During this period, say 3 months, we simply chart its growth. This establishes a **baseline** of behavior, a measure of behavior as it normally occurs without the experimental manipulation. In the second phase of the experiment, we introduce the experimental manipulation (condition *B*): For the second 3-month period, we talk to the plant for 2 hours a day. "Talking" is operationally defined as reading aloud from Euell Gibbons's *Stalking the Wild Asparagus.*[4] We continue to chart the plant's growth throughout this phase of the experiment. If talking aids growth, the plant should grow more during the second part of the experiment. If talking has no effect on growth, the plant should continue to grow about as much as it did in the baseline condition.

So far this procedure looks very much like what we do when we carry out a two-group design: We use a control group to establish a baseline of behavior; we compare behavior in the experimental condition with what we see in the control condition. The procedures are similar in those respects, but there is also an important difference. Since we are using only one subject, we are looking at that subject at different points in time. Our rubber plant is 3 months older by the time we finish the first set of observations. The season has changed. The plant now gets a different amount of light each day. The humidity has probably changed too. Of course, some of these extraneous variables can be controlled. We can raise our plant in a laboratory in which light, temperature, and moisture are always the same. But we cannot discount the fact that the plant has aged. Any differences in the amount of growth we see during the experimental manipulation might be due to natural changes in the growth cycle of this plant. In other words, we may have confounding. For this reason, the small *N* experiment includes one additional, crucial step. After completing the experimental manipulation, we remove the independent variable and return to the original control condition (*A*). We do not talk to the subject at all during the last 3 months of the experiment; we simply continue to monitor its growth.

We verify the effect of our independent variable in the small *N* experiment by returning to the original baseline condition. Our hypothesis is that talking to a plant makes it grow faster. Suppose that our plant did grow faster in the second phase of the experiment: Compared to the baseline condition, the plant grew faster when we talked to it. If the change in growth rate was produced by some extraneous variable such as maturation, the growth rate probably will not change much after we stop talking to the plant. On the other hand, if talking caused the plant to grow faster, we would expect a decline in the growth rate after we stop. But under some circumstances, the change in behavior caused by an experimental manipulation may persist even after the experimental manipulation has been discontinued. If the target behavior does not return to the baseline level, we cannot automatically rule out the effect of the independent variable. One problem is that no matter how hard we try, we may not be able to recreate the original baseline conditions perfectly. This is especially true in experiments outside the laboratory. In these cases, we may want to repeat the procedures more than once. We can return to the baseline condition and reapply the experimental manipulation many times if we wish. Often we need to do that several times to make sure our findings were not produced by some chance variation in the testing situation.

[4] Gibbons, E. (1970). *Stalking the wild asparagus.* New York: David McKay.

When to Use Small *N* Designs

Like all within-subjects designs, the small *N* design is appropriate when we want good control over subject variables. It is also appropriate when we are interested in the behavior of a particular subject. The small *N* design is applied to many behavior-modification problems, which often concern a single person (see Box 8-1).

We have focused on the importance of returning to the baseline conditions to verify the impact of our independent variable. However, in many behavior modification studies, researchers choose not to return to the control condition. This is often true in experiments done to modify self-injurious behaviors. Suppose you were working with a disturbed child who hit his head against the wall, kicked himself, and punched himself with his fists. Tate and Baroff (1966) reported their work with just such a boy. When the boy, Sam, harmed himself, Tate and Baroff stopped talking to him and stopped holding his hand. With these and other interventions, Sam's self-destructive behaviors decreased.

How do we know that not talking to Sam and not holding his hand actually caused the change in behavior? Perhaps the change was just a coincidence. Would we want to find out? Would we want to return to an original set of conditions that might make Sam hurt himself again? No. Even though the experimental procedures require a return to the baseline conditions, psychologists sacrifice some scientific precision for ethical reasons. When we make an intervention that we hope will be therapeutic, our primary goal is helping the patient. If we succeed in changing his or her behavior to something more adaptive, we have accomplished that goal.

When to Use Large *N* Designs

The small *N* design is appropriate when studying a particular subject, such as a disturbed child. It is also useful when very few subjects are available. You can actually carry out an entire experiment with just one subject, although this is not often ideal. A small *N* study may have little external validity. When we do experiments, we usually want to be able to **generalize** from our results—we want to be able to make statements about people or rats that were not actually subjects in an experiment. Many researchers prefer to do large *N* studies because they believe that they can then generalize from their results more successfully. All other things being equal, an experiment with more subjects has greater generalizability.

In a large *N* study, we may form separate groups of subjects for each treatment condition. The subjects run through their assigned conditions, and we then measure them on the dependent variable. We pool data from each group and evaluate them statistically to see if the groups behaved differently. In a small *N* experiment, we watch one or two subjects over an extended period of time. We record baseline data. We introduce the experimental intervention and monitor the changes in the dependent variable

BOX **8-1**
A behavior-
modification
example:
Picking up
after Jim

Hall (1971) reports on the case of a new bride who was having a problem with her husband: "According to the wife, Jim's jacket was a permanent fixture on the back of the couch and his shoes could usually be found close by. Occasionally he would decorate the back of the chair with a sweater" (p. 43). The bride did not want to pick up after Jim or continue nagging him to put his clothes away. The solution was found through a simple behavior-modification experiment. In these kinds of experiments, researchers try to change behaviors by applying various rewards and punishments as the independent variable. Rewards and punishments are presented as a consequence of the target behaviors to be modified. Researchers often use small N designs to do this. How did a small N design get a husband to pick up his clothes?

First, of course, the experimenters needed a baseline of behavior. We need to know how often the husband left his clothes in the living room under the usual circumstances. Records were made of how many items of clothing remained in the living room for more than 15 minutes; the average was two per day. During the experimental phase of the study, husband and wife agreed that whoever left more clothing in the living room during the week would have to do the dishes the following week. Leaving clothing in the living room then had a specific consequence. The husband could avoid that consequence by putting his clothes away. During the 2-week experimental period, the husband left no clothing in the living room. (Presumably the tidy wife did the same, so it is not clear who actually did the dishes during that time.)

Did the threat of doing the dishes (the independent variable) really produce the change in behavior? Perhaps the husband just became more aware of his wife's concern for the appearance of the house. The wife thought the problem was solved, so she let her husband know that the threat of dishwashing was lifted; nothing more would happen if he left his clothes in the living room. The outcome is illustrated on the following page in Figure 8-2. You can see that the husband went back to leaving his clothes in the room when the threat of doing the dishes was removed. It seemed that the threat really did affect his behavior. Still, you can also see from the figure that he did not leave quite as many clothes around as before. It may be that the second baseline period was not exactly identical to the first. For instance, if the weather had warmed up, Jim's jacket may have stayed in the closet during that time. This story had a happy ending. As you can see from the figure, after additional training (doing dishes contingent$_2$), Jim put his clothes away.

throughout the experimental condition. Typically, we take several measurements. We can see whether the effect of the experimental intervention is instant or whether it builds over time. We continue to measure after the intervention is removed. We can verify that the independent variable

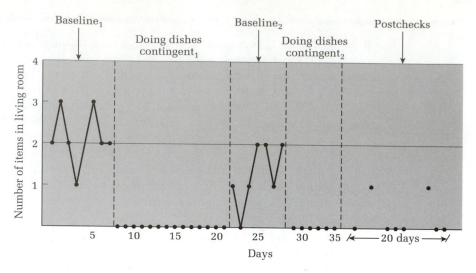

FIGURE **8-2** A record of the number of clothing items left in the living room by a newlywed husband. From "Managing behavior. 3: Applications in school and home," by R. V. Hall, S. J. Alley, and L. Cox. Copyright © 1971 by PRO-ED, Inc. Reprinted with permission.

causes changes in behavior because we can see what happens when that variable is removed. In short, we may get a more complete and accurate picture from a small *N* study than from a large *N* study that tests the same hypothesis. Usually, the impact of the independent variable is so apparent in small *N* studies that statistical tests are not needed to evaluate the results.

Then why not use a small *N* design for every experiment? We would certainly save a lot of time recruiting subjects and doing statistics. But is it safe to generalize from a small *N* study? Small *N* researchers say yes, as long as we can evaluate how "typical" our small sample is. One *ficus elastica* might be much like another; one laboratory rat might or might not be. We could compare the behavior of our rat during the baseline condition with the many records of other rats in the research literature. If our rat seems to behave about the same as other rats, we would probably assume it is a typical subject. However, even if the subject behaves typically in our baseline conditions, we still cannot be sure this particular subject is not unusually sensitive to the independent variable.

Generalizing from the results of one or two subjects is particularly risky when the subjects are people. No two people would be expected to react in exactly the same way. Pooling the responses of many individual subjects makes it more likely that the effects are generalizable to people outside the experiment.

Generalizing also depends on the type of process that is being measured. Some psychophysical (sensation and perception) processes are quite similar in most people. We all react in much the same way to a loud, unexpected sound, such as a gunshot, by displaying a startle reaction. Other psychological processes—such as whether we will laugh in relief or get angry at an experimenter who fired off a gun close to our head—show large individual differences. If we are measuring a process that is relatively *in*variant, the results from a small *N* experiment would have greater generalizability than if we were measuring a behavior for which we expected large differences among people.

In a small *N* study, we also cannot be sure that the results are not due to some unseen accident. For instance, our plant study could be contaminated by a well-meaning cleaning person who gives fertilizer to our subject just at the time we begin talking to it. For these reasons, it is especially important to replicate the findings of a small *N* experiment before generalizations are made. An experiment with multiple applications of a treatment and multiple returns to baseline is more convincing than a single application.

It is impossible to say whether small or large *N* studies always have greater generality. All things rarely are equal. A large *N* study with a badly biased sample may tell us little about behavior in the population. However, the findings of a well-controlled experiment with a single subject might be successfully replicated again and again on different subjects. By gathering baseline data, applying the experimental manipulation, and then returning to the baseline condition, we can get a very clear idea of the impact of the independent variable.

ABA DESIGNS

The small *N* experiments we have discussed so far have all used an **ABA design.** *ABA* refers to the order of the conditions of the experiment: *A* (the control condition) is presented first, followed by *B* (the experimental condition). Finally, we return to the control condition (*A*) to verify that the change in behavior is linked to the independent variable. Typically, small *N* experiments use the *ABA* design. Some are variations of the *ABA* format (for example, Figure 8-2 shows an *ABABA* sequence). If we want to use several *different* experimental conditions in a small *N* experiment, we can extend the *ABA* format. We can proceed as follows: AB_1 AB_2 AB_3, and so on. What is important is that we collect baseline data before any experimental intervention and that we return to the baseline (control) condition after each experimental treatment.

Instead of looking at the behavior of a single subject across conditions, we can also look at the across-conditions behavior of an entire *group* using an *ABA* design. We can study changes in the group without much concern for how individual subjects change. The *ABA* within-subjects design enables us to do this. The basics of this design are the same; the only difference is that we test a group rather than only one or two subjects. The main limitation of this approach is that the experimental treatment must be reversible: We must be able to return to the control condition. If treatment conditions are not reversible, we cannot use an *ABA* design. (We will look at some alternative procedures in the next chapter.)

Pedalino and Gamboa (1974) wanted to study the behavior of workers in a large manufacturing and distribution center. Specifically, they wanted to see how they could get more people to come to work regularly. They hypothesized that attendance would improve if people were rewarded for coming to work. Their independent variable was reinforcement; their dependent variable was absenteeism. How would we test this hypothesis with a between-subjects design? The obvious choice is a two-group design. We would begin by taking a random sample of workers. We would randomly place half our sample in the control condition, their usual work situation. The other half would be in the experimental condition—they would receive reinforcement for coming to work regularly. Can you foresee any problems with this approach?

Of course, various workers may have very different work environments. On the one hand, Kathy's supervisor, Ms. Merkle, is a known tyrant, who stands over people's desks and points out their errors as they work. John is supervised by Mr. Albert, who is equally irritating. Both Kathy and John get frequent headaches and often find themselves unable to come to work. On the other hand, Robert and Joan work with Mr. Solomon, whose philosophy is that people really want to do a good job and will if you encourage them. Ms. Murphy feels the same. She and Mr. Solomon praise their staffs whenever they do well. Besides having different supervisors, our subjects may also be different ages. If absenteeism is related to age, that could make a difference. Of course, we assume that randomization takes care of things like age, supervisors, and other subject variables. Our randomly formed groups should be about the same age and the same general health, have supervisors who are equally awful, and so on. If we are especially concerned about any of these variables, we can form matched groups.

But there are still other disadvantages in using two or more separate groups. We may not be able to get as much control over the experiment as we can with a within-subjects design. If our random groups are spread over several offices, we may not be able to monitor all the changes in working conditions that occur during our experiment: Supervisors are rotated; workers get raises; some quit and others take their places. We also do not have the chance to see what happens to the same workers before, during, and after the experimental intervention. But with an *ABA* design, we get that chance. We can nail down the effect of our independent variable by observing the same group before, during, and after the experimental treatment.

For these reasons, Pedalino and Gamboa tested their hypothesis using an *ABA* design. First, they collected baseline data: They measured the amount of absenteeism under the usual working conditions. The experimental condition was a lottery poker game. During this condition, each employee was allowed to pick a card from a deck of playing cards on each day he or she came to work on time. At the end of the 5-day work week, the employee with the best poker hand won $20. During the time the lottery was in effect, absenteeism dropped 18%. When the lottery was stopped, people began skipping work more often. Pedalino and Gamboa concluded that the lottery poker game had reduced absenteeism.

You can see that switching back to the baseline condition was essential. Something else might have happened about the same time the lottery was started. Maybe everyone had just gotten a raise and felt better about coming to work. Maybe the flu season ended. But we know that the lottery produced a change in attendance because absenteeism rose again when the lottery ended. As a further check, Pedalino and Gamboa started up the lottery again and absenteeism dropped again.

PRETEST/POSTTEST DESIGNS

Sometimes we want to assess more simply whether an experimental treatment increases or decreases the existing level of a behavior. We can measure the level of behavior before and after treatment and compare these levels using a **pretest/posttest design**—one of the most frequently used group designs in the social sciences (Cook & Campbell, 1979). It is a repeated-measures design (subjects are measured more than once on the dependent variable), but there is only one treatment condition. All subjects receive the same level of the independent variable, and the treatment is not reversed. Because only one level of an independent variable is tested (it is always present), this is typically considered a quasiexperimental design. Subjects may be tested in a single group session, or they may be tested one at a time in different experimental sessions. In a pretest/posttest design, subjects are assessed once with the dependent measure (pretest), then given a treatment, and then retested on the same measure (posttest). The effect of the independent variable is shown by changes between scores at the first and second testing.

Suppose a school counselor wanted to assess the effectiveness of a preparation course for college admissions tests that she had developed for college-bound students. Sixty students have signed up to take the course from her. Optimally, she would like to compare admissions test scores of students who received the training with scores of those who did not. She could randomly assign half the students who signed up for the course to the training condition and the other half to a control group and compare their scores. But she sees an ethical problem with this: She would have to deny the course to half the people who want it, and that is out of the question. Alternatively, she could use some other group of students (such as those who did not sign up) as the control group. But she worries that these students might have different characteristics than the ones who want to take the course. Because she cannot think of a suitable control group, she decides to use a pretest/posttest design.

The first day of the course, she gives all 60 students in the course a pretest—a practice S.A.T.—to establish a baseline score for each student. She is hopeful that at the end of the 6-week preparation course, students will get higher scores than they did the first time around. At the end of the course, she tests them again. She finds that, on the average, their scores improved by 20 points. Should she keep the training program? This is an internal validity question. How confident can she be with this design that her training program caused the improvement? Not as confident as she could have been had she used a two-group design that included a control group.

There are simply too many other things that could have caused the improvement—practice effects, for example. Anastasi (1958) has shown that people do better the second time they take an intelligence test, even without any special training in between. Familiarity with a test can improve performance. Test takers may be less anxious the second time around; they also may have learned new information (in their other classes, reading the paper, watching TV) that improves their scores the second time. Without a group that receives no training to control for other things that might occur with the passage of time, it is clear that a pretest/posttest design lacks internal validity. Even so, it has been widely used in situations where a control group is impossible or unethical.

Sometimes a pretest/posttest design is used in circumstances where the treatment time is short, as in a single experimental session. A researcher who wants to test the benefits of subliminal self-help tapes designed to increase self-esteem could use a pretest/posttest design. He might test 30 subjects, one at a time. Using a standard test, he could measure each subject's self-esteem when they first arrive at the laboratory. Subjects could listen to the 45-minute tape, and the researcher could measure self-esteem again. If extraneous variables had been carefully controlled during all 30 experimental sessions, we would be *somewhat* more confident that an increase in self-esteem after the treatment was really attributable to the tape. (We will look at some important extraneous variables and how to control them in the next chapter.) However, without a control group, we still could not be certain that the rise in self-esteem was not brought about by practice with the test,[5] because people also seem to get better scores on personality and adjustment tests with practice (Windle, 1954).

HOW CAN YOU CHOOSE?

How do you decide whether to use a within-subjects or a between-subjects design? First, as always, think about the hypothesis of the experiment. How many treatment conditions do you need to test the hypothesis? Would it be possible to have each subject in more than one of these conditions? If so, you may be able to use a within-subjects design. Do your treat-

---

[5] In fact, this explanation is quite plausible. Greenwald, Spangenberg, Pratkanis, and Eskenazi (1991) used a more complex pretest/posttest design to test subliminal self-esteem tapes. After replicating the study on three different subject samples, they concluded that the tapes had no effect on self-esteem; however, with or without the self-esteem tapes, posttest self-esteem scores were somewhat higher than pretest scores.

ment conditions interfere with one another? Yes? Then you ought to use a between-subjects design. Can you reverse your experimental treatment? You may want to consider an *ABA* design. Do you want to test the effect of an IV that is not reversible, but a control group is impractical or unethical? You might think about a pretest/posttest design, even though it is not as high in internal validity as other designs.

Consider the practical advantages of each approach. Is it simpler to run the experiment one way or the other? Which will be more time-consuming? If you can get only a few subjects, the within-subjects design may be better. Remember that there is a tradeoff: The longer the experiment takes, the harder it may be to find willing subjects.

You can control subject variables best in a within-subjects design. If there are likely to be large individual differences in the way subjects respond to the experiment, the within-subjects approach is usually better.

Remember to review the research literature. If other experimenters have used within-subjects designs for similar problems, it is probably because that approach works best.

If all other things seem equal, use the within-subjects design. It is better from a statistical standpoint; you maximize your chances of detecting the effect of the independent variable.

SUMMARY

Within-subjects designs are designs in which each subject takes part in more than one condition of the experiment. These designs are advantageous because they enable us to compare the behavior of the same subjects under different treatment conditions. We can often get a more precise picture of the effects of the independent variable from a within-subjects design than we can from a between-subjects design. Subject variables are better controlled in the within-subjects experiment. We eliminate the error produced by differences between subjects and thus make a more precise assessment of the impact of the independent variable.

The *small* N *design* is used to study the behavior of only one or two subjects at a time. This approach requires very careful control over the conditions of the experiment. A typical small *N* experiment begins with observing and recording the subject's behavior under the control conditions. This is the *baseline*. The experimental intervention is then introduced, and the subject's behavior is monitored throughout the experimental period. This behavior is then compared with the baseline records. To rule out the possibility of confounding by extraneous variables, there is a return to the original control condition. Multiple applications of the treatment and multiple returns to baseline are most convincing. In addition, small *N* experiments should be replicated.

Most small *N* studies use an *ABA design. ABA* refers to the order of the treatment conditions. We can use the *ABA* approach or some variation in many experiments with groups of subjects as well as with individuals. The main limitation on this approach is that we can use it only with experimental treatments that are completely reversible.

When a control group is impractical or unethical, researchers often use a *pretest/posttest design*. Unless all extraneous variables can be carefully controlled during the entire time the treatment is applied, this design has little internal validity. Even then, treatment effects on the posttest can be confounded by practice effects due to previous testing.

Whether to choose a within-subjects or a between-subjects design depends on several factors. Practical and methodological considerations come into play. A within-subjects design requires fewer subjects; it is less time-consuming when each subject requires extensive training; and it controls well for subject variables. Statistically, a researcher stands a better chance of detecting the effect of the independent variable using a within-subjects design. However, we cannot use within-subjects designs if experimental conditions will interfere with one another, as in various learning tasks. In addition, these designs are sometimes impractical because they take longer to run than a corresponding between-subjects experiment.

KEY TERMS

ABA design   A type of within-subjects design in which the control condition (*A*) is presented first, followed by the experimental condition (*B*), followed by a return to the control condition (*A*).

Baseline   A measure of behavior as it normally occurs without the experimental manipulation; used to assess the impact of the experimental intervention.

Generalizing   The process of extending the results of a specific study to individuals and situations not directly tested; an inductive process.

Large *N* design   Similar to a small *N* design, except that groups of subjects are required.

Mixed design   A factorial design that combines within-subjects and between-subjects factors.

Pretest/posttest design   A repeated-measures design with only one treatment condition; subjects are assessed once with the dependent measure (pretest); given a treatment; then retested on the same measure (posttest).

Repeated-measures design   A design in which subjects are measured more than once on the dependent variable; same as a within-subjects design.

Small *N* design   A within-subjects design in which just one or two subjects are used; typically, the experimenter collects baseline data during an initial control condition; applies the experimental treatment; then reinstates the original control condition to verify that changes observed in behavior were caused by the experimental intervention.

Subject variables   The characteristics of the subjects in an experiment that cannot be manipulated; independent variables, in the sense that a researcher can select subjects for their particular values.

Within-subjects design   A design in which each subject takes part in more than one condition of the experiment.

REVIEW AND STUDY QUESTIONS

1. What is a within-subjects experiment? How is it different from a between-subjects experiment?
2. Discuss three advantages of using a within-subjects design.
3. Discuss three disadvantages of using a within-subjects design.
4. What is a small N design?
5. Discuss the relative advantages and disadvantages of small N versus large N designs.
6. Outline an experiment to test this hypothesis: Children who are given weaponlike toys (for example, toy guns and knives) become more aggressive.
   a. What are your independent and dependent variables?
   b. How would you operationally define "aggression"?
   c. How would you test this hypothesis using a small N design?
   d. What are the disadvantages of using a small N design for this experiment?
7. Mary is very excited about the within-subjects approach. "Now I'll never need to run large numbers of subjects again," she says. What has she forgotten?
8. For each of the following dependent measures, evaluate the pros and cons of using a within-subjects approach:
   a. The taste of a new toothpaste
   b. The cavity-preventing properties of a new toothpaste
   c. The readability of a new typeface
   d. The impact of good and bad news
9. One student is still looking for shortcuts. He says: "Running through the control condition of an experiment twice is silly. I'll just run through A and B and draw my conclusions from that." What would you say to him to convince him that carrying out the entire ABA design would be a better idea?
10. Explain how the levels of your independent variable can influence your decision to use a within- or between-subjects design.
11. What requirements must be met to make the within-subjects approach feasible?
12. Ms. Perkins, a school principal, is interested in this question: Does having breakfast improve children's school performance? She would like to gather some scientific data on this question. You are invited in as a consultant because Ms. Perkins is not sure how to proceed. Help her out by doing the following:

a. Identify the independent and dependent variables for her.
b. Formulate a workable operational definition for each variable.
c. Outline two different approaches to the research question: one a between-subjects approach, one a within-subjects approach.
d. Explain to Ms. Perkins the relative advantages and disadvantages of these approaches for her problem.
e. Which approach would you recommend and why?
f. What potential problems can you anticipate in carrying out this study?

13. When is a pretest/posttest design used? What are the limitations of this design?

REFERENCES

ANASTASI, A. (1958). *Differential psychology* (3rd ed.). New York: Macmillan.

BOWER, G. H. (1972). Mental imagery and associative learning. In L. W. Gregg (Ed.), *Cognition in learning and memory.* New York: Wiley.

COOK, T. D., & CAMPBELL, D. T. (1979). *Quasi-experimentation: Design and analysis for field settings.* Chicago: Rand McNally.

COREN, S., & GIRGUS, J. (1972). Illusion decrement in intersecting line figures. *Psychonomic Science, 26,* 108–110.

FAVREAU, O. E. (1977). Psychology in action: Disillusioned. *American Psychologist, 32*(7), 568–571.

GACKENBACH, J., & SCHILLIG, B. (1983). Lucid dreams: The content of conscious awareness of dreaming during the dream. *Journal of Mental Imagery, 7*(2), 1–14.

GREENWALD, A., SPANGENBERG, E., PRATKANIS, A., & ESKENAZI, J. (1991). Double-blind tests of subliminal self-help audiotapes. *Psychological Science, 2*(2), 119–122.

HALL, R. V. (1971). *Managing behavior. 3: Applications in school and home.* Austin, TX: PRO-ED, Inc.

PEDALINO, E., & GAMBOA, V. (1974). Behavior modification and absenteeism: Intervention in one industrial setting. *Journal of Applied Psychology, 59,* 694–698.

TATE, B. G., & BAROFF, G. S. (1966). Aversive control of self-injurious behavior in a psychotic boy. *Behavior Research and Therapy, 4,* 281–287.

WINDLE, C. (1954). Test-retest effect on personality questionnaires. *Educational Psychology Measurement, 14,* 617–633.

9

Controlling Extraneous Variables: Physical Variables

When we experiment, we want to create treatment conditions that will let us see the effects of the independent variables clearly. Our experiments should be internally valid: Only the independent variable should change systematically from one condition to another. In the last several chapters, you saw how we can control for some subject variables that might lead to confounding: We can use random assignment to different treatment groups. We can match subjects on variables that are related to the dependent variable before randomly assigning them to groups. We can run the experiment using a within-subjects design. In this chapter and the one that follows, we will look closely at some techniques for handling three types of extraneous variables: physical, personality, and social. Each poses special problems in an experiment. Many can be controlled by the same procedures, but some require special procedures. In this chapter we will look at the first type, the physical variables.

PHYSICAL VARIABLES

Poor Janice Johnson was trying to run an experiment on riddles that were tricky and required a lot of thought. On Thursday, her first day of testing, Janice recruited subjects in the library and tested them on the spot in a quiet reading room. The next day she came back to run the rest of the experiment. To her dismay, Janice found that the reading room closed early on Fridays. The only place she could test her subjects was in the lobby of the building. It was fairly quiet there, but people walked by now and then, laughing and talking about plans for the weekend. Janice cried, "What a dummy I am! These testing conditions will confound my experiment! Why did I run all my control group subjects yesterday?"

The day of the week, the testing room, the noise, the distractions are all **physical variables,** aspects of the testing conditions that need to be controlled. Janice's experiment was in real trouble because she ran all her control subjects on a Thursday and all her experimental subjects on a Friday (and we all know that Fridays are different!).[1] The control group was tested under quiet conditions. The experimental group was tested in a different

[1] Many of our colleagues try to avoid running *any* experiments on Fridays. We are not sure if it is because they are worried that subjects will be less motivated to participate or whether they themselves are just looking forward to the weekend.

place with more noise and distractions. Clearly, there was confounding in Janice's experiment: The testing conditions changed along with the independent variable. Her problems could have been avoided by using one of the three general techniques for controlling physical variables: elimination, constancy of conditions, and balancing. We cannot possibly identify all the extraneous variables that influence the outcome of a study—but we try to find as many as we can. By using control techniques, we increase the chances of an internally valid experiment.

Elimination and Constancy

To make sure that an extraneous variable does not affect an experiment, sometimes we just take it out—we **eliminate** it. If noise might confound the results, we test in a soundproof room. If we do not want interruptions, we hang a sign on the door saying "Do not disturb. Experiment in progress."

We want to eliminate all potential sources of error in our measurements. Campbell and Stanley (1963), for example, said that *instrumentation* was a threat to the internal validity of an experiment. By instrumentation they meant any changes that might occur in the measuring instrument across conditions. Often the measuring device is a person. Observers gathering data may become fatigued as the observations continue and miss important data as the experiment goes on. Their subjective ratings may also shift. Researchers try to eliminate these sources of error by using objective measures whenever possible. Videotaping subjects has become relatively common, allowing for reviews and cross checking of observers' ratings.

Even an automated recording device can introduce fluctuations in measurements because of changes in temperature and humidity. Calibration can vary slightly from trial to trial. Increasingly, researchers are relying on computerized equipment to achieve precision (see Figure 9-1).

Ideally, we would like to eliminate all extraneous variables from an experiment. But this is easier said than done. Sometimes there is no soundproof room. Things like the weather, the lighting, and the paint on the walls are simply there; we cannot eliminate them. Instead, we use the second control procedure—constancy of conditions.

Constancy of conditions means simply that we keep treatment conditions as nearly similar as possible. If we cannot eliminate a variable, we try to make sure that it stays the same in all treatment conditions. We cannot take the paint off the walls, but we can test all subjects in the same room. That way we make sure that the pea-green walls offend all subjects equally in all conditions. The same goes for lighting, the comfort of the chairs, the mustiness of the drapes; all stay the same for all the subjects. We also try to keep the mechanics of the testing procedures the same. For instance, it is helpful to write out instructions to subjects before beginning the experiment. The written instructions are then *read* to subjects to guarantee that all subjects in each condition get exactly the same instructions. Exactly the

FIGURE **9-1** Microprocessor-based laboratory equipment for computer acquisition of
psychophysiological data.

same amount of time is allowed for each subject to complete each task—
unless time is the independent or dependent variable.

Many physical variables like time of testing, testing place, and
mechanical procedures can be kept constant with a little effort. An experimenter may end up controlling some variables that would not have
affected the results anyway, but it is better to use the controls than to have
regrets later. If someone can punch holes in the results simply by pointing
out that the experimental group had lunch but the control group did not,
the experimenter will have a hard time making a strong case for the effects
of the independent variable.

Balancing

Sometimes neither elimination nor constancy can be used. Perhaps some
variables cannot be eliminated. For example, we would like to test in a
soundproof room but we do not have access to one. We would like to test
all subjects together at the same time, but they cannot come at once. What
can we do in these situations? Confounding occurs when something in the
experiment changes systematically along with the independent variable. If
we cannot eliminate extraneous variables or keep them constant throughout an experiment, we can still make sure that they do not confound the
results. The key to the problem is the *way* the variables change. If they
change in a way that is *systematically linked to the levels of the independent variable,* we are in trouble. If we test experimental subjects in one
room and control subjects in another, we have created an orderly change
in many of the variables that make up the testing conditions. We will not
be able to tell for sure whether the independent variable or something

TABLE **9-1**

Balancing the effects of the testing room across two treatment conditions, control (*C*) and experimental (*E*)	
Green Testing Room: Subjects	*Pink Testing Room: Subjects*
C_1	C_4
C_2	C_5
C_3	C_6
E_1	E_4
E_2	E_5
E_3	E_6

NOTE: *Half the subjects are randomly assigned to each testing room. Half the subjects in each room are then randomly assigned to the control condition, half to the experimental condition.*

about the different testing rooms produced changes in the groups. The control group might do better if it is tested in the same sunny room as the experimental group. The key to controlling variables that cannot be eliminated or held constant is the third technique for physical variables, balancing.

We know that ideally we should not test subjects in two different rooms. But perhaps we have no choice; it is two rooms or nothing. We want to be sure testing conditions do not change in a way that is related to the independent variable. We can do this through **balancing,** distributing the effects of an extraneous variable across the different treatment conditions of the experiment. A way in which we might do this with room assignment is shown in Table 9-1.

We begin by randomly assigning half the subjects to the first testing room. The other half will be tested in the second room. Next, we randomly assign half the subjects *in each room* to the experimental condition; the remaining subjects will be in the control condition. Notice that we have not wiped out the differences between the two testing rooms; they are just as different as ever. However, the hope is that the effects of the rooms are the same, or balanced, for both treatment conditions. For every control subject tested in the green room, there is an experimental subject tested in that room. For every control subject tested in the pink room, there is an experimental subject tested in that room.

Janice could have salvaged her riddle experiment by using balancing. Instead of testing all control subjects on the first day, she should have randomly assigned each subject to either the experimental or the control condition. Then by chance, she would have tested roughly half the control subjects and half the experimental subjects on Thursday. Roughly half the control subjects would have taken part in the quiet reading room, along with roughly half the experimental subjects. On the second day, Janice would have continued assigning subjects to the two treatment conditions at random. She then would have tested about half the control subjects and half the experimental subjects in the noisy lobby. Notice that she still would have had subjects who were tested under two different testing conditions. But the effects of these conditions would have been about the same for the two treatments in the experiment, so the testing conditions would not have confounded the results of her experiment.

We can use balancing for many other variables as well. For example, if we cannot test all subjects at the same time of day, we can arrange things so that we test equal numbers of experimental and control subjects before and after lunch. Many physical variables will be balanced across conditions automatically as we assign our subjects to treatment conditions at random. Time of testing, weather conditions, and the day of the week are typically controlled in this way. Usually, we do not even think about these sorts of extraneous variables. As long as there is no systematic change in an extraneous variable, things are fine. If we assign subjects to treatment conditions at random, we can be reasonably sure (but not positive) that we will not accidentally test all control subjects on a cool, comfortable day and all experimental subjects on a hot, muggy day. We can, of course, easily improve control by using block randomization (see Chapter 6).

At this point you may be wondering whether there is a limit on the number of extraneous variables that must be controlled. There may indeed be many possibilities, but you can set up a reasonably good experiment by taking precautions: Eliminate extraneous variables when you can. Keep treatment conditions as similar as possible. Balance out the effects of other variables, like the testing room, by making sure that the effects are distributed evenly across all treatment conditions. As always, be sure to assign individual subjects to treatment conditions at random. The experimental literature will also help you plan a strategy. If other experimenters have carefully controlled the size of the testing room, you will want to be more cautious with that variable than with some others, such as the day of the week. If you can avoid it, do not let extraneous variables change along with the independent variable. You can never completely rule out the possibility of confounding if you let that happen.

CONTROLLING WITHIN-SUBJECTS DESIGNS

The procedures we have discussed so far—elimination, constancy of conditions, and balancing—are needed in most experiments. However, there are special problems in using a within-subjects design. The fact that subjects take part in more than one condition of the experiment leads to some snags that do not occur when we test different subjects in each condition. The problems that arise can be grouped into two categories: order effects and carryover effects.

Controlling for Order Effects: Counterbalancing

Suppose we want to do some market research on a new brand of cola. We know that people differ a great deal in how they rate things like foods and beverages, so we decide to use a within-subjects design. We would like to get people to compare their present brand of cola with our new brand. We will get ratings on how good our cola tastes compared to the old brands. That information will tell us whether we can expect the new product to compete with well-known brands. Our hypothesis is that our new cola will get better ratings than the old brands.

We recruit cola drinkers and bring them to our testing center. For 2 hours before the taste test, we keep them in a lounge in which they can relax and read magazines—but they cannot eat or drink. Then we give a glass of the new cola to each subject. We give each person time to drink it and then ask each person to indicate on a rating scale how much he or she liked the taste. Since we want to compare subjects' ratings of the new cola with their ratings of their regular brands, we carry out a second condition. We ask the subjects to drink a glass of their favorite cola. After, we get them to rate their favorite drinks on the rating scale. Now we have ratings of the two types of colas, new and old. We can compare the average ratings and see how our product competes.

Would it surprise you to learn that the average rating of our new brand was much higher than the average rating of the old brands? What is wrong with this experiment? The problem is that *any* cola might taste good after you have not had anything to drink for several hours. The first cola will taste better than the second.

In this experiment we varied the brand of cola that people were asked to drink. There were two conditions, New Brand and Old Brand. Unfortunately, in addition to varying the brand of cola, we varied an important extraneous variable—order. We created confounding by always giving subjects the new cola first. Subjects might have rated New Brand higher because it really is delicious, but the ratings were probably distorted because subjects had not had anything to drink for a full 2 hours before they tasted the new product. The subjects may have given the old brands lower ratings because they had just had something else to drink and were no longer thirsty. In this experiment we see that the *order* in which we presented the treatment conditions (that is, the different colas) may have changed the subjects' responses. We have confounding due to **order effects,** the changes in performance that occur when a condition falls in different places in a series of treatments.

Order effects are important in within-subjects experiments, which require that each subject be in more than one condition. Subjects will naturally receive some treatments before others. If the order of the treatments alters their effects, we can get some very distorted data. Two kinds of changes occur when subjects run in more than one condition. (1) Performance can decline as the experiment goes on: Subjects get tired. As they solve more and more word problems, for instance, they may begin to make mistakes. They may also become bored or irritated by the experiment and merely "go through the motions" until it is over. (2) Other factors may lead to improvement as the experiment proceeds—that is, to **practice effects.** As subjects become familiar with the experiment, they may relax and do a little better. They get better at using the apparatus, develop strategies for solving problems, or even catch on to the real purpose of the study.

All these changes, *both positive and negative,* are called **progressive error:** As the experiment progresses, results are distorted. The changes in subjects' responses are not caused by the independent variable; they are order effects produced when we run subjects through more than one treatment condition. Progressive error includes any changes in the subjects' responses that are caused by testing in multiple-treatment conditions. It includes order effects such as the effects of practice.

We control for any extraneous variable by making sure it affects all treatment conditions in the same way. We can do that by eliminating the variable completely, by holding it constant, or by balancing it out across treatment conditions. However, in a within-subjects experiment, we cannot eliminate order effects. Neither can we hold them constant, giving all subjects the treatments in the same order, because we are trying to avoid just this kind of systematic effect. But we can balance them out—distribute them across the conditions—so that they affect all conditions equally.

Think about the cola experiment. We did a poor job of setting it up because we let the order of the colas stay the same for all subjects. Everyone tasted the New Brand first. How could we redo the experiment so that progressive error would affect the results for both kinds of colas in the same way? We want to be sure that subjects' ratings reflect accurate taste judgments, not merely a difference between the first and second glass of cola. Suppose we modify our procedures a little. We run the first condition the same as before: Subjects do not eat or drink for 2 hours; then they drink a glass of New Brand cola and give their ratings. But instead of having them drink the Old Brand immediately, we have them return to the lounge for another 2 hours. At the end of that time, we give them the Old Brand cola and get the second set of ratings. Does this help? We avoid the problem of having subjects drink New Brand after 2 hours in the lounge and Old Brand when they are not as thirsty. However, our data may still be contaminated by the order of the conditions. When the subjects drink New Brand, they have been in the lounge a total of 2 hours. When they drink Old Brand, they have spent 4 hours in the lounge. By this time, they may be tired of hanging around. They may be getting hungry. They have also had practice filling out the rating scale, as well as time to think about what they said before.

Fortunately, researchers have worked out several procedures for controlling for order effects. These procedures are called **counterbalancing,** and they all have the same function: to distribute progressive error across the different treatment conditions of the experiment. By using these procedures, we can guarantee that the order effects that alter results on one condition will be offset, or counterbalanced, by the order effects operating on other conditions.

Let us assume that we can actually graph the effects of progressive error in our cola experiment. With each subject, error accumulates as the experiment progresses. Subjects get better at filling out the rating scale, they develop criteria for evaluating taste, and so on. Their responses change relative to their responses on the first trial. Figure 9-2 illustrates what progressive error in this experiment might look like. You can see that it is low in the early part of the experiment and increases gradually as the experiment continues. If everyone tastes New Brand first, there will be less progressive error affecting that condition than any other. The experiment will be invalidated.

Subject-by-subject counterbalancing.   We can control for progressive error through one of two general approaches. First, we can control it by using **subject-by-subject counterbalancing.** The idea is to divide up the effects of progressive error so that they will be the same for all conditions that each subject completes. How can we do this? Think carefully about what Figure 9-2 illustrates. The amount of progressive error (that is, the net outcome of fatigue, practice, and so on) in an experiment changes as the experiment continues. We can never expect progressive error to be the same for both conditions as long as we always run one condition first. Progressive error will always be less for the condition we run first. Somehow, we have to set up a procedure to make sure both conditions include some trials when progressive error is relatively low and others when it is relatively high.

If we try different ways of presenting two treatments, we will find one effective way to handle progressive error: Present each treatment more than once. We give each subject two glasses of each cola instead of one, but we do it in a particular order. Let us call New Brand "condition A" and Old Brand "condition B." We can equalize progressive error for these two conditions by presenting them in the order ABBA. If you refer to Figure 9-2, you can gain some insight into how the ABBA procedure works.

The values of progressive error are depicted on the vertical axis for each of four successive trials. For the first trial, progressive error is equal to 1 unit; for the second trial, 2 units; for the third and fourth trials, 3 and 4 units, respectively. If we run treatment conditions in the ABBA order, we can add up the units of progressive error for condition A and condition B. Progressive error works out to be 5 units for condition A (1 unit plus 4 units) and 5 units for condition B (2 plus 3 units). Of course, these numerical quantities are hypothetical, but you can see the logic behind the counterbalancing procedure. Now both conditions contain some trials in which progressive error is relatively high and others in which it is relatively low, but the total units of error are the same for both conditions.

Using subject-by-subject counterbalancing, each subject gets the ABBA sequence. This guarantees that progressive error affects conditions A and B about equally for each subject, assuming progressive error follows the

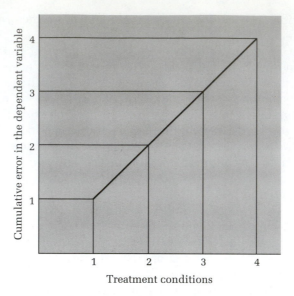

FIGURE **9-2** The impact of progressive error on responses in an experiment. The later trials (conditions) are affected more than the earlier ones.

pattern shown in Figure 9-2. If there are more than two treatment conditions, we can counterbalance for each subject by continuing the pattern. With three conditions, each subject gets *ABCCBA;* with four, each subject gets *ABCDDCBA;* and so on.

Progressive error is not necessarily this easy to control completely. Figure 9-2 illustrates error that is *linear;* that is, described by one straight line. But suppose true error has a more complex distribution across trials. Subjects get a little better with practice; they also fatigue to some extent. But on a long series of trials, they may catch their second wind and do a bit better as the experiment draws to a close. Suppose the impact of progressive error looks more like that represented in Figure 9-3. If we use the *ABBA* procedure, progressive error will be 3 units (1 + 2) for condition *A* and 5 units (2 + 3) for condition *B*. This is little better than testing everyone on *A* first, then *B*.

The effects of progressive error are not always linear. They may be curvilinear or nonmonotonic (changing direction), as in Figure 9-3. In reality, we rarely know precisely what progressive error will look like. Therefore it is especially important to be cautious when planning a design involving repeated measures for each subject. The available control procedures may not be adequate to distribute the effects of progressive error equally across all conditions. We rely on prior research to guide our decisions. Occasionally, progressive error itself must become a variable for study. When we clarify its impact beforehand, we can set up the most effective controls.

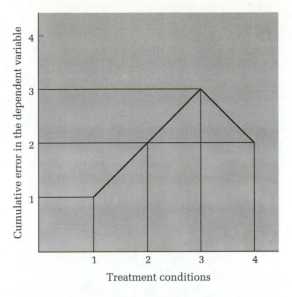

FIGURE **9-3** Nonlinear impact of progressive error in a hypothetical experiment.

Across-subjects counterbalancing. One of the drawbacks of counterbalancing within each subject is that we have to present each condition to each subject more than once. As the number of conditions increases, the length of the sequence also increases. Depending on the experiment, the procedures can become time-consuming, expensive, or just plain boring for the subjects as well as the experimenter. As an alternative, we can often use another set of procedures, **across-subjects counterbalancing.** These procedures serve the same basic purpose as subject-by-subject counterbalancing: They are used to distribute the effects of progressive error so that, theoretically, the effects will be the same for all conditions of the experiment. We are not always concerned about the individual subject's responses, but we still want to be sure that progressive error affects the various treatment conditions equally. These across-subjects techniques are complete and partial counterbalancing.

Complete counterbalancing. If we always present treatment conditions in the same order, progressive error will affect some conditions more than others. Complete counterbalancing controls for this by using all possible sequences of the conditions and using every sequence the same number of times. If we had only two treatments, *A* and *B,* we would give half the subjects *A* and then *B.* We would give the other subjects *B* first and then *A.* You can see that this is very similar to what we did to control order effects within each subject by giving each subject both sequences, *AB* and *BA.* But when we counterbalance across subjects, we need to give each subject only one sequence. Different subjects are assigned to the different sequences at random. Some subjects go through condition *A* without any practice; others go through *B* without any practice. The effects of progressive error should turn out to be about the same for each condition if we pool the data from all subjects.

It is easy to counterbalance when there are only two conditions, but suppose there are more. What if we are testing the hypothesis that people remember happy faces better than sad ones? In our experiment we have three sets of photographs. One set (*A*) shows smiling faces. The second set (*B*) shows frowning faces. The third set (*C*) is used as a control; it shows faces that appear to be neutral. We plan to show subjects each set of photographs once. Then we will ask them to go through another much larger set, say 100 in all, and pick out the ones they have seen before. The large set will contain faces of all types so that subjects will not be able to select the correct faces simply by picking out all those that are smiling, frowning, or expressionless. Our dependent variable is the number of faces subjects can recognize in each treatment condition. Clearly, we should not show all the happy faces first. We know, for instance, that when subjects are asked to remember things, the ones they learn first may interfere with later items. Thus subjects might recognize the first set of faces more efficiently than later ones. We can control for this kind of error by using complete counterbalancing. We use all the possible sequences of the treatment conditions; we also use each sequence the same number of times.

Table 9-2 shows complete counterbalancing for an experiment with three treatment conditions. There are six possible sequences of the three conditions. For our face-recognition experiment, we would need sequences like happy, neutral, sad (*ACB*) and sad, happy, neutral (*BAC*). To counterbalance completely, we must use all the sequences and use each one the same number of times. For six sequences, we would need at least six subjects. Ideally, we should have more than one subject for each sequence, so we need a number of subjects that is a multiple of 6. Remember that we have to use all the sequences an equal number of times. We can use 6, or 12, or 18 subjects but not 9, 11, or 17 because these are not multiples of 6.

Can we tell in advance how many sequences and how many subjects we will need? How can we be sure we did not miss a sequence? You can find the number of possible sequences by computing *n* factorial, represented by *n*!. We get *n*! by computing the following product:

$$n! = 1 \times 2 \times 3 \cdots (n - 1)(n)$$

This may look difficult, but it is really very simple. The *n* stands for the number we are working with. We begin with 1 and simply multiply each successive number together until we have gone through *n*. Let us see how it works by computing 4!:

$$4! = 1 \times 2 \times 3 \times 4 = 24$$

TABLE **9-2**

The six sequences of three treatment conditions						
A	B	C		B	A	C
B	C	A		C	B	A
C	A	B		A	C	B

4! is equal to 24. This tells us that when we have 4 treatment conditions, there are 24 possible orders in which to present them.

Earlier we saw that there are six possible sequences if we have only three conditions. You can verify that by the formula too:

$$3! = 1 \times 2 \times 3 = 6$$

The number of possible sequences clearly increases very quickly as the number of treatment conditions rises. To counterbalance an experiment completely, we need at least one subject for each possible sequence. That means we need at least four times as many subjects for a four-condition experiment as we do for a three-condition experiment (24 versus 6 possible sequences). We also need to present each sequence an equal number of times. If we want more than one subject per sequence, we will need multiples of 24 for a four-condition experiment—a minimum of 48 subjects.

Partial counterbalancing.   You can see that it is economical to keep the number of treatments to a minimum. If we double the number of conditions from 3 to 6, we increase the minimum number of subjects needed to counterbalance completely from 6 to 720. Of course, it makes sense to omit any condition that is not necessary for a good test of the hypothesis. Still, sometimes 6 or even more conditions are essential. In those cases we may use **partial counterbalancing** procedures. The basic idea is the same. We use these procedures when we cannot do complete counterbalancing but still want to have some control over progressive error. Partial counterbalancing controls progressive error by using some subset of the available sequences; these sequences are chosen through special procedures.

The simplest partial counterbalancing procedure is **randomized counterbalancing:** When there are many possible sequences, we randomly select out as many sequences as we have subjects for the experiment. Suppose we have 120 possible sequences (five treatment conditions) and only 30 subjects. We would randomly select 30 sequences, and each subject would get one of those sequences. You can see that this procedure may not control for order effects quite as effectively as complete counterbalancing, but it is better than simply using the same order for all subjects. If possible, use complete counterbalancing because it is safer. If you must use partial counterbalancing, be realistic about it. If there are 720 possible sequences in the experiment, running three subjects just does not make sense. You will not be able to get good control over order effects. *As a rule of thumb, use at least as many randomly selected sequences as there are values of the independent variable.*

Another procedure commonly used to select a subset of sequences is called **Latin square counterbalancing.** A matrix, or square, of sequences is constructed that satisfies the following condition: Each treatment appears only once in any order position in the sequences. Table 9-3 shows a basic Latin square for an experiment with four treatment conditions. Each row represents a different order sequence. Notice that each of the four treatment conditions appears in the first, second, third, and fourth position only once. This method controls adequately for progressive error due to order effects because each treatment condition occurs equally often in each position.

Once you have selected your sequences, you would assign subjects at random to receive the different orders. Remember that each sequence is used equally often. With four sequences, you would need to run at least four subjects. If you have more subjects available, it is always better to run more than one subject in each order condition. For the four-condition experiment, any multiple of 4 subjects could be used: 8, 12, 16, and so on.

Using a Latin square to determine treatment sequences will provide protection against order effects, but it cannot control for other kinds of *systematic interference* between two treatment conditions. Notice that some parts of the sequences tend to repeat themselves. For instance, in Table 9-3, condition *A* comes right before *B* in two out of four of the sequences. If exposure to condition *A* affects how subjects will respond to condition *B*, the Latin square will not provide enough control. The experiment can still be confounded. This kind of systematic interference is called a "carryover effect."

Carryover Effects

Perry Mason, the great fictional defense attorney, always wins his cases (except once, when the client was actually guilty). He always finds a way to get to the truth before the end of the trial. Imagine him in court, cross-examining a witness. His large, imposing frame commands respect. A witness has just identified the defendant as the woman who passed close by him in the hallway outside the murder victim's apartment. The witness vividly recalls the defendant's rare and expensive perfume. No, he could not be mistaken about it. Perry wants to test the man's ability to identify other scents. He presents the witness with a small vial. "It is essence of lilac," says the witness confidently. The witness sniffs a second vial and correctly states, "This smells like gasoline!" Now Mason presents the critical test—a vial containing the defendant's perfume. A dismayed and confused witness is unable to identify it. His testimony crumbles. He breaks down and confesses to the crime.

TABLE **9-3**

Latin square counterbalancing for four treatment conditions			
A	B	C	D
B	A	D	C
C	D	A	B
D	C	B	A

A dramatic and fanciful story indeed, but it illustrates another key problem in the within-subjects design. Mason was using a within-subjects approach when he presented the witness with the vials. What the witness did not know was that Mason was playing with **carryover effects:** The effects of some treatments will persist, or carry over, after the treatments are removed. A few whiffs of gasoline spoiled the witness's ability to identify any other scents for a time. The guilty witness panicked and confessed. On a smaller scale, imagine how carryover effects could sabotage experiments. In the last chapter we saw how some combinations of treatments are impossible to administer to the same subjects because one treatment precludes another. For instance, we cannot both do and not do surgery on the same animal. Similarly, we do not want to allow one experimental condition to interfere with a subsequent condition. For example, we do not want to give subjects treatments that will give them clues to what they should do in later conditions. We do not want one experimental treatment to make a later treatment easier (or harder). We do not want the effects of early conditions to contaminate later conditions.

Researchers studying emotions are forced to work around this problem all the time. Suppose we are interested in studying facial-muscle movement during different emotional states. Smiling, for example, is accompanied by movement of the *zygomaticus major,* the muscle that lifts up the corners of the mouth; frowning comes about when the *corrugator supercilii* pulls the brows together and down (Ekman, Friesen, & Ancoli, 1980). In this area of research, within-subjects designs are preferred because there are large individual differences in facial-muscle activity. A researcher might use a series of film clips to induce several different emotions in an experiment, while several pairs of electrodes are connected to the subject's face.

Ordinarily, a very funny film sketch brings on a wide smile in viewers, and a lot of electrical activity is recorded from the pair of electrodes placed above the *zygomaticus.* Conversely, the *corrugator* typically shows a lot of activity during a very sad scene. However, we cannot apply one of these treatment conditions right after another because of carryover effects. A funny scene does not seem nearly as funny as it should if a subject has just watched a tragic death scene. If we were recording the facial muscles, we would find that the activity of the *zygomaticus* was dampened by the previous emotion. When inducing different emotions within subjects, researchers have to take precautions to ensure that one emotion has completely passed before they begin each new treatment. In this case they must wait until all activity from the facial muscles has stopped before they apply a new treatment condition.

Note that carryover effects differ from order effects in an important way. Order effects emerge as a result of the *position* of a treatment in a sequence. It does not matter what the specific treatment is; if it occurs first in a sequence, subjects will handle it differently than if it occurs last. Carryover, however, is a function of the *treatment* itself. Gasoline will produce changes in the ability to detect odor no matter whether the subject smells it first, second, or last. Feeling sadness will carry over to the next emotion regardless of whether sadness is the first, second, or fourth condition in the experiment.

We can control for carryover effects to some extent. If treatments affect each other about equally, an experimenter can get reasonably good control by using some of the same procedures that control for order effects—counterbalancing. Subject-by-subject counterbalancing and complete counterbalancing will usually control carryover effects adequately. Control is less assured with randomized counterbalancing and it may not be controlled at all if Latin square counterbalancing is used.[2] Sometimes, though, as we saw with Perry Mason and the gasoline, the effect of one condition is much greater than that of others. Gasoline altered the witness's performance more than lilacs did or onions would. When one condition has more impact than the others, we say that the carryover effects are *asymmetrical*—or more simply, lopsided. When one condition carries over more than the others, control is extremely difficult, if not impossible. In such situations an experimenter should reconsider the design of the experiment and switch to a between-subjects design if possible.

Choosing Among Counterbalancing Procedures

Every experiment with a within-subjects design will need some form of counterbalancing. Deciding whether to use subject-by-subject or across-subjects counterbalancing can be a problem in itself. We need to counterbalance for each subject when we expect large differences in the pattern of progressive error from subject to subject. In a weight-lifting experiment, we might expect subjects to fatigue at different rates. In that sort of experiment, it makes sense to counterbalance conditions for each person in the study because that would give the most control over order and carryover effects. In some experiments we do not expect large differences in the way

[2] Using mathematical techniques, it is possible to construct special Latin squares (called "balanced Latin squares") that can control for both systematic treatment effects and order effects. These techniques are demonstrated in Elmes, D. G., Kantowitz, B. H., & Roediger, H. L. (1985).

progressive error affects each subject. To put it another way, if we could graph progressive error for each subject, in some experiments the graphs might look about the same. We do not need to worry about progressive error within each subject when we know the effects will be about the same for everyone.

There are practical things to consider too. You may not have the time to run through all the conditions more than once for each subject. You may not have enough subjects to make across-subjects procedures feasible. The same considerations that come into play as you select a within- or between-subjects design can also limit your choice of controls in the within-subjects experiment. Again, you should look at the procedures that have been used in similar experiments. If prior researchers have had success with across-subjects counterbalancing, it is probably all right to use it. Avoid randomized and Latin square counterbalancing if you expect carry-over effects. When in doubt, counterbalance subject by subject if you can. The worst that can happen is that you may "overcontrol" the experiment. It is always a good idea to use the procedures that give the most control simply because you may not know what the extraneous variables are or whether progressive error really will be the same for all subjects.

Although we have talked about counterbalancing mainly in the context of within-subjects designs, counterbalancing procedures can be useful in between-subjects experiments too. For example, in an experiment on list learning, a researcher might compare two different study conditions on people's ability to memorize a list of ten words. The researcher would want both groups to memorize the same ten words to make sure that the lists were equally difficult in both study conditions. In addition, it might be desirable to use several different random orders of the items on each list and randomly assign some number of subjects in each group to each different list. If just one order were used, the possibility exists that the list contained some logical sequence that was easier to learn under one set of conditions than another. Whenever subjects are presented with an experimental *stimulus* that is really a group of items (words, pictures, stories, and the like), the order of the items should be counterbalanced to avoid confounding. You may find other opportunities to apply the counterbalancing procedures you have learned as you design your own experiments.

SUMMARY

One of the major goals in setting up experiments is to avoid confounding. The independent variable should be the only thing that changes systematically across the conditions of the experiment; extraneous variables must be controlled so that they will not alter the results. Several different control procedures can be used to handle extraneous *physical variables*—aspects of the testing conditions that need to be controlled, such as the nature of the testing room, the time of day, and the mechanics of running the experiment.

The three general techniques for dealing with physical variables are *elimination, constancy of conditions,* and *balancing.* These are essential to all good experiments. However, complicated control problems occur in experiments using within-subjects designs because each subject takes part in more than one condition of the experiment. In these experiments we have to control for two kinds of extraneous variables, order effects and carryover effects.

Order effects are the positive and negative changes in performance that occur when a treatment condition falls in different places in a series of treatments. All these changes, both positive and negative, are called *progressive error:* Results are distorted as the experiment *progresses.* We looked at three forms of *counterbalancing* procedures for controlling order effects. All have the same basic function, to distribute progressive error across the different treatment conditions of the experiment.

Subject-by-subject counterbalancing controls for progressive error for each individual subject; it consists of presenting all treatment conditions twice, first in one order, then in reverse order. With two treatment conditions, for example, each subject will get the sequence *ABBA. Across-subjects counterbalancing* (complete and partial counterbalancing) can accomplish some of the same goals by pooling all subjects' data together to equalize the effects of progressive error for each condition. *Complete counterbalancing* requires using all the possible sequences that can be formed out of the treatment conditions and using each sequence the same number of times. The number of subjects needed for a completely counterbalanced experiment increases very rapidly as the number of treatment conditions increases. With three conditions, there must be a minimum of 6 subjects (3 factorial, or 3!); with six conditions, there must be a minimum of 720 subjects (6!). When complete counterbalancing is not feasible, we may use a *partial counterbalancing* procedure such as *randomized counterbalancing.* This involves selecting a subset of all the available sequences at random. A second partial counterbalancing technique, *Latin square counterbalancing,* is a particularly effective procedure for controlling order effects.

In addition to order effects, there may also be *carryover effects* in a within-subjects experiment. These occur when the treatment conditions affect each other. Most carryover effects can be controlled adequately by using within-subjects counterbalancing or complete counterbalancing.

Deciding on the particular form of counterbalancing to use may be difficult. Subject-by-subject counterbalancing offers the most control and should be used whenever possible. If this cannot be done, across-subjects counterbalancing has many practical advantages. Counterbalancing of some form must be used in every experiment that has a within-subjects design. The procedures may also be useful in between-subjects experiments containing series of trials. It is always better to err on the side of controlling too much; there is more danger in failing to control something that could affect the results.

KEY TERMS

Across-subjects counterbalancing A technique for controlling progressive error that pools all subjects' data together to equalize the effects of progressive error for each condition.

Balancing A technique used to control the impact of extraneous variables by distributing their effects equally across treatment conditions.

Carryover effect The persistence of the effect of a treatment condition after the condition ends.

Complete counterbalancing A technique for controlling progressive error that uses all possible sequences that can be formed out of the treatment conditions and uses each sequence the same number of times.

Constancy of conditions A control procedure used to avoid confounding; keeping all aspects of the treatment conditions identical except for the independent variable that is being manipulated.

Counterbalancing A technique for controlling order effects by distributing progressive error across the different treatment conditions of the experiment; may also control carryover effects.

Elimination A technique to control extraneous variables by removing them from an experiment.

Latin square counterbalancing A partial counterbalancing technique in which a matrix, or square, of sequences of treatment conditions is constructed to which subjects are assigned at random.

Order effects The changes in performance that occur when a condition falls in different places in a series of treatments.

Partial counterbalancing A technique for controlling progressive error by using some subset of the available sequences of treatment conditions.

Physical variables Aspects of the testing conditions that need to be controlled.

Practice effects Changes in subjects' performance resulting from practice.

Progressive error Fatigue, practice, and other extraneous sequence effects producing changes in subjects' responses during within-subjects experiments.

Randomized counterbalancing The simplest partial counterbalancing procedure in which the experimenter randomly selects as many sequences of treatment conditions as there are subjects for the experiment.

Subject-by-subject counterbalancing A technique for controlling progressive error for each individual subject by presenting all treatment conditions twice, first in one order, then in reverse order.

REVIEW AND STUDY QUESTIONS

1. What are physical variables in an experiment?
2. How is elimination used as a control procedure? Give two examples of variables that could be controlled by elimination.
3. What is constancy of conditions? Give two examples of variables that could be controlled through constancy of conditions.
4. What is balancing? Give two examples of variables that could be controlled by balancing.
5. Explain the difference between a control group and the control procedures used in an experiment.
6. Suppose a classmate says, "Constancy of conditions does not eliminate extraneous variables from an experiment. So why bother with it?" How would you convince this person that constancy of conditions is an important control procedure?
7. You are doing a study at a local school. Because of the way things are scheduled, you can have one small testing room in the morning and another much larger testing room in the afternoon. If you have two treatment conditions (experimental and control), how can you assign subjects to the testing rooms so that the type of room will not lead to confounding in your experiment?
8. You are planning an experiment on anagrams (jumbled words). You want to test whether different scramble patterns lead to different solution rates. For instance, the letter order 54321 might be easier to solve than 41352 (12345 represents the actual word). You want to use the same words in all conditions so that the type of word will not be a confounding variable. People solve anagrams at different rates, so you are thinking about using a within-subjects design.
    a. If you use a within-subjects design for this experiment, will you have to worry about order effects? Why or why not?
    b. Review the three counterbalancing techniques (subject-by-subject, complete, and partial) for handling order effects discussed in this chapter. Which would help you most in this experiment? Why?
    c. What are the carryover effects? Would they be a problem in this experiment? How would you handle them?
9. You have just bought two new pairs of shoes and are wondering which will wear better. Design a within-subjects experiment that would answer your question. What extraneous variables would you want to control? Would counterbalancing be useful in this study? How?
10. A researcher has the hypothesis that subjects will overestimate the speed of a light moving in a circular path and underestimate the speed of a light moving in a square path. Because of the time it will take to

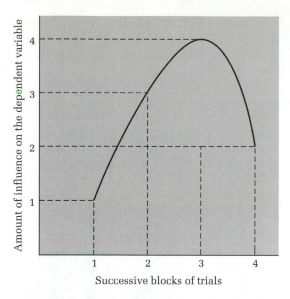

FIGURE **9-4** Progressive error in an experiment on breathing rate during weight lifting.

set up the apparatus for each subject, she would like to run the experiment using a within-subjects design.

    a. What problems will arise if she runs all trials with the circular path first?

    b. How would you control for progressive error in this study?

11. A television commercial showed people tasting and choosing between two colas. One was labeled "*R*"; the other was labeled "*Q*." The majority of people said they liked cola *R* better than cola *Q*. Given what you know about experimental design, would you accept the ad's claim that cola *R* tastes better than cola *Q*? Why or why not? How might you change the procedures to get more acceptable data?

12. Figure 9-4 illustrates progressive error measured in an experiment on breathing rate during weight lifting. Because of warm-up and fatigue effects across subjects, progressive error was curvilinear. Based on the figure, what strategy would you recommend for handling progressive error in this experiment and why?

REFERENCES

CAMPBELL, D. T., & STANLEY, J. C. (1963). *Experimental and quasi-experimental designs for research.* Chicago: Rand McNally.

EKMAN, P., FRIESEN, W., & ANCOLI, S. (1980). Facial signs of emotional experience. *Journal of Personality and Social Psychology, 39*(6), 1125–1134.

ELMES, D. G., KANTOWITZ, B. H., &
ROEDIGER, H. L. (1985). *Research
methods in psychology.* St. Paul,
MN: West.

UNDERWOOD, B. J. (1966). *Experimental psychology.* New York:
Appleton-Century-Crofts.

10

Controlling Extraneous Variables: Personality and Social Variables

By now you should be feeling more and more optimistic about research. If a researcher plans carefully, keeps the treatment conditions as constant as possible, and uses counterbalancing, he or she is sure to have an airtight experiment. Well, this is not exactly true. Earlier in the text, we touched on **subject variables:** all the characteristics of the subjects themselves that might influence the outcome of the experiment. In this chapter, we will look more closely at some important subject variables—response style and response set. We will also consider some of the social factors that affect subjects' responses, as well as the experimenter's role in shaping the outcome of the experiment. Like physical variables, these personality and social variables must be controlled in order to obtain valid results.

If personality and social variables are not controlled, we may have experiments that are invalid. A valid experiment measures the true effect of our independent variable. When an experiment has **internal validity,** the changes in the dependent variable across treatment conditions are produced by the experimental manipulations: All the relevant extraneous variables have been controlled so that there is no confounding. However, we are also concerned with **external validity;** that is, whether the findings describe events outside the experiment. Is it possible to extend the results of the experiment to other situations, to other groups of subjects, or to the real world? Both issues can be affected by the experimenter's ability to control for personality and social variables.

PERSONALITY VARIABLES

We can often control for many subject variables like intelligence by assigning subjects to treatment conditions at random. Random assignment helps us form groups of subjects who are about the same on personal characteristics that affect the results of the experiment. When we do not want to rely on randomization (for example, when the number of available subjects is small), we may measure and match subjects on a variable that is known to be related to the dependent variable. Through matching, we can form treatment groups that are roughly the same on critical variables. We use these procedures to be sure the experiment will really tell us what we want to know. Sometimes, however, we can accidentally measure *the wrong thing.* This is a special problem when we gather data through interviews, questionnaires, surveys, or other written tests to which the subject can respond selectively.

Response Style

There are a variety of ways in which subjects' own characteristics may inadvertently alter a research outcome. In this section we will look at response styles, which are some of the ways subjects can cause errors in an experiment. **Response styles** are tendencies to respond to questionnaire items in specific ways, regardless of the content. We will discuss willingness to answer, position preferences, yea-saying and nay-saying, and guarding against response style.

Willingness to answer.   Let us unobtrusively observe Steve and Sarah, two students taking a final exam for a course in experimental psychology. Both students have studied hard for the exam and have completed all the practice exercises in their textbooks. Steve is having trouble with some of the questions. He is not sure of the answers, so he leaves them blank. Sarah is also unsure of some answers, but she opts for inserting some educated guesses. She earns extra points because of her **willingness to answer** and obtains a higher total score than Steve.

Sarah and Steve differ in their exam scores. They also differ in *response style* (Rorer, 1965), the way they handle questions regardless of the content. Response styles are most likely to affect responding when the correct answers are in doubt. Sarah is more willing to answer even though she is guessing, and that works to her advantage on any test that has no penalty for guessing. This is true for classroom exams as well as for some standard IQ and achievement tests that are often used in research. To discourage guessing, some tests are scored by subtracting a portion of the number answered incorrectly from the number answered correctly. An unwillingness to answer is often a problem in questionnaire or survey research. Subjects may omit key questions, making both scoring and interpretation difficult.

Position preference.   Response styles can influence the selection of multiple-choice answers too. When in doubt, perhaps you always answer *b*. This is a **position preference.** If your professor happens to share your preference and puts most of the correct answers in the *b* slot, your guesses will yield extra points.[1] Because of position preferences, sophisticated test builders vary the arrangement of correct answers throughout a test.

Yea-saying and nay-saying.   Take a few moments to look at the statements in Table 10-1. Would you say that each is true or false for you? The

---

[1] Even rats learning to run mazes are known to show position preferences. For example, if a food reward always requires a right turn into a white corridor, animals with a preference to turn right will have a clear advantage. Researchers control for this by varying the location of the white corridor so that the animal must sometimes go left, sometimes right.

TABLE **10-1**

Possible items on a personality scale

1. I feel happy most of the time.
2. I enjoy being with other people.
3. I dislike paying attention to details.
4. When I can, I avoid noisy places.
5. Sometimes I feel frightened for no apparent reason.

items are similar to ones you might find on the Minnesota Multiphasic Personality Inventory (MMPI), which is made up of a long series of items of this type. The way you answer the items on the test can tell a psychologist various things about your personality—for instance, whether you are anxious or depressed. At first glance the way people answer such questions seems straightforward. A person who feels happy ought to answer true to the first item. We would expect subjects to respond to the **manifest content** of the questions, the plain meaning of the words that actually appear on the page. If a question asks about noisy places, the manifest content of the question is noisy places. Subjects should answer each question truthfully based on its manifest content. A subject who never wants to go to another noisy place should say, "I really don't like noisy places at all," and answer true to item 4.

When we give a questionnaire or other paper-and-pencil test, we are usually interested in the manifest content of the items. "Have you ever visited another country?" means just that; the manifest content of the item is simply foreign travel. Most people would answer based on their actual travel histories. However, researchers have noticed that some interesting things can happen when subjects fill out questionnaires—especially when the questionnaires ask about feelings or attitudes. Some subjects seem to respond to questions in a consistent way: They will answer yes or true to most items, or they will say no or false to most items. Some subjects are yea-sayers; others are nay-sayers. **Yea-sayers** are apt to agree with a question regardless of its manifest content. **Nay-sayers** tend to disagree no matter what they are asked. This is another example of response style (Rorer, 1965).

Guarding against response style. Experiment results can be distorted if we do not guard against response styles. Imagine a simple perception experiment. We have some moving lights on a dark screen. One light moves in a square path; the other moves in a circular path. Both move at the same actual speed. But based on some prior research, we predict that subjects will judge that the light in the circular path moves faster. After subjects watch the lights for a while, we ask them this question: "Did the circular light move faster than the light moving in the square?" By phrasing the question this way, we can expect the yea-sayers to say yes and support our hypothesis. Of course, all the nay-sayers ought to say no. What is the problem? Some subjects say yes and others say no. Doesn't it all balance out? Well, the yea-sayers and nay-sayers may be of equal numbers. But now the problem becomes one of validity: Are we really measuring what we set out to measure? We want to know something about how subjects perceive lights that move along paths of different shapes. Instead, we seem to be measuring the way that subjects answer questions.

How can we avoid a problem with response style? In the perception experiment, we can measure the dependent variable (what the subjects saw) in a better way. Instead of just asking whether the circular light moved faster, we might ask this: "Did the circular light move faster, slower, or about the same as the square light?" This question poses its own problems, as we will see later in this chapter. However, it is a cut above the original question because it cannot be answered with a simple yes or no. It forces the subject to think more about the answer. This helps to control the effects of yea-saying and nay-saying. Warwick and Lininger (1975) recommend this approach when writing a series of questions. They suggest giving each option some specific content. For instance, think about the difference between these two items:

"Do you agree or disagree that the cost of living has gone up in the last year?"
"In your opinion have prices gone up, gone down, or stayed about the same the past year, or don't you know?" (p. 146)

When we phrase questions to have simple yes/no or agree/disagree answers, we make it easy for subjects to respond based on response style. By building some specific content into the options, we encourage subjects to give more thought to each choice.

If we must use yes/no questions, we can still take some precautions. Table 10-2 shows two versions of the Unfounded Optimism Inventory (UOI). The "optimistic" choice is underlined for each item. We would say that a person who makes many optimistic choices has more unfounded optimism than one who makes few of those choices. Notice that the two versions of our test are quite different. The manifest content of the items is the same for both versions; we are asking about the same things in both sets of questions. The difference is in the way the items are keyed. To get a high

TABLE **10-2**

The Unfounded Optimism Inventory					
Version A: No Control for Response Style			*Version B: Controlling for Response Style**		
1. I know that everything will be all right.	<u>Yes</u>	NO	1. I know that everything will be all right.	<u>Yes</u>	NO
2. I can pick the fastest line at the bank.	<u>Yes</u>	NO	2. I always stand in the slowest line at the bank.	YES	<u>No</u>
3. I often smile at nothing.	<u>Yes</u>	NO	3. I rarely smile, even when provoked.	YES	<u>No</u>
4. If I lose money, I expect it to be returned.	<u>Yes</u>	NO	4. If I lose money, I expect it to be returned.	<u>Yes</u>	NO

* The yes/no responses are also counterbalanced to control for order effects.

Unfounded Optimism score on version *A*, a person would have to answer most of the items by saying yes. All the items in version *A* are written so that the optimistic response is a yes response. Subjects who are yea-sayers would score high on unfounded optimism—even if they happen to be somewhat pessimistic.

Now look at version *B*. Some questions from version *A* have been rewritten so that the optimistic response can be either yes or no, depending on the question. (The optimistic responses are underlined.) To get a high Unfounded Optimism score, a subject would have to give both yes and no answers. Using a version like this, we would know that subjects who turned up high on Unfounded Optimism are probably not pessimistic yea-sayers. In other words, by controlling for the effects of response style in the questions, we can develop more valid measures. We can come closer to getting the information we are seeking.

Response Set

Someone with a response style will answer questions without paying much attention to the manifest content of each item. The person will answer yes or no depending on whether he or she is a yea-sayer or a nay-sayer. Other subjects may answer questions based on **latent content,** the meaning behind the question. When we try to "read between the lines," we are looking for latent content.

We often try to respond to latent content with a particular goal in mind. That goal can be called a **response set,** a picture we want to create of ourselves.

There are many practical examples of the response set. The job interview is one of the most common (see Figure 10-1). On the one hand, few prospective applicants would say they want to work as little as possible. On the other hand, many people fantasize about winning state lotteries and never working again. Applicants often feign enthusiasm for jobs of little interest only because they need to earn some money. A response set is clearly operating, with applicants striving hard to create the impression of dedicated, hard-working employees. Similarly, few employers emphasize the boring, tedious aspects of jobs with no prospects for advancement, preferring to present the plusses of employment, such as good fringe benefits.

Take a moment to answer the questions in Table 10-3. Can you tell what the latent content of each item is? What are the questions really asking?

The questions are taken from a scale developed to demonstrate response set, that some people respond to the latent rather than the manifest content of an item. They reply based on what they think their answers will show. Crowne and Marlowe (1964) developed this particular set of questions to test whether subjects have the response set called "social desirability." In order to look good on many of the items, you would have to lie. For instance, few of us would find it easy to get along with "loud-mouthed, obnoxious people," although it is socially desirable, or nice, to

FIGURE **10-1** Job applicant discussing prospective employment. Brooks/Cole photo.

be able to get along with everyone. Subjects who have the social-desirability response set will lie in order to make themselves look better in the eyes of the experimenter. They may not lie on all questions, but they will distort the truth enough to make themselves look better. For instance, Carol might say true to the first question, indicating that she looks into the qualifications of all the candidates running for office. In reality, Carol studies only the qualifications of the major party candidates. She may or may not feel that she is actually lying. She may believe that she is just bending the question a little.

Whether or not the subject feels a sense of guilt or remorse for making a better-than-true impression is not usually critical to the experiment. What does concern us is the way a response set can alter the data we get. We can never be completely sure that subjects have given us accurate data. In any number of experiments, subjects may distort the truth in order to

TABLE 10-3

The Marlowe-Crowne Social Desirability Scale Personal Reaction Inventory*

Listed below are a number of statements concerning personal attitudes and traits. Read each item and decide whether the statement is true or false as it pertains to you personally.

1. Before voting I thoroughly investigate the qualifications of all the candidates. (T)
2. I never hesitate to go out of my way to help someone in trouble. (T)
3. It is sometimes hard for me to go on with my work if I am not encouraged. (F)
4. I have never intensely disliked anyone. (T)
5. On occasion I have had doubts about my ability to succeed in life. (F)
6. I sometimes feel resentful when I don't get my way. (F)
7. I am always careful about my manner of dress. (T)
8. My table manners at home are as good as when I eat out in a restaurant. (T)
9. If I could get into a movie without paying and be sure I was not seen, I would probably do it. (F)
10. On a few occasions, I have given up doing something because I thought too little of my ability. (F)
11. I like to gossip at times. (F)
12. There have been times when I felt like rebelling against people in authority even though I knew they were right. (F)
13. No matter who I'm talking to, I'm always a good listener. (T)
14. I can remember "playing sick" to get out of something. (F)
15. There have been occasions when I took advantage of someone. (F)
16. I'm always willing to admit it when I make a mistake. (T)
17. I always try to practice what I preach. (T)
18. I don't find it particularly difficult to get along with loud-mouthed, obnoxious people. (T)
19. I sometimes try to get even, rather than forgive and forget. (F)
20. When I don't know something, I don't at all mind admitting it. (T)
21. I am always courteous, even to people who are disagreeable. (T)
22. At times I have really insisted on having things my own way. (F)
23. There have been occasions when I felt like smashing things. (F)
24. I would never think of letting someone else be punished for my wrongdoings. (T)
25. I never resent being asked to return a favor. (T)
26. I have never been irked when people expressed ideas very different from my own. (T)
27. I never make a long trip without checking the safety of my car. (T)
28. There have been times when I was quite jealous of the good fortune of others. (F)
29. I have almost never felt the urge to tell someone off. (T)
30. I am sometimes irritated by people who ask favors of me. (F)
31. I have never felt that I was punished without cause. (T)
32. I sometimes think when people have a misfortune they only got what they deserved. (F)
33. I have never deliberately said something that hurt someone's feelings. (T)

*The responses shown are the socially desirable ones. *Source:* From The Approval Motive, *by D. P. Crowne and D. Marlowe, 1964. Copyright © 1964 John Wiley & Sons, Inc. Reprinted by permission.*

improve their images. For instance, a subject might report that she is "very confident" about a particular task, whereas she really feels very uneasy about it. If subjects' confidence ratings are the dependent variable, the experiment may lead to some inaccurate conclusions.

What can we do about response sets? A person with a response set will answer based on the latent content of questions. Some subjects may try to give the most socially desirable response; others will try to give a deviant response. To counteract a response set, we can develop alternative questions that have the same latent content. For example, which of the following best describes your attitudes toward pets?

____ Everyone should have a pet.
____ I think pets are a waste of time.

    or

____ Pets are fun but not everyone wants the responsibility.
____ Pets make good companions.

You can see how the implications of the choices differ. In the first pair, one answer seems to be more socially desirable than the other. John might feel pressured to pick the first choice so that he will appear to be an animal lover. In the second pair, the choices are about equally acceptable. John can show that he likes animals by selecting either item. He can also express his feeling that pets can be a nuisance without worrying that his response will stigmatize him in some way. The second set of alternatives is more likely to lead to accurate data.

Minimizing socially desirable responses is an important part of any research strategy because it is a common response set, particularly in psychological research. It is only natural that most people will try to create a positive impression when they *feel* their psychological behavior is being evaluated by a researcher. (We will return to this topic later in the chapter.) One of the added benefits of using standard questionnaires and tests is that the test developers (or others who have used the measures in their research) have usually addressed the problem of social-desirability response sets for you. Typically, as part of the test-standardization procedure, the social-desirability score of a test is measured by correlating people's responses on the test with their responses on the Marlowe-Crowne or a similar measure of social desirability. A significant r means that scores on the test are likely to be related to social desirability. If the test you want to use shows a strong correlation with the Marlowe-Crowne, you will need to be particularly concerned about minimizing the response set. You will want to set up the experimental situation to minimize socially desirable responding. It helps if subjects feel anonymous—that no one will be able to associate their responses with them. *Never* ask them to put their name on their questionnaires! In addition, it often helps if you test subjects in a group, rather than alone, because it increases feelings of anonymity.

We also want to minimize the impact of response set in interview situations. Lengthy interviews with multiple interviewers is a technique currently in vogue with some employers. The logic is that no one can sustain a false front indefinitely. The pressure interview is another approach; here, the interviewer deliberately sets out to create a stressful situation that will prompt the applicant to behave spontaneously and honestly. Neither approach is necessarily ethical or even effective in scientific research. Ideally, researchers prefer to have interview data supported by independent observations of the subjects' actions.

The same is true for the results of questionnaires. For example, Haas and Sherman (1982) reported sex differences in self-reported topics of conversation. Women talking with other women reportedly talk more about family, relationship problems, health, pregnancy, menstruation, food, and men. Men talking with men reportedly talk more about women, sex, money, news, sports, hunting, and fishing. The researchers rightly pointed out that these data need to be confirmed through actual systematic observations of conversations. Respondents to a questionnaire may not be able to assess their own behavior accurately. Recall of past behavior may simply be incomplete. In addition, a response set could influence men and women to intentionally distort the data in favor of sex-role stereotypes by assuming that is what the researcher is attempting to find.

SOCIAL VARIABLES

In addition to controlling subject variables that might alter the outcome of the experiment, researchers are concerned about **social variables,** qualities of the relationships between subjects and experimenters that may influence results. Two principal social variables, demand characteristics and experimenter bias, can be controlled through single- and double-blind experiments.

Demand Characteristics

Response set and response style are important in many experiments, especially those in which we obtain data through questionnaires. But there is another more general source of error affecting experiments in which we have human subjects: These are **demand characteristics,** aspects of the situation itself that *demand* that people behave in a particular way. Have you ever walked along a busy street and noticed someone looking up at the sky or at a building? You may have found yourself looking up too. This is a good example of what we mean by demand characteristics. What we do is often shaped by what we think we are expected to do. When you enter a classroom, even on the first day of the term, you probably walk in and take a seat. When the professor begins talking, you listen. Of course, you are fulfilling a role you learned in your earliest days at school, the role of the "good student" in the classroom. The cue of being in the classroom leads you to behave in a predictable way. Most research subjects want to be good subjects. They want to conform to what they think is the proper role of "subject." They may not even be consciously aware of the ways in which they alter their behavior when they come into an experiment. For example, subjects may assume a very active role. They may try to guess the hypothesis of the experiment and adjust their responses accordingly.

Let us return to the perception experiment in which two lights move at the same speed but in different paths. We are looking for a difference in the way subjects perceive the movement of these lights. Specifically, we expect subjects to perceive the light in the circular path as moving faster. We ask: "Did the light in the circular path move faster, slower, or about the same as the light in the square path?" If you were a subject in this experiment, what would you think about this question? The experimenter has gone to a lot of trouble to set up these lights and recruit subjects. Suppose you really could not see any difference in the speed of the lights. But why would anyone go to the bother of showing you two lights that move at the same speed and then ask you whether one moved faster? You might begin to suspect that there really was some subtle difference in the speeds and somehow you did not notice it. But you want to be a good subject. You do not want to tell the experimenter that you were not paying attention or that you are not very good at judging speed. So you guess. You say, "Well, maybe the round one really was moving a little faster because it didn't make all those turns. So I'll say the round one was faster even though I'm not sure that's what I saw."

An experimenter generally wants subjects to be as naive as possible. They should understand the nature and purpose of the experiment but not the exact hypothesis. The reason for this is simple. If subjects know what we expect to find, they may produce data that will support the hypothesis. On the surface that may seem like a good thing. Wouldn't it be wonderful if experiments always confirmed their hypotheses? It would—if the experiments were valid. We want to be able to say that the independent variable caused a change in behavior. If behavior changes simply because subjects think the researcher wants an experiment to turn out in a particular way, the experiment has not measured what it was intended to measure.

Subjects often try to guess the hypotheses. This is a problem, especially in within-subjects experiments; since the subjects take part in more than one treatment condition, they usually have a better chance of guessing the hypothesis. Of course, subjects sometimes guess incorrectly. They may think they are helping by responding in a particular way, but their "help" produces data that make it impossible to confirm the hypothesis. Occasionally, subjects will actually try to produce data that conflict with the hypothesis. They may guess the hypothesis, disagree with it, and set out to disprove it. Again, they may be wrong; they may actually wind up supporting the predictions. But either way, our problem is that this kind of data is not worth much. We want to set up experiments in which we can test the effect of an independent variable, not the subjects' skill at "psyching out" experiments.

Does this sort of thing really happen? Do subjects' experiences and answers change depending on what they think is supposed to happen in the experiment? Can the demand characteristics of an experiment lead to changes in subject behavior? What if subjects simply do what they think they are supposed to do? Orne and Scheibe (1964) devised a clever experiment to evaluate the effects of demand characteristics on research on sensory deprivation.

Traditionally, subjects in sensory-deprivation experiments were isolated from sensory experiences of all kinds. They wore translucent goggles so that they could not see shapes clearly; they were typically restricted to lying on a soft bed; they wore coverings over their arms to minimize sensations from movement and touch. White noise (noise of all frequencies that sounds very much like static on a radio) was played to mask ordinary sounds. With these procedures, prolonged sensory deprivation led to emotional upset, disorientation, and even hallucinations. Orne and Scheibe followed a very different procedure. They placed their experimental and control subjects alone in a room that hardly created any deprivation at all. The room was 6 × 7 × 8 feet in size and was furnished with a desk and two chairs. The subjects could easily hear sounds from the hallway and birds chirping outside. They did not wear goggles and so had their normal vision. There was water and a sandwich in case they got hungry. They were given a set of arithmetic problems to work on if they wanted something to do, and they could move around as much as they wanted to within the room.

The difference between the experimental and control groups in this study was the way the experiment was presented to each group. Experimental-group subjects were interviewed by a man in a white medical coat. A tray of drugs and medical instruments, labeled "Emergency Tray," was in the room. Subjects were told that there was an alarm button in the "deprivation chamber." If they became upset, they were advised to press the alarm button. They were also told that a physician was present. Pulse and blood pressure readings were taken. Everything possible was done to create an atmosphere of seriousness and preparation for a possible crisis. Subjects were also read some instructions for reporting their experiences while in the chamber, including possible visual imagery, unusual feelings, and disorientation—the typical sensory-deprivation effects. Control-group subjects were told that they were control subjects. The experimenter wore regular business clothes. There was no emergency tray or alarm button. Subjects were told that if they wanted to leave the chamber, they could simply knock on the window. They were given the same general instructions to report their experiences, but everything was done to create a relaxed impression. When the blood pressure and pulse readings were made, the control subjects were told that the readings were being taken simply because they had been taken for the experimental subjects.

If we compare the two procedures, we see that Orne and Scheibe manipulated demand characteristics in their experiment. All subjects were placed in the same "deprivation" setting. But the experimental subjects were given every reason to expect that something awful, or at least out of the ordinary, might happen to them. The control group was treated in a more casual way that probably communicated something like "You'll be in this room for a while." What would you expect to happen in this experiment? Would subjects show the usual effects of sensory deprivation? If we look just at the physical layout of this experiment, we can see that there is little reason to expect anyone to become disoriented or show any other unusual symptoms in a short period of time. The subjects had full use of all their senses. Their movements were not restricted, they could eat, and they had a task to do if they got bored.

Orne and Scheibe's findings implicated demand characteristics as a cause of some of the prior sensory-deprivation findings: Their experimental subjects, those led to expect some strange experience, showed significantly more signs of disturbance. Compared to the controls, the experimental subjects gave the "impression of almost being tortured" (p. 11). All the subjects in Orne and Scheibe's experiment experienced the same "deprivation," but only the experimental group showed the usual effects of sensory deprivation. For the experimental group, the researchers had created the impression that something unusual would happen to them. The subjects' expectations were confirmed: They experienced a variety of changes that did not occur for the control subjects, who had a different set of expectations. The changes were varied and at times dramatic: "The buzzing of the fluorescent light is growing alternately louder and softer so that at times it sounds like a jackhammer"; "There are multicolored spots on the wall"; "The numbers on the number sheets are blurring and assuming various inkblot forms" (p. 10). Indeed, one subject hit the panic button and listed "disorganization of senses" as one of his reasons for stopping. These findings do not rule out the possibility that some genuine changes occur when subjects undergo an actual restriction of sensory experience. They do, however, illustrate the importance of demand characteristics in shaping the outcome of such studies.

Controlling demand characteristics: Single-blind experiments.   When we run experiments, we try not to give subjects clues to what may happen to them because of the independent variable. We do not want to influence the outcome of the experiment by having subjects know the hypothesis. A good way to control some effects of demand characteristics is through a **single-blind experiment,** an experiment in which subjects do not know which treatment they are getting.

When we do a single-blind experiment, we can disclose some but not all information about the experiment to subjects. We can disclose what is going to happen to them in the experiment; we can also keep them fully informed about the purpose of the study. But we keep them "blind" to one thing: We do not tell them what treatment condition they are in. This approach is very common in experiments with drugs. If we give a subject some substance, the subject might react based on what he or she *expects* the drug to do. For instance, suppose we want to test a new headache remedy. If we give the new drug to several people with headaches, some of them will report that they feel better after taking the medicine. Did the medicine help? We don't know. To answer this question, we need a control group of people who do not receive the drug. Researchers know that if you give a person *any* pill, the person is apt to say the pill helped. We call this the **placebo effect.**

When we test a drug, we give the control group a placebo—a pill, injection, or other treatment that contains none of the actual medication. And, we only disclose partial information. We do not tell subjects which treat-

FIGURE **10-2** An advertisement for Dr. R. C. Flower's Nerve Pills. The success of some patent medicines can be attributed in part to placebo effects. However, a large measure of alcohol in some preparations may have helped too. National Library of Medicine

ment they are receiving. The subject is blind to that aspect of the experiment. We can eliminate some of the effects of demand characteristics by ensuring that subjects do not know exactly what changes (if any) they should expect. They cannot be sure whether they are in the control group or in an experimental group. If we see changes in their behavior, those changes are more likely to be caused by the independent variable. Subjects will not be able to report what they think the experimenter wants to hear (for example, that the new medication made them feel better). They will not know what the experimenter expects because they will not know which treatment they are getting.

However, as Leavitt (1974) points out, subjects typically know they are getting *some kind of treatment,* and so we may rarely be able to measure the actual effects of a drug by itself. Instead, we see the effects of the treatment plus placebo effects that are shaped by the subjects' expectations. We then compare those effects with the effects of the placebo alone on the control group.

In other kinds of experiments, we can get placebo effects too. Suppose we want to conduct a simple learning study; we want to see whether the brightness of a room influences how easily people learn. We hypothesize that people will learn more quickly under bright lighting conditions. We form two groups: an experimental group and a control group. Both groups will be asked to memorize a list of ten nonsense words—like *bragzap* and *crumdip* (in several different random orders, of course). Subjects will be tested individually in the same small office, which is furnished with a desk, chair, and reading lamp. The control group will learn the list under normal illumination conditions (a 75-watt reading light); the experimental group will learn it under brighter-than-normal conditions (a 150-watt light). The length of time it takes subjects to memorize all ten words will be the dependent measure.

We want to conduct a single-blind study. We might tell subjects: "We are investigating the effects of room lighting on learning. We are asking people to learn a list of ten made-up words as quickly as possible. Different people will learn the list under different lighting conditions, and we will see whether lighting makes a difference." We have given subjects information about the purpose of the experiment and told them what would happen to them during the experiment. Notice that we have not disclosed our expectations about their performance, and we have not told them which condition they are in. But have we structured the situation so that these are fairly simple to figure out? Probably we have. Subjects are quite likely to figure out our hypothesis—and behave accordingly. If they believe the light is normal or even a bit dim, they may take longer to learn the list simply because they expect it to take longer. If the light seems bright, they may learn the list more quickly because they expect the added light makes learning easier. This could confound the experiment because their expectation varies systematically with the independent variable—it would take them longer in the control than in the experimental condition, just as we predicted, but the difference might not be due to the light levels at all.

What alternatives do we have? We could give them less information. We could simply say that we are investigating the influence of different study environments on learning. This might keep them from guessing our true hypothesis or it might not. Perhaps some experimental subjects guess that we are testing quiet versus noisy spaces or different kinds of chairs or different colored walls. Whatever they guess, there is always the possibility that their guess will be confirmed by the way they behave. Whatever they guess may alter the time it would normally take to learn the list. Nevertheless, most researchers would agree that this situation is somewhat better than the first. Chances are that individual subjects would guess different things and behave in different ways, but their behavior would not change systematically along with the independent variable. It would not be a confound, but it would certainly make the impact of the independent variable difficult to detect. It would introduce large individual differences in responding, which is something we work hard to avoid when we can.

Controlling demand characteristics: Cover stories. There is another alternative for controlling the possibility that subjects might guess the experimental hypothesis—we could use a cover story. When we create an experimental situation, we want subjects to respond as normally as possible. At the very least, we do not want their expectations to alter their responses on the dependent measure. Sometimes the best control over demand characteristics is gained through the use of a **cover story,** which is a plausible but false explanation for the procedures used in the study. It is told to disguise the actual research hypothesis so that subjects cannot guess what it is.

Consider the following situation. Wells and Petty (1980) noticed that people nod their heads up and down when they are exposed to something they find agreeable and shake their heads from side to side in the presence of something they find disagreeable. They wondered if this could be reversed. Would people tend to find something agreeable if they were nodding their heads when they were exposed to it? Would they find something disagreeable if they were shaking their heads when exposed to it?

In order to test their hypothesis, the researchers would have to get some subjects to nod their heads when they were exposed to a stimulus and other subjects to shake their heads when they were exposed to the same stimulus. They could then ask all the subjects how agreeable or disagreeable they found the stimulus. They predicted that subjects who were nodding their heads would find it agreeable and those who were shaking their heads would find it disagreeable.

They could have instructed subjects to nod or shake their heads and told them of the experimental hypothesis. But if the results had come out the way Wells and Petty predicted, would you have been convinced? Probably not! What if the researchers did not disclose the hypothesis but simply instructed subjects to either nod or shake their heads? Would you have been convinced if the data came out as predicted? No, because there is a strong chance that subjects might figure out such a simple hypothesis: "You told me to shake my head because you want me to find this thing disagreeable, so I'll tell you that I find it disagreeable."

How can the researchers get around this problem? They can't instruct subjects to move their heads, because the subjects will probably use the instructions to figure out the hypothesis. Yet they must get the subjects to either shake or nod their heads in order to test the hypothesis. This is the type of situation in which a cover story must be developed. And we have to be clever because the cover story has to give the subjects an explanation for what we want them to do—move their heads—without tipping them off to the hypothesis being tested. Wells and Petty came up with a cover story that was clever indeed. They told subjects they would be listening to a message (the experimental stimulus) through a set of headphones. They told subjects that the purpose of the experiment was to test the headphones—to see whether the headphones worked efficiently if listeners were moving their heads while listening. Their cover story provided subjects with an explanation for the head-moving instructions that had nothing to do with the experimental hypothesis. Given this plausible explanation, subjects would not look for another explanation and would be unlikely to discover the real experimental hypothesis. Wells and Petty explained the real purpose of the head movements to subjects at the end of the experimental session.

Why not always use a cover story such as one devised by Wells and Petty? Quite simply, cover stories involve deception. Deception is a departure from fully informed consent. As we discovered in Chapter 5, researchers must increasingly be concerned about the rights of the participant as the departure from fully informed consent becomes more dramatic. For this reason, cover stories should be used sparingly. Remember that debriefing is required for all subjects in such experiments. If you believe your experiment can have internal validity without a cover story, do not use one.

Experimenter Bias

Perhaps without realizing it, an experimenter can give subjects cues that tell them how he or she would like them to respond. Subjects will often comply with these subtle requests and give the data the experimenter is seeking. Imagine the experimenter running the earlier perception experiment. She asks, "Does the light in the circular path move faster, slower, or at the same speed as the light in the square path?" As she says "faster," she leans forward slightly, raises her eyebrows, and speaks a little louder. Most of her subjects say that the light in the circular path moved "faster."

We call this sort of influence **experimenter bias;** the experimenter does something that creates confounding in the experiment. The experimenter may give a cue to respond in a particular way, or he or she may behave differently in different treatment conditions. Dr. R. might be warm and friendly in the experimental condition, but he may seem indifferent in the control condition. That is all right if the experimenter's demeanor is the independent variable. If it is not, it may confound the results. Subjects might feel more at ease in the experimental condition and so perform better.

Sometimes, as in the case of Dr. R., the nature of the experimental treatment can bring on experimenter bias. Dr. R. may have found the experimental condition much more interesting than the control condition. If so, then Dr. R. probably found it much more fun to run experimental than control sessions, and this showed up as increased warmth toward subjects in the experimental condition. But experimenter bias doesn't always work in this way.

Imagine that Dr. R.'s experimental condition was particularly noxious for subjects and Dr. R. knew it. Researchers do not enjoy putting subjects through unpleasant procedures! Every time Dr. R. knew that a subject would be undergoing the noxious procedure, he became somewhat anxious, and he transmitted this anxiety to subjects. As you can imagine, his behavior would be a particular problem if the dependent variable was anxiety. If Dr. R.'s hypothesis was that the noxious procedure would make subjects more anxious than the control procedure, his experiment would be confounded. Subjects could have picked up the cue from Dr. R. that there was something to be anxious about, and so they were. Effects on subjects' anxiety may have had every bit as much to do with Dr. R.'s demeanor as with the independent variable.[2]

The characteristics an experimenter brings to the experimental setting can be very important. An experimenter who is warm and friendly can elicit very different responses from subjects than one who is cold and aloof: Subjects sometimes learn better, talk more, get better scores on intelligence and adjustment tests, and are typically more compliant and eager to please when the experimenter acts in a friendly manner (Rosenthal, 1976). Clearly, an experimenter who appeared hostile would get less than optimal performance from research subjects. However, one should not come across as *too* friendly. The research setting is a novel one for most subjects, and they are often a bit anxious. We want to establish rapport with subjects so that they will feel at ease, but (unless the experimenter's demeanor is the independent variable) we do not want to make subjects behave in an atypical way. So be pleasant, but remember that you can affect the outcome of your experiment. However you act toward subjects, do it *consistently* across all the treatment conditions. If your behavior is different in the experimental and control conditions, for example, you are a potential confound.

So far it seems that experimenter effects can be a problem only with human subjects. After all, a rat will not notice a smile and then learn faster. Probably not, but experimenters may handle rats more and handle them more gently if they think the rats are special.

Experimenter effects can be just as important in animal studies as they are in human ones. Experimenters may treat subjects differently depending on what they expect from them. They may give more time to subjects that have gone through a particular treatment. This outcome is called the **Rosenthal effect** after the man who first reported it (Rosenthal, 1976). (It is also called the "Pygmalion effect," after the legend in which the sculptor Pygmalion fell in love with his own statue of the perfect woman.) Box 10-1 summarizes some of Rosenthal's key findings. The Rosenthal effect can be another source of confounding in an experiment.

Experimenter bias occurs in other ways too. The experimenter may also make errors in recording the data from the experiment. He or she may "misread" a scale or score an item incorrectly. Coincidentally, Rosenthal (1978) reported that researchers are more likely to make errors that favor the hypothesis. In a sample of 21 published studies, he found that about 1% of all observations made were probably wrong. Of those, two-thirds favored the experimenters' hypotheses. By chance, we would expect only about 50% of the errors to support the researchers' hypotheses.

Controlling experimenter bias: Double-blind experiments.   How can we eliminate experimenter effects from research? The first step, of course, is

---

[2] This actually happened to one of the authors in the first experiment she ran in graduate school. The experiment was ruined, but it taught her a valuable lesson—one that both authors hope you will not learn through your own personal experience.

BOX **10-1**
The Rosenthal effect

In a variety of laboratory and nonlaboratory studies, researchers have documented the self-fulfilling prophecy: Expectations can alter the behavior of others, even animals (Rosenthal & Fode, 1963). As Rosenthal explained:

Fode and I told a class of 12 students that one could produce a strain of intelligent rats by inbreeding them to increase their ability to run mazes quickly. To demonstrate, we gave each student five rats, which had to learn to run to the darker of two arms of a T-maze. We told half of our student-experimenters that they had the "maze-bright" intelligent rats; we told the rest that they had the stupid rats. Naturally, there was no real difference among any of the animals.

But, they certainly behaved differently in their performance. The rats believed to be bright improved daily in running the maze—they ran faster and more accurately—while the apparently dull animals did poorly. The "dumb" rats refused to budge from the starting point 29 percent of the time, while the "smart" rats were recalcitrant only 11 percent of the time.

Then we asked our students to rate the rats and to describe their own attitudes toward them. Those who believed they were working with intelligent animals *liked* them better and found them more pleasant. Such students said they felt more relaxed with the animals; they treated them more gently and were more enthusiastic about the experiment than students who thought they had dull rats to work with. Curiously, the students with "bright" rats said they handled them more but talked to them less. One wonders what students with "dull" rats were saying to those poor creatures. (p. 58)

In a later study, Rosenthal and Jacobson (1966) found a similar effect in the classroom. They gave children an IQ test at the start of the school

(continued)

FIGURE **10-3**   Robert Rosenthal.

BOX **10-1**
continued

year. Randomly selected children in each class were labeled "intellectual bloomers." "We gave each teacher the names of these children, who, we explained, could be expected to show remarkable gains during the coming year on the basis of their test scores. In fact the difference between these experimental children and the control group was solely in the teacher's mind" (p. 248). Eight months later they found greater gains in the IQ scores of the "bloomers" relative to the other children. Based on this and many other studies, Rosenthal proposed a fourfold explanation for the phenomenon.

People who have been led to expect good things from their students, children, clients, or what-have-you appear to:

- create a warmer social-emotional mood around their "special" students (climate);
- give more feedback to these students about their performance (feedback);
- teach more material and more difficult material to their special students (input);
- give their special students more opportunities to respond and question (output). (p. 60)*

* From "The Pygmalion Effect Lives" by R. Rosenthal, in R.E. Schell (Ed.), 1973, *Readings in Developmental Psychology Today, 2nd Ed.,* pp. 247–252. Copyright © 1973 by Ziff-Davis Publishing Company. Reprinted by permission of *Psychology Today* Magazine.

to be aware of them. We want to be sure we do not do anything that will contaminate the data. By following a set of written directions, timing all phases of the experiment, and being as consistent as possible, we can avoid some mistakes. We make our observations as objective as possible. We try to set up experiments to minimize the amount of personal contact between an experimenter and a subject so that unintentional bias does not happen. But sometimes we just cannot anticipate how bias might creep into an experiment.

Let us say we are doing a study of cartoons and children's art. We want to see whether children who have just watched a cartoon will draw more abstract pictures than children who have just watched a filmed version of the same story. The cartoon group sees animated drawings of people; the film group sees actual people acting out the same story. We show the children the cartoon or film. Then we ask them to draw pictures.

We have developed a way of scoring the children's drawings for abstractness. Our measure includes a number of specific dimensions, such as whether objects are colored in their true-to-life colors. We will score each child's picture on the abstractness scale. If our hypothesis is correct, the drawings of the children who saw the cartoon will be more abstract than the drawings of children who saw the film.

As we sit down to score the pictures, we notice different features in the drawings. We may also notice that we tend to score somewhat differently depending on which child drew the picture. Sometimes it is not clear how we should score a particular item. Melanie drew what appears to be a green orange. Oranges really are green before they get ripe, but they are usually orange in pictures. Should we score this as "abstract" or not? Scoring the dependent measures is no time to be making subjective judgments. We should have worked out these kinds of issues before running the experiment. But if these questions do arise in scoring, we might find ourselves deciding in favor of the more abstract rating if we were scoring a picture drawn by a child who saw the cartoon. We might distort the scoring a little by being inconsistent. In doing so, we would bias the data so that they would support our own hypothesis. It is easy to do this without even realizing it.

One of the best ways of controlling for experimenter bias is to run a **double-blind experiment,** one in which the subjects do not know which treatment they are in and the experimenter does not know either. The value of the double-blind experiment is this: If the experimenter does not know which treatment the subject is getting, he or she cannot bias the responses in any systematic way. Since the subject is kept in the dark too, the effects of demand characteristics are controlled along with experimenter bias.

If we are running a nutrition experiment and want to use the double-blind procedure, we get an assistant to assign subjects to treatment conditions. Experimental subjects receive a dietary supplement (for example, vitamin E). Control subjects receive a placebo. The subjects are not told which treatment they will receive; they only know they are part of an experiment on nutrition and that they may or may not receive a vitamin supplement that is thought to produce various effects. The assistant administers the treatments. When we measure the subjects on the dependent variable (for example, interview them, observe them in a waiting room, or score them on a written test), we also do not know which treatment each received. We are "blind" to that information. After the data have been collected and scored, the assistant lets us know who belonged to each treatment group. We can then go on to evaluate the impact of the independent variable.

Wasson et al. (1984) followed this same basic procedure in a study of the effects of continuity of outpatient health care in elderly men. They randomly assigned patients to a "continuous" or "discontinuous" condition. In the continuous condition, subjects saw the same health-care provider (physician, nurse practitioner, or physician's assistant) each time they visited the clinic. Subjects in the discontinuous condition were assigned for treatment in such a way that on each visit there was a 33% chance of seeing a different provider, and no provider could be seen more than three consecutive times.

Only 10% of the clinic patients participated in the study. They were not identified to the health-care providers and changes in patient assignments were made gradually so that patients would not suspect the pattern of assignments. Although we can easily question whether patients caught on to the nature of the study, it was in principle a double-blind experiment. The outcome was that patients in the continuous group had fewer hospital admissions, had shorter stays, and perceived that providers were more knowledgeable, competent, and interested in patient education.

In some experiments the subjects always know what treatment condition they are getting. For instance, in our study of cartoons and children's art, each child would know whether he or she saw a cartoon or a film. The children would not know the exact hypothesis of the study. Still, we could not really say that they are "blind" to the treatment conditions. In these experiments we may not be able to use a truly double- or even single-blind procedure. Even so, we can build in some controls for experimenter bias. We can try not to assign subjects to their conditions until after we have finished interacting with them. We can make sure that the person who scores the subjects' responses does not know which treatment each subject received. We might have an independent rater score subjects' drawings. We do not tell the rater which subjects belonged to which group. If we are doing our own scoring, it is more difficult to remain naive. However, with some planning we can skirt the most serious temptations. We standardize the testing and scoring procedures as much as possible. We try to be consistent in the way we handle the experiment from one subject to another. We avoid giving subjects extraneous clues as to how to behave.[3] As you design experiments, you will work very hard to control sources of confounding. Do not forget that *you* may be the biggest extraneous variable of all.

Personality and social variables can affect experiments. As you think about an experiment, try to anticipate subjects' reactions. Put yourself in the subject's place. How would you feel about answering your own questions? Would you be inclined to distort your answers because you would be too embarrassed to answer honestly? Would the experimental hypothesis be obvious to you? Think about your own behavior and the design of the experiment. Have you stacked the deck in any way? Do your instructions suggest the changes you expect to observe? Have you taken precautions to keep your own behavior as consistent as possible from one treatment condition to another? Are your instructions written down so that you will follow the same procedures each time? Are you prepared to introduce yourself and interact with all your subjects in the same way? You may find it useful to make a dry run before you start testing subjects. You might even consider a pilot study so that any bugs in the procedures can be worked out before you actually collect data for the experiment.

This chapter brings us to the close of the method section of the text. We have covered many techniques for designing and running solid experiments. In the next section, we will look at results and our next important question: What do we do with our data once we have them?

---

[3] When the experimenter *does* know the subject's condition (which happens if there isn't an assistant available), researchers often find a way to standardize the instructions that need to be given to subjects. There are several good ways to do this: You can give subjects written instructions or you can have them listen to the instructions on tape. If these methods are not practical, you can read the instructions word for word to all subjects. Avoid relying on memory; remember, it is important that the words *and* your voice stay the same each time.

SUMMARY

An experiment should measure what it is intended to measure: It should be valid. An *internally valid* experiment is one in which the researcher is confident that the changes in behavior across treatments were caused by the independent variable. An experiment is *externally valid* if the results can be applied to other situations. A variety of personality and social variables may lead to invalidity in an experiment; these are response style, response set, demand characteristics, and experimenter bias.

A subject with a *response style* has a characteristic way of answering questions, regardless of content. *Willingness to answer, position preferences,* and *yea-saying* are examples of response styles. To control for response style, experimenters can write questions that cannot be answered with a simple yes or no. They try to build specific content into each choice and vary the wording of questions so that subjects will be forced to think about their responses.

Experimenters also want to avoid measuring a *response set.* Subjects with a response set respond in terms of *latent content,* the meaning behind the questions. Social desirability is the best-known response set. Subjects who have the social-desirability response set will lie (or at least distort the truth) in order to look better in the eyes of the experimenter. This response set can be controlled to some extent by wording questions so that alternative answers have roughly the same social value. Subjects should then be able to answer the *manifest content* (the plain meaning) of the questions.

Demand characteristics can also create problems in experiments. Just being in an experiment can lead to changes in a subject's behavior that may have nothing to do with the experimental manipulation. Subjects may want to be "good" subjects; they may try to provide data that confirm the hypothesis. Their expectations about what will happen to them in the experiment can also shape their responses. One way of controlling demand characteristics is to run a *single-blind experiment.* Here, the experimenter tells subjects everything about the experiment except which treatment they will receive. This is a common approach to drug and nutrition experiments. Subjects are told that they may receive a drug or vitamin or a placebo. The *placebo* is a pill, injection, or other treatment that contains none of the actual substance being tested. Because the subjects in a single-blind experiment do not know for sure which treatment condition they are in, they are less likely to provide data that are distorted to conform to their notion of what the researcher expects to find. Another way to reduce demand characteristics is to use a *cover story,* which disguises the real research hypothesis.

The last potential source of error discussed in this chapter is *experimenter bias.* Without realizing it, an experimenter may give subtle cues that tell subjects how they are expected to behave. If an experimenter smiles at subjects every time they give the predicted response, he or she may not be getting an accurate picture of the way the independent variable operates. One way to control for experimenter bias is the *double-blind experiment,* in which the experimenter does not know which treatment the subjects are getting, and the subjects do not know either. This approach enables the experimenter to measure the dependent variable more objectively.

KEY TERMS

Cover story   A plausible but false explanation of the procedures in an experiment told to disguise the actual research hypothesis so that subjects cannot guess what it is.

Demand characteristics   The aspects of the experimental situation itself that demand or elicit particular behaviors; may lead to distorted data by compelling subjects to produce responses that conform to what subjects believe is expected of them in the experiment.

Double-blind experiment   An experiment in which neither the subjects nor the experimenter know which treatment the subjects are in; used to control experimenter bias.

Experimenter bias   Any behavior of the experimenter that can create confounding in an experiment.

External validity   The degree to which the findings of an experiment apply to situations not tested directly; their generalizability to the real world.

Internal validity   The degree to which a researcher is able to establish a causal relationship between a specified set of antecedent conditions (treatments) and the subsequent observed behavior.

Latent content   The implicit meaning of a question, sentence, dream, statement, and the like.

Manifest content   The explicit meaning of a question, sentence, dream, statement, and the like.

Nay-saying   A response style in which subjects show a tendency to disagree with a question regardless of its manifest content.

Placebo effect   The result of giving subjects a pill, injection, or other treatment that actually contains none of the independent variable but that elicits a change in subjects' behavior regardless.

Position preference   A response in which subjects show a tendency to choose answers appearing in the same position (say, the *b* slot) in multiple-choice questions.

Response set   The tendency to respond to the latent meaning of a question rather than its manifest content in an attempt to create a certain impression.

Response style   The tendency to respond in a particular way regardless of the latent or manifest content of the question asked.

Rosenthal effect   The phenomenon of experimenters treating subjects differently depending on what they expect from the subjects; also called the "Pygmalion effect."

Single-blind experiment   An experiment in which subjects are not told which of the treatment conditions they are in; a procedure used to control demand characteristics.

Social variables   The qualities of the relationships between subjects and experimenters that may influence the results of an experiment.

Subject variables   The characteristics of the subjects in an experiment that cannot be manipulated; independent variables, in the sense that a researcher can select subjects for their particular values.

Willingness to answer   A response style in which subjects show an inclination to answer questions even when the answers are in doubt.

Yea-saying   A response style in which subjects show a tendency to agree with a question regardless of its manifest content.

REVIEW AND STUDY QUESTIONS

1. Define and give an example of each of the following terms:
   a. Manifest content
   b. Latent content
   c. Response style
   d. Response set
2. You are preparing a questionnaire on attitudes toward childrearing practices: Are parents permissive or strict?
   a. What would you do to control for response style?
   b. Make up a set of four simple questions, controlling for response style.
   c. Would you worry about response set? How might response set affect subjects' responses to the questionnaire?
3. What are demand characteristics? How do they affect our data?
4. What is a single-blind experiment?
5. Outline a single-blind experiment to test this hypothesis: A new drug, Elate, makes hospital patients less depressed.
   a. What is the independent variable?
   b. What is the dependent variable?
   c. What is a placebo? Will you use one in this experiment? Why?
6. A researcher says, "I want my experiment to be a success. I'm sure my hypothesis is correct. So I'll just give my subjects a couple of hints here and there. You know, maybe a wink now and then if they give a good answer. That way I'll really be able to show that my independent variable had an effect."
   a. How would you convince her that her plan is faulty?
   b. What is a double-blind experiment? Would you recommend that she use it? Why or why not?
7. Dr. R. is planning a large-scale learning experiment. He would like to have 100 rats in the experimental group and another 100 in the control group. Because he needs so many rats, he says, "Well, I can't test all these animals by myself. I'll ask Dr. G. to help me. She can run the animals in the control group while I test the animals in the experimental group."

a. Knowing what you know about experimenter bias, is Dr. R.'s solution a good one? What may happen if one experimenter tests all the experimental subjects while another tests all the control subjects?

b. Given what you know about balancing procedures, work out a better plan for Dr. R.

8. Discuss the ways in which response set and response style might influence the validity of an experiment.

9. A researcher doing a survey on political beliefs finds that several subjects skipped one or more items on the questionnaire they were given. Since it will be inconvenient to analyze the data with different numbers of responses to the various questions, the researcher decides to discard all the incomplete questionnaires. Discuss the implications of the researcher's decision for interpreting the results of this study. Will the results be valid? Why or why not?

10. Allan is planning his first date with Cindy. He will try to be especially polite and witty. He will wear his best black shirt and a new gold chain. His roommate (who happens to be taking an experimental psychology course) says, "We're talking response set." Explain what he means.

11. What are demand characteristics? Describe two ways of controlling for them in an experiment.

12. When should a cover story be used? When shouldn't one be used? Discuss the ethical problem raised by the use of cover stories.

REFERENCES

CROWNE, D. P., & MARLOWE, D. (1964). *The approval motive.* New York: Wiley.

HAAS, A., & SHERMAN, M. (1982). Reported topics of conversation among same-sex adults. *Communication Quarterly, 30*(4), 332–342.

LEAVITT, P. (1974). *Drugs and behavior.* Philadelphia: Saunders.

ORNE, M. T., & SCHEIBE, K. E. (1964). The contribution of nondeprivation factors in the production of sensory deprivation effects: The psychology of the "panic button." *Journal of Abnormal and Social Psychology, 68,* 3–12.

RORER, L. G. (1965). The great response-style myth. *Psychological Bulletin, 63,* 129–156.

ROSENTHAL, R. (1973, September). The Pygmalion effect lives. *Psychology Today,* pp. 56–63.

ROSENTHAL, R. (1976). *Experimenter effects in behavioral research* (2nd ed.). New York: Halsted.

ROSENTHAL, R. (1978). How often are our numbers wrong? *American Psychologist, 33*(11), 1005–1008.

ROSENTHAL, R., & FODE, K. L. (1963). The effect of experimenter bias on the performance of the albino rat. *Behavioral Science, 8,* 183–189.

ROSENTHAL, R., & JACOBSON, L. (1966). Teachers' expectancies: Determinants of pupils' IQ gains. *Psychological Reports, 19,* 115–118.

WARWICK, D. P., & LININGER, C. A. (1975). *The sample survey: Theory and practice.* New York: McGraw-Hill.

WASSON, J. H., SAUVIGNE, A. E., MOGIELNICKI, R. P., GAUDETTE, C., & ROCKWELL, A. (1984). Continuity of outpatient medical care in elderly men. *Journal of the American Medical Association, 252*(17), 2413–2417.

WELLS, G. L., & PETTY, R. E. (1980). The effects of overt head-movements on persuasion: Compatibility and incompatibility of responses. *Journal of Basic and Applied Social Psychology, 1,* 219–230.

PART**THREE**

Results: Coping with Data

11

Weighing the Evidence

Statistical Inference: An Overview
Defining Variability
Testing the Null Hypothesis

Applying Statistical Inference: An Example
Choosing a Significance Level
Type 1 and Type 2 Errors

The Odds of Finding Significance
The Importance of Variability
One-Tailed and Two-Tailed Tests

Test Statistics

Summary

Key Terms

Review and Study Questions

References

Somehow the word *statistics* brings terror to the eyes of even the most dedicated student. You may be feeling the same. If you glance through this chapter, however, you will find that there are very few numbers. There are no computations. Instead, the chapter is intended to give you a general understanding of why we use statistics in research. We will also cover some basic terms that you need in order to understand how statistics are applied.

Statistics are quantitative measurements of samples. Through statistics we can quantify the phenomenon we observe. Vesselo (1965) summed it up this way:

> Loose phrases such as "miles away," "poles apart," "a giant's stride," "minute," "pinpoint," "in a nutshell," though picturesque, are notably inaccurate. Though this is unimportant in conversational or literary activity, these impressions persist; when transferred to fields of serious thought, where important and far-reaching decisions are being made, leading to a choice of alternative lines of actions, or when planning for the future, with a great expenditure of time and money and even life at stake, vague impressions will not do. Accurate measurement and comparison, and estimation in a scientific form are vital. (p. 189)

There are many different kinds of statistics that can be computed on any given sample. A statistic may be thought of as a numerical index of some characteristic of the data. Each *statistic* describes something different about the data, much as miles per gallon and compression ratios each tell us something different about our cars. Some statistics can be used to make comparisons between different samples.

The point of working with statistics is that they enable us to evaluate objectively the data we worked so hard to collect. Let us look at a hypothetical mystery to illustrate the kind of evaluation that takes place.

WEIGHING THE EVIDENCE

Ms. Adams has just been arrested for murder. Detective Katz has found the victim's car keys, footprints, and bifocals in Ms. Adams' apartment. Witnesses say the victim and Ms. Adams were having dinner together at the local coffee shop a short time before the crime was committed. Yes, there is evidence against her. But did she actually commit the crime? Detective Katz knows he must establish her guilt beyond a reasonable doubt. Can he do that? Yes, he has the keys, the footprints, and even the bifocals that were found in Ms. Adams' apartment. He has witnesses who will swear they saw the suspect and victim dining calmly on hot pastrami sandwiches a short time before the murder. But is this proof? What Detective Katz has put together is a case based largely on circumstantial evidence. The evidence suggests that Ms. Adams knew the victim well enough to share pastrami sandwiches and that the victim visited her apartment sometime before the murder. The evidence implicates Ms. Adams in the crime, but it does not *prove* that she did it. Other people may have known the victim well enough to share sandwiches too. And other people may have committed the murder. Given the evidence, the best Detective Katz can do is attempt to establish Ms. Adams' guilt beyond a reasonable doubt. He can show that she, more than anyone else, is likely to be the murderer.

When we carry out a psychological experiment, we find ourselves in a plight similar to the one Detective Katz is in. Katz has investigated a case. We have run an experiment. Katz has collected evidence. We have gathered some data. Katz would like to prove his suspect committed the crime. We would like to prove our independent variable caused the changes we see in our dependent variable.

Given all you have learned about experimentation, you will not be too surprised to learn that we can never actually *prove* an independent variable caused the changes we see in a dependent variable. Proving something means establishing the truth of it by presenting evidence and logical arguments. Do you remember doing proofs in geometry? You began with a premise such as this: In every right triangle, the square of the hypotenuse is equal to the sum of the squares of the legs. You would then use all the facts you knew about geometry to construct a logical argument that would prove the premise true. Your proof would show that the premise is true because there would be no logical alternative. You would come down to a final step that would look something like this: $AB = AB$. Unfortunately, outside of mathematics, proving things is not always so straightforward. Detective Katz would like to prove Ms. Adams guilty. He believes she is. But can he develop a proof as airtight as $AB = AB$? Since his evidence is circumstantial, the best he can do is show that she is *probably* guilty.

When we evaluate the data from a psychological experiment, we do a very similar thing. We carry out statistical tests to determine whether the independent variable *probably* caused changes in the dependent variable from one treatment condition to another. We cannot really prove that it did. Other factors like coincidence or chance can also lead to differences. However, we can make some statements about how likely it is that the independent variable had an effect. We base those statements on the statistical tests that we do.

STATISTICAL INFERENCE: AN OVERVIEW

As we evaluate the results of an experiment, we naturally want to be able to come to conclusions about the impact of the independent variable. We could just look at our results and see which groups did better. But that would not be very precise. When we run an experiment, we typically start with a sample of subjects drawn from a population. The population consists of all people, animals, or objects that have at least one characteristic in common, and the sample is a group that *represents* the larger population. Remember that we typically test samples, but we want to be able to make inferences about the entire population we have sampled. Fortunately, the way statistics work allows us to do exactly that.

Within any population, the scores on a dependent variable will differ somewhat. Because the members of a population are different individuals, we do not expect everyone to score exactly the same. The scores of the subjects we sampled will also differ. The question we ask with statistics is this: Are the differences we see between treatment groups significantly greater than what we would expect to see between *any* samples of scores drawn from this population? Answering this question involves a **statistical inference,** making a statement about the population and all its samples based on what we see in the samples we have.

Suppose two groups of students in a class are asked to report their weights. To make a statistical inference about the two groups (samples), we must first calculate the **mean,** or arithmetical average, of each group by adding up the students' weights and then dividing the sum by the total number of weights. The mean weight of the 12 students on the window side of the room is 152 pounds. The mean weight of the 12 students on the opposite side of the room is 147 pounds, an absolute difference of 5 pounds. Would you conclude from these measurements that students on the two sides of the room do not belong to the same population? Perhaps they belong to different species. Or perhaps sitting near the windows causes students to gain weight. More likely, you are thinking that it is silly to make anything of a difference of 5 pounds. After all, not everybody has the same weight; the weight of any two groups will differ somewhat. You have made a statistical inference based on your knowledge of the weight of these groups. You conclude they probably belong to the same population—even though you have not measured everyone in that population.

Defining Variability

When we measure subjects on any variable, we do not expect everyone to come out with exactly the same score. If we measure two or more groups on almost any dimension, we can expect some variability or fluctuation in their scores. Variability is one of the most important concepts you need to understand and to analyze the results of experiments. In a commonsense way, **variability** is the amount of fluctuation we see in something. The altitude of Italy varies from places at sea level along the coast to Mt. Rosa, which is 15,203 feet high.[1] We could say there is a lot of variability in the altitude of places in Italy. There is relatively little variability in the altitude of Brooklyn, New York; all of Brooklyn lies very close to sea level.

[1] *Hammond citation world atlas* (1974). Maplewood, NJ: Hammond, p. 35.

When we do a statistical test, we are asking whether our pattern of results is significantly different from what we would expect to see because of the usual variability among people in the population. Since we are using the scientific method, we do not want to answer this question in a subjective way. A researcher may wish to argue that their results are obviously significant. You may disagree. Instead of leaving the choice up to the individual, statistical tests have been set up so that we have *standards*—conventions or guidelines about what is significant so that everyone can agree on whether results are significant or not. In law we accept the verdict of the jury as our standard of guilt or innocence. In psychology we accept the outcome of statistical tests to establish whether an independent variable had an effect in a particular experiment. We can summarize the overall process of statistical inference with a few steps. In each experiment, the researcher (1) samples from a population, (2) states a null hypothesis, (3) chooses a significance level, and (4) evaluates the results of the experiment for statistical significance, retaining or rejecting the null hypothesis.

Testing the Null Hypothesis

In our legal system, a person is presumed innocent until proved guilty. We assume that the person did not do anything wrong until there is convincing evidence to show otherwise. We make a similar assumption about the independent variable as we set up statistical tests. Until we can determine otherwise, we assume an independent variable has no effect.

We do not actually test the research hypothesis of an experiment directly. Instead, we formulate and test the **null hypothesis (H_0)**, which states that the performance of the treatment groups is so similar that the scores must have been sampled from the same population. In effect, the null hypothesis says that any differences we see between treatments amount to nothing. We assume that a suspect is innocent until the evidence leads us to conclude that he or she is guilty. Similarly, we assume that the data from different treatment groups came from the same population and any differences between them amount to nothing more than the ordinary variability in scores we would expect in any population. We hold to the assumption that the null hypothesis is correct until the evidence shows the assumption can be rejected.

At this point, you may be feeling a bit confused. "Don't we get our samples from the same population to begin with? Why do we have to assume that the data came from the same population?" Actually, the null hypothesis is not as strange as it seems. We do take our sample of subjects from the same population, at least as far as we know. Ideally, we take random samples and use random assignment to avoid creating treatment groups that differ from each other before the experiment even begins. However, in the experiment we manipulate the independent variable so that the treatment groups are exposed to different conditions. When the experiment is over, we would like to be able to *reject the null hypothesis* by showing that the effect produced by the independent variable led to real differences in the responses of the groups. We reject the null hypothesis by showing that our treatments produced differences that are sufficiently large that they are unlikely to be encountered within the same population even if we take normal variability into account. And in a sense, even though we test only a sample, the experiment is testing whether the population of untreated subjects' scores now differs from the population of treated subjects' scores.

We use statistical tests to tell us if we can reject the null hypothesis or not. If we reject the null hypothesis, we are confirming a change between the groups that occurred as a result of the experiment: Our results are **statistically significant.** If we can reject the null hypothesis, we are saying that the data from the treatment groups are now so different that they look as if they came from different populations; the normal *variability* of scores on the dependent measure is not enough to account for our results. However, when we retain the null hypothesis, we are saying that the scores from the treatment groups are still so similar that the experimental manipulation must have had little impact; the pattern can be explained by normal variability in a single population.

There is no way to directly test the **alternative hypothesis (H_1)**—the research hypothesis—which states that the data came from different populations. There is no way to *prove* that this is so or that the independent variable caused the pattern of results. The best we can do is show it is unlikely that the pattern occurred from chance variation within the population we sampled: We can only show that the null hypothesis is probably wrong.

Let us suppose our experiment deals with the effects of background music on job performance. We form two random groups of subjects and place them in identical testing rooms. We give them sets of purchase invoices and instruct them to write a seven-digit account number on each one, separate out the carbon copies, and order them alphabetically. The task is routine and similar to many office jobs. We want to test the research hypothesis that background music enhances job performance. We can only test this alternative hypothesis *indirectly* by attempting to show that the null hypothesis is probably false. We predict that the experimental group that hears background music will process more invoices in a set period of time than a control group that does not hear background music. So that we will not create experimenter effects during the testing, we operate all our equipment controls from outside the testing rooms. After playing taped instructions over an intercom, we turn on the music for the experimental group by flipping a switch on a control panel. The control group performs in an identical but quiet room.

When the testing hour is over, we return to collect our materials. We debrief the subjects, explaining the purpose of the experiment and what we expected to find. To our dismay, subjects in the experimental group become uneasy. They are concerned about their hearing because it seems that they did not hear any music at all. With a little checking, we discover that the control switch is not working. When we thought we turned on the music, nothing happened. The music affected our experimental group as much as it did the control group—not at all.

What do you think would happen if we went ahead and counted up the number of invoices each group processed anyway? Our treatment groups were randomly selected from the same population and randomly assigned to the two conditions. Thus we would expect both groups to have processed about the same average number of invoices. Our independent variable had no effect on the experimental group, so there is no reason to expect the performance of the two groups to be very different. We expect their performance will continue to look like the performance of two groups drawn from the same population.

When we do a statistical test, we begin by doing essentially the same thing: We formulate the null hypothesis by stating that the performance of the treatment groups is so similar that the groups must belong to the same population. We reject the null hypothesis when the difference between treatments is so large that chance variations cannot explain it. A series of *frequency distributions* in Figure 11-1 illustrates the general way this process would work in an experiment in which the independent variable has a large effect.

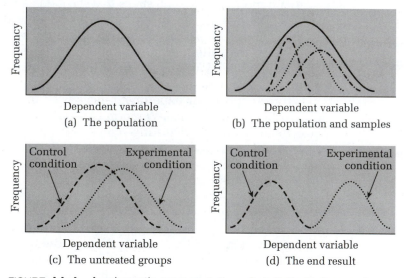

FIGURE **11-1** A schematic representation of statistical inference in an experiment in which the independent variable had a large effect.

Process of Statistical Inference

1. Consider the population to be sampled: Because of variability, individual scores on the dependent variable will differ.
2. Consider different random samples within the population: Their scores on the dependent variable will also differ because of normal variability. Assume the null hypothesis is correct.
3. Apply the treatment conditions to randomly selected, randomly assigned samples.

We often represent a group of individual scores on a dependent variable by graphing the distribution of scores in the form of frequency distributions, or frequency polygons. You will be seeing many of these in the pages to come. When graphing a frequency distribution, possible values of the dependent variable are marked off along the *abscissa,* the X or horizontal axis at the bottom. Frequencies (numbers of individuals) are marked off on the *ordinate,* the Y or vertical axis.

Suppose you have a data set consisting of subjects' scores on a 7-point rating scale—a scale with numbers from 0 to 6 used as the dependent measure. The possible values of the scale would be listed at equidistant points along the abscissa. The leftmost mark along the abscissa would be the smallest possible value—0. This would be followed by a mark for 1, 2, 3, and so on, up to 6.

Frequency would be marked off on the ordinate, beginning with a frequency of 0 near the bottom of the ordinate, then 1, 2, and so on, until you get to the number representing the *maximum frequency* for any score. Let's say that the number 4 on the scale was chosen by more people than any other number and that it was chosen by 10 subjects. The maximum frequency for any score, then, will be 10. So the last value you would mark off near the top of the ordinate is a 10. Now that you have labeled the graph, you simply plot the frequency for each value of the dependent variable. Because the dependent variable has 7 values, you would end up with 7 points on the graph. Finally, you simply connect the dots. Your distribution is now represented by a curve, sometimes called a frequency *polygon.* You will notice that the frequency distributions illustrating general concepts rather than actual sets of data usually do not have the abscissa or ordinate completely labeled. Of course, graphs do need to be completely labeled if an actual data set is used.

A frequency polygon makes it easy to examine an entire data set at a glance. You can plot one experimental group or several on the same graph (see Figure 11-1). You can visually inspect the data to see whether the curve resembles the shape of the normal curve depicted in Figure 11-2. While we will not cover the procedure in this book, statistics courses teach ways that you can *transform* a data set so that it more closely approximates a normal curve. This sometimes makes it easier to reject the null hypothesis.

4. After the treatment, the samples now appear to belong to different populations: Reject the null hypothesis.

Whether or not we will reject the null hypothesis depends to a large extent on variability. When there is a great deal of variability in the population, large differences between samples will be common. The more variability there is on the dependent measure, the greater the difference between treatment groups has to be before we may say that the data look like they belong to different populations. *The more variability, the harder it will be to reject the null hypothesis.* In an experiment we want to be precise; we want to know exactly how much variability there is in the data. Then we can estimate the exact odds that we would see such large differences between treatment groups even if the independent variable had no effect. There is always some chance that the null hypothesis is true; even very large differences can occasionally appear between two samples from the same population.

The reasoning is the same when we evaluate the data from a within-subjects experiment. If the difference in the data from various treatment conditions is large in relation to variability, then we may be able to reject the null hypothesis. We may conclude that the data of subjects under different treatments look like data that probably came from different populations: The odds are that something in the experiment produced a significant change in subjects' behavior from one condition to another. The null hypothesis (H_0) states that the means (average scores) for the treatment conditions come from the same population. Thus the difference we see between two treatments merely reflects sampling error: We have drawn two samples from a population in which there is variability on the dependent measure. Let us turn to another example so we can look at these principles in a more concrete way.

APPLYING STATISTICAL INFERENCE: AN EXAMPLE

Imagine we are running another experiment. This is our hypothesis: Time passes quickly when you are having fun. This is a **directional hypothesis;** it predicts the way the difference between groups will go. We are saying that time will go faster, not slower, for people who are having fun than for people who are not having fun. We have decided to use a two-group, between-subjects design. We operationally define "having fun" as looking at a collection of cartoons. Our experimental group will be given the cartoons and instructed to examine them to see how funny they are. We will not tell subjects that they will be given 10 minutes for the task. The control group will also be given 10 minutes to examine the same cartoons, minus the captions. Control subjects will see the drawings, but they will miss the punch lines and will not have much fun. The independent variable is fun. The dependent variable is subjects' estimates of the amount of time that elapses during the experiment. A small deception is used in this experiment: We do not tell the subjects the true purpose of the experiment beforehand. After subjects examine the cartoons for 10 minutes, we ask them to estimate the amount of time that has passed since they started. The null hypothesis (H_0) is that the time estimates of the two groups are similar and were sampled from the same population. Note that this is different from the research hypothesis (H_1), which says that the fun group will make shorter estimates.

Suppose we have actually run the experiment and computed the means. The mean estimated elapsed time for the control group is 12.5 minutes. The mean estimated elapsed time for the experimental group is 8.4 minutes. On the face of it, it appears that the experimental group really did experience the time as going more quickly than the control group. On average, the members of the experimental group thought that only about 8 minutes had passed. To them it seemed they had been at their task for less time than the actual clock time. The control group on average estimated the elapsed time to be longer than it really was. Can we conclude that fun makes the time pass more quickly?

No. You know that we have to consider the variability of the data before we can draw any conclusions about the differences we find between two treatment groups. We need to evaluate our data with statistical tests. Our first step was to state a null hypothesis: The time estimates came from the same population. Now if we could measure the population from which our samples were drawn—say, all college sophomores—we would find that ability to estimate elapsed time varies. Some people are very accurate; others are inaccurate. Some overestimate time; others underestimate. If we could somehow test all sophomores and ask them to estimate the length of a 10-minute interval, we might get a frequency distribution that looks something like the one shown in Figure 11-2. This distribution is a **normal curve**—a symmetrical, bell-shaped curve. The bulk of the scores represented by this distribution fall close to the center. (Most students' estimates will be fairly accurate.) Many of the statistical tests you will do include the assumption that the population you have sampled is normally distributed on the dependent variable. If you could somehow measure everyone in the population on that variable, the graph of all those measurements would be a normal curve.

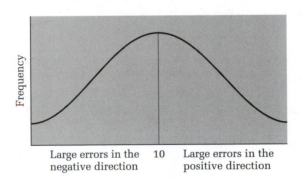

Large errors in the   10   Large errors in the
negative direction   positive direction

FIGURE **11-2** A normal curve: Hypothetical distribution of time estimates of all college sophomores estimating the length of a 10-minute time interval.

Since we are rarely able to measure the whole population we want to study, we make inferences about what goes on in the population. We base those inferences on what we see in our samples. Keep in mind that what we want to know about our data is whether the differences we observe between treatment groups are significant. The means of different samples of subjects will vary when they are measured on just about any variable, but can we reject the null hypothesis? In reality, we are rarely able to work with the normal curve that represents the actual population of interest. However, the sample means have a distribution too. It is called the *sampling distribution of the mean.* The larger the sample size, the more closely this distribution will resemble a normal curve.

It is possible to construct the distribution of other statistics too, such as the difference between means of samples drawn two at a time from the same population. Because of variability, any two samples will differ from one another. Some will differ a great deal, some very little. The question is whether they differ enough to allow us to conclude that the null hypothesis is not a likely explanation for what we have observed. In our time-passage experiment, the null hypothesis says that although the time estimates of our groups are different, they just reflect sampling error. The greater the variability in the population, the less likely it is that we will be able to reject the null hypothesis. If the population varies greatly, then occasionally we would even expect to see very large differences between samples from that population. Those large differences could occur by chance and would have nothing to do with the independent variable.

The figures we are using to illustrate these relationships are, of course, hypothetical. We cannot measure everyone in the population. So although the figures help us understand the logic of what we expect to happen in an experiment, they do not help us make decisions about our data. Fortunately, mathematicians have worked out other methods.

The test statistics we will cover later are mathematical representations of the relationship between observed differences between groups and variability. Test statistics have known distributions that we *can* use to make inferences about our data. In the next chapter, you will find some examples of how that is done. The process requires some knowledge of probability theory.

We make our decisions about the null hypothesis on the basis of probabilities. How likely is it that a difference so large occurred just by chance? What are the odds that the usual variability in the population led to treatment groups that differ so much on the dependent variable? We test the null hypothesis (H_0) for two reasons. First, it is the most likely explanation of what has occurred. When we measure different samples, or even the same sample at different times, we expect some variation between them. It would actually be very unusual to get exactly the same data from different groups. So when groups differ, we are most likely observing variations that would occur even if there had been no experimental intervention. Second, there is no way we can verify the alternative to the null hypothesis directly. The alternative hypothesis (H_1) states that the treatment means are so different that they come from distinct populations. H_1 is actually what we would like to show. We would like to be able to say that the treatment groups differ because of our experimental manipulation. Unfortunately, no matter how different the groups are, there is always some chance that the results were caused by sampling error. Like Detective Katz, the best we can do is show that our explanation for what happened is *probably* true.

Choosing a Significance Level

In order to decide whether the differences between our treatment conditions are significant or important, we need a **significance level,** a criterion for deciding whether to accept or reject the null hypothesis. How much of a difference between treatments do we require? If the differences between treatments are probably caused by the chance variation in the population, we cannot talk about a treatment effect. You know that there is always a possibility that even extreme differences between treatments occurred by chance.

Now suppose you knew that, by chance, the odds of getting a difference as large as we found are about 2 out of 3. The treatment means were likely to be different—even if the independent variable had no effect at all. Would you be willing to scrap the null hypothesis? If we rejected the null hypothesis against those odds, we would probably be wrong 2 out of 3 times. We would be saying that the means came from different populations when they actually came from the same one.

Naturally, we would like to be reasonably sure about our conclusions. If we reject the null hypothesis, we would like to know that our decision is probably correct. How sure we need to be can vary depending on the circumstances: Suppose you are at a sidewalk sale and you find a good-looking, cheap shirt. However, because it is a sidewalk sale, you cannot try on the shirt, and if you buy it, you cannot return it. You guess there is a 1 in 10 chance that the shirt will not fit. Will you buy it anyway? Your decision will be based on what you stand to lose. If the shirt costs $5, you might risk it. But you might not risk $20. If you are short of cash, you might not be willing to risk anything. Similarly, when we evaluate the results of an experiment, we evaluate the risks involved in making the wrong decision. If we are dealing with life-and-death research on new drug therapies or suicide prevention, we will be much less willing to risk being wrong. We might be somewhat more relaxed in a taste test of a new beverage. What an experimenter does in a particular experiment depends on what he or she is testing. However, there are conventions for deciding whether to accept or reject the null hypothesis. In psychology, by convention, we can generally reject the null hypothesis if the probability of obtaining this pattern of data by chance alone is less than 5%. Then we say the significance level is $p < .05$ (read "p less than .05"). A significance level of $p < .05$ would be appropriate for our time-estimation experiment.

When we choose a significance level of .05, we are saying that we will reject the null hypothesis if we get a pattern of data so unlikely that it could have occurred by chance less than 5 times out of 100. That is actually less than the odds of tossing a coin four times and getting four consecutive heads.[2] It is possible to get four heads in a row—but it just is not likely. If we saw it happen, we would probably ask to see the coin. If we see such unlikely differences between treatment groups, we reject the null hypothesis and say that our results are statistically significant.

In some experiments we may want a stricter criterion. We may choose a significance level of $p < .01$. That means the odds of getting such large treatment effects by chance are less than 1 in 100—that is a little less than the odds of tossing a coin six times and getting six consecutive heads. Pharmaceutical research, for example, generally adopts this criterion. Even stricter criteria, such as $p < .001$ (less than one in a thousand), might be chosen for some medical research or other projects in which being wrong about a treatment effect could have disastrous human consequences.

In order to make a valid test of a hypothesis, think ahead and decide what the significance level will be before running the experiment. It is not legitimate to collect all the data and then pick the significance level depending on how the results turned out. The experiment would yield significant results—but only because we stacked the deck in our favor. For instance, we might find that the difference between performance of two treatment groups is significant at the .20 level. That would mean a difference this large could have occurred by chance about 20 times out of 100. We could accept this as a meaningful difference, but we would not be making a very rigorous test of the hypothesis. (And by convention, p values greater than .05 in psychological research would not be considered statistically significant by other researchers.) Now that precise probability levels can be obtained using computer data-analysis programs, many researchers simply report the significance levels of the results they obtained so that readers can evaluate them on their own. Reporting obtained probability levels is also commonly done when the results did not reach the significance level the researcher had chosen.

In the time-estimation experiment, we are testing the notion that time passes quickly when a person is having fun. Assume we had chosen $p < .05$ as the significance level for this experiment. We would evaluate the results against this criterion. If the results could have occurred by chance more than 5% of the time, we could not reject the null hypothesis: The data are too similar to say that they probably came from different populations, and the results are not statistically significant. However, if the results could have occurred by chance less than 5% of the time, we are able to reject the null hypothesis: The data are statistically significant—they look as if they came from different populations. This is just another way of saying that the independent variable apparently had an effect: It altered the behavior of the treatment groups. Our groups started out the same, but their scores on time estimation now look as if they came from different populations. Figure 11-3 illustrates the way the distributions of sample means from those populations might look. The figure represents what we would find if we were able to test all possible samples from both popula-

---

[2] For the curious reader, the actual probability of four heads in a row is $p = .0675$ (.5 $\times$ .5 $\times$ .5 $\times$ .5).

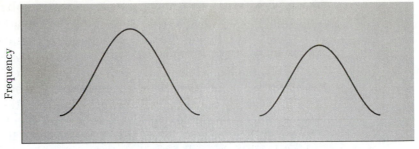

FIGURE **11-3** Hypothetical distributions of populations having fun and not having fun. The independent variable had a large effect on subjects' time estimates.

tions (people who are having fun and people who are not). Of course, there is variability among the samples drawn from both populations; some samples give more accurate estimates than others. However, in this idealized situation, you can see that the populations do not overlap. On time estimation, people who are having fun are distinctly different from people who are not. On the average, people who are having fun consistently say that time passes more quickly than it does for the control subjects who are not having fun. If that were really so, we would expect to obtain large differences between treatment groups exposed to different levels of the independent variable (fun). We would expect a significant difference between treatment groups if the independent variable had such a large effect on subjects' behaviors.

In reality, the picture is rarely so perfect. Many extraneous variables can affect the outcome of an experiment, and the data may not be a true reflection of the impact of the independent variable. Also, although the experimental manipulation is effective, its impact may not be as powerful as the one we have drawn here. More typically, we expect some overlap between treatment populations. But we cannot be sure exactly how much overlap there is because we usually cannot measure every possible sample. And because of this overlap, our conclusions about the results may be wrong.

Type 1 and Type 2 Errors

Even though our results were statistically significant, the null hypothesis could still be true. It could be that we have somehow obtained treatment means that really do belong to the same population. They seem to be significantly different even though the independent variable had no effect. What are the odds of making that mistake? After all, we reject the null hypothesis only if the treatment groups are very different. Is this really a problem? How serious the error is depends on the actual experiment. If the decision involves a life-and-death issue, the consequences could be very serious. However, from a practical standpoint, making the wrong decision about the null hypothesis is always serious. Why bother to run a carefully controlled experiment only to draw the wrong conclusions at the end?

If we reject the null hypothesis when it really is true, we have made a **Type 1 error:** We say that chance differences between treatments were caused by the experiment; although the independent variable had little or no effect, we claim its effect was significant. The odds of making a Type 1 error are exactly equal to the value we choose for the significance level. If we are using a .05 significance level, the probability of a Type 1 error is .05. If our significance level is .05, then 5 times out of 100 (or 5% of the time), we will reject the null hypothesis when we should not. There will be 5 times out of 100 when the extreme differences we see really occurred by chance. If we choose a .01 significance level, the probability of a Type 1 error is .01, or 1 chance in 100.

Could we minimize the odds of a Type 1 error simply by choosing a more extreme significance level? Yes, but there is a tradeoff in doing that. We can make a second kind of error, a **Type 2 error:** We fail to reject the null hypothesis even though it is really false. We have missed a treatment effect that was real. If we conclude that the pattern of results was caused by chance variations when it was really caused by the independent variable, we have made a Type 2 error.

The more extreme the significance level, the more likely we are to make a Type 2 error. But how does this happen? Won't the differences between treatments be so extreme that we will surely find them? Not necessarily. If the independent variable has a very dramatic effect (and if there is not much variability between subjects on the dependent variable), we might wind up sampling from two completely distinct populations, such as people having fun and people not having fun (as in Figure 11-3). There might be no similarity between them at all. *But more typically, the responses of the populations will overlap.* Figure 11-4 illustrates that possibility for the experiment on time estimation.

When data from two populations look very similar, there is no sure way we can tell that they come from different populations. These are the cases that lead to a Type 2 error. Because there is overlap between the responses we sample, we are sometimes unable to show a significant difference between the treatments, even though the independent variable had some effect. Instead, we accept the null hypothesis. We say that the differences between the treatment means occurred simply by chance. The probability of making a Type 2 error is affected by the amount of overlap between the populations being sampled. If the responses of people having fun are very similar to those of people not having fun, it will be hard to show that fun altered the responses in any way. The more overlap there is, the harder it is to detect the effect of the independent variable. The probability of making a Type 2 error is represented by the Greek letter β (*beta*). We would be able to find the exact value of β only if we could measure all possible samples of both populations. But say we knew that the odds of making a Type 2 error were equal to exactly .75 in our experiment. Then the odds of making a correct decision would be equal to $1 - .75$, or .25. If we are likely to be wrong 3 out of 4 times (.75), then we should be right 1

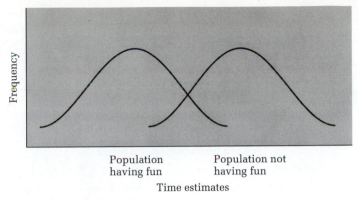

Frequency

Population
having fun

Population not
having fun

Time estimates

FIGURE **11-4** Hypothetical distribution of populations having fun
and not having fun. The independent variable had a moderate
effect on subjects' time estimates.

out of 4 times (.25). The odds of correctly rejecting the null hypothesis
when it is false are always equal to $1 - \beta$.

This last quantity $(1 - \beta)$ is also referred to as the *power* of the statistical test.[3] We touched on this concept in Chapter 6 in connection with
sample size. Although we cannot measure the precise value of β, we can
reduce it by increasing our sample size. We stand a better chance of correctly rejecting H_0 with a sample of 50 than with a sample of 20. As you
know, the ability to detect a treatment effect is also related to how much
variability there is in the population; therefore we can reduce β by reducing the variability in our sample data (by controlling extraneous variables
or using a within-subjects or matched-groups design). We can also use the
more powerful statistical tests. The tests explained in this text are called
"parametric tests." They require certain assumptions about the data (normally distributed, comparable variability across groups, interval or ratio
data). Tests known as "nonparametric tests" are used when these assumptions cannot be met. They are somewhat less powerful.

We can also accept a less extreme significance level. We are more likely
to detect a difference using a significance level of $p < .05$ than one of $p <
.01$. However, remember that adopting a less extreme significance level
also increases the chance of a Type 1 error.

The probability of making a Type 1 error is always equal to the value
chosen as the significance level. This is represented by the Greek letter α
(*alpha*). There is some chance (α) that we will reject the null hypothesis
when we should have retained it. There is a $1 - \alpha$ chance that we will
accept the null hypothesis when that is the correct decision. Altogether,
there are four possible decisions we can make when we evaluate the data
from an experiment. These are summarized in Table 11-1.

[3] Even though *beta* cannot be precisely measured, there are useful charts and tables for estimating statistical power $(1 - \beta)$. Power charts can be found in many statistics textbooks, but
the classic source book is Cohen, J. (1969). *Statistical power analysis for the behavioral sciences*. New York, NY: Academic Press.

TABLE **11-1**

		Your Decision	
		Accept the Null Hypothesis	*Reject the Null Hypothesis*
The Real Story	Null hypothesis is true. (The data came from the same population.)	You are correct: $p = 1 - \alpha$	You have made a Type 1 error: $p = \alpha$
	Null hypothesis is false. (The data belong to different populations.)	You have made a Type 2 error: $p = \beta$	You are correct: $p = 1 - \beta$

Evaluating results: The four possible outcomes and the odds that they will occur

NOTE: p *stands for probability;* α *represents the significance level of the experiment.*

When we make a Type 2 error, we accept the null hypothesis. We fail to confirm the research hypothesis of the experiment. The independent variable had an effect, but we are unable to detect it. A Type 2 error is like acquitting a suspect who is guilty: We allow the suspect to go free although he or she really did commit the crime. When we make a Type 1 error, our mistake has greater implications for the suspect. We reject the null hypothesis and conclude that the differences between treatment means are so great that they confirm our predictions. For instance, we may conclude that the time estimates of people having fun are significantly less than the time estimates of people not having fun. Remember, that does not prove the research hypothesis; it suggests that it is *probably* true. Of course, we are always pleased to confirm our predictions. We can begin to speculate on all the important consequences of having demonstrated a significant effect. But think about what is happening in this case. When we make a Type 1 error, we explain an effect that does not really exist, and this can often be a more serious error than failing to detect an effect. A Type 1 error is like putting an innocent person in jail. We attribute a crime to someone who did nothing at all. The possibility of making a Type 1 error makes it especially important that we replicate the findings of experiments.

THE ODDS OF FINDING SIGNIFICANCE

In addition to choosing and applying a significance level, it is important to understand how the odds of finding significance are affected by two factors: the amount of variability in the data and whether we have a directional or a nondirectional hypothesis. Let us take a closer look at how these factors influence the outcome of an experiment.

The Importance of Variability

Suppose we could somehow measure all possible samples of college sophomores on time estimation. We would see that the distribution of means of those samples is a normal distribution—a symmetrical, bell-shaped curve. Like individual subjects, some samples perform better than others. Most are about average; but some do well and some do poorly. Suppose we could take all possible pairs of samples and find the differences between their means. We would get another distribution. The outcome would resemble Figure 11-5. You can see that many of the differences between sample means fall right around zero. Because time estimation is normally distributed, the means of most samples will be close to the mean of the population on that variable. The differences between those means will be very small. However, some differences are very large; they occur at the extremes of the distribution. They represent differences between means of groups that are very far apart on time estimation. As you can see, there are relatively few differences that are so extreme. We find fewer and fewer instances as we move away from zero. There is variability in the differences between means just as there is variability between samples.[4]

Some differences between means are more likely than others. For normal distributions, it is possible to calculate the odds that each difference will occur (and statisticians have spent a lot of time calculating these odds for us). The odds of getting very small differences—close to zero—between the means of any two samples are high. Most sample means fall close to the mean of the population, so if you subtract one sample mean from another, the difference will be close to zero. We should not be too surprised if the groups in our experiment turn out to be very close together on the

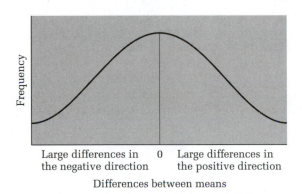

FIGURE **11-5** Hypothetical distribution of the differences between all possible pairs of means drawn from a distribution.

[4] The first statistical tests we will look at are tests to evaluate differences between treatment means directly. Other characteristics of treatment groups, such as their variability, can be compared and evaluated by using different tests.

dependent variable. But the odds of seeing much larger differences are less. The exact odds depend on the amount of variability in the population.

Large differences are more likely in populations that have high variability on the dependent measure. Figure 11-6 shows you three distributions of differences between sample means. The distributions are similar except for the amount of variability in the populations sampled. The first distribution shows differences between the means of samples from a population in which there was little variability on the variable that was measured. Since the sample means are all relatively close to each other (that is, there was little variability in them), the differences between them also tend to be small. The second distribution is based on a population in which there was a moderate amount of variability on the variable that was mea-

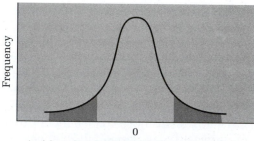

(a) A distribution with low variability

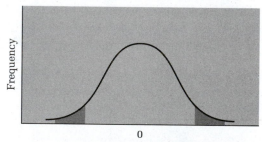

(b) A distribution with moderate variability

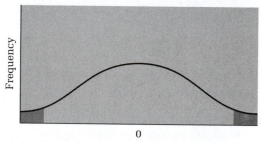

(c) A distribution with high variability

FIGURE **11-6** Three hypothetical distributions of differences between sample means. Shaded areas represent the most extreme 5% of each distribution.

sured. You can see that the differences between means of samples from this population tend to be larger than the differences in the first distribution. The third distribution is based on a population in which there was a great deal of variability on the variable that was measured. You can see that this distribution is the widest. The differences between the means of the samples from this population tend to be very large because there is a great deal of variability in the population.

The shaded areas of the curves in Figure 11-6 are the **critical regions** ($p < .05$), the parts of each distribution that make up the most extreme 5% of the differences between means. Differences large enough to fall within these areas will occur by chance less than 5% of the time. If our significance level is $p < .05$, we will reject the null hypothesis if the treatment groups differ by amounts that fall within these critical regions. Do you notice anything special about where the cutoffs for the 5% levels are? You will find that they fall in a different place for each distribution. Actually, as the amount of variability in the distribution goes up, the critical regions are farther from the center of the distribution. *When there is more variability, larger differences are required to reject the null hypothesis.*

Ideally, we want our treatment conditions to be the only source of variability in an experiment. We control variables such as testing conditions and practice time that might create differences between subjects' scores and therefore introduce unwanted variability. For instance, in the time-estimation experiment, we must be careful to give everyone exactly 10 minutes to look at the cartoons. Remember, we will be making inferences about the population on the basis of the samples we observe. If our samples produce highly variable data, we must assume that the population is also highly variable on the dependent measure. If the population has high variability, finding a statistically significant effect requires very large differences between the scores from different treatment groups in the experiment. Any unnecessary sources of variation in an experiment will reduce the chances of rejecting the null hypothesis. They will increase the chances of a Type 2 error. It will be difficult to get significant results if extraneous variables are not carefully controlled.

One-Tailed and Two-Tailed Tests

In Figure 11-6 you will also notice that the critical regions of the distributions have been divided up between both ends of the curves. For each curve, the 5% critical region includes 2.5% on the low end and an additional 2.5% on the high end. These curves have been marked to illustrate a **two-tailed test** of a hypothesis: The critical region of the distribution is divided between its two tails.

We use a two-tailed test whenever we have a **nondirectional hypothesis,** one that does not predict the exact pattern of results—the direction of the effect we will produce through the experimental manipulation. For example, cars driven on oil *A* perform differently from cars driven on oil *B*. Notice that the hypothesis predicts there will be a difference between the performance of cars driven on two different brands of oil. However,

"Darling, you have made a significant difference in my life ($p < .01$)."

FIGURE **11-7**

there is no indication of what the pattern of results will be. Will cars driven on *A* perform better than those driven on *B*? The researcher has not made a prediction on that. The hypothesis is nondirectional.

You can understand why we use a two-tailed test with such a hypothesis if you think about what we mean by significance level and critical region. We want to know if our pattern of results is so unlikely that it was probably not caused by chance variations in the population; we want to know whether differences between treatment groups fall within the critical region. When a researcher states a nondirectional hypothesis, he or she is willing to accept extreme differences that go in either direction. It does not matter whether *A* is better than *B* or vice versa; the researcher has only postulated that the independent variable produces a difference. Since differences in either direction are acceptable, the critical region, the most extreme 5% of the distribution, has to be split between both tails of the curve. Suppose we did not split it, but instead included 5% on each end of the distribution. If we did that, we would be changing the significance level—we would have doubled it. We would be saying we would reject the null hypothesis if the difference fell in the most extreme 10% of the distribution.

Often we are able to make a more precise prediction about the effects of the independent variable. These may be based on our own pilot studies or on our review of prior research. A nondirectional hypothesis can often be transformed into one that is directional: Cars driven on oil *A* perform better than cars driven on oil *B*. Now we are predicting exactly what we will see when we evaluate the performance of cars driven on oils *A* and *B;* we predict that *A* will fare better than *B*.

When we have a directional hypothesis, we make a **one-tailed test:** The critical region is located in just one tail of the distribution. The hypothesis that time passes quickly when you are having fun is a directional hypothesis. It requires a one-tailed test. Figure 11-8 shows the relative locations of the critical regions of the same distribution using a one-tailed and a two-tailed test.[5] The advantage of using a one-tailed test is obvious. The size of the critical region is larger and closer to the center of the distribution, making it easier for differences between means to be large enough to fall there. You can see from the figure that the *critical value,* the minimum value needed for significance, will be smaller when we do a one-tailed test. Treatment effects do not need to be as dramatic when we have a directional hypothesis; we can get significant results more easily when we use a directional hypothesis and a one-tailed test.

You may be thinking that it will be easy to get significance now. We can just state our hypothesis in a directional way. Then if the data go in the other direction, we will change the hypothesis and still have significant results. It is a reasonable idea, but unfortunately we cannot handle things that way. Just as you need to choose a significance level in advance, you need to decide on the hypothesis in advance and stick to it. Otherwise, you have not tested anything. If you write a hypothesis to fit results you already have, you are actually describing a set of data after the fact. Of course, there

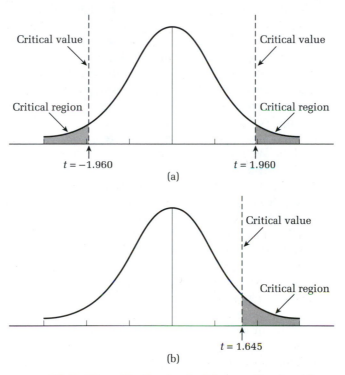

FIGURE **11-8** The critical region for (a) a nondirectional (two-tailed) test and (b) a directional (one-tailed) test.

[5] The distribution shown depicts locations of critical regions for the *t* statistic, which will be discussed in Chapter 12.

is nothing inherently wrong with offering explanations for observations. That is how we generate new hypotheses. However, we cannot call that experimentation. By definition, when we experiment we make a controlled test of a hypothesis that has already been stated.

So far we have looked at hypothetical distributions based on the means of all the samples that could be drawn from a population. These make wonderful illustrations of the concepts we are discussing. However, to draw these figures, we had to assume we were somehow able to take huge numbers of samples. In the real world, that is nearly always impossible. We do not have the actual distributions of all sample means when we run an experiment. We rarely even know the average score for the whole population. Instead, we have to draw conclusions on the basis of the few samples of subjects that we do have. To do that, we compute inferential statistics.

TEST STATISTICS

Inferential statistics are statistics that can be used as indicators of what is going on in the population. They are also called **test statistics** because they can be used to evaluate results. A test statistic is a numerical summary of what is going on in our data. When we compute a test statistic, we transform the relationship between treatment differences and variability into a simple quantitative measure. Generally speaking, the larger the test statistic, the more likely it is that the independent variable produced a change in subjects' responses. A large test statistic indicates that the differences we see across treatments are large relative to the amount of variability in the data. We are more likely to be able to reject the null hypothesis if we obtain a large test statistic.

You know there is always *some* chance that the null hypothesis really is true. It is always possible that even a large test statistic is within the range of events that could occur by chance. But think about a throw of the dice. You know that the odds of rolling 7 are greater than the odds of rolling snake eyes. How do you know? You can calculate the odds of each event. There are more ways to make 7 than there are to make 2. Similarly, researchers have worked hard to calculate just how likely every value of a test statistic would be. Each test statistic has its own distribution of values. For each value, statisticians have calculated the probability that the value could occur just by chance due to random sampling. Those values and probability levels are summarized in tables like the ones you will find at the back of this book.

Although we have anchored our discussion of statistics to examples of particular experiments, we have not dealt with many of the details of doing the actual statistical tests. In the next two chapters, we will look at how we decide which test to use. We will also look closely at the actual procedures used to compute and evaluate test statistics.

SUMMARY

In principle, experimenters would like to prove that the independent variable caused the changes observed in the behavior of subjects under different conditions. In practice, however, the best they can do is show that the differences observed were *probably* caused by the experiment. Experimenters carry out statistical tests to determine whether the independent variable probably caused the changes in the dependent variable. They really cannot prove that it did, but they can make statements about how likely it is that the independent variable had an effect.

The first step in a statistical analysis of data is setting up the *null hypothesis* (H_0), which states that the differences between treatments amount to nothing. We assume the null hypothesis is true until the evidence shows it can be rejected. The null hypothesis is necessary because we cannot automatically conclude that a difference between treatments is meaningful. Variability in the data is expected. *Variability* is the amount of fluctuation observed in scores on a dependent variable. In order to know whether to accept or reject the null hypothesis, an experimenter needs to know how much variability there is on the dependent measure. The more variability there is, the greater the difference between groups has to be before we may say that the data probably came from different populations. Since we cannot actually measure the populations, we make *statistical inferences* from the samples we do measure.

Some differences between treatments are more likely than others, and it is possible to calculate the odds that each difference will occur. The *means* (averages) of most samples are close to the mean of the population. Thus the odds of getting treatment means that are fairly similar are high. The odds of seeing much larger differences are less. The exact odds depend on the amount of variability in the population. We decide whether the differences between treatments are statistically *significant* or important on the basis of probabilities. In psychology, by convention, we usually reject the null hypothesis if the difference between treatments is so extreme that it could have occurred by chance less than 5 times out of 100. This is called a .05 *significance level.* In effect, it says that the probability of getting so large a difference just by chance is less than .05 ($p < .05$).

If we have chosen a .05 significance level and the difference between treatments is so large that it could have occurred by chance less than 5% of the time, we reject the null hypothesis. When we reject the null hypothesis, we confirm the *alternative hypothesis* (H_1), which states that the treatment data are sampled from different populations. When we reject the null hypothesis, we are saying that the experiment is the most likely explanation for the differences we have observed.

There are two types of decision errors, Type 1 and Type 2 errors. A *Type 1 error* means the experimenter has incorrectly rejected the null hypothesis: The conclusion is that the differences between treatment means were probably not caused by chance, although, in fact, they were. *Type 2 errors* occur when the independent variable really did have an effect, but the experimenter fails to detect it: The null hypothesis is accepted when the treatment means were actually drawn from different populations. A Type 1 error is usually more serious because it confirms an effect that does not exist.

The decision about the null hypothesis must take variability into account. *Test statistics,* numerical summaries of what is going on in the data, must be computed. For each test statistic, statisticians have calculated the probability of each possible value. Those probabilities are used to judge the significance of the results.

KEY TERMS

Alternative hypothesis (H_1) A statement that the data came from different populations; the research hypothesis, which cannot be tested directly.

Critical region Portion(s) of the distribution of a test statistic extreme enough to satisfy the researcher's criterion for rejecting the null hypothesis—for instance, the most extreme 5% of a distribution where $p < .05$ is the chosen significance level.

Directional hypothesis A statement that predicts the exact pattern of results that will be observed, such as which treatment group will perform best.

Inferential statistics Statistics that can be used as indicators of what is going on in a population; also called "test statistics."

Mean An arithmetical average computed by dividing the sum of a group of scores by the total number of scores.

Nondirectional hypothesis A statement that predicts a difference without predicting the exact pattern of results.

Normal curve The distribution of data in a symmetrical, bell-shaped curve.

Null hypothesis (H_0) A statement that the performance of treatment groups is so similar that the groups must belong to the same population; a way of saying that the experimental manipulation had no important effect.

One-tailed test A statistical procedure used when a directional prediction has been made; the critical region of the distribution of the test statistic (t, for instance) is measured in just one tail of the distribution.

Significance level The statistical criterion for deciding whether to accept or reject the null hypothesis.

Statistical inference A statement made about a population and all its samples based on the samples observed.

Statistical significance Meeting the set criterion for significance; the data do not support the null hypothesis; confirming a change between the groups that occurred as a result of the experiment.

Statistics Quantitative measurements of samples; quantitative data.

Test statistics   Statistics that can be used as indicators of what is going on in a population and can be used to evaluate results; also called "inferential statistics."

Two-tailed test   A statistical procedure used when a nondirectional prediction has been made; the critical region of the distribution of the test statistic (t, for instance) is divided over both tails of the distribution.

Type 1 error   An error made by rejecting the null hypothesis even though it is really true.

Type 2 error   An error made by accepting the null hypothesis even though it is really false.

Variability   Fluctuation data; can be defined numerically as the range, variance, or standard deviation.

REVIEW AND STUDY QUESTIONS

1. What is variability? Give three examples of dependent measures that you would expect to have high variability.

2. Jack is still looking for a shortcut. After running an experiment, he says: "Oh, wow. The difference between my two treatment means is 60 points. I mean, like, that's such a large difference that I'm sure my independent variable had an effect." What is Jack forgetting? Explain how you could account for his findings without assuming that his independent variable produced the difference between his treatment means.

3. What is a null hypothesis?

4. You have run an experiment to test the effects of noise on motor dexterity. It was a three-group experiment. Your three conditions were a control condition in which there was no noise, a low-noise condition, and a high-noise condition. Your three treatment means are different. State the null hypothesis for your experiment.

5. a. Julie is going to run an experiment tomorrow in which her significance level will be $p < .05$. What does that mean?
   b. If she decides to use $p < .01$ as her significance level, will it be easier or harder for her to detect the effect of the independent variable? Why?

6. For each of the following examples, explain whether the researcher has committed a Type 1 or Type 2 error and why.
   a. Dr. G. rejects the null hypothesis although the independent variable had no effect.
   b. Dr. R. correctly accepts the null hypothesis.
   c. Although the independent variable had an effect, Dr. G. accepts the null hypothesis.

7. a. What are the odds that you will make a Type 1 error in an experiment?
   b. How could you reduce those odds?

8. Given what you know about Type 1 and Type 2 errors, explain why it is important to replicate the results of an experiment.

9. For each of the following hypotheses, tell whether they are directional or nondirectional and whether they would require a one-tailed or two-tailed statistical test:
   a. Adversity builds character.
   b. Television viewing alters children's attention span.
   c. Recall of nonsense syllables improves with repeated presentations.
   d. Newborns behave differently under bright versus dim lights.
10. Mary is a little discouraged. She says: "If we cannot prove that our independent variable had an effect, why bother doing an experiment?" Explain to Mary what we do accomplish when we evaluate the results of an experiment.

REFERENCES

COHEN, J. (1969). *Statistical power analysis for the behavioral sciences.* New York: Academic Press.

VESSELO, I. R. (1965). *How to read statistics.* London: George G. Harrap.

12

Analyzing Results: Two-Group Examples

Organizing Data

Summarizing Data: Using Descriptive Statistics
Measures of Central Tendency
Measuring Variability
Computing the Variance

Which Test Do I Use?
Levels of Measurement
Selecting a Test for a Two-Group Experiment

The *t* Test
Effects of Sample Size
Degrees of Freedom
The Critical Value of *t*
Using the *t* Test
The *t* Test for Independent Groups
The *t* Test for Matched Groups

Summary

Key Terms

Review and Study Questions

References

I n Chapter 11 we discussed the principles of statistical inference. We focused on the logic behind statistical tests. By now you may be thinking, "Okay, I have all these principles. But I also have some data, and I still do not know what to do with them." By the end of this chapter, you will know how to begin your data analysis and how to carry it through when you have a two-group experiment.

We will begin by looking at the results of an experiment that has two independent groups. We will go through the basic stages of data analysis. We will organize and summarize the data and trace the process of selecting a statistical test for them. Then we will actually carry out that test. Finally, we will apply some of the same principles to handle a two-condition experiment that was run within subjects.

In Chapter 11 we considered a hypothetical experiment to compare the time estimates of two groups of subjects, those having fun and those not having fun. One group saw cartoons with captions for 10 minutes. The other group saw the same cartoons but without the captions. Our assumption was that the incomplete cartoons would not be nearly as much fun as the complete ones. Compared to subjects who saw the incomplete cartoons, we predicted that subjects who saw the complete cartoons would estimate that less time had passed. This experiment had a two-independent-groups design. Subjects were assigned at random to one of the two treatments. The exact hypothesis of the experiment was disguised. Subjects were merely told that they should examine the cartoons carefully and that they would be asked to rate them for "funniness" later. Because there were no strong arguments against it, we chose the conventional $p < .05$ significance level for this experiment.

Suppose we have actually run the experiment and we have the data. What do we do with them? Where do we begin? There are three basic steps in analyzing any set of data: First, we organize it. Second, we summarize it. Third, we apply a statistical test to interpret our results. We will look at each of these steps in detail.

If you have access to computers, you may wish to obtain packaged software to carry out the statistical procedures covered in this and the next chapter. Minitab, SPSSX, BMDP, SYSTAT, and SAS are some software programs that are currently used by psychologists. However, you will develop a greater understanding of what the procedures accomplish if you follow the examples in the chapters and work out the practice exercises yourself first.

ORGANIZING DATA

We start by organizing the data. The hypothetical data from our time-estimation experiment have been organized in Table 12-1. You can see that these data have been laid out in columns. Subjects' responses are divided into two columns, one for each of the two treatment groups. Each subject in each group is listed by number next to his or her datum. Statistical work will go more quickly and be more accurate if you begin by organizing the data and labeling them in a clear and orderly way. Especially with more complex designs, you will avoid a great deal of confusion if you take the time to prepare data tables. Many students find it easiest to use columnar paper, such as bookkeeping paper. At the very least, do your work on lined paper so you will be sure which datum belongs to which subject. You can simplify the task by preparing an orderly data sheet that you can use to record subjects' responses throughout the experiment.

SUMMARIZING DATA: USING DESCRIPTIVE STATISTICS

Published articles rarely contain the data obtained from every single subject in the experiment. The data we record as we run an experiment are called **raw data.** Like raw potatoes, they are unprocessed and sometimes hard to swallow.

Whenever we report the results of an experiment, we report **summary data** rather than raw data. Usually readers are not interested in the scores of individual subjects, and neither are we. Rather, we want to compare treatment effects, and we do that by comparing group data. (The only exception is a small N experiment.) When we have group data, we summarize them with **descriptive statistics,** shorthand ways of describing data: They represent standard procedures for summarizing results. For example, when we want to order a window shade, we do not carry the window frame to the hardware store. Instead, we summarize its character-

TABLE **12-1**

Laying out organized data			
Group 1 (Incomplete Cartoons)		Group 2 (Complete Cartoons)	
Subject	Time Estimate (min)	Subject	Time Estimate (min)
S_1	11.2	S_6	13.6
S_2	16.2	S_7	10.9
S_3	13.3	S_8	5.5
S_4	12.1	S_9	8.8
S_5	18.2	S_{10}	9.2

istics using the standard dimensions of length and width. Similarly, we summarize and describe data by using some of the standard descriptive statistics: measures of central tendency (mean, median, and mode) and measures of variability (range, variance, and standard deviation).

Measures of Central Tendency

As you know, statistics are quantitative indexes of the characteristics of our samples. Some of the most commonly computed and reported statistics are **measures of central tendency,** summary statistics that describe what is typical of a distribution of scores. The **mode** is the score that occurs most often. The **median** is the score that divides the distribution in half so that half the scores in the distribution fall above the median, half below. The **mean** is the arithmetic average: Add all the scores together and divide by the total number of scores, and you have the mean. The mean is the most commonly reported measure of central tendency. Only the mean can be manipulated algebraically (an important feature in statistical analysis).

Together, the mean, median, and mode are useful indicators of the *shape* of the distribution of values we have. If the distribution is symmetrical and has only one mode (no scores tied for most frequent), the mean, median, and mode will coincide. Distributions of scores are rarely perfectly symmetrical. More often they are asymmetrical, or *skewed*—one tail of the distribution will be longer than the other, representing more extreme low or high scores. In a skewed distribution, the mean, median, and mode will be different, and each may lead to different impressions about the data. The mean is particularly sensitive to skew; it is pulled in the direction of extreme scores. Consider this set of scores:

3 4 5 6 6 6 7 8 9

These data form a symmetrical distribution. The mean is 6, the mode is 6, and the median is also 6. Suppose we substitute a higher score into the set:

3 4 5 6 6 6 7 8 18

The distribution of scores is no longer symmetrical. Substituting the single extreme score has altered the shape of the distribution; to accommodate the extreme score, one tail is now longer than the other, so the curve has become skewed. The mode and median are still 6. However, the mean is now 7. The mean has increased because of one exceptionally large score. Alternatively, if our distribution had been skewed in the direction of an extreme low score rather than an extreme high score, the mean would have been less than the mode and median.

Even when the means of two distributions are the same, the distributions may be quite different. Reichmann (1961) cited these examples:

a. 5 5 6 6 6 6 7 7

b. 1 2 4 9 10 10

In (a) the mean is 6 and truly is typical of the data because the distribution is symmetrical. In (b) the mean is also 6, but clearly 6 is not a usual score. Note that the mode can be useful to describe distributions that contain many identical scores. The mode of (a) is 6 and the mode of (b) is 10, but obviously the mode would be more representative of (a) than (b).

Clearly, the particular statistic we choose to report can make a difference in the impression we create through our data. Wages are often cited as one category of data that is subject to distortion. The distribution of wages in the United States is not symmetrical but is skewed to the right: Lots of people earn relatively small amounts of money, whereas a few earn a great deal. The mean income is thus always higher than the median or the mode. Millionaires pull the mean up. Corporate management would prefer to use means in salary negotiations; labor would prefer to talk in terms of median or modal salaries. When evaluating any descriptive data, it is important to ask who is reporting what statistic and for what purpose. (Huff's *How to Lie with Statistics* [1954] is a delightful treatise on this topic.) Figure 12-1 shows the relationship between the mean, median, and mode for various distributions. Panel (a) illustrates a symmetrical distribution (the mean, median, and mode are the same). Panel (b) illustrates a *bimodal* distribution (two scores are tied for most frequent). Panels (c) and (d) represent two types of skewed distributions in which the mean, median, and mode are three different values.

Measuring Variability

We also use descriptive statistics to measure the amount of variability in data. So far we have talked about variability in a commonsense way: We say that anything that fluctuates has variability. When we do statistical tests, **variability** has more specific meanings. It is defined numerically by one of several descriptive statistics: the range, the variance, and the standard deviation. By using these statistics, we can compare the variability of one sample with that of another. The simplest measure of variability is the **range,** the difference between the largest and smallest scores in a set of data. If the scores on an exam varied from a high of 100 points to a low of 74, we would say that the range is 26. (Just subtract 74 from 100.) If the price of a 6-ounce bag of potato chips varies from 39 cents in one store to 53 cents in another, we would say that the price range is 14 cents. The range is often a useful measure. It can be computed quickly, and it gives a

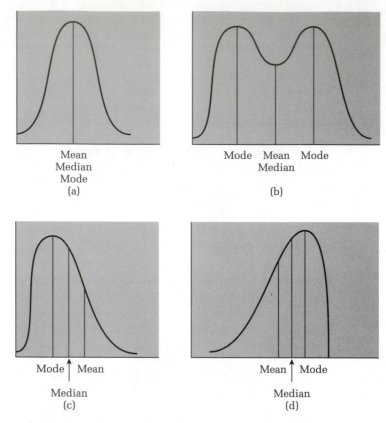

FIGURE **12-1** Mean, median, and mode in different distributions.

straightforward indication of the spread between the high and low scores in a distribution.

The problem with using the range is that it does not reflect the amount of variability in all the scores. Figure 12-2 shows you two distributions of test scores that have the same range. However, you can see that the distributions are really very different from each other. The distribution for class 1 indicates that the test scores varied a great deal from student to student. In class 2, however, most students got similar scores: One extreme score accounts for the relatively large size of the range in this case. Knowing that these distributions have the same range tells us very little about them.

Computing the Variance

When we measure variability, we would like to be able to compare different samples in a more meaningful way. Computing the statistic we call the variance enables us to do that. Computing the variance is a way of transforming variability into a standard form that provides a good but simple description of how much individual scores differ from one another. By

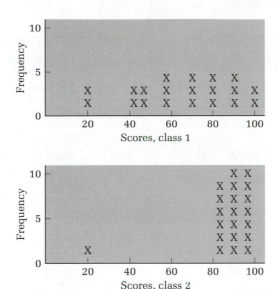

FIGURE **12-2** Two distributions with the same range (80 points).

using the variance, we can talk about the variability of all our scores without having to present an entire set of data each time, just as we can order a window shade without carrying the window frame to the shop.

The **variance** tells us something about how much scores are spread out, or *dispersed,* around the mean of the data. Are they spread out a great deal around some central value or are they tightly clustered around the mean? This can be useful information. Merchants sometimes use the concept of variance when they select stock for their stores. Let's take the example of figuring out how many pairs of women's shoes to order in a particular style. We know that the average shoe size of American women is 8½. But clearly, an individual woman's shoe size can vary considerably from this mean. But how much do sizes typically vary? Are most women going to wear a size close to an 8½ or will many women wear sizes far away from this average? Knowing how much variability to expect would help the store owner know how many pairs of each size to keep on hand. If shoe sizes vary only a little, most customers will wear a size close to 8½, and the owner could safely stock only sizes that are close to the average without missing too many sales. But if there is a lot of variance in shoe size, the owner would want to stock some number of all the smaller and larger sizes too, because it is likely that the next customer who walks through the door could have either very small or very large feet!

The variance is the average squared deviation of scores from their mean. The easiest way to explain this is to show you how we get the variance. Table 12-2 shows the steps we follow to compute the variance of the scores of one group of subjects. The scores are those of the hypothetical group of subjects who estimated the time that passed while they were look-

TABLE 12-2

Computing the variance: Time estimates of subjects who saw incomplete cartoons (in minutes)

Step 1. List each subject's score (X_i):

Subject	X_i
S_1	11.2
S_2	16.2
S_3	13.3
S_4	12.1
S_5	18.2

Step 2. Add the scores together:
$\Sigma X_i = 71.0$

Step 3. Compute the mean:

$$\overline{X} = \frac{\Sigma X_i}{N}$$

$$\overline{X} = \frac{71.0}{5}$$

$\overline{X} = 14.2$ min

Step 4. Compute the deviation from the mean for each subject ($X_i - \overline{X}$):

$11.2 - 14.2 = -3.0$
$16.2 - 14.2 = 2.0$
$13.3 - 14.2 = -0.9$
$12.1 - 14.2 = -2.1$
$18.2 - 14.2 = 4.0$

Step 5. Square the deviation from the mean for each subject ($X_i - \overline{X})^2$:

$(-3.0)(-3.0) = 9.00$
$(2.0)(2.0) = 4.00$
$(-0.9)(-0.9) = 0.81$
$(-2.1)(-2.1) = 4.41$
$(4.0)(4.0) = 16.00$

Step 6. Add the squared deviations together:
$\Sigma(X_i - \overline{X})^2 = 34.22$

Step 7. Compute the variance:

$$s^2 = \frac{\Sigma(X_i - \overline{X})^2}{N - 1}$$

$$s^2 = \frac{34.22}{5 - 1} \text{ or } 8.6 \text{ min}$$

---

ing at a series of cartoons with missing captions. The steps are numbered so that you can follow them more easily. One way or another, you will be computing the variance in just about every statistical test that you do, so it is important to master this concept.

Step 1. We have already listed each subject's score, so step 1 has been completed. Note that each subject's score is represented by X_i.

Step 2. If we have not already done so, we must compute the group mean by first adding together the scores of all the subjects in the group. The total is represented in mathematical notation by the Greek letter *sigma* (Σ).

Step 3. Once you have the total of all the scores in the group, compute the mean. Divide the total of all the scores in the sample (ΣX_i) by the number of scores you have (N). The mean is represented by $\overline{X}$. The mean, an average, gives us an idea of what the overall sample is like. The mean time estimate of this sample is 14.2 minutes. You can see that some subjects gave estimates that are above the mean and others gave estimates that are below it. In fact, in this sample there are no subjects whose estimates are exactly equal to the mean. The mean is an overall description, but how representative it is of the sample depends on other factors, such as the variance.

Step 4. We now compute the deviations from the mean for each subject. Deviations are differences between what we see and what is typical. If someone behaves in an unusual way, we say that his or her behavior deviates, or is deviant from the norm.

A sample of data has a mean—that is, an average that gives us an idea of what the sample is like. The mean of this particular sample is 14.2 minutes. This tells us that when we added up the estimates of all the subjects in the sample and divided by the number of subjects, we got 14.2 minutes. It does not say that *each* subject estimated 14.2 minutes. Actually, we know that no one in this sample said that exactly 14.2 minutes had passed: All the subjects deviated from the group mean. But by how much? We can find out simply by calculating the difference between each subject's estimate and the group mean. We subtract 14.2 ($\overline{X}$) from the actual estimate each subject gave.

Step 5. Next, we square the deviations from the mean. Remember that when we multiply a negative number (for example, -30) by itself, the result is a positive number. That means that all squared deviations from the mean will be positive numbers even though some of the subjects fell below the mean and so had negative deviations from the mean.

Step 6. Now we add all the deviations together to get a total of squared deviations from the mean.

Step 7. Finally, we compute the variance. You can see that we need the results of steps 1 through 6 before we can do step 7. The formula is just a shorthand way of writing all the operations we perform to get the variance. The variance for a sample is represented by s^2. The s comes from the Greek letter *sigma,* used to represent the variance of a population. The formula tells us that to get the variance of a sample, we must divide the sum of the squared deviations from the mean by $N - 1$. N is the number of scores.

The variance formula actually tells us to compute an average—the *average of the squared deviations from the mean.* That is exactly what we mean by variance. The variance is an indicator of how much variability there is in our data. The more variability, the larger the variance. You may be wondering why the variance formula tells us to divide by $N - 1$, not simply by N: When we compute the mean, we divide by N. When we compute the variance for a sample, we are actually trying to estimate how much variability there is in the population we are sampling. Since we cannot measure the whole population, we draw inferences from samples. Statisticians have shown that samples typically *underestimate* the variance of the population because small samples can miss some very extreme scores that would be likely to occur if the entire population were tested. So we correct for this in the variance formula. We get a more accurate estimate of how much variability there is in the population if we compute the variance of a sample by dividing by $N - 1$ instead of by N.

The variance for the subjects who were shown the incomplete cartoons is 8.6 minutes.[1] This tells us that, on average, the *square* of each subject's deviation from the group mean is 8.6 minutes. If we take the *square root* of the variance (s^2), we have another useful measure of variability, the **standard deviation,** or *s*. It reflects the average deviation of scores about the mean. We cannot compute that average directly by adding up the deviations; the total of the deviations from the mean is always zero. So we use the square root of the variance to return to the original unsquared units of measurement. The standard deviation of our "no-fun" group means that, on average, we can expect each individual subject to deviate from the group mean by 2.93 minutes. We use the same procedures for each treatment group. To save time, we will tell you that those computations yield a group mean of 9.6 minutes and a variance of 8.8 minutes for the "fun group," subjects who saw cartoons complete with caption. You may want to verify those figures by working through the formulas on your own.

When we report the results of our experiments, we usually report these summary statistics in place of raw data. Typically, we give the mean and the variance or standard deviation of each treatment group. We may also report the range, although the range is often not given in published reports because of its limited use. We have now completed the first two stages of analyzing our results: We have organized and summarized the data. We will use the summary data again when we do the statistical tests.

WHICH TEST DO I USE?

The discussion of how to choose a statistical test was postponed until now so that the various aspects of data analysis could be presented first. However, in practice, it is best to select a test (and a significance level) as you plan the design of the experiment.

When we looked at experimental designs, we developed a set of questions to help us choose the best design for an experiment. We can make decisions about which statistical tests to use in much the same way. The number of independent variables is still important. How many do you have? How many treatment groups? Is the experiment within or between subjects? Did you use matching? As you become more familiar with selecting and using statistics, you will not need to go through all these steps. But you will find it much easier to choose the right test if you begin with these questions. In addition to the number of independent variables and treatment conditions, we need to consider the type of data we are analyzing. The way we measured the dependent variable makes a difference in the way we handle the results. There are different statistical tests for different kinds of data.

---

[1] We have rounded this off to the nearest tenth. Remember the conventions used for rounding: We round down if the last digit is less than 5; we round up if the last digit is more than 5. If the last digit is 5, we follow this rule: Round up if the digit to be rounded off is an odd number; simply drop the 5 if the digit to be rounded is an even number. Thus 8.35 becomes 8.4, and 4.65 becomes 4.6.

Levels of Measurement

Recall from Chapter 4 that the **level of measurement** is the kind of scale used to measure a variable. There are four levels of measurement: ratio, interval, ordinal, and nominal. To review quickly, a **ratio scale** has equal intervals between all its values and an absolute zero point. These attributes enable us to express relationships between values on these scales as ratios: We can say 2 pounds are twice as heavy as 1 pound.

An **interval scale** also measures magnitude, or quantitative size, and has equal intervals between values. However, it has no true zero point.

An **ordinal scale** reflects differences only in magnitude, where magnitude is measured in the form of ranks. We cannot be sure that the intervals between values are equal, and the scale has no absolute zero.

A **nominal scale** classifies items into distinct categories that have no quantitative relationship to one another. Nominal scaling provides the least information. It tells nothing about magnitude, nor does it have equal intervals between values.

Variables may be measured by using one of these four types of scales. We have looked mainly at ratio and interval data in our examples because these scales yield the most information and researchers tend to prefer them. But remember that different techniques are needed for different types of data.

Selecting a Test for a Two-Group Experiment

To select the appropriate statistical test, first decide which level of measurement you will use to measure the dependent variable and then answer the other questions summarized in Table 12-3. You now have all the information you need to select a statistical test.

Let us return to our time-estimation example. How will we know which statistical test to use? First, let's answer the questions from Table 12-3.

1. There is one independent variable (fun).
2. There are two treatment conditions (fun versus no fun).
3. The experiment is run between subjects. (There are different subjects in each treatment condition.)
4. The subjects are not matched.
5. The dependent variable is measured by a ratio scale. (Time estimates have magnitude, equal intervals, and an absolute zero—there is no way to score below zero.)[2]

---

[2] It can be argued that time estimates do not constitute a *true* ratio scale because we have no way of knowing whether subjects use equal intervals between values. The 1st minute of waiting in line, for example, might seem longer or shorter than the 31st. The same argument can be made regarding other dependent measures that rely on subjects' perceptions, such as ratings of attractiveness. This difficulty is often ignored by researchers because the statistical tests commonly used are reasonably accurate in spite of it.

TABLE **12-3**

**The parameters
of data analysis**

1. How many independent variables are there?
2. How many treatment conditions are there?
3. Is the experiment run between or within subjects?
4. Are the subjects matched?
5. What is the level of measurement of the dependent variable?

With this information, we can select a possible test to use for the data. Table 12-4 shows the most common statistical tests, organized by the number of independent variables they can handle, the level of measurement of the dependent variable, and whether the experiment is within or between subjects. We will not discuss all the tests in detail; the table note supplies sources to consult for further information.

There are other tests that we do not even list, but they are used less often and you may not need them until you take more advanced courses. Here and in the next chapter we will focus on the tests you are most likely to need for your first experiments.

The table indicates "possible" tests; it does not tell us what we will definitely need in all cases. That is because it may be possible to use more than one test. Also, before using any test, we must be sure we have the kind of data the test was designed to handle. This goes beyond asking whether our level of measurement is appropriate. As you learn about the tests, you will also learn that each test has its own additional requirements.

THE *t* TEST

For our hypothetical experiment, Table 12-4 suggests the *t* test for independent groups. When we want to evaluate interval or ratio data from a two-group experiment, we compute the test statistic *t*, which is a computational way of relating differences between treatment means to the amount of variability we would expect to see between any two sets of data drawn from the same population. When we evaluate the likelihood of obtaining a particular value of *t*, we are performing a **t test.**

The exact probabilities of each value of *t* have been calculated for us. However, the distribution of these values changes depending on the number of subjects in the samples. Before actually computing *t* for the time-estimation example, let us examine the family of *t* distributions and the effects of sample size.

TABLE **12-4**

Selecting a possible statistical test by number of independent variables and level of measurement						
	One Independent Variable				Two Independent Variables	
	Two Treatments		More Than Two		Factorial Designs	
Level of Measurement of Dependent Variable	Two Independent Groups	Two Matched Groups (or Within Subjects)	Multiple Independent Groups	Multiple Matched Groups (or Within Subjects)	Independent Groups	Matched Groups (or Within Subjects)
Interval or ratio	t test for independent groups	t test for matched groups	One-way ANOVA (randomized)	One-way ANOVA (repeated measures)	Two-way ANOVA	Two-way ANOVA (repeated measures)
Ordinal	Mann-Whitney U test	Wilcoxon test	Kruskal–Wallis test	Friedman test	—	—
Nominal	Chi square test	—	Chi square test	—	—	—

NOTE: *Shaded boxes list tests not discussed in this text. You can find explanations of them in most standard texts on statistics. A good source is McCall, R. B. (1980),* Fundamental statistics for psychology *(3rd ed.), New York: Harcourt Brace Jovanovich. See Winer, B. J. (1971),* Statistical principles in experimental design, *New York: McGraw-Hill, for repeated measures procedures.*

Effects of Sample Size

Size of sample is very important. If we take both small and large samples from the same population, we will generally find that small samples vary more from the mean of the population than large samples do. You know that test statistics represent a relationship between treatment effects and variability. If sample size affects variability, it also affects the size of the test statistics.

For a test statistic such as *t,* sample size is critical because the exact shape of the distribution of *t* changes depending on the size of the samples. The *t* statistic has a whole family of distributions, some of which are shown in Figure 12-3. The *t* distributions resemble the normal curve we looked at in Chapter 11. They are symmetrical, with the greatest concentration of values around the mean. The shape of the *t* distribution becomes more and more like the normal curve as the sample size increases. With small samples, the *t* distribution has a flatter and wider shape.

Sample size is also important because of the assumptions we make whenever we apply *t.* One of the requirements of a *t* test is that the data to be analyzed (interval or ratio) come from populations that are normally distributed. We must be able to assume that if we could somehow measure

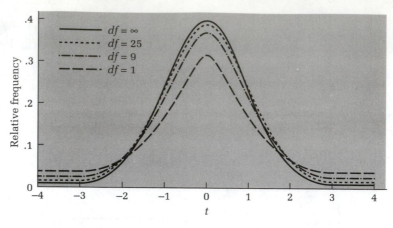

FIGURE **12-3** Some members of the family of *t* distributions. Adapted from *Quantitative Methods in Psychology,* by D. Lewis. Copyright © 1960 by McGraw-Hill, Inc. Reprinted by permission.

all the members of the population, their scores on the dependent variable would form a normal curve. If the data come from populations that are not normally distributed, we have a problem. The odds of getting each individual *t* value were worked out for populations that are normally distributed. If the data do not come from such populations, the odds that have been worked out for *t* will be wrong for those data. Of course, we can hardly ever measure all the members of a population. We get around this problem by using large samples so that the correct odds of each *t* value are very close to what they would be if the population were normally distributed. This is rarely a problem because the *t* test is relatively **robust**—the assumption of a normal distribution of population values can be violated without creating serious errors. If there are at least 10 to 20 subjects in each treatment group, a *t* test is probably safe; with 30 subjects in a group, most researchers would not worry at all.

Degrees of Freedom

We select the appropriate *t* distribution based on **degrees of freedom (df)**. (Figure 12-3 refers to degrees of freedom [*df*] rather than number of subjects.) The degrees of freedom tell us how many members of a set of data could vary or change value without changing the value of a statistic we already know for those data. Samples that are the same size can have different degrees of freedom depending on the way the experiment is designed and on the statistic being computed. Let us say we know the mean of the data. Then the degrees of freedom tell us how many members of that set of data could change without altering the value of the mean.

Imagine that a phone number is a set of data. It has seven digits. Suppose that the total of the seven digits in the number is 37 and that the first six digits of the number are 8, 9, 4, 3, 9, and 2. Can you find the last digit? Of course you can. Since you know the total and six of the digits, you can easily compute the value of the last digit, which is *not free to vary*. Different combinations of the first six digits are possible. But once their values have been set, the value of the last digit is also set if the total must equal 37. If we tried to substitute any other value for the seventh digit, the total, or the known statistic, would no longer be correct. The degrees of freedom for this phone number therefore equal 6. If we include an area code in the data, say 2, 1, 2, we would say that the telephone number has 10 digits. It now totals 42. Its degrees of freedom now equal $10 - 1$, or 9. Clearly, the degrees of freedom are related to the number of digits, or data, in a sample.

Similarly, the degrees of freedom in the distribution of a statistic vary in a way related to the number of subjects sampled. However, we compute degrees of freedom differently for different test statistics. Sometimes all but one value of a set of data can change, sometimes fewer. The way we compute the degrees of freedom can also be different for different applications of the same statistic. The way we compute the degrees of freedom for *t*, for instance, changes depending on what we are testing with *t*. If we are using different statistics or the same statistic applied in different ways, we may have different degrees of freedom, even though sample sizes are identical. That is why the critical values of test statistics are always presented and organized by degrees of freedom rather than by number of subjects.

The Critical Value of *t*

Let us look more closely at two distributions of *t* to get a clearer idea of how degrees of freedom will affect the critical value of *t*. The **critical value of *t*** is the *minimum* value necessary to reject the null hypothesis at our chosen significance level. Figure 12-4 shows distributions of *t* for 25 and 9 degrees of freedom. It also shows the critical values of *t* for the $p < .05$ significance level using a two-tailed test. What is the relationship between these levels?

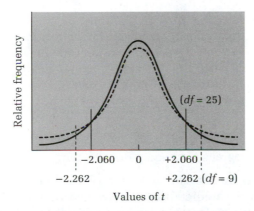

FIGURE **12-4**   The *t* distribution for 25 and 9 degrees of freedom and critical values at $p < .05$.

As the t distribution changes shape, the critical value of t needed to reject the null hypothesis also changes. Remember that the significance level, or critical level, refers to probabilities. We are looking to see whether the value of t that we compute from our data is more or less likely than our chosen critical value. If the experimental manipulation was effective, the computed value of t should be more extreme than the chosen critical value. In terms of probabilities, this means that the computed value of t is so extreme that it is unlikely it could have occurred by chance less than 5% of the time.

It is easy to see that the distribution for 9 degrees of freedom is flatter and wider than the other curve shown. In terms of probabilities, you can see that the most extreme 5% of this distribution falls relatively far out on the curve. Smaller degrees of freedom mean more variability between samples. That means that more and more cases will be far from the mean of the population; large differences between samples can be expected to occur relatively often just by chance. Thus the tails of the t distribution will get fatter as sample size (and degrees of freedom) get smaller. With 25 degrees of freedom, the tails of the t distribution are thinner: The most extreme 5% of the distribution falls closer to the mean.

Can you see what this means for our decision about the null hypothesis? We will reject the null hypothesis if the computed value of t is more extreme than the most extreme 5% of the distribution. Because the distribution changes shape as the degrees of freedom change, the critical value of t also changes. In fact, the critical value of t (the value needed to reject the null hypothesis) gets larger as the degrees of freedom get smaller. The fewer the subjects, the less likely it is that we will be able to reject the null hypothesis. The fewer the subjects, the higher the critical value of t needed to demonstrate a statistically significant effect from an experimental manipulation. And with fewer subjects, we also have a greater chance of making a Type 2 error.

Using the t Test

Before we can use the t test, we have to know how to find the critical values of t. Fortunately, they have been worked out for us and organized into tables in which we can find them quickly and easily. To use the statistical tables, we need three pieces of information.

1. Will we use a directional or nondirectional test (that is, a one- or two-tailed test)?
2. What is our significance level?
3. How many degrees of freedom do we have?

In our experiment on fun, we have a directional hypothesis. Our directional hypothesis predicts that the average time estimate of the no-fun group will be greater than the average time estimate of the fun group. That means that we may use a one-tailed test. We chose a $p < .05$ significance level. The degrees of freedom (df) for this experiment equal the total number of subjects in both groups minus the number of groups. Here, $df = 5 + 5 - 2$, or 8. Now turn to Appendix B and find Table B2, which shows the critical values of t for both one- and two-tailed tests and several degrees of freedom. Find the critical value of t for 8 df, a one-tailed test, and $p < .05$.

The critical value of t for this experiment is 1.86.[3] If our *observed value of* t (the value we compute) is less than 1.86, we must accept the null hypothesis. Computed values of t that are less extreme than the critical value indicate that differences between our treatment groups are not large enough to be significant. They were probably caused by chance variations between the samples. If the computed value of t is equal to or greater than 1.86, we reject the null hypothesis. If the computed value of t is more extreme than the critical value in the table, it is unlikely that the differences between treatment groups can be explained simply by chance; and in a well-controlled experiment, the most likely explanation is that differences were produced by the independent variable.[4]

The *t* Test for Independent Groups

We cannot just compare raw data or absolute differences between treatment groups; we must evaluate the results by taking variability into account. Just by chance, treatment groups are likely to differ somewhat even if the independent variable had no effect. Computing a test statistic gives a numerical index of this relationship; t is just one of many test statistics we can compute. We use the ***t* test for independent groups** when we have two different, randomly selected samples of subjects, randomly assigned to two treatments, and interval or ratio data. Let us use t to analyze the results of the time-estimation experiment. The hypothetical data from that experiment are summarized in Table 12-5.

The table tells us at a glance that the performance of the groups is different. The mean time estimate of subjects in the no-fun group is 14.2 minutes; that of subjects in the fun group is 9.6 minutes. Of course, we know that this absolute difference may not be significant. We have to evaluate the difference in terms of the amount of variability we find between any samples drawn from the population. We have to decide whether to retain or reject the null hypothesis. To do that, we must compute the observed value of t (t_{obs}) for these data using the formula below:

$$t_{obs} = \frac{\overline{X}_1 - \overline{X}_2}{\sqrt{\left(\frac{(N_1 - 1)s_1^2 + (N_2 - 1)s_2^2}{(N_1 + N_2 - 2)}\right) \cdot \left(\frac{1}{N_1} + \frac{1}{N_2}\right)}}$$

[3] You already know that it is easier to get statistical significance with a one-tailed test. If we had not made a directional prediction, the critical value of t (two-tailed, $p < .05$) would have been 2.306.

[4] Computed and critical values of t will be negative numbers in cases where the $\overline{X}$ of group 2 is larger than the $\overline{X}$ of group 1.

TABLE **12-5**

Summary data for a hypothetical experiment on fun and time estimation	
No-Fun Group (Group 1)	Fun Group (Group 2)
$\overline{X}_1 = 14.2$ min	$\overline{X}_2 = 9.6$ min
$s_1{}^2 = 8.6$ min	$s_2{}^2 = 8.8$ min
$N_1 = 5$	$N_2 = 5$

NOTE: *Since we predicted that the no-fun group will make larger time estimates, we labeled that group "group 1." Given our prediction, $\overline{X}_1 - \overline{X}_2$ should be a positive number and our computed value of t should be positive. It does not really matter which way the groups are labeled as long as we set up the critical value of t (in a positive or negative direction) consistent with our predictions and our computations of t. We are using hypothetical data here to keep things simple. If you were actually running this experiment, you would want to have more than five subjects in each treatment group.*

The computation of *t* for these data is shown in Table 12-6. The formula is just a shorthand way of writing the steps to get *t*. If you take it slowly and step by step, you should have no trouble.

When we first talked about test statistics in a general way, we said that they represent a relationship between treatment effects and variability. If you think about what is shown in the formula for *t,* you will see very clearly how that principle is applied. The numerator (the top) tells us to find the difference between the means of the two treatment groups. If the independent variable had a large effect, we would expect this difference to be relatively large. Notice that the denominator of the formula (the bottom) is a collection of terms that represents the variances of the treatment groups and the number of subjects in each group. The denominator is an estimate of variability. If the ratio between the two components is relatively large, we may be able to reject the null hypothesis. We will reject it if the computed value of *t* is more extreme than 1.86. If the value of t_{obs} is more extreme than that, the odds are good that the difference between the groups did not occur by chance.

The computed value of *t* turns out to be 2.47. Since a value of 2.47 is more extreme than the critical value, we reject the null hypothesis: There is a significant difference between the time estimates of subjects who had fun and subjects who did not. How much importance we wish to attach to these findings depends partly on our assessment of the quality of this experiment. Were control procedures adequate? Were variables defined appropriately? These issues will influence our final judgment. The possibility of a Type 1 error must be considered. Before we can draw any sweeping conclusions from the findings, we should replicate the experiment. We will return to these issues when we discuss the interpretation of results.

TABLE **12-6**

Computation of t for the data presented in Table 12-5, the hypothetical experiment on fun and time estimation

Step 1. Lay out the formula.

$$t_{obs} = \frac{\overline{X}_1 - \overline{X}_2}{\sqrt{\left(\dfrac{(N_1 - 1)s_1{}^2 + (N_2 - 1)s_2{}^2}{(N_1 + N_2 - 2)}\right) \cdot \left(\dfrac{1}{N_1} + \dfrac{1}{N_2}\right)}}$$

Step 2. Put in all the quantities needed.

$$t_{obs} = \frac{14.2 - 9.6}{\sqrt{\left(\dfrac{(5 - 1)8.6 + (5 - 1)8.8}{(5 + 5 - 2)}\right) \cdot \left(\dfrac{1}{5} + \dfrac{1}{5}\right)}}$$

Step 3. Calculate the difference between treatment means; begin simplifying the denominator.

$$t_{obs} = \frac{4.6}{\sqrt{\left(\dfrac{(4)8.6 + (4)8.8}{(8)}\right) \cdot \left(\dfrac{1}{5} + \dfrac{1}{5}\right)}}$$

Step 4. Continue simplifying the denominator.

$$t_{obs} = \frac{4.6}{\sqrt{\left(\dfrac{34.4 + 35.2}{(8)}\right) \cdot \left(\dfrac{1}{5} + \dfrac{1}{5}\right)}}$$

Step 5. Remember to complete all operations inside the parentheses first.

$$t_{obs} = \frac{4.6}{\sqrt{\left(\dfrac{69.6}{8}\right) \cdot \left(\dfrac{2}{5}\right)}}$$

Step 6. Convert all fractions in the denominator to decimals.

$$t_{obs} = \frac{4.6}{\sqrt{(8.7) \cdot (.40)}}$$

Step 7. Complete the multiplication.

$$t_{obs} = \frac{4.6}{\sqrt{(3.48)}}$$

Step 8. Remember to take the square root of the denominator.

$$t_{obs} = \frac{4.6}{1.86}$$

Step 9. Divide the numerator by the denominator and you have the computed value of t. Compare it with the critical value.

$$t_{obs} = 2.47$$

NOTE: df $= N_1 + N_2 - 2$; df $= 5 + 5 - 2$, or 8.

The *t* Test for Matched Groups

The procedures we have discussed so far assume that the two samples of subjects are independent, randomly selected groups. We need different procedures when we look at the data for matched groups of subjects. If we did statistical tests for these experiments in the same way as for an independent-groups experiment, we would overestimate the amount of variability in the population sampled.

You know that subjects are apt to differ on a dependent variable simply because subjects are not all the same. Even if we are testing rats, we find that some run faster than others. One source of variability is individual differences. Subjects' scores vary because subjects differ from one another.

BOX **12-1**
A two-group, within-subjects example

Robert Yin had already done research showing that people had trouble recognizing photographs of faces they had seen upside down (Yin, 1969). (Figure 12-5 shows an upside-down example.) Now he wanted to test whether inversion would affect recognition of line drawings as well. He showed the same subjects two sets of drawings of faces.* After each set, he showed subjects pairs of drawings and asked them to pick out the drawing they had seen before in each pair. Subjects saw one set of drawings and test pairs in the usual upright position; the other set was shown to them upside down. The order of presentation was counterbalanced across subjects to control for order effects.

FIGURE **12-5** Do you recognize this person? © NBC Photography

* Yin tested for effects on the memory of costumed figures as well as faces. Since he used the same procedures to handle both kinds of pictures, we will focus only on faces. Yin's results for the costumed figures were similar but less dramatic than the results for the inverted faces.

Even the scores of the *same* subjects measured at different times vary, but they usually do not vary quite as much as the responses of different subjects. Neither do the scores of subjects who are matched on a relevant variable. For these reasons, the way that we compute variability changes when we use matched groups or a within-subjects design. You will get a better sense of how these procedures compare by looking at an example of a within-subjects experiment done with two treatment conditions. The research problem is summarized in Box 12-1.

What statistical test would you use for the Yin experiment? (See Table 12-4.) This experiment is similar to the time-estimation example. We are looking at one independent variable, two treatment conditions, and a ratio scale of measurement (that is, number of correct identifications). However, this experiment is also quite different because it was run with only one group of subjects: It was a within-subjects experiment. The appropriate statistical test is a *t* test for matched groups. Obviously, the treatment groups were not matched per se in this experiment; they are simply the same subjects, and there may be no better match than that.

The *t* **test for matched groups** uses the same family of *t* distributions you have already seen. It also applies to interval and ratio data and requires the assumption that the population sampled is normally distributed on the dependent variable. But because it is used to evaluate data from an experiment in which the treatment groups are not independent, the computations are handled differently.

Table 12-7 shows how data and computations from a within-subjects (or matched-groups) experiment would look, based on the inverted-faces experiment. The data are hypothetical and are presented just to illustrate the procedures simply; Yin used many more subjects. The scores for each subject represent the number of correct responses each made under each treatment condition. The table also illustrates the computation of *t* for matched groups: We use exactly the same procedures for within-subjects and matched-groups experiments with two treatment conditions.

From the table, you can see that we compute *t* for these data by looking at differences between each subject's performance under the two treatment conditions. This reflects the logic behind the design we are using. We are evaluating the effect of the independent variable *within* each subject. Similarly, when we have matched pairs of subjects, we want to look at the effects of our independent variable within each matched pair. The observed value of *t* for these data is $t_{obs} = 4.81$. How does that compare to the critical value of *t*? Can we reject the null hypothesis? Who knows? Unfortunately, we never bothered to figure out what the critical value of *t* would be. Of course, we need to look at Table B2 (see Appendix B). Assume that the researcher had decided to use a $p < .05$ significance level. Should we use a one- or a two-tailed test? Although Yin (1969) might have made a directional prediction based on prior evidence, he was simply testing the notion that inversion would affect line drawings of faces. He did not specify the direction of the effect, so a two-tailed test is appropriate.

Since we computed *t* for this experiment with different procedures, we also have to compute *df* differently. Because we are looking at differences between pairs of scores, our *df* is based on the number of pairs. The *df* for two matched groups is $N - 1$, where N is the number of pairs. The *df* for this experiment is $5 - 1$, or 4. If you look at Table B2, you will see that the critical value of *t* for 4 *df* and a two-tailed test ($p < .05$) is 2.776. Since the computed value of *t* (4.81) is more extreme than the critical value, we reject the null hypothesis, which says that these data were sampled from the same population. (The actual data from Yin's experiment also yielded a

TABLE **12-7**

Evaluating data from a within-subjects experiment on memory for inverted faces (scores represent number recalled correctly)

Subject (or Pair)	Upright Faces (X_1)	Inverted Faces (X_2)	Difference Scores $(X_1 - X_2) = D_i$	D_i^2
S_1	5	3	$(5 - 3) = 2$	4
S_2	3	2	$(3 - 2) = 1$	1
S_3	4	3	$(4 - 3) = 1$	1
S_4	5	3	$(5 - 3) = 2$	4
S_5	3	0	$(3 - 0) = 3$	9
			$\Sigma D_i = 9$	$\Sigma D_i^2 = 19$

Computing t

Step 1. This formula for *t* requires difference scores (D_i). The computation of *t* is based on differences between pairs of scores rather than group means. (Note how difference scores were computed above.)

$$t_{obs} = \frac{\Sigma D_i}{\sqrt{\dfrac{N\Sigma D_i^2 - (\Sigma D_i)^2}{N - 1}}}$$

Step 2. Put in all the required values. Note that *N* stands for the number of pairs of data.

$$t_{obs} = \frac{9}{\sqrt{\dfrac{5(19) - (9)^2}{5 - 1}}}$$

Step 3. Simplify the denominator. Remember to take the square root.

$$t_{obs} = \frac{9}{\sqrt{\dfrac{(95) - (81)}{4}}} \text{ or } \frac{9}{\sqrt{\dfrac{14}{4}}}$$

Step 4. Our computed *t*. We are now ready to make a decision on the null hypothesis.

$$t_{obs} = 4.81$$

$df = N - 1$, where *N* is the number of pairs of scores.

NOTE: *A* t *test for matched groups, to be used for two matched groups or a two-condition within-subjects design, ratio or interval data only. These hypothetical scores represent the number of drawings correctly recognized out of five presented in each condition.*

significant difference: Subjects had significantly more difficulty recognizing drawings presented upside down.)

Notice that using the within-subjects procedures affects the critical value of *t*. In the last example, we had five subjects in each treatment group for a total of ten scores—just as we have here—but when we use the within-subjects or matched-groups *t*, we end up with many fewer degrees of freedom. Even though we have the same number of actual scores in both examples, we have about half as many degrees of freedom when we use the *t* test for matched groups. And if you look at Table B2, you will notice that the critical value of *t* needed to reject the null hypothesis increases as the degrees of freedom get smaller. The fewer degrees of freedom we have, the more difficult it will be to reject the null hypothesis. It takes a more extreme *t* to reach significance in the matched-groups or within-subjects experiment. Compare the two-tailed critical values of *t* ($p < .05$) for 4 *df* and 8 *df* and you will see that you need a larger *t* when you have fewer degrees of freedom.

If we need a larger value of t in a within-subjects or matched-groups experiment, why would we bother to match subjects or use a within-subjects design at all? It seems as though it would be easier to find a significant difference with the independent-groups design. But actually, it would not. We have not yet discussed all the reasons for variability in data, but one thing should be clear: If we measure the responses of *different* subjects, we are likely to get much more variability than if we measure the same subjects, or matched subjects. Using the matched-groups design lowers the amount of variability in the data. Look at the formulas for t: The denominator (the bottom) of each formula reflects variability. When we reduce variability among individual subjects, we make the denominator of the t formula smaller. That in turn makes the computed value of t a great deal larger. To put it more simply, when we use a matched-groups or a within-subjects design, we have a tradeoff: We lower the degrees of freedom for the experiment, but we also lower the amount of variability produced by factors other than the independent variable. And as you already know, that can give us a more precise measure of the effect of the experimental manipulation.[5]

SUMMARY

There are four basic steps in analyzing results: (1) *organize the data;* (2) *summarize them;* (3) *apply the appropriate statistical test;* (4) *interpret the outcome of the test.* We organize data by making sure that all subjects' responses are labeled clearly and separated by treatment condition. We summarize data by computing *descriptive statistics,* shorthand representations of data. Some commonly used descriptive statistics are the *measures of central tendency* (mean, median, and mode) and *measures of variability* (range, variance, and standard deviation).

The *mean* is the arithmetic average of all scores in a group. The *mode* is the most frequent score. The *median* is the score that divides the distribution in half.

We also want to know how much variability there is among subjects' scores: how much they differ from one another. The *range* is the difference between the largest and the smallest scores in a set of data. Two distributions with the same range can look quite different; the range shows only how much the highest and lowest scores differ. The *variance* is a more precise indication of the amount of variability. It reflects the amount of variability among all the scores in a distribution, and so it is a more useful indicator than the range. The larger the variance, the more subjects' scores differ from one another. The *standard deviation* is the square root of the variance. It reflects the average deviation of scores about the mean. Finding the standard deviation converts "squared deviations" back to the original unsquared units of measurement. The larger the standard deviation, the more each individual subject is apt to differ from the group mean.

[5] Don't forget the other benefit of the within-subjects design—you have only used half as many subjects as you did in the matched-groups or independent-groups design.

Five basic questions help us choose an appropriate statistical test: (1) How many independent variables are there? (2) How many treatment conditions are there? (3) Is the experiment run between or within subjects? (4) Are the subjects matched? (5) What is the level of measurement of the dependent variable?

A common statistical test is the t *test for independent groups.* We use *t* tests to evaluate interval or ratio data from two-group experiments. The *t* statistic is a computational way of relating differences between treatment means to the amount of variability expected between any two samples of data from the same population. One of the assumptions of the test is that the data come from populations that are normally distributed on the dependent variable. A *t* test is done by computing a *t* statistic for the data. The computed value of *t* is compared to the *critical value of t* based on the chosen significance level. If the computed value of *t* is more extreme than the critical value, the null hypothesis is rejected; the difference between treatment means is statistically significant.

The *t* statistic has a whole family of distributions. The appropriate distribution is selected based on the *degrees of freedom* for the experiment. The degrees of freedom indicate how many members of a set of data could vary or change value without changing the value of a statistic already known for that data. With two independent groups, the degrees of freedom for *t* are equal to the total number of subjects minus 2. As the degrees of freedom of *t* get larger, the critical value of *t* gets less extreme. In addition to the degrees of freedom, the critical value of *t* also depends on whether the hypothesis is directional or nondirectional.

A within-subjects design or matching in a two-group experiment requires a different statistical procedure, the t *test for matched groups.* The same family of *t* distributions that apply to the independent-groups procedures are used for this test. However, *t* for matched or within-subjects data is computed by looking at the differences between each pair of responses. This procedure decreases the degrees of freedom, making it somewhat harder to reject the null hypothesis. However, using the matched-groups procedures to compute *t* greatly reduces the estimate of variability in the data and results in a more precise measure of the effect of the independent variable.

KEY TERMS

Critical value of *t*   The minimum value of the test statistic necessary to reject the null hypothesis at the chosen significance level.

Degrees of freedom (*df*)   The number of members of a set of data that can vary or change value without changing the value of a known statistic for those data.

Descriptive statistics   The standard procedures used to summarize and describe data quickly and clearly; summary statistics reported for an experiment, including mean, range, and standard deviation.

Interval scale   The measurement of magnitude, or quantitative size, having equal intervals between values but no true zero point.

Level of measurement   The type of scale of measurement—either ratio, interval, ordinal, or nominal—used to measure a variable.

Mean   An arithmetical average computed by dividing the sum of a group of scores by the total number of scores.

Measures of central tendency   Summary statistics that describe what is typical of a distribution of scores.

Median   The score that divides a distribution in half so that half the scores in the distribution fall above the median, half below; a measure of central tendency.

Mode   The most frequently occurring score in a distribution; a measure of central tendency.

Nominal scale   The simplest level of measurement; classifies items into two or more distinct categories on the basis of some common feature.

Ordinal scale   A measure of magnitude in which each value is measured in the form of ranks.

Range   The difference between the largest and smallest scores in a set of data; a rough indication of the amount of variability in the data.

Ratio scale   A measure of magnitude having equal intervals between values and having an absolute zero point.

Raw data   Data recorded as an experiment is run; the responses of individual subjects.

Robust   The assumption of a normal distribution of population values can be violated without creating serious errors.

Standard deviation   The square root of the variance; measures the average deviation of scores about the mean, thus reflecting the amount of variability in the data.

Summary data   Descriptive statistics computed from the raw data of an experiment, including the measures of central tendency.

***t* test**   The procedure used to evaluate the likelihood of a particular difference between treatment means by computing the test statistic *t;* used to analyze the results of a two-condition experiment with one independent variable and interval or ratio data.

***t* test for independent groups**   The procedure used to evaluate the likelihood of a particular difference between treatment means by computing the test statistic *t;* used to analyze the results of a two-group experiment with independent groups of subjects.

***t* test for matched groups**   The procedure used to evaluate the likelihood of a particular difference between treatment means by computing the test statistic *t;* used to analyze two-group experiments using matched-subjects or within-subjects designs. Sometimes referred to as a within-subjects *t* test.

Variability   Fluctuation in data; can be defined numerically as the range, variance, or standard deviation.

Variance   The average squared deviation of scores from their mean; a more precise measure of variability than the range.

REVIEW AND STUDY QUESTIONS

1. What are the four basic stages of analyzing the results of an experiment?
2. What are descriptive statistics? Why do we need them in an experiment?
3. Define each of the following and explain what each tells us about a set of data:
   a. The mean
   b. The range
   c. The variance
   d. The standard deviation
4. Two families have the same average income per person. Does this mean that each person in both families earns the same amount of money? Explain.
5. Below are two distributions of scores on a memory test. Find the mean, range, variance, and standard deviation of each group.

Group 1	Group 2
5	3
6	1
8	3
3	2
1	5

6. What five basic questions must we answer before we can select the appropriate statistical test for an experiment?
7. What is a t test? When is it used?
8. Briefly outline the difference between the t test for independent groups and the t test for matched groups.
9. Our computed value of t is more extreme than the critical value. What does that mean? Do we accept or reject the null hypothesis?
10. Our computed value of t is less extreme than the table value. What does that mean? Do we accept or reject the null hypothesis?
11. Our computed value of t is $+3.28$. Our critical value of t is $+2.048$. We have 28 degrees of freedom and we are using a two-tailed (nondirectional) test. Draw a simple figure to illustrate the relationship between the critical and the computed values of t for this result.
12. Poor Jack is getting more and more confused. He says: "Anyone can see that my group means are different. Why do I have to go through all the trouble of making all these computations of t?" Can you explain to him why these procedures are necessary? What advantage do they have over simply doing Jack's "eye test"?
13. Our computed value of t is -1.07. We have made a directional prediction and our critical value is -1.734. Make a rough illustration of the relationship between the computed and table values of t in this case. Is there a significant difference between the treatment means?
14. Suppose that we had *not* made a directional prediction in the time-estimation experiment. Would the results still have been statistically significant if we had used a two-tailed test?
15. A researcher has studied subjects' ability to learn to translate words

into Morse code. He has experimented with two treatment conditions: In one condition, the subjects are given massed practice. They spend 8 full hours working on the task. In the other condition, subjects are given distributed practice. They also spend 8 hours practicing, but their practice is spread over 4 days; they practice 2 hours each day. After the subjects have completed their practice, they are given a test message to encode. The dependent variable is the number of errors made in encoding the test message. Since intelligence may affect the learning of this new skill, the researcher has matched the subjects on that variable. The results are given below. Decide which statistical test would be appropriate for these data, carry out the test, and evaluate the outcome. Assume that the researcher has chosen a $p < .01$ level of significance and that the direction of the outcome has not been predicted.

Massed Practice		Distributed Practice	
S_1	6	S_1	5
S_2	4	S_2	3
S_3	3	S_3	2
S_4	5	S_4	2
S_5	2	S_5	3

16. Assume that the Morse code researcher did not match the subjects.
    a. Which statistical test would be appropriate? Carry out that test and evaluate the outcome for $p < .01$ and a nondirectional prediction.
    b. Follow the same procedure as in (a) but assume that the researcher has now predicted that the massed-practice group will make more errors.
17. Alice has decided that the procedures for finding t for a matched-groups design are a little easier to do, so she will just make sure she can match her subjects on some variable. That way she can save a little time on the computations. What is wrong with her approach? What is she forgetting?

REFERENCES

HUFF, D. (1954). *How to lie with statistics.* New York: Norton.

LEWIS, D. (1960). *Quantitative methods in psychology.* New York: McGraw-Hill.

McCALL, R. B. (1980). *Fundamental statistics for psychology* (3rd ed.). New York: Harcourt Brace Jovanovich.

REICHMANN, W. J. (1961). *Use and abuse of statistics.* London: Methuen.

WINER, B. J. (1971). *Statistical principles in experimental design* (2nd ed.). New York: McGraw-Hill.

YIN, R. (1969). Perception of inverted faces. *Journal of Experimental Psychology, 81,* 141–145.

13

Analyzing Results:
Multiple-Group and Factorial Experiments

Analysis of Variance

Sources of Variability

A One-Way Analysis of Variance
Within-Groups Variability
Between-Groups Variability
Computing and Evaluating the F Ratio

Analyzing Data from a Factorial Experiment

A Two-Way Analysis of Variance
Assumptions Behind the Two-Way Analysis of Variance
Evaluating the F Ratios

Summary

Key Terms

Review and Study Questions

References

$\mathcal{S}$o far we have covered some of the techniques for data from experiments with only two groups. The *t* tests for matched and independent groups are used when we have interval or ratio data in two-group experiments. However, very often we need to test more than two levels of an independent variable. We may need three or more groups to give an adequate idea of the way that a particular variable operates. We may even want to study more than one independent variable at a time. For those experiments, we need other kinds of statistical procedures.

In this chapter we will look at procedures that can be used for interval or ratio data from multiple-group and factorial experiments.[1] These procedures fall under the general heading of "analysis of variance." By the end of this chapter, you will know how these procedures work and why they are needed; you will also be ready to carry them out. We will begin by taking a general look at analysis of variance.

ANALYSIS OF VARIANCE

The **analysis of variance (ANOVA)** is a statistical procedure used to evaluate differences among two or more treatment means.[2] The name reflects the basic nature of the test—the variance in the data is analyzed into component parts, which are then compared and evaluated for statistical significance. Treatment means are not compared directly. In Chapter 12 the *t* test was used to evaluate the data from a two-group experiment. You may be wondering why we need another procedure at all. After all, a multiple-group experiment is just a continuation of a two-group design. We could use *t* tests to compare all the treatment means. We could analyze one pair, and then the next, and just keep doing that until we did all the pairs. But computing several *t* tests for each experiment is very bothersome. With five treatment levels, you would need ten different *t* tests to account for all possible pairs of means.

---

[1] Other forms of the basic analysis of variance (ANOVA) can be used for noninterval data. However, in this chapter we will talk about ANOVA only in its most common form. We will also assume that we have different subjects in each of our treatment groups.

[2] In a two-group experiment, a researcher can actually use either a *t* test or an analysis of variance, and both are found in the psychological literature. When statistics must be calculated by hand, the *t* test has been preferred because it is somewhat easier to calculate. However, for a two-group experiment, *t* values and ANOVA values (called *F*s) are directly related. In fact, $F = t^2$ when only two groups are being tested.

There is also a more serious problem. The more t tests in one experiment, the more apt you are to make a Type 1 error. Remember that when you do a single test, the odds of rejecting the null hypothesis by mistake are equal to your significance level (for example, 5%). Doing many t tests in the same experiment distorts those odds and increases the possibility that you will reject a null hypothesis that is really true. Although it would be inappropriate to use several t tests in a multiple-group experiment, many of the principles of statistical analysis in the last two chapters still apply. We are still testing a null hypothesis. From the samples we have tested, we draw inferences about the population. We also use distribution curves to evaluate the results according to the significance levels we have chosen.

Still, there are many differences. The analysis of variance does not work like a t test. When we computed t, we calculated differences between treatment groups—differences between treatment means for the independent-groups design and differences between pairs of scores in the matched-groups design. We looked at those differences in relation to our estimates of the amount of variability in the populations sampled. The analysis of variance enables us to test the null hypothesis in a slightly different way. It breaks up the variability in the data into component parts. Each part represents variability produced by a different combination of factors in the experiment.

In the simplest analysis of variance, all the variability in the data can be divided into two parts: within-groups variability and between-groups variability. **Within-groups variability** is the degree to which the scores of subjects in the *same* treatment group differ from one another (that is, how much subjects vary from others in the group). **Between-groups variability** is the degree to which the scores of *different* treatment groups differ from one another (that is, how much subjects vary under different levels of the independent variable). The proportions of the within-groups and between-groups variability differ from one experiment to another. Sometimes between-groups variability is larger than within-groups variability; sometimes the two parts are about the same. Their relative proportions vary depending on the impact of the independent variable. When we carry out the analysis of variance, we are actually evaluating the likelihood that the proportions we observe could occur by chance. To understand how this process works, we need to look more closely at the sources of variability that produce these components.

SOURCES OF VARIABILITY

Ideally, when we run an experiment we would like to be able to show that the pattern of data obtained was caused by the experimental manipulation. However, you already know that if we observe changes in the dependent variable across treatment conditions, those changes may not be entirely due to the effects of the independent variable. But what else accounts for changes in the dependent variable? What else might produce variability in the scores of subjects across treatment conditions?

One common source of variability is individual differences. Whether we test children or chimps, we find that some do better than others. Within each treatment group, subjects' scores will differ from one another because subjects are different from one another. We use random assignment or matching in each experiment so that these differences do not confound the results of the experiment. We do not want differences between groups to be produced solely by extraneous subject variables. However, no two groups will be identical in every respect, so individual differences may lead to variability between groups as well as within the same group.

There are other sources of variability in data. Some differences between scores will be due to things we did not handle well in the experiment. For instance, we may have made small mistakes in measuring lines that subjects drew or in timing their answers. Extraneous variables of all kinds can produce more variability. They may cause changes in subjects' behavior that we may not detect. One subject is tested when the room is cool and so does a little better than the others. As with individual differences, these factors can lead to variability within the same group of subjects, as well as between different treatment groups. We can lump all these factors together in a single category called **error:** Individual differences, undetected mistakes in recording data, variations in testing conditions, and a host of extraneous variables are all aspects of error that produce variability in subjects' data both within and between treatment groups.

Another major source of variability in the data is the experimental manipulation. We test subjects under different treatment conditions (that is, various levels of an independent variable). We predict that these conditions will alter subjects' behavior; we expect subjects under different treatment conditions to behave differently from one another. In other words, we expect our treatment conditions to create variability among the responses of subjects who are tested under different levels of an independent variable.

But the experimental manipulation does not operate the same as other sources of variability in the experiment. Error leads to variability between different treatment groups; it also produces variability within the same group. Unlike those sources of variability, treatment conditions produce variability *only* between the responses of different treatment groups. Subjects within the same treatment group are all treated in the same manner. Their scores may differ because of individual differences or error but not because they were exposed to different levels of the independent variable: Subjects in the same treatment group all receive the same level of the independent variable.

When we do an analysis of variance, we break the variability in our data into parts that reflect the sources of variability in the experiment: within-groups variability and between-groups variability. *Within-groups variability is the extent to which subjects' scores differ from one another under the same treatment conditions.* The factors that we call error explain the variability that we see within groups. *Between-groups variability is the*

TABLE **13-1**

Sources of variability in an experiment with one independent variable	
Variability Within Groups	*Variability Between Groups*
Error	Error
Individual differences	Individual differences
Extraneous variables	Extraneous variables
	Treatment effects

extent to which group performance differs from one treatment condition to another. Between-groups variability is made up of error and the effects of the independent variable. These components are summarized above in Table 13-1.

We can evaluate the effect of the independent variable by comparing the relative size of these components of variability. The logic behind this is straightforward. The variability within groups comes from error and nothing else. The variability between groups comes from both error and treatment effects. If the independent variable had an effect, the between-groups variability should be larger than the within-groups variability. We compare the relative sizes of these components by computing a ratio between them called the **F ratio.** Conceptually, it looks like this:

$$F = \frac{\text{Variability from treatment effects} + \text{error}}{\text{Variability from error}}$$

or

$$F = \frac{\text{Variability between groups}}{\text{Variability within groups}}$$

Theoretically, if the independent variable had no effect, the F ratio should equal 1. There should be just as much variability within groups as there is between them: The same sources of variability would be operating both within and between treatments. However, the larger the effect of the independent variable, the larger the F ratio should be. The independent variable will lead to greater differences between the scores of subjects who receive different levels of the independent variable. Figure 13-1 represents both possibilities graphically.

We use the distribution of F to evaluate the significance of the F ratio that we compute. F, like t, is actually a whole family of distributions. The shape of the distribution changes as the size of the samples changes. We will use the degrees of freedom to choose the correct distribution and critical value for each experiment. If the F ratio is statistically significant, the amount of between-groups variability is large compared to the amount of within-groups variability. It is so large that it is unlikely that all the group

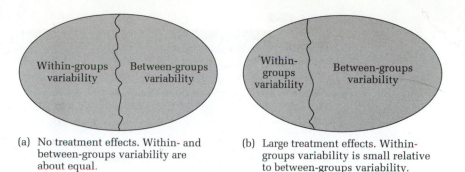

(a) No treatment effects. Within- and between-groups variability are about equal.

(b) Large treatment effects. Within-groups variability is small relative to between-groups variability.

FIGURE **13-1** The components of variability in an experiment with two possible outcomes.

means belong to the same population. If F is significant, we reject the null hypothesis that all the treatment means were drawn from the same population: We confirm the existence of differences across the groups that were probably produced by the independent variable.

Now that you have a general idea of how ANOVA works, let us turn to an example of a multiple-group experiment. We will look at some hypothetical data obtained from three groups of subjects who learned high-, medium-, and low-frequency words. We will proceed step by step through the computation of the F ratio. We will test F with a $p < .05$ significance level. Since this experiment has only one independent variable, the statistical test we do is called a "one-way analysis of variance."

A ONE-WAY ANALYSIS OF VARIANCE

Assume that we have done a very simple experiment on learning. We have made up three lists of words that occur with varying frequencies in the English language. We know that frequency is likely to affect subjects' ability to learn lists of words: Words that occur with greater frequencies are apt to be easier to learn because they are more familiar and also more meaningful to us. We have made up lists of high-, medium-, and low-frequency two-syllable nouns. We defined these categories on the basis of Howes's (1966) count of the frequency of words in spoken English. Our high-frequency words occurred at least 50 times in Howes's sample of 250,000 words. Our medium-frequency words occurred more than once but less than 50 times. The low-frequency words occurred only once in Howes's sample. By these criteria, words like *hundred, mother,* and *question* are high frequency; *coffee* and *paper* are medium frequency; *turtle* and *textbook* are low frequency. Our hypothesis is that a list of words that has higher frequency in the spoken language will be recalled with greater accuracy than a list that has lower frequency. We ran the experiment using a between-subjects design: Our subjects were randomly assigned to three different treatment

TABLE **13-2**

	Group 1 (Low Frequency)	Group 2 (Medium Frequency)	Group 3 (High Frequency)
Hypothetical data from an experiment on word frequency and learning			
S_1	2	1	3
S_2	2	3	4
S_3	1	3	2
S_4	0	3	3
S_5	1	3	4
	$\overline{X}_1 = 1.2$	$\overline{X}_2 = 2.6$	$\overline{X}_3 = 3.2$
	$s_1{}^2 = .7$	$s_2{}^2 = .8$	$s_3{}^2 = .7$

NOTE: *Scores represent the number of words recalled from a list. All subjects saw the same number of items.*

groups, one for each of the three word frequencies. The procedures for presenting the lists and testing recall were identical for all the groups.

This is a three-group experiment. It has one independent variable—the frequency of the words on each list. The dependent variable is the number of words subjects are able to recall, a ratio scale measure. As in any experiment, we will test the null hypothesis: The means of the three groups were sampled from the same population. Let us use a significance level of $p < .05$ for the data. Table 12-4 (from the previous chapter) indicates that the data from this experiment may be analyzed by using a one-way analysis of variance. Table 13-2 shows some hypothetical data. As you can see, there are three groups. Their scores represent the number of words they recalled from the list they were shown. We have already begun our analysis of the data by organizing and summarizing it in table form.

Certain assumptions about our data must be met if we are to use analysis-of-variance procedures appropriately. First, the procedures we will use here require that treatment groups are independent from each other and that the samples have been selected at random. They also require that the populations from which the groups are sampled are normally distributed on the dependent variable and that the variances of those populations are roughly equal, or *homogeneous.* However, the F test is relatively robust. If we have fairly large groups of subjects, the assumptions can be violated without serious errors. The computations shown here are for illustration only. We are looking at very few subjects so that the procedures will be clear. In practice, it would be better to have larger treatment groups because of the assumptions of the ANOVA procedures.

Within-Groups Variability

In order to compute an F ratio for these data, we need two pieces of information: the within-groups variability and the between-groups variability. We begin with the procedures for finding within-groups variability because they are a little simpler.

Think about the definition of within-groups variability—the extent to which subjects' scores vary from the scores of other subjects within the same group. If we had only one group, we could measure its variability by computing the variance. We would use the formula

$$s^2 = \frac{\Sigma(X - \overline{X})^2}{N - 1}$$

We would begin by finding the sum of squared deviations from the group mean. For each score in the group, we would calculate the difference between that score and the group mean $(X - \overline{X})$. We would square each of those differences $(X - \overline{X})^2$, then add them together (Σ). To get a good estimate of the amount of variability in the population sampled, we would find the variance by dividing the sum of the squared deviations by $N - 1$, the degrees of freedom.

The variance we compute for one group is the average squared deviation from the mean of that group. Of course, when we do an analysis of variance, we are working with several groups at the same time. We need to get an estimate of within-groups variability. That estimate must *pool,* or combine, the variability in all treatment groups. We do that in two stages that are exactly parallel to the way we find the variance of a single group. First, we compute the **sum of squares (SS),** which is just a shorthand way of talking about the sum of squared deviations from the group mean. To get the sum of squares for within-groups variability, we compute the squared deviation of each score from its group mean.[3] Then we simply add them all together.

We can summarize all those steps with the formula

$$\mathbf{SS_W} = \Sigma(X_1 - \overline{X}_1)^2 + \Sigma(X_2 - \overline{X}_2)^2 \cdots + \Sigma(X_p - \overline{X}_p)^2$$

The letter p stands for the number of groups in our experiment. In our example we have only three groups, but the analysis-of-variance procedures can be used with any number of groups. We simply keep adding up the squared deviations of scores from their group means until we have accounted for all the scores in all the groups.

Once we have the sum of squares within groups, we are ready to find the within-groups variance. With only one group, we know that we get a good estimate of the variance in the population if we divide our sum of squared deviations by $N - 1$, which is actually the degrees of freedom for one group. When we compute within-groups variance for several groups, we also need to divide by the degrees of freedom. For one group, the degrees of freedom are $N - 1$. For more than one group, the degrees of freedom are $N - p$. N is the total number of scores; p is the total number of

[3] The formulas throughout this chapter are definitional formulas—direct statements of the operations they define. They are presented to clarify the logic behind the ANOVA procedures. Computational formulas are shown in Appendix A. They are derived from the definitional formulas; and although computational formulas are sometimes easier to use, the rationale behind them is less clear.

groups. We divide through by that number (df_W) to get the within-groups variance. The W stands for within groups.

Note that although we are calculating the variance within groups, analysis of variance has its own peculiar terminology. You have learned sum of squares, which is an understandable abbreviation. However, when we finally obtain what we would otherwise call a variance estimate, we change terms rather abruptly. Dividing the SS_W by df_W gives us the mean square. This is actually an abbreviation too, although its origin is not as clear. The mean is an average. The variance is the average squared deviation from the mean. So the **mean square (MS)** is an average squared deviation. The existence of a plot to confuse students on this point has been suggested many times, but it has never been confirmed. The important point is this: We are still talking about variance in the data. The mean square within groups (MS_W) is one estimate of the amount of variability in the population sampled. It represents one portion of the variability in the data, the portion produced by the combination of sources that we call "error." The value of MS_W will constitute the denominator, or bottom, of the F ratio. Table 13-3 shows how to compute SS_W and MS_W for our three-group example.

Between-Groups Variability

Once we have MS_W, we are ready to calculate the second component of the F ratio, a measure of the variability between groups of subjects. It is a measure that reflects both error and treatment effects: Between-groups variability is the extent to which group performance differs from one treatment condition to another. Let us look a little more closely at the implications of that definition.

If the independent variable had no effect in this experiment, the subjects in all the groups would have done about equally well. We would not expect to see any dramatic difference in recall from one group to another; the only differences we would see would be due to error. If that were the case, the means of the individual treatment groups would all be about the same. We could compute one overall mean, or **grand mean,** an average of all the treatment means. If our independent variable had no effect, the grand mean would describe the data about as well as three separate means, one for each of the three separate groups. But imagine what would happen if the independent variable really did have an effect on subjects' recall. We could still compute an overall grand mean that would represent the average of all the subjects' scores. However, the means of the individual groups would be quite different from the grand mean. They would also be quite different from one another.

You already know that we measure the amount of variability *within* groups by finding the total variance of scores from the individual group means. Similarly, we can measure the variability *between* groups by finding the variance of the group means from their mean, the grand mean of the experiment. Now that you are familiar with the logic behind the pro-

TABLE **13-3**

Computing within-groups variance for a three-group example			
Step 1. Compute the deviation of each score from its group mean.	*Group 1* *(Low Frequency)*	$(X_1 - \overline{X}_1)$	$(X_1 - \overline{X}_1)^2$
	S_1 2	.8	.64
	S_2 2	.8	.64
	S_3 1	− .2	.04
	S_4 0	−1.2	1.44
	S_5 1	− .2	.04
	$\overline{X}_1 = 1.2$		$\Sigma(X_1 - \overline{X}_1)^2 = 2.80$
Step 2. Square the deviation of each score from its group mean.	*Group 2* *(Medium Frequency)*	$(X_2 - \overline{X}_2)$	$(X_2 - \overline{X}_2)^2$
	S_1 1	−1.6	2.56
	S_2 3	.4	.16
	S_3 3	.4	.16
	S_4 3	.4	.16
	S_5 3	.4	.16
	$\overline{X}_2 = 2.6$		$\Sigma(X_2 - \overline{X}_2)^2 = 3.20$
Step 3. Total the squared deviation scores for each group.	*Group 3* *(High Frequency)*	$(X_3 - \overline{X}_3)$	$(X_3 - \overline{X}_3)^2$
	S_1 3	− .2	.04
	S_2 4	.8	.64
	S_3 2	−1.2	1.44
	S_4 3	− .2	.04
	S_5 4	.8	.64
	$\overline{X}_3 = 3.2$		$\Sigma(X_3 - \overline{X}_3)^2 = 2.80$

Step 4. Add all the group totals together to find $\mathbf{SS_W}$.

$$\boxed{\mathbf{SS_W} = \Sigma(X_1 - \overline{X}_1)^2 + \Sigma(X_2 - \overline{X}_2)^2 + \Sigma(X_3 - \overline{X}_3)^2 = 8.80}$$

Step 5. Find df_W.

$$\boxed{df_W = N - p}$$

N = Number of scores
p = Number of groups

$df_W = 15 - 3$
$df_W = 12$

Step 6. Find $\mathbf{MS_W}$.

$$\boxed{\mathbf{MS_W} = \frac{\mathbf{SS_W}}{df_W}}$$

$$\mathbf{MS_W} = \frac{8.80}{12}$$

$$\mathbf{MS_W} = .73$$

NOTE: *The same procedures apply when the groups are unequal in size.*

cedures, let us compute the between-groups variance. The process is carried out in Table 13-4 for our three-group example. We begin by computing the grand mean, the average of all the treatment means. We then compute deviations of the group means from the grand mean, and then we obtain the squared deviations. Notice, however, that the formula for $\mathbf{SS_B}$ (*B* stands for between groups) is a little different from the one for $\mathbf{SS_W}$. Instead of simply adding together all the squared deviations, each one is first multiplied by n_j, the number of subjects in each respective treatment group.

TABLE **13-4**

Finding the between-groups variance for our three-groups example

	Group 1 (Low Frequency)	Group 2 (Medium Frequency)	Group 3 (High Frequency)
Step 1. Compute the grand mean, the mean of all the group means.	$\overline{X}_1 = 1.2$	$\overline{X}_2 = 2.6$	$\overline{X}_3 = 3.2$

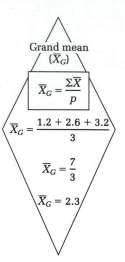

Step 2. Compute the differences between each group and the grand mean.

$\overline{X}_1 - \overline{X}_G =$	$\overline{X}_2 - \overline{X}_G =$	$\overline{X}_3 - \overline{X}_G =$
$1.2 - 2.3 = -1.1$	$2.6 - 2.3 = .3$	$3.2 - 2.3 = .9$

Step 3. Put those differences in the $\mathbf{SS_B}$ formula; n is the number of subjects in each group; p is the number of groups—this general formula can handle any number of groups.

$$\boxed{\mathbf{SS_B} = n_1(\overline{X}_1 - \overline{X}_G)^2 + n_2(\overline{X}_2 - \overline{X}_G)^2 + n_3(\overline{X}_3 - \overline{X}_G)^2 \cdots n_p(\overline{X}_p - \overline{X}_G)^2}$$

$$\mathbf{SS_B} = 5(-1.1)^2 + 5(.3)^2 + 5(.9)^2$$

Step 4. Square all deviations from the grand mean.

$$\mathbf{SS_B} = 5(1.21) + 5(.09) + 5(.81)$$

Step 5. Carry out all multiplications.

$$\mathbf{SS_B} = 6.05 + .45 + 4.05$$

Step 6. Obtain the total $\mathbf{SS_B}$.

$$\mathbf{SS_B} = 10.55$$

Step 7. Calculate the degrees of freedom; p is the number of groups.

$$\boxed{df_\mathrm{B} = p - 1}$$

$$df_\mathrm{B} = 3 - 1, \text{ or } 2$$

TABLE **13-4** *(continued)*

Step 8. Divide SS_B by df_B to find the mean square between groups, the second estimate of population variance.	$$\boxed{MS_B = \frac{SS_B}{df_B}}$$ $$MS_B = \frac{10.55}{2}$$ $$MS_B = 5.28$$

NOTE: *At this point you can check your work by computing SS_T, which represents the total sum of squares for the data. Since we are simply dividing the variability into two components, $SS_B + SS_W$ should equal SS_T. You can compute SS_T with this formula: $SS_T = \Sigma(X^2) - \frac{(\Sigma X)^2}{N}$. N is the number of scores. For this example,*

$$SS_T = 101 - \frac{(35)^2}{15}$$

$$SS_T = 101 - \left(\frac{1225}{15}\right)$$

$$SS_T = 101 - 81.67$$

$$SS_T = 19.33$$
Check:
$$SS_T = SS_B + SS_W$$
$$19.33 = 10.55 + 8.80$$
(The small discrepancy is due to rounding error.)

Next, we find the variance about the grand mean, the mean square between groups (MS_B). To get MS_B, we divide SS_B by its degrees of freedom. We are now working with group means rather than individual subjects' scores. Hence, our degrees of freedom for SS_B (df_B) are equal to $p - 1$, where p is the number of groups. The MS_B gives us a second estimate of the amount of variability in the population. MS_B reflects the amount of variability produced by error *and* treatment effects in the experiment. This variability estimate will form the numerator, or top, of the F ratio.

Computing and Evaluating the *F* Ratio

We now have both components of variability that we need to compute our F ratio. As you already know, the F ratio represents this relationship:

$$F = \frac{\text{Variability from treatment effects } + \text{ error}}{\text{Variability from error}}$$

We have transformed the components of this formula into the numerical terms MS_B and MS_W. Thus the statistical form of the F ratio is as follows:

$$F = \frac{MS_B}{MS_W}$$

If we substitute our computed values into this formula, we find that for our three-group example,

$$F = \frac{5.28}{.73} \text{ or } 7.23$$

To test our F ratio for significance, we need to find the critical value. As you know, F is a whole family of distributions. We use our degrees of freedom to locate the appropriate distribution. But is there a problem? As we computed F, we actually calculated two different degrees of freedom, one to get MS_B and another to get MS_W. Which do we use? Since the F test can be used with any number of groups as well as any number of subjects, we need both. The F distribution changes as the size of treatment groups changes; it also changes as the number of treatment conditions changes. If you look in Appendix B, you will find that Table B3 lists critical values of F. The table is organized by the degrees of freedom. The values listed across the top refer to the degrees of freedom of the numerator of the F ratio—here, df_B. Values listed vertically down the side of the table indicate the degrees of freedom of the denominator of the F ratio—here, df_W. To find the appropriate critical value, first locate df_B along the top of the table, then locate df_W along the side. Now find the place in the table where those two lines meet. We are looking for $df_B = 2$ and $df_W = 12$. (These are simply the df values we computed to get mean squares.) If we look at a portion of the table, we see this:

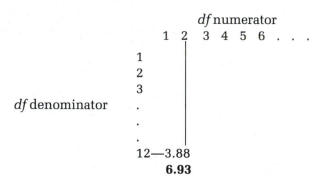

The value in light type, 3.88, is the critical value of F at the .05 level; **6.93**, shown in boldface, is the critical value of F at the .01 level. Remember, these values apply *only* to an F test with 2 and 12 degrees of freedom. We have to look up the critical values for each experiment. Figure 13-2 illustrates the distribution of F with 2 and 12 degrees of freedom. It also shows the distribution of F with 2 and 6 degrees of freedom. As you can see, the critical values change dramatically as the degrees of freedom change.

We chose a significance level of $p < .05$ for our three-group experiment. To be statistically significant, we need a computed value of F that is greater than the table value for our level of significance. Our computed value of F was 7.23. The table value of F is 3.88 at the .05 level: Therefore

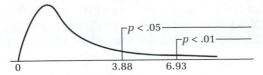

(a) The distribution of F with 2 (numerator) and 12 (denominator) degrees of freedom

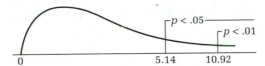

(b) The distribution of F with 2 (numerator) and 6 (denominator) degrees of freedom

FIGURE **13-2** The distribution of F with varying degrees of freedom.

our computed F is significant. We reject the null hypothesis that the treatment means came from the same population. Our computed F is large enough, in fact, that it is also significant at the .01 level: It is greater than 6.93, the critical value of F at the .01 level.

Preparing a summary table. By now it may seem that we have gone through a thousand steps to evaluate the data from this study. The count is actually slightly less than that, but you can understand why we need to prepare a simple, comprehensive summary of the findings. We would not present all the steps and calculations in an actual report. Instead, we sometimes summarize our computations in a summary table. A summary table for our example is shown in Table 13-5. The table includes all the basic information needed to compute F, along with the actual computed value.[4] However, we do not include the table values of F. Since we have given the degrees of freedom, readers can always consult their own tables to get the critical value if they need it. The format of the table is used by convention, and you should follow it exactly; list between-groups variance first, and so on.

Graphing the results. Another useful way of summarizing the results of an experiment is graphing. We can transform our findings into a picture that shows the reader the overall results at a glance. Look closely at Figure 13-3, which presents the results of our experiment as a graph.

The figure illustrates several general points you should keep in mind. Notice that the figure is well proportioned; the vertical axis is roughly three-fourths the size of the horizontal axis. Notice also that the indepen-

---

[4] Complete summary tables are not always found in published articles. Even so, it is good to include them, and many instructors will want to see a summary table as part of your research report.

TABLE **13-5**

Analysis-of-variance summary table				
Source	*df*	**SS**	**MS**	*F*
Between groups	2	10.55	5.28	$\dfrac{\text{MS}_\text{B}}{\text{MS}_\text{W}} = 7.23^*$
Within groups	12	8.80	.73	
Total	14	19.35		

$^*p < .01$

dent variable is plotted on the horizontal axis; the dependent variable is plotted on the vertical axis. Finally, note that the data points represent group means. We usually do not graph the data of individual subjects unless we have a small N design. Of course, the axes are labeled clearly so that readers will know exactly what the figure represents.

Interpreting the results.   We know that the computed F was significant for these data. We will have more to say about interpreting the meaning of significant outcomes in the next chapter. However, there are some points about the F test that should be made before we go further.

From the graph of our results (Figure 13-3), you can see quite clearly that subjects in different groups performed differently from one another in this experiment. Subjects in the high-frequency group recalled the most items; subjects in the low-frequency group recalled the least. You can also see clearly from the figure that the variation between different groups was not uniform. The high- and low-frequency groups differed more from each other than from the medium-frequency group. It is very important to keep

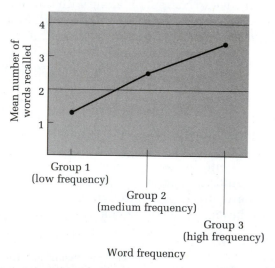

FIGURE **13-3**   The mean number of words recalled as a function of word frequency.

in mind that when we compute F, we test only the *overall* pattern of treatment means. Our significant F in this example tells us that across all the group means, there is a significant difference. If we had only two treatment groups, we would know immediately that one group mean was significantly higher than another. But when three or more groups are being compared, as they are in our experiment, the F test does not test the differences between each pair of means, and we do not know exactly where the difference is. From the graph, it seems likely that the high and the low groups are significantly different from each other. After all, they differ the most. However, the difference between, say, the low- and the medium-frequency groups may or may not be significant. After a significant F has been obtained, further statistics are needed to determine which groups are really different from each other. (If an F is nonsignificant, we would not need to go any further.) When we need to pinpoint the exact source of the differences across several treatment groups, we can use follow-up tests. There are two basic types of follow-up tests: post hoc tests and a priori comparisons.[5]

There are several different **post hoc tests**—tests done after the overall analysis indicates a significant difference. We will not go into the details of these tests here, but some of the names you will see are the Tukey and the Scheffé tests. These tests have essentially the same function: They can be used to make pair-by-pair comparisons to pinpoint the source of a significant difference across several treatments. For instance, by comparing each treatment group with every other group in our word frequency experiment, post hoc tests would tell us whether high-frequency words were significantly easier to recall than medium-frequency words or only easier than low-frequency words. They would also tell us whether medium-frequency words were significantly easier to recall than low-frequency words.

Couldn't we just use a series of t tests to make these pairwise comparisons? No, because (as we mentioned at the beginning of this chapter) we would be increasing our odds of making a Type 1 error. With three treatment groups, our chances of making a Type 1 error could be as high as three times our significance level ($3 \times .05 = .15$). Post hoc tests, however, are more *conservative* statistical tests. They are conservative because they are specifically designed to guard against increasing the chances of rejecting the null hypothesis when it is really true. These kinds of post hoc tests, however, can result in less power to detect treatment effects. They can increase the chances of making a Type 2 error. One way around this is to use another statistical procedure for pinpointing significant effects, a priori comparisons.

A priori comparisons are tests between specific treatment groups that were anticipated, or planned, before the experiment was conducted. For this reason, they are also called "planned comparisons." A priori comparisons are often used to test specific predictions. For example, in our word-

---

[5] For additional information about follow-up tests and how to compute them, we suggest you consult Lehman's *Statistics and Research Design in the Behavioral Sciences* (1991).

frequency experiment, we might have made the following two predictions before we conducted the study: (1) High-frequency words will be easier to recall than medium-frequency words, and (2) medium-frequency words will be easier to learn than low-frequency words. If the overall ANOVA is significant, we would conduct two a priori comparisons. Unlike post hoc tests, a priori comparisons are considered part of the original analysis of variance. Typically, we do not worry about increasing the odds of a Type 1 error as long as the number of planned comparisons is *less than* the number of treatment groups in the experiment. Planned comparisons can also be used to test predictions that one group will be different from all the others in the experiment. For instance, we might have planned to contrast the high-frequency conditions with all others. The manner of computing a priori comparisons is less conservative than post hoc tests, making them more powerful.

Wouldn't we always use planned comparisons then? Not necessarily. Sometimes we have too many predictions, making the chances of a Type 1 error unacceptable. Other times (particularly when things do not turn out exactly the way we expected), we want to explore group differences that we did not predict in advance. Just as we cannot change our hypotheses or our significance levels to suit the way the data come out, it is always inappropriate to use planned comparisons to pinpoint *unplanned* effects.

Let us briefly summarize what we have accomplished in this chapter so far. We took a multiple-group experiment and selected a suitable statistical test on the basis of three dimensions: We considered the number of independent variables, the number of treatment groups, and the level of measurement in making our choice. The experiment had one independent variable (word frequency) and three treatment groups (low, medium, and high frequency). The dependent variable (number of words recalled) was measured by a ratio scale. The data therefore required a one-way analysis of variance, or F test, which we carried out and evaluated. We also prepared a summary table of our analysis and graphed the group means.

The basic principles of the analysis of variance apply in many multiple-group experiments. However, those principles can also be extended to handle more complex research designs. We will carry them further in our next example, an experiment with a factorial design.

ANALYZING DATA FROM A FACTORIAL EXPERIMENT

Factorial experiments are designed to look at the effects of more than one independent variable at a time. They also enable us to look at the interaction between variables. The impact of one independent variable may differ depending on the values of the other independent variables in the experiment. When we analyze the data from a factorial experiment, we evaluate both kinds of effects. We look at the impact of each independent variable; we assess whether there is a main effect of each independent variable. We also measure the size of any interaction between the variables. Let us look

Word frequency (Factor 1)

Low   High

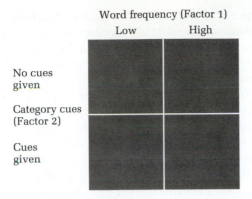

No cues
given

Category cues
(Factor 2)

Cues
given

FIGURE **13-4** Diagram of a 2 × 2 factorial
experiment on the effects of word frequency and cuing on recall.

at an example of a simple factorial experiment and see which statistical
procedures are used to accomplish these goals.

Assume we have set up and run another experiment to explore the
relationship between word frequency and recall. Half the subjects saw
high-frequency words, and half saw low-frequency words. This time
though, we have run a factorial experiment. In addition to evaluating the
effect of frequency, we have manipulated our testing procedures in a 2 × 2
design. The design is diagrammed in Figure 13-4. Half the subjects have
been asked simply to recall the words they saw on the original list. The
other half have given cues to aid them in remembering the words they
saw. For instance, suppose subjects saw the word *camel* on the original list.
If they were in the "no-cue" condition, they were simply asked to recall
the word. If they were in the "cue" condition, we provided the name of the
category the word belongs to—animal. Category cues were given for all
words on the list.

Our hypothesis, which is based on prior research (such as Tulving &
Pearlstone, 1966), is that cuing will enhance recall. Frequency will also
affect recall, with the more frequent words being easier to recall. We have
two independent variables in this experiment—word frequency and category cues. Our dependent variable is the number of words correctly
recalled from each list, a ratio measure. We will use $p < .05$ as our significance level. If you consult Table 12-4, you will find that the statistical test
indicated for these data is a two-way analysis of variance.

You already know how to do the basic, or one-way, ANOVA. The same
principles apply to all ANOVA procedures. But when we have a factorial
design, additional complexities arise. The procedures for the one-way
ANOVA are not designed to give us as much information as we want to get
from a factorial experiment. We want to be able to evaluate the effect of
each independent variable: We need to know whether the word frequency
and category cues affect ability to recall words. Of course, we also want to
know whether there was any interaction between the two variables. We
want to assess whether the effects of using different frequencies might dif-

fer depending on whether cues are given—or perhaps the effect of cues varies depending on whether the word to be recalled is relatively frequent or infrequent.

To answer all these questions with an analysis of variance, we need to break down the variance in the data into more components than we had before. In the one-way ANOVA, we had one independent variable. We divided all the variability in the data into just two parts: within-groups and between-groups variability. Within-groups variability is created by all those sources of error in the experiment: individual differences, the experimenter's mistakes, and other extraneous variables. Between-groups variability is created by all those sources of error plus the effect of the independent variable.

The same is true in a factorial experiment. We can separate variability into within-groups and between-groups variance. However, the picture is more complex. Between-groups variability comes from error and treatment effects, but there are several sources of treatment effects in the factorial experiment. Every independent variable may produce its own unique treatment effects; each can produce a portion of the between-groups variability or a main effect. The interaction of the independent variables can produce another portion. This is represented graphically in Figure 13-5, which compares the components of variability for the one-way analysis of variance against a two-way analysis of variance for a two-factor experiment.

We can begin our analysis of variance for the factorial experiment by finding within- and between-groups variability. However, we will also need to break between-groups variability into its component parts: the variability associated with each of the independent variables and the variability associated with the interaction between them.

When we did the one-way ANOVA, we used a summary table to organize our computations. When we do a two-way ANOVA, it is helpful to plan the summary table in advance. We can use it to keep track of computations as we do them. The outline of the summary table for a two-factor

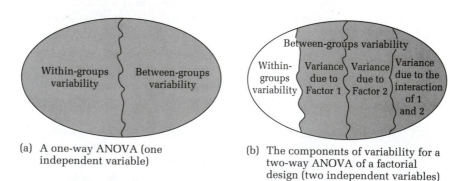

(a) A one-way ANOVA (one independent variable)

(b) The components of variability for a two-way ANOVA of a factorial design (two independent variables)

FIGURE **13-5** The components of variability for (a) a one-way analysis of variance (one independent variable) and (b) a two-way analysis of variance (two independent variables).

TABLE **13-6**

<table>
<tr><td colspan="6">**Summarizing the analysis of variance for a two-factor experiment**</td></tr>
<tr><td>*Source*</td><td>*df*</td><td>**SS**</td><td>**MS**</td><td>$F = \dfrac{\text{MS}}{\text{MS}_\text{W}}$</td></tr>
<tr><td>Between groups</td><td></td><td></td><td></td><td></td></tr>
<tr><td>   Factor 1</td><td></td><td></td><td></td><td></td></tr>
<tr><td>   Factor 2</td><td></td><td></td><td></td><td></td></tr>
<tr><td>   Interaction 1 × 2</td><td></td><td></td><td></td><td></td></tr>
<tr><td>Within groups</td><td></td><td></td><td></td><td></td></tr>
<tr><td>   Total</td><td></td><td></td><td></td><td></td></tr>
</table>

experiment is shown in Table 13-6. You can see that all the sources of variability in the experiment are represented. We must find all these components in order to compute the F ratios needed to judge significance. We will calculate a different F ratio for every source of between-groups variability in the experiment and use those ratios to decide whether the effects of each independent variable are significant. We will also decide whether there is a significant interaction.

A TWO-WAY ANALYSIS OF VARIANCE

Table 13-7 presents some hypothetical data from our experiment to test the effect of word frequency and category cues on recall. Since this is a 2 × 2 factorial design, the data are divided into four treatment groups. We have

TABLE **13-7**

Hypothetical data from a two-factor experiment: The effects of word frequency and category cues on recall in a list-learning task

		Word Frequency (Factor 1)			
		Low		High	
	No cues given	2 3 1 4 5	$\overline{X}_1 = 3$	4 5 4 6 6	$\overline{X}_2 = 5$
Category Cues (Factor 2)	Cues given	4 6 5 6 9	$\overline{X}_3 = 6$	7 6 9 8 10	$\overline{X}_4 = 8$

NOTE: *Scores represent number of words correctly recalled from a list.*

already begun the data analysis by computing the mean number of words correctly recalled by each treatment group. Let us take an overall look at the steps required to complete the analysis of variance. The actual computations are shown in Tables 13-8 through 13-12, which follow our written description.

Assumptions Behind the Two-Way Analysis of Variance

The procedures and formulas for a two-way ANOVA require the same basic assumptions as the one-way ANOVA procedures we examined earlier. They assume that the treatment groups are independent from each other and that the observations were randomly sampled. They also assume that the population from which each treatment group is sampled is normally distributed on the dependent variable. Finally, they assume that the variances of the populations are all about equal (homogeneous). The computations here are done just for the sake of illustration, so we have only five subjects per treatment group. However, the assumptions behind the ANOVA procedures are more likely to be met with larger groups of subjects. In addition, the procedures shown here assume equal number of subjects (n) in each group and more than one subject per group. If you have unequal ns, you will need more complicated procedures. The same is true if you have used within-subjects procedures. In either case, consult your instructor or see Winer's *Statistical Principles in Experimental Design* (1971).

Finally, these procedures are set for fixed models, experiments in which the values of the independent variables are fixed by the experimenter. In other words, the experimenter chooses to run subjects at certain levels of each independent variable. In our example the experimenter has chosen to use high and low word frequencies and two levels of the category-cue variable—cues versus no cues. However, in experiments with random models (randomly selected values of the independent variables) or mixed models, different statistical procedures are required. Most experiments follow the fixed model, as we do here.

Step 1: Computing within-groups variability. We begin the ANOVA by filling in the within-groups section of the summary table. We need the degrees of freedom (df), the sum of squares within groups (SS_W), and the mean square within groups (MS_W). To get them, we follow the same basic procedures that we used for the one-way ANOVA. The calculations for our 2×2 experiment are shown in Table 13-8. Remember that the mean square within groups represents variability produced by individual differences, extraneous variables, and other sources of error in the experiment. We will use MS_W to evaluate the impact of the independent variables and their interaction in the experiment.

Step 2: Computing between-groups variability. We continue our ANOVA by finding the total sum of squares between groups, SS_B. We need

TABLE **13-8**

Step 1: Computing within-groups variability (MS_W) for a 2 × 2 factorial experiment

Word Frequency
(Factor 1)

Category Cues (Factor 2)

		Low			High	
	X_1	$(X_1 - \overline{X}_1)$	$(X_1 - \overline{X}_1)^2$	X_2	$(X_2 - \overline{X}_2)$	$(X_2 - \overline{X}_2)^2$
No cues given	2	−1	1	4	−1	1
	3	0	0	5	0	0
	1	−2	4	4	−1	1
	4	1	1	6	1	1
	5	2	4	6	1	1
	$\overline{X}_1 = 3$		$\Sigma(X_1 - \overline{X}_1)^2 = 10$	$\overline{X}_2 = 5$		$\Sigma(X_2 - \overline{X}_2)^2 = 4$
	X_3	$(X_3 - \overline{X}_3)$	$(X_3 - \overline{X}_3)^2$	X_4	$(X_4 - \overline{X}_4)$	$(X_4 - \overline{X}_4)^2$
Cues given	4	−2	4	7	−1	1
	6	0	0	6	−2	4
	5	−1	1	9	1	1
	6	0	0	8	0	0
	9	3	9	10	2	4
	$\overline{X}_3 = 6$		$\Sigma(X_3 - \overline{X}_3)^2 = 14$	$\overline{X}_4 = 8$		$\Sigma(X_4 - \overline{X}_4)^2 = 10$

$$\boxed{SS_W = \Sigma(X_1 - \overline{X}_1)^2 + \Sigma(X_2 - \overline{X}_2)^2 + \Sigma(X_3 - \overline{X}_3)^2 + \Sigma(X_4 - \overline{X}_4)^2 + \cdots + \Sigma(X_{pq} - \overline{X}_{pq})^2}$$

$SS_W = 10 + 4 + 14 + 10$

$SS_W = 38$

$\boxed{df_W = N - pq}$ N = Number of scores; pq = Number of rows × number of columns

$df_W = 20 - 4$, or 16

$$\boxed{MS_W = \frac{SS_W}{df_W}}$$

$MS_W = \dfrac{38}{16}$

$MS_W = 2.38$

the SS_B because it represents all the variability we have among treatment groups. To complete our ANOVA, we will have to divide the SS_B into its main components: the parts associated with each of the independent variables and the part associated with the interaction between them. Table 13-9 illustrates the procedures for finding SS_B for our factorial example.

Step 3: Computing main effects.   As you know, the ANOVA procedures have some special terms associated with them. *Sum of squares* and *mean square* refer to variability in the data. When we want to discuss the variability associated with a single independent variable in a factorial design, we call it a **main effect,** the change in the dependent variable produced by the various levels of a single independent variable. In our 2 × 2 example,

TABLE **13-9**

Step 2: Computing the between-groups variability (SS_B) for a 2×2 factorial experiment

	Group 1	Group 2	Group 3	Group 4	Grand Mean ($\overline{X}_G$)
	$\overline{X}_1 = 3$ $n_1 = 5$	$\overline{X}_2 = 5$ $n_2 = 5$	$\overline{X}_3 = 6$ $n_3 = 5$	$\overline{X}_4 = 8$ $n_4 = 5$	$\overline{X}_G = \dfrac{\text{Total of all group means}}{\text{Number of groups}}$
Step 1. Compute the grand mean, the mean of all the group means.					$\overline{X}_G = \dfrac{3 + 5 + 6 + 8}{4}$ $\overline{X}_G = \dfrac{22}{4}$ $\overline{X}_G = 5.5$
Step 2. Compute the deviation of each group mean from the grand mean.	$\overline{X}_1 - \overline{X}_G =$ $3 - 5.5$ or -2.5	$\overline{X}_2 - \overline{X}_G =$ $5 - 5.5$ or $-.5$	$\overline{X}_3 - \overline{X}_G =$ $6 - 5.5$ or $.5$	$\overline{X}_4 - \overline{X}_G =$ $8 - 5.5$ or 2.5	

$$SS_B = n_1(\overline{X}_1 - \overline{X}_G)^2 + n_2(\overline{X}_2 - \overline{X}_G)^2 + n_3(\overline{X}_3 - \overline{X}_G)^2 + \cdots + n_{pq}(\overline{X}_{pq} - \overline{X}_G)^2$$

Step	Group 1	Group 2	Group 3	Group 4
Step 3. Put the deviations in the SS_B formula; n is the number of subjects in each group.	$SS_B = 5(-2.5)^2 +$	$5(-.5)^2 +$	$5(.5)^2 +$	$5(2.5)^2$
Step 4. Square all deviations from the grand mean.	$SS_B = 5(6.25) +$	$5(.25) +$	$5(.25) +$	$5(6.25)$
Step 5. Complete all computations.	$SS_B = 31.25 +$	$1.25 +$	$1.25 +$	31.25
	$SS_B = 65$			

we are looking for a main effect of word frequency. We are also looking for a main effect of category cues. The number of main effects to be tested in a factorial experiment is determined by the number of independent variables in the experiment.

When we carry out our ANOVA, we evaluate whether each main effect in the experiment is significant: We compute an F ratio to test the impact of each independent variable. When we test for a significant main effect, we are simply asking again whether subjects' scores on the dependent variable differ depending on the levels of one independent variable that we have manipulated. To measure the total between-groups variability, we calculated the deviation of group means around their grand mean. In effect, we asked how much individual treatment groups differed from the average of all the groups. When we measure a main effect, we want to look only at a particular portion of the total variability. We want to measure how much variability occurs between groups because of the impact of one independent variable.

We can ask a straightforward question: How much do the means of groups under different levels of one variable, say, word frequency, differ from the grand mean of all the groups? This is like the logic we followed in doing the one-way ANOVA: The larger the effect of the independent variable, the larger the differences from the grand mean. In our example a large main effect of word frequency would mean that subjects' recall varied depending on whether the words to be learned were relatively common or uncommon. When we evaluate the main effect of one independent variable, we treat the data as if that variable is the only one in the experiment. We simply ignore all the other experimental manipulations that were done: We say *we collapse the data across the other conditions of the experiment.* In effect, we pretend that those conditions did not exist. Table 13-10 shows how this is done as we compute SS_1 for our first independent variable, word frequency.

We also need to test for a main effect of the second variable. We know that this second variable may have contributed to the total variability between treatment groups. We can evaluate the main effect of the second variable by using the same basic procedures we followed to get the main effect of word frequency. In effect, we ask whether subjects' recall differed depending on whether they were given category cues or not: Did it differ regardless of whether they were shown high- or low-frequency words? We look at the effects of our second independent variable by simply disregarding the word-frequency manipulation. *We collapse the data across the word-frequency conditions.* Table 13-11 shows the procedures.

Step 4: Computing the interaction. The variability associated with the interaction of the two independent variables is simply what remains after the main effects of the independent variables have been taken into account. The variability between groups that is not explained by either independent variable may be explained by their **interaction.**

Since we have two independent variables, the SS_B must be divided into three parts: the variability associated with the first independent vari-

TABLE **13-10**

		Word Frequency (Factor 1)	
		Low	High
Step 1. Find the mean at each level of Factor 1: Ignore Factor 2 (rows) and find the mean of each column. N is the number of scores.	No cues given	$\overline{X}_1 = 3$ $(N = 5)$	$\overline{X}_2 = 5$ $(N = 5)$
	Cues given	$\overline{X}_3 = 6$ $(N = 5)$	$\overline{X}_4 = 8$ $(N = 5)$
	Column means	$\overline{X}_{col\ 1} = 4.5$	$\overline{X}_{col\ 2} = 6.5$
Step 2. Find the difference between each column mean and the grand mean.	Column mean − Grand mean $\overline{X}_G = 5.5$	$\overline{X}_{col\ 1} - \overline{X}_G =$ $4.5 - 5.5 = -1.0$	$\overline{X}_{col\ 2} - \overline{X}_G =$ $6.5 - 5.5 = 1.0$

Category Cues (Factor 2)

Step 3. Put those differences in the **SS₁** formula; n is the number of subjects in each group; p is the number of rows; q is the number of columns. This general formula will handle any number of columns.

$$\mathbf{SS_1} = np\ \Sigma[(\overline{X}_{col\ 1} - \overline{X}_G)^2 + (\overline{X}_{col\ 2} - \overline{X}_G)^2 + \cdots + (\overline{X}_{col\ q} - \overline{X}_G)^2]$$

$\mathbf{SS_1} = 5(2)\Sigma[(-1.0)^2 + (1.0)^2]$

$\mathbf{SS_1} = 10[(1) + (1)]$

$\mathbf{SS_1} = 10(2)$

$\mathbf{SS_1} = 20$

Step 4. To get **MS₁**, divide **SS₁** by df_1.

$$\mathbf{MS_1} = \frac{\mathbf{SS_1}}{df_1} \qquad \begin{array}{l} df_1 = q - 1 \\ df_1 = 2 - 1,\ \text{or}\ 1 \end{array}$$

$\mathbf{MS_1} = \dfrac{20}{1}$

$\mathbf{MS_1} = 20$

able (**SS₁**); the variability associated with the second independent variable (**SS₂**); and the variability associated with the interaction of the two (**SS₁×₂**). Once we have computed the total **SS_B**, **SS₁**, and **SS₂**, the simplest way to find **SS₁×₂** is by subtracting:

$$\mathbf{SS_{1 \times 2}} = \mathbf{SS_B} - \mathbf{SS_1} - \mathbf{SS_2}$$

The sum of squares for the interaction is entered in the summary table, Table 13-12.

Step 5: Computing the *F* ratios. We have now completed nearly all the computations that we need to evaluate the results of our experiment. We summarize our calculations in a summary table (Table 13-12). The table is similar to the one we prepared for the simple ANOVA. The only difference

TABLE **13-11**

Step 3: Finding the main effect for Factor 2 (category cue) in a 2 × 2 factorial experiment

Step 1. Find the mean at each level of Factor 2: Ignore Factor 1 (columns) and find the mean of each row.

Step 2. Find the difference between each row mean and the grand mean.

		Word Frequency (Factor 1)			
		Low	High	Row means	Row mean − grand mean
Category Cues (Factor 2)	No cues given	$\overline{X}_1 = 3$	$\overline{X}_2 = 5$	$\overline{X}_{\text{row 1}} = 4$	$\overline{X}_{\text{row 1}} - \overline{X}_G =$ 4 − 5.5 or −1.5
	Cues given	$\overline{X}_3 = 6$	$\overline{X}_4 = 8$	$\overline{X}_{\text{row 2}} = 7$	$\overline{X}_{\text{row 2}} - \overline{X}_G =$ 7 − 5.5 or 1.5

$(\overline{X}_G = 5.5)$

Step 3. Put those differences in the SS_2 formula; n is the number of subjects in each group; q is the number of columns; p is the number of rows. This general formula will handle any number of rows.

$$SS_2 = nq \, \Sigma[(\overline{X}_{\text{row 1}} - \overline{X}_G)^2 + (\overline{X}_{\text{row 2}} - \overline{X}_G)^2 + \cdots + (\overline{X}_{\text{row } p} - \overline{X}_G)^2]$$

$SS_2 = 5(2)[(-1.5)^2 + (1.5)^2]$

$SS_2 = 10[2.25 + 2.25]$

$SS_2 = 10(4.50)$ or 45

Step 4. To get MS_2, divide SS_2 by df_2.

$$MS_2 = \frac{SS_2}{df_2}$$ 　　$df_2 = p - 1$
　　　　　　　　$df_2 = 2 - 1$, or 1

$$MS_2 = \frac{45}{1}$$

$MS_2 = 45$

is in the way we represent the sources of variability. Because we have two independent variables in this experiment, we have three sources of variability: Factor 1, Factor 2, and their interaction. The within-groups variability (MS_W) is used as the denominator of all three F ratios required to evaluate the significance of these sources. The three F ratios have been computed and are also shown in the summary table.

EVALUATING THE *F* RATIOS

To judge whether the computed F ratios are significant, we compare them to the table values of F. We get those values from our table of F values in Appendix B, Table B3. The procedures are the same as those used for the simple ANOVA. We locate the proper value of F by using the degrees of freedom of the F ratio. We look across the top of Table B3 to find the degrees of freedom that belong to the top, or numerator, of the F ratio. We look along the side of the table to find the degrees of freedom of the denom-

TABLE **13-12**

Steps 4 and 5: Summary table; analysis of variance for a 2 × 2 factorial experiment and computed *F* ratios				
Source	*df*	**SS**	**MS**	*F*
Between groups		65^a		
Factor 1 (word frequency)	$q - 1 = 1$	20	20	$F_1 = \dfrac{20}{2.38}$ or 8.40*
Factor 2 (category cues)	$p - 1 = 1$	45	45	$F_2 = \dfrac{45}{2.38}$ or 18.91**
Interaction 1 × 2	$(p - 1)(q - 1) = 1$	0^b	0	$F_{1 \times 2} = \dfrac{0}{2.38}$ or 0
Within groups	$N - pq = 16$	38	2.38	
Total	$N - 1 = 19$			

*$p < .05$
**$p < .01$
^{a}**SS$_B$** is usually not shown in published articles.
^{b}We find the sum of squares for the interaction of our two variables by subtracting:

$$\mathbf{SS_{1 \times 2} = SS_B - SS_1 - SS_2}$$

The **SS$_{1 \times 2}$** represents all the between-groups variability that is not explained by the main effect of either independent variable. Its degrees of freedom depend on the degrees of freedom for the main effects. Here, there is no interaction.

inator of our *F* ratio. Each *F* ratio we compute has its own degrees of freedom. That means that each ratio has its own critical value or table value of *F*. When we evaluate each *F* ratio, we must be sure we are using the correct degrees of freedom and the correct critical value.

Practice finding the correct critical value by looking up the table values of *F* for the *F* ratios we have computed. The *F* ratio for Factor 1 (word frequency) has 1 degree of freedom for the numerator (**MS$_1$**); it has 16 degrees of freedom for the denominator (**MS$_W$**). The table value of $F(1, 16)$ is 4.49 at $p < .05$ and 8.53 at $p < .01$. Our computed value of *F* for Factor 1 is 8.40. Therefore the effect of Factor 1 is significant at $p < .05$. Our computed value of *F* is more extreme than the table value at $p < .05$. This means the main effect of word frequency is so large that it is probably not due to chance. Whether the lists contained high- or low-frequency words made a significant difference in subjects' recall. We reject the null hypothesis that the means of the high- and low-frequency groups were sampled from the same population.

The *F* ratio for Factor 2 (category cues) also has 1 degree of freedom for the numerator (**MS$_2$**); it has 16 degrees of freedom for the denominator (**MS$_W$**). We know that the table value of $F(1, 16)$ is 4.49 at $p < .05$ and 8.53 at $p < .01$. (They turn out to be the same as they were for Factor 1 because we had the same number of treatment levels and subjects for both word frequency and category cues.) Our computed value of *F* for Factor 2 is 18.91. The main effect of Factor 2 is significant at $p < .01$: Our computed value of *F* for Factor 2 is more extreme (that is, larger) than the table value at $p < .01$. Subjects who received category cues recalled significantly more items than subjects who did not receive cues. We reject the null hypothesis that the means of the groups under the two levels of Factor 2 were sampled from the same population.

The computed F for the interaction is 0. This is clearly not significant. In effect, this tells us that the variability between treatment groups can be explained by the effect of either word frequency or category cues acting separately on subjects' scores. Also, the impact of each independent variable was unrelated to the value of the other independent variable: The effect of word frequency was the same whether or not subjects received category cues. Similarly, the effect of giving category cues was the same whether subjects saw high- or low-frequency words.

If the interaction had been significant, we would be limited in what we could conclude about the main effects in this experiment. Generally, the existence of a significant interaction makes a discussion of simple main effects unnecessary. If there is a significant interaction, it is usually more useful to discuss the impact of the independent variables in combination with each other. A significant interaction means that the impact of one independent variable differs depending on the value of the other. We can make accurate predictions about subjects' performance only when we know the subjects' position with respect to both variables. For instance, in this example a significant interaction would mean that we could accurately predict the approximate number of items the average subject would recall—but only if we knew both that the subject saw high-frequency words and that the subject received cues. Without the interaction, we can make a reasonably good prediction if we know the subject's position on only one variable. If we know that Carl was given category cues, we automatically also know that he probably did better than the subjects who did not get cues, regardless of whether he saw high- or low-frequency words.

Graphing the results.   When we had only one independent variable, we had only one line to graph. However, in a factorial experiment, we need to do more. The results of our experiment are presented graphically in Figure 13-6. Notice that the vertical axis still represents the dependent variable. The horizontal axis represents the different levels of one independent variable. Each line that is graphed presents the data from a different level of the other independent variable. One line represents the recall of subjects who were given category cues; the other stands for recall under the no-cues condition. You can see from the location of the lines that there are differences between the scores of subjects under the various conditions of this experiment.

Our example yielded two significant main effects. The distance between the two lines (cues versus no cues) reflects the impact of the category cues variable. If giving category cues had no effect on the number of items that subjects recalled, the two lines would fall in the same place on the graph. Similarly, the impact of the word-frequency variable is indicated by the relative position of the data points along the vertical axis. If

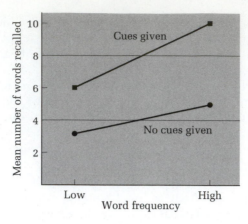

FIGURE **13-6** Graphing the results of a two-factor experiment: Recall of word lists as a function of word frequency and category cues.

word frequency had no effect on recall, subjects would recall about the same number of items in both the high- and low-frequency conditions. These and other possible outcomes are illustrated in Figure 13-7.

Notice that interactions appear on the graphs as lines that are not parallel. If the lines converge, diverge, or intersect, we may have a significant interaction effect. Such graphs are useful for summarizing the results of an experiment to give an overall view of the findings. They are especially useful in constructing summaries of findings for experimental reports. But they are not substitutes for statistical analysis. Even though the results look impressive, we need to carry out all the statistical procedures before we can make precise statements of whether we will accept them as significant findings.

SUMMARY

The *analysis of variance (ANOVA)* procedures are used in experiments having more than two treatment conditions and interval or ratio data. An analysis of variance evaluates the effect of treatment conditions by looking at the variability in data. In the one-way ANOVA, all the variability in the data can be divided into two parts: within-groups variability and between-groups variability. *Within-groups variability* is the degree to which the scores of subjects in the same treatment group differ from one another; *between-groups variability* is the degree to which different treatment groups differ from one another.

Variability is caused by all the sources of *error* in the experiment: differences between subjects as well as measurement errors and other extraneous variables. Error also contributes to within-groups and between-groups variability. Between-groups variability, however, reflects variability due to error and treatment conditions. If the independent variable had

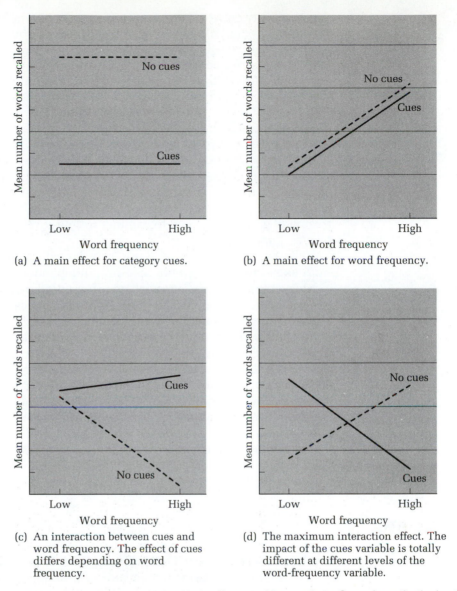

(a) A main effect for category cues.

(b) A main effect for word frequency.

(c) An interaction between cues and word frequency. The effect of cues differs depending on word frequency.

(d) The maximum interaction effect. The impact of the cues variable is totally different at different levels of the word-frequency variable.

FIGURE **13-7** Illustrating other main effects and interactions: Some hypothetical outcomes of an experiment on the effects of word frequency and category cues on list recall.

an effect, there should be more variability between treatment groups than there is within them: Between-groups variability should be large relative to the amount of variability within each group.

The relationship of within- and between-groups variability is evaluated by computing the statistic called F, which represents the ratio between the variability observed *between* treatment groups and the variability *within* the groups. The larger the F ratio, the more likely it is that the variability between groups was caused by the independent variable. F is found by computing these quantities: sum of squares between groups (SS_B) and sum of squares within groups (SS_W). Each of these quantities is divided by its respective degrees of freedom (df) to obtain the mean square between groups (MS_B) and mean square within groups (MS_W). The degrees of freedom of the experiment are used to locate the critical values of F in standardized tables. If the computed value of F is more extreme than the table value at the chosen level of significance, the null hypothesis that treatment means were sampled from the same population is rejected.

The analysis of variance tests the overall pattern of means in the different treatment groups. When there are more than two treatment groups tested, the F test does not test for significant differences between each pair of means. To pinpoint the exact location of the differences across several treatment groups, we need to conduct follow-up tests: *post hoc tests* or *a priori comparisons*.

The basic ANOVA procedures may be extended to handle the data from experiments with more than one independent variable. In factorial experiments the variability in data may be caused by several sources: It can be produced by error; it may also be produced by each independent variable in the experiment. The effects of each independent variable are called *main effects*. In addition, there may be variability due to the *interaction* or combination of variables in the experiment. There is an interaction when the effect of one independent variable changes depending on the value of another independent variable in the experiment. In analyzing data from a factorial experiment, an F ratio is computed to evaluate each main effect and each possible interaction. The basic computational procedures for a two-factor experiment (two-way ANOVA) are similar to those for a one-way analysis of variance.

KEY TERMS

Analysis of variance (ANOVA)   The statistical procedure used to evaluate differences among two or more treatment means by breaking the variability in the data into components that reflect the influence of error and error plus treatment effects; also called the "F test."

A priori comparisons   Statistical tests between specific treatment groups that were anticipated, or planned, before the experiment was conducted; also called "planned comparisons."

Between-groups variability   The degree to which the scores of *different* treatment groups differ from one another (that is, how much subjects vary under different levels of the independent variable); a measure of variability produced by treatment effects and error.

Error   The variability within and between treatment groups that is not produced by changes in the independent variables; variability produced by individual differences and other extraneous variables.

F ratio   A test statistic used in the analysis of variance; the ratio between the variability observed *between* treatment groups and the variability observed *within* treatment groups.

Grand mean   An average of all the treatment means.

Interaction   The change in the effect of one independent variable when another independent variable in the experiment changes value.

Main effect   The action of a single independent variable in an experiment; the change in the dependent variable produced by the various levels of a single independent variable.

Mean square (MS)   An average squared deviation; a variance estimate used in analysis-of-variance procedures and found by dividing the sum of squares by the degrees of freedom.

Post hoc tests   Statistical tests performed after the overall analysis indicates a significant difference; used to pinpoint which differences are significant.

Sum of squares (SS)   The sum of the squared deviations from the group mean; an index of variability used in the analysis-of-variance procedures.

Within-groups variability   The degree to which the scores of subjects in the *same* treatment group differ from one another (that is, how much subjects vary from others in the group); an index of the degree of fluctuation among scores that is attributable to error.

REVIEW AND STUDY QUESTIONS

1. When do we use a one-way analysis of variance?
2. What is within-groups variability?
3. What are the sources of within-groups variability?
4. What is between-groups variability?
5. What are the sources of between-groups variability in an experiment with one independent variable?
6. Explain how the one-way analysis of variance works: How do we use within- and between-groups variability?
7. Briefly explain each of these terms:
   a. Sum of squares within groups (SS_W)
   b. Sum of squares between groups (SS_B)
   c. Mean square within groups (MS_W)
   d. Mean square between groups (MS_B)
   e. The F ratio
8. A researcher computed the F ratio for a four-group experiment. The computed F is 4.86. The degrees of freedom are 3 for the numerator and 16 for the denominator.

a. Is the computed value of F significant at $p < .05$? Explain.

b. Is it significant at $p < .01$? Explain.

9. Suppose we have done a one-way analysis of variance for a three-group experiment, and our computed F is significant. What can we say about the means of the treatment groups of our experiment?

10. Explain why $SS_T = SS_W + SS_B$ in the one-way ANOVA.

11. In addition to the basic requirements (several treatments and so on) for using the analysis of variance, what assumptions must we make about our data in order to use the test?

12. Jack is still unconvinced. "I'd rather use a bunch of t tests than try to figure out this analysis of variance." Explain to him why the analysis of variance is more appropriate when we have more than two treatment groups.

13. Some of the ANOVA terminology is different from the terms used in earlier chapters. However, the concepts are similar. Test your understanding of the concepts by matching the following items on the right with the appropriate concept on the left. (Use each term only once.)

Choice

a. Within-groups variability
b. Mean square
c. Null hypothesis
d. Sum of squares
e. Between-groups variability
f. F
g. Critical value

1. A test statistic _____
2. Total of squared deviations _____
3. A variance estimate _____
4. Treatment means sampled from the same population _____
5. The table value of the test statistic at the chosen significance level _____
6. Reflects variability due to error _____
7. Reflects variability due to error plus treatment effects _____

14. Practice carrying out the one-way ANOVA procedures by calculating the F ratio for these data. The hypothetical scores below represent the responses of subjects in four treatment groups who were given four different driver-education programs. The dependent variable is the subjects' errors on their state examination for a driver's license:

Group 1	Group 2	Group 3	Group 4
3	1	1	2
3	2	1	3
1	1	3	2
3	4	1	5
1	2	2	1

a. What is the computed value of F for these data?

b. Is F significant at $p < .05$?

c. Prepare a summary table for your data.

d. Graph the results.

e. Do you need follow-up tests to pinpoint the location of significant group differences? Explain.

15. Take the data from question 14. Add 10 to the score of each subject in group 1.

a. If you now carried through the ANOVA again, would you expect the computed values of SS_B and SS_W to change? Explain.

b. Would the computed value of F change? If so, how?

c. Carry out the computations on the new data and see whether your predictions are confirmed.

16. Define these terms:

a. Main effect

b. Interaction

17. In the one-way ANOVA, we divide all the variability in our data into just two components. Explain how the ANOVA procedures differ when we are dealing with a factorial experiment.

18. Explain what the components of variability will be in a two-way ANOVA to evaluate the data from a factorial experiment with two independent variables.

19. Identify each of these terms. What does each represent?

a. SS_1 e. MS_1 i. F_1

b. SS_2 f. MS_2 j. F_2

c. $SS_{1 \times 2}$ g. $MS_{1 \times 2}$ k. $F_{1 \times 2}$

d. SS_W h. MS_W

20. When we carry out the ANOVA for a factorial experiment, we compute an F ratio for each independent variable and for each possible interaction. Explain why we do not compute F_W, an F ratio to evaluate the size of the within-groups variability.

21. An experimenter has studied the effects of cigarette smoking on learning. Two levels of the smoking variable were used: All the subjects are smokers, but only half are given cigarettes to smoke during the half-hour before the experiment; the other half are not allowed to smoke after they arrive at the laboratory. There are also two levels of the learning variable. Subjects are all given the same materials to study. However, half the subjects are told they will be asked to recall the words they see (intentional-learning condition). The remaining subjects are told they will be asked to rate various types of printing for readability. They are *not* told they will be asked to recall the actual words they see (this is the incidental-learning condition).

a. Here are some hypothetical data from the learning and smoking experiment. Practice the two-way ANOVA on these data.

| | Factor 1 (Smoking) | |
	Smoked	Did not smoke
Intentional	4	5
	1	3
	3	5
	5	1
	2	2
Factor 2 (Learning)		
Incidental	3	4
	5	3
	4	2
	1	1
	2	4

b. Explain what would happen if we added 10 to the score of each subject in the intentional-learning groups.

c. Explain what would happen if we added 10 to the score of each subject in the incidental-learning, no-smoking group.

22. Prepare a simple graph to illustrate each of the following possible outcomes of the experiment in question 21:

a. There is a main effect for cigarette smoking only: Subjects who smoked remember more. There is no interaction.

b. There is a main effect for learning: Subjects learned more in the intentional-learning condition. There was no main effect for cigarette smoking and no interaction.

c. There was a strong interaction between smoking and the learning conditions. Illustrate at least two forms this interaction might take.

REFERENCES

HOWES, D. (1966). A word count of spoken English. *Journal of Verbal Learning and Verbal Behavior, 5,* 572–604.

LEHMAN, R. S. (1991). *Statistics and research design in the behavioral sciences.* Belmont, CA: Wadsworth.

TULVING, E., & PEARLSTONE, Z. (1966). Availability versus accessibility of information in memory for words. *Journal of Verbal Learning and Verbal Behavior, 5,* 381–391.

WINER, B. J. (1971). *Statistical principles in experimental design* (2nd ed.). New York: McGraw-Hill.

PART**FOUR**
4

Discussion

**Drawing
Conclusions:
The Search for
the Elusive
Bottom Line**

**Writing the
Research
Report**

14

Drawing Conclusions:
The Search for the Elusive Bottom Line

Evaluating the Experiment from the Inside: Internal Validity

Classic Threats to Internal Validity

Taking a Broader Perspective: The Problem of External Validity

Generalizing from the Results

Generalizing Across Subjects

Generalizing from Procedures to Concepts: Research Significance

Generalizing Beyond the Laboratory

Increasing External Validity

Handling a Nonsignificant Outcome

Faulty Procedures

Faulty Hypothesis

Summary

Key Terms

Review and Study Questions

References

We have now discussed all the major steps for setting up and running a psychological experiment and evaluating the results using statistical tests. The goal of an experiment is to establish a cause and effect relationship between an independent and a dependent variable. In this text we have covered a variety of experimental designs and control procedures that enable us to do this in a legitimate way. After the data are analyzed through statistics, however, two questions remain: What does it all mean? Have we accomplished our goal?

Even when there is a significant treatment effect, we have only established a statistical outcome. We have found that, for the data collected, there were differences between treatments so large that they could occur by chance only a small percentage of the time. We have not tested the experimental hypothesis directly. Whether or not the results are statistically significant tells us nothing about the quality of the experiment; statistically significant results may or may not have any practical or theoretical implications. You could, in fact, invent data that show significant treatment effects. Of course, we would like to find statistically significant differences. We would like results to be consistent with predictions. But in addition, we would like findings to be convincing and to have applications in settings outside the particular experiment. When interpreting the results of experiments, we look beyond the simple question of whether they are statistically significant; we evaluate the pros and cons of accepting them at face value. The discussion and evaluation of findings are included in research reports: Besides telling others what we did, we want to tell them what we think it means.

This chapter contains a discussion of some of the problems of drawing conclusions from the results of an experiment. We will review some of the criteria—internal and external validity—used to evaluate the worth of an experiment. We will also focus on some aspects of the generality of particular research findings beyond the context of an experiment. Finally, we will zero in on special problems that arise when our predictions are not confirmed.

EVALUATING THE EXPERIMENT FROM THE INSIDE: INTERNAL VALIDITY

When evaluating an experiment, we begin by judging it from the inside: Is the experiment methodologically sound? Is it *internally valid?* An experiment is internally valid when the effects of an extraneous variable—a variable not the focus of the experiment—have not been mistaken for the effects of the independent variable. An internally valid experiment is free of confounding: Effects on the dependent variable can be attributed solely to the experimental treatment. You will not find many obvious examples of internally invalid experiments in the research literature. All the articles published in major journals (for example, those published by the American Psychological Association, the American Psychological Society, or other professional organizations) are carefully reviewed before they are accepted. Only the best get published. An experiment that contained an obvious source of confounding probably would not make it into print. However, as you read the literature, be on the lookout for more subtle problems. Perhaps a researcher overlooked something that may be important. Perhaps there is an alternative explanation of the findings if we view them in the context of another theoretical approach. If you can make a good case for your criticism, you may have the beginning of your own study to settle the question. Box 14-1 presents an interesting example of a series of studies done to explore possible confounding in a researcher's own published results.

Of course, the best way to assure internal validity is to plan ahead. As you design experiments, you must be sure that your procedures incorporate the appropriate control techniques. Use standard techniques like random assignment, constancy of conditions, and counterbalancing throughout your research. But when you are ready to evaluate the outcome of the experiment, do not forget to consider what *actually* happened. You will need to ask yourself whether the experimental set-up created the conditions you intended? Did subjects follow instructions properly? Was the drug actually in the solution that was injected? Did you manipulate the independent variable successfully? Did the sad film really make the subjects feel sad? Were subjects in the low-anxiety condition really less anxious than subjects in the high-anxiety condition? To be sure, some researchers include an assessment of this as part of their experimental procedures. This is called a "manipulation check" because it checks on how successfully the experimenter manipulated the situation he or she intended to produce.

But even the most careful plans can go awry. You may have designed a tight set of procedures before you began testing subjects, but in practice, you may have been forced to deviate from the plan. Did these small changes affect the way subjects responded? You want to be certain that all your procedures accomplished what you intended. Did you find that sub-

---

BOX **14-1**
Isolating variables in
free recall
In the first of a series of experiments, Ritchey (1982) reported the findings of a study on children's recall. Age was treated as one independent variable: Third-graders, sixth-graders, and adults were the three levels of this variable. The type of stimulus was another independent variable: Words, outline drawings, and detailed drawings were used, as shown in Figure 14-1.

Ritchey found that, contrary to predictions, children remembered outline drawings better in a subsequent recall task. This was unexpected since the detailed drawings included more features that could be encoded in memory. However, even though outline drawings are less elaborate, they are more distinctive (unusual) because they differ from the drawings we usually see.

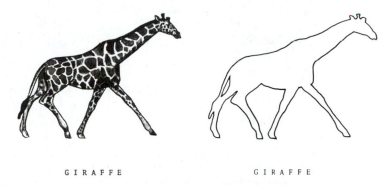

GIRAFFE   GIRAFFE

FIGURE **14-1**   Stimuli used to test pictorial detail and recall: detailed (left) and outline (right) drawings. The figure on the right is less elaborate but more distinctive than the figure on the left. Drawings furnished by Gary H. Ritchey. Used with permission.

In later experiments Ritchey and Armstrong (1982) showed that subjects recalled detailed drawings better than less elaborate drawings—when the degree of distinctiveness was controlled. Distinctiveness, as in the caricature in Figure 14-2, made items easier to recall when the amount of elaboration (detail) was controlled.

Thus the original confounding between elaboration and distinctiveness led to further research. This in turn helped clarify the relationship between the two variables as they influence free recall.

FIGURE **14-2**   Stimuli used to separate effects of elaboration and distinctiveness. Left to right: detailed, outline, caricature drawings. The figures on the left and the right are equally elaborate, but the right-hand figure is more distinctive. Drawings furnished by Gary H. Ritchey. Used with permission.

jects in your control group did not understand directions? Did they keep asking questions to clarify their task in the experiment? Your instructions may have been confusing under that condition. Can you be sure, then, that those subjects really did what you wanted them to do?

Many researchers incorporate an informal interview (or a written questionnaire) at the end of the experiment to get at this kind of information. They ask subjects to talk about their thoughts and feelings during the experiment. They also ask about any questions that subjects might have had during the procedures. If subjects did not follow instructions, the experimental manipulation may not be the best explanation of the findings. In an informal interview, the researcher can also try to get a sense of whether subjects guessed the experimental hypothesis by asking them what they thought the experiment was trying to show. If a group of subjects guessed the hypothesis, their data may be of limited value. It can be advantageous to spend a little extra time interviewing the first few subjects in depth, so that any potential problems in the procedures can be corrected before you run a large number of subjects through the experiment, wasting your time and theirs.

Some of these validity issues are difficult to resolve because of the demand characteristics of the experiment itself. For instance, Orne (1969) suggested that a "pact of ignorance" forms between subjects and experimenter. Subjects may be aware that if they guess the hypothesis of the experiment, their data will be discarded. If you ask them what they understood about the purpose of the experiment, they may not reveal all they know. Subjects need to believe that you really want a truthful answer. Some researchers have gone as far as offering subjects an incentive for guessing the experimental hypothesis during informal interviews. Orne also pointed out that experimenters may not really press subjects for much information, because it may mean that some data may not be usable. Most researchers do not want to spend unnecessary time testing additional subjects. They may be tempted to accept subjects' reports at face value instead of requesting additional information that might provide a more objective evaluation. Avoid this temptation if you want to be sure your experiment is internally valid.

Always review the experimental procedures after the experiment. Did any extraneous variables change along with the independent variable? Did testing conditions change midstream? Were there any other unplanned changes that might have altered subjects' responses? Remember that if something other than the independent variable can explain the results, the experiment is not internally valid. Before concluding that your experiment is internally valid, there are several threats to internal validity that need to be reviewed.

Classic Threats to Internal Validity

Psychologist Donald Campbell (Campbell, 1957; Campbell & Stanley, 1966; Cook & Campbell, 1979) identified eight kinds of extraneous variables that can threaten the internal validity of experiments and quasi-experiments. Since that time, Campbell's listing of these potential sources of confounding has become required course material for successive classes of experimental psychology students; hence, they have become known as the "classic" threats to internal validity. You already know some of them from previous chapters.

A confound is present whenever effects could plausibly be explained by an extraneous variable that occurs in some treatment conditions but not in others. Remember that a confound is an extraneous variable that *varies systematically* along with experimental conditions. An extraneous variable that pops up randomly across conditions is not a confound—it simply increases the amount of variance in the scores that we call error, making it harder to detect a significant treatment effect. Between-subjects designs may be confounded if an extraneous variable affects *some experimental groups but not others* with regularity. Within-subjects designs may be confounded if an extraneous variable is present only in *certain experimental treatments but not in others.* Whenever you evaluate experimental research, consider each of the eight classic threats. You can never be sure that the effects produced on the dependent variable were really due to the experimental manipulation if any of these threats are present.

The first threat is called **history,** and it refers to the history of the experiment. Ask yourself whether the experimental effects could have been caused by any outside event or occurrence rather than the independent variable. (It need not be a great historical event, although it could be.) History is most often a problem when a whole group of individuals are tested together in the same experimental condition. Some outside event that occurred prior to their group testing session could influence responses of the entire group, and effects produced by the event could be mistaken for effects of the IV. Suppose you were testing two different weight-loss programs in which subjects were exposed to your treatment during daily group meetings. You assessed the benefits of the program by measuring how much weight each person lost at the end of a 7-day program. After weighing subjects in both groups, you discover that individuals who received treatment *B* lost an average of 2 pounds that week; whereas the mean for treatment *A* was 4 pounds. You want to make sure that the history of both groups prior to weighing was the same. Imagine the confound in your experiment if individuals in group *B* were weighed right after lunch, but the subjects in group *A* were weighed just before lunch. You would not know if the differences you observed were caused by your diet program or by the fact that one group had just eaten and the other had not.

The second classic threat, **maturation,** refers to any internal (physical *or* psychological) changes in subjects that might have affected scores on the dependent measure (not only "maturing" in the way we typically think of it). The kinds of internal changes that we usually worry about are things like boredom and fatigue that can occur during a single testing session. Boredom or fatigue are more likely in within-subjects designs that require lengthy testing sessions. If you have counterbalanced for the order of treatments, you should not have to worry about a maturation threat, because whatever boredom or fatigue exists will be spread evenly across all the conditions of the experiment. The informal interview is a useful way to discover maturation threats.

Maturation effects can also be a problem in studies that take months or even years to finish. For example, when researchers working with children conduct *longitudinal studies* (evaluating the same groups over a long time period), maturation can be a confound. Young children can make cognitive and physical leaps during certain ages, so researchers must take steps to control for effects produced by these kinds of internal changes. Otherwise, effects produced by the independent variable may be confounded by this extraneous variable. Another kind of maturation can occur even in brief experiments whenever university students are the subjects. Just as you are now more sophisticated about research than you were when you first opened your textbook, other students are gaining knowledge over the course of the semester too. In psychology experiments, the subjects are often students taking a course in introductory psychology, and they may be much more sophisticated about correctly guessing your hypotheses later in the semester than they are in the beginning. You would not want to run condition *A* in September and October and leave condition *B* for November and December!

A **testing** threat refers to effects on the dependent variable produced by a previous administration of the same test or other measuring instrument. It is not uncommon to measure subjects on a dependent variable (anxiety, depression, extraversion) at the beginning of the experiment and then remeasure them using the same test after a treatment is given. Unfortunately, this procedure introduces a testing threat, because individuals frequently perform differently the second time they are tested—even without any intervening experimental treatment. This is one reason that *test-retest reliability* can be an important piece of information for a researcher. Low test-retest reliability can mean that the researcher can expect large differences in scores from one testing session to the next even without any experimental manipulation. Even the most reliable tests that psychologists use—standardized intelligence tests like the Wechsler Adult Intelligence Scale, Revised—do not have perfect test-retest reliability. Performance tends to improve with practice even without any special treatment.

You already know about the fourth threat, **instrumentation.** Whenever some feature of the measuring instrument itself changes over the course of the experiment, internal validity is threatened. The example most often used to illustrate this concept is the case of the "rubber ruler." Imagine that your dependent measure was the length of a line drawn by subjects. To measure it, you use the only ruler you have—a rubber ruler. Unknown to you, it stretches a bit every time you use it. Each consecutive measurement is a little more inaccurate, and successive measurements tend to underestimate line length. If you measure lines drawn by subjects in one treatment condition before you measure lines drawn in a different condition, your measurements in one group will systematically underestimate line length to a greater extent than your measurements in another group.

We are certain you will never use a rubber ruler to measure your dependent variable, but instrumentation threats are not always this obvious. Mechanical measuring instruments can break or become less accurate. A speedometer could falter at high speeds but not at low, underestimating how fast subjects are pedaling an exercise bike in your "high-motivation" condition. But instrumentation is also a potential problem whenever human observers are used to record behavior or when people score questionnaires by hand. The behavior of subjects in one condition can be inherently more interesting than in another, and observers might pay much less attention in a control condition, making more errors in recording. Instrumentation can even be a problem when we use written measures. Are all your questions equally easy to read in all conditions? Are the intervals you typed on all the scales really equal? When you ran out of questionnaires, were your new copies as good as the first set? Did you allow subjects in all conditions the same amount of space to write stories? Seemingly small things like these can alter subjects' responses; if they vary systematically with your treatment conditions, your experiment loses internal validity.

The threat of **statistical regression** (also called "regression toward the mean") can occur whenever subjects are assigned to conditions on the basis of extreme scores on a test. Statistically, extreme scores tend to be less reliable than moderate scores (those closer to the mean). If the same extreme scorers are retested, their scores are likely to be closer to the mean the second time around. Extreme high scores tend to go down a bit, and extreme low scores tend to rise somewhat; scores at both extremes typically get closer to the mean *without any treatment at all.*

Selection is a threat to internal validity whenever a procedure other than true random assignment was used to assign subjects to conditions. How were members of the treatment groups chosen? If nonrandom assignment procedures were used, the subjects in one treatment condition may begin the experiment with different characteristics than the subjects in another condition. And there is always a chance that these characteristics—not your IV—might be the cause of observed effects on the DV.

Did significantly more subjects drop out of one experimental condition than others? If so, consider the threat of **subject mortality.** Drop-out rates should always be stated in a research report, so that the reader can be on the lookout for this threat. Whenever the drop-out rate in a particular treatment condition is high, it should be a red flag: Something about the treatment is making subjects drop out. Usually, it means that the treatment is frightening, painful, or distressing. If the drop-out rate is very high, it can mean that the treatment is sufficiently obnoxious that *typical* subjects would choose to leave, and the ones who remain could be unusual in some respect. You have to ask yourself: "Why did so many subjects drop out?" (Maybe the experimental tasks were too repetitive or the weight-loss regimen was too difficult.) "What does this tell me about the subjects who finished this condition of the experiment?" (They were probably more patient than most people or they were more motivated than most dieters.) Your answers are likely to uncover a confounding variable. Effects on the dependent measure might have been produced by this characteristic, not by the independent variable. The last threat is really a family of threats. A selection threat can combine with another threat to form a **selection interaction.** If subjects were not randomly assigned to groups, one of the other threats may have affected some experimental groups but not others. Selection can interact with history, maturation, mortality, and so on to produce effects on the dependent variable. Suppose you had accidentally assigned people who were more obese to the harder of two diet programs. At the end of your experiment, you found that many individuals in this group dropped out before completing the program. Clearly, your experiment would not be internally valid; you would be faced with the possibility of a selection × mortality threat.

Statistical-conclusion validity.   Let us hope your experiment will be free of confounding variables like the eight classic threats to internal validity. But confounding is not the only threat to an experiment's internal validity. Other kinds of problems can lead to false conclusions about cause and effect relationships between experimental variables. We also need to evaluate the experiment in terms of the results we obtained from statistical tests. We want to be certain that any inferences we make about the relationship between independent and dependent variables have **statistical-conclusion validity,** the validity of drawing conclusions about a treatment effect from the statistical results that were obtained (Cook & Campbell, 1979). Whenever the assumptions of a statistical test are violated, statistical-conclusion validity is in doubt. Clearly, if we used a test statistic inappropriately (a t test using nominal data), there would be some doubt about the validity of conclusions we could draw from a "statistically significant" effect. But less obvious factors can influence statistical-conclusion validity too: the number of statistical tests computed and the power of the statistical test are two common sources of low validity.

You already know the problem created by too many pairwise comparisons—a higher chance of making a Type 1 error (concluding that your treatment had an effect when it really did not). If the chances of making a Type 1 error have been increased, then statistical-conclusion validity has been lowered. Inferring a cause and effect relationship is much riskier. You also know that it is easier to get statistical significance with a large than with a small sample because small samples reduce the power of statistical tests. If your experimental results were barely significant even though you tested 400 subjects, you probably should be cautious about drawing conclusions. We will return to the notion of statistical power and validity when we discuss null findings later in the chapter.

TAKING A BROADER PERSPECTIVE: THE PROBLEM OF EXTERNAL VALIDITY

So far we have talked about evaluating an experiment within itself. Did extraneous variables contaminate the results? Is the study free of confounding? But in addition, we want to look beyond the experiment to broader questions. We want to know whether the experiment has *external validity:* Do the findings have implications outside the experiment? Can we make any general statements about the impact of the independent variable? An experiment is externally valid if the results can be extended to other situations accurately. However, external validity is not an either/or matter; it is a continuum. Some experiments are more externally valid than others.

Generalizing from the Results

When an experiment has some degree of external validity, we may generalize from the results. One definition of generalizing is "making vague." We make our findings more universal than they actually are by ignoring the specific details of the experiment. Instead of speaking in terms of a particular sample (for example, 30 female undergraduates) and a specific set of operational definitions (for example, scores on the Manifest Anxiety Scale), we draw broader inferences from the findings through inductive thinking. When we think inductively, we reason from specific facts to more general principles. Early in the text, you saw how we can use induction to formulate research hypotheses. We also use induction when we make generalizations on the basis of a specific set of findings. Whether our generalizations will be accurate depends on a variety of factors that affect the external validity of an experiment.

An externally valid experiment meets two basic requirements. First, the experiment is internally valid; it demonstrates a cause and effect relationship. The results of the experiment were produced by the independent variable. The experiment is free of confounding. Second, findings that are externally valid can be *replicated.* We (or other researchers) can replicate or duplicate the original findings in other experiments. If we get statistically significant results again, we can be more sure that the findings were not just flukes of our sampling procedures, or Type 1 errors. Valid experimental findings appear again and again. Similar effects should reappear in similar studies. Findings that appear once and cannot be replicated have limited scientific importance, and any general conclusions that we draw from such findings may be inaccurate.

Of course, when you complete a single experiment, you do not know whether the findings can be replicated, unless you are actually replicating some earlier findings. Partly for that reason, you will often see single articles that contain reports of several experiments. These series of experiments typically extend the findings of one principal study. They provide data on alternative explanations and applications of those findings; they also serve to provide evidence that the findings can be replicated. If a researcher consistently obtains confirmation of a hypothesis throughout a series of experiments, the findings have some degree of external validity.

In addition to the overall requirements of internal validity and replicability, we can also look at external validity as it applies to several important issues: generalizability across subjects, across procedures, and beyond the laboratory.

Generalizing Across Subjects

How much can we generalize from one group of subjects to another? How much can we generalize from a sample to the population that interests us? There are no hard and fast answers to these questions. Experiments may have different outcomes when they are run on different samples. For that reason, we try to get samples from the population we want to discuss. If we want to make statements about college students, we ought to sample college students. It makes sense to assume that all college students have some characteristics in common that enable us to speak of them as a group. Nevertheless, we need to be cautious in drawing conclusions about all students on the basis of one study. What is true for students in Kansas may not be true for students in New York.

In addition, practical problems prevent us from obtaining truly random samples. There is typically *bias* in the way human subjects are chosen, if only in that they are all volunteers. The student (or homemaker or salesperson) who volunteers may not be typical. As a group, volunteers may be quite different from nonvolunteers. In fact, some researchers have found that volunteers may differ from nonvolunteers on a variety of factors. These include intelligence, education, and attitudes toward psychological testing (see, for instance, Rosenthal & Rosnow, 1975).

The problem becomes even more acute when we try to extend our findings to a larger group, such as all people. Other writers have commented on the fact that a rather large proportion of research findings in psychology has come from studies of white rats and college students. Of course, many of these findings have been replicated in studies with different species and with a variety of human subjects too. But the fact remains that the generality of our research is often constrained by practical problems. College students are intrinsically interesting. Perhaps more important, they are also more available for research than the average adult who spends the better part of the day at a regular job. White rats are relatively easy to keep, and they cost less than monkeys. These mundane factors shape the research that we do. When we have trouble finding subjects, we will also have trouble getting samples that are typical of the population we are trying to study. Therefore the external validity of the experiment will be limited.

How far can we go in generalizing from a study? Clearly, the further from the population actually sampled, the shakier our position becomes, at least until we do more testing. As research findings are duplicated in subsequent studies with different types of subjects, their generality is supported. Findings that appeared only with red-headed 19-year-old Stanford University students would not have much generality.

At times, it makes sense to explore some of the questions of generality across subjects *within the same experiment.* For instance, if we suspect that age or social class will alter the impact of an independent variable, we may treat those subject variables as additional independent variables. We might, for example, include several different age groups for testing. When that is not feasible, we may be forced to rely on later studies to clarify the role of those additional variables. However, we may accept the generality of some findings for ethical reasons. Manufacturers often use laboratory animals to test the safety of new products such as drugs, shampoos, and cosmetics. A product that proved harmful to nonhuman subjects would not be marketed, even though there was no *direct* evidence that it was dangerous to humans.

Generalizing from Procedures to Concepts: Research Significance

Ideally, our findings also illustrate the operation of general principles: They are not unique to the particular procedures used in the experiment. For instance, Hess (1975) showed that pupil size affected the ratings men gave to photographs. A picture of the same woman received more favorable ratings when she was shown with larger pupils. If this finding has generality across procedures, we would expect to get similar results with different sets of photographs. We would not expect the findings to be peculiar to the photos of one particular person. If the findings also have generality across subjects, we would expect that different types of men would give similar data. We might also expect to see similar responses from women rating photos of men.

Sometimes attempts to generalize across procedures raise theoretical issues that are hard to resolve. These issues arise when we study variables that can have multiple operational definitions. An operational definition, in principle, defines a variable in terms of observable operations, procedures, and measurements. As we saw in an earlier chapter, some variables, like anxiety, may be defined in various ways. When we generalize from the results of an experiment, we face the problem of going from a specific operational definition of a concept to conclusions about the concept itself. We do not want to talk about the number of errors that subjects made; instead, we want to talk about "learning." We may not be interested in the effects of difficult mazes per se; we want to talk about "frustration." Naturally, it is desirable to view findings from this more abstract perspective; we would like to discover principles that explain behavior in general. Ultimately, we would like to use induction to build new theories and to apply our findings to practical problems.

But typically, it is risky to generalize from the findings of a single experiment in this way. The reasons are closely related to some of the issues we discussed earlier. We cannot always be certain of how reliable or valid our procedures are. For example, is your definition of "learning" tapping into the same phenomenon Dr. D. used in his study? One experiment may be suggestive, but we go far beyond our data when we expand our findings to explain all possibilities. For these reasons, researchers "hedge" a bit when they discuss results. The discussion sections of research reports are dotted with qualifying statements: "These findings suggest . . . ," "It seems reasonable that . . . ," "It appears that. . . ." Such statements often distress new researchers who would prefer to be able to say that something occurred with certainty. However, keep these points in mind: First, statistical tests allow us to make probability statements only. We never confirm our research hypothesis directly, and we certainly never "prove" it. We are able to say only that the null hypothesis is an unlikely explanation for what we have observed. That restricts the kinds of statements we may make about our findings.

In addition, as we formulate general conclusions, we move further away from the actual observations that we made. We can make some statements with confidence: We can report exactly what we did and what we observed in the experiment. When we begin to interpret results, we go beyond what we actually did and what we actually observed. As we do so, we are on increasingly shaky ground. Researchers qualify the conclusions they draw because there is no way to be certain their generalizations will always be true. Perhaps the findings describe the effects of the independent variable only under a very specific set of circumstances—namely, those defined in one experiment. Perhaps other operational definitions of the variables would lead to other outcomes. As we know, testing different sorts of subjects might do the same.

Still, if our findings have some degree of generality, we expect them to be consistent with the findings of prior researchers who have studied the same variables. Thus, as we evaluate the generality of our results, we look at them in the context of the work that has already been done in the field.

We have talked about evaluating statistical significance. But findings also have research significance. As we evaluate them, we ask several pertinent questions. First, are they consistent with prior studies? If so, how do they clarify or extend our knowledge? Do they have any implications for broader theoretical issues? At this stage, we are coming full circle on the research process. We began our experimental plan by reviewing the research literature. We used findings of prior researchers as a guide to the important issues and the most suitable procedures for the area we studied. Now, with our results in hand, we consider the place of our findings in the context of prior work in that area.

If our findings do not mesh with earlier findings, our experiment may be suspect. For instance, we know that newborn babies prefer patterns over solid-colored forms (Fantz, 1963). If we have devised a testing system that leads us to conclude that babies actually prefer unpatterned figures, we have a problem. We must be able to reconcile our findings with what has already been shown. Novel findings are suspicious when the prior findings have been replicated; the burden of explanation usually falls on the researcher who claims the novel findings. The possibility of an undetected flaw in the experiment must be evaluated with special caution.

You will occasionally read reports of findings that appear to be conflicting. Often the apparent contradictions result from subtle differences in the operational definitions, the procedures, and the subjects used in various experiments. These inconsistencies may lead researchers into new studies to discover more general principles.

This is part of the process of theory building we discussed in Chapter 1. A theory is meant to make sense of many bits of data. The theory can stand as long as it is adequate to explain observed results. However, as conflicting data appear, more and more supporting assumptions may be needed to explain new findings. Ultimately, the theory may become so burdened by assumptions and exceptions that it must be discarded.

Generalizing Beyond the Laboratory

So far we have talked about using induction to extend the results of specific experiments to other samples, other populations and procedures, and more general concepts. You know by now that we have some difficulty generalizing from one set of experimental procedures to another with accuracy. As you can imagine, we come up against an even greater problem when we extend the results of a laboratory experiment to what we might observe in the real world. Remember that a laboratory experiment is carried out under specific, controlled conditions. The laboratory researcher tries to eliminate all the extraneous influences that might affect the outcome of the experiment. The laboratory experiment is the most precise tool we have for measuring the effect of an independent variable as it varies under controlled conditions. The problem in extending laboratory findings is simple in principle: The variables we study usually do not occur under the same controlled conditions in real life. All sorts of extraneous factors may affect the influence of any one particular variable.

Increasing External Validity

The degree of control we get in a laboratory experiment gives us a great deal of precision. However, some researchers have argued that it may also provide data that have little relevance to our everyday lives. Results obtained in the laboratory may not match those obtained in the field. Hanson (1980) reviewed the literature on attitudes and behavior. He found more laboratory than field studies reporting a positive correlation between reported attitudes and behavior. In the laboratory it seems that people are more likely to think and act consistently. More field than laboratory studies in the literature supported the conclusion that people's reported attitudes do not predict what they will do in their everyday lives.

How safe is it to extend the results of a laboratory experiment to everyday life? There is no clear-cut answer to that question. It is often impossible to know whether the findings of a particular experiment are externally valid until we do additional studies. However, researchers use at least five general approaches to increase and verify the external validity of laboratory findings: aggregation, multivariate designs, nonreactive measurements, field experiments, and naturalistic observation. Let us look at each in turn.

Aggregation. If experiments create a limited, artificial context for behavior, we can begin to increase the generality and external validity of our findings by combining the results of experiments done in different ways.

This is the logic behind meta-analysis, discussed in Chapter 3. Meta-analysis uses statistics to combine and quantify data obtained from many similar experiments.

Epstein (1980) called this approach **aggregation,** the grouping together and averaging of data gathered in various ways. Epstein described four types of aggregation that can be used to increase the external validity of our data and broaden the scope of our experimental findings.

Aggregation over subjects. Combining data of several subjects is already typical of psychology studies. Rather than relying on one or two subjects who may be unusual, we sample greater numbers. Their data are pooled, and our conclusions are based on group averages, as we saw in the last two chapters. Presumably, the larger sample is more representative of the population. These group data in principle should have greater external validity.

Aggregation over stimuli and/or situations. In addition to generalizing to a population, researchers commonly wish to generalize their results across a range of stimuli. For instance, an experiment on color matching that uses only 20 pairs of colors may be used to draw conclusions about the full range of 7500 different colors. In what sense do the 20 selected colors represent the overall range of 7500?

Epstein argued that stimuli must be sampled as effectively as we sample subjects. So must the context of the experiment. A social psychological experiment on helpfulness, for instance, might yield different results during the holiday season when subjects may feel especially cooperative and helpful. We should not assume that such seemingly irrelevant factors do not alter experimental outcomes. Having sampled in a variety of situations, we can have more confidence in our results.

Aggregation over trials and/or occasions. By using many trials and combining multiple testing sessions, we minimize the effects associated with specific trials. If an experimenter unwittingly gives a cue to the correct response on a particular trial, combining data from many trials will cancel out the distortion.[1]

Testing on various occasions also minimizes the effects created by the uniqueness of each testing session. Barber (1976) pointed out that experimental procedures are often not sufficiently standardized. The researcher may be more enthusiastic one time than the next; he or she may use slightly different words to introduce the experiment each time. Aggregating occasions provides data on the replicability of findings obtained in specific testing sessions.

Aggregation over measures. Finally, Epstein recommended using multiple measuring procedures. When we select a measure, such as one achievement test, we are sampling from all the measures available. But our

---

[1] This is analogous to the use of grade-point averages (GPA) to represent academic achievement. Occasionally, you may feel you received too low a grade; another instructor may surprise you with a grade higher than you expect. These differences tend to cancel out. The more courses you take, the better the chances that your GPA reflects your true level of achievement.

one selection may not be the best. Measuring in more than one way will offset the errors we may make using one inadequate instrument.

The different forms of aggregation provide converging lines of evidence for an explanation of behavior. The relative importance of the various forms of aggregation is still open to empirical verification. However, it is clear that we can have more confidence in results that can be reproduced using different subjects, in different situations, on different occasions, and measured in more than one way.

Multivariate Designs. In this text we have focused on research designs that have one independent and one dependent variable. However, since variables do not usually occur separately, we also looked at factorial designs in which we explore the effects of more than one independent variable at a time. As complicated as those designs may have seemed at first, there are other designs that are even more elaborate. They are called **multivariate designs** because they deal with multiple variables. These designs have become increasingly important in psychological research as computer technology has become more widely available. Without computers, multivariate statistical analysis is impractical.

Multivariate designs enable us to look at many variables in combination. Typically, they are designs in which there is more than one dependent variable.[2] Measurements may be made on one or several samples (Cooley & Lohnes, 1971). The procedures used to evaluate the results of these studies are extensions of the basic techniques you have already learned. Some of the more common multivariate designs are multiple correlation and factor analysis, which were discussed in Chapter 2, and multivariate analysis of variance. Here, we will take a brief look at the multivariate analysis of variance so you will have some idea of why multivariate procedures are desirable.

The multivariate analysis of variance is an extension of the analysis of variance described in Chapter 13. We used the ANOVA to study the effect of more than one independent variable in a factorial design. However, those designs had only one dependent variable. By using a **multivariate analysis of variance (MANOVA),** the researcher can measure the effects of independent variables as they affect *sets* of dependent variables. He or she can evaluate whether the independent variables influence subjects' scores on the dependent variables as they occur in combination.

Through this type of design, a researcher interested in "improvement after psychotherapy" could approach the problem in a more comprehensive way than would be possible through a simpler factorial design. For instance, he or she could explore the effects of several independent variables: type of therapy, type of patient, sex of patient, sex of therapist. He or she could also measure several aspects of improvement instead of just one. The researcher might measure the patients' self-reports, the therapists' reports, and symptoms as rated by objective observers. This could provide

---

[2] Cooley and Lohnes (1971) point out that a factorial design is also "multivariate" in the sense that it has more than one independent variable. However, it is customary to restrict the term *multivariate* to designs with several dependent measures.

a more comprehensive index of "improvement" than any single measure. The MANOVA tests the effects of the independent variables on the whole set of measures at once. As with the simpler ANOVA procedures, the researcher would also be able to test for interactions among the independent variables on this set of improvement measures. Type of therapy and type of patient might interact to affect improvement. Higher-order interactions would be possible too; several independent variables may operate together to affect improvement.

With a MANOVA, the researcher also has the option of analyzing differences in trends among the various dependent measures. Effects produced by independent variables may be stronger on some measures than on others. Perhaps patients' reports show greater improvement than symptom ratings. In short, a MANOVA provides much more information than the simpler analysis of variance.

The advantage of this and other multivariate procedures is that they allow us to look at combinations of variables that can be more representative of reality. Instead of focusing on one aspect of improvement in therapy, such as self-report, the researcher can evaluate a spectrum of behavior. This provides a perspective on behavior that can have greater external validity than the simpler univariate approach. For that reason, there are now special journals devoted primarily to multivariate research—for example, *Multivariate Behavioral Research* and *Journal of Multivariate Experimental Personality and Clinical Psychology*. We may be able to increase the external validity of some studies by using multivariate rather than univariate approaches. We can also extend earlier findings by applying these new techniques to old questions.

Nonreactive measurements.   We can also increase external validity by working to minimize **reactivity** in an experiment. Subjects react to being subjects. They react to being observed. Their responses may not be the same as the responses of others who are not observed. Thus they may not have external validity.

We dealt with the problem of reactivity implicitly when we discussed the demand characteristics of an experiment. If an experiment has obvious demand characteristics, the results may not have much generality. They may not reflect what we would see outside the laboratory. When a subject comes into an experiment, the subject assumes an active role. The subject has certain expectations about what will happen in the experiment. If the researcher inadvertently gives cues that tell the subject what to do, the problem is even more serious. Subjects may actively try to generate data that support the reseacher's predictions. The opposite may also happen: A subject may "guess" the hypothesis and then try to produce data to refute it.

We try to control demand characteristics and thus reactivity in part by being careful not to give subjects unnecessary cues. However, as Orne (1969) suggested, it may be difficult to get accurate information about our procedures. The pact of ignorance that forms between subjects and experimenters can affect external as well as internal validity. We can make better assessments of the impact of experimental manipulations through single- and double-blind experiments because the results will be less influenced by subjects' reactivity.

Since some subjects react differently from others, we need controls for other social and personality variables as well. An experiment that does not contain the appropriate controls for response set and response style may not have external validity: The subjects in the experiment may have responded in idiosyncratic ways. We have to be especially wary of variables like social desirability. We know, for instance, that subjects in interviews are apt to present a more favorable picture of themselves, distorting their responses to "look good" in the eyes of the researcher. Results distorted in this way may have little generality; they may not reflect what is true of behavior outside the laboratory.

Developing unobtrusive measures. As long as subjects know they are being observed and measured, their responses may be distorted in some way. If nothing else, they may be a little nervous. For that reason, researchers have also tried to develop specific procedures to measure subjects' behavior without letting them know they are being measured. These **unobtrusive measures** are not influenced by subjects' reactions. They have greater external validity because they yield data more similar to what we expect to see outside an experiment.

For example, in Chapter 2 we discussed the Bechtol and Williams (1977) study of littering, which was done partly through unobtrusive measures. They counted up cans on a beach to obtain an index of littering. Many unobtrusive measures depend on physical aspects of the environment. We could evaluate the popularity of several attractions in a national park by comparing the condition of the trails leading to those sites; the more popular attractions would have well-worn trails. Similarly, we could judge the seating preferences of patrons of a theater by the condition of the seats.

We can also gather data by observing subjects unobtrusively. For example, Marston, London, Cooper, and Cohen (1977) made unobtrusive observations of obese and thin diners in a restaurant. Without diners' knowledge, they recorded behaviors such as toying with food, size of bites, and rate of biting. They identified a "thin eating" pattern among women: smaller bites, a generally slower rate of eating, and more extraneous behaviors, such as putting down the fork now and then. The unobtrusive approach seems to have greater external validity than bringing subjects into a laboratory to observe their eating behavior.

Unobtrusive measures have often been used ingeniously to minimize reactivity. You can find more detailed discussions of nonreactive measures in Webb, Campbell, Schwartz, and Sechrest (1966) and in Willems and Raush (1969).

Field experiments.   Most unobtrusive measures are used outside the laboratory. Perhaps the most obvious way of dealing with the whole problem of external validity is simply to take the experiment out of the laboratory. If we suspect that subjects will behave differently under more realistic conditions, we can try it and see. Clearly, some experimental problems do not lend themselves to this approach. But those that do can lead us into fruitful new tests of our hypotheses.

The **field experiment** meets the basic requirements of an experiment: We manipulate antecedent conditions and observe the outcome on dependent measures of behavior. But instead of studying subjects in the laboratory, we observe them in a natural setting. This approach has greater external validity. For instance, Mann (1977) studied social influence and line-joining behavior. He did his experiment at a bus stop in Jerusalem. Baseline data collected in the control condition showed that people there do not typically form lines to wait for buses. In the experimental condition, confederates of the experimenter took their places at the empty bus stop soon after a bus had stopped there. The experimental manipulations consisted of varying the number of confederates waiting and their positions at the bus stop. Mann found that lines of at least six confederates were required to produce significant levels of line-joining behavior among the first commuters to arrive at the stop.

This approach clearly illustrates the advantages of the field approach. It would be difficult to set up a laboratory situation that would be a credible representation of "waiting for a bus." However, field experiments also have certain limitations. One potential problem is that the researcher often has little control over who participates in the experiment: Whoever came to the bus stop during the experiment was included. Thus samples may not be random. In addition, we may have more difficulty specifying the characteristics of these samples than we do in a laboratory experiment, where we are usually able to get more information about subject variables. Assigning subjects in the field to treatment conditions at random provides some control for subject variables, but we are usually less able to control extraneous variables in a field setting.

Field experiments can be used to validate findings obtained in the laboratory. If results under controlled laboratory conditions have some degree of external validity, we should observe similar outcomes when we study behavior in more realistic settings. Doob and Gross (1968) used this approach to verify data obtained through questionnaires. College students were asked to say whether they would be likely to honk sooner at a stalled new car or a stalled old car in the street. Men predicted they would honk sooner at a newer car. Women predicted they would honk sooner at an older car. In a field experiment, drivers were blocked in traffic by either a new expensive car or an old car. Observers recorded the time before honking. They found that, in general, subjects of both genders actually waited longer before honking at the new expensive car.

The inconsistencies in the Doob and Gross data highlight the importance of verifying evidence (particularly evidence based on subject reports) in more realistic settings. The logical extension of this process is evaluating findings in the context of ongoing behavior, without experimental intervention. This takes us back to one of the basic methods of gathering psychological data— naturalistic observation.

Naturalistic observation.   When we first discussed naturalistic observation in Chapter 2, we looked at Miller's (1977) suggestions for the application of naturalistic observation in psychological research. In particular, he suggested that "naturalistic observation can be used to validate or add substance to previously obtained laboratory findings" (p. 214). Miller also suggested that the process of laboratory research and naturalistic observation may be used in a complementary way. We can use naturalistic observation to suggest specific hypotheses about behavior and then test those hypotheses under the controlled conditions of the laboratory. We can return to the naturalistic setting to verify our findings.

The important implication of Miller's statement is quite simply this: Although we often think of the experiment as a unique, perhaps isolated method of research, we can use it to best advantage when we combine it with other modes of research. Psychologists try to discover principles and applications that will ultimately benefit humanity. Since most of us do not live in laboratories, our research must have some link to everyday life. Psychologists can strengthen that link by using a variety of research methods in combination: They can thus maintain precision without sacrificing relevance.

HANDLING A NONSIGNIFICANT OUTCOME

Up to this point, we have approached the problems of interpreting data from a fairly optimistic perspective. We have more or less assumed that the results we are trying to evaluate were statistically significant and that they supported the predictions. But suppose we have run a well-planned experiment that did not work: Our predictions were not confirmed. Our treatment means are embarrassingly similar. Can anything be gained from such an experiment?

Research journals give the impression that all experiments yield significant results. Unfortunately, we do not see all the studies that were carried out and did not make it into print. The occasional negative outcome reported in the literature is there because that outcome has implications for a theoretical position that predicts there *should* be significant differences. In reality, many studies do not turn out exactly the way the researcher expected.

If you ran an experiment and your results were not significant, don't be discouraged; even the best researchers have an occasional dud. One of the characteristics of a good researcher is that he or she uses nonsignificant findings in a constructive way. A good researcher asks, "Why didn't things go as expected?" and uses the answers to generate better studies. If your experiment did not support your predictions, you should evaluate it from two perspectives. First, were the procedures right? Second, was the hypothesis reasonable?

Faulty Procedures

We may not confirm our predictions because our procedures were faulty. Of course, we are always on the lookout for confounding. For instance, we may have inadvertently allowed control subjects a little more practice time, which compensated for the effects of the special training procedures used in the experimental condition. Review everything you did. Did you apply all the appropriate control procedures? Did you use random assignment? Counterbalancing? Are there problems with demand characteristics or experimenter bias?

Another possibility is that although there were no confounding variables in the experiment, numerous uncontrolled variables increased the amount of variability between individual subjects' scores. If there was a lot of uncontrolled variability in scores on the dependent measure, treatment effects might not have been detectable. Perhaps your reading of the instructions varied from time to time. Maybe some of the subjects were recruited in the laundromat, whereas others came from a factory. Perhaps your measuring instrument was unreliable. Even though the effects of these variables tend to "randomize out" across treatment conditions, they still have the net effect of increasing the amount of within-groups or error variance. If we happen to be studying an independent variable that has a relatively weak effect, we may be in trouble. Our experimental manipulation may not be powerful enough to override the effect of all the other sources of variation in the experiment. We may be unable to reject the null hypothesis even though the independent variable had an effect. That is, we may be making a Type 2 error. You can also see that when an experiment produces a large error variance, statistical-conclusion validity is lowered. In this case, a decision not to reject the null hypothesis based on the results of the statistical test may be an invalid conclusion.

When you get null findings, always ask yourself whether your sample was large enough. It can be difficult to get statistically significant effects using very small samples unless your treatment effects are strong. You may simply not have had enough *power* in your statistical test if only a small number of subjects were used. Low power reduces the statistical-conclusion validity: It can produce a Type 2 error. The technique for assessing power can be found in Cohen (1969).

Another possible cause of null results is that the experimental manipulation was inadequate: The independent variable might have had a powerful effect if we had defined treatment levels in a better way. Our "hungry" rats were deprived of food for only 6 hours. Perhaps 24 hours would have been a more effective fast. We instructed our experimental subjects to form mental images of the words on a screen. Perhaps our control subjects did the same even though we told them not to. Better procedures may be needed. Of course, the only way to check these possibilities is by running new experiments.

We also look for problems in the way we measured the dependent variable. Did we measure what we intended? Was the measure valid? Suppose we are trying to assess the effect of different camera angles on the sexual appeal of photographs. We ask subjects to rate a series of photographs, some of which are mildly erotic. Subjects' ratings may be contaminated by their need to give socially desirable responses. We may end up measuring social desirability rather than the appeal of the photos.

If the experimental procedures are faulty, we have not made a valid test of our hypothesis. The best time to deal with faulty procedures is *before* running the experiment. It seems to be quite easy to formulate after-the-fact explanations: "I did not get significant results because there were flies in the room when I tested my experimental group." Perhaps.

No one enjoys coming to the end of a data analysis only to find that there are no significant differences between the treatment groups. All that work and so little to show for it. At best, it is disappointing. It is not easy to justify so much effort. Perhaps to save face, we sometimes get caught up in attempts to explain that what we did was fine: We designed sound procedures that are internally valid. Is it our fault that a fire drill was called in the middle of the experiment? Of course not. But few of us like to consider the possibility that the experiment was doomed from the start.

Faulty Hypothesis

When we evaluate the outcome of an experiment, we must look at it from the standpoint of all of the internal components we have discussed. In addition to procedural aspects, we want to be sure that the experiment represents good thinking. If we have what seems to be a flawless procedure for studying a hypothesis, we have executed the experiment carefully and the results are not significant, we must at least consider the possibility that the hypothesis was faulty. We need to go back and rethink the problem. Perhaps we overlooked some key feature of prior studies. Perhaps our reasoning was confused. The good researcher uses this evaluation process to decide where to go next.

Be cautious in drawing conclusions from nonsignificant results. They usually are not justified, even if the data are close to being significant. The null hypothesis may be correct. We treat as new knowledge only statistically significant disconfirmations of the null hypothesis. Consider the possibility that the hypothesis needs to be reworked. Use what you learned in this experiment to plan a better one the next time.

SUMMARY

Some of the problems of evaluating and drawing conclusions from the results of an experiment have to do with whether or not an experiment is valid. An experiment that is *internally valid* is free of confounding. In evaluating the internal validity of an experiment, the researcher considers both the plan for running the experiment and what actually happened. If extraneous variables affected the results, they may not be interpretable. Threats to internal validity, such as *history, maturation, testing, instrumentation, statistical regression, selection, subject mortality,* and *selection interactions* are potential confounding variables. An experiment is *externally valid* if the results can be extended to other situations with accuracy. Inductive thinking can be used to generalize from the results of the particular experiment to broader principles and implications.

To be externally valid, an experiment must first be internally valid. However, external validity is a continuum not an either/or situation. Some studies have greater external validity than others. Findings that are externally valid can be replicated. They can be extended to different samples of subjects and to the larger population. They can also be extended across different experimental procedures and discussed in terms of general concepts.

A major part of the interpretation of research is placing it in the context of prior work. If findings are not consistent with prior studies, the discrepancy must be explained. These inconsistencies may form the basis of new experiments.

Results can also have implications outside the experimental setting. It is usually difficult to make this determination within the context of a single study. Researchers use at least five approaches to increase as well as verify the degree of external validity of their findings: aggregation of data, multivariate designs, nonreactive measures, field experiments, and naturalistic observation. Data may be *aggregated,* or combined, over subjects, stimuli, and/or situations. Findings may also be verified through multiple trials and/or testing occasions and by measuring outcomes through more than one measuring instrument. *Multivariate designs* test multiple variables. Measurements may be made on one or more samples of subjects, and relationships between combinations of variables may be assessed. Researchers also try to decrease *reactivity* in their studies; they measure behavior in such a way that the outcome will not be affected by subjects' reactions to the experiment. Reactivity is reduced by controlling the demand characteristics of the experiment. *Unobtrusive measures* of behavior can also be used to control reactivity. The *field experiment* is another means of increasing external validity. Finally, researchers may confirm the validity of laboratory findings through *naturalistic observation.* Using research methods in combination is another fruitful way to study behavior.

There is also the practical dilemma of dealing with nonsignificant findings. Experimental procedures must always be reviewed for sources of internal invalidity, such as uncontrolled extraneous variables. Low statistical power or a weak manipulation of the independent variable should be considered. The thinking that led to the hypothesis should be reviewed to be sure the predictions were reasonable.

KEY TERMS

Aggregation   The grouping together and averaging of data gathered in various ways; including aggregation over subjects, over stimuli and/or situations, over trials and/or occasions, and over measures.

Field experiment   An experiment conducted outside the laboratory; used to increase external validity, verify earlier laboratory findings, and investigate problems that cannot be studied successfully in the laboratory.

History threat   Any outside event or occurrence that could confound an experiment; a classic threat to internal validity.

Instrumentation threat   Any change in some feature of the measuring instrument itself over the course of an experiment; a classic threat to internal validity.

Maturation threat   Any internal (physical or psychological) change in subjects that might affect scores on the dependent measure; a classic threat to internal validity.

Multivariate analysis of variance (MANOVA)   The statistical procedure used to study the impact of independent variables on two or more dependent variables; an extension of analysis of variance.

Multivariate designs   Research designs and statistical procedures used to evaluate the effects of many variables in combination; including multiple correlation, factor analysis, and multivariate analysis of variance.

Reactivity   The tendency of subjects to alter responses or behaviors when they are aware of the presence of an observer.

Selection-interaction threat   The combination of a selection threat with another threat to cause confounding of an experiment; a classic threat to internal validity.

Selection threat   The possibility of confounding in an experiment whenever subjects are assigned to conditions by a procedure other than true random assignment; a classic threat to internal validity.

Statistical-conclusion validity   The degree to which conclusions about a treatment effect can be drawn from the statistical results obtained.

Statistical-regression threat   The possibility of confounding in an experiment whenever subjects are assigned to conditions on the basis of extreme scores on a test; a classic threat to internal validity.

Subject-mortality threat   The possibility of confounding in an experiment whenever the drop-out rate among subjects is related to the treatment condition itself; a classic threat to internal validity.

Testing threat   The effects on the dependent variable produced by a previous administration of the same test or other measuring instrument; a classic threat to internal validity.

Unobtrusive measure A procedure used to assess subjects' behaviors without their knowledge; used to obtain more objective data.

REVIEW AND STUDY QUESTIONS

1. Discuss three potential sources of internal invalidity in an experiment. How would you control each one?
2. How does internal validity affect the conclusions that may be drawn from the results of an experiment?
3. What are the classic threats to internal validity? Why are they potential confounds?
4. What factors influence statistical-conclusion validity?
5. What is external validity?
6. An experiment that is not internally valid cannot be externally valid. Why?
7. Why is replicability a requirement for external validity?
8. Explain how we use inductive thinking to extend the findings of an experiment beyond the particular study.
9. What issues affect the decision to generalize the findings of an experiment to other samples of subjects? To other populations?
10. The operational definition of a particular variable may be changed from one experiment to another. Explain how and why this affects the generality of research findings.
11. In writing up a research report, a psychologist concluded by saying: "These results prove my hypothesis. They provide conclusive evidence that working crossword puzzles improves vocabulary." Without knowing the details of the researcher's procedures, what could you say about each of the following:
    a. Assuming that the findings are statistically significant, are the researcher's conclusions justified? Explain.
    b. Assume that several researchers have conducted similar experiments. The previous findings have been inconclusive. What can be said about the conclusion in view of prior research?
    c. Given your answers to (a) and (b), reword the experimenter's conclusions appropriately.
    d. If you chose to conduct a similar study, what extraneous variables might affect the internal validity of the experiment?
    e. Explain how aggregation could be used to broaden the implications of these findings.
12. What are multivariate procedures?
13. How can multivariate procedures be used to increase the external validity of an experiment?
14. How does the reactivity of subjects influence the external validity of an experiment?

15. Discuss three techniques for reducing reactivity.
16. Pick one of the laboratory experiments we have discussed in this text; devise a way to confirm the findings of that experiment either through a field experiment or through naturalistic observation.
17. Deanna is not quite sure how to interpret the results of an experiment she did. She found that her data were not quite significant ($p < .07$). What advice would you give her about explaining her findings?
18. Jack is skeptical of this whole chapter: "If we have to put so many limits on what we can say about an experiment, why bother? Let's just talk about what we found and leave it at that." Explain to Jack the purpose of generalizing from our findings. What do we accomplish when we generalize correctly?

REFERENCES

BARBER, T. X. (1976). *Pitfalls in human research*. New York: Pergamon Press.

BECHTOL, B. E., & WILLIAMS, J. R. (1977). California litter. *Natural History, 86*(6), 62–65.

CAMPBELL, D. T. (1957). Factors relevant to the validity of experiments in social settings. *Psychological Bulletin, 54,* 297–312.

CAMPBELL, D. T., & STANLEY, J. C. (1966). *Experimental and quasi-experimental designs for research*. Chicago: Rand McNally.

COHEN, J. (1969). *Statistical power analysis for the behavioral sciences*. New York: Academic Press.

COOK, T. D., & CAMPBELL, D. T. (1979). *Quasi-experimentation: Design and analysis issues for field settings*. Chicago: Rand McNally.

COOLEY, W. W., & LOHNES, P. R. (1971). *Multivariate data analysis*. New York: Wiley.

DOOB, A. N., & GROSS, A. N. (1968). Status of frustrator as an inhibitor of horn-honking responses. *Journal of Social Psychology, 76*(2), 213–218.

EPSTEIN, S. (1980). The stability of behavior. II. Implications for psychological research. *American Psychologist, 35*(9), 790–806.

FANTZ, R. L. (1963). Pattern vision in newborn infants. *Science, 140,* 296–297.

HANSON, D. J. (1980). Relationship between methods and findings in attitude-behavior research. *Psychology, 17,* 11–13.

HESS, E. (1975). Role of pupil size in communication. *Scientific American, 233*(5), 110*ff*.

MANN, L. (1977). The effect of stimulus queues on queue-joining behavior. *Journal of Personality and Social Psychology, 35*(6), 437–442.

MARSTON, A. R., LONDON, P., COOPER, L., & COHEN, N. (1977). In vivo observation of the eating behavior of obese and nonobese subjects. *Journal of Consulting and Clinical Psychology, 45,* 335–336.

MILLER, D. B. (1977). Roles of naturalistic observation in comparative psychology. *American Psychologist, 32,* 211–219.

ORNE, M. T. (1969). Demand characteristics and the concept of quasicontrols. In R. Rosenthal & R. L. Rosnow (Eds.), *Artifact in behavioral research*. New York: Academic Press.

RITCHEY, G. H. (1982). Pictorial detail and recall in adults and children. *Journal of Experimental Psycholoy: Learning, Memory, and Cognition, 8*(2), 139–141.

RITCHEY, G. H., & ARMSTRONG, E. L. (1982). *Elaboration, distinctiveness, and recognition time in free recall*. Paper presented at the meeting of the Psychonomic Society, Minneapolis, MN.

ROSENTHAL, R., & ROSNOW, R. L. (1975). *The volunteer subject*. New York: Wiley.

WEBB, E. J., CAMPBELL, D. T., SCHWARTZ, R. D., & SECHREST, L. (1966). *Unobtrusive measures: Nonreactive research in the behavioral sciences*. Chicago: Rand McNally.

WILLEMS, E. P., & RAUSH, H. L. (Eds.). (1969). *Naturalistic viewpoints in psychological research*. New York: Holt, Rinehart and Winston.

15

Writing the Research Report

The Written Report: Purpose and Format

Major Sections
Descriptive Title
Abstract
Introduction
Method
Results
Discussion
References

Looking at a Journal Article
General Orientation
A Sample Journal Article

Preparing Your Manuscript: Procedural Details

Making Revisions

Summary

Key Terms

Review and Study Questions

References

Report writing is a major part of the research process. For that reason, you may find that your instructor shows little sympathy for your reluctance to write up dull results. Most likely, you will be required to write a report, whether or not your findings will change the direction of psychology. In this chapter we will discuss the purpose and structure of psychological **research reports.** As you know, the overall structure of this text parallels the general structure of these reports. In each report we find an introduction, a method section, a section on results, and a discussion. Each report also has an abstract or summary and a list of references. We will begin by reviewing the basic content of each section. Then we will look at an example of an actual research article to see how these ideas are put into practice. We will also focus on specific aspects of preparing the manuscript of a report and on points that often cause problems for beginners.

THE WRITTEN REPORT: PURPOSE AND FORMAT

The primary purpose of a written report is *communication.* Through our report we tell others what we did and what we found. In addition to reporting findings, we should also provide enough information to enable other researchers to make a critical evaluation of procedures and a reasonable judgment about the quality of the experiment. In addition, we want to provide enough information to enable others to replicate and extend the findings.

Research reports are written in a **scientific writing style.** You have probably noticed that the style of writing in published articles seems fact-filled and dry compared to other kinds of writing. It is supposed to be. The goal of an experimental report is to provide information, not to entertain the reader or express opinions. You already know that all facts need to be documented by citing the published sources where you read about them. In addition, when you write a research report, avoid seeming opinionated about your topic: Keep your personal feelings out of the report. It is a scientific document for public communication, not an essay or personal statement. Authors try to avoid personal pronouns like *I* or *we* whenever possible (their occasional use is acceptable to avoid awkward sentences). The scientific style is also parsimonious—an author attempts to give complete information in as few words as possible. The amount of publication space in journals is limited, so authors write as concisely as possible, selecting their words carefully. It takes practice for most of us to write this way, because it is very different from more common writing styles. If you can avoid writing any sentences that seem "flowery," you will be on your way to a scientific writing style. Always avoid slang; it lacks exact meaning and may not be universally familiar.

When you write your research report, be careful to use unbiased language. The American Psychological Association (APA) and other journal publishers are committed to encouraging language free of gender or ethnic bias in their publications. There are several techniques for avoiding bias: When writing about ethnic groups, use the term that is currently preferred by most members of that group. Always use nonsexist language in your report. Whenever you are writing about individuals (research participants, people in general), select words that are free of gender bias. Because some sexist words are so embedded in our language, this can seem awkward at first. For example, do not talk about the benefits of psychological research for "man" or "mankind" when you really mean "all people"—say "people" instead. Don't refer to a subject as "he" (unless all your subjects really were male); use "he or she" or "they," instead. Never assume that a researcher is male; 50% of those currently graduating with Ph.Ds in psychology are women.

One of the other difficulties people encounter when they write their first reports is that they take too much for granted. After you have worked on a study for some time, what you did may seem quite obvious. The difficulty is that although it is obvious to you, your readers will not understand it unless you explain it. Remember that the whole point of writing a report is to communicate information. A reader should be able to understand what you did and why without having to come to you and ask questions about it.

Psychological reports are expected to follow the format set by the APA. It is presented in detail in the *Publication Manual* (1983), which was prepared to make the job of reporting easier for researchers as well as readers. As early as 1928, psychologists and other social scientists recognized the need for standards for presenting research data. The first "manual" was a seven-page article that appeared in the *Psychological Bulletin* in 1929. The present manual spans 208 pages and contains material on all aspects of appropriate content, as well as detailed explanations of specific layout and style requirements. Our presentation here will be brief; if you have questions about specific problems, you should refer to the manual.

The need for a standard format for reports becomes clear when you consider the tremendous volume of research going on today. The APA alone publishes about 20 journals, which translates to about 1500 articles per year. Many thousands more are reviewed and not accepted for publication. Others are published in numerous non-APA, psychology-related journals. If everyone used a different format for writing reports, reviewers would have a hard time evaluating the work; writers would agonize over its presentation; and readers would have trouble locating the information they need. The design of your experiment is the place for creativity, not the format of your report—*it* should conform to the APA standards. Although some of the details of format vary from one journal to another, most follow the overall structure outlined here.

MAJOR SECTIONS

Every research report must contain these major components: a descriptive title, an abstract, an introduction, a method section, a results section, a discussion section, and a list of references. We will look at each part in turn so that you will have a clear idea of the basic requirements of each. Many reports contain additional components, such as footnotes, tables, or figures (graphs, pictures, or drawings). For now we will focus on the content of the major sections. Try to develop a feel for what we accomplish through each section. Later, we will look at layout requirements and additional components.

Descriptive Title

Reports need a **descriptive title** that gives readers an idea of what the report is about. The simplest way to guarantee this is by naming both the independent and dependent variables of the study in the title, stating the relationship between them. Here are some examples from articles we have discussed in prior chapters: "Effect of Initial Selling Price on Subsequent Sales" (Doob et al., 1969); "Anxiety, Fear, and Social Affiliation" (Sarnoff & Zimbardo, 1961); "Social Enhancement and Impairment of Performance in the Cockroach" (Zajonc, Heingartner, & Herman, 1969). Titles like "A Psychological Experiment" are far too vague to be of much use to a reader who is trying to track down specific information. However, titles should be limited to about 15 words; leave something to be said in the body of the report.

Abstract

An **abstract** is a summary of the report. It should be 100 to 150 words long for an empirical study. Write it in the same general style you use in the report. Here and elsewhere in the report, write in the *past tense* (because the research has already happened). The abstract should be a concise synopsis of the experiment. It should be written so that it makes sense and can stand by itself. It should contain a statement of the problem studied, the method, the results, and the conclusions. Unless you are replicating a particular published experiment, leave out citations. Tell your readers what sorts of subjects you used (for example, 30 adult macaque monkeys). Describe the design (for example, a 2×2 factorial design). Summarize the procedures used in the experiment and state the results briefly. You should also state the important and interesting conclusions you reached.

At this point you may be thinking, "All that in 150 words or less? You must be kidding!" Actually, we're quite serious. But it may help you to know that abstracts are notoriously difficult to write; they require a technique few of us practice very often. For that reason, many people find it easiest to write the abstract after they write the report. You may want to do the same.

The practical value of the abstract. You will have a better appreciation for the content of abstracts if you understand how and why abstracts are used. With so many articles coming out each year, information on a selected topic can be very hard to track down. It would be quite tedious for a researcher to have to search through the indexes of a dozen different publications, many of which appear monthly. It would also be very time-consuming to read every article. Fortunately, we have other publications, such as *Psychological Abstracts* and *Social Science Citation Index,* which are guides to the literature in psychology. If you ask, your reference librarian will direct you to available sources and show you how to use them if you need help.

Psychological Abstracts is the major reference source in psychology. You will find it in the reference section of your library. Many university libraries also have a computerized program for searching through abstracts (PsycLIT). As the name implies, *Psychological Abstracts* contains the abstracts from journal articles. We can locate articles that will help us without having to scan every report in every journal. *Psychological Abstracts* also includes some book listings and references to other kinds of psychology-related documents, such as government reports. You should become familiar with *Psychological Abstracts* and other guides to the literature, because they save a lot of time. Using *Psychological Abstracts* efficiently, however, requires a bit of practice.

Using *Psychological Abstracts*: Locating reference information. We are going to briefly describe how to use *Psychological Abstracts*. (On your own, you can check on the availability of a computer literature search; some libraries, however, do charge for this service.) *Psychological Abstracts* is made up of several distinct parts. First, monthly issues are self-contained. They include the abstracts and references, an author index, and a brief subject index. Twice a year an index is published that lists articles by both subject and author. These index volumes are more efficient to use when locating articles because they organize the information from six monthly issues into one volume—but they will be missing abstracts from the most recent articles, which were published after the index was compiled. Each year the abstracts themselves are bound into two separate volumes. For 1976, for example, your library has two large, bound volumes of abstracts and two bound volumes of indexes—one of each for January–June 1976 and one of each for July–December 1976. Every 3 years, cumulative subject and author indexes are also published.

Unless you are researching a problem of historical interest, it is usually most efficient to start your review of the literature by looking in the most recent *Abstracts*. Journal articles contain lists of references that can be used to go farther back into a problem if necessary. (Review articles are especially useful for this purpose.) How far you will have to go depends on the problem and your purposes. Usually, you will be looking for information related to a particular problem area. Let us say we are planning an experiment on what happens when you pay people different salaries for doing the same job, and we would like to see what other researchers have done in this area.[1] We look in the subject index under the appropriate topic headings. Usually, the more precise we are about what we are seeking, the easier it will be to find. For instance, *salaries* is a fairly specific term. Under this heading, we find several numbers listed; these numbers pertain to abstracts from different studies that relate to "salaries." The numbers in the index tell us where the abstract for each study is located, and we can look them up. If the abstract sounds like the study might be useful to us, we can find and read the whole article. As you search through the indexes, you will develop a sense of what terms to check out. The indexes also suggest alternative terms to check. The *Thesaurus of Psychological Index Terms* published by the APA (1981) is also a useful guide to subject terminology.

If you were searching for the work of a particular researcher, you would simply look for that person's name in the author indexes. You can also begin to check the author index as you identify key people in your field of interest. You can quickly see whether they have done anything lately.

Figure 15-1 shows a portion of a page from *Psychological Abstracts Index,* 1991, Volume 78, to illustrate what we may find under "salaries." We look through the items listed to see whether any are relevant to our work. There is one on temporary pay reductions for manufacturing employees beside the number 7467. It sounds promising, so we would like to read the abstract of the article on that topic. To find it, look in the *Abstracts* volume that corresponds to this particular index volume (Volume 78). However, note that the numbers given in the index volumes are not page numbers. Instead, they are numbers of the abstract entries contained in the *Abstracts* volumes. For instance, 7467 refers to entry 7467 in Volume 78 of *Psychological Abstracts.* We look for entry 7467 in that volume and find it on page 743. A portion of that page is shown in Figure 15-2.

As you can see, the entry in *Psychological Abstracts* contains the full journal title of the article. It contains the journal reference so we will be able to locate the actual article. And it contains the journal abstract itself. We can read the abstract and decide whether the article is relevant to what we are doing. If it is, we can find and read the article. If it is not, we can simply move on to something else. The abstract is probably the most frequently read part of any article. If the abstract is poor, uninteresting, or uninformative, readers may not go on to read the entire article. That is why

[1] Information on locating reference material is included here to demonstrate the importance of writing good abstracts. The research literature should always be reviewed before designing and conducting a study. Additional information on library research can be found in *Library Use: A Handbook for Psychology* (Reed & Baxter, 1983).

temporary pay reduction, theft rates, manufacturing employees, 7467

FIGURE **15-1** A sample from *Psychological Abstracts Index,*
1991, *78.* Copyright © 1991 by the American Psychological
Association. Reprinted with permission.

it is especially important to include all the pertinent facts of an experiment
in the abstract.

Good abstracts make our research more accessible to our readers. Good
titles do the same, since the title determines the way that an article will be
indexed in *Psychological Abstracts.* As you use *Psychological Abstracts* in
your review of the research literature, you are also preparing for the next
major section of your research report, the introduction.

Introduction

The **introduction** sets the stage for what follows. A good introduction tells
readers what you are doing and why: It introduces your hypothesis and
how you will test it. As you write your introduction, think about what
readers should get out of it. The focus should be the hypothesis. After reading the introduction, readers should have answers to the following questions: What problem are you studying? What does the prior literature in
the area say about the problem? What is your hypothesis? What thinking
led up to that hypothesis? What is the overall plan for testing the hypothesis? Do you make any specific predictions about the outcome of the
study?

7467. Greenberg, Jerald. (Ohio State U. Faculty of Management & Human
Resources, Columbus) Employee theft as a reaction to underpayment inequity: The hidden cost of pay cuts. *Journal of Applied Psychology.*
1990(Oct), Vol 75(5), 561–568. —Employee theft rates were measured in
manufacturing plants during a period in which pay was temporarily reduced
by 15%. Compared with pre- or postreduction pay period (or with control
groups whose pay was unchanged), groups whose pay was reduced had
significantly higher theft rates. When the basis for the pay cuts was thoroughly and sensitively explained to employees, feelings of inequity were
lessened, and the theft rate was reduced as well. The data support equity
theory's predictions regarding likely responses to underpayment and extend
recently accumulated evidence demonstrating the mitigating effects of adequate explanations on feelings of inequity. [An erratum for this article
appears in *Journal of Applied Psychology,* 1990 (Fall), Vol 75(6).]

FIGURE **15-2** A sample item from *Psychological Abstracts,*
1991, *78,* p. 743. This citation is reprinted with permission
(fee paid) of the American Psychological Association, publisher of *Psychological Abstracts* and the *PsychINFO Data-
base* (Copyright © 1991 by the American Psychological
Association) and may not be reproduced without its prior
permission.

The introduction is the proper place to include the review of the research literature that led to your hypothesis or that lends support to it. For instance, you might show how prior findings have been inconsistent or ambiguous. Explain how your experiment may clarify the problem. It is not necessary to cite every bit of research that has ever been done in an area; cite only what is most essential to understanding the nature of the problem. Be careful to show how you got to your hypothesis. Readers should be able to follow the thinking that took you there. Do not assume that anything is obvious.

State your hypothesis explicitly at some point in the introduction. Usually, it should appear toward the end of the introduction, after you have explained the research and the thinking behind it. Identifying independent and dependent variables is appropriate. Then say something about general procedures if that seems warranted. You may want to include a sentence or two about operational definitions to prepare readers for what follows in the report. If you have made predictions about the outcome of the study, by all means say so. Be sure you also say why you expect these results; do not expect readers to guess what you are thinking.

Method

The **method section** tells readers how you went about doing the experiment. It should be detailed enough to allow another researcher to read it and replicate your experiment. It is customary to subdivide the method section into several labeled subsections: subjects, apparatus (or materials), procedure, and design.[2] You may not need every subsection; you should adjust the format according to the kind of study you are presenting.

Subjects. The subsection on subjects (sometimes called "participants") should tell readers the important characteristics of your sample. It should answer these key questions: How many subjects did you have? What are their relevant characteristics (age, sex, species, weight, and so on)? How were subjects recruited and/or selected? Were they paid or given course credit? How did you assign them to conditions? Give any additional information that may be important to understanding your experiment. If any subjects dropped out of the study, report that too and explain the circumstances.

Apparatus. This section is sometimes called the "materials" section. Use your judgment to decide which label is more appropriate for your study. In this subsection you should provide readers with a description of any equipment used in the study. Standard things like stopwatches or pencils do not have to be described in detail. However, refer to any ready-made,

---

[2] From time to time, authors deviate from the customary subheadings when they feel it is appropriate. For example, *Participants* sometimes replaces *Subjects*. Unusual manipulations, experimental stimuli, or complex dependent measures are sometimes placed in separately labeled subsections.

specialized equipment by name, manufacturer, size, and model number—for example, "The film clip was presented on an RCA 19-inch color monitor, model #318482." Identify standardized tests by name and include a citation—for instance, "Subjects filled out the Social Desirability Scale (Crowne & Marlowe, 1964)." If you built your own equipment or prepared your own stimulus figures or questionnaire, give the details. Sometimes an illustration or sample items need to be included. Be sure to provide all the information essential for replication, including physical dimensions like length, width, and color if appropriate. Unless another measure is standard (as in TV screens), give measurements in metric units.

Procedure.   This section should provide readers with a clear description of all the procedures followed in your experiment. After reading this section, a person should know how to carry out the experiment just as you did it. "Subjects were seated in a comfortable chair located approximately 2.85m from the television monitor." Any special control procedures you used should be identified here—for instance, "The film clips were presented in counterbalanced order to control for order effects." You may want to include the exact instructions you gave to subjects, particularly if the instructions constituted your experimental manipulation. Otherwise, simply summarize them.

One easy way to write a procedure section is to report everything step by step in chronological order. Use some discretion in reporting commonplace details; the reader does not need to be told obvious things about the procedures. For instance, if you gave subjects a written test, it would be unnecessary to report that they were seated during the test. However, do report anything unusual about your procedures. (Having to use the experimenter's back as a writing surface would be unusual, and you would need to report it.) Be sure to identify your experimental manipulations carefully. Spell out the way you measured the dependent variable. Always ask yourself whether someone could replicate your experiment based on what you have said.

Design.   This section is usually optional. If your design is fairly straightforward (for example, two independent groups), it probably does not require a separate section. You can easily give all the necessary information elsewhere. However, in your first reports, you may find it helpful to write a design section anyway to keep the plan of your experiment in focus.

Identify the independent and dependent variables in this section. Indicate the kind of research design you have. If it is a factorial design, it is always helpful to the reader if you include the factor labels (as you learned in Chapter 7). For instance, in a $6 \times 4 \times 3$ factorial design, write out the factor names along with the design. Tell whether the design was a between-subjects, within-subjects, or a mixed design—for example, "The experiment was a $6 \times 4 \times 3$ (reinforcement $\times$ food deprivation $\times$ age) between-subjects factorial design." In mixed designs, be sure to specify the within- and between-subjects factors, because they might not be obvious to the reader. For example, if reinforcement had been a within-subjects factor in this experiment, you could say instead, "Level of reinforcement was a within-subjects factor; food deprivation and age were between-subjects factors." As the design becomes more complicated, readers usually need more explicit help in structuring the plan of the experiment. Do what makes the most sense to clarify your study. Finally, specify the dependent variable: "The dependent variable was the amount of time it took to learn the maze."

Results

The **results section** of a report should tell readers what you found. Findings are easier to understand if you begin with a brief summary of your principal findings stated *in words.* Then report the results of your statistical tests (F or t values, results from post hoc tests, and so on) and summary data (for example, means, standard deviations, or range, as appropriate). Remember that we usually do not report individual scores unless we have a small N design. Tell readers what statistical tests you used to evaluate the data, along with computed values of test statistics. Indicate degrees of freedom and significance levels. Be sure that you have stated all group means included in important findings.

Suppose a student researcher tested a previous finding from the literature (Greeson & Williams, 1986) that violent music videos can increase people's acceptance of violent behavior. The student conducted a two-independent-groups experiment testing the effects of watching violent versus nonviolent music videos on subjects' attitudes toward violence. She designed a questionnaire to measure attitudes toward violence; the higher the score, the more accepting an individual was of violent behavior. A between-subjects t test showed that the prediction was confirmed by her experiment, and she was able to reject the null hypothesis. Her results section would begin by stating, in words, what she found: "As predicted, subjects expressed more positive attitudes toward violence after viewing violent music videos than after viewing nonviolent videos." Then she would report the results of her statistical tests and relevant summary data—for example, "A t test indicated that attitude scores were significantly different after violent videos than after nonviolent ones, $t(34) = 3.12$, $p < .01$. Subjects shown a violent music video were more accepting of violence ($M = 7.89$, $SD = 2.10$) than subjects who watched a nonviolent video ($M = 4.20$, $SD = 1.89$)." There are no hard and fast rules for presenting statistics—as long as the presentation is clear to the reader.

In a simple two-group experiment, the results section would probably not be very long. But if you have a factorial design, you will have more results to report (main effects, interactions, post hoc tests, and the like). If you have more than one dependent measure, you may wish to present the results for each measure separately. As with the simpler experiment, begin by stating, in words, what you found. Then report all the effects produced by your statistical tests and relevant summary data for each kind of effect.

Typically, we report main effects first, then go on to the interaction(s). Finally, give the results of post hoc tests or other group comparisons if you used them. Be sure that the reader can understand one effect completely before going on to the next. If you have presented a lot of statistics, it is helpful to the reader if you summarize the effects in words at some point.

Sometimes results can be summarized most easily through figures or tables, but these should be used sparingly. They should enhance what you have to say about the data. Avoid reporting the same statistics or summary data in the text *and* in a table or graph. If your *F* values, means, and *SD*s are in a table, simply refer the reader to the table at the appropriate time—for instance, "Results of the statistical tests and group means are shown in Table 1." If you use figures and tables, they must be referred to within the text. They should be an integral part of the presentation, not ornaments dangling in space. (Later in the chapter, you will learn how to include them in your written report.) The results section is used only to present the objective data as they appeared in the experiment. Interpretation of the results belongs in the next section.

Discussion

The overall purpose of the **discussion section** is to evaluate and interpret the results. Your discussion should tie things together for readers. In the introduction you reviewed the literature and showed readers how you arrived at your hypothesis and predictions. In the method section, you described the details of what you did. In the results section, you presented what you found. Now in the discussion, you need to pull everything together. You need to explain what you have accomplished: How do your findings fit in with the original problem stated in the introduction? How do they fit in with prior research in the area? Are they consistent? If not, can any discrepancies be reconciled? The discussion section is also the place to talk about what you think your results mean: What are the implications of the research? Can you generalize from the findings? Does further research suggest itself?

Begin the discussion section with a clear summary sentence or two restating your results (in words only). Any sources of confounding that might influence the interpretation of the data should be reported. But be reasonable. It is not necessary to mention things that are probably irrelevant: Whether or not all subjects had breakfast probably is not critical, especially if you assigned them to conditions at random. However, if half the experimental subjects walked out on the experiment before it was over because they were faint from hunger, your readers should know that, as well as how it may have affected the data.

Do not get caught up in offering excuses for why your results were not significant. Rethink both your procedures and your hypothesis if necessary. Apologies for small samples often lead to this common error: "If more subjects had been tested, the results would have been significant." Avoid being tempted to make something out of nonsignificant findings, even if they go in the direction you predicted. *A trend in the right direction does not guarantee a significant outcome with a larger sample.* Very small samples are unreliable; the trend could even reverse itself if you had a large sample! Running the experiment with more subjects is the only way to validate your hunch.

Keep in mind that when readers finish the discussion section, they should have a sense of closure. They should know where you were going and why. They should know how you got there, what you found, and where it fits in the context of what was already known about the problem.

References

Any articles or books mentioned in the report should be listed in your **references** at the end. These enable readers to go back and make their own evaluation of the literature. Be sure that the references are accurate and that they follow the APA procedures for listing them.

LOOKING AT A JOURNAL ARTICLE

Now let us take a detailed look at the requirements of a research report by going through an actual journal article. We have selected an article that is relatively short; many journal articles are considerably longer. First, we will examine the basic content of the article; then we will look at the procedures to follow when preparing the manuscript. We will do this in separate steps just as you should when writing your own manuscript. Work on the content first. Then put in the procedural details as you create your final draft. Keeping these stages separate will simplify your task. For our example we will use the same article we already located in *Psychological Abstracts.* The article will appear on the following right-hand pages with our comments on the left-hand pages so that you may shift back and forth easily between the two.

General Orientation

Journal articles are usually written for informed audiences. They are also written with strict constraints on the amount of space that can be devoted to any single topic. That is why you may find some articles difficult to follow unless you have already read somewhat extensively in the field. Therefore, before we launch into our examination of the article, let us review some general concepts you need in order to understand it.

The article (Greenberg, 1990) is a report of an experiment on the effects of a temporary pay cut on employee theft. Greenberg hypothesized that pay cuts would lead to increased theft from the workplace. He also predicted that the amount of stealing would be related to workers' feelings about how unfairly, or inequitably, they were being treated by the company; people who felt that the temporary pay cut was fair would steal less than people who felt it was unfair.

Greenberg's hypotheses were predictions that he made on the basis of equity theory as proposed by Adams (1965). You might recall that we discussed a later version of equity theory (Walster, Walster, & Berscheid, 1978) in Chapter 3. The theory is a simple one: People who feel that they are not being fairly rewarded for their contributions will react by trying to increase their rewards in some way. Equity theory predicts that workers who feel that their pay is unfair, or inequitable, will attempt to increase their outcomes (rewards minus costs) in order to restore feelings of equity. One way they can do this, Greenberg predicted, is by stealing from the workplace.

Greenberg also hypothesized that feelings of inequity over a pay cut could be reduced if the reasons for the pay cut were adequately explained to workers. Workers who were not given a good explanation for the pay cut would feel that they were being treated more unfairly than workers who were given adequate reasons. To support this prediction, Greenberg cited several recent experiments showing results that seemed to come to similar conclusions.

Unanticipated business circumstances provided the opportunity for Greenberg to test these hypotheses in a real-world setting. His experiment was conducted using workers in three different manufacturing plants owned by the same company. Two of the plants (plant A and plant B) had recently been affected by lost contracts, but the third (plant C) had not. In the case of plants A and B, management was faced with a dilemma: They could lay off some of the employees or they could institute a temporary (10–week) pay cut of 15% for all the employees in these two plants. They chose the latter alternative. Because plant C had not lost contracts, no action was necessary there. It was decided that workers in plant A would be given a lengthy explanation of the reasons for the pay cut; workers in plant B would be informed about the pay cut, but they would not be given an explanation. The workers in plant C, whose pay was unchanged, provided a control group condition for the experiment.

Data on employee theft were collected before, during, and after the 10-week period. Information on employees' feelings about the reasons for the pay cut and its fairness was also collected (in essence, these answers provided information on how equitably treated the workers felt). The data supported Greenberg's hypotheses and equity theory: (1) In general, theft increased when workers had to take a cut in pay, but (2) there was less theft among workers who had been provided with an adequate explanation for the pay cut than among those not given an adequate explanation.

A Sample Journal Article[3]

① **Descriptive title.** Note that the title identifies the main focus of the study. Without reading further, we know that the researcher studied employee theft, underpayment inequity, and pay cuts, and that he investigated how inequity influences theft.

② **Names and affiliation.** The author's name is given as it would ordinarily be written; titles (Dr., Mr., Ms.) are not stated. The university, agency, or business affiliation of the author (or authors) is also listed.

③ **Abstract.** In the published article, the abstract is usually not labeled. It is conspicuously indented and set off by smaller type. (Your typed manuscript, of course, will not look like this. Your abstract will be typed on its own page and labeled, as you will see a little later.) Notice that the abstract summarizes what was done and what was found; all the main points of the article are presented.

④ **Author Notes.** Notes are included to provide information about special circumstances surrounding the study; for instance, if the results were presented elsewhere or were part of a dissertation or thesis project. (However, when you type your manuscript, author notes will go on a separate page.) Author notes are also used to acknowledge special contributions from individuals or granting organizations who facilitated the research. Author notes always include a correspondence address, where readers can write for a copy of the experiment (called a "reprint") or for further information.

⑤ **Introduction.** The introduction begins immediately after the abstract. Like the abstract, the introduction is never labeled. Notice how the author presents the logic and background research that suggested this study. The theoretical basis for the hypotheses is presented, and supporting research is clearly cited. The author tells us the pertinent facts about the field and how these facts relate to the hypotheses of the experiment. The author states his two hypotheses explicitly in the final two paragraphs of the introduction.

   Note the format for citing prior research: "Recent research in the area of procedural justice (Lind & Tyler, 1988) has shown that. . . ." Factual statements must always carry citations of this type. Full credit must be given to the source of ideas, procedures, or phrases to avoid any form of plagiarism. Note that the full references for all citations are given in the list of references at the end of the article; we rarely use footnotes to cite references.

[3] From "Employee Theft As A Reaction to Underpayment Inequity: The Hidden Cost of Pay Cuts," by J. Greenberg, 1990 *Journal of Applied Psychology, 75,* 5, pp. 561–568. Copyright © 1990 by The American Psychological Association. Reprinted by permission.

Journal of Applied Psychology
1990, Vol. 75, No. 5, 561–568

(1)

Employee Theft as a Reaction to Underpayment Inequity: The Hidden Cost of Pay Cuts

(2)

Jerald Greenberg
Faculty of Management and Human Resources
Ohio State University

(3)

Employee theft rates were measured in manufacturing plants during a period in which pay was temporarily reduced by 15%. Compared with pre- or postreduction pay periods (or with control groups whose pay was unchanged), groups whose pay was reduced had significantly higher theft rates. When the basis for the pay cuts was thoroughly and sensitively explained to employees, feelings of inequity were lessened, and the theft rate was reduced as well. The data support equity theory's predictions regarding likely responses to underpayment and extend recently accumulated evidence demonstrating the mitigating effects of adequate explanations on feelings of inequity.

(5)

Employee theft constitutes one of the most pervasive and serious problems in the field of human resource management. Although exact figures are difficult to come by, the American Management Association (1977) has estimated that employee theft cost American businesses from $5 billion to $10 billion in 1975, representing the single most expensive form of nonviolent crime against businesses.

Traditionally, social scientists have considered several plausible explanations for employee theft. Among the most popular are theories postulating that theft is the result of attempts to ease financial pressure (Merton, 1938), moral laxity among a younger workforce (Merriam, 1977), available opportunities (Astor, 1972), expressions of job dissatisfaction (Mangione & Quinn, 1975), and the existence of norms tolerating theft (Horning, 1970). More recently, Hollinger and Clark (1983) conducted a large-scale survey and interview study designed to explore these and other explanations of employee theft. Interestingly, they found that the best predictor was employee attitudes: "When employees felt exploited by the company . . . these workers were more involved in acts against the organizations as a mechanism to correct perceptions of inequity or injustice" (Hollinger & Clark, 1983, p. 142).

Hollinger and Clark's (1983) suggestion that employee theft is related to feelings of injustice is consistent with several schools of sociological and anthropological thought. For example, in studies of hotel dining room employees (Mars, 1973) and maritime dock workers (Mars, 1974), Mars found that employees viewed theft *not* as inappropriate but "as a morally justified addition to wages; indeed, as an entitlement due from exploiting employers" (Mars, 1974, p. 224). Similarly, Kemper (1966)

argued that employee theft may be the result of "reciprocal deviance," that is, employees' perceptions that their employers defaulted on their obligations to them, thereby encouraging them to respond with similar acts of deviance. Fisher and Baron (1982) made a similar argument in presenting their equity-control model of vandalism. They claimed that vandalism is a form of inequity reduction in that an individual vandal's breaking the rules regarding property rights follows from his or her feelings of mistreatment by authorities. Recent evidence in support of this idea is found in a study by DeMore, Fisher, and Baron (1988). In that study, university students claimed to engage in more vandalism the less fairly they felt they had been treated by their university and the less control they believed they had over such treatment.

Such conceptualizations are in keeping with current theoretical positions in the field of organizational justice (Greenberg, 1987). These formulations allow more precise hypotheses to be developed regarding when employee theft is likely to occur. For example, consider equity theory's (Adams, 1965) claim that workers who feel inequitably underpaid (i.e., those who believe that the rewards they are receiving relative to the contributions they are making are less than they should be) may respond by attempting to raise their outcomes (i.e., raise the level of rewards received). Although research has supported this claim (for a review, see Greenberg, 1982), studies have been limited to situations in which persons paid on a piece-work basis produce more goods of poorer quality to raise their outcomes without effectively raising their inputs. Given earlier conceptual claims and supporting evidence associating student vandalism with inequitable treatment (DeMore et al., 1988), it may be reasoned analogously that employee theft is a specific reaction to underpayment inequity and constitutes an attempt to bring outcomes into line with prevailing standards of fair pay.

Recent research in the area of procedural justice (Lind & Tyler, 1988) has shown that perceptions of fair treatment and outcomes depend not only on the relative level of one's outcomes but also on the explanations given for those outcomes (for a review, see Folger & Bies, 1989). For example, researchers have found that decision outcomes and procedures were better

(4)

A preliminary report of the research reported in this article was presented at the annual meeting of the Academy of Management, San Francisco, August 1990.

I gratefully acknowledge the helpful comments of Robert J. Bies and three anonymous reviewers on an earlier draft of this article.

Correspondence concerning this article should be addressed to Jerald Greenberg, Faculty of Management and Human Resources, Ohio State University, 1775 College Road, Columbus, Ohio 43210-1399.

(6) **Method.** This section gives the details of how the experiment was carried out. Notice that the author has adapted the format of the subsections to fit the kind of information he needs to present; each subsection is clearly labeled. In this article the subjects ("participants") subsection is relatively long because subjects were not randomly selected or randomly assigned to conditions. Because random procedures were not used, the author needed to show that subjects in the three groups did not differ on potentially confounding extraneous variables. Demographic data about subjects (such as age, gender, or education level) is important information for the reader whenever subject characteristics might be a confound. Loss of data during the experiment also was explained.

Notice that the author chose to omit an apparatus or materials subsection because the experiment did not require any special equipment or nonstandard materials. The procedures used in this study were described in detail. The wording of statements made to subjects was a critical component of the experimental manipulation, so the explanations used in each condition were reported *verbatim*. The author chose to include a separate subsection to describe the measures used in the study, which needed extensive description. Notice that enough detail is given to permit replication.

accepted when (a) people were assured that higher authorities were sensitive to their viewpoints (Tyler, 1988), (b) the decision was made without bias (Lind & Lissak, 1985), (c) the decision was applied consistently (Greenberg, 1986), (d) the decision was carefully justified on the basis of adequate information (Shapiro & Buttner, 1988), (e) the decisionmakers communicated their ideas honestly (Bies, 1986), and (f) persons influenced by the decision were treated in a courteous and civil manner (Bies & Moag, 1986). Such findings suggest that interpersonal treatment is an important determinant of reactions to potentially unfair situations (Tyler & Bies, 1990).

It is an interesting idea that perceptions of inequity (and corresponding attempts to redress inequities) may be reduced when explanations meeting the criteria presented in the preceding paragraph are offered to account for inequitable states. This notion was tested in the present study by capitalizing on a naturalistic manipulation—a temporary pay reduction for employees of selected manufacturing plants. Data were available for 30 consecutive weeks: 10 weeks before a pay reduction occurred, 10 weeks during the pay-reduction period, and 10 weeks after normal pay was reinstated. Following from equity theory, it was hypothesized that ratings of payment fairness would be lower during the pay-reduction period than during periods of normal payment (i.e., before and after the pay reduction). It was similarly hypothesized that rates of employee theft would be higher during the reduced-pay period than during periods of normal payment. Such actions would be consistent with equity theory's claim that one likely way of responding to underpayment inequity is by attempting to raise the level of rewards received. Although not previously studied in this connection, employee theft is a plausible mechanism for redressing states of inequity (Hollinger & Clark, 1983).

Additional hypotheses were derived from recent research (e.g., Cropanzano & Folger, 1989; Folger & Martin, 1986; Shapiro & Buttner, 1988; Weiner, Amirkham, Folkes, & Varette, 1987) showing that explanations for negative outcomes mitigate people's reactions to those outcomes (for a review, see Folger & Bies, 1989; Tyler & Bies, 1990). Generally speaking, in these studies the use of adequate explanations (i.e., ones that relied on complete, accurate information presented in a socially sensitive manner) tended to reduce the negative reactions that resulted from such outcomes and facilitated acceptance of the outcomes. From the perspective of Folger's (1986) referent cognitions theory, adequate explanations help victimized parties place their undercompensation in perspective by getting them to understand that things could have been worse. As such, adequate explanations were expected in the present study to lessen the feelings of inequity that accompanied the pay cut. Thus, it was reasoned that employees' feelings of payment inequity, and attempts to reduce that inequity (such as by pilfering), would be reduced when adequate explanations were given to account for the pay reduction. Specifically, it was hypothesized that the magnitude of the expressed inequity—and the rate of employee theft—would be lower when pay reductions were adequately explained than when they were inadequately explained.

Method

Participants

Participants in the study were nonunion employees working for 30 consecutive weeks in three manufacturing plants owned by the same

Table I
Distribution of Attrition and Turnover Across Conditions

Condition	Starting n	Missing data	Resignations Before pay cut	Resignations During pay cut	Resignations After pay cut	Final n
Adequate explanation (Plant A)	64	6	1	1	1	55
Inadeaute explanation (Plant B)	53	8	1	12	2	30
Control (Plant C)	66	5	1	0	2	58

parent company. The plants were located in different sections of the midwestern United States and manufactured small mechanical parts mostly for the aerospace and automotive industries. The employees' average age (M = 28.5 years), level of education (M = 11.2 years), and tenure with the company (M = 3.2 years) did not significantly differ among the three plants, $F < 1.00$, in all cases. The local unemployment rates in the communities surrounding the three plants were not significantly different from each other (overall M = 6.4%), $F < 1.00$. It is important to establish this equivalence of characteristics across research sites because the assignment of individuals to conditions was not random across sites, thereby precluding the assumption of equivalence afforded by random assignment (Cook & Campbell, 1976).

As the study began, Plant A employed 64 workers in the following jobs: 5 salaried low-level managerial employees (4 men, 1 woman); 47 hourly-wage semiskilled and unskilled production workers (38 men, 9 women); and 12 hourly-wage clerical workers (all women). Almost identical proportions with respect to job type (and sex of employees within job type) existed in Plant B (n = 53) and Plant C (n = 66). Because some employees failed to complete questionnaires during some weeks, and because some employees voluntarily left their jobs during the study period, complete sets of questionnaires were available from 55 employees of Plant A, 30 employees of Plant B, and 58 employees of Plant C. This constituted a total sample of 143 employees, distributed to conditions as summarized in Table 1. The demographic characteristics of the 40 workers who were not included in the study did not differ significantly from the characteristics of the 143 who remained in the study (in all cases, $F < 2.00$), minimizing the possibility that those who remained in the study were a select group.

Procedure

Because of the loss of two large manufacturing contracts, the host company was forced to reduce its payroll by temporarily cutting wages by 15% across the board in two of its manufacturing plants (Plants A and B). This was done in lieu of laying off any employees. After this decision was made, I was asked to help assess the impact of the wage cuts in several key areas, including employee theft. Each of the payment-group manipulations was carried out in a separate plant. The assignment of Plant A to one experimental condition and Plant B to another experimental condition was determined at random. Assignment to the control group was determined by the host company's decision that pay cuts were not necessary in Plant C.[1]

---

[1] Admittedly, conducting the study in this manner meant that the two randomly assigned groups may have been nonequivalent with respect to some unknown variables that might have otherwise affected the results (Cook & Campbell, 1976). However, some reassurance of

Method (continued).   All independent and dependent variables are described carefully in the method section. A complete description of the explanations is provided. This enables the reader to see how the three explanation conditions constituted a between-subjects manipulation of the independent variable. Theft rates were the primary dependent measure, but Greenberg also measured subjects' knowledge about the basis for their pay and their attitudes toward pay equity. Procedures for obtaining scores for each measure were carefully explained; each questionnaire item was provided. A design subsection was not included in the method section. The theft and questionnaire measures required different kinds of statistical procedures; therefore the design structure is given later in the next section, where each analysis can be completely explained.

The *adequate explanation* condition was created in Plant A. To effect this, a meeting (lasting approximately 90 min) was called at the end of a work week. At that meeting, all employees were told by the company president that their pay was going to be reduced by 15%, effective the following week, for a period expected to last 10 weeks. During this meeting several types of explanations were provided. On the basis of recent research (Folger & Bies, 1989; Tyler & Bies, 1990), I hypothesized that these explanations would mitigate reactions to the pay cut. The workers were told that company management seriously regretted having to reduce their pay but that doing so would preclude the need for any layoffs. They were further assured that all plant employees would share in the pay cuts and that no favoritism would be shown.[2] A relevant verbatim passage follows:

> Something we hate to do here at [company name] is lay off any of our employees. But, as you probably know, we've lost our key contracts with [company names], which will make things pretty lean around here for a little while. As a result, we need to cut somewhere, and we've come up with a plan that will get us through these tough times. I've been working on it with [name of person] in accounting, and we're sure it will work. The plan is simple: Starting Monday, we will each get a 15% cut in pay. This applies to you, to me, to everyone who works here at [name of plant]. If we do it this way, there'll be no cut in benefits and no layoffs—just a 15% pay reduction. So, either your hourly wages or your salary will be reduced by 15%. Will it hurt? Of course! But, it will hurt us all alike. We're all in it together. Let me just add that it really hurts me to do this, and the decision didn't come easily. We considered all possible avenues, but nothing was feasible. I think of you all as family, and it hurts me to take away what you've worked so hard for. But, for the next 10 weeks, we'll just have to tough it out.

In addition to these remarks, the basis for the decision was clearly explained and justified by presenting charts and graphs detailing the temporary effects of the lost contracts on cash-flow revenues. Projections verified that the cash-flow problem dictating the need for the pay cuts was only temporary, and this was clearly explained. All employees were assured that the pay cut was designed to last only 10 weeks.[3] Specifically, the employees were told the following:

> The reason I'm sharing all this information with you is that I want you to understand what is happening here. It's just a temporary problem we're facing, and one that I hope will never happen again. At least the best course of action from our accounting department is clear: The pay cuts will work, and they will not have to last longer than 10 weeks. The new jobs we'll be picking up from [name of company] will really help get us back on our feet. Hopefully, by then we'll be stronger than ever. Of course, I know we're no stronger than our people, and I personally thank each and every one of you for your strength.

The tone of the presentation was such that a great deal of respect was shown for the workers, and all questions were answered with sensitivity. Approximately 1 hr was spent answering all questions. Each response brought an expression of remorse at having to take such action (e.g., "Again, I really wish this weren't necessary."). The good intent of

this message was reinforced by the fact that the president issued the message in person.

Plant B was the site of the *inadequate explanation* condition. Here, a meeting lasting approximately 15 min was called at the end of a work week. All employees were told by a company vice president that their pay was going to be reduced by 15%, effective the following week, for a period expected to last 10 weeks. The only additional information that was provided indicated that the lost contracts dictated the need for the pay cut. No expressions of apology or remorse were shared, and the basis for the decision was not clearly described. The following verbatim remarks characterize this condition:

> It is inevitable in a business like ours that cost-cutting measures are often necessary to make ends meet. Unfortunately, the time has come for us to take such measures here at [company name]. I know it won't be easy on anyone, but [name of company president] has decided that a 15% across-the-board pay cut will be instituted effective Monday. This is largely the result of the fact that we've lost our contracts with [name of companies]. However, soon we'll be picking up jobs with [name of company], so we're sure the pay cuts will last only 10 weeks. I realize this isn't easy, but such reductions are an unfortunate fact of life in the manufacturing business. On behalf of [company president's name] and myself, we thank you for bearing with us over these rough times. I'll answer one or two questions, but then I have to catch a plane for another meeting.

Finally, because the parts manufactured at Plant C were unaffected by the lost contracts, no pay cuts were mandated there. Plant C constituted the *control* condition for the study.

Measures

Two categories of dependent measures were used: actuarial data on employee theft, and self-report measures tapping some of the processes assumed to be underlying the theft behavior.

---

between-group similarity is provided by the demonstrated equivalence between worker characteristics, economic conditions, and job duties for both plants. Moreover, the deliberate assignment of Plant C to the control condition raises the possibility that something besides the lack of manipulation may have been responsible for the results (Cook & Campbell, 1976). However, informal postexperiment interviews with plant officials and employees confirmed that no unusual "local history" events occurred during the study period. Further assurance that this was not a problem comes from the fact that, before and after the pay cut, the control group's responses were identical to the other groups' responses for all measures used in the study.

[2] Before the meetings scheduled in each plant, the individuals involved (i.e., company president in Plant A and a vice president in Plant B) met with me to develop outlines of their presentations. Several carefully crafted sentences conveying salient aspects of the manipulation were prepared for inclusion in the speaker's notes. Because local company norms dictated using informal meetings instead of formal presentations, complete scripts for the entire sessions could not be prepared in advance. As a result, it was necessary to establish that key differences in the manipulated variables were actually communicated in the meetings. With this in mind, each session was videotaped, and the videotapes were played back to a group of 112 undergraduate students after all identifying information was deleted. The students were asked to indicate in which of the two tapes (Tape A for Plant A; Tape B for Plant B) the speaker (a) presented more information about the pay cuts and (b) expressed greater remorse about the pay cuts. The order of presentation of the tapes was randomized. Virtually all of the students agreed that the speaker on Tape A presented more information and expressed greater remorse. Taken together with my in-person confirmation that the manipulations were conducted as desired, these findings suggest that differentially adequate explanations were given to the two groups. Unfortunately, it was not possible to conduct further analyses on these tapes because the host company insisted that they be destroyed to prevent the unwanted dissemination of sensitive company information.

[3] Because of the sensitive and privileged nature of the internal accounting information, I was not permitted to divulge these data. Indeed, although I helped company officials present this information in understandable form, these charts and graphs were never made part of my file.

(7) **Results.** Analysis of the primary dependent measure (employee theft rates) required several steps in this experiment. Both experimental hypotheses were tested in a 3 × 3 mixed-design ANOVA. The author first presents the results of the analysis of variance and then refers us to a figure that summarizes the findings clearly and quickly. Notice that the figure adds to the information presented in the text by depicting the means for each of the nine conditions of the experiment. Since the findings include an interaction effect, the visual presentation helps us understand the complex patterns that emerged. The figure also sets the stage for presenting the results of additional statistical tests (simple-effects tests[4] and post hoc tests).

You can see that the figure is well proportioned and pleasing to look at. The lines are clearly labeled by a legend that appears within the figure. The axes are also clearly labeled and marked off, and units of measurement (percentages) are given.

Notice how the author used two tables to present summary data and test results; he referred to each table in the text. Because multiple measures were used, the significant effects are considerably easier to understand when shown in tables. For instance, the reader can easily compare effects obtained on both questionnaire measures just by looking at Table 2. In addition, the tables eliminated the need for a wordier presentation of the findings.

---

[4] After a significant two-way interaction, a one-way ANOVA within each level of one of the factors can be performed; these are known as simple-effects tests (Winer, 1971). In essence, the author tested the (simple) effects of the three pay periods on theft among workers in the separate explanation conditions. When pay period produced a significant effect on theft in one of the explanation conditions, post hoc tests were needed to ascertain whether theft was greater during the pay cut than before or after.

Employee theft rates. The measure of employee theft used for this study was the company accounting department's standard formula for computing "shrinkage." The formula yielded the percentage of inventory (e.g., tools, supplies, etc.) unaccounted for by known waste, sales, use in the conduct of business, or normal depreciation. (For a discussion of the difficulties attendant to deriving such measures, see Hollinger & Clark, 1983.) These measures were obtained unobtrusively (during nonwork hours) by representatives of the company's headquarters on a weekly basis during the study period. The persons taking inventory were aware of any legitimate factors that contributed to accounted-for changes in inventory levels (such as shipments received, supplies used during projects, etc.) but were blind to the experimental hypotheses.[4]

Because no single standard for computing shrinkage is uniformly used (Hollinger & Clark, 1983), it was not possible to compare the base rates of employee theft in the present sample to any industry-wide average. However, evidence that the employee theft rate studied here was not atypical was provided by showing that the mean theft rate for the 10-week period before the pay cut was not significantly different from the overall theft rate for all three plants for the prior year, $F <$ 1.00. These data are important in that they provide some assurance that the changes in theft rates observed were not simply deviations from unusual patterns that later merely regressed to the mean.[5]

Questionnaire measures. Two types of questionnaire measures were needed to establish the validity of the study and to facilitate interpretation of the theft data—one group of questions to verify differences in familiarity with the basis for establishing pay (the manipulation check), and another group of questions to establish differences in perceived payment equity. The questionnaires were administered biweekly (during odd-numbered weeks in the study period) at the plant sites during nonworking hours. Because a larger, unrelated study had been going on for several months, the workers were used to completing questionnaires, making it unlikely that any suspicions were aroused by the questions inserted for this study. Participants were assured of the anonymity of their responses.

The "pay basis" measure was designed to provide a check on the validity of the payment-group variable. Participants answered four items on a 5-point scale ranging from *not at all* (1), to *slightly* (2), to *moderately* (3), to *highly* (4) to *extremely* (5). The questions were (a) "How adequate was your employer's explanation regarding the basis of your current pay?" (b) "How familiar are you with the way your employer determines your pay?" (c) "How thoroughly did your employer communicate the basis for your current pay to you?" and (d) "How much concern did your employer show about your feelings when communicating your pay?" A high degree of internal consistency was found for these items (coefficient alpha = .89).

The "pay equity" measure consisted of four items, three of which were anchored with the same scale points as the pay basis items. Specifically, participants responded to the following items: (a) "To what extent do you believe your current pay reflects your actual contributions to the job?" (b) "How fairly paid do you feel you currently are on your job?" and (c) "How satisfied are you with your current overall pay level?" The fourth item asked, "Relative to what you feel you should be paid, do you believe your current pay is: ____ much too low, ____ a little too low, ____ about right, ____ a little too high, ____ much too high?" Because only the first 3 points of this bidirectional scale were actually used, responses to this 3-point scale were combined with the 5-point unidirectional scales for the other items. Coefficient alpha was high (.84), justifying combining the individual items. The option of using existing standardized scales tapping reactions to pay (e.g., the Pay Satisfaction Questionnaire; Heneman & Schwab, 1985) was rejected in favor of ad hoc measures because these were judged to be much more sensitive to the measurement objectives of the present study (cf. Heneman, 1985).

Results ⑦

Preliminary Analyses

Prior to the principal data analyses, preliminary analyses were conducted to determine whether to separate the 15 biweekly questionnaire responses into three equal groups, reflecting responses before, during, and after the pay cut. The five 2-week response periods were treated as a repeated measure in mixed-design analyses of variance (ANOVAs) in which the payment group was the between-subjects factor (adequate explanation, inadequate explanation, no pay cut). Separate analyses were conducted for each of the three groups. Because no significant main effects or interactions involving the response periods were obtained in analyses for either questionnaire measure (all Fs < 1.00), the decision was made to combine the observations into three groups composed of more reliable observations (before, during, or after the pay cut).

Because only one employee-theft-rate figure was reported for each week (the figure was aggregate, as opposed to individual, data), it was not possible to conduct a parallel set of ANOVAs for this measure. However, separate tests were performed within each payment group to compare each week's theft rate to the mean for all 10 weeks. This process was repeated separately for each of the three response periods (i.e., before, during, and after the pay cut). Because no significant effects emerged in any of these analyses (all values of $t < .50$, $df = 9$), the decision was made (paralleling that for the questionnaire measures) to group the weekly scores into three 10-week response periods.

Employee Theft Rate

Analyses of theft rates were based on a 3×3 mixed-design ANOVA in which payment group was the between-subjects variable, response period was the within-subjects variable, and the 10 weekly theft rates within each cell constituted the data. A significant Payment Period × Response Period interaction was found, $F(4, 56) = 9.66$, $p < .001$. Figure 1 summarizes the means contributing to this interaction.

For each payment group, simple effects tests were performed to determine whether the means differed significantly across response periods. Any significant effects were followed up with the Tukey honestly significant difference (HSD) procedure (with alpha set at .05). In addition, tests for quadratic trend components were performed using orthogonal polynomials (Hays, 1963). This analysis was performed to note trends in the data over time in a situation in which the number of available

---

[4] Although the theft-rate figures (i.e., percentage of inventory loss unaccounted for) were used internally to compute dollar-loss figures, data substantiating a specific dollar-loss amount caused by the thefts were not made available to me. Again, this decision was prompted by the company's desire to avoid potential embarrassment.

[5] Unfortunately, week-by-week theft-rate data were not available prior to the study period. As a result, it was impossible to compare the weekly theft rates during the study to earlier weekly theft rates. Thus, it was not possible to rule out the possibility raised by one reviewer that the results may reflect some seasonal fluctuations in theft that coincided with the manipulation period.

Note the format used to report the test statistics. The statistic (for example, F) is indicated first, in italics. (All test statistics should be italicized; indicate italics in your typed manuscript by underlining.) Degrees of freedom are shown in parentheses. The computed value and the significance level that was obtained are given:

$F(2, 27) = 9.15, p < .001$

(For F values, it is customary to show the df for the numerator first.) Note that we never give the critical values from the statistical tables—the reader can look them up if necessary. The null hypothesis is not stated either. However, you should indicate the use of a one-tailed test.

In addition to analyses of variance and follow-up tests, the researcher used more sophisticated statistical procedures (quadratic trends) to measure how closely the theft results for the three pay periods resemble a straight line in each explanation condition. As you can see from the figure, the lines representing the three explanation conditions are not simply straight and they do not have the same shape. They go up and down depending on the pay period *and* the type of explanation workers received.

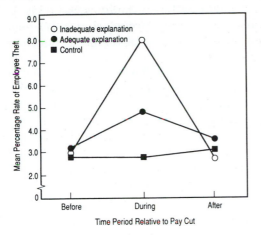

Figure 1. Mean percentage of employee theft as a function of time relative to pay cut.

data points was too small to use time series analyses (Zuwaylif, 1970).

A simple effects test within the inadequate-explanation condition was significant, $F(2, 27) = 9.15$, $p < .001$. Post hoc tests revealed that significantly higher levels of theft were observed during the pay reduction than before or after the pay reduction. Consistent with this configuration, the quadratic trend was highly significant, $F(1, 27) = 12.18$, $p < .001$.

Within the adequate-explanation condition, the overall simple effects test was weaker but still significant, $F(2, 52) = 3.76$, $p < .05$. This effect was the result of a similar, though less pronounced, pattern of means showing theft to be higher during the pay cut than either before or after the pay cut. Tests for a quadratic trend component failed to reach conventional levels of significance, $F(2, 52) = 2.10$, $p < .15$.

Finally, within the control group, simple effects tests revealed that the means did not differ from each other significantly across the three response periods, $F(2, 55) < 1.00$.

To establish pre- and postmanipulation equivalence, it was useful to compare means between payment groups (adequate explanation, inadequate explanation, no pay cut) within response periods. Simple effects tests showed no significant simple main effects of payment group before or after the pay cut, $F < 1.00$ in both cases. However, the effect of payment group was highly significant during the pay cut, $F(2, 27) = 10.71$, $p < .001$. Tukey HSD tests revealed that the three means were significantly different from each other. In other words, within the pay-reduction period, the theft rate in the inadequate-explanation condition ($M = 8.9$) was significantly higher than that in the adequate-explanation condition ($M = 5.7$), which was in turn higher than that in the control condition ($M = 3.7$).

Questionnaire Responses

Responses to the pay basis and pay equity questionnaires were analyzed with ANOVA designs identical to that used for the

employee-theft measure. For these dependent variables, however, the data consisted of individual responses to the summed items constituting each questionnaire within each cell. The two questionnaire measures were not significantly correlated, $r = .07$.

For the pay basis measure, a significant Payment Group × Response Period interaction was obtained, $F(4, 280) = 256.10$, $p < .0001$. The corresponding means and standard deviations are summarized at the top of Table 2. As shown, post hoc tests revealed that employees in the adequate-explanation condition demonstrated greater understanding of the basis for pay determination than employees in the other two conditions once the explanation occurred (i.e., during and after the pay cut). The adequate-explanation manipulation successfully enhanced employees' understanding of the basis for pay determination.

A significant interaction effect also was obtained for the pay equity measure, $F(4, 280) = 29.05$, $p < .001$. The corresponding means and standard deviations are summarized at the bottom of Table 2. As shown, post hoc tests revealed that during the pay cut, employees in the inadequate-explanation condition expressed the greatest perceptions of pay inequity. Workers whose pay reductions were adequately explained to them did not express heightened payment inequity while their pay was reduced.

Turnover

A summary of missing data and data lost because of voluntary turnover appears in Table 1. Not surprisingly, the majority of the turnover occurred among employees experiencing inadequately explained pay reductions (12 of the 52 workers, or 23.1% of those still on the job at that time). Resignations in other conditions were uniformly 5% or less. Consistent with this, the distribution of resignations over conditions during the pay-cut period was highly significant, $\chi^2(2, N = 13) = 20.48$, $p < .001$—a result of the fact that 12 of the 13 resignations occurred in the inadequate-explanation group. By contrast, the distribution of resignations across conditions was equal before the pay cut, $\chi^2(2, N = 3) < 0.5$, and after the pay cut, $\chi^2(2, N = 5) < 0.5$.

Discussion

The data support the hypothesis derived from equity theory (Adams, 1965) that workers experiencing underpayment inequity would attempt to redress that inequity by raising their inputs—in the present case, by pilfering from their employer. Indeed, while workers experienced a 15% pay reduction, they reported feeling underpaid and stole over twice as much as they did when they felt equitably paid. Two distinct interpretations of these theft data may be offered, both of which are consistent with equity theory (Adams, 1965). First, it is possible that the pay reduction led to feelings of frustration and resentment, which motivated the aggressive acts of theft. This possibility is in keeping with recent research findings demonstrating that pay cuts are associated with negative affective reactions to organizational authorities (Greenberg, 1989) and that increases in vandalism correlate positively with perceptions of mistreatment by authorities (DeMore et al., 1988). Such an interpretation follows from a reciprocal deviance orientation to inequity

8 **Discussion.** Note that the author begins by restating his major findings. He goes on to offer his explanations for the findings, referring back to the theories that formed the basis for the experiment. Notice that he relates his findings to the broader theoretical issues of underpayment inequity. In addition, he carefully discusses factors that might limit the conclusions that can be drawn from the experiment. The author does not make vast leaps from his data to grand conclusions, but he does explain the implications of his experimental findings for reducing the problem of employee theft.

Table 2

Data Summaries for Questionnaire Measures

| | | Response period | | | | | |
| | | Before | | During | | After | |
Measure/payment group	n	M	SD	M	SD	M	SD
Pay basis[a]							
Inadequate explanation	30	40.70ₐ	4.38	42.39ₐ	3.40	43.74ₐ	4.93
Adequate explanation	55	43.22ₐ	5.58	76.10_b	6.48	73.73_b	5.70
Control	58	42.36ₐ	6.49	40.72ₐ	3.83	41.90ₐ	4.46
Pay equity[b]							
Inadequate explanation	30	56.87ₐ	5.54	40.20_b	7.56	57.43ₐ	6.70
Adequate explanation	55	61.22ₐ	9.57	59.56ₐ	9.52	56.03ₐ	9.37
Control	58	61.29ₐ	8.67	60.98ₐ	9.18	58.02ₐ	8.57

Note. Within each row and each column, means not sharing a common subscript are significantly different from each other beyond the .05 level on the basis of the Tukey honestly significant difference technique corrected for confounded comparisons with the Cicchetti (1972) approximation.
[a] Mean scores for the pay basis measure could range from 20 to 100. Higher scores reflect greater degrees of familiarity with the basis for establishing pay.　[b] Mean scores for the pay equity measure could range from 20 to 90. Higher scores reflect greater degrees of perceived payment equity.

reduction, which suggests that employees' acts of deviance are encouraged by their beliefs that their employers defaulted on their obligations to them by reducing their pay (Kemper, 1966). From this perspective, acts of theft may be understood as a manifestation of feelings of mistreatment.

It is also possible to interpret the thefts as direct attempts to correct underpayment inequity by adjusting the balance of valued resources between the worker and the specific source of that inequity. As such, acts of theft may be interpreted as unofficial transfers of outcomes from the employer to the employee. Because no direct evidence is available suggesting that the stolen items had any positive valence to the employees, it is impossible to claim unambiguously that the theft rates represented employees' attempts to increase their own outcomes. Although such an interpretation is consistent with a considerable amount of evidence on the distribution of rewards and resources (for reviews, see Freedman & Montanari, 1980; Leventhal, 1976), it is also possible that disgruntled employees may have been content to reduce the valued resources available to the agent of their discontent. That is, they may have been motivated to reduce the employer's worth whether or not doing so directly benefited themselves. Unfortunately, the questionnaire items that would have been necessary to provide more refined interpretations of the present data might also have aroused subjects' suspiciousness that theft was being studied, thereby creating the potential for subject reactance (Webb, Campbell, Schwartz, Sechrest, & Grove, 1981). As a result, no such self-report data were collected. Nevertheless, the results are clearly in keeping with equity theory.

The present data also reveal a critical moderator of the tendency to pilfer to restore equity with one's employer—namely, the use of an adequate explanation for the pay cut. Pay cuts that were explained in an honest and caring manner were not seen by employees as being as unfair as pay cuts that were not explained carefully. Accordingly, reactions to carefully explained underpayment also were less severe (i.e., the pilferage rates were lower). These findings add to a recently developing body of

research showing that the use of adequately reasoned explanations offered with interpersonal sensitivity tends to mitigate the negative effects associated with the information itself (for reviews, see Folger & Bies, 1989; Tyler & Bies, 1990). The explanations used in the present study were obviously quite successful in reducing costs, both to employees (in terms of inequity distress) and employers (in terms of pilferage and turnover).

An interesting and important aspect of the present study is that a sizeable portion of the participants in the inadequate-explanation condition voluntarily left their jobs during the pay-reduction period; in fact, a much larger proportion resigned than did so in any other condition (or within the same condition at other times). It is tempting to take this finding as support for the idea that quitting one's job is an extreme form of reaction to underpayment inequity (Finn & Lee, 1972) and that the voluntary turnover found here was another form of reaction to inequity. However, because of the nonrandom design of the study, it is not possible to rule out factors other than the experimental manipulation—a difficulty common to quasi-experimental studies (Cook & Campbell, 1976). Despite this problem, several facts lend support to the inequity interpretation. First, the finding that the theft rate immediately before the manipulations did not differ significantly from the previous year's theft rate suggests that nothing out of the ordinary was happening that may have been responsible for the results. Second, because the theft rate was highest precisely under the only conditions in which feelings of inequity were high (i.e., during the pay-cut period following an inadequate explanation), feelings of inequity and theft rate probably are related, both resulting from the manipulated variable exactly as predicted by equity theory (Adams, 1965) and referent cognitions theory (Folger, 1986). Because this interpretation is theoretically supported, its position is strengthened relative to alternatives that may be raised in the absence of random assignment.

Generalizing from the present findings, it appears that adequately explaining inequitable conditions may be an effective means of reducing potentially costly reactions to feelings of

9 **References.** Here, the researcher cites all the sources mentioned in the article. Note that the references follow a set format. Use all underlining and punctuation as shown:

For journal articles with one author

Author's surname, and initial(s). The year of publication (in parentheses). Title of the article with only the first word capitalized. *The Name of the Journal, Volume number,* page numbers.

For books

Author's surname, and initial(s). The year of publication (in parentheses). *Title of the book with only the first word capitalized.* City of publication: Publisher's name.

underpayment inequity. To be effective, however, such explanations must be perceived as honest, genuine, and not manipulative (Tyler, 1988). Still, to the extent that underpayment conditions are acknowledged and justified by employers (as opposed to ignored or minimized by them), it appears that both workers and their organizations may stand to benefit. Given the high costs of employee theft (American Management Association, 1977), it appears that explaining the basis for inequities may be a very effective (and totally free) mechanism for reducing the costs of employee theft.

Practical implications notwithstanding, the present findings raise some important questions for equity theory (Adams, 1965) about the use of various modes of inequity reduction. Whereas the focus of this study was on pilferage, turnover was another type of response that occurred. Unfortunately, the nature of the present data makes it impossible to determine the trade-offs between various modes of inequity reduction. Did some employees resign in response to underpayment while others (perhaps those with fewer options for alternative employment) stayed on and expressed their negative feelings by stealing? Or was it that the most aggrieved employees stole company property before leaving, while others simply lowered their inputs? Because the theft rates were aggregate, actuarial data and could not be traced to particular employees, and because performance data were not collected, it was not possible to determine when and how different forms of inequity-reduction behavior are likely to occur. As a result, serious questions remain regarding how different inequity-resolution tactics may be used in conjunction with each other.

Confidence in interpretations of the present findings is limited because actuarial-level dependent measures (theft and turnover) were collected in conjunction with an individual-level variable (perceived payment equity), thereby making it impossible to conduct mediational analyses of the results. Exacerbating this problem is the fact that the use of a quasi-experimental design does not allow the discounting of alternative explanations (as noted earlier). Thus, although it is plausible that inequity leads to stealing unless mitigated by an adequate explanation, it is impossible to statistically discount the alternative possibility that unknown preexisting differences between the plants constituting the payment groups (e.g., different norms against stealing or differential acceptance of management's promise that the pay cut would be temporary) may have been responsible for the results. However, in support of the present findings, it is important to note that such limitations are inherent to some degree in all quasi-experimental research designs (Cook & Campbell, 1976).

Although nonrandom assignment precludes the discounting of alternative explanations, support for the present interpretation of the data may be derived from converging sources of theoretically based data. In this case, several lines of analogous research converge with my claim that adequate explanations enhanced the acceptance of undesired outcomes. For example, Folger and his associates (e.g., Folger & Martin, 1986; Folger, Rosenfield, & Robinson, 1983) measured laboratory subjects' feelings of discontent in reaction to procedural changes that created unfavorable conditions for them. Consistent with referent cognitions theory (Folger, 1986), Folger and his colleagues found that these feelings of discontent were reduced only when

the need to make procedural changes was adequately explained. Similarly, in another line of investigation, Weiner et al. (1987) found that persons victimized by another's harmdoing expressed less anger toward the harmdoer when claims of mitigating circumstances were offered for the harmdoer's actions. Both lines of investigation show that negative affective reactions are reduced by the presentation of adequate explanatory information. As such, they provide good convergent evidence for the my claim that adequately explained pay cuts mitigated feelings of inequity and reactions to underpayment inequity.

Finally, an important question may be raised about the compound nature of the explanation manipulation used in the present study. Because the adequate-explanation condition and the inadequate-explanation condition differed along several dimensions (postulated a priori to contribute to mitigation of the effects of the inequity), it was not possible to determine the individual effects of the various contributing factors. Specifically, the explanations differed in terms of several factors. Some of these, such as the quality of the information and the interpersonal sincerity of its presentation, have been recognized as mitigating reactions to undesirable outcomes (Shapiro & Buttner, 1988). Other differences between conditions, such as possible differences in the credibility of the source (the president versus the vice president) have not yet been studied. Clearly, the unique effects of these factors are prime candidates for future research efforts.

To conclude, the results of the present study shed new light on employee theft—one of the most important problems in the field of human-resource management. The evidence confirms that employee theft is a predictable response to underpayment inequity and reveals that such reactions can be substantially reduced by the inexpensive tactic of explaining the basis for the inequity in clear, honest, and sensitive terms.

 References

Adams, J. S. (1965). Inequity in social exchange. In L. Berkowitz (Ed.), *Advances in experimental social psychology* (Vol. 2, pp. 267–299). San Diego, CA: Academic Press.

American Management Association. (1977, March). *Summary overview of the "state of the art" regarding information gathering techniques and level of knowledge in three areas concerning crimes against business: Draft report*. Washington, DC: National Institute of Law Enforcement and Criminal Justice, Law Enforcement Assistance Administration.

Astor, S. D. (1972, March). Twenty steps to preventing theft in business. *Management Review, 61*(3), 34–35.

Bies, R. J. (1986, August). *Identifying principles of interactional justice: The case of corporate recruiting*. Symposium conducted at the annual meeting of the Academy of Management, Chicago, IL.

Bies, R. J., & Moag, J. S. (1986). Interactional justice: Communication criteria of fairness. In R. J. Lewicki, B. H. Sheppard, & B. H. Bazerman (Eds.), *Research on negotiation in organizations* (Vol. 1, pp. 43–55). Greenwich, CT: JAI Press.

Cicchetti, D. V. (1972). Extension of multiple-range tests to interaction tables in the analysis of variance: A rapid approximate solution. *Psychological Bulletin, 77*, 405–408.

Cook, T. D., & Campbell, D. T. (1976). The design and conduct of quasi-experiments and true experiments in field settings. In M. D. Dunnette (Ed.), *Handbook of industrial and organizational psychology* (pp. 223–326). Chicago: Rand McNally.

References (continued).   Other references listed in Greenberg's article illustrate additional procedures for sources with multiple authors and for articles that appear in edited volumes. For more unusual problems, see the APA *Publication Manual*.

Cropanzano, R., & Folger, R. (1989). Referent cognitions and task decision autonomy: Beyond equity theory. *Journal of Applied Psychology, 74,* 293–299.

DeMore, S. W., Fisher, J. D., & Baron, R. M. (1988). The equity-control model as a predictor of vandalism among college students. *Journal of Applied Social Psychology, 18,* 80–91.

Finn, R. H., & Lee, S. M. (1972). Salary equity: Its determination, analysis and correlates. *Journal of Applied Psychology, 56,* 283–292.

Fisher, J. D., & Baron, R. M. (1982). An equity-based model of vandalism. *Population and Environment, 5,* 182–200.

Folger, R. (1986). Rethinking equity theory: A referent cognitions model. In H. W. Bierhoff, R. L. Cohen, & J. Greenberg (Eds.), *Justice in social relations* (pp. 145–162). New York: Plenum Press.

Folger, R., & Bies, R. J. (1989). Managerial responsibilities and procedural justice. *Employee Responsibilities and Rights Journal, 2,* 79–90.

Folger, R., & Martin, C. (1986). Relative deprivation and referent cognitions: Distributive and procedural justice effects. *Journal of Applied Psychology, 22,* 531–546.

Folger, R., Rosenfield, D., & Robinson, T. (1983). Relative deprivation and procedural justification. *Journal of Personality and Social Psychology, 45,* 268–273.

Freedman, S. M., & Montanari, J. R. (1980). An integrative model of managerial reward allocation. *Academy of Management Review, 5,* 381–390.

Greenberg, J. (1982). Approaching equity and avoiding inequity in groups and organizations. In J. Greenberg & R. L. Cohen (Eds.), *Equity and justice in social behavior* (pp. 389–435). San Diego, CA: Academic Press.

Greenberg, J. (1986). Determinants of perceived fairness of performance evaluations. *Journal of Applied Psychology, 71,* 340–342.

Greenberg, J. (1987). A taxonomy of organizational justice theories. *Academy of Management Review, 12,* 9–22.

Greenberg, J. (1989). Cognitive re-evaluation of outcomes in response to underpayment inequity. *Academy of Management Journal, 32,* 174–184.

Hays, W. L. (1963). *Statistics.* New York: Holt, Rinehart, & Winston.

Heneman, H. G., III. (1985). Pay satisfaction. In K. Rowland & G. Ferris (Eds.), *Research in personnel and human resources management* (Vol. 3, pp. 115–139). Greenwich, CT: JAI Press.

Heneman, H. G., III, & Schwab, D. P. (1985). Pay satisfaction: Its multidimensional nature and measurement. *International Journal of Psychology, 20,* 129–141.

Hollinger, R. D., & Clark, J. P. (1983). *Theft by employees.* Lexington, MA: Lexington Books.

Horning, D. (1970). Blue collar theft: Conceptions of property, attitudes toward pilfering, and work group norms in a modern indus-

trial plant. In E. O. Smigel & H. L. Ross (Eds.), *Crimes against bureaucracy* (pp. 46–64). New York: Van Nostrand Reinhold.

Kemper, T. D. (1966). Representative roles and the legitimization of deviance. *Social Problems, 13,* 288–298.

Leventhal, G. S. (1976). The distribution of rewards and resources in groups and organizations. In L. Berkowitz & E. Walster (Eds.), *Advances in experimental social psychology* (Vol. 9, pp. 91–131). San Diego, CA: Academic Press.

Lind, E. A., & Lissak, R. (1985). Apparent impropriety and procedural fairness judgments. *Journal of Experimental Social Psychology, 21,* 19–29.

Lind, E. A., & Tyler, T. (1988). *The social psychology of procedural justice.* New York: Plenum Press.

Mangione, T. W., & Quinn, R. P. (1975). Job satisfaction, counter-productive behavior, and drug use at work. *Journal of Applied Psychology, 11,* 114–116.

Mars, G. (1973). Chance, punters, and the fiddle: Institutionalized pilferage in a hotel dining room. In M. Warner (Ed.), *The sociology of the workplace* (pp. 200–210). New York: Halsted Press.

Mars, G. (1974). Dock pilferage: A case study in occupational theft. In P. Rock & M. McIntosh (Eds.), *Deviance and social control* (pp. 209–228). London: Tavistock Institute.

Merriam, D. (1977). Employee theft. *Criminal Justice Abstracts, 9,* 380–386.

Merton, R. T. (1938). Social structure and anomie. *American Sociological Review, 3,* 672–682.

Shapiro, D. L., & Buttner, E. H. (1988, August). *Adequate explanations: What are they, and do they enhance procedural justice under severe outcome circumstances?* Paper presented at the annual meeting of the Academy of Management, Anaheim, CA.

Tyler, T. R. (1988). What is procedural justice? *Law and Society Review, 22,* 301–335.

Tyler, T. R., & Bies, R. J. (1990). Beyond formal procedures: The interpersonal context of procedural justice. In J. Carroll (Ed.), *Applied social psychology and organizational settings* (pp. 77–98). Hillsdale, NJ: Erlbaum.

Webb, E. J., Campbell, D. T., Schwartz, R. D., Sechrest, L., & Grove, J. B. (1981). *Nonreactive measures in the social sciences* (2nd ed.). Boston: Houghton Mifflin.

Weiner, B., Amirkhan, J., Folkes, V. S., & Varette, J. A. (1987). An attributional analysis of excuse giving: Studies of a naive theory of emotion. *Journal of Personality and Social Psychology, 52,* 316–324.

Zuwaylif, F. H. (1970). *General applied statistics.* Reading, MA: Addison-Wesley.

Received January 2, 1990
Revision received March 26, 1990
Accepted March 27, 1990 ■

PREPARING YOUR MANUSCRIPT: PROCEDURAL DETAILS

By now you have a good idea of what we accomplish through a research paper. You have also seen some of the specific techniques used to achieve these goals. Now that we understand the content of each section, let us look at the details of setting up the typed copy. Journal articles contain special typefaces, and some journals use a two-column layout that you cannot create easily on your typewriter or word processor. Thus your actual written report will not look like a published article. Your job is to put together a draft that could easily be turned into the published form. A typed version of the Greenberg article is reproduced for you in Appendix C so that you can refer to it as you prepare your own report. Be careful to follow the format for spacing and underlining carefully.

Here, we will look at the layout of sections and headings as shown in Figure 15-3. Your manuscript should be laid out exactly like the sample pages shown.

On the first page, give the title, your name, and your affiliation. Also show a **running head** in the bottom half of the page. The *running head* is a brief version of your title. (Greenberg used the running head "Employee theft and underpayment inequity.") The head should take no more than 60 spaces, including spaces between words. If your full title is short, your running head may be the same as your full title.

Type the word *Abstract* as a centered heading on the next page. Type the abstract and use double spacing.

Type the complete title, centered, at the top of the next page. Then type the introduction. Do not label it; everyone will know what it is. Continue to use double spacing throughout the report.

You do not need a new page to start the method section; begin it wherever the introduction ends. Type the word *Method* as a centered heading. Label each subsection of the method section with the appropriate subheading. Start each subheading (such as *Subjects*) flush with the margin of the page. Underline the subheadings.

Your results section may also be started within a page. Start it where the method section ends. Simply type the word *Results* as a centered heading. Be sure to follow the correct format for reporting statistical data.

Graphs, drawings, or pictures are called "figures." Rows and columns of numbers are called "tables." If you wish to use a table or figure, be sure to refer to it in words in the text—for instance: "See Table 1"; "The group means are shown in Table 1"; or "Figure 1 illustrates the significant interaction." Tables are numbered consecutively: Your first table is called "Table 1"; your second table is called "Table 2," and so on. Figures are numbered the same way: Your first figure is always called "Figure 1," your second is "Figure 2," and so forth. Use the insert format to tell the printer where each table or figure would go in the body of the report for publication:

Insert Table 1 about here

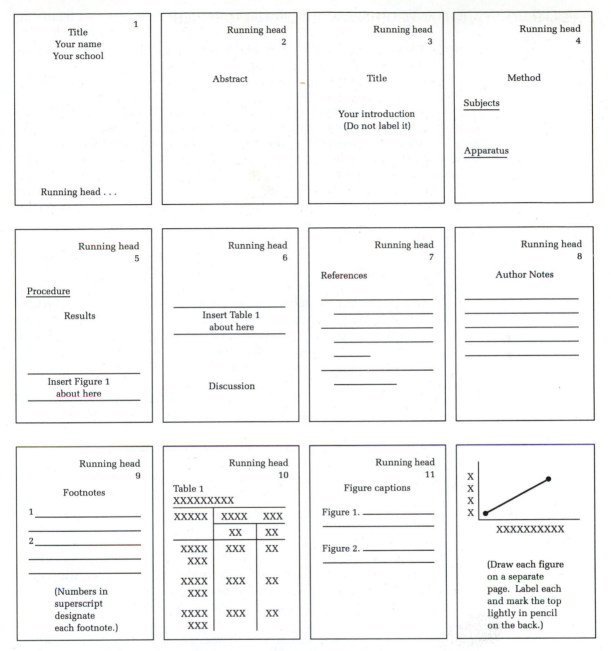

FIGURE **15-3** The general layout of a research report. Use 1½-inch (4-centimeter) margins on all sides. Double space throughout. Do not hyphenate.

Follow the same procedure for inserting figures. Prepare each table and each figure on a separate page. Write the figure number and article title lightly on the back of each figure; also indicate the top of each figure by writing the word *top* at the top of the page (lightly on the back). Figure captions do not go on the figures themselves; the captions to all figures go on a separate page labeled "Figure captions." With tables, all written information (including the title) is typed right in the table. Remember that everything is double-spaced—even tables and figure captions.

Continue on to the discussion. Type the word *Discussion* as a centered heading. Then type your discussion.

On a new page, type the centered heading *References.* List all your references in alphabetical order by authors' last names. Start each reference flush with the margin of the page. If a reference runs to more than one line, indent additional lines three spaces. Begin the next reference again flush with the margin.

Author notes, containing acknowledgments and your corresponding address, go on a new page after the references. Any footnotes will go on the following page. Center these headings as in Figure 15-3.

Now put in the pages of tables in the order they will appear in the text. Put in the page (or pages) of figure captions next. Be sure the captions are in order according to the way they will appear in the text. Last, put in all the figures.

Assign a number to each page, beginning with the title page. The title page is page 1. Type the running head at the top of each subsequent numbered page, above the page number. Notice that a page number and running head are typed on all pages *except* those containing figures. (Refer to Appendix C to see how all these details come together in an actual manuscript.)

We use the procedures discussed here so that our reports can be turned into published versions fairly easily. The procedures have become standard because they work. Although they may seem somewhat arbitrary and unnecessarily rigid, the alternative is a chaotic situation in which no one knows what to do or what to expect. The value of these procedures is that in the long run they make our work easier.

MAKING REVISIONS

Now that we understand most of the major reporting principles, we should spend a bit more time looking at the overall picture. Scientific writing can seem dry and tedious, through little fault of the authors. Remember that your task in writing a report is to communicate exactly what you did in the experiment. You must do that as clearly and concisely as possible. Authors are often forced to cut articles down to save journal space.

Try to model your writing style after the precise language of a journal article. Try to say exactly what you mean. That is not as simple as it sounds. One technique some students use is reading aloud. How does it sound? Your own ear can be a guide. Would you be able to understand it if you had not written it? Try to put yourself in your reader's place. Better yet, try to get the opinion of a naive reader. Can your reader follow what you did? Can you make it clearer? Then *revise your report.*

One of the things that often surprises people is that when researchers sit down to write reports, they do not usually stop at a first draft. They may continue to revise and rework the same paper several times before they feel it is acceptable. Somehow the thought of rewriting seems to unnerve many people. But even the best writers make revisions. They need editors too. Good writing takes work. The first draft of your report should be just that—a first draft. Work on improving it, polishing it, refining it. Put as much care into writing your report as you put into doing the study. A good study merits a good presentation. Evaluate your draft to make sure you have accomplished the goals of each section of the report. Make the necessary changes or additions.

As you work on revisions, be aware of some common errors that can detract from your report. First, be sure you understand the difference between *affect* and *effect. Affect* is a verb: The powerful heat *affected* their thinking. *Effect* is a noun: The *effect* of food deprivation was transient. But food deprivation *affects* learning. Be careful of other spelling errors too. They detract from the overall quality of your work. Note that the word *data* is a plural noun: The data are convincing. Double-check for biased or sexist language. As with any writing, try to form each paragraph around a single main idea, but avoid paragraphs that are comprised of only one or two sentences. If an idea is important enough for a report, it probably deserves at least three sentences! You can often combine several points in the same paragraph (as we did in this one).

It is inaccurate as well as disappointing to say, "I got no results in this experiment." You *always* get results, although they may not be what you predicted. Conversely, do not make grand statements based on the data of one experiment. Your results may enable you to reject the null hypothesis. However, you have not "proved" anything; you simply confirmed your predictions. You could be making a Type 1 error. Avoid words like *true* and *absolutely.*

Finally, keep in mind that this process is part of a scientific venture. We are looking for observable data that can be evaluated on the basis of objective criteria. This is not the place to talk about personal experiences, popular knowledge, or common sense. All your statements need to be documented. Stick to the literature and the facts. Present and discuss data. Pay particular attention to your discussion section. Remember that your discussion should wrap things up; readers should finish your report with an understanding of what the study was about and where it fits. You may offer suggestions for future research, but try to view each report as a document that has a beginning and an end.

SUMMARY

The purpose of a *research report* is communication. A *scientific writing style* is used in research reports. Through a report we tell others what we did and what we found. A report should contain enough information to permit other researchers to evaluate the findings and replicate them if they choose. The language used is objective, unbiased, and nonsexist.

The *Publication Manual of the American Psychological Association* includes detailed information regarding the format, content, and layout of reports. We follow these standards by convention so that writers as well as readers will have a consistent model for dealing with psychological research.

The psychological research report has these main components: a *descriptive title,* an *abstract,* an *introduction,* a *method* section, a *results* section, a *discussion,* and a list of *references.* Additional components include author notes, footnotes, and tables or figures.

Abstracts are especially important because they are used in the major reference for psychological information, *Psychological Abstracts,* which organizes information from many journals, books, and psychology-related publications into one handy source.

There are many specific procedural details for carrying out the goals of each section of the report. Some of these can be seen in published articles; they are also seen in a typed manuscript. Reports are written in several stages: The first is a draft, which is then revised and polished to give the experiment the best possible presentation.

KEY TERMS

Abstract   A 100- to 150-word summary of the report, which precedes the four major sections.

Descriptive title   The title of the report, which describes what the report is about; typically includes the variables tested and the relationship between them.

Discussion section   The final major section of the report; it evaluates and interprets results and discusses implications of the research.

Introduction   The first major section of the report; it explains the research, what led up to it, and states the research hypothesis.

Method section   The second major section of the report; it explains in detail how the research was conducted and who the subjects were.

References   A list of books and articles cited in the report; placed at the end of the report.

Research report   Written report of psychological research, which contains four major sections: Introduction, Method, Results, and Discussion.

Results section   The third major section of the report; it describes the findings and presents results of statistical tests and summary data.

Running head   A short version of the title, usually placed at the top of each page of the report.

Scientific writing style   A concise, impersonal, and unbiased form of writing used in research reports.

REVIEW AND STUDY QUESTIONS

1. What is the purpose of a research report?
2. What is scientific writing style? How is it different from writing a letter to a friend?
3. What are the major sections that should be included in each report?
4. Think of three terms that are ethnically biased and three that are sexist. Think of some alternative, unbiased terms and practice them in everyday conversation.
5. A title should be "descriptive." What do we mean by that? What is the importance of using a descriptive title?
6. Practice writing report titles by suggesting a good descriptive title that might be used for a report on each of the following sets of independent and dependent variables:
   a. Food deprivation; the speed of maze running
   b. Practice; time required to solve a word problem
   c. Maturation; fear of strangers
   d. Printer's type; reading rate
7. What is the function of the abstract of a research report?
8. What basic information should be contained in an abstract?
9. What is *Psychological Abstracts?*
10. Practice using *Psychological Abstracts* by carrying out each of the following:
    a. Find three references for articles on delayed recall.
    b. Locate an article published in 1990 on the effects of rock music videos.
    c. Obtain references for at least two articles authored by Linda A. Jackson.
11. What is the *Publication Manual of the American Psychological Association?* Why is it important?
12. What is the function of the introduction of a report? What basic information should you include in an introduction?
13. What is the function of the method section of a report? What basic information should you include in the method section?
14. You want to divide a method section into subsections. What common subsections are often used? What information would you include in each?
15. What information would you include in the results section?
16. The discussion section of a report serves several functions. What are they?
17. Why do we need to include references at the end of a report?
18. Jack is not pleased with this chapter. He says: "If I have to follow all these silly rules for writing a report, I won't have any chance to be creative." Tell him why a standard format for writing reports is important.
19. Explain how you would show each of the following in a report:
    a. The results of a t test with 38 degrees of freedom, where the computed value of t was 1.38.

b. The results of an ANOVA with 1 and 12 degrees of freedom, where the computed value of F was 3.78.
c. The proper placement of a figure within the text.
d. The proper placement of a table within the text.
e. The proper reference for this book.
f. The proper references for the articles located for question 10.
20. Explain the major differences between the manuscript of an article and the printed version we might see in a journal.

REFERENCES

ADAMS, J. S. (1965). Inequity in social exchange. In L. Berkowitz (Ed.) *Advances in experimental social psychology* (Vol. 2, pp. 267–299). San Diego, CA: Academic Press.

AMERICAN PSYCHOLOGICAL ASSOCIATION (1981). *Thesaurus of Psychological Index Terms*. Washington, DC: Author.

AMERICAN PSYCHOLOGICAL ASSOCIATION (1983). *Publication Manual of the American Psychological Association* (3rd ed.), Washington, DC: Author.

CROWNE, D. P., & MARLOWE, D. (1964). *The approval motive*. New York: Wiley.

DOOB, A. N., CARLSMITH, J. M., FREEDMAN, J. L., LANDAUER, T. K., & TOM, S. (1969). Effect of initial selling price on subsequent sales. *Journal of Personality and Social Psychology, 11,* 345–350.

GREENBERG, J. (1990). Employee theft as a reaction to underpayment inequity: The hidden cost of pay cuts. *Journal of Applied Psychology, 75,* 561–568.

GREESON, L. E., & WILLIAMS, R. A. (1986). Social implications of music videos for youth. *Youth and Society, 18,* 177–189.

REED, J. G., & BAXTER, P. M. (1983). *Library use: A handbook for psychology*. Washington, DC: American Psychological Association.

SARNOFF, I., & ZIMBARDO, P. G. (1961). Anxiety, fear, and social affiliation. *Journal of Abnormal and Social Psychology, 62,* 356–363.

WALSTER (HATFIELD), E., WALSTER, G., & BERSHEID, E. (1978). *Equity: Theory and research*. Boston: Allyn and Bacon.

WINER, B. J. (1971). *Statistical principles in experimental design* (2nd ed.). New York: McGraw-Hill.

Table A1 A one-way analysis of variance for a three-group example: Computational formulas

	Group 1	X_1^2	Group 2	X_2^2	Group 3	X_3^2
Step 1. Square each score.	2	4	1	1	3	9
	2	4	3	9	4	16
	1	1	3	9	2	4
	0	0	3	9	3	9
	1	1	3	9	4	16
Step 2. Total the scores and squared scores of each group.	$\Sigma X_1 = 6$ $N_1 = 5$	$\Sigma X_1^2 = 10$	$\Sigma X_2 = 13$ $N_2 = 5$	$\Sigma X_2^2 = 37$	$\Sigma X_3 = 16$ $N_3 = 5$	$\Sigma X_3^2 = 54$

Step 3. Total all scores.

$$\Sigma X = 6 + 13 + 16$$
$$= 35$$

Step 4. Total all squared scores.

$$\Sigma X^2 = 10 + 37 + 54$$
$$= 101$$

Step 5. Find sum of squares total. N is the total number of scores.

$$\boxed{SS_T = \Sigma X^2 - \frac{(\Sigma X)^2}{N}}$$

$$= 101 - \frac{(35)^2}{15}$$

$$= 101 - \frac{(1225)}{15}$$

$$= 101 - 81.67$$

$$= 19.33$$

Step 6. Find sum of squares between groups (p is the number of groups).

$$SS_B = \frac{(\Sigma X_1)^2}{N_1} + \frac{(\Sigma X_2)^2}{N_2} + \ldots + \frac{\Sigma X_p)^2}{N_p} - \frac{(\Sigma X)^2}{N}$$

$$= \frac{(6)^2}{5} + \frac{(15)^2}{5} + \frac{(16)^2}{5} - \frac{(35)^2}{15}$$

$$= 7.20 + 33.80 + 51.20 - 81.67$$

$$= 92.20 - 81.67$$

$$= 10.53$$

Step 7. Find sum of squares within groups.

$$SS_W = SS_T - SS_B$$

$$= 19.33 - 10.53$$

$$= 8.80$$

Step 8. Complete the summary table and compute F.

Source	df	SS	MS	F
Between groups	$(p - 1) = 2$	10.53	5.26	7.21*
Within groups	$(N - p) = 12$	8.80	.73	
Total	14	19.33		

* $p < 0.1$

NOTE: Table 13-3 in this text shows the analysis using definitional formulas. Discrepancies between the computed values found through the two methods are due to rounding errors. The two approaches are mathematically equivalent.

Table A2 A two-way analysis of variance: Computational formulas

Step 1. Total scores in each treatment group.

Step 2. Find row and column totals and means.

	Factor 1 (Word Frequency)			Row Totals	Row Means
	Low		**High**		
No cues	X_1 X_1^2 2 4 3 9 1 1 4 16 5 25 $\Sigma X_1 = 15$ $\Sigma X_1^2 = 55$ $N_1 = 5$		X_2 X_2^2 4 16 5 25 4 16 6 36 6 36 $\Sigma X_2 = 25$ $\Sigma X_2^2 = 129$ $N_2 = 5$	40	20
Factor 2 (Category cues) **Cues**	X_3 X_3^2 4 16 6 36 5 25 6 36 9 81 $\Sigma X_3 = 30$ $\Sigma X_3^2 = 194$ $N_3 = 5$		X_4 X_4^2 7 49 6 36 9 81 8 64 10 100 $\Sigma X_4 = 40$ $\Sigma X_4^2 = 330$ $N_4 = 5$	70	35
Column totals	45		65	Grand total $\Sigma X = 110$	
Column means	22.5		32.5	Grand mean $\dfrac{\Sigma X}{N} = 5.5$	

Step 3. Total all scores and compute grand mean. N is the total number of scores.

Step 4. Find the total of all squared scores.

$$\Sigma X^2 = 55 + 129 + 194 + 330$$
$$= 708$$

Step 5. Find the sum of squares total.

$$\boxed{SS_T = \Sigma X^2 - \frac{(\Sigma X)^2}{N}}$$

$$= 708 - \frac{(110)^2}{20}$$

$$= 708 - 605$$

$$= 103$$

Step 6. Find sum of squares between groups (p is the number of levels of Factor 2; q is the number of levels of Factor 1; pq is the number of groups).

$$\boxed{SS_B = \frac{(\Sigma X_1)^2}{N_1} + \frac{(\Sigma X_2)^2}{N_2} + \dots + \frac{\Sigma X_{pq}{}^2}{N_{pq}} - \frac{(\Sigma X)^2}{N}}$$

$$= \frac{(15)^2}{5} + \frac{(25)^2}{5} + \frac{(30)^2}{5} + \frac{(40)^2}{5} - \frac{(110)^2}{20}$$

$$= 45 + 125 + 180 + 320 - 605$$

$$= 670 - 605$$

$$= 65$$

Step 7. Find sum of squares within groups.

$$SS_W = SS_T - SS_B$$

$$= 103 - 65$$

$$= 38$$

Step 8. Find sum of squares for Factor 1; total (Σ) across all columns.

$$SS_1 = \Sigma \left[\frac{(\text{Total of each column})^2}{(N \text{ in each column})} \right] - \frac{(\Sigma X)^2}{N}$$

$$= \Sigma \left(\frac{(45)^2}{10} + \frac{(65)^2}{10} \right) - \frac{(110)^2}{20}$$

$$= (202.5 + 422.5) - 605$$

$$= 625 - 605$$

$$= 20$$

Step 9. Find sum of squares for Factor 2; total (Σ) across all rows.

$$SS_2 = \Sigma \left[\frac{(\text{Total each row})^2}{(N \text{ in each row})} \right] - \frac{(\Sigma X)^2}{N}$$

$$= \Sigma \left(\frac{(40)^2}{(10)} + \frac{(70)^2}{(10)} \right) - \frac{(110)^2}{20}$$

$$= (160 + 490) - 605$$

$$= 650 - 605$$

$$= 45$$

Step 10. Find sum of squares for the interaction.

$$SS_{1 \times 2} = SS_B - SS_1 - SS_2$$

$$= 65 - 20 - 45$$

$$= 0$$

Step 11. Complete the summary table and compute F (p is the number of levels of Factor 2; q is the number of levels of Factor 1).

Source	df	SS	MS	F
Between groups				
Factor 1	$q - 1 = 1$	20	20	$F_1 = \frac{20}{2.38}$ or 8.40*
Factor 2	$p - 1 = 1$	45	45	$F_2 = \frac{45}{2.38}$ or 18.91**
Interaction 1 × 2	$(p - 1)(q - 1) = 1$	0	0	$F_{1 \times 2} = \frac{0}{2.38}$ or 0
Within groups	16	38	2.38	
Total	$N - 1 = 19$	65		

*$p \leq .05$
**$p \leq .01$

NOTE: Tables 13-2 through 13-12 in this text illustrate the definitional formulas for these procedures. The two approaches *are mathematically equivalent.*

Table B1 Random numbers

03 47 43 73 86	36 96 47 36 61	46 98 63 71 62	33 26 16 80 45	60 11 14 10 95
97 74 24 67 62	42 81 14 57 20	42 53 32 37 32	27 07 36 07 51	24 51 79 89 73
16 76 62 27 66	56 50 26 71 07	32 90 79 78 53	13 55 38 58 59	88 97 54 14 10
12 56 85 99 26	96 96 68 27 31	05 03 72 93 15	57 12 10 14 21	88 26 49 81 76
55 59 56 35 64	38 54 82 46 22	31 62 43 09 90	06 18 44 32 53	23 83 01 30 30
16 22 77 94 39	49 54 43 54 82	17 37 93 23 78	87 35 20 96 43	84 26 34 91 64
84 42 17 53 31	57 24 55 06 88	77 04 74 47 67	21 76 33 50 25	83 92 12 06 76
63 01 63 78 59	16 95 55 67 19	98 10 50 71 75	12 86 73 58 07	44 39 52 38 79
33 21 12 34 29	78 64 56 07 82	52 42 07 44 38	15 51 00 13 42	99 66 02 79 54
57 60 86 32 44	09 47 27 96 54	49 17 46 09 62	90 52 84 77 27	08 02 73 43 28
18 18 07 92 46	44 17 16 58 09	79 83 86 19 62	06 76 50 03 10	55 23 64 05 05
26 62 38 97 75	84 16 07 44 99	83 11 46 32 24	20 14 85 88 45	10 93 72 88 71
23 42 40 64 74	82 97 77 77 81	07 45 32 14 08	32 98 94 07 72	93 85 79 10 75
52 30 28 19 95	50 92 26 11 97	00 56 76 31 38	80 22 02 53 53	86 60 42 04 53
37 45 94 35 12	83 39 50 08 30	42 34 07 96 88	54 42 06 87 98	35 85 29 48 39
70 29 17 12 13	40 33 20 38 26	13 89 51 03 74	17 76 37 13 04	07 74 21 19 30
56 62 18 37 35	96 83 50 87 75	97 12 25 93 47	70 33 24 03 54	97 77 46 44 80
99 49 57 22 77	88 42 95 45 72	16 64 36 16 00	04 43 18 66 79	94 77 24 21 90
16 08 15 04 72	33 27 14 34 09	45 59 34 68 49	12 72 07 34 45	99 27 72 95 14
31 16 93 32 43	50 27 89 87 19	20 15 37 00 49	52 85 66 60 44	38 68 88 11 80
68 34 30 13 70	55 74 30 77 40	44 22 78 84 26	04 33 46 09 52	68 07 97 06 57
74 57 25 65 76	59 29 97 68 60	71 91 38 67 54	13 58 18 24 76	15 54 55 95 52
27 42 37 86 53	48 55 90 65 72	96 57 69 36 10	96 46 92 42 45	97 60 49 04 91
00 39 68 29 61	66 37 32 20 30	77 84 57 03 29	10 45 65 04 26	11 04 96 67 24
29 94 98 94 24	68 49 69 10 82	53 75 91 93 30	34 25 20 57 27	40 48 73 51 92
16 90 82 66 59	83 62 64 11 12	67 19 00 71 74	60 47 21 29 68	02 02 37 03 31
11 27 94 75 06	06 09 19 74 66	02 94 37 34 02	76 70 90 30 66	38 45 94 30 38
35 25 20 16 20	33 32 51 26 38	79 78 45 04 91	16 92 53 56 16	02 76 59 95 98
38 23 16 86 38	42 38 97 01 50	87 75 66 81 41	40 01 74 91 62	48 51 84 08 32
31 96 25 91 47	96 44 33 49 13	34 86 82 53 91	00 52 43 48 85	27 55 26 89 62
66 67 40 67 14	64 05 71 95 86	11 05 65 09 68	76 83 20 37 90	57 16 00 11 66
14 90 84 45 11	75 73 88 05 90	52 27 41 14 86	22 98 12 22 08	07 52 74 95 80
68 05 51 18 00	33 96 02 75 19	07 60 62 93 55	59 33 82 43 90	49 37 38 44 59
20 46 78 73 90	97 51 40 14 02	04 02 33 31 08	39 54 16 49 36	47 95 93 13 30
64 19 58 97 79	15 06 15 93 20	01 90 10 75 06	40 78 78 89 62	02 67 74 17 33

(continued)

```
05 26 93 70 60    22 35 85 15 13    92 03 51 59 77    59 56 78 06 83    52 91 05 70 74
07 97 10 88 23    09 98 42 99 64    61 71 62 99 15    06 51 29 16 93    58 05 77 09 51
68 71 86 85 85    54 87 66 47 54    73 32 08 11 12    44 95 92 63 16    29 56 24 29 48
26 99 61 65 53    58 37 78 80 70    42 10 50 67 42    32 17 55 85 74    94 44 67 16 94
14 65 52 68 75    87 59 36 22 41    26 78 63 06 55    13 08 27 01 50    15 29 39 39 43

17 53 77 58 71    71 41 61 50 72    12 41 94 96 26    44 95 27 36 99    02 96 74 30 83
90 26 59 21 19    23 52 23 33 12    96 93 02 18 39    07 02 18 36 07    25 99 32 70 23
41 23 52 55 99    31 04 49 69 96    10 47 48 45 88    13 41 43 89 20    97 17 14 49 17
60 20 50 81 69    31 99 73 68 68    35 81 33 03 76    24 30 12 48 60    18 99 10 72 34
91 25 38 05 90    94 58 28 41 36    45 37 59 03 09    90 35 57 29 12    82 62 54 65 60

34 50 57 74 37    98 80 33 00 91    09 77 93 19 82    74 94 80 04 04    45 07 31 66 49
85 22 04 39 43    73 81 53 94 79    33 62 46 86 28    08 31 54 46 31    53 94 13 38 47
09 79 13 77 48    73 82 97 22 21    05 03 27 24 83    72 89 44 05 60    35 80 39 94 88
88 75 80 18 14    22 95 75 42 49    39 32 82 22 49    02 48 07 70 37    16 04 61 67 87
90 96 23 70 00    39 00 03 06 90    55 85 78 38 36    94 37 30 69 32    90 89 00 76 33

53 74 23 99 67    61 32 28 69 84    94 62 67 86 24    98 33 41 19 95    47 53 53 38 09
63 38 06 86 54    99 00 65 26 94    02 82 90 23 07    79 62 67 80 60    75 91 12 81 19
35 30 58 21 46    06 72 17 10 94    25 21 31 75 96    49 28 24 00 49    55 65 79 78 07
63 43 36 82 69    65 51 18 37 88    61 38 44 12 45    32 92 85 88 65    54 34 81 85 35
98 25 37 55 26    01 91 82 81 46    74 71 12 94 97    24 02 71 37 07    03 92 18 66 75

02 63 21 17 69    71 50 80 89 56    38 15 70 11 48    43 40 45 86 98    00 83 26 91 03
64 55 22 21 82    48 22 28 06 00    61 54 13 43 91    82 78 12 23 29    06 66 24 12 27
85 07 26 13 89    01 10 07 82 04    59 63 69 36 03    69 11 15 83 80    13 29 54 19 28
58 54 16 24 15    51 54 44 82 00    62 61 65 04 69    38 18 65 18 97    85 72 13 49 21
34 85 27 84 87    61 48 64 56 26    90 18 48 13 26    37 70 15 42 57    65 65 80 39 07

03 92 18 27 46    57 99 16 96 56    30 33 72 85 22    84 64 38 56 98    99 01 30 98 64
62 95 30 27 59    37 75 41 66 48    86 97 80 61 45    23 53 04 01 63    45 76 08 64 27
08 45 93 15 22    60 21 75 46 91    98 77 27 85 42    28 88 61 08 84    69 62 03 42 73
07 08 55 18 40    45 44 75 13 90    24 94 96 61 02    57 55 66 83 15    73 42 37 11 61
01 85 89 95 66    51 10 19 34 88    15 84 97 19 75    12 76 39 43 78    64 63 91 08 25

72 84 71 14 35    19 11 58 49 26    50 11 17 17 76    86 31 57 20 18    95 60 78 46 75
88 78 28 16 84    13 52 53 94 53    75 45 69 30 96    73 89 65 70 31    99 17 43 48 76
45 17 75 65 57    28 40 19 72 12    25 12 74 75 67    60 40 60 81 19    24 62 01 61 16
96 76 28 12 54    22 01 11 94 25    71 96 16 16 88    68 64 36 74 45    19 59 50 88 92
43 31 67 72 30    24 02 94 08 63    38 32 36 66 02    69 36 38 25 39    48 03 45 15 22

50 44 66 44 21    66 06 58 05 62    68 15 54 35 02    42 35 48 96 32    14 52 41 52 48
22 66 22 15 86    26 63 75 41 99    58 42 36 72 24    58 37 52 18 51    03 37 18 39 11
96 24 40 14 51    23 22 30 88 57    95 67 47 29 83    94 69 40 06 07    18 16 36 78 86
31 73 91 61 19    60 20 72 93 48    98 57 07 23 69    65 95 39 69 58    56 80 30 19 44
78 60 73 99 84    43 89 94 36 45    56 69 47 07 41    90 22 91 07 12    78 35 34 08 72

84 37 90 61 56    70 10 23 98 05    85 11 34 76 60    76 48 45 34 60    01 64 18 39 96
36 67 10 08 23    98 93 35 08 86    99 29 76 29 81    33 34 91 58 93    63 14 52 32 52
07 28 59 07 48    89 64 58 89 75    83 85 62 27 89    30 14 78 56 27    86 63 59 80 02
10 15 83 87 60    79 24 31 66 56    21 48 24 06 93    91 98 94 05 49    01 47 59 38 00
55 19 68 97 65    03 73 52 16 56    00 53 55 90 27    33 42 29 38 87    22 13 88 83 34
```

Table B1   Random numbers *(continued)*

53	81	29	13	39	35	01	20	71	34	62	33	74	82	14	53	73	19	09	03	56	54	29	56	93
51	86	32	68	92	33	98	74	66	99	40	14	71	94	58	45	94	19	38	81	14	44	99	81	07
35	91	70	29	13	80	03	54	07	27	96	94	78	32	66	50	95	52	74	33	13	80	55	62	54
37	71	67	95	13	20	02	44	95	94	64	85	04	05	72	01	32	90	76	14	53	89	74	60	41
93	66	13	83	27	92	79	64	64	72	28	54	96	53	84	48	14	52	98	94	56	07	93	89	30
02	96	08	45	65	13	05	00	41	84	93	07	54	72	59	21	45	57	09	77	19	48	56	27	44
49	83	43	48	35	82	88	33	69	96	72	36	04	19	76	47	45	15	18	60	82	11	08	95	97
84	60	71	62	46	40	80	81	30	37	34	39	23	05	38	25	15	35	71	30	88	12	57	21	77
18	17	30	88	71	44	91	14	88	47	89	23	30	63	15	56	34	20	47	89	99	82	93	24	98
79	69	10	61	78	71	32	76	95	62	87	00	22	58	40	92	54	01	75	25	43	11	71	99	31
75	93	36	57	83	56	20	14	82	11	74	21	97	90	65	96	42	68	63	86	74	54	13	26	94
38	30	92	29	03	06	28	81	39	38	62	25	06	84	63	61	29	08	93	67	04	32	92	08	00
51	29	50	10	34	31	57	75	95	80	51	97	02	74	77	76	15	48	49	44	18	55	63	77	09
21	31	38	86	24	37	79	81	53	74	73	24	16	10	33	52	83	90	94	76	70	47	14	54	36
29	01	23	87	88	58	02	39	37	67	42	10	14	20	92	16	55	23	42	45	54	96	09	11	06
95	33	95	22	00	18	74	72	00	18	38	79	58	69	32	81	76	80	26	92	82	80	84	25	39
90	84	60	79	80	24	36	59	87	38	82	07	53	89	35	96	35	23	79	18	05	98	90	07	35
46	40	62	98	82	54	97	20	56	95	15	74	80	08	32	16	46	70	50	80	67	72	16	42	79
20	31	89	03	43	38	46	82	68	72	32	14	82	99	70	80	60	47	18	97	63	49	30	21	30
71	59	73	05	50	08	22	23	71	77	91	01	93	20	49	82	96	59	26	94	66	39	67	08	60

SOURCE: Fisher and Yates. From Table XXXIII in Statistical Tables for Biological, Agricultural and Medical Research, *published by Longman Group Ltd., London. (Previously published by Oliver and Boyd, Edinburgh.) Reprinted with permission of the authors and publishers.*

Table B2 Critical Values of *t*

	LEVEL OF SIGNIFICANCE FOR ONE-TAILED TEST			
	.05	.025	.01	.005
	LEVEL OF SIGNIFICANCE FOR TWO-TAILED TEST			
df	.10	.05	.02	.01
1	6.314	12.706	31.821	63.657
2	2.920	4.303	6.965	9.925
3	2.353	3.182	4.541	5.841
4	2.132	2.776	3.747	4.604
5	2.015	2.571	3.365	4.032
6	1.943	2.447	3.143	3.707
7	1.895	2.365	2.998	3.499
8	1.860	2.306	2.896	3.355
9	1.833	2.262	2.821	3.250
10	1.812	2.228	2.764	3.169
11	1.796	2.201	2.718	3.106
12	1.782	2.179	2.681	3.055
13	1.771	2.160	2.650	3.012
14	1.761	2.145	2.624	2.977
15	1.753	2.131	2.602	2.947
16	1.746	2.120	2.583	2.921
17	1.740	2.110	2.567	2.898
18	1.734	2.101	2.552	2.878
19	1.729	2.093	2.539	2.861
20	1.725	2.086	2.528	2.845
21	1.721	2.080	2.518	2.831
22	1.717	2.074	2.508	2.819
23	1.714	2.069	2.500	2.807
24	1.711	2.064	2.492	2.797
25	1.708	2.060	2.485	2.787
26	1.706	2.056	2.479	2.779
27	1.703	2.052	2.473	2.771
28	1.701	2.048	2.467	2.763
29	1.699	2.045	2.462	2.756
30	1.697	2.042	2.457	2.750
40	1.684	2.021	2.423	2.704
60	1.671	2.000	2.390	2.660
120	1.658	1.980	2.358	2.617
∞	1.645	1.960	2.326	2.576

SOURCE: *Fisher and Yates. From Table III in* Statistical Tables for Biological, Agricultural and Medical Research, *published by Longman Group Ltd., London. (Previously published by Oliver and Boyd, Edinburgh.) Reprinted with permission of the authors and publishers.*

Table B3 Critical Values of F (.05 level in roman type, .01 level in **boldface**)

DEGREES OF FREEDOM FOR GREATER MEAN SQUARE [NUMERATOR]

Each cell lists the .05 level value (roman) over the .01 level value (**boldface**).

Denom. df	1	2	3	4	5	6	7	8	9	10	11	12	14	16	20	24	30	40	50	75	100	200	500	∞
1	161 / **4,052**	200 / **4,999**	216 / **5,403**	225 / **5,625**	230 / **5,764**	234 / **5,859**	237 / **5,928**	239 / **5,981**	241 / **6,022**	242 / **6,056**	243 / **6,082**	244 / **6,106**	245 / **6,142**	246 / **6,169**	248 / **6,208**	249 / **6,234**	250 / **6,261**	251 / **6,286**	252 / **6,302**	253 / **6,323**	253 / **6,334**	254 / **6,352**	254 / **6,361**	254 / **6,366**
2	18.51 / **98.49**	19.00 / **99.00**	19.16 / **99.17**	19.25 / **99.25**	19.30 / **99.30**	19.33 / **99.33**	19.36 / **99.36**	19.37 / **99.37**	19.38 / **99.39**	19.39 / **99.40**	19.40 / **99.41**	19.41 / **99.42**	19.42 / **99.43**	19.43 / **99.44**	19.44 / **99.45**	19.45 / **99.46**	19.46 / **99.47**	19.47 / **99.48**	19.47 / **99.48**	19.48 / **99.49**	19.49 / **99.49**	19.49 / **99.49**	19.50 / **99.50**	19.50 / **99.50**
3	10.13 / **34.12**	9.55 / **30.82**	9.28 / **29.46**	9.12 / **28.71**	9.01 / **28.24**	8.94 / **27.91**	8.88 / **27.67**	8.84 / **27.49**	8.81 / **27.34**	8.78 / **27.23**	8.76 / **27.13**	8.74 / **27.05**	8.71 / **26.92**	8.69 / **26.83**	8.66 / **26.69**	8.64 / **26.60**	8.62 / **26.50**	8.60 / **26.41**	8.58 / **26.35**	8.57 / **26.27**	8.56 / **26.23**	8.54 / **26.18**	8.54 / **26.14**	8.53 / **26.12**
4	7.71 / **21.20**	6.94 / **18.00**	6.59 / **16.69**	6.39 / **15.98**	6.26 / **15.52**	6.16 / **15.21**	6.09 / **14.98**	6.04 / **14.80**	6.00 / **14.66**	5.96 / **14.54**	5.93 / **14.45**	5.91 / **14.37**	5.87 / **14.24**	5.84 / **14.15**	5.80 / **14.02**	5.77 / **13.93**	5.74 / **13.83**	5.71 / **13.74**	5.70 / **13.69**	5.68 / **13.61**	5.66 / **13.57**	5.65 / **13.52**	5.64 / **13.48**	5.63 / **13.46**
5	6.61 / **16.26**	5.79 / **13.27**	5.41 / **12.06**	5.19 / **11.39**	5.05 / **10.97**	4.95 / **10.67**	4.88 / **10.45**	4.82 / **10.29**	4.78 / **10.15**	4.74 / **10.05**	4.70 / **9.96**	4.68 / **9.89**	4.64 / **9.77**	4.60 / **9.68**	4.56 / **9.55**	4.53 / **9.47**	4.50 / **9.38**	4.46 / **9.29**	4.44 / **9.24**	4.42 / **9.17**	4.40 / **9.13**	4.38 / **9.07**	4.37 / **9.04**	4.36 / **9.02**
6	5.99 / **13.74**	5.14 / **10.92**	4.76 / **9.78**	4.53 / **9.15**	4.39 / **8.75**	4.28 / **8.47**	4.21 / **8.26**	4.15 / **8.10**	4.10 / **7.98**	4.06 / **7.87**	4.03 / **7.79**	4.00 / **7.72**	3.96 / **7.60**	3.92 / **7.52**	3.87 / **7.39**	3.84 / **7.31**	3.81 / **7.23**	3.77 / **7.14**	3.75 / **7.09**	3.72 / **7.02**	3.71 / **6.99**	3.69 / **6.94**	3.68 / **6.90**	3.67 / **6.88**
7	5.59 / **12.25**	4.74 / **9.55**	4.35 / **8.45**	4.12 / **7.85**	3.97 / **7.46**	3.87 / **7.19**	3.79 / **7.00**	3.73 / **6.84**	3.68 / **6.71**	3.63 / **6.62**	3.60 / **6.54**	3.57 / **6.47**	3.52 / **6.35**	3.49 / **6.27**	3.44 / **6.15**	3.41 / **6.07**	3.38 / **5.98**	3.34 / **5.90**	3.32 / **5.85**	3.29 / **5.78**	3.28 / **5.75**	3.25 / **5.70**	3.24 / **5.67**	3.23 / **5.65**
8	5.32 / **11.26**	4.46 / **8.65**	4.07 / **7.59**	3.84 / **7.01**	3.69 / **6.63**	3.58 / **6.37**	3.50 / **6.19**	3.44 / **6.03**	3.39 / **5.91**	3.34 / **5.82**	3.31 / **5.74**	3.28 / **5.67**	3.23 / **5.56**	3.20 / **5.48**	3.15 / **5.36**	3.12 / **5.28**	3.08 / **5.20**	3.05 / **5.11**	3.03 / **5.06**	3.00 / **5.00**	2.98 / **4.96**	2.96 / **4.91**	2.94 / **4.88**	2.93 / **4.86**
9	5.12 / **10.56**	4.26 / **8.02**	3.86 / **6.99**	3.63 / **6.42**	3.48 / **6.06**	3.37 / **5.80**	3.29 / **5.62**	3.23 / **5.47**	3.18 / **5.35**	3.13 / **5.26**	3.10 / **5.18**	3.07 / **5.11**	3.02 / **5.00**	2.98 / **4.92**	2.93 / **4.80**	2.90 / **4.73**	2.86 / **4.64**	2.82 / **4.56**	2.80 / **4.51**	2.77 / **4.45**	2.76 / **4.41**	2.73 / **4.36**	2.72 / **4.33**	2.71 / **4.31**
10	4.96 / **10.04**	4.10 / **7.56**	3.71 / **6.55**	3.48 / **5.99**	3.33 / **5.64**	3.22 / **5.39**	3.14 / **5.21**	3.07 / **5.06**	3.02 / **4.95**	2.97 / **4.85**	2.94 / **4.78**	2.91 / **4.71**	2.86 / **4.60**	2.82 / **4.52**	2.77 / **4.41**	2.74 / **4.33**	2.70 / **4.25**	2.67 / **4.17**	2.64 / **4.12**	2.61 / **4.05**	2.59 / **4.01**	2.56 / **3.96**	2.55 / **3.93**	2.54 / **3.91**
11	4.84 / **9.65**	3.98 / **7.20**	3.59 / **6.22**	3.36 / **5.67**	3.20 / **5.32**	3.09 / **5.07**	3.01 / **4.88**	2.95 / **4.74**	2.90 / **4.63**	2.86 / **4.54**	2.82 / **4.46**	2.79 / **4.40**	2.74 / **4.29**	2.70 / **4.21**	2.65 / **4.10**	2.61 / **4.02**	2.57 / **3.94**	2.53 / **3.86**	2.50 / **3.80**	2.47 / **3.74**	2.45 / **3.70**	2.42 / **3.66**	2.41 / **3.62**	2.40 / **3.60**
12	4.75 / **9.33**	3.88 / **6.93**	3.49 / **5.95**	3.26 / **5.41**	3.11 / **5.06**	3.00 / **4.82**	2.92 / **4.65**	2.85 / **4.50**	2.80 / **4.39**	2.76 / **4.30**	2.72 / **4.22**	2.69 / **4.16**	2.64 / **4.05**	2.60 / **3.98**	2.54 / **3.86**	2.50 / **3.78**	2.46 / **3.70**	2.42 / **3.61**	2.40 / **3.56**	2.36 / **3.49**	2.35 / **3.46**	2.32 / **3.41**	2.31 / **3.38**	2.30 / **3.36**
13	4.67 / **9.07**	3.80 / **6.70**	3.41 / **5.74**	3.18 / **5.20**	3.02 / **4.86**	2.92 / **4.62**	2.84 / **4.44**	2.77 / **4.30**	2.72 / **4.19**	2.67 / **4.10**	2.63 / **4.02**	2.60 / **3.96**	2.55 / **3.85**	2.51 / **3.78**	2.46 / **3.67**	2.42 / **3.59**	2.38 / **3.51**	2.34 / **3.42**	2.32 / **3.37**	2.28 / **3.30**	2.26 / **3.27**	2.24 / **3.21**	2.22 / **3.18**	2.21 / **3.16**

DEGREES OF FREEDOM FOR LESSER MEAN SQUARE [DENOMINATOR]

NOTE: Find the critical value of F for each of your F ratios. Locate the degrees of freedom associated with the numerator of your F ratio along the top of the table. Locate the degrees of freedom associated with the denominator of your F ratio along the side of the table. The place where the correct row and column meet indicates the appropriate critical values. The numbers in light type give you the values at the .05 level; the numbers in dark type give you the values at the .01 level. Reject the null hypothesis when the computed value of F is equal to or greater than the table value.

(continued)

Table B3 Critical Values of F (continued)

DEGREES OF FREEDOM FOR GREATER MEAN SQUARE [NUMERATOR]

Each cell lists the .05 value (top) over the .01 value (bottom). Row labels are DEGREES OF FREEDOM FOR LESSER MEAN SQUARE [DENOMINATOR].

df	1	2	3	4	5	6	7	8	9	10	11	12	14	16	20	24	30	40	50	75	100	200	500	∞
14	4.60 / 8.86	3.74 / 6.51	3.34 / 5.56	3.11 / 5.03	2.96 / 4.69	2.85 / 4.46	2.77 / 4.28	2.70 / 4.14	2.65 / 4.03	2.60 / 3.94	2.56 / 3.86	2.53 / 3.80	2.48 / 3.70	2.44 / 3.62	2.39 / 3.51	2.35 / 3.43	2.31 / 3.34	2.27 / 3.26	2.24 / 3.21	2.21 / 3.14	2.19 / 3.11	2.16 / 3.06	2.14 / 3.02	2.13 / 3.00
15	4.54 / 8.68	3.68 / 6.36	3.29 / 5.42	3.06 / 4.89	2.90 / 4.56	2.79 / 4.32	2.70 / 4.14	2.64 / 4.00	2.59 / 3.89	2.55 / 3.80	2.51 / 3.73	2.48 / 3.67	2.43 / 3.56	2.39 / 3.48	2.33 / 3.36	2.29 / 3.29	2.25 / 3.20	2.21 / 3.12	2.18 / 3.07	2.15 / 3.00	2.12 / 2.97	2.10 / 2.92	2.08 / 2.89	2.07 / 2.87
16	4.49 / 8.53	3.63 / 6.23	3.24 / 5.29	3.01 / 4.77	2.85 / 4.44	2.74 / 4.20	2.66 / 4.03	2.59 / 3.89	2.54 / 3.78	2.49 / 3.69	2.45 / 3.61	2.42 / 3.55	2.37 / 3.45	2.33 / 3.37	2.28 / 3.25	2.24 / 3.18	2.20 / 3.10	2.16 / 3.01	2.13 / 2.96	2.09 / 2.88	2.07 / 2.86	2.04 / 2.80	2.02 / 2.77	2.01 / 2.75
17	4.45 / 8.40	3.59 / 6.11	3.20 / 5.18	2.96 / 4.67	2.81 / 4.34	2.70 / 4.10	2.62 / 3.93	2.55 / 3.79	2.50 / 3.68	2.45 / 3.59	2.41 / 3.52	2.38 / 3.45	2.33 / 3.35	2.29 / 3.27	2.23 / 3.16	2.19 / 3.08	2.15 / 3.00	2.11 / 2.92	2.08 / 2.86	2.04 / 2.79	2.02 / 2.76	1.99 / 2.70	1.97 / 2.67	1.96 / 2.65
18	4.41 / 8.28	3.55 / 6.01	3.16 / 5.09	2.93 / 4.58	2.77 / 4.25	2.66 / 4.01	2.58 / 3.85	2.51 / 3.71	2.46 / 3.60	2.41 / 3.51	2.37 / 3.44	2.34 / 3.37	2.29 / 3.27	2.25 / 3.19	2.19 / 3.07	2.15 / 3.00	2.11 / 2.91	2.07 / 2.83	2.04 / 2.78	2.00 / 2.71	1.98 / 2.68	1.95 / 2.62	1.93 / 2.59	1.92 / 2.57
19	4.38 / 8.18	3.52 / 5.93	3.13 / 5.01	2.90 / 4.50	2.74 / 4.17	2.63 / 3.94	2.55 / 3.77	2.48 / 3.63	2.43 / 3.52	2.38 / 3.43	2.34 / 3.36	2.31 / 3.30	2.26 / 3.19	2.21 / 3.12	2.15 / 3.00	2.11 / 2.92	2.07 / 2.84	2.02 / 2.76	2.00 / 2.70	1.96 / 2.63	1.94 / 2.60	1.91 / 2.54	1.90 / 2.51	1.88 / 2.49
20	4.35 / 8.10	3.49 / 5.85	3.10 / 4.94	2.87 / 4.43	2.71 / 4.10	2.60 / 3.87	2.52 / 3.71	2.45 / 3.56	2.40 / 3.45	2.35 / 3.37	2.31 / 3.30	2.28 / 3.23	2.23 / 3.13	2.18 / 3.05	2.12 / 2.94	2.08 / 2.86	2.04 / 2.77	1.99 / 2.69	1.96 / 2.63	1.92 / 2.56	1.90 / 2.53	1.87 / 2.47	1.85 / 2.44	1.84 / 2.42
21	4.32 / 8.02	3.47 / 5.78	3.07 / 4.87	2.84 / 4.37	2.68 / 4.04	2.57 / 3.81	2.49 / 3.65	2.42 / 3.51	2.37 / 3.40	2.32 / 3.31	2.28 / 3.24	2.25 / 3.17	2.20 / 3.07	2.15 / 2.99	2.09 / 2.88	2.05 / 2.80	2.00 / 2.72	1.96 / 2.63	1.93 / 2.58	1.89 / 2.51	1.87 / 2.47	1.84 / 2.42	1.82 / 2.38	1.81 / 2.36
22	4.30 / 7.94	3.44 / 5.72	3.05 / 4.82	2.82 / 4.31	2.66 / 3.99	2.55 / 3.76	2.47 / 3.59	2.40 / 3.45	2.35 / 3.35	2.30 / 3.26	2.26 / 3.18	2.23 / 3.12	2.18 / 3.02	2.13 / 2.94	2.07 / 2.83	2.03 / 2.75	1.98 / 2.67	1.93 / 2.58	1.91 / 2.53	1.87 / 2.46	1.84 / 2.42	1.81 / 2.37	1.80 / 2.33	1.78 / 2.31
23	4.28 / 7.88	3.42 / 5.66	3.03 / 4.76	2.80 / 4.26	2.64 / 3.94	2.53 / 3.71	2.45 / 3.54	2.38 / 3.41	2.32 / 3.30	2.28 / 3.21	2.24 / 3.14	2.20 / 3.07	2.14 / 2.97	2.10 / 2.89	2.04 / 2.78	2.00 / 2.70	1.96 / 2.62	1.91 / 2.53	1.88 / 2.48	1.84 / 2.41	1.82 / 2.37	1.79 / 2.32	1.77 / 2.28	1.76 / 2.26
24	4.26 / 7.82	3.40 / 5.61	3.01 / 4.72	2.78 / 4.22	2.62 / 3.90	2.51 / 3.67	2.43 / 3.50	2.36 / 3.36	2.30 / 3.25	2.26 / 3.17	2.22 / 3.09	2.18 / 3.03	2.13 / 2.93	2.09 / 2.85	2.02 / 2.74	1.98 / 2.66	1.94 / 2.58	1.89 / 2.49	1.86 / 2.44	1.82 / 2.36	1.80 / 2.33	1.76 / 2.27	1.74 / 2.23	1.73 / 2.21
25	4.24 / 7.77	3.38 / 5.57	2.99 / 4.68	2.76 / 4.18	2.60 / 3.86	2.49 / 3.63	2.41 / 3.46	2.34 / 3.32	2.28 / 3.21	2.24 / 3.13	2.20 / 3.05	2.16 / 2.99	2.11 / 2.89	2.06 / 2.81	2.00 / 2.70	1.96 / 2.62	1.92 / 2.54	1.87 / 2.45	1.84 / 2.40	1.80 / 2.32	1.77 / 2.29	1.74 / 2.23	1.72 / 2.19	1.71 / 2.17
26	4.22 / 7.72	3.37 / 5.53	2.98 / 4.64	2.74 / 4.14	2.59 / 3.82	2.47 / 3.59	2.39 / 3.42	2.32 / 3.29	2.27 / 3.17	2.22 / 3.09	2.18 / 3.02	2.15 / 2.96	2.10 / 2.86	2.05 / 2.77	1.99 / 2.66	1.95 / 2.58	1.90 / 2.50	1.85 / 2.41	1.82 / 2.36	1.78 / 2.28	1.76 / 2.25	1.72 / 2.19	1.70 / 2.15	1.69 / 2.13

Table B3 Critical Values of F (continued)

DEGREES OF FREEDOM FOR LESSER MEAN SQUARE [DENOMINATOR] (rows) × DEGREES OF FREEDOM FOR GREATER MEAN SQUARE [NUMERATOR] (columns)

	1	2	3	4	5	6	7	8	9	10	11	12	14	16	20	24	30	40	50	75	100	200	500	∞
27	4.21 / 7.68	3.35 / 5.49	2.96 / 4.60	2.73 / 4.11	2.57 / 3.79	2.46 / 3.56	2.37 / 3.39	2.30 / 3.26	2.25 / 3.14	2.20 / 3.06	2.16 / 2.98	2.13 / 2.93	2.08 / 2.83	2.03 / 2.74	1.97 / 2.63	1.93 / 2.55	1.88 / 2.47	1.84 / 2.38	1.80 / 2.33	1.76 / 2.25	1.74 / 2.21	1.71 / 2.16	1.68 / 2.12	1.67 / 2.10
28	4.20 / 7.64	3.34 / 5.45	2.95 / 4.57	2.71 / 4.07	2.56 / 3.76	2.44 / 3.53	2.36 / 3.36	2.29 / 3.23	2.24 / 3.11	2.19 / 3.03	2.15 / 2.95	2.12 / 2.90	2.06 / 2.80	2.02 / 2.71	1.96 / 2.60	1.91 / 2.52	1.87 / 2.44	1.81 / 2.35	1.78 / 2.30	1.75 / 2.22	1.72 / 2.18	1.69 / 2.13	1.67 / 2.09	1.65 / 2.06
29	4.18 / 7.60	3.33 / 5.42	2.93 / 4.54	2.70 / 4.04	2.54 / 3.73	2.43 / 3.50	2.35 / 3.33	2.28 / 3.20	2.22 / 3.08	2.18 / 3.00	2.14 / 2.92	2.10 / 2.87	2.05 / 2.77	2.00 / 2.68	1.94 / 2.57	1.90 / 2.49	1.85 / 2.41	1.80 / 2.32	1.77 / 2.27	1.73 / 2.19	1.71 / 2.15	1.68 / 2.10	1.65 / 2.06	1.64 / 2.03
30	4.17 / 7.56	3.32 / 5.39	2.92 / 4.51	2.69 / 4.02	2.53 / 3.70	2.42 / 3.47	2.34 / 3.30	2.27 / 3.17	2.21 / 3.06	2.16 / 2.98	2.12 / 2.90	2.09 / 2.84	2.04 / 2.74	1.99 / 2.66	1.93 / 2.55	1.89 / 2.47	1.84 / 2.38	1.79 / 2.29	1.76 / 2.24	1.72 / 2.16	1.69 / 2.13	1.66 / 2.07	1.64 / 2.03	1.62 / 2.01
32	4.15 / 7.50	3.30 / 5.34	2.90 / 4.46	2.67 / 3.97	2.51 / 3.66	2.40 / 3.42	2.32 / 3.25	2.25 / 3.12	2.19 / 3.01	2.14 / 2.94	2.10 / 2.86	2.07 / 2.80	2.02 / 2.70	1.97 / 2.62	1.91 / 2.51	1.86 / 2.42	1.82 / 2.34	1.76 / 2.25	1.74 / 2.20	1.69 / 2.12	1.67 / 2.08	1.64 / 2.02	1.61 / 1.98	1.59 / 1.96
34	4.13 / 7.44	3.28 / 5.29	2.88 / 4.42	2.65 / 3.93	2.49 / 3.61	2.38 / 3.38	2.30 / 3.21	2.23 / 3.08	2.17 / 2.97	2.12 / 2.89	2.08 / 2.82	2.05 / 2.76	2.00 / 2.66	1.95 / 2.58	1.89 / 2.47	1.84 / 2.38	1.80 / 2.30	1.74 / 2.21	1.71 / 2.15	1.67 / 2.08	1.64 / 2.04	1.61 / 1.98	1.59 / 1.94	1.57 / 1.91
36	4.11 / 7.39	3.26 / 5.25	2.86 / 4.38	2.63 / 3.89	2.48 / 3.58	2.36 / 3.35	2.28 / 3.18	2.21 / 3.04	2.15 / 2.94	2.10 / 2.86	2.06 / 2.78	2.03 / 2.72	1.98 / 2.62	1.93 / 2.54	1.87 / 2.43	1.82 / 2.35	1.78 / 2.26	1.72 / 2.17	1.69 / 2.12	1.65 / 2.04	1.62 / 2.00	1.59 / 1.94	1.56 / 1.90	1.55 / 1.87
38	4.10 / 7.35	3.25 / 5.21	2.85 / 4.34	2.62 / 3.86	2.46 / 3.54	2.35 / 3.32	2.26 / 3.15	2.19 / 3.02	2.14 / 2.91	2.09 / 2.82	2.05 / 2.75	2.02 / 2.69	1.96 / 2.59	1.92 / 2.51	1.85 / 2.40	1.80 / 2.32	1.76 / 2.22	1.71 / 2.14	1.67 / 2.08	1.63 / 2.00	1.60 / 1.97	1.57 / 1.90	1.54 / 1.86	1.53 / 1.84
40	4.08 / 7.31	3.23 / 5.18	2.84 / 4.31	2.61 / 3.83	2.45 / 3.51	2.34 / 3.29	2.25 / 3.12	2.18 / 2.99	2.12 / 2.88	2.07 / 2.80	2.04 / 2.73	2.00 / 2.66	1.95 / 2.56	1.90 / 2.49	1.84 / 2.37	1.79 / 2.29	1.74 / 2.20	1.69 / 2.11	1.66 / 2.05	1.61 / 1.97	1.59 / 1.94	1.55 / 1.88	1.53 / 1.84	1.51 / 1.81
42	4.07 / 7.27	3.22 / 5.15	2.83 / 4.29	2.59 / 3.80	2.44 / 3.49	2.32 / 3.26	2.24 / 3.10	2.17 / 2.96	2.11 / 2.86	2.06 / 2.77	2.02 / 2.70	1.99 / 2.64	1.94 / 2.54	1.89 / 2.46	1.82 / 2.35	1.78 / 2.26	1.73 / 2.17	1.68 / 2.08	1.64 / 2.02	1.60 / 1.94	1.57 / 1.91	1.54 / 1.85	1.51 / 1.80	1.49 / 1.78
44	4.06 / 7.24	3.21 / 5.12	2.82 / 4.26	2.58 / 3.78	2.43 / 3.46	2.31 / 3.24	2.23 / 3.07	2.16 / 2.94	2.10 / 2.84	2.05 / 2.75	2.01 / 2.68	1.98 / 2.62	1.92 / 2.52	1.88 / 2.44	1.81 / 2.32	1.76 / 2.24	1.72 / 2.15	1.66 / 2.06	1.63 / 2.00	1.58 / 1.92	1.56 / 1.88	1.52 / 1.82	1.50 / 1.78	1.48 / 1.75
46	4.05 / 7.21	3.20 / 5.10	2.81 / 4.24	2.57 / 3.76	2.42 / 3.44	2.30 / 3.22	2.22 / 3.05	2.14 / 2.92	2.09 / 2.82	2.04 / 2.73	2.00 / 2.66	1.97 / 2.60	1.91 / 2.50	1.87 / 2.42	1.80 / 2.30	1.75 / 2.22	1.71 / 2.13	1.65 / 2.04	1.62 / 1.98	1.57 / 1.90	1.54 / 1.86	1.51 / 1.80	1.48 / 1.76	1.46 / 1.72
48	4.04 / 7.19	3.19 / 5.08	2.80 / 4.22	2.56 / 3.74	2.41 / 3.42	2.30 / 3.20	2.21 / 3.04	2.14 / 2.90	2.08 / 2.80	2.03 / 2.71	1.99 / 2.64	1.96 / 2.58	1.90 / 2.48	1.86 / 2.40	1.79 / 2.28	1.74 / 2.20	1.70 / 2.11	1.64 / 2.02	1.61 / 1.96	1.56 / 1.88	1.53 / 1.84	1.50 / 1.78	1.47 / 1.73	1.45 / 1.70

(continued)

Table B3 Critical Values of F (continued)

DEGREES OF FREEDOM FOR LESSER MEAN SQUARE [DENOMINATOR] / DEGREES OF FREEDOM FOR GREATER MEAN SQUARE [NUMERATOR]

Each cell shows two critical values (upper = roman, lower = bold).

den \ num	1	2	3	4	5	6	7	8	9	10	11	12	14	16	20	24	30	40	50	75	100	200	500	∞
50	4.03 / **7.17**	3.18 / **5.06**	2.79 / **4.20**	2.56 / **3.72**	2.40 / **3.41**	2.29 / **3.18**	2.20 / **3.02**	2.13 / **2.88**	2.07 / **2.78**	2.02 / **2.70**	1.98 / **2.62**	1.95 / **2.56**	1.90 / **2.46**	1.85 / **2.39**	1.78 / **2.26**	1.74 / **2.18**	1.69 / **2.10**	1.63 / **2.00**	1.60 / **1.94**	1.55 / **1.86**	1.52 / **1.82**	1.48 / **1.76**	1.46 / **1.71**	1.44 / **1.68**
55	4.02 / **7.12**	3.17 / **5.01**	2.78 / **4.16**	2.54 / **3.68**	2.38 / **3.37**	2.27 / **3.15**	2.18 / **2.98**	2.11 / **2.85**	2.05 / **2.75**	2.00 / **2.66**	1.97 / **2.59**	1.93 / **2.53**	1.88 / **2.43**	1.83 / **2.35**	1.76 / **2.23**	1.72 / **2.15**	1.67 / **2.06**	1.61 / **1.96**	1.58 / **1.90**	1.52 / **1.82**	1.50 / **1.78**	1.46 / **1.71**	1.43 / **1.66**	1.41 / **1.64**
60	4.00 / **7.08**	3.15 / **4.98**	2.76 / **4.13**	2.52 / **3.65**	2.37 / **3.34**	2.25 / **3.12**	2.17 / **2.95**	2.10 / **2.82**	2.04 / **2.72**	1.99 / **2.63**	1.95 / **2.56**	1.92 / **2.50**	1.86 / **2.40**	1.81 / **2.32**	1.75 / **2.20**	1.70 / **2.12**	1.65 / **2.03**	1.59 / **1.93**	1.56 / **1.87**	1.50 / **1.79**	1.48 / **1.74**	1.44 / **1.68**	1.41 / **1.63**	1.39 / **1.60**
65	3.99 / **7.04**	3.14 / **4.95**	2.75 / **4.10**	2.51 / **3.62**	2.36 / **3.31**	2.24 / **3.09**	2.15 / **2.93**	2.08 / **2.79**	2.02 / **2.70**	1.98 / **2.61**	1.94 / **2.54**	1.90 / **2.47**	1.85 / **2.37**	1.80 / **2.30**	1.73 / **2.18**	1.68 / **2.09**	1.63 / **2.00**	1.57 / **1.90**	1.54 / **1.84**	1.49 / **1.76**	1.46 / **1.71**	1.42 / **1.64**	1.39 / **1.60**	1.37 / **1.56**
70	3.98 / **7.01**	3.13 / **4.92**	2.74 / **4.08**	2.50 / **3.60**	2.35 / **3.29**	2.23 / **3.07**	2.14 / **2.91**	2.07 / **2.77**	2.01 / **2.67**	1.97 / **2.59**	1.93 / **2.51**	1.89 / **2.45**	1.84 / **2.35**	1.79 / **2.28**	1.72 / **2.15**	1.67 / **2.07**	1.62 / **1.98**	1.56 / **1.88**	1.53 / **1.82**	1.47 / **1.74**	1.45 / **1.69**	1.40 / **1.62**	1.37 / **1.56**	1.35 / **1.53**
80	3.96 / **6.96**	3.11 / **4.88**	2.72 / **4.04**	2.48 / **3.56**	2.33 / **3.25**	2.21 / **3.04**	2.12 / **2.87**	2.05 / **2.74**	1.99 / **2.64**	1.95 / **2.55**	1.91 / **2.48**	1.88 / **2.41**	1.82 / **2.32**	1.77 / **2.24**	1.70 / **2.11**	1.65 / **2.03**	1.60 / **1.94**	1.54 / **1.84**	1.51 / **1.78**	1.45 / **1.70**	1.42 / **1.65**	1.38 / **1.57**	1.35 / **1.52**	1.32 / **1.49**
100	3.94 / **6.90**	3.09 / **4.82**	2.70 / **3.98**	2.46 / **3.51**	2.30 / **3.20**	2.19 / **2.99**	2.10 / **2.82**	2.03 / **2.69**	1.97 / **2.59**	1.92 / **2.51**	1.88 / **2.43**	1.85 / **2.36**	1.79 / **2.26**	1.75 / **2.19**	1.68 / **2.06**	1.63 / **1.98**	1.57 / **1.89**	1.51 / **1.79**	1.48 / **1.73**	1.42 / **1.64**	1.39 / **1.59**	1.34 / **1.51**	1.30 / **1.46**	1.28 / **1.43**
125	3.92 / **6.84**	3.07 / **4.78**	2.68 / **3.94**	2.44 / **3.47**	2.29 / **3.17**	2.17 / **2.95**	2.08 / **2.79**	2.01 / **2.65**	1.95 / **2.56**	1.90 / **2.47**	1.86 / **2.40**	1.83 / **2.33**	1.77 / **2.23**	1.72 / **2.15**	1.65 / **2.03**	1.60 / **1.94**	1.55 / **1.85**	1.49 / **1.75**	1.45 / **1.68**	1.39 / **1.59**	1.36 / **1.54**	1.31 / **1.46**	1.27 / **1.40**	1.25 / **1.37**
150	3.91 / **6.81**	3.06 / **4.75**	2.67 / **3.91**	2.43 / **3.44**	2.27 / **3.14**	2.16 / **2.92**	2.07 / **2.76**	2.00 / **2.62**	1.94 / **2.53**	1.89 / **2.44**	1.85 / **2.37**	1.82 / **2.30**	1.76 / **2.20**	1.71 / **2.12**	1.64 / **2.00**	1.59 / **1.91**	1.54 / **1.83**	1.47 / **1.72**	1.44 / **1.66**	1.37 / **1.56**	1.34 / **1.51**	1.29 / **1.43**	1.25 / **1.37**	1.22 / **1.33**
200	3.89 / **6.76**	3.04 / **4.71**	2.65 / **3.88**	2.41 / **3.41**	2.26 / **3.11**	2.14 / **2.90**	2.05 / **2.73**	1.98 / **2.60**	1.92 / **2.50**	1.87 / **2.41**	1.83 / **2.34**	1.80 / **2.28**	1.74 / **2.17**	1.69 / **2.09**	1.62 / **1.97**	1.57 / **1.88**	1.52 / **1.79**	1.45 / **1.69**	1.42 / **1.62**	1.35 / **1.53**	1.32 / **1.48**	1.26 / **1.39**	1.22 / **1.33**	1.19 / **1.28**
400	3.86 / **6.70**	3.02 / **4.66**	2.62 / **3.83**	2.39 / **3.36**	2.23 / **3.06**	2.12 / **2.85**	2.03 / **2.69**	1.96 / **2.55**	1.90 / **2.46**	1.85 / **2.37**	1.81 / **2.29**	1.78 / **2.23**	1.72 / **2.12**	1.67 / **2.04**	1.60 / **1.92**	1.54 / **1.84**	1.49 / **1.74**	1.42 / **1.64**	1.38 / **1.57**	1.32 / **1.47**	1.28 / **1.42**	1.22 / **1.32**	1.16 / **1.24**	1.13 / **1.19**
1000	3.85 / **6.66**	3.00 / **4.62**	2.61 / **3.80**	2.38 / **3.34**	2.22 / **3.04**	2.10 / **2.82**	2.02 / **2.66**	1.95 / **2.53**	1.89 / **2.43**	1.84 / **2.34**	1.80 / **2.26**	1.76 / **2.20**	1.70 / **2.09**	1.65 / **2.01**	1.58 / **1.89**	1.53 / **1.81**	1.47 / **1.71**	1.41 / **1.61**	1.36 / **1.54**	1.30 / **1.44**	1.26 / **1.38**	1.19 / **1.28**	1.13 / **1.19**	1.08 / **1.11**
∞	3.84 / **6.64**	2.99 / **4.60**	2.60 / **3.78**	2.37 / **3.32**	2.21 / **3.02**	2.09 / **2.80**	2.01 / **2.64**	1.94 / **2.51**	1.88 / **2.41**	1.83 / **2.32**	1.79 / **2.24**	1.75 / **2.18**	1.69 / **2.07**	1.64 / **1.99**	1.57 / **1.87**	1.52 / **1.79**	1.46 / **1.69**	1.40 / **1.59**	1.35 / **1.52**	1.28 / **1.41**	1.24 / **1.36**	1.17 / **1.25**	1.11 / **1.15**	1.00 / **1.00**

SOURCE: George W. Snedecor and William G. Cochran. Statistical Methods © 1967, Sixth Edition by Iowa State University Press, Ames, Iowa 50010. Reprinted with permission.

Appendix C
A Journal Article
in Manuscript
Form *

Note:

Some procedures for preparing and submitting a manuscript vary from journal to journal. Consult the correct APA publication manual and the specific journal before submitting any manuscript for publication.

Employee Theft as a Reaction to Underpayment Inequity:

The Hidden Cost of Pay Cuts

Jerald Greenberg

Faculty of Management and Human Resources

Ohio State University

Abstract

Employee theft rates were measured in manufacturing
plants during a period in which pay was temporarily
reduced by 15%. Compared with pre- or postreduction pay
periods (or with control groups whose pay was unchanged),
groups whose pay was reduced had significantly higher
theft rates. When the basis for the pay cuts was
thoroughly and sensitively explained to employees,
feelings of inequity were lessened, and the theft rate was
reduced as well. The data support equity theory's
predictions regarding likely responses to underpayment and
extend recently accumulated evidence demonstrating the
mitigating effects of adequate explanations on feelings of
inequity.

Employee Theft as a Reaction to Underpayment Inequity:

The Hidden Cost of Pay Cuts

Employee theft constitutes one of the most pervasive and serious problems in the field of human resource management. Although exact figures are difficult to come by, the American Management Association (1977) has estimated that employee theft cost American businesses from $5 billion to $10 billion in 1975, representing the single most expensive form of nonviolent crime against businesses.

Traditionally, social scientists have considered several plausible explanations for employee theft. Among the most popular are theories postulating that theft is the result of attempts to ease financial pressure (Merton, 1938), moral laxity among a younger workforce (Merriam, 1977), available opportunities (Astor, 1972), expressions of job dissatisfaction (Mangione & Quinn, 1975), and the existence of norms tolerating theft (Horning, 1970). More recently, Hollinger and Clark (1983) conducted a large-scale survey and interview study designed to explore these and other explanations of employee theft. Interestingly, they found that the best predictor was employee attitudes: "When employees felt exploited by the company ... these workers were more involved in acts against the organizations as a mechanism to correct perceptions of inequity or injustice" (Hollinger & Clark, 1983, p. 142).

Hollinger and Clark's (1983) suggestion that employee theft is related to feelings of injustice is consistent with several schools of sociological and anthropological thought. For example, in studies of hotel dining room employees (Mars, 1973) and maritime dock workers (Mars, 1974), Mars found that employees viewed theft <u>not</u> as inappropriate but "as a morally justified addition to wages: indeed, as an entitlement due from exploiting employers" (Mars, 1974, p. 224). Similarly, Kemper (1966) argued that employee theft may be the result of "reciprocal deviance," that is, employees' perceptions that their employers defaulted on their obligations to them, thereby encouraging them to respond with similar acts of deviance. Fisher and Baron (1982) made a similar argument in presenting their equity-control model of vandalism. They claimed that vandalism is a form of inequity reduction in that an individual vandal's breaking the rules regarding property rights follows from his or her feelings of mistreatment by authorities. Recent evidence in support of this idea is found in a study by

DeMore, Fisher, and Baron (1988). In that study, university students claimed to engage in more vandalism the less fairly they felt they had been treated by their university and the less control they believed they had over such treatment.

Such conceptualizations are in keeping with current theoretical positions in the field of organizational justice (Greenberg, 1987). These formulations allow more precise hypotheses to be developed regarding when employee theft is likely to occur. For example, consider equity theory's (Adams, 1965) claim that workers who feel inequitably underpaid (i.e., those who believe that the rewards they are receiving relative to the contributions they are making are less than they should be) may respond by attempting to raise their outcomes (i.e., raise the level of rewards received). Although research has supported this claim (for a review, see Greenberg, 1982), studies have been limited to situations in which persons paid on a piece-work basis produce more goods of poorer quality to raise their outcomes without effectively raising their inputs. Given earlier claims and supporting evidence associating student vandalism with inequitable treatment (DeMore et al., 1988), it may be reasoned analogously that employee theft is a specific reaction to underpayment inequity and constitutes an attempt to bring outcomes into line with prevailing standards of fair pay.

Recent research in the area of procedural justice (Lind & Tyler, 1988) has shown that perceptions of fair treatment and outcomes depend not only on the relative level of one's outcomes but also on the explanations given for those outcomes (for a review, see Folger & Bies, 1989). For example, researchers have found that decision outcomes and procedures were better accepted when (a) people were assured that higher authorities were sensitive to their viewpoints (Tyler, 1988), (b) the decision was made without bias (Lind & Lissak, 1985), (c) the decision was applied consistently (Greenberg, 1986), (d) the decision was carefully justified on the basis of adequate information (Shapiro & Buttner, 1988), (e) the decisionmakers communicated their ideas honestly (Bies, 1986), and (f) persons influenced by the decision were treated in a courteous and civil manner (Bies & Moag, 1986). Such findings suggest that interpersonal treatment is an important determinant of reactions to potentially unfair situations (Tyler & Bies, 1990).

It is an interesting idea that perceptions of

inequity (and corresponding attempts to redress inequities) may be reduced when explanations meeting the criteria presented in the preceding paragraph are offered to account for inequitable states. This notion was tested in the present study by capitalizing on a naturalistic manipulation—a temporary pay reduction for employees of selected manufacturing plants. Data were available for 30 consecutive weeks: 10 weeks before a pay reduction occurred, 10 weeks during the pay-reduction period, and 10 weeks after normal pay was reinstated. Following from equity theory, it was hypothesized that ratings of payment fairness would be lower during the pay-reduction period than during periods of normal payment (i.e., before and after the pay reduction). It was similarly hypothesized that rates of employee theft would be higher during the reduced-pay period than during periods of normal payment. Such actions would be consistent with equity theory's claim that one likely way of responding to underpayment inequity is by attempting to raise the level of rewards received. Although not previously studied in this connection, employee theft is a plausible mechanism for redressing states of inequity (Hollinger & Clark, 1983).

Additional hypotheses were derived from recent research (e.g., Cropanzano & Folger, 1989; Folger & Martin, 1986; Shapiro & Buttner, 1988; Weiner, Amirkham, Folkes, & Varette, 1987) showing that explanations for negative outcomes mitigate people's reactions to those outcomes (for a review, see Folger & Bies, 1989; Tyler & Bies, 1990). Generally speaking, in these studies the use of adequate explanations (i.e., ones that relied on complete, accurate information presented in a socially sensitive manner) tended to reduce the negative reactions that resulted from such outcomes and facilitated acceptance of the outcomes. From the perspective of Folger's (1986) referent cognitions theory, adequate explanations help victimized parties place their undercompensation in perspective by getting them to understand that things could have been worse. As such, adequate explanations were expected in the present study to lessen the feelings of inequity that accompanied the pay cut. Thus, it was reasoned that employees' feelings of payment inequity, and attempts to reduce that inequity (such as by pilfering), would be reduced when adequate explanations were given to account for the pay reduction.

Specifically, it was hypothesized that the magnitude of the expressed inequity—and the rate of employee theft— would be lower when pay reductions were adequately explained than when they were inadequately explained.

Method

Participants

Participants in the study were nonunion employees working for 30 consecutive weeks in three manufacturing plants, owned by the same parent company. The plants were located in different sections of the midwestern United States and manufactured small mechanical parts mostly for the aerospace and automotive industries. The employees' average age ($\underline{M}$ = 28.5 years), level of education ($\underline{M}$ = 11.2 years), and tenure with the company ($\underline{M}$ = 3.2 years) did not significantly differ among the three plants, $\underline{F}$ < 1.00, in all cases. The local unemployment rates in the communities surrounding the three plants were not significantly different from each other (overall $\underline{M}$ = 6.4%), $\underline{F}$ < 1.00. It is important to establish this equivalence of characteristics across research sites because the assignment of individuals to conditions was not random across sites, thereby precluding the assumption

of equivalence afforded by random assignment (Cook &
Campbell, 1976).

As the study began, Plant A employed 64 workers in
the following jobs: 5 salaried low-level managerial
employees (4 men, 1 woman); 47 hourly-wage semiskilled and
unskilled production workers (38 men, 9 women); and 12
hourly-wage clerical workers (all women). Almost identical
proportions with respect to job type (and sex of employees
within job type) existed in Plant B ($\underline{n}$ = 53) and Plant C
($\underline{n}$ = 66). Because some employees failed to complete
questionnaires during some weeks, and because some
employees voluntarily left their jobs during the study
period, complete sets of questionnaires were available
from 55 employees of Plant A, 30 employees of Plant B, and
58 employees of Plant C. This constituted a total sample
of 143 employees, distributed to conditions as summarized
in Table 1. The demographic characteristics of the 40
workers who were not included in the study did not differ
significantly from the characteristics of the 143 who
remained in the study (in all cases, $\underline{F}$ < 2.00), minimizing
the possibility that those who remained in the study were
a select group.

Insert Table 1 about here

Procedure

Because of the loss of two large manufacturing
contracts, the host company was forced to reduce its
payroll by temporarily cutting wages by 15% across the
board in two of its manufacturing plants (Plants A and B).
This was done in lieu of laying off any employees. After
this decision was made, I was asked to help assess the
impact of the wage cuts in several key areas, including
employee theft. Each of the payment-group manipulations
was carried out in a separate plant. The assignment of
Plant A to one experimental condition was determined at
random. Assignment to the control group was determined by
the host company's decision that pay cuts were not
necessary in Plant C.[1]

The adequate explanation condition was created in
Plant A. To effect this, a meeting (lasting approximately
90 min) was called at the end of a work week. At that
meeting, all employees were told by the company president
that their pay was going to be reduced by 15%, effective
the following week, for a period expected to last 10
weeks. During this meeting several types of explanations

were provided. On the basis of recent research (Folger &
Bies, 1989), I hypothesized that these explanations would
mitigate reactions to the pay cut. The workers were told
that company management seriously regretted having to
reduce their pay but that doing so would preclude the need
for any layoffs. They were further assured that all plant
employees would share in the pay cuts and that no
favoritism would be shown.[2] A relevant verbatim passage
follows:

> Something we hate to do here at [company name] is lay
> off any of our employees. But, as you probably know,
> we've lost our key contracts with [company names],
> which will make things pretty lean around here for a
> little while. As a result, we need to cut somewhere,
> and we've come up with a plan that will get us through
> these tough times. I've been working on it with [name
> of person] in accounting, and we're sure it will work.
>
> The plan is simple: Starting Monday, we will each
> get a 15% cut in pay. This applies to you, to me, to
> everyone who works here at [name of plant]. If we do it
> this way, there'll be no cut in benefits and no
> layoffs—just a 15% pay reduction. So, either your
> hourly wages or your salary will be reduced by 15%.

Will it hurt? Of course! But, it will hurt us all alike. We're all in it together. Let me just add that it really hurts me to do this, and the decision didn't come easily. We considered all possible avenues, but nothing was feasible. I think of you all as family, and it hurts me to take away what you've worked so hard for. But, for the next 10 weeks, we'll just have to tough it out.

In addition to these remarks, the basis for the decision was clearly explained and justified by presenting charts and graphs detailing the temporary effects of the lost contracts on cash-flow revenues. Projections verified that the cash-flow problem dictating the need for the pay cuts was temporary, and this was clearly explained. All employees were assured that the pay cut was designed to last only 10 weeks.[3] Specifically, the employees were told the following:

The reason I'm sharing all this information with you is that I want you to understand what is happening here. It's just a temporary problem we're facing, and one that I hope will never happen again. At least the best course of action from our accounting department is clear. The pay cuts will work, and they will not have to last longer than 10 weeks. The new jobs we'll be picking up from [name of company] will really help get us back on our feet. Hopefully, by then we'll be stronger than ever. Of course, I know we're no stronger than our people, and I personally thank each and every one of you for your strength.

The tone of the presentation was such that a great deal of respect was shown for the workers, and all questions were answered with sensitivity. Approximately 1 hr was spent answering all questions. Each response brought an expression of remorse at having to take such action (e.g., "Again, I really wish this weren't necessary."). The good intent of this message was reinforced by the fact that the president issued the message in person.

Plant B was the site of the inadequate explanation condition. Here, a meeting lasting approximately 15 min was called at the end of a work week. All employees were told by a company vice president that their pay was going to be reduced by 15%, effective the following week, for a period expected to last 10 weeks. The only additional information that was provided indicated that the lost contracts dictated the need for the pay cut. No expressions of apology or remorse were shared, and the basis for the decision was not clearly described. The following verbatim remarks characterize this condition: It is inevitable in a business like ours that cost-cutting measures are often necessary to make ends meet. Unfortunately, the time has come for us to take such measures here at [company name]. I know it won't be easy on anyone, but [name of company president] has decided that a 15% across-the-board pay cut will be instituted effective Monday. This is largely the result of the fact that we've lost our contracts with [names of companies]. However, soon we'll be picking up jobs with [name of company], so we're sure the pay cuts will last only 10 weeks. I realize this isn't easy, but such reductions are an unfortunate fact of life in the manufacturing business. On behalf of [company president's name] and myself, we thank you for bearing with us over these rough times. I'll answer one or two questions, but then I have to catch a plane for another meeting.

Finally, because the parts manufactured at Plant C were unaffected by the lost contracts, no pay cuts were mandated there. Plant C constituted the control condition for the study.

Measures

Two categories of dependent measures were used: actuarial data on employee theft, and self-report measures tapping some of the processes assumed to be underlying the theft behavior.

Employee theft rates. The measure of employee theft used for this study was the company accounting department's standard formula for computing "shrinkage." The formula yielded the percentage of inventory (e.g., tools, supplies, etc.) unaccounted for by known waste, sales, use in the conduct of business, or normal depreciation. (For a discussion of the difficulties attendant to deriving such measures, see Hollinger & Clark, 1983.) These measures were obtained unobtrusively (during nonwork hours) by representatives of the company's headquarters on a weekly basis during the study period. The persons taking inventory were aware of any legitimate factors that contributed to accounted-for changes in inventory levels (such as shipments received, supplies used during projects, etc.) but were blind to the experimental hypotheses.[4]

Because no single standard for computing shrinkage is uniformly used (Hollinger & Clark, 1983), it was not possible to compare the base rates of employee theft in the present sample to any industry-wide average. However, evidence that the employee theft rate studied here was not atypical was provided by showing that the mean theft rate for the 10-week period before the pay cut was not significantly different from the overall theft rate for all three plants for the prior year, $F < 1.00$. These data are important in that they provide some assurance that the changes in theft rates observed were not simply deviations from unusual patterns that later merely regressed to the mean.[5]

Questionnaire measures. Two types of questionnaire measures were needed to establish the validity of the study and to facilitate interpretation of the theft data—one group of questions to verify differences in familiarity with the basis for establishing pay (the manipulation check), and another group of questions to establish differences in perceived payment equity. The questionnaires were administered biweekly (during odd-numbered weeks in the study period) at the plant sites during nonworking hours. Because a larger, unrelated study had been going on for several months, the workers were used to completing questionnaires, making it unlikely that any suspicions were aroused by the questions inserted for this study. Participants were assured of the anonymity of their responses.

The "pay basis" measure was designed to provide a check on the validity of the payment-group variable. Participants answered four items on a 5-point scale ranging from not at all (1), to slightly (2), to moderately (3), to highly (4), to extremely (5). The questions were (a) "How adequate was your employer's explanation regarding the basis of your current pay?" (b) "How familiar are you with the way your employer determines your pay?" (c) "How thoroughly did your employer communicate the basis for your current pay to you?" and (d) "How much concern did your employer show about your feelings when communicating your pay?" A high degree of internal consistency was found for these items (coefficient alpha = .89).

The "pay equity" measure consisted of four items, three of which were anchored with the same scale points as the pay basis items. Specifically, participants responded to the following items: (a) "To what extent do you believe your current pay reflects your actual contributions to the job?" (b) "How fairly paid do you feel you currently are on your job?" and (c) "How satisfied are you with your current overall pay level?" The fourth item asked, "Relative to what you feel you should be paid, do you believe your current pay is: ___ much too low, ___ a little too low, ___ about right, ___ a little too high, ___ much too high?" Because only the first 3 points of this bidirectional scale were actually used, responses to this 3-point scale were combined with the 5-point unidirectional scales for the other items. Coefficient alpha was high (.84), justifying combining the individual items. The option of using existing standardized scales tapping reactions to pay (e.g., the Pay Satisfaction Questionnaire; Heneman & Schwab, 1985) was rejected in favor of ad hoc measures because these were judged to be much more sensitive to the measurement objectives of the present study (cf. Heneman, 1985).

Results

Preliminary Analyses

Prior to the principal data analyses, preliminary analyses were conducted to determine whether to separate the 15 biweekly questionnaire responses into three equal groups, reflecting responses before, during, and after the pay cut. The five 2-week response periods were treated as a repeated measure in mixed-design analyses of variance (ANOVAS) in which the payment group was the between-subjects factor (adequate explanation, inadequate explanation, no pay cut). Separate analyses were conducted for each of the three groups. Because no significant main effects or interactions involving the response periods were obtained in analyses for either questionnaire measure (all Fs < 1.00), the decision was made to combine the observations into three groups composed of more reliable observations (before, during, or after the pay cut).

Because only one employee-theft-rate figure was reported for each week (the figure was aggregate, as opposed to individual, data), it was not possible to conduct a parallel set of ANOVAS for this measure. However, separate tests were performed within each payment group to compare each week's theft rate to the mean for all 10 weeks. This process was repeated separately for each of the three response periods (i.e., before, during, and after the pay cut). Because no significant effects emerged in any of these analyses (all values of t < .50,

$\underline{df}$ = 9), the decision was made (paralleling that for the questionnaire measures) to group the weekly scores into three 10-week response periods.

Employee Theft Rate

Analyses of theft rates were based on a 3 × 3 mixed-design ANOVA in which payment group was the between-subjects variable, response period was the within-subjects variable, and the 10 weekly theft rates within each cell constituted the data. A significant Payment Period × Response Period interaction was found, $\underline{F}(4, 56) = 9.66$, $\underline{p} < .001$. Figure 1 summarizes the means contributing to this interaction.

Insert Figure 1 about here

For each payment group, simple effects tests were performed to determine whether the means differed significantly across response periods. Any significant effects were followed up with the Tukey honestly significant difference (HSD) procedure (with alpha set at .05). In addition, tests for quadratic trend components were performed using orthogonal polynomials (Hays, 1963). This analysis was performed to note trends in the data over time in a situation in which the number of available data points was too small to use time series analyses (Zuwaylif, 1970).

A simple effects test within the inadequate-explanation condition was significant, $F(2, 27) = 9.15$, $p < .001$. Post hoc tests revealed that significantly higher levels of theft were observed during the pay reduction than before or after the pay reduction. Consistent with this configuration, the quadratic trend was highly significant, $F(1, 27) = 12.18$, $p < .001$.

Within the adequate-explanation condition, the overall simple effects test was weaker but still significant, $F(2, 52) = 3.76$, $p < .05$. This effect was the result of a similar, though less pronounced, pattern of means showing theft to be higher during the pay cut than either before or after the pay cut. Tests for a quadratic trend component failed to reach conventional levels of significance, $F(2, 52) = 2.10$, $p < .15$.

Finally, within the control group, simple effects tests revealed that the means did not differ from each other significantly across the three response periods, $F(2, 55) < 1.00$.

To establish pre- and postmanipulation equivalence, it was useful to compare means between payment groups

(adequate explanation, inadequate explanation, no pay cut)
within response periods. Simple effects tests showed no
significant simple main effects of payment group before or
after the pay cut, $F < 1.00$ in both cases. However, the
effect of payment group was highly significant during the
pay cut, $F(2, 27) = 10.71$, $p < .001$. Tukey HSD tests
revealed that the three means were significantly different
from each other. In other words, within the pay-reduction
period, the theft rate in the inadequate-explanation
condition ($M = 8.9$) was significantly higher than that in
the adequate explanation condition ($M = 5.7$), which was in
turn higher than that in the control condition ($M = 3.7$).

Questionnaire Responses

Responses to the pay basis and pay equity
questionnaires were analyzed with ANOVA designs identical
to that used for the employee-theft measure. For these
dependent variables, however, the data consisted of
individual responses to the summed items constituting each
questionnaire within each cell. The two questionnaire
measures were not significantly correlated, $r = .07$.

For the pay basis measure, a significant Payment
Group × Response Period interaction was obtained,
$F(4, 280) = 256.10$, $p < .0001$. The corresponding means and

standard deviations are summarized at the top of Table 2.
As shown, post hoc tests revealed that employees in the
adequate-explanation condition demonstrated greater
understanding of the basis for pay determination than
employees in the other two conditions once the explanation
occurred (i.e., during and after the pay cut). The
adequate-explanation manipulation successfully enhanced
employees' understanding of the basis for pay
determination.

_____

Insert Table 2 about here

_____

A significant interaction effect also was obtained
for the pay equity measure, $F(4, 280) = 29.05$, $p < .001$.
The corresponding means and standard deviations are
summarized at the bottom of Table 2. As shown, post hoc
tests revealed that during the pay cut, employees in the
inadequate-explanation condition expressed the greatest
perceptions of pay inequity. Workers whose pay reductions
were adequately explained to them did not express
heightened payment inequity while their pay was reduced.

Turnover

A summary of missing data and data lost because of
voluntary turnover appears in Table 1. Not surprisingly,

the majority of the turnover occurred among employees experiencing inadequately explained pay reductions (12 of the 52 workers, or 23.1% of those still on the job at that time). Resignations in other conditions were uniformly 5% or less. Consistent with this, the distribution of resignations over conditions during the pay-cut period was highly significant, $\underline{x}^2(2, \underline{N} = 13) = 20.48$, $\underline{p} < .001$—a result of the fact that 12 of the 13 resignations occurred in the inadequate-explanation group. By contrast, the distribution of resignations across conditions was equal before the pay cut, $\underline{x}^2(2, \underline{N} = 3) < 0.5$, and after the pay cut, $\underline{x}^2(2, \underline{N} = 5) < 0.5$.

Discussion

The data support the hypothesis derived from equity theory (Adams, 1965) that workers experiencing underpayment inequity would attempt to redress that inequity by raising their inputs—in the present case, by pilfering from their employer. Indeed, while workers experienced a 15% pay reduction, they reported feeling underpaid and stole over twice as much as they did when they felt equitably paid. Two distinct interpretations of these theft data may be offered, both of which are consistent with equity theory (Adams, 1965). First, it is possible that the pay reduction led to feelings of frustration and resentment, which motivated the aggressive acts of theft. This possibility is in keeping with recent research findings demonstrating that pay cuts are associated with negative affective reactions to organizational authorities (Greenberg, 1989) and that increases in vandalism correlate positively with perceptions of mistreatment by authorities (DeMore et al., 1988). Such an interpretation follows from a reciprocal deviance orientation to inequity reduction, which suggests that employees' acts of deviance are encouraged by their beliefs that their employers defaulted on their obligations to them by reducing their pay (Kemper, 1966). From this perspective, acts of theft may be understood as a manifestation of feelings of mistreatment.

It is also possible to interpret the thefts as direct attempts to correct underpayment inequity by adjusting the balance of valued resources between the worker and the specific source of that inequity. As such, acts of theft may be interpreted as unofficial transfers of outcomes from the employer to the employee. Because no direct evidence is available suggesting that the stolen items had any positive valence to the employees, it is impossible to claim unambiguously that the theft rates represented employees' attempts to increase their own outcomes. Although such an interpretation is consistent with a considerable amount of evidence on the distribution of rewards and resources (for reviews, see Freedman & Montanari, 1980; Leventhal, 1976), it is also possible that disgruntled employees may have been content to reduce the valued resources available to the agent of their discontent. That is, they may have been motivated to reduce the employer's worth whether or not doing so directly benefited themselves. Unfortunately, the questionnaire items that would have been necessary to provide more refined interpretations of the present data might also have aroused subjects' suspiciousness that theft was being studied, thereby creating the potential for subject reactance (Webb, Campbell, Schwartz, Sechrest, & Grove, 1981). As a result, no such self-report data were collected. Nevertheless, the results are clearly in keeping with equity theory.

The present data also reveal a critical moderator of the tendency to pilfer to restore equity with one's employer—namely, the use of an adequate explanation for the pay cut. Pay cuts that were explained in an honest and caring manner were not seen by employees as being as unfair as pay cuts that were not explained carefully. Accordingly, reactions to carefully explained underpayment also were less severe (i.e., the pilferage rates were lower). These findings add to a recently developing body of research showing that the use of adequately reasoned explanations offered with interpersonal sensitivity tends to mitigate the negative effects associated with the information itself (for reviews, see Folger & Bies, 1989; Tyler & Bies, 1990). The explanations used in the present study were obviously quite successful in reducing costs, both to employees (in terms of inequity distress) and employers (in terms of pilferage and turnover).

An interesting and important aspect of the present study is that a sizeable portion of the participants in the inadequate-explanation condition voluntarily left their jobs during the pay-reduction period; in fact, a much larger proportion resigned than did so in any other condition (or within the same condition at other times). It is tempting to take this finding as support for the idea that quitting one's job is an extreme form of reaction to underpayment inequity (Finn & Lee, 1972) and that the voluntary turnover found here was another form of reaction to inequity. However, because of the nonrandom design of the study, it is not possible to rule out factors other than the experimental manipulation—a difficulty common to quasi-experimental studies (Cook & Campbell, 1976). Despite this problem, several facts lend support to the inequity interpretation. First, the finding that the theft rate immediately before the manipulations did not differ significantly from the previous year's theft rate suggests that nothing out of the ordinary was happening that may have been responsible for the results. Second, because the theft rate was highest precisely under the only conditions in which feelings of inequity were high (i.e., during the pay-cut period following an inadequate explanation), feelings of inequity and theft rate probably are related, both resulting from the manipulated variable exactly as predicted by equity theory (Adams, 1965) and referent cognitions theory (Folger, 1986). Because this interpretation is theoretically supported, its position is strengthened relative to alternatives that may be raised in the absence of random assignment.

Generalizing from the present findings, it appears

that adequately explaining inequitable conditions may be an effective means of reducing potentially costly reactions to feelings of underpayment inequity. To be effective, however, such explanations must be perceived as honest, genuine, and not manipulative (Tyler, 1988). Still, to the extent that underpayment conditions are acknowledged and justified by employers (as opposed to ignored or minimized by them), it appears that both workers and their organizations may stand to benefit. Given the high costs of employee theft (American Management Association, 1977), it appears that explaining the basis for inequities may be a very effective (and totally free) mechanism for reducing the costs of employee theft.

Practical implications notwithstanding, the present findings raise some important questions for equity theory (Adams, 1965) about the use of various modes of inequity reduction. Whereas the focus of this study was on pilferage, turnover was another type of response that occurred. Unfortunately, the nature of the present data makes it impossible to determine the trade-offs between various modes of inequity reduction. Did some employees resign in response to underpayment while others (perhaps

those with fewer options for alternative employment)
stayed on and expressed their negative feelings by
stealing? Or was it that the most aggrieved employees
stole company property before leaving, while others simply
lowered their inputs? Because the theft rates were
aggregate, actuarial data and could not be traced to
particular employees, and because performance data were
not collected, it was not possible to determine when and
how different forms of inequity-reduction behavior are
likely to occur. As a result, serious questions remain
regarding how different inequity-resolution tactics may be
used in conjunction with each other.

Confidence in interpretations of the present findings
is limited because actuarial-level dependent measures
(theft and turnover) were collected in conjunction with an
individual-level variable (perceived payment equity),
thereby making it impossible to conduct mediational
analyses of the results. Exacerbating this problem is the
fact that the use of a quasi-experimental design does not
allow the discounting of alternative explanations (as
noted earlier). Thus, although it is plausible that
inequity leads to stealing unless mitigated by an adequate
explanation, it is impossible to statistically discount

the alternative possibility that unknown preexisting differences between the plants constituting the payment groups (e.g., different norms against stealing or differential acceptance of management's promise that the pay cut would be temporary) may have been responsible for the results. However, in support of the present findings, it is important to note that such limitations are inherent to some degree in all quasi-experimental research design (Cook & Campbell, 1976).

Although nonrandom assignment precludes the discounting of alternative explanations, support for the present interpretation of the data may be derived from converging sources of theoretically based data. In this case, several lines of analogous research converge with my claim that adequate explanations enhanced the acceptance of undesired outcomes. For example, Folger and his associates (e.g., Folger & Martin, 1986; Folger, Rosenfield, & Robinson, 1983) measured laboratory subjects' feelings of discontent in reaction to procedural changes that created unfavorable conditions for them. Consistent with referent cognitions theory (Folger, 1986), Folger and his colleagues found that these feelings of discontent were reduced only when the need to make procedural changes was adequately explained. Similarly, in another line of investigation, Weiner et al. (1987) found that persons victimized by another's harmdoing expressed less anger toward the harmdoer when claims of mitigating circumstances were offered for the harmdoer's actions. Both lines of investigation show that negative affective reactions are reduced by the presentation of adequate explanatory information. As such, they provide good convergent evidence for my claim that adequately explained pay cuts mitigated feelings of inequity and reactions to underpayment inequity.

Finally, an important question may be raised about the compound nature of the explanation manipulation used in the present study. Because the adequate-explanation condition and the inadequate-explanation condition differed along several dimensions (postulated a priori to contribute to mitigation of the effects of the inequity), it was not possible to determine the individual effects of the various contributing factors. Specifically, the explanations differed in terms of several factors. Some of these, such as the quality of the information and the interpersonal sincerity of its presentation, have been recognized as mitigating reactions to undesirable outcomes

(Shapiro & Buttner, 1988). Other differences between conditions, such as possible differences in the credibility of the source (the president versus the vice president) have not yet been studied. Clearly, the unique effects of these factors are prime candidates for future research efforts.

To conclude, the results of the present study shed new light on employee theft—one of the most important problems in the field of human-resource management. The evidence confirms that employee theft is a predictable response to underpayment inequity and reveals that such reactions can be substantially reduced by the inexpensive tactic of explaining the basis for the inequity in clear, honest, and sensitive terms.

References

Adams, J. S. (1965). Inequity in social exchange. In L.
Berkewitz (Ed.), Advances in experimental social
psychology (Vol. 2, pp. 267-299). San Diego, CA:
Academic Press.

American Management Association. (1977, March). Summary
overview of the "state of the art" regarding
information gathering techniques and level of knowledge
in three areas concerning crimes against business:
Draft report. Washington, DC: National Institute of Law
Enforcement and Criminal Justice, Law Enforcement
Assistance Administration.

Astor, S. D. (1972, March). Twenty steps to preventing
theft in business. Management Review, 61(3), 34-45.

Bies, R. J. (1986, August). Identifying principles of
interactional justice: The case of corporate
recruiting. Symposium conducted at the annual meeting
of the Academy of Management, Chicago, IL.

Bies, R. J., & Moag, J. S. (1986). Interactional justice:
Communication criteria of fairness. In R. J. Lewicki,
B. H. Sheppard, & B. H. Bazerman (Eds.), Research on
negotiation in organizations (Vol. 1, pp. 43-55).
Creenwich, CT: JAI Press.

Cicchetti, D. V. (1972). Extension of multiple-range tests to interaction tables in the analysis of variance: A rapid approximate solution. Psychological Bulletin, 77, 405-408.

Cook, T. D., & Campbell, D. T. (1976). The design and conduct of quasi-experiments and true experiments in field settings. In M. D. Dunnette (Ed.), Handbook of industrial and organizational psychology (pp. 223-326). Chicago: Rand McNally.

Cropanzano, R., & Folger, R. (1989). Referent cognitions and task decision autonomy: Beyond equity theory. Journal of Applied Psychology, 74, 293-299.

DeMore, S. W., Fisher, J. D., & Baron, R. M. (1988). The equity-control model as a predictor of vandalism among college students. Journal of Applied Social Psychology, 18, 80-91.

Finn, R. H., & Lee, S. M. (1972). Salary equity: Its determination, analysis and correlates. Journal of Applied Psychology, 56, 283-292.

Fisher, J. D., & Baron, R. M. (1982). An equity-based model of vandalism. Population and Environment, 5, 182-200.

Folger, R. (1986). Rethinking equity theory: A referent

cognitions model. In H. W. Bierhoff, R. L. Cohen, & J. Greenberg (Eds.), Justice in social relations (pp. 145-162). New York: Plenem Press.

Folger, R., & Bies, R. J. (1989). Managerial responsibilities and procedural justice. Employee Responsibilities and Rights Journal, 2, 79-90.

Folger, R., & Martin, C. (1986). Relative deprivation and referent cognitions: Distributive and procedural justice effects. Journal of Applied Psychology, 22, 531-546.

Folger, R., Rosenfield, D., & Robinson, T. (1983). Relative deprivation and procedural justification. Journal of Personality and Social Psychology, 45, 268-273.

Freedman, S. M., & Montanari, J. R. (1980). An integrative model of managerial reward allocation. Academy of Management Review, 5, 381-390.

Greenberg, J. (1982). Approaching equity and avoiding inequity in groups and organizations. In J. Greenberg & R. L. Cohen (Eds.) Equity and justice in social behavior (pp. 389-435). San Diego, CA: Academic Press.

Greenberg, J. (1986). Determinants of perceived fairness

of performance evaluations. Journal of Applied
Psychology, 71, 340-342.

Greenberg, J. (1987). A taxonomy of organizational justice
theories. Academy of Management Review, 12, 9-22.

Greenberg, J. (1989). Cognitive re-evaluation of outcomes
in response to underpayment inequity. Academy of
Management Journal, 32, 174-184.

Hays, W. L. (1963). Statistics. New York: Holt, Rinehart,
& Winston.

Heneman, H. G., III (1985). Pay satisfaction. In K.
Rowland & G. Ferris (Eds.), Research in personnel and
human resources management (Vol. 3, pp. 115-139).
Greenwich, CT: JAI Press.

Heneman, H. G., III, & Schwab, D. P. (1985). Pay
satisfaction: Its multidimensional nature and
measurement. International Journal of Psychology, 20,
129-141.

Hollinger, R. D., & Clark, J. P. (1983). Theft by
employees. Lexington, MA: Lexington Books.

Horning, D. (1970). Blue collar theft: Conceptions of
property, attitudes toward pilfering, and work group
norms in a modern industrial plant. In E. O. Smigel &

H. L. Ross (Eds.), Crimes against bureaucracy (pp. 46-64). New York: Van Nostrand Reinhold.

Kemper, T. D. (1966). Representative roles and the legitimization of deviance. Social Problems, 13, 288-298.

Leventhal, G. S. (1976). The distribution of rewards and resources in groups and organizations. In L. Berkowitz & E. Walster (Eds.), Advances in experimental social psychology (Vol. 9, pp. 91-131). San Diego, CA: Academic Press.

Lind, E. A., & Lissak, R. (1985). Apparent impropriety and procedural fairness judgments. Journal of Experimental Social Psychology, 21, 19-29.

Lind, E. A., & Tyler, T. (1988). The social psychology of procedural justice. New York: Plenum Press.

Mangione, T. W., & Quinn, R. P. (1975). Job satisfaction, counter-productive behavior, and drug use at work. Journal of Applied Psychology, 11, 114-116.

Mars, G. (1973). Chance, punters, and the fiddle: Institutionalized pilferage in a hotel dining room. In M. Warner (Ed.), The sociology of the workplace (pp. 200-210). New York: Halsted Press.

Mars, G. (1974). Dock pilferage: A case study in

occupational theft. In P. Rock & M. McIntosh (Eds.),

Deviance and social control (pp. 209-228). London:

Tavistock Institute.

Merriam, D. (1977). Employee theft. Criminal Justice

Abstracts, 9, 380-386.

Merton, R. T. (1938). Social structure and anomie.

American Sociological Review, 3, 672-682.

Shapiro, D. L., & Buttner, E. H. (1988, August). Adequate

explanations: What are they, and do they enhance

procedural justice under severe outcome circumstances?

Paper presented at the annual meeting of the Academy of

Management, Anaheim, CA.

Tyler, T. R. (1988). What is procedural justice? Law and

Society Review, 22, 301-335.

Tyler, T. R., & Bies, R. J. (1990). Beyond formal

procedures: The interpersonal context of procedural

justice. In J. Carroll (Ed.), Applied social psychology

and organizational settings (pp. 77-98). Hillsdale,

NJ: Erlbaum.

Webb, E. J., Campbell, D. T., Schwartz, R. D., Sechrest,

L., & Grove, J. B. (1981). Nonreactive measures in the

social sciences (2nd ed.). Boston: Houghton Mifflin.

Weiner, B., Amirkhan, J., Folkes, V. S., & Varette, J. A.

(1987). An attributional analysis of excuse giving: Studies of a naive theory of emotion. <u>Journal of Personality and Social Psychology</u>, <u>52</u>, 316-324.

Zuwaylif, F. H. (1970). <u>General applied statistics</u>. Reading, MA: Addison-Wesley.

Author Notes

A preliminary report of the research reported in this article was presented at the annual meeting of the Academy of Management, San Francisco, August, 1990.

I gratefully acknowledge the helpful comments of Robert J. Bies and three anonymous reviewers on an earlier draft of this article.

Correspondence concerning this article should be addressed to Jerald Greenberg, Faculty of Management and Human Resources, Ohio State University, 1775 College Road, Columbus, Ohio 43210-1399.

Footnotes

[1] Admittedly, conducting the study in this manner meant that the two randomly assigned groups may have been nonequivalent with respect to some unknown variables that might have otherwise affected the results (Cook & Campbell, 1976). However, some reassurance of between-group similarity is provided by the demonstrated equivalence between worker characteristics, economic conditions, and job duties for both plants. Moreover, the deliberate assignment of Plant C to the control condition raises the possibility that something besides the lack of manipulation may have been responsible for the results (Cook & Campbell, 1976). However, informal postexperiment interviews with plant officials and employees confirmed that no unusual ''local history'' events occurred during the study period. Further assurance that this was not a problem comes from the fact that, before and after the pay cut, the control group's responses were identical to the other groups' responses for all measures used in the study.

[2] Before the meetings scheduled in each plant, the individuals involved (i.e., company president in Plant A and a vice president in Plant B) met with me to develop outlines of their presentations. Several carefully crafted sentences conveying salient aspects of the manipulation were prepared for inclusion in the speaker's

notes. Because local company norms dictated using informal meet-ings instead of formal presentations, complete scripts for the entire sessions could not be prepared in advance. As a result, it was necessary to establish that key differences in the manipulated variables were actually communicated in the meetings. With this in mind, each session was videotaped, and the videotapes were played back to a group of 112 undergraduate students after all identifying information was deleted. The students were asked to indicate in which of the two tapes (Tape A for Plant A; Tape B for Plant B) the speaker (a) presented more information about the pay cuts and (b) expressed greater remorse about the pay cuts. The order of presen-tation of the tapes was randomized. Virtually all of the students agreed that the speaker on Tape A presented more information and expressed greater remorse. Taken together with my in-person con-firmation that the manipulations were conducted as desired, these findings suggest that differentially adequate explanations were given to the two groups. Unfortunately, it was not possible to con-duct further analyses on these tapes because the host company insisted that they be destroyed to prevent the unwanted dissemi-nation of sensitive company information.

[3] Because of the sensitive and privileged nature of the internal accounting information, I was not permitted to divulge these data.

Indeed, although I helped company officials present this information in understandable form, these charts and graphs were never made part of my file.

[4] Although the theft-rate figures (i.e., percentage of inventory loss unaccounted for) were used internally to compute dollar-loss figures, data substantiating a specific dollar-loss amount caused by the thefts were not made available to me. Again, this decision was prompted by the company's desire to avoid potential embarrassment.

[5] Unfortunately, week-by-week theft-rate data were not available prior to the study period. As a result, it was impossible to compare the weekly theft rates during the study to earlier weekly theft rates. Thus, it was not possible to rule out the possibility raised by one reviewer that the results may reflect some seasonal fluctuations in theft that coincided with the manipulation period.

Table 1

Distribution of Attrition and Turnover Across Conditions

Condition	Starting n	Missing data	Resignations Before pay cut	Resignations During pay cut	Resignations After pay cut	Final n
Adequate explanation (Plant A)	64	6	1	1	1	55
Inadequate explanation (Plant B)	53	8	1	12	2	30
Control (Plant C)	66	5	1	0	2	58

Table 2

Data Summaries for Questionnaire Measures

Measurement/payment group		Response Period					
		Before		During		After	
	$\underline{n}$	$\underline{M}$	$\underline{SD}$	$\underline{M}$	$\underline{SD}$	$\underline{M}$	$\underline{SD}$
Pay basis							
Inadequate explanation	30	40.70	4.38	42.39	3.40	43.74	4.93
Adequate explanation	55	43.22	5.58	76.10	6.48	73.73	5.70
Control	58	42.36	6.49	40.72	3.83	41.90	4.46
Pay equity							
Inadequate explanation	30	56.87	5.54	40.20	7.56	57.43	6.70
Adequate explanation	55	61.22	9.57	59.56	9.52	56.03	9.37
Control	58	61.29	8.67	60.98	9.18	58.02	8.57

$\underline{Note}$. Within each row and each column, means not sharing a common subscript are significantly different from each other beyond the .05 level on the basis of the Tukey honestly significant difference technique corrected for confounded comparisons with the Cicchetti (1972) approximation.

FIGURE 1 Mean percentage of employee theft as a function of time relative to pay cut.

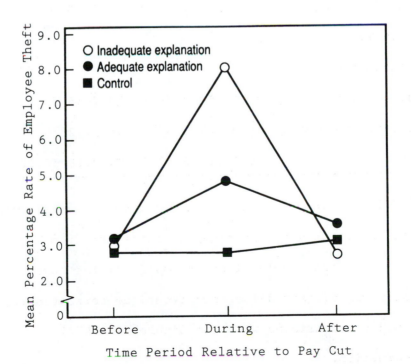

ABA **design** A type of within-subjects design in which the control condition (*A*) is presented first, followed by the experimental condition (*B*), followed by a return to the control condition (*A*).

Abstract A 100- to 150-word summary of the report, which precedes the four major sections.

Accidental sampling A form of nonprobability sampling that selects subjects from any available group.

Across-subjects counterbalancing A technique for controlling progressive error that pools all subjects' data together to equalize the effects of progressive error for each condition.

Aggregation The grouping together and averaging of data gathered in various ways; including aggregation over subjects, over stimuli and/or situations, over trials and/or occasions, and over measures.

Alternative hypothesis (H_1) A statement that the data came from different populations; the research hypothesis, which cannot be tested directly.

Analysis of variance (ANOVA) The statistical procedure used to evaluate differences among two or more treatment means by breaking the variability in the data into components that reflect the influence of error and error plus treatment effects; also called the *F test*.

Analytic statement A statement that is always true.

Antecedent conditions All circumstances that occur or exist before the event or behavior to be explained; also called *antecedents*.

A priori comparisons Statistical tests between specific treatment groups that were anticipated, or planned, before the experiment was conducted; also called *planned comparisons*.

At minimal risk The subject's odds of being harmed are not increased by the research.

At risk The likelihood of a subject being harmed in some way because of the nature of the research.

Balancing A technique used to control the impact of extraneous variables by distributing their effects equally across treatment conditions.

Baseline A measure of behavior as it normally occurs without the experimental manipulation; used to assess the impact of the experimental intervention.

Between-groups variability The degree to which the scores of *different* treatment groups differ from one another (that is, how much subjects vary under different levels of the independent variable); a measure of variability produced by treatment effects and error.

Between-subjects design A design in which different subjects take part in each condition of the experiment.

Block randomization The procedure used to assign equal numbers of subjects at random to each treatment condition of an experiment. Subjects are assigned to treatment blocks, where each block represents the condition of the experiment listed in random order.

Carryover effect The persistence of the effect of a treatment condition after the condition ends.

Case study The descriptive record of an individual's experiences and/or behaviors kept by an outside observer that may be used to make inferences about developmental processes, the impact of life events, a person's level of functioning, and the origin of disorders.

Cause and effect relationship The relation between a particular behavior and a set of antecedents that always precedes it— whereas other antecedents do not—so that the set is inferred to *cause* the behavior.

Cluster sampling The random selection of subjects by groups that occur in the population of interest; used when the population is very large.

Complete counterbalancing A technique for controlling progressive error that uses all possible sequences that can be formed out of the treatment conditions and uses each sequence the same number of times.

Confounding An error that occurs when the value of an extraneous variable changes systematically along with the independent variable in an experiment.

Constancy of conditions A control procedure used to avoid confounding; keeping all aspects of the treatment conditions identical except for the independent variable that is being manipulated.

Construct validity The degree to which a measurement device accurately assesses the hypothetical construct it is intended to measure.

Content validity The degree to which the content of a measure reflects the content of what is measured.

Continuous dimension The concept that traits, attitudes, and preferences can be viewed as continuous dimensions (i.e. sociability can be viewed as a continuous dimension ranging from very unsociable to very sociable).

Contradictory statement A statement that is always false.

Control condition The determination of the value of a dependent variable without the presence of the independent variable.

Control group The subjects in a control condition.

Correlation The degree of relationship between two or more traits, behaviors, or events.

Correlational study A study designed to determine the correlation between two or more traits, behaviors, or events.

Counterbalancing A technique for controlling order effects by distributing progressive error across the different treatment conditions of the experiment; may also control carryover effects.

Cover story A plausible but false explanation of the procedures in an experiment told to disguise the actual research hypothesis so that subjects cannot guess what it is.

Critical region Portion(s) of the distribution of a test statistic extreme enough to satisfy the researcher's criterion for rejecting the null hypothesis—for instance, the most extreme 5% of a distribution where $p < .05$ is the chosen significance level.

Critical value of *t* The minimum value of the test statistic necessary to reject the null hypothesis at the chosen significance level.

Debriefing The principle of full disclosure at the end of an experiment; that is, explaining to the subject the nature and purpose of the study.

Deductive model The process of reasoning from general principles to specific instances; most useful for testing the principles of a theory.

Degrees of freedom (*df*) The number of members of a set of data that can vary or change value without changing the value of a known statistic for those data.

Demand characteristics The aspects of the experimental situation itself that demand or elicit particular behaviors; may lead to distorted data by compelling subjects to produce responses that conform to what subjects believe is expected of them in the experiment.

Dependent variable (DV) The particular behavior that a researcher tries to explain in an experiment.

Descriptive statistics The standard procedures used to summarize and describe data quickly and clearly; summary statistics reported for an experiment, including mean, range, and standard deviation.

Descriptive title The title of the report, which describes what the report is about; typically includes the variables tested and the relationship between them.

Deviant case analysis An extension of the evaluative case study in which deviant individuals are compared with those who are not to isolate the significant variations between them and perhaps explain the origin of the deviance.

Directional hypothesis A statement that predicts the exact pattern of results that will be observed, such as which treatment group will perform best.

Discussion section The final major section of the report; it evaluates and interprets results and discusses implications of the research.

Double-blind experiment An experiment in which neither the subjects nor the experimenter know which treatment the subjects are in; used to control experimenter bias.

Elimination A technique to control extraneous variables by removing them from an experiment.

Environmental variable An independent variable that the experimenter can bring under direct control.

Error The variability within and between treatment groups that is not produced by changes in the independent variables; variability produced by individual differences and other extraneous variables.

Experimental condition A treatment condition in which the researcher applies a particular value of an independent variable to subjects and then measures the dependent variable.

Experimental design The general structure of an experiment (but not its specific content).

Experimental group The subjects in an experimental condition.

Experimental hypothesis A statement that predicts the effects of specified antecedent conditions on a measured behavior.

Experimental method The controlled test of a hypothesis about behavior.

Experimental operational definition The explanation of the meaning of independent variables; defines *exactly* what was done to create the various treatment conditions of the experiment.

Experimentation The process undertaken to discover something new or to demonstrate that events that have already occurred will occur again under a specified set of conditions; a principal tool of the scientific method.

Experimenter bias Any behavior of the experimenter that can create confounding in an experiment.

Explanation The specifying of the antecedent conditions of an event or behavior.

Ex post facto study A study in which a researcher systematically examines the effects of preexisting subject characteristics (often called *subject variables*) by forming treatment groups on the basis of the differences that already exist between subjects.

External validity The degree to which the findings of an experiment apply to situations not tested directly; their generalizability to the real world.

Extraneous variable A variable other than an independent or dependent variable; a variable that is not the main focus of an experiment and that may confound the results if not controlled.

Face validity The degree to which a measurement technique is self-evident.

Factor An independent variable in a factorial design.

Factorial design An experimental design in which more than one independent variable is manipulated.

Field experiment An experiment conducted outside the laboratory; used to increase external validity, verify earlier laboratory findings, and investigate problems that cannot be studied successfully in the laboratory.

Field study A nonexperimental research method used in the field or in a real-life setting, typically employing a variety of techniques including naturalistic observation, unobtrusive measures, and interviews.

***F* ratio** A test statistic used in the analysis of variance; the ratio between the variability observed *between* treatment groups and the variability observed *within* treatment groups.

Fruitful statement A statement that leads to new studies.

Generalizing The process of extending the results of a specific study to individuals and situations not directly tested; an inductive process.

Good thinking Organized and rational thought, characterized by openmindedness and objectivity, and including application of the principle of parsimony; a principal tool of the scientific method.

Grand mean An average of all the treatment means.

Higher-order interaction An interaction effect involving more than two independent variables.

History threat Any outside event or occurrence that could confound an experiment; a classic threat to internal validity.

Hypothesis The thesis, or main idea, of an experiment consisting of a statement that predicts the relationship between at least two variables.

Hypothetical construct Unseen processes, such as hunger or learning, postulated to explain observable behavior.

Independent variable (IV) The variable (antecedent condition) that the experimenter intentionally manipulates.

Inductive model The process of reasoning from specific cases to more general principles to form a hypothesis.

Inferential statistics Statistics that can be used as indicators of what is going on in a population; also called *test statistics.*

Informed consent A subject's voluntary agreement to participate in a research project after the nature and purpose of the study have been explained.

Instrumentation threat Any change in some feature of the measuring instrument itself over the course of an experiment; a classic threat to internal validity.

Interaction The change in the effect of one independent variable when another independent variable in the experiment changes value.

Interitem reliability The degree to which different items measuring the same variable attain the same results.

Internal validity The degree to which a researcher is able to establish a causal relationship between a specified set of antecedent conditions (treatments) and the subsequent observed behavior; the soundness of the procedures within an experiment.

Interrater reliability The degree of agreement among different observers or raters.

Interval scale The measurement of magnitude, or quantitative size, having equal intervals between values but no true zero point.

Introduction The first major section of the report; it explains the research, what led up to it, and states the research hypothesis.

Intuition The development of ideas from hunches; knowing directly without reasoning from objective data.

Large *N* design Similar to a small *N* design, except that groups of subjects are required.

Latent content The implicit meaning of a question, sentence, dream, statement, and the like.

Latin square counterbalancing A partial counterbalancing technique in which a matrix, or square, of sequences of treatment conditions is constructed to which subjects are assigned at random.

Laws General scientific principles that explain our universe and predict events.

Level of measurement The type of scale of measurement—either ratio, interval, ordinal, or nominal—used to measure a variable.

Main effect The action of a single independent variable in an experiment; the change in the dependent variable produced by the various levels of a single independent variable.

Manifest content The explicit meaning of a question, sentence, dream, statement, and the like.

Maturation threat Any internal (physical or psychological) change in subjects that might affect scores on the dependent measure; a classic threat to internal validity.

Mean An arithmetical average computed by dividing the sum of a group of scores by the total number of scores.

Mean square (MS) An average squared deviation; a variance estimate used in analysis-of-variance procedures and found by dividing the sum of squares by the degrees of freedom.

Measured operational definition The description of *exactly* how a variable in an experiment is measured.

Measurement The systematic estimation of the quantity, size, or quality of an observable event; a principal tool of the scientific method.

Measures of central tendency Summary statistics that describe what is typical of a distribution of scores.

Median The score that divides a distribution in half so that half the distribution lies above the median, half below; a measure of central tendency.

Method section The second major section of the report, it explains in detail how the research was conducted and who the subjects were.

Methodology The scientific techniques used to collect and evaluate psychological data (facts and figures).

Mixed design A factorial design that combines one independent variable that is manipulated within subjects with a nonmanipulated independent variable (or subject variable).

Mode The most frequently occurring score in a distribution; a measure of central tendency.

Multiple-group design A between-subjects design with one independent variable, in which there are more than two treatment conditions.

Multiple-independent-groups design The most commonly used multiple-group design in which the subjects are assigned to the different treatment conditions at random.

Multivariate analysis of variance (MANOVA) The statistical procedure used to study the impact of independent variables on two or more dependent variables; an extension of analysis of variance.

Multivariate designs Research designs and statistical procedures used to evaluate the effects of many variables in combination; including multiple correlation, factor analysis, and multivariate analysis of variance.

Naturalistic observation A descriptive technique used in nonexperimental research of observing behaviors as they occur spontaneously in natural settings.

Nay-saying A response style in which subjects show a tendency to disagree with a question regardless of its manifest content.

Negative correlation The relationship existing between two variables such that an increase in one is associated with a decrease in the other; also called an *inverse relationship*.

Nominal scale The simplest level of measurement; classifies items into two or more distinct categories on the basis of some common feature.

Nondirectional hypothesis A statement that predicts a difference without predicting the exact pattern of results.

Nonexperimental hypothesis A statement of predictions of how events, traits, or behavior might be related, but not a statement about cause and effect.

Nonprobability sampling A selection of subjects that is not random; the probability of selecting any individual subject is unknown.

Normal curve The distribution of data in a symmetrical, bell-shaped curve.

Null hypothesis (H_0) A statement that the performance of treatment groups is so similar that the groups must belong to the same population; a way of saying that the experimental manipulation had no important effect.

Observation The systematic noting

and recording of events; a principal tool of the scientific method.

One-tailed test A statistical procedure used when a directional prediction has been made; the critical region of the distribution of the test statistic (t, for instance) is measured in just one tail of the distribution.

Operational definition The specification of the precise meaning of a variable within an experiment; defines a variable in terms of observable operations, procedures, and measurements.

Order effects The changes in performance that occur when a condition falls in different places in a series of treatments.

Ordinal scale A measure of magnitude in which each value is measured in the form of ranks.

Oversampling In stratified random sampling, the selection of a larger than actual proportion of a particular subgroup in a population.

Partial counterbalancing A technique for controlling progressive error by using some subset of the available sequences of treatment conditions.

Phenomenology A nonexperimental method of gathering data by attending to and describing one's own immediate experience.

Physical variables Aspects of the testing conditions that need to be controlled.

Placebo effect The result of giving subjects a pill, injection, or other treatment that actually contains none of the independent variable but that elicits a change in subjects' behavior regardless.

Placebo group A control condition in which subjects are treated exactly the same as subjects who are in the experimental group, except for the presence of the independent variable.

Plagiarism The representation of someone else's ideas, words, or written work as one's own; a serious breach of ethics that can result in legal action.

Population In psychology experiments, all people, animals, or objects that have at least one characteristic in common.

Position preference A response style in which subjects show a tendency to choose answers appearing in the same position (say, the b slot) in multiple-choice questions.

Positive correlation The relationship between two measures such that an increase in the value of one is associated with an increase in the value of the other; also called a *direct relationship*.

Post hoc tests Statistical tests performed after the overall analysis indicates a significant difference; used to pinpoint which differences are significant.

Practice effects Changes in subjects' performance resulting from practice.

Precision matching Creating pairs whose subjects have identical scores on the matching variable.

Predictive validity The degree to which a measure, definition, or experiment yields information that allows prediction of behavior.

Pretest/posttest design A repeated-measures design with only one treatment condition; subjects are assessed once with the dependent measure (pretest); given a treatment; then retested on the same measure (posttest).

Principle of parsimony An aspect of good thinking, stating that the simplest explanation is preferred until ruled out by conflicting evidence; also known as *Occam's razor*.

Probability The study of the likelihood of events; a quantitative discipline that counts events and possible outcomes.

Probability sampling The selection of subjects in such a way that the odds of their being in a study are known or can be calculated.

Progressive error Fatigue, practice, and other extraneous sequence effects producing changes in subjects' responses during within-subjects experiments.

Psychology experiment A controlled procedure in which at least two different treatment conditions are applied to subjects whose behaviors are then measured and compared to test a hypothesis about the effects of the treatments on behavior.

Quota sampling A form of nonprobability sampling that selects subjects by preset target numbers intended to reflect the makeup of the population of interest.

Random assignment The technique of assigning subjects to treatments so that each subject has an equal chance of being assigned to each treatment condition.

Randomized counterbalancing The simplest partial counterbalancing procedure in which the experimenter randomly selects as many sequences of treatment conditions as there are subjects for the experiment.

Random number table A table of numbers generated by a computer so that every number has an equal chance of being selected for each position in the table.

Random selection The selection of subjects without bias; the outcome of the sampling procedure cannot be predicted ahead of time by any known law.

Range The difference between the largest and smallest scores in a set of data; a rough indication of the amount of variability in the data.

Range matching Creating pairs of subjects whose scores on the matching variable fall within a previously specified range of scores.

Rank-ordered matching Creating matched pairs by placing subjects in order of their scores on the matching variable; subjects with adjacent scores become pairs.

Ratio scale A measure of magnitude having equal intervals between values and having an absolute zero point.

Raw data Data recorded as an experiment is run; the responses of individual subjects.

Reactivity The tendency of subjects to alter responses or behaviors when they are aware of the presence of an observer.

References A list of books and articles cited in the report; placed at the end of each report.

Regression line The line of best fit; represents the equation that best describes the mathematical relationship between two variables measured in a correlational study.

Reliability The consistency and predictability of experimental procedures and measurements.

Repeated-measures design A design in which the subjects are measured more than once on the dependent variable; same as a within-subjects design.

Replication The process of repeating research procedures to verify that the outcome will be the same as before; a principal tool of the scientific method.

Representativeness How closely the responses of a sample of subjects reflect those responses that would be obtained if the entire population were sampled.

Research report Written report of psychological research, which contains four major sections: Introduction, Method, Results, and Discussion.

Response set The tendency to respond to the latent meaning of a question rather than its manifest content in an attempt to create a certain impression.

Response style The tendency to respond in a particular way regardless of the latent or manifest content of the question asked.

Results section The third major section of the report; it describes the findings and presents results of statistical tests and summary data.

Retrospective data The data collected in the present based on recollections of past events; apt to be inaccurate because of faulty memory, bias, mood, and situation.

Robust The assumption of a normal distribution of population values can be violated without creating serious errors.

Rosenthal effect The phenomenon of experimenters treating subjects differently depending on what they expect from the subjects; also called the *Pygmalion effect*.

Running head A short version of the title, usually placed at the top of each page of the report.

Sample of subjects A part of a population of interest assumed to be representative of the whole.

Scale of measurement The type of precise, quantitative measurement used to measure variables.

Scatterplot A graph of data created by plotting the value of one variable on the X (horizontal) axis and the other variable on the Y (vertical) axis for each subject in a correlational study.

Science The systematic gathering of data to provide descriptions of events taking place under specific conditions, enabling researchers to explain, predict, and control events.

Scientific writing style A concise, impersonal, and unbiased form of writing used in research reports.

Selection-interaction threat The combination of a selection threat with another threat to cause confounding of an experiment; a classic threat to internal validity.

Selection threat The possibility of confounding in an experiment whenever subjects are assigned to conditions by a procedure other than true random assignment; a classic threat to internal validity.

Serendipity The knack of finding things that are not being sought.

Shorthand notation A system that uses numbers to describe the design of a factorial experiment.

Significance level The statistical criterion for deciding whether to accept or reject the null hypothesis.

Simple random sample The most basic form of probability sampling; all members of a population have an equal chance of being selected.

Single-blind experiment An experiment in which subjects are not told which of the treatment conditions they are in; a procedure used to control demand characteristics.

Small N design A within-subjects design in which just one or two subjects are used; typically the experimenter collects baseline data during an initial control condition; applies the experimental treatment; then reinstates the original control condition to verify that changes observed in behavior were caused by the experimental intervention.

Social variables The qualities of the

relationships between subjects and experimenters that may influence the results of an experiment.

Standard deviation The square root of the variance; measures the average deviation of scores about the mean, thus reflecting the amount of variability in the data.

Statistical-conclusion validity The degree to which conclusions about a treatment effect can be drawn from the statistical results obtained.

Statistical inference A statement made about a population and all its samples based on the samples observed.

Statistical-regression threat The possibility of confounding in an experiment whenever subjects are assigned to conditions on the basis of extreme scores on a test; a classic threat to internal validity.

Statistical significance Meeting the set criterion for significance; the data do not support the null hypothesis; confirming a change between the groups that occurred as a result of the experiment.

Statistics Quantitative measurements of samples; quantitative data.

Stratified random sampling The random sampling of known subsets, or subgroups, of the population; can improve the representativeness of the sample and increase the accuracy of the experimental results for the entire population.

Subject-by-subject counterbalancing A technique for controlling progressive error for each individual subject by presenting all treatment conditions twice, first in one order, then in reverse order.

Subject-mortality threat The possibility of confounding in an experiment whenever the drop-out rate among subjects is related to the treatment condition itself; a classic threat to internal validity.

Subject variable The characteristics of the subjects in an experiment that cannot be manipulated; an independent variable, in the sense that a researcher can select subjects for their particular values.

Summary data Descriptive statistics computed from the raw data of an experiment, including the measures of central tendency.

Sum of squares (SS) The sum of the squared deviations from the group mean; an index of variability used in the analysis-of-variance procedures.

Synthetic statement A statement that can be either true or false, a condition necessary to form an experimental hypothesis.

Task variable An aspect of a task that the experimenter intentionally manipulates.

Testable Capable of being tested; typically used in reference to a hypothesis. Two requirements must be met in order to have a testable hypothesis: procedures for manipulating the setting must exist, and the predicted outcome must be observable.

Testing threat The effects on the dependent variable produced by a previous administration of the same test or other measuring instrument; a classic threat to internal validity.

Test-retest reliability Consistency between an individual's scores on the same test taken at two or more different times.

Test statistics Statistics that can be used as indicators of what is going on in a population and can be used to evaluate results; also called *inferential statistics*.

Theory A set of general principles that attempts to explain and predict behavior.

Treatment A specific set of antecedent conditions created by the experimenter and presented to subjects to test its effect on behavior.

t **test** The procedure used to evaluate the likelihood of a particular difference between treatment means by computing the test statistic *t*; used to analyze the results of a two-condition experiment with one independent variable and interval or ratio data.

t **test for independent groups** The procedure used to evaluate the likelihood of a particular difference between treatment means by computing the test statistic *t*; used to analyze the results of a two-group experiment with independent groups of subjects.

t **test for matched groups** The procedure used to evaluate the likelihood

of a particular difference between treatment means by computing the test statistic *t*; used to analyze two-group experiments using matched-subjects or within-subjects designs. Sometimes referred to as a within-subjects *t* test.

Two-factor experiment The simplest factorial design, having two independent variables.

Two-group design The simplest experimental design, used when only two treatment conditions are needed.

Two-independent-groups design An experimental design in which randomly selected subjects are placed in each of two treatment conditions through random assignment.

Two-matched-groups design An experimental design with two treatment conditions and with subjects who are matched on a subject variable thought to be highly related to the dependent variable. Generally, subjects are first measured on the matching variable, then divided into pairs having the most similar scores; members of each pair are then assigned to treatment conditions at random.

Two-tailed test A statistical procedure used when a nondirectional prediction has been made; the critical region of the distribution of the test statistic (*t*, for instance) is divided over both tails of the distribution.

Type 1 error An error made by rejecting the null hypothesis even though it is really true.

Type 2 error An error made by accepting the null hypothesis even though it is really false.

Unobtrusive measure A procedure used to assess subjects' behaviors without their knowledge; used to obtain more objective data.

Validity The soundness of a statement; its ability to withstand criticism; in experiments, the principle of actually studying the variables intended to be measured.

Variability Fluctuation in data; can be defined numerically as the range, variance, or standard deviation.

Variance The average squared deviation of scores from their mean; a more precise measure of variability than the range.

Willingness to answer A response style in which subjects show an inclination to answer questions even when the answers are in doubt.

Within-groups variability The degree to which the scores of subjects in the *same* treatment group differ from one another (that is, how much subjects vary from others in the group); an index of the degree of fluctuation among scores that is attributable to error.

Within-subjects design A design in which each subject takes part in more than one condition of the experiment.

Yea-saying A response style in which subjects show a tendency to agree with a question regardless of its manifest content.

*Page numbers in bold face indicate the first mention of a Key Term; those in italic
  designate the page where the Key Term is defined.

501

5+5